SOFTWARE ENGINEERING
WITH JAVA

The following
are registered
trademarks:

Access	Motif
ADF	MS-DOS
ADW	MVS/360
Aide-de-Camp	Natural
Analyst/Designer	New York Times
AT & T	Newton
Apple	Nomad
Bachman Product Set	Object C
Battlemap	Objective-C
Borland	OMTool
Bull	1-800-FLOWERS
CA-Tellaplan	ORB Plus
CCC	OS/360
Coca Cola	OS/370
CVS	OS/VS2
Demo II	Powerhouse
Emeraude	QAPartner
Excel	RAMIS-II
Excelerator	Rational
Focus	Rose
Foundation	SoftBench
Ford	Software through Pictures
FoxBASE	SPARCstation
Guide	SQL
Hewlett-Packard	Statemate
Honeywell	Sun
Hypercard	Sun Microsystems
Hypertalk	System Architect
IBM	Teamwork
IEW	The Design Machine
IMS/360	UNIX
Informix	VAX
Java	VM/370
Lotus 1-2-3	VMS
Lucent Technologies	Wall Street Journal
Macintosh	Windows 95
MacProject	X11
Method/1	XRunner
Microsoft	

To Sharon, David, and Lauren

© Richard D. Irwin, a Times Mirror Higher Education Group, Inc. company,
1997

Irwin Book Team

Publisher: *Tom Casson*
Senior sponsoring editor: *Elizabeth A. Jones*
Editorial coordinator: *Bradley Kosirog*
Director of marketing: *Kurt L. Strand*
Senior project supervisor: *Rebecca Dodson*
Production supervisor: *Karen Thigpen*
Designer: *Matthew Baldwin*
Cover Illustration: *Hamish Mac Ewan/Super Stock*
Prepress Buyer: *Heather D. Burbridge*
Compositor: *Weimer Graphics, Inc., Division of Shepard Poorman Communications Corp.*
Typeface: *10/12 Times Roman*
Printer: *R. R. Donnelley & Sons Company*

◤▼◣ **Times Mirror**
M **Higher Education Group**

Library of Congress Cataloging-in-Publication Data

Schach, Stephen R.
    Software engineering with Java / Stephen R. Schach.
        p.   cm.
    Includes index.
    ISBN 0-256-24167-8
    1. Java (Computer program language)   2. Software engineering.
    I. Title.
    QA76.73.J38S3   1997
005.13'3—dc20   96-35285

Printed in the United States of America
1 2 3 4 5 6 7 8 9 0 DO 3 2 1 0 9 8 7 6

SOFTWARE ENGINEERING
WITH JAVA

Stephen R. Schach
Vanderbilt University

IRWIN

Chicago • Bogotá • Boston • Buenos Aires • Caracas
London • Madrid • Mexico City • Sydney • Toronto

PREFACE

Java is the premier language of the World Wide Web and hence of the Internet and the Information Super Highway. It is also the programming language du jour, the darling of the columnists in computer newspapers and e-zines (online magazines). Furthermore, as a consequence of the vast economic potential of the Information Super Highway, Java is probably the best known programming language among investors who may know nothing about computers; the name "Java" appears in *The Wall Street Journal* nearly as frequently as "pork-belly futures" and "selling short against the box."

These are most definitely *not* the reasons why I chose to bring out a Java version of *Classical and Object-Oriented Software Engineering,* Third Edition. On the contrary, the reason why I selected Java is that Java embodies the principles of software engineering. This is described in greater detail in the epilogue of this book, entitled "Java: A Case Study in Software Engineering."

Java is much more than just a language for World Wide Web applets (small application programs) that can be accessed over the Web and then run on one's own computer. On the contrary, Java is a general-purpose programming language that can be used for software for all kinds and, in addition, on the Web.

At the end of each chapter in the Third Edition of *Classical and Object-Oriented Software Engineering* there is a continuing major Case Study implemented in C++. In this book, that Case Study is implemented in Java, demonstrating that Java can be used for serious software. Certain of the problems in this book require the student to modify the Case Study in some way. The source code of the Case Study (Appendixes C and I) is available by anonymous ftp from ftp.vuse.vanderbilt.edu (address 129.59.100.10) in directory /pub /Software_Eng/Java, or on a diskette from Richard D. Irwin, 1333 Burr Ridge Parkway, Burr Ridge, IL 60521.

Also, students are required to use Java to implement the 14-part Term Project of this book. The detailed solution of the Term Project in the Instructor's Manual (available from Richard D. Irwin, at the address given at the end of the previous paragraph) is an additional demonstration that Java is indeed a general-purpose programming language.

Acknowledgments

I am grateful to Rob Bland of IBM, co-author of the Instructor's Manual for this book, for his many helpful and insightful suggestions, especially regarding Chapter 6.

I should also like to thank the many individuals at Richard D. Irwin who have worked on this book. I am especially grateful to senior sponsoring editor Betsy Jones and senior project supervisor Becky Dodson.

Finally, I thank my family for their encouragement and unquestioning support throughout the writing of this book. After five other books, they fully appreciate that

I write best when I am alone in my study, even though I would far rather be with them. As always, I lovingly dedicate this book to my wife, Sharon, and my children, David and Lauren.

Stephen R. Schach

PREFACE TO THE THIRD EDITION OF *CLASSICAL AND OBJECT-ORIENTED SOFTWARE ENGINEERING*

The Second Edition of *Software Engineering* was published in 1993. At that time there were two major approaches to software development, namely the structured paradigm and the object-oriented paradigm. The structured paradigm was a tried and trusted approach, but it was not always successful. On the other hand, the object-oriented paradigm seemed promising, but no more than that. The Second Edition reflected this attitude. The book certainly included material on objects and on object-oriented design, but at that time it was premature to stress a new paradigm that had not been proven to be superior to the structured paradigm.

In the 3 years since the Second Edition was published, evidence has been steadily mounting that the object-oriented paradigm is superior to classical software engineering approaches. In fact, a textbook exclusively devoted to object-oriented software engineering would now be justified.

If that is so, then why is this book entitled *Classical and Object-Oriented Software Engineering?* Why are the classical techniques even mentioned? There are two reasons for this.

First, this book is a textbook at the senior undergraduate or first year graduate level, and it is likely that many students who use this book will be employed by organizations that still use classical software engineering techniques. Furthermore, even if an organization is now using the object-oriented approach for developing new software, existing software still has to be maintained, and this existing software is not object-oriented. Thus, excluding classical material would not be fair to students using this text.

The second reason why both classical and object-oriented techniques are included is that it is impossible to understand why object-oriented technology is superior to classical technology without fully understanding classical approaches and how they differ from the object-oriented approach. Thus, the classical and object-oriented approaches are not merely both described in this book, they are compared, contrasted, and analyzed. This ensures that the reader will fully appreciate why so many software professionals feel that the object-oriented approach is superior to classical approaches. Furthermore, if the student is employed at an organization that has not yet adopted object-oriented technology, he or she will be able to advise that organization regarding both the strengths and the weaknesses of the new paradigm.

Thus, the major change in this edition is that the object-oriented paradigm is emphasized. Objects are introduced in the very first chapter and are discussed throughout the book. Chapter 6, entitled "Introduction to Objects," provides clear definitions of basic object-oriented concepts such as classes, objects, inheritance, polymorphism, and dynamic binding (the chapter is an extended version of Chapter 9 of the second edition). There is a new chapter on object-oriented analysis, a topic that was not covered in the second edition. Particular attention is also paid to object-oriented life-cycle models, object-oriented design, management implications of the object-oriented paradigm, and to the testing and maintenance of object-oriented software. Metrics for objects and cohesion and coupling of objects are also covered. In addition, there are many briefer references to objects, usually only a paragraph or even a sentence in length. The reason is that the object-oriented paradigm is not just concerned with how the various phases are performed, but rather permeates the way we think about software engineering. As a result, object-oriented technology pervades this book.

The software process is still the concept that underlies the book as a whole. In order to control the process, we have to be able to measure what is happening to the project. Accordingly, the stress on metrics is maintained.

The third edition continues and extends other themes of the previous editions. For instance, the second edition contained a discussion of the Capability Maturity Model (CMM) and how it was being used to improve the software process and thereby boost productivity. In this edition, the ISO 9000-series is also discussed and is contrasted with the CMM.

There have been a number of developments within the area of Computer-Aided Software Engineering (CASE). On the one hand, some organizations have become disillusioned with CASE, whereas others have introduced CASE and have observed a marked improvement in areas such as productivity, software quality, and employee morale. This book gives a balanced view of CASE and explains why organizations have had such differing experiences with it. CASE tools for the object-oriented paradigm are also included.

Topics that continue to be emphasized throughout the book include the importance of maintenance and the need for complete and correct documentation at all times. The importance of software reuse is still stressed, but now within the context of objects.

The book is still essentially language-independent. The few code examples are in C++. To be more precise, wherever possible the "C subset of C++" has been used. In addition, care has been taken to use as few C idioms as possible so that the material can also be understood by readers with little or no knowledge of C. The only chapter where C++ (rather than C) is employed is Chapter 6, and detailed explanations of specific C++ constructs have been provided there. In addition, the implementation of the Case Study in Appendix I uses some C++ constructs.

With regard to prerequisites, it is assumed that the reader is familiar with one high-level programming language such as Pascal, C, BASIC, COBOL, or FORTRAN. Although most of the examples are in C, no previous knowledge of C is needed. In addition, the reader is expected to have taken a course in data structures.

How the Third Edition Is Organized

The order of the chapters reflects the order of the phases of the software life cycle. Specifically, Part Two of this book (Chapters 7 through 14) consists of a phase-by-phase treatment of the software life cycle, starting with the requirements phase and ending with the maintenance phase. In order to prepare the reader for this material, Part One contains the background material needed to understand the second part of the book. For example, Part One introduces the reader to CASE, metrics, and testing because each chapter of Part Two contains a section on CASE tools for that phase, a section on metrics for that phase, and a section on testing during that phase.

In order to ensure that the key software engineering techniques of Part Two are truly understood, each is presented twice. First, whenever a technique is introduced, it is illustrated by means of the elevator problem. The elevator problem is the correct size for the reader to be able to see the technique applied to a complete problem, and it has enough subtleties to highlight both the strengths and weaknesses of the technique being taught. Then, at the end of each chapter there is a continuing major Case Study. A detailed solution to the Case Study is presented. The material for each phase of the Case Study is generally too large to appear in the chapter itself. Instead, only key points of the solution are presented in the chapter itself and the complete material appears at the end of the book (Appendices C through I).

The Problem Sets

In this edition, there are four types of exercises. First, as before, at the end of each chapter there are a number of exercises intended to highlight key points. These exercises are self-contained; the technical information for all of the exercises can be found in this book.

Second, there is a software term project. It is designed to be solved by students working in teams of three, the smallest number of team members that cannot confer over a standard telephone. The term project comprises 14 separate components, each tied to the relevant chapter. For example, design is the topic of Chapter 11, so in that chapter the component of the term project is concerned with designing the software for the project. By breaking a large project into smaller, well-defined pieces, the instructor can monitor the progress of the class more closely. The structure of the term project is such that instructors may freely apply the 14 components to any other project they choose.

Because this book is written for use by graduate students as well as upperclass undergraduates, the third type of problem is based on research papers in the software engineering literature. In each chapter an important paper has been chosen; wherever possible, a paper related to object-oriented software engineering has been selected. The student is asked to read the paper and to answer a question relating to its contents. Of course, the instructor is free to assign any other research paper; the "For Further Reading" section at the end of each chapter includes a wide variety of relevant papers.

New to this edition is the fourth type of problem, namely, problems related to the Case Study. A number of instructors have told me that they believe their students learn more by modifying an existing product than by developing a product from scratch. Many senior software engineers in the industry with whom I have discussed the issue agree with that viewpoint. Accordingly, each chapter in which the Case Study is presented has at least three problems that require the student to modify the Case Study in some way. For example, in one chapter the student is asked to redesign the Case Study using a different technique from the one used for the Case Study. In another chapter, the student is asked what the effect would have been of performing the steps of object-oriented analysis in a different order. In order to make it easy to modify the source code of the Case Study (Appendices C and I), the source code is available by anonymous CD from **ftp.vuse.vanderbilt.edu** (129.59.100.10) in directory **/pub/Software_Eng/Third_Edition**, or on a diskette from Richard D. Irwin, 1333 Burr Ridge Parkway, Burr Ridge, Illinois 60521.

The Instructor's Manual contains detailed solutions to all the exercises, as well as to the term project. The Instructor's Manual is also available from Richard D. Irwin, and so are transparency masters for all the figures in this book.

Acknowledgments

I am indebted to those who reviewed this edition, including:

Dan Berry
The Technion

Doug Bickerstaff
Eastern Washington University

Richard J. Botting
California State University–San Bernardino

Buster Dunsmore
Purdue University

E.B. Fernandez
Florida Atlantic University

Donald Gotterbarn
East Tennessee State University

Greg Jones
Utah State University

Peter E. Jones
University of Western Australia–Nedlands, Perth

David Notkin
University of Washington

Hal Render
University of Colorado–Colorado Springs

Bob Schuerman
State College, Pennsylvania

K.C. Tai
North Carolina State University

Laurie Werth
University of Texas–Austin

Lee White
Case Western Reserve University

George W. Zobrist
University of Missouri–Rolla

Jeff Gray, co-author of the Instructor's Manual for this edition, has made many helpful suggestions. In particular, I thank him for his ideas regarding the Z specification of Section 8.8.1. I am grateful to Saveen Reddy for his comments on Sections 6.4 through 6.6. I should also like to thank Keith Pierce, University of Minnesota, Duluth, for his helpful suggestions regarding test plans. Some of the material of the MSG Case Study, presented at the end of Chapters 7 through 13 and in Appendices C through I, has been taken from the Term Project in the Second Edition of this book and from the Instructor's Manual for the Second Edition (co-authored by Santhosh R. Sastry).

I should like to single out three individuals at Richard D. Irwin to whom I am especially grateful. I thank senior sponsoring editor Betsy Jones, project editor Becky Dodson, and copy editor June Waldman for their many valuable contributions to this book.

Finally, I thank my family for their wholehearted support and encouragement throughout the writing of this edition. As with all my previous books, I have done my utmost to ensure that family commitments took precedence over writing. However, when deadlines loomed, this was sometimes not possible. At such times, they were always understanding, and for this I am most grateful. As always, I dedicate this book to my wife, Sharon, and my children, David and Lauren, with love.

Stephen R. Schach

BRIEF CONTENTS

CONTENTS

PART 2

The Phases of the Software Process   195

CHAPTER 7

Requirements Phase   197

CHAPTER 8

Specification Phase   222

CHAPTER 9

Object-Oriented Analysis Phase   268

WHY JAVA?

Java is not just a language for World Wide Web applets (small application programs). On the contrary, Java is an all-purpose programming language that can be successfully used for all kinds of software, including data processing software, scientific software, systems programming, and real-time software, as well as for portable Web software.

The reason why Java was chosen as the primary language for this book is because Java can be considered to be a case study in software engineering. In other words, the design of the Java language reflects good software engineering practice.

Before we can show this, we must first describe software engineering in depth; that is done in the 14 chapters of this book. Throughout those chapters we use Java to highlight specific issues. Then, in the epilogue, we return to the subject of Java as a case study in software engineering and show that the various principles and practices described in this book are embodied in the programming language Java.

1

INTRODUCTION TO THE SOFTWARE PROCESS

The first six chapters of this book serve a dual role. They introduce the reader to the software process, and they also provide an overview of the book. The software process is the way we produce software. It starts with concept exploration and ends when the product is finally decommissioned. During this period the product goes through a series of phases such as requirements, specification, planning, design, implementation, integration, maintenance, and, ultimately, retirement. The software process also includes the tools and techniques we use to develop and maintain software, as well as the software professionals involved.

In Chapter 1, "Scope of Software Engineering," it is pointed out that techniques for software production must be cost-effective and must also promote constructive interaction between the members of the software production team. The importance of objects is stressed throughout the book, starting with this chapter.

"The Software Process and Its Problems" is the title of Chapter 2. Many problems of software engineering are described, but no solutions are put forward in this chapter. Instead, the reader is informed where in the book each problem is tackled. In this way, the chapter serves as a guide to the entire book.

A variety of different software life-cycle models are discussed in detail in Chapter 3, "Software Life-Cycle Models." These include the waterfall model, the rapid prototyping model, the incremental model, and the spiral model. To enable the reader to decide on an appropriate life-cycle model for a specific project, the various life-cycle models are compared and contrasted.

Chapter 4 is entitled "Stepwise Refinement, CASE, and Other Tools of the Trade." A software engineer needs to be able to use a number of different tools, both theoretical and practical. In this chapter the reader is introduced to a variety of software engineering tools. One such tool is stepwise refinement, a technique for decomposing a large problem into smaller, more tractable problems. Another tool is cost–benefit analysis, a technique for determining whether a software project is financially feasible. Then computer-aided software engineering (CASE) tools are described. A CASE tool is a software product that assists software engineers to develop and maintain software. Finally, in order to manage the software process, it is necessary to measure various quantities to determine whether the project is on track. These measures (metrics) are critical to the success of a project. The last two topics of Chapter 4, namely CASE tools and metrics, are treated in detail in Chapters 7 through 14, which describe the specific phases of the software life cycle. There is a discussion of the CASE tools that support each phase, as well as a description of the metrics needed to manage that phase adequately.

An important theme of this book is that testing is not a separate phase to be carried out just before delivering the product to the client, or even at the end of each phase of the software life cycle. Instead, testing is performed in parallel with all software production activities. In Chapter 5, "Testing Principles," the concepts underlying testing are discussed. Testing techniques specific to the individual phases of the software life cycle are deferred until Chapters 7 through 14.

Chapter 6, "Introduction to Objects," is the last chapter of Part One. There is a detailed explanation of classes and objects, and why the object-oriented paradigm is proving to be more successful than the structured paradigm. The ideas of this chapter are then utilized in the rest of the book, particularly Chapter 9, "Object-Oriented Analysis Phase," and Chapter 11, "Design Phase," in which object-oriented design is presented.

1

SCOPE OF SOFTWARE ENGINEERING

A well-known story is told of the executive who received a computer-generated bill for $0.00. After having a good laugh with friends about "idiot computers," the executive tossed the bill away. A month later a similar bill arrived, this time marked 30 days. Then came the third bill. The fourth bill arrived a month later, accompanied by a message hinting at possible legal action if the bill for $0.00 was not paid at once.

The fifth bill, marked 120 days, did not hint at anything—the message was rude and forthright, threatening all manner of legal actions if the bill was not immediately paid. Fearful of his organization's credit rating in the hands of this maniacal machine, the executive called an acquaintance who was a software engineer and related the whole sorry story. Trying not to laugh, the software engineer told the executive to mail a check for $0.00. This had the desired effect, and a receipt for $0.00 was received a few days later. The executive carefully filed it away in case the computer at some future date might allege that $0.00 was still owing.

This well-known story has a less well-known sequel. A few days later the executive was summoned by his bank manager. The banker held up a check and asked, "Is this your check?"

The executive agreed that it was.

"Would you mind telling me why you wrote a check for $0.00?" asked the banker.

So the whole story was retold. When the executive had finished, the banker turned to him and quietly asked, "Have you any idea what your check for $0.00 did to *our* computer system?"

A computer professional can laugh at this story, albeit somewhat nervously. After all, every one of us has designed or implemented a product that, in its original form, would have resulted in the equivalent of sending dunning letters for $0.00. Up to now, we have always caught this sort of fault during testing. But our laughter has a hollow ring to it, because at the back of our minds there is the fear that someday we will not detect the fault before the product is delivered to the customer.

A decidedly less humorous software fault was detected on November 9, 1979. The Strategic Air Command had an alert scramble when the world-wide military monitoring command and control system (WWMCCS) computer network reported that the Soviet Union had launched missiles aimed toward the United States [Neumann, 1980]. What actually happened was that a simulated attack was interpreted as the real thing, just as in the movie *WarGames* some 5 years later. Although the U.S. Department of Defense has understandably not given details about the precise mechanism by which test data were taken for actual data, it seems reasonable to ascribe the problem to a software fault. Either the system as a whole was not designed to

---

JUST IN CASE YOU WANTED TO KNOW

In the case of the WWMCCS network, disaster was averted at the last minute. However, the consequences of other software faults have sometimes been tragic. For example, between 1985 and 1987 at least two patients died as a consequence of severe overdoses of radiation delivered by the Therac-25 medical linear accelerator [Leveson and Turner, 1993]. The cause was a fault in the control software.

During the 1991 Gulf War, a Scud missile penetrated the Patriot anti-missile shield and struck a barracks near Dhahran, Saudi Arabia. In all 28 Americans were killed, and 98 wounded. The software for the Patriot missile contained a cumulative timing fault. The Patriot was designed to operate for only a few hours at a

time, after which the clock was reset. As a result, the fault never had a significant effect and, therefore, was not detected. In the Gulf, however, the Dhahran Patriot missile battery ran continuously for over 100 hours. This caused the accumulated time discrepancy to become large enough to render the system inaccurate.

During the Gulf War, the United States shipped Patriot missiles to Israel for protection against the Scuds. Israeli forces detected the timing problem after only 8 hours and immediately reported it to the manufacturer in the United States. They corrected the fault as quickly as they could, but tragically, the new software arrived the day after the direct hit by the Scud [Mellor, 1994].

---

differentiate between simulations and reality, or the user interface did not include the necessary checks for ensuring that users of the system would be able to distinguish fact from fiction. In other words, a software fault, if indeed the problem was caused by software, could have brought civilization as we know it to an unpleasant and abrupt end. (See the Just in Case You Wanted to Know box on this page for information on disasters caused by other software faults.)

Whether we are dealing with billing or air defense, software is being delivered late, over budget, and full of residual faults. Software engineering is an attempt to solve these problems. In other words, software engineering is a discipline whose aim is the production of fault-free software, delivered on time and within budget, that satisfies the user's needs. Furthermore, the software must be easy to modify when the user's needs change. In order to achieve these goals, a software engineer has to acquire a broad range of skills, both technical and managerial. These skills have to be applied not just to programming but to every phase of software production, from requirements to maintenance.

The scope of software engineering is extremely broad. Some aspects of software engineering can be categorized as mathematics or computer science; other aspects fall into the areas of economics, management, or psychology. In order to display the wide-reaching realm of software engineering, five different aspects will now be examined.

1.1 HISTORICAL ASPECTS

It is a fact that electric power generators fail, but far less frequently than payroll products. It is true that bridges sometimes collapse, but considerably less often than operating systems do.

In the belief that software design, implementation, and maintenance could be put on the same footing as traditional engineering disciplines, a NATO study group in 1967 coined the term "software engineering." The claim that building software is similar to other engineering tasks was endorsed by the 1968 NATO Software Engineering Conference held in Garmisch, Germany [Naur, Randell, and Buxton, 1976]. This endorsement is not too surprising; the very name of the conference reflected the belief that software production should be an engineeringlike activity. A conclusion of the conferees was that software engineering should use the philosophies and paradigms of established engineering disciplines to solve what they termed the *software crisis,* namely, that the quality of software was generally unacceptably low and that deadlines and cost limits were not being met.

The fact that the crisis is still with us, more than 25 years later, tells us two things. First, the software production process, while resembling traditional engineering in many respects, has its own unique properties and problems. Second, the software crisis should be renamed the *software depression,* in view of its long duration and poor prognosis.

It is certainly true that bridges collapse less frequently than operating systems. Why then cannot bridge-building techniques be used to build operating systems? What the NATO conferees overlooked is that bridges are as different from operating systems as ravens are from writing desks.

A major difference between bridges and operating systems lies in the attitudes of the civil engineering community and the software engineering community to the act of collapsing. When a bridge collapses, as the Tacoma Narrows bridge did in 1940, the bridge almost always has to be redesigned and rebuilt. The original design was faulty and posed a threat to human safety; certainly the design requires drastic changes. In addition, the effects of the collapse will in almost every instance have caused so much damage to the bridge fabric that the only reasonable thing to do is to demolish what is left of the faulty bridge and rebuild it. Furthermore, other bridges built to the same design have to be carefully inspected and, in the worst case, rebuilt.

In contrast, an operating system crash is not considered unusual and rarely triggers an immediate investigation into its design. When a crash occurs, it may be possible simply to reboot the system in the hope that the set of circumstances that caused the crash will not recur. This may be the only remedy if, as is often the case, there is no evidence as to the cause of the crash. The damage caused by the crash will usually be minor: a database partially corrupted, a few files lost. Even when damage to the file system is considerable, back-up data can often restore the file system to a state not too far removed from its precrash condition. Perhaps if software engineers treated an operating system crash as seriously as civil engineers treat a bridge collapse, the overall level of professionalism within software engineering would rise.

Now consider a real-time system, that is, a system able to respond to inputs from the real world as fast as they occur. An example is a computer-controlled intensive care unit. Irrespective of how many medical emergencies occur virtually simultaneously, the system must continue to alert the medical staff to every new emergency without ceasing to monitor those patients whose condition is critical but stable. In general, the failure of a real-time system, whether it controls an intensive care unit, a nuclear reactor, or the climatic conditions aboard a future space station, has significant effects. Most real-time systems, therefore, include some element of fault tolerance to minimize the effects of a failure. That is, the system is designed to attempt an automatic recovery from any failure.

The very concept of fault tolerance highlights a major difference between bridges and operating systems. Bridges are engineered to withstand every reasonably anticipated condition, such as high winds, flash floods, and so on. An implicit assumption of all too many software builders is that we cannot hope to anticipate all possible conditions that the software must withstand, so we must design our software to try to minimize the damage that an unanticipated condition might cause. In other words, bridges are assumed to be perfectly engineered. In contrast, most operating systems are assumed to be imperfectly engineered; many are designed in such a way that rebooting is a simple operation that the user may perform whenever needed. This difference is a fundamental reason why so much software today cannot be considered *engineered*, in the classical sense of the word.

It might be suggested that this difference is only temporary. After all, we have been building bridges for thousands of years, and we therefore have considerable experience and expertise in the types of conditions a bridge must withstand. We have less than 50 years of experience with operating systems. Surely with more experience, the argument goes, we will understand operating systems as well as we understand bridges and will eventually be able to construct operating systems that will not fail.

The flaw in this argument is that hardware, and hence the associated operating system, is growing more complex faster than we can master it. In the 1960s, we had multiprogramming operating systems, in the 1970s we had to deal with virtual memory, and now we are attempting to come to terms with multiprocessor and distributed (network) operating systems. Until we can handle the complexity caused by the interconnections of the various components of a software product such as an operating system, we cannot hope to understand it fully, and if we do not understand it, we cannot hope to engineer it.

Part of the reason for the complexity of software is that, as it is executed, software goes through discrete states. Changing even one bit causes the software to change state. The total number of such states can be vast, and many of them have not been considered by the development team. If the software enters such an unanticipated state, the result will often be software failure. In contrast, bridges are continuous (analog) systems. They are described using continuous mathematics, essentially calculus. However, discrete systems such as operating systems have to be described using discrete mathematics [Parnas, 1990]. Software engineers therefore have to be skilled in discrete mathematics, a primary tool in trying to cope with this complexity.

A second major difference between bridges and operating systems is maintenance. Maintaining a bridge is generally restricted to painting it, repairing minor cracks, resurfacing the road, and so on. A civil engineer, if asked to rotate a bridge through 90° or to move it hundreds of miles, would consider the requester to be bereft of his or her senses. However, we think nothing of asking a software engineer to convert a batch operating system into a time-sharing one or to port it from one machine to another machine with totally different architectural characteristics. It is not unusual for 50 percent of the source code of an operating system to be rewritten over a 5-year period, especially if it is ported to new hardware. But no engineer would consent to replacing half a bridge; safety requirements would dictate that a new bridge be built. The area of maintenance is thus a second fundamental aspect in which software engineering differs from conventional engineering. Further maintenance aspects of software engineering are described in Section 1.3. But first, economic-oriented aspects are presented.

1.2 ECONOMIC ASPECTS

An insight into the relationship between software engineering and computer science can be obtained by comparing and contrasting the relationship between chemical engineering and chemistry. After all, computer science and chemistry are both sciences, and both have a theoretical component and a practical component. In the case of chemistry, the practical component is laboratory work; in the case of computer science, the practical component is programming.

Consider the process of extracting gasoline from coal. During World War II, the Germans used this process to make fuel for their war machine because they were largely cut off from oil supplies. While the anti-apartheid oil embargo was in effect, the government of the Republic of South Africa poured billions of dollars into SASOL (an Afrikaans acronym standing for "South African coal into oil"). About half of South Africa's liquid fuel needs were met in this way.

From the viewpoint of a chemist, there are many possible ways to convert coal into gasoline, and all are equally important. After all, no one chemical reaction is more important than any other. But from the chemical engineer's viewpoint, there is, at any one time, exactly one important mechanism for synthesizing gasoline from coal—namely, the reaction that is economically the most attractive. In other words, the chemical engineer evaluates all possible reactions, then rejects all but that one reaction for which the cost per liter is the lowest.

A similar relationship holds between computer science and software engineering. The computer scientist investigates a variety of ways to produce software, some good and some bad. But the software engineer is interested in only those techniques that make sound economic sense.

For instance, a software organization that is currently using coding technique CT_1 discovers that new coding technique CT_2 would result in code being produced in only nine-tenths of the time needed by CT_1. Common sense seems to dictate that CT_2 is the appropriate technique to use. In fact, although common sense certainly dictates that the faster technique is the technique of choice, the economics of software engineering may imply the opposite. For example, coding technique CT_2 may indeed be 10 percent faster than CT_1, and the resulting code may be of comparable quality from the viewpoint of satisfying the client's current needs. But the use of technique CT_2 may result in code that is difficult to maintain, thereby making the cost of CT_2 higher over the life of the product. Of course, if the software developer is not

---

1. Requirements phase (Chapter 7)

2. Specification (analysis) phase (Chapters 8 and 9)

3. Planning phase (Chapter 10)

4. Design phase (Chapter 11)

5. Implementation phase (Chapters 12 and 13)

6. Integration phase (Chapter 13)

7. Maintenance phase (Chapter 14)

8. Retirement

Figure 1.1   The phases of the software life cycle, and the chapters in this book in which they are presented.

responsible for any maintenance, then, from the viewpoint of that developer, CT_2 is a most attractive proposition. After all, use of CT_2 would cost 10 percent less. The client should insist that technique CT_1 be used and pay the higher initial cost, with the expectation that the total lifetime cost of the software will be lower. Unfortunately, it is often the case that the sole aim of both the client and the software provider is to produce code as quickly as possible. The long-term effects of using a particular technique are generally ignored in the interests of short-term gain. Applying economic principles to software engineering requires the client to choose techniques that reduce long-term costs.

The inclusion of maintenance cost when calculating software costs leads directly to the next section.

1.3   MAINTENANCE ASPECTS

The series of steps that software undergoes, from concept exploration through final retirement, is termed the *life cycle*. During this period the product goes through a series of phases: requirements, specification, planning, design, implementation, integration, maintenance, and retirement. Life-cycle models are discussed in detail in Chapter 3; the topic is introduced at this point so that the concept of maintenance can be defined.

Until the end of the 1970s most organizations were producing software using as their life-cycle model what is now termed the *waterfall model*. There are many variations of this model, but by and large the product goes through eight broad phases. These phases probably do not correspond exactly to the phases of any one particular organization, but they are sufficiently close to most practices for the purposes of this book. Similarly, the precise name of each phase varies from organization to organization. The names used here for the various phases have been chosen to be as general as possible in the hope that the reader will feel comfortable with them. For easy reference, the phases are summarized in Figure 1.1, which also indicates the chapters in this book in which they are presented.

1. *Requirements Phase:* The concept is explored and refined, and the client's requirements are elicited.

2. *Specification (Analysis) Phase:* The client's requirements are analyzed and presented in the form of the *specification document,* "what the product is supposed to do." This phase is sometimes called the analysis phase.

3. *Planning Phase:* A plan is drawn up, the *software project management plan,* describing the proposed software development in detail.

4. *Design Phase:* The specifications undergo two consecutive design processes. First comes *architectural design* in which the product as a whole is broken down into components, called *modules.* Then each module in turn is designed; this process is termed *detailed design.* The two resulting *design documents* describe "how the product does it."

5. *Implementation Phase:* The various components are coded and tested.

6. *Integration Phase:* The components of the product are combined and tested as a whole. When the developers are satisfied with the product, it is tested by the client *(acceptance testing).* This phase ends when the product is accepted by the client and goes into operations mode. (We will see in Chapter 13 that the integration phase should be performed in parallel with the implementation phase.)

7. *Maintenance Phase:* Maintenance includes all changes to the product once the client has agreed that it satisfies the specification document. Maintenance includes *corrective maintenance* (or software repair), which consists of the removal of residual faults while leaving the specifications unchanged, as well as *enhancement* (or software update), which consists of changes to the specifications and the implementation of those changes. There are, in turn, two types of enhancement. The first is *perfective maintenance,* changes that the client thinks will improve the effectiveness of the product, such as additional functionality or decreased response time. The second is *adaptive maintenance,* changes made in response to changes in the environment in which the product operates, such as new government regulations. Studies have indicated that, on average, maintainers spend approximately 17.5 percent of their time on corrective maintenance, 60.5 percent on perfective maintenance, and 18 percent on adaptive maintenance [Lientz, Swanson, and Tompkins, 1978].

8. *Retirement:* The product is removed from service.

Returning to the topic of maintenance, it is sometimes said that only bad software products undergo maintenance. In fact, the opposite is true; bad products are thrown away, whereas good products are repaired and enhanced, perhaps for 10 or 15 years. Furthermore, a software product is a model of the real world, and the real world is perpetually changing. As a consequence, software has to be maintained constantly in order to remain an accurate reflection of the real world.

For instance, if the sales tax rate changes from 6 percent to 7 percent, almost every software product that deals with buying or selling has to be changed. Suppose the product contains the Java statement

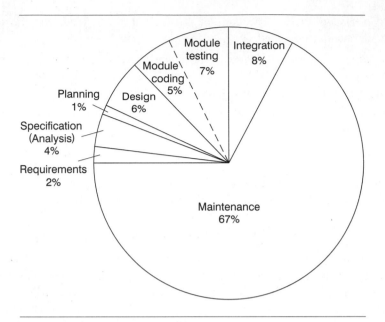

Figure 1.2 Approximate relative costs of the phases of the software life cycle.

public static final float salesTax = (**float**) 6.0;

declaring that salesTax is a floating-point constant, and is initialized to the value 6.0. In this case maintenance is relatively simple. With the aid of a text editor the value 6.0 is replaced by 7.0, and the code is recompiled and relinked. However, if instead of using the name salesTax, the actual value 6.0 has been used in the product wherever the value of the sales tax is invoked, then such a product will be extremely difficult to maintain. For example, there may be occurrences of the value 6.0 in the source code that should be changed to 7.0 but are overlooked, or instances of 6.0 that do not refer to sales tax, but will incorrectly be changed to 7.0. Finding these faults is almost always difficult and time-consuming. In fact, with some software it might be less expensive in the long run to throw the product away and recode it, rather than try to determine which of the many constants need to be changed and how to make the modifications.

The real-time real world is also constantly changing. The missiles with which a jet fighter is armed may be replaced by a new model, requiring a change in the weapons control component of the associated avionics system. A six-cylinder engine is to be offered as an option in a popular four-cylinder automobile; this implies changing the on-board computer that controls the carburetor, timing, and so on.

Healthy organizations change; only dying organizations are static. This means that maintenance in the form of enhancement is a positive part of an organization's activities, reflecting that the organization is on the move.

But just how much time is devoted to maintenance? The pie chart in Figure 1.2 was obtained by averaging data from various sources, including [Elshoff, 1976],

	Various Projects between 1976 and 1981	132 More Recent Hewlett-Packard Projects
Requirements, specification, and planning phases	21%	18%
Design phase	18	19
Implementation phase	36	34
Integration phase	24	29

Figure 1.3 Comparison of approximate average percentages of time spent on the development phases for various projects between 1976 and 1981 and for 132 more recent Hewlett-Packard projects.

[Daly, 1977], [Zelkowitz, Shaw, and Gannon, 1979], and [Boehm, 1981]. Figure 1.2 shows the approximate percentage of time (= money) spent on each phase of the software life cycle. Currently, the proportion of time spent on the various development phases is remarkably similar. This is shown in Figure 1.3, which compares the data in Figure 1.2 with more recent data on 132 Hewlett-Packard projects [Grady, 1994]. The data from Figure 1.2 has been grouped to make it comparable to the newer data.[1]

As can be seen from Figure 1.2, about two-thirds of total software costs is devoted to maintenance. Newer data confirms the continuing emphasis on maintenance. For example, in 1992 between 60 percent and 80 percent of research and development personnel at Hewlett-Packard was involved in maintenance, and maintenance constituted between 40 percent and 60 percent of the total cost of software [Coleman, Ash, Lowther, and Oman, 1994]. However, there are many organizations that currently devote as much as 80 percent of their time and effort to maintenance [Yourdon, 1992]. Thus maintenance is an extremely time-consuming and expensive phase of the software life cycle.

Consider again the software organization that is currently using coding technique CT_1, but a salesperson promises that CT_2 will reduce coding time by 10 percent. Even if CT_2 has no adverse effect on maintenance, an astute software manager will think twice before changing coding practices. The entire staff will have to be retrained, new software development tools purchased, and perhaps additional staff hired who are experienced in the new technique. All this expense and disruption will have to be endured for a possible 0.5 percent decrease in software costs because, as shown in Figure 1.2, module coding consumes on average only 5 percent of total software costs.

Now suppose a new technique that reduces maintenance by 10 percent is developed. This should be introduced at once because, on average, it will reduce overall costs by 6.7 percent. The overhead involved in changing to this technique is a small price to pay for such a large overall savings.

[1]Figure 1.3 reflects only the development phases. Thus the proportion of development time devoted to the requirements, specification, and planning phases in Figure 1.2 is $(2 + 4 + 1)/33$, or 21 percent, as shown in Figure 1.3.

Figure 1.4 Relative cost of fixing a fault at each phase of the software life cycle. The solid line is the best fit for the data relating to the larger software projects, and the dashed line is the best fit for the smaller software projects.
SOURCE: Barry Boehm, *Software Engineering Economics*, © 1981, p. 40. Adapted by permission of Prentice-Hall, Inc., Englewood Cliffs, NJ.

Because maintenance is so important, a major aspect of software engineering consists of those techniques, tools, and practices that lead to a reduction in maintenance costs.

1.4 SPECIFICATION AND DESIGN ASPECTS

Software professionals are human, and therefore sometimes we make an error while developing a product. As a result, there will be a fault in the software. If the error is made during the requirements phase, then the resulting fault will probably also appear in the specifications, the design, and the code. It is clear that the earlier we correct a fault, the better.

The relative costs of fixing a fault at various phases in the software life cycle are shown in Figure 1.4 [Boehm, 1981]. The figure reflects data from IBM [Fagan, 1974], GTE [Daly, 1977], the Safeguard project [Stephenson, 1976], and some smaller TRW projects [Boehm, 1980]. The solid straight line in Figure 1.4 is the best fit for the data relating to the larger projects, and the dashed line is the best fit for the

Figure 1.5   Solid line depicts points on solid line of Figure 1.4 plotted on a linear scale. Dashed line depicts newer data.

smaller projects. For each of the phases of the software life cycle, the corresponding relative cost to detect and correct a fault is depicted in Figure 1.5. Each step on the solid line in Figure 1.5 is constructed by taking the corresponding point on the solid straight line of Figure 1.4 and plotting the data on a linear scale.

Suppose that it costs $40 to detect and correct a specific fault during the design phase. From the solid line in Figure 1.5 (projects between 1974 and 1980), that same fault would cost only about $20 to fix during the specification phase. But during the maintenance phase, that fault would cost around $2,000 to detect and correct. Newer data show that it is now even more important to detect faults early. The dashed line in Figure 1.5 shows the cost of detecting and correcting a fault during the development of system software for the IBM AS/400 [Kan et al., 1994]. On average, the same fault would cost $3,680 to fix during the maintenance phase of the AS/400 software.

The reason that the cost of correcting a fault increases so steeply is related to what has to be done to correct a fault. Early in the development life cycle the product essentially exists only on paper and correcting a fault may simply mean using an eraser and pencil. At the other extreme is a product that has already been delivered to a client. At the very least, correcting a fault will mean editing the code, recompiling and relinking it, and then carefully testing. Next, it is critical to check that making the change has not created a new problem elsewhere in the product. All the relevant documentation, including manuals, then needs to be updated. Finally, the corrected product must be delivered and installed. The moral of the story is: We must find faults early, or else it will cost us money. We should therefore employ techniques for detecting faults during the requirements and specification phases.

There is a further need for such techniques. Studies have shown [Boehm, 1979] that between 60 percent and 70 percent of all faults detected in large-scale projects are specification or design faults. Newer results bear out this preponderance of specification and design faults. An *inspection* is a careful examination of a document by a team (Section 5.2.3). During 203 inspections of Jet Propulsion Laboratory software for the NASA unmanned interplanetary space program, on average about 1.9 faults were detected per page of a specification document, 0.9 faults per page of a design, but only 0.3 faults per page of code [Kelly, Sherif, and Hops, 1992].

Thus it is important that we improve our specification and design techniques not only so that faults can be found as early as possible, but also because specification and design faults constitute such a large proportion of all faults. Just as the example in the previous section showed that reducing maintenance costs by 10 percent will reduce overall costs by nearly 7 percent, reducing specification and design faults by 10 percent will reduce the overall number of faults by 6 percent to 7 percent.

Newer data on a number of projects are reported in [Bhandari et al., 1994]. For example, a compiler was undergoing extensive changes. At the end of the design phase, the faults detected during the project were categorized. Only 13 percent of the faults were carry-overs from previous versions of the compiler. Of the remaining faults, 16 percent were introduced during the specification phase, and 71 percent were introduced during the design phase. The fact that so many faults are introduced early in the software life cycle highlights another important aspect of software engineering, namely, techniques that yield better specifications and designs.

Most software is produced by a team of software engineers, rather than by a single individual who is responsible for every phase of the development and maintenance life cycle. We now consider the implications of this.

1.5   TEAM PROGRAMMING ASPECTS

The performance–price factor of a computer may be defined as follows:

$$\text{performance–price factor} = \text{time to perform } 1,000,000 \text{ additions} \times \text{cost of CPU and main memory}$$

This quantity has decreased by an order of magnitude with each succeeding generation of computers. That is to say, the performance–price factor has decreased by an order of magnitude six times over the past 30 years. This decrease has been a consequence of discoveries in electronics, particularly the transistor, and very large scale integration (VLSI).

The result of these discoveries has been that organizations can easily afford hardware that can run large products, that is, products too large to be written by one person within the allowed time constraints. For example, if a product has to be delivered within 18 months, but would take a single programmer 15 years to complete, then the product must be developed by a team. However, team programming leads to interface problems among code components and communications problems among team members.

For example, Joe and Freda code modules p and q respectively, where module p calls module q. When Joe codes p, he writes a call to q with five arguments in the argument list. Freda codes q with five arguments, but in a different order from those of Joe. Unless function prototypes are used, this will not be detected by an ANSI C compiler. A few software tools such as the Java compiler and interpreter, *lint* for C (Section 12.10.4), or an Ada linker will detect such a type violation, but only if the interchanged arguments are of different types; if they are of the same type, then the problem may not be detected for a long period of time. It may be debated that this is a design problem; and that if the modules had been more carefully designed, this problem would not have happened. That may be true, but what happens in practice is that the design is often changed after coding commences, but notification of a change is sometimes not distributed to all members of the development team. Thus, when a design that affects two or more programmers has been changed, poor communications can lead to the interface problems Joe and Freda experienced. This sort of problem does not occur when only one individual is responsible for every aspect of the product, as was the case before powerful computers that can run huge products became affordable.

But interfacing problems are merely the tip of the iceberg when it comes to problems that can arise when software is developed by teams. Unless the team is properly organized, an inordinate amount of time can be wasted in conferences between team members. Suppose that a product takes a single programmer 1 year to complete. If the same task is assigned to a team of three programmers, the time for completing the task is frequently closer to 1 year than the expected 4 months, and the quality of the resulting code may well be lower than if the task is assigned to one individual. Because a considerable proportion of today's software is being developed and maintained by teams, the scope of software engineering must also include techniques for ensuring that teams are properly organized and managed.

As has been shown in the preceding sections, the scope of software engineering is extremely broad. It includes every phase of the software life cycle, from requirements to retirement. It also includes human aspects, such as team organization; economic aspects; and legal aspects, such as copyright law. All these aspects are implicitly incorporated in the definition of software engineering given at the beginning of this chapter, namely, that software engineering is a discipline whose aim is the production of fault-free software, that is delivered on time, within budget, and that satisfies the user's needs.

1.6 THE OBJECT-ORIENTED PARADIGM

Since 1967 a wide variety of techniques have been suggested to help solve the software crisis. Major breakthroughs were made between approximately 1975 and

1985 with the development of the so-called structured paradigm. The techniques constituting the structured paradigm include structured systems analysis (Section 8.3), composite/structured design (Section 6.1), structured programming (Section 12.3), and structured testing (Section 12.16.2). These techniques seemed extremely promising when first used. However, as time passed they proved to be somewhat less successful in two respects. First, the techniques were sometimes unable to cope with the increasing size of software products. That is to say, the structured techniques were adequate when dealing with products of (say) 5,000 or even 50,000 lines of code. Today, however, products containing 500,000 lines of code are not considered large; even products of 5,000,000 or more lines of code are not that unusual. However, it turned out that the structured techniques frequently could not scale up sufficiently to be able to handle today's larger products.

The maintenance phase is the second area in which the structured paradigm has not lived up to earlier expectations. The major driving force behind the development of the structured paradigm 20 years ago was the fact that, on average, two-thirds of the software budget was being devoted to maintenance (see Figure 1.2). Unfortunately, the structured paradigm has not solved this problem; as pointed out in Section 1.3, there are still many organizations today that spend up to 80 percent of their time and effort on maintenance [Yourdon, 1992].

The introduction of the structured paradigm led to major improvements in the software industry. Before the structured paradigm was utilized, most software organizations did not use any specific techniques; each individual worked in his or her own way. The introduction of the structured paradigm within the industry was a major reason for the wide-scale adoption of software engineering practices. Nevertheless, the structured paradigm did not solve all the problems of software production.

The reason for the limited success of the structured paradigm is that the structured techniques are either action oriented or data oriented, but not both. The basic components of a software product are the actions[2] of the product and the data on which those actions operate. For example, **determine average height** is an action that operates on a collection of heights (data) and returns the average of those heights (data). Some structured techniques, such as data flow analysis (Section 11.3), are action oriented. That is to say, such techniques concentrate on the actions of the product; the data are of secondary importance. Conversely, techniques such as Jackson system development (Section 11.6) are data oriented. The emphasis here is on the data; the actions that operate on the data are of less significance.

In contrast, the object-oriented paradigm considers both data and actions to be of equal importance. A simplistic way of looking at an object is as a unified software component that incorporates both the data and the actions that operate on that data. This definition is incomplete and will be fleshed out later in the book, once *inheritance* has been defined (Section 6.7). Nevertheless, the definition captures much of the essence of an object.

A bank account is one example of an object (see Figure 1.6). The data component of the object is the **account balance.** The actions that can be performed

---

| [2]The word *action* is used here rather than *process* in order to avoid confusion with the term *software process.*

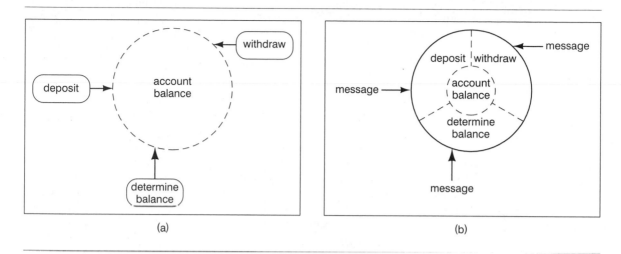

(a)   (b)

Figure 1.6 Comparison of implementations of a bank account using (a) structured paradigm and (b) object-oriented paradigm. Solid black line surrounding object denotes that details as to how account balance is implemented are not known outside object.

on that account balance include **deposit** money, **withdraw** money, and **determine balance**. From the viewpoint of the structured paradigm, a product that deals with banking would have to incorporate a data element, namely the **account balance**, and three actions, namely, **deposit**, **withdraw**, and **determine balance**. From the object-oriented viewpoint, a bank account is an object. This object combines a data element together with the three actions performed on that data element in a single unit.

Up to now, there seems to be little difference between the two approaches. However, a key point is the way in which an object is implemented. Specifically, details as to how the data element of an object is stored are not known from outside the object. This is an instance of "information hiding" and is discussed in more detail in Section 6.6. Thus, in the case of the bank account object shown in Figure 1.6(b), the rest of the software product is aware of the fact that there is such a thing as a balance within a bank account object, but it has no idea as to the format of **account balance**. That is to say, there is no knowledge outside the object as to whether the account balance is implemented as an integer or a floating-point number, or whether it is a field (component) of some larger structure. This information barrier surrounding the object is denoted by the solid black line in Figure 1.6(b), which depicts an implementation using the object-oriented paradigm. In contrast, there is a dashed line surrounding **account balance** in Figure 1.6(a), because all details of **account balance** are known to the modules in the implementation using the structured paradigm, and the value of **account balance** can therefore be changed by any of them.

Returning to Figure 1.6(b), the object-oriented implementation: If a customer deposits $10 in an account, then a message is sent to the **deposit** action (*method*) of the relevant object telling it to increment the **account balance** data element (*instance* *voriable*) by $10. The **deposit** method is within the bank account object and knows how the **account balance** instance variable is implemented; this is denoted by the dashed line inside the object. But there is no need for any entity external to the object to have this knowledge. The fact that the three methods in Figure 1.6(b) shield **account balance** from the rest of the product symbolizes this localization of knowledge.

At first sight, the fact that implementation details are local to an object may not seem to be terribly useful. The payoff comes during maintenance. First, suppose that the banking product has been constructed using the structured paradigm. If the way that an **account balance** is represented is changed from (say) an integer to a field of a structure, then every part of that product that has anything to do with an **account balance** has to be changed, and these changes have to be made consistently. In contrast, if the object-oriented paradigm is used, then the only changes that need be made are within the bank account object itself. No other part of the product has knowledge of how an **account balance** is implemented, so no other part can have access to an **account balance**. Consequently, no other part of the banking product needs to be changed. Thus, the object-oriented paradigm makes maintenance quicker and easier, and the chance of introducing a regression fault (that is, a fault inadvertently introduced into one part of a product as a consequence of making an apparently unrelated change to another part of the product) is greatly reduced.

In addition to maintenance benefits, the object-oriented paradigm makes development easier. In many instances, an object has a physical counterpart. For example, the object **bank account** in the bank product corresponds to an actual bank account in the bank for which this product is being written. As will be shown in Chapter 9, modeling plays a major role in the object-oriented paradigm. The close correspondence between the objects in a product and their counterparts in the real world promotes better software development.

There is yet another way of looking at the benefits of the object-oriented paradigm. Well-designed objects are independent units. As has been explained, an object consists of both data and the actions that are performed on that data. If all the actions that are performed on the data of an object are included in that object, then the object can be considered a conceptually independent entity. Everything in the product that relates to the portion of the real world modeled by that object can be found in the object itself. This conceptual independence is sometimes termed *encapsulation* (Section 6.4.1). But there is an additional form of independence, namely, physical independence. In a well-designed object, information hiding ensures that implementation details are hidden from everything outside that object. The only allowable form of communication is the sending of a message to the object to carry out a specific action. The way that the action is carried out is entirely the responsibility of the object itself. For this reason, object-oriented design is sometimes referred to as *responsibility-driven design* [Wirfs-Brock, Wilkerson, and Wiener, 1990] or *design by contract* [Meyer 1992a]. (For another view of responsibility-driven design, see the Just in Case You Wanted to Know box on page 21.)

A product that has been built using the structured paradigm is essentially a single unit. This is one reason why the structured paradigm has been less successful when applied to larger products. In contrast, when the object-oriented paradigm is

---

JUST IN CASE YOU WANTED TO KNOW

Suppose that you live in New Orleans, and you want to have a floral arrangement delivered to your aunt in Iowa City on her birthday [Budd, 1991]. One way would be to try to obtain a list of all the florists in Iowa City and then determine which one is located closest to your aunt's home. An easier way is to call 1-800-FLOWERS and leave the entire responsibility for delivering the floral arrangement to that organization.

You do not need to know the identity of the Iowa City florist who will deliver the flowers.

In exactly the same way, when a message is sent to an object, not only is it entirely irrelevant how the request is carried out, but the unit that sends the message is not even allowed to know the internal structure of the object. The object itself is totally responsible for every detail of carrying out the message.

---

correctly used, the resulting product consists of a number of smaller, essentially independent units. The object-oriented paradigm reduces the level of complexity of a software product and simplifies both development and maintenance.

Another positive feature of the object-oriented paradigm is that it promotes reuse; because objects are independent entities, they can be utilized in future products. This reuse of objects reduces the time and cost of both development and maintenance, as explained in Chapter 6.

When the object-oriented paradigm is utilized, the software life cycle (Figure 1.1) has to be modified somewhat. Figure 1.7 shows the software life cycles of both the structured and object-oriented paradigms. To appreciate the difference, first consider the design phase of the structured paradigm. As stated in Section 1.3, this phase is divided into two subphases, namely, architectural design followed by detailed design. In the architectural design subphase, the product is decomposed into components, called modules. Then, during the detailed design subphase, the data structures and algorithms of each module are designed in turn. Finally, during the implementation phase, these modules are implemented.

If the object-oriented paradigm is used instead, one of the steps during the analysis phase is to determine the objects. Because an object is a kind of module, architectural design is therefore performed during the object-oriented analysis phase. Thus, object-oriented analysis goes further than the corresponding specification (analysis) phase of the structured paradigm. This is shown in Figure 1.8.

This difference between the two paradigms has major consequences. When the structured paradigm is used, there is almost always a sharp transition between the analysis (specification) phase and the design phase. After all, the aim of the specification phase is to determine *what* the product is to do, whereas the purpose of the design phase is to decide *how* to do it. In contrast, when object-oriented analysis is used, objects enter the life cycle at the very beginning. The objects are extracted in the analysis phase, designed in the design phase, and coded in the implementation phase. Thus, the object-oriented paradigm is an integrated approach; the transition from phase to phase is far smoother than with the structured paradigm, thereby reducing the number of faults during development.

Structured Paradigm	Object-Oriented Paradigm
1. Requirements phase	1. Requirements phase
2. Specification (analysis) phase	2′. Object-oriented analysis phase
3. Planning phase	3. Planning phase
4. Design phase	4′. Object-oriented design phase
5. Implementation phase	5′. Object-oriented programming phase
6. Integration phase	6. Integration phase
7. Maintenance phase	7. Maintenance phase
8. Retirement	8. Retirement

Figure 1.7 Comparison of life cycles of structured paradigm and object-oriented paradigm.

As already mentioned, it is inadequate to define an object merely as a software component that encapsulates both data and actions and implements information hiding. A more complete definition is given in Chapter 6 when objects are examined in depth. But first, the terminology used in this book must be considered in greater detail.

1.7 TERMINOLOGY

Since the 1970s the difference between a *program* and a *system* has become blurred. In the "good old days" the distinction was clear. A program was an autonomous piece of code, generally in the form of a deck of punched cards, that could be executed. A system was a related collection of programs. Thus a system might consist of programs P, Q, R, and S. Magnetic tape T_1 was mounted, then program P was run. It caused a deck of data cards to be read in and produced as output tapes T_2 and T_3. Tape T_2 was then rewound, and program Q was run, producing tape T_4 as

Structured Paradigm	Object-Oriented Paradigm
2. Specification (analysis) phase	2′. Object-oriented analysis phase
• Determine what the product does	• Determine what the product does • Extract the objects
4. Design phase	4′. Object-oriented design phase
• Architectural design (extract the modules) • Detailed design	• Detailed design
5. Implementation phase	5′. Object-oriented programming phase
• Implement in appropriate programming language	• Implement in appropriate object-oriented programming language

Figure 1.8 Differences between structured paradigm and object-oriented paradigm.

output. Program R now merged tapes T_3 and T_4 into tape T_5; T_5 served as input for program S, which printed a series of reports.

Compare that situation with a product, running on a machine with a front-end communications processor and a back-end database manager, that performs real-time control of a steel mill. The single piece of software controlling the steel mill does far more than the old-fashioned system, but in terms of the classic definitions of program and system, this software is undoubtedly a program. To add to the confusion, the term *system* is now also used to denote the hardware–software combination. For example, the flight control system in an aircraft consists of both the in-flight computers and the software running on them. Depending on who is using the term, the flight control system may also include the controls, such as the joystick, that send commands to the computer, and the parts of the aircraft, such as the wing flaps, that are controlled by the computer.

A word that is used on almost every page of this book is *software*. Software consists of not just code in machine-readable form, but also all the documentation that is an intrinsic component of every project. Thus software includes the specification document, the design document, legal and accounting documents of all kinds, the software project management plan and other management documents, as well as all types of manuals.

In order to minimize confusion, this book uses the term *product* to denote a nontrivial piece of software. There are two reasons for this convention. The first is simply to obviate the program versus system confusion by using a third term. The second reason is more important: This book deals with the process of software production, and the end result of a process is termed a *product. Software production* then consists of two phases: *software development* followed by *maintenance*. Finally, the term *system* is used in its modern sense, that is, the combined hardware and software; or as part of universally accepted phrases, such as operating system and management information system.

Two words that are widely used within the context of software engineering are *methodology* and *paradigm*. Both are used in the same sense, namely, a collection of techniques that cover the life cycle. This usage offends language purists; after all, "methodology" means the science of methods, and a "paradigm" is a model or a pattern. Notwithstanding the best efforts of the author and others to encourage software engineers to use the words correctly, the practice is now so widespread that, in the interests of clarity, both words are used in this book in the sense of a *collection of techniques*. Erudite readers who are offended by this corruption of the English language are warmly invited to take up the cudgels of linguistic accuracy on the author's behalf; he is tired of tilting at windmills!

One term that is avoided as far as possible is *bug* (the history of this word is in the Just in Case You Wanted to Know box on page 24). The term *bug* nowadays is simply a euphemism for error. Although there is generally no real harm in using euphemisms, the word bug has overtones that are not conducive to good software production. Specifically, instead of saying, "I made an error," a programmer will say, "A bug crept into the code" (not *my* code, but *the* code), thereby transferring responsibility for the error from the programmer to the bug. No one blames a

---

JUST IN CASE YOU WANTED TO KNOW

The first use of the word *bug* to denote a fault is attributed to the late Rear Admiral Grace Murray Hopper, one of the designers of COBOL. On September 9, 1945, a moth flew into the Mark II computer that Hopper and her colleagues used at Harvard, and lodged between the contact plates of a relay. Thus there was literally a bug in the system. Hopper taped the bug to the log book and wrote, "First actual case of bug being found." The log book, with moth still attached, is in the Naval Museum at the Naval Surface Weapons Center, in Dahlgren, Virginia.

While this may have been the first use of "bug" within a computer context, the word was used in engineering slang in the nineteenth century [Shapiro, 1994]. For example, Thomas Alva Edison wrote on November 18, 1878, "This thing gives out and then that—'Bugs'—as such little faults and difficulties are called . . . " [Josephson, 1992]. One of the definitions of a bug in the 1934 Edition of *Webster's New English Dictionary* is "A defect in apparatus or its operation." It is clear from Hopper's remark that she, too, was familiar with the use of the word in that context, otherwise she would have explained what she meant.

---

programmer for coming down with a case of influenza, because flu is caused by the flu bug. Referring to an error as a bug is a way of casting off responsibility. In contrast, the programmer who says, "I made an error," is a computer professional who takes responsibility for his or her actions.

There is considerable confusion regarding object-oriented terminology. For example, in addition to the term *attribute* for a data component of an object, the term *state variable* is sometimes used in the object-oriented literature. In Java, the term is *instance variable;* in C++ the term *field* is used. With regard to the actions of an object, the term *method* is usually used; in C++, however, the term is *member function*. In C++, a *member* of an object refers to either an attribute ("field") or a method. In Java, the term *field* is used to denote either an attribute ("instance variable") or a method. In order to avoid confusion, wherever possible the generic terms *attribute* and *method* are used in this book.

Thankfully, some terminology is widely accepted. For example, when a method within an object is invoked, this is almost universally termed *sending a message* to the object.

The last item in this chapter is the Just in Case You Wanted to Know box on page 25 explaining the origin of the name *Java*.

Chapter Review

Software engineering is defined (Section 1.1) as a discipline whose aim is the production of fault-free software that satisfies the user's needs and that is delivered on time and within budget. In order to achieve this goal, appropriate techniques have to be used in all phases of software production, including specification and design (Section 1.4) and maintenance (Section 1.3). Software engineering addresses all phases of the software life cycle and incorporates aspects of many different areas of

---

JUST IN CASE YOU WANTED TO KNOW

In 1991 James Gosling of Sun Microsystems developed Java. While he was developing the language, he frequently stared out the window at a large oak tree outside his office. In fact, he did this so often that he decided to name his new language *Oak*. However, his choice of name was unacceptable to Sun becaue it could not be copyrighted, and without a copyright Sun would lose control of the language, as explained in Section 12.10.4.

After an intensive search for a name that was both copyrightable and easy to remember, Gosling's group came up with *Java*. During the 18th century, much of the coffee imported into England was grown in Java, the most populous island in the Dutch East Indies (now Indonesia). As a result, *Java* is now a slang word for coffee, the third most popular beverage among software engineers. Unfortunately, the names of the Big Two carbonated cola beverages have already been copyrighted.

---

human knowledge, including economics (Section 1.2) and the social sciences (Section 1.5). In Section 1.6, objects are introduced, and a brief comparison between the structured and object-oriented paradigms is made. In the final section (Section 1.7), the terminology used in this book is explained.

For Further Reading

Boehm is a valuable source of further information on the scope of software engineering [Boehm, 1976; Boehm and Papaccio, 1988]. Other excellent papers on that topic include [Goldberg, 1986], [Mathis, 1986], and [Card, McGarry, and Page, 1987]. [DeMarco and Lister, 1989] is a report on the extent to which software engineering techniques are actually used in practice. For an analysis of the extent to which software engineering can be considered to be a true engineering discipline, see [Shaw, 1990].

The current practice of software engineering is described in [Yourdon, 1992]. For a view on the importance of maintenance in software engineering and how to plan for it, see [Parnas, 1994]. A forecast of the future of software engineering is given in [Basili and Musa, 1991].

The unreliability of software and the resulting risks (especially in safety-critical systems) are discussed in [Littlewood and Strigini, 1992] and [Mellor, 1994]. A modern view on the software crisis appears in [Gibbs, 1994].

The fact that mathematics underpins software engineering is stressed in [Parnas, 1990]. For an introduction to the importance of economics in software engineering, consult [Boehm, 1981].

The two classics on the social sciences and software engineering are [Weinberg, 1971] and [Shneiderman, 1980]. Neither book requires prior knowledge of psychology or the behavioral sciences in general. A newer book on the topic is [DeMarco and Lister, 1987].

Brooks's classic book, *The Mythical Man-Month* [Brooks, 1975], is a highly recommended introduction to the realities of software engineering. The book includes sections on all the topics mentioned in this chapter.

An excellent introduction to the object-oriented paradigm is [Budd, 1991]. Three successful projects carried using the object-oriented paradigm are described in [Capper, Colgate, Hunter, and James, 1994]. [Scholtz et al., 1993] is a report on a workshop held in April 1993 on the state of the art and the practice of object-oriented programming. Important articles on the object-oriented paradigm are found in the October 1992 issue of *IEEE Computer*, the January 1993 issue of *IEEE Software*, and the January 1993 and November 1993 issues of the *Journal of Systems and Software*.

Problems

1.1   You are in charge of developing a package that will handle all aspects of billing for a cable television company and ensuring that the package will be delivered on time and within budget. Your development budget is $320,000. Approximately how much money should you devote to each phase of the software life cycle?

1.2   You are a software-engineering consultant. The vice-president for sales of a major regional shoe retailing chain wants you to develop a product that will carry out all the accounting functions of the company and will also provide online information regarding orders and inventory in the various company warehouses. Terminals are required for 12 accounting clerks, 35 order clerks, and 40 warehouse clerks. In addition, 15 managers must be able to access data. The president is willing to pay $35,000 for the hardware and the software together and wants the complete product in 3 weeks. What do you tell him? Bear in mind that as a consultant you want his business, no matter how unreasonable his request.

1.3   You are an admiral in the Velorian Navy. It has been decided to call in a software development organization to develop the control software for a new generation of ship-to-ship missiles. You are in charge of supervising the project. In order to protect the government of Veloria, what clauses do you include in the contract with the software developers?

1.4   You are a software engineer and your job is to supervise the development of the software in Problem 1.3. List ways that your company can fail to satisfy the contract with the Navy. What are the probable causes of such failures?

1.5   Eighteen months after delivery, a fault is detected in a chemical engineering product that determines the optimal temperature for brewing beer. The cost of fixing the fault is $12,400. The cause of the fault is an ambiguous sentence in the specification document. Approximately how much would it have cost to have corrected the fault during the specification phase?

Suppose that the fault in Problem 1.5 had been detected during the implementation **1.6** phase. Approximately how much would it have cost to have fixed it then?

You are the president of an organization that builds large-scale software. You show **1.7** Figure 1.5 to your employees, urging them to find faults early in the software life cycle. Someone responds that it is unreasonable to expect anyone to remove faults before they have entered the product. For example, how can anyone remove a fault during the design phase if the fault in question is a coding fault? What do you reply?

Look up the word *system* in a dictionary. How many different definitions are there? **1.8** Write down those definitions that are applicable within the context of software engineering.

It is your first day at your first job. Your manager hands you a listing and says, "See if **1.9** you can find the bug." What do you reply?

You are in charge of developing the product in Problem 1.1. Will you use the object- **1.10** oriented paradigm or the structured paradigm? Give reasons for your answer.

(Term Project) Suppose that the Osbert Oglesby product described in Appendix A **1.11** has been implemented exactly as described. Now a more accurate formula for estimating the value of a masterwork is discovered. In what ways will the existing product have to be changed? Would it be better to discard everything and start again from scratch?

(Readings in Software Engineering) Your instructor will distribute copies of [Snyder, **1.12** 1993]. Why do you think that there are so many different terms for the various object-oriented concepts?

References

[Basili and Musa, 1991] V. R. BASILI AND J. D. MUSA, "The Future Engineering of Software: A Management Perspective," *IEEE Computer* **24** (September 1991), pp. 90–96.

[Bhandari et al., 1994] I. BHANDARI, M. J. HALLIDAY, J. CHAAR, R. CHILLAREGE, K. JONES, J. S. ATKINSON, C. LEPORI-COSTELLO, P. Y. JASPER, E. D. TARVER, C. C. LEWIS, AND M. YONEZAWA, "In-Process Improvement through Defect Data Interpretation," *IBM Systems Journal* **33** (No. 1, 1994), pp. 182–214.

[Boehm, 1976] B. W. BOEHM, "Software Engineering," *IEEE Transactions on Computers* **C-25** (December 1976), pp. 1226–1241.

[Boehm, 1979] B. W. BOEHM, "Software Engineering, R & D Trends and Defense Needs," in: *Research Directions in Software Technology*, P. Wegner (Editor), The MIT Press, Cambridge, MA, 1979.

[Boehm, 1980] B. W. BOEHM, "Developing Small-Scale Application Software Products: Some Experimental Results," *Proceedings of the Eighth IFIP World Computer Congress*, October 1980, pp. 321–326.

[Boehm, 1981] B. W. BOEHM, *Software Engineering Economics*, Prentice-Hall, Englewood Cliffs, NJ, 1981.

[Boehm and Papaccio, 1988] B. W. BOEHM AND P. N. PAPACCIO, "Understanding and Controlling Software Costs," *IEEE Transactions on Software Engineering* **14** (October 1988), pp. 1462–1477.

[Brooks, 1975] F. P. BROOKS, JR., *The Mythical Man-Month: Essays on Software Engineering*, Addison-Wesley, Reading, MA, 1975.

[Budd, 1991] T. A. BUDD, *An Introduction to Object-Oriented Programming*, Addison-Wesley, Reading, MA, 1991.

[Capper, Colgate, Hunter, and James, 1994] N. P. CAPPER, R. J. COLGATE, J. C. HUNTER, AND M. F. JAMES, "The Impact of Object-Oriented Technology on Software Quality: Three Case Histories," *IBM Systems Journal* **33** (No. 1, 1994), pp. 131–157.

[Card, McGarry, and Page, 1987] D. N. CARD, F. E. MCGARRY, AND G. T. PAGE, "Evaluating Software Engineering Technologies," *IEEE Transactions on Software Engineering* **SE-13** (July 1987), pp. 845–851.

[Coleman, Ash, Lowther, and Oman, 1994] D. COLEMAN, D. ASH, B. LOWTHER, AND P. OMAN, "Using Metrics to Evaluate Software System Maintainability," *IEEE Computer* **27** (August 1994), pp. 44–49.

[Daly, 1977] E. B. DALY, "Management of Software Development," *IEEE Transactions on Software Engineering* **SE-3** (May 1977), pp. 229–242.

[DeMarco and Lister, 1987] T. DEMARCO AND T. LISTER, *Peopleware: Productive Projects and Teams*, Dorset House, New York, 1987.

[DeMarco and Lister, 1989] T. DEMARCO AND T. LISTER, "Software Development: The State of the Art vs. State of the Practice," *Proceedings of the 11th International Conference on Software Engineering*, Pittsburgh, May 1989, pp. 271–275.

[Elshoff, 1976] J. L. ELSHOFF, "An Analysis of Some Commercial PL/I Programs," *IEEE Transactions on Software Engineering* **SE-2** (June 1976), 113–120.

[Fagan, 1974] M. E. FAGAN, "Design and Code Inspections and Process Control in the Development of Programs," Technical Report IBM-SSD TR 21.572, IBM Corporation, December 1974.

[Gibbs, 1994] W. W. GIBBS, "Software's Chronic Crisis," *Scientific American* **271** (September 1994), pp. 86–95.

[Goldberg, 1986] R. GOLDBERG, "Software Engineering: An Emerging Discipline," *IBM Systems Journal* **25** (No. 3/4, 1986), pp. 334–353.

[Grady, 1994] R. B. GRADY, "Successfully Applying Software Metrics," *IEEE Computer* **27** (September 1994), pp. 18–25.

[Josephson, 1992] M. JOSEPHSON, *Edison, A Biography*, John Wiley and Sons, New York, 1992.

[Kan et al., 1994] S. H. KAN, S. D. DULL, D. N. AMUNDSON, R. J. LINDNER, AND R. J. HEDGER, "AS/400 Software Quality Management," *IBM Systems Journal* **33** (No. 1, 1994), pp. 62–88.

[Kelly, Sherif, and Hops, 1992] J. C. KELLY, J. S. SHERIF, AND J. HOPS, "An Analysis of Defect Densities Found during Software Inspections," *Journal of Systems and Software* **17** (January 1992), pp. 111–117.

[Leveson and Turner, 1993] N. G. LEVESON AND C. S. TURNER, "An Investigation of the Therac-25 Accidents," *IEEE Computer* **26** (July 1993), pp. 18–41.

[Lientz, Swanson, and Tompkins, 1978] B. P. LIENTZ, E. B. SWANSON, AND G. E. TOMPKINS, "Characteristics of Application Software Maintenance," *Communications of the ACM* **21** (June 1978), pp. 466–471.

[Littlewood and Strigini, 1992] B. LITTLEWOOD AND L. STRIGINI, "The Risks of Software," *Scientific American* **267** (November 1992), pp. 62–75.

[Mathis, 1986] R. F. MATHIS, "The Last 10 Percent," *IEEE Transactions on Software Engineering* **SE-12** (June 1986), pp. 705–712.

[Mellor, 1994] P. MELLOR, "CAD: Computer-Aided Disaster," Technical Report, Centre for Software Reliability, City University, London, UK, July 1994.

[Meyer, 1992a] B. MEYER, "Applying 'Design by Contract'," *IEEE Computer* **25** (October 1992), pp. 40–51.

[Naur, Randell, and Buxton, 1976] P. NAUR, B. RANDELL, AND J. N. BUXTON (Editors), *Software Engineering: Concepts and Techniques: Proceedings of the NATO Conferences*, Petrocelli-Charter, New York, 1976.

[Neumann, 1980] P. G. NEUMANN, Letter from the Editor, *ACM SIGSOFT Software Engineering Notes* **5** (July 1980), p. 2.

[Parnas, 1990] D. L. PARNAS, "Education for Computing Professionals" *IEEE Computer* **23** (January 1990), pp. 17–22.

[Parnas, 1994] D. L. PARNAS, "Software Aging," *Proceedings of the 16th International Conference on Software Engineering*, Sorrento, Italy, May 1994, pp. 279–287.

[Scholtz et al., 1993] J. SCHOLTZ, S. CHIDAMBER, R. GLASS, A. GOERNER, M. B. ROSSON, M. STARK, AND I. VESSEY, "Object-Oriented Programming: The Promise and the Reality," *Journal of Systems and Software* **23** (November 1993), pp. 199–204.

[Shapiro, 1994] F. R. SHAPIRO, "The First Bug," *Byte* **19** (April 1994), p. 308.

[Shaw, 1990] M. SHAW, "Prospects for an Engineering Discipline of Software," *IEEE Software* **7** (November 1990), pp. 15–24.

[Shneiderman, 1980] B. SHNEIDERMAN, *Software Psychology: Human Factors in Computer and Information Systems*, Winthrop Publishers, Cambridge, MA, 1980.

[Snyder, 1993] A. SNYDER, "The Essence of Objects: Concepts and Terms," *IEEE Software* **10** (January 1993), pp. 31–42.

[Stephenson, 1976] W. E. STEPHENSON, "An Analysis of the Resources Used in Safeguard System Software Development," Bell Laboratories, Draft Paper, August 1976.

[Weinberg, 1971] G. M. WEINBERG, *The Psychology of Computer Programming*, Van Nostrand Reinhold, New York, 1971.

[Wirfs-Brock, Wilkerson, and Wiener, 1990] R. WIRFS-BROCK, B. WILKERSON, AND L. WIENER, *Designing Object-Oriented Software*, Prentice-Hall, Englewood Cliffs, NJ, 1990.

[Yourdon, 1992] E. YOURDON, *Decline and Fall of the American Programmer*, Yourdon Press, Englewood Cliffs, NJ, 1992.

[Zelkowitz, Shaw, and Gannon, 1979] M. V. ZELKOWITZ, A. C. SHAW, AND J. D. GANNON, *Principles of Software Engineering and Design*, Prentice-Hall, Englewood Cliffs, NJ, 1979.

2

THE SOFTWARE PROCESS AND ITS PROBLEMS

The software process is the way we produce software. It incorporates the software life-cycle model (Section 1.3), the tools we use (Section 4.3), and the individuals building the software.

Different organizations have different software processes. For example, consider the issue of documentation. Some organizations consider the software they produce to be self-documenting; that is, the product can be understood simply by reading the source code. Other organizations, however, are documentation intensive. They perform careful design activities, check and recheck designs before coding commences, and give detailed descriptions of each module to the programmers. Test cases are preplanned, the result of each test run is logged, and the test data are carefully filed. Once the product enters the maintenance phase, any suggested change must be proposed in writing, with detailed reasons for making the change. The proposed change can be made only with written authorization, and the modification is not integrated into the product until the documentation has been updated and the changes to the documentation approved.

Intensity of testing is another measure by which organizations can be compared. Some organizations devote up to half their software budgets to the testing of software, whereas others feel that only the user can thoroughly test a product. Consequently, some companies devote minimal time and effort to testing the product, but spend a considerable amount of time fixing faults detected by the user.

Maintenance is a major preoccupation of many software organizations. Software that is 5, 10, or even 20 years old is continually enhanced to meet changing needs; in addition, residual faults continue to appear, even after the software has been in successful operations mode for many years. In contrast, other organizations are essentially concerned with research, leaving development, let alone maintenance, to others. This applies particularly to university computer science departments, where graduate students build software to prove that a particular design or technique is feasible. The commercial exploitation of the validated concept is then left to other organizations. (See the Just in Case You Wanted to Know box on page 31 regarding the wide variation in the ways different organizations develop software.)

However, regardless of the exact procedure, the software process broadly follows the phases outlined in Section 1.3, namely, requirements, specification, planning, design, implementation, integration, maintenance, and retirement. Some of these phases are known by other names. One example is that the requirements and specification phases together are sometimes called *systems analysis*. Another example is the maintenance

JUST IN CASE YOU WANTED TO KNOW

Why does the software process vary so drastically from organization to organization? A major reason is lack of software engineering skills. All too many software professionals simply do not keep up-to-date. They continue to develop software the Olde Fashioned Way, because they do not know any other way.

Another reason for differences in the software process is that many software managers are excellent managers, but know precious little about software development or maintenance. Their lack of technical knowledge can result in the project slipping so badly behind schedule that there is no point in continuing. This is frequently the reason that many software projects are never completed.

Another reason for differences among processes is management outlook. For example, one organization may decide that it is better to deliver a product on time, even if it is not adequately tested. Given the identical circumstances, a different organization might conclude that the risk of delivering that product without comprehensive testing would be far greater than taking the time to test the product thoroughly.

The bottom line is that software is developed by people, and the process within a given organization depends first and foremost on the individuals working in that organization. If those individuals are ethical, hard-working, intelligent, sensible, and up-to-date, then the chances are good that the software process within that organization will be satisfactory. Unfortunately, the converse is equally true.

phase. Once the client agrees that the product has passed its acceptance test, the product can be used to perform useful work. For this reason, the maintenance phase is sometimes referred to as *operations mode*. Furthermore, certain phases may be subdivided; for instance, the design phase is almost always broken down into *architectural design* and *detailed design*.

In the preceding list of phases there is no separate testing phase. This omission is deliberate. Testing is not a separate phase, but rather an activity that takes place all the way through software production. The requirements have to be tested, the specification document has to be tested, the design has to be tested, and so on. There are times in the process when testing is carried out to the almost total exclusion of other activities. This occurs toward the end of each phase (*verification*) and is especially true before the product is handed over to the client (*validation*). Although there are times when testing predominates, there should never be times when no testing is being performed. If testing is treated as a separate phase, then there is a very real danger that testing will not be carried out constantly through every phase of the product development and maintenance process.

There is also no separate documentation phase. It is important that each phase be fully documented before the next phase begins. First, the pressures to deliver a product on time are such that postponed documentation may never be completed. Second, the individual responsible for an early phase in the software process may have been transferred to a different area of responsibility or be working for another organization by the time the documentation has to be produced. Third, a product is constantly changing during development. For example, the design will usually have to be modified during the implementation phase to take into account new information about the product. Unless the design has been fully documented by the design team,

---

JUST IN CASE YOU WANTED TO KNOW

In practice, software development does not always progress as smoothly as suggested here. That is to say, the various phases of the life cycle can overlap. Instead of a clean division into eight separate phases, what frequently happens is: "Specify some, design some, code some, then specify some more, design some more, and so on."

Such an incremental process (Section 3.4) can be most productive, provided that the process is strictly followed. What happens all too often, however, is that some pieces are coded before they have been properly designed, and some parts are designed before they have been properly specified.

For this reason, I advocate phasewise software development, unless your organization is well managed and can handle an incremental process. But many organizations cannot work incrementally, and for them I strongly recommend a strict phasewise approach.

---

modifications to the design will be extremely difficult to achieve. Furthermore, it will not be easy for the original designers to document their design after it has been modified. For all these reasons, the documentation for each phase of the software development process must be completed by the team responsible for that phase— before the next phase starts. Furthermore, the documentation must always be updated to reflect the current version of the product.

In this chapter the phases through which a product passes are described (but see the Just in Case You Wanted to Know box on this page), together with potential difficulties that may arise during each phase. In addition, testing procedures appropriate to each phase are described. Finally, in Section 2.10 inherent difficulties of software production as a whole are presented. Solutions to the difficulties associated with the production of software are usually nontrivial, and the rest of this book is devoted to describing suitable techniques. In this chapter, then, only the difficulties are highlighted, but the reader is guided to the relevant sections or chapters for solutions. Thus this chapter is not only an overview of the software process, but it is also a guide to much of the rest of this book.

2.1   CLIENT, DEVELOPER, AND USER

Some preliminary definitions are needed here. The *client* is the individual or organization who wants a product to be developed. The *developers* are the members of the organization responsible for producing that product. The developers may be responsible for every aspect of the process, from the requirements phase onwards, or they may be responsible for only the implementation of an already designed product. The term *software development* covers all aspects of software production before the product enters the maintenance phase. Any task that is a step toward building a piece of software, including specifying, planning, designing, testing, or documenting, constitutes software development. And after it has been developed, the software is maintained.

The client and developers may both be part of the same organization. For example, the client may be the head actuary of an insurance company, and the developers a team headed by the vice-president for management information systems of that insurance company. This is termed *internal* software development. On the other hand, with *contract* software the client and developers are two totally independent organizations. For instance, the client may be the Department of Defense, and the developers a major defense contractor specializing in software for weapons systems. On a much smaller scale, the client may be an accountant in a one-person practice, and the developer a student who earns income by writing software on a part-time basis.

The third party involved in software production is the *user*. The user is the person or persons on whose behalf the client has commissioned the product and who will utilize the software. In the insurance company example, the users may be insurance agents who will use the software to select the most appropriate policy. In some instances the client and the user will be the same person (for example, the accountant discussed previously).

The rest of this chapter presents the eight phases of the software life cycle, and carefully analyzes the role played by testing in each phase. The first phase is the requirements phase.

2.2 REQUIREMENTS PHASE

Software development is an expensive process. The development process usually begins when the client approaches a development organization with regard to a piece of software that, in the opinion of the client, is either essential to the profitability of his or her enterprise or can somehow be economically justified. At any stage of the process, if the client stops believing that the software is cost-effective, development will immediately terminate. Throughout this chapter the assumption is made that the client feels that the cost is justified.

At an initial meeting between client and developers, the client will outline the product as he or she conceptualizes it. From the viewpoint of the developers, the client's description of the product may be vague, unreasonable, contradictory, or simply impossible to achieve. The task of the developers at this stage is to determine exactly what it is that the client needs and to find out from the client what constraints exist. Typical constraints are cost and deadline (for example, the finished product must cost less than $370,000 and must be completed within 14 months), but a variety of other constraints are often present, such as reliability (the product must be operational 99% of the time) or the size of the object code (it has to run on the client's personal computer). This preliminary investigation is sometimes called *concept exploration*. In subsequent meetings between members of the development team and the client team, the functionality of the proposed product is successively refined and analyzed for technical feasibility and financial justification.

Up to now, everything seems to be straightforward. Unfortunately, the requirements phase is frequently carried out improperly. When the product is finally delivered to the user, perhaps a year or two after the specifications have been signed off by the client, the client may call the developers and say, "I know that this is what

I asked for, but it isn't really what I wanted." What the client asked for, and therefore, what the developers thought the client wanted, was not what the client actually *needed*. There can be a number of reasons for this predicament. First, the client may not truly understand what is going on in his or her own organization. For example, it is no use asking the software developers for a faster operating system if the cause of the current slow response is a badly designed database. Or, if the client operates an unprofitable chain of retail stores, the client may ask for a financial management information system that reflects such items as sales, salaries, accounts payable, and accounts receivable. Such a product will be of little use if the real reason for the losses is shrinkage (shoplifting, and theft by employees). If that is the case, then a stock control product rather than a financial control product is required.

But the major reason that the client frequently asks for the wrong product is that software is complex. If it is difficult for a software professional to visualize a piece of software and its functionality, the problem is far worse for a client who is barely computer literate. There are a number of ways of coping with this; one of them is rapid prototyping.

A *rapid prototype* is a piece of software hurriedly put together that incorporates much of the functionality of the target product, but omits those aspects generally invisible to the client, such as file updating or error handling. The client and users then experiment with the prototype to determine whether it indeed meets their needs. The rapid prototype can be changed until the client and users are satisfied that it encapsulates the functionality they desire. Rapid prototyping and other requirements analysis techniques are discussed in detail in Chapter 7.

2.2.1 REQUIREMENTS PHASE TESTING

Within every software development organization there should be a group whose primary responsibility is to ensure that the delivered product is what the client ordered—that the product has been correctly built in every way. This group is called the software quality assurance (SQA) group. The quality of software is the extent to which it meets its specifications. Quality and software quality assurance are described in more detail in Chapter 5, as is the role of SQA in setting up and enforcing standards.

The SQA group must play a role right from the start of the development process. In particular, it is vital that the product satisfy the client's needs. The SQA group must, therefore, verify with the client that the final version of the rapid prototype is totally satisfactory.

It is essential that the rapid prototype be carefully checked by both client and users to be certain that it reflects their current needs. Nevertheless, no matter how meticulously this is done, there is always the possibility that forces beyond the control of the development team will necessitate changes in the requirements while the product is being developed. Further development will then have to be put on hold until the necessary modifications have been made to the partially completed product.

A major issue in software development is this so-called moving target problem when the client changes the requirements during development. One reason this occurs is an unforeseeable change in circumstances. For example, if a company expands its operations, or is taken over by another company, then many products will have to be modified, including those still under development. However, the major cause of the moving target problem is a client who keeps changing his or her mind. As explained in Section 14.4.4, there is nothing that can be done about it if the client has sufficient clout.

2.3 SPECIFICATION PHASE

Once the client agrees that the developers understand the requirements, the *specification document* is drawn up by the specification team. As opposed to the informal requirements phase, the specification document (or *specifications*) explicitly describes the functionality of the product, that is, precisely what the product is supposed to do, and lists any constraints that the product must satisfy. The specification document will include the inputs to the product and the required outputs. For example, if the client needs a payroll product, then the inputs will include the pay scale of each employee, data from a time clock, as well as information from personnel files so that taxes can be computed correctly. The outputs will be paychecks and reports such as Social Security deductions. In addition, the specification document will include stipulations that the product must be able to handle correctly a wide range of deductions such as medical insurance payments, union dues, and pension fund contributions.

The specification document of the product constitutes a contract. The software developers will be deemed to have completed the contract when they deliver a product that satisfies the acceptance criteria of the specification document. For this reason, the specification document should not include imprecise terms like suitable, convenient, ample, or enough, or other terms that sound exact but which in practice are equally imprecise, such as optimal, or 98 percent complete. Whereas contract software development can lead to a lawsuit, there is no chance of the specification document forming the basis for legal action when the client and developers are from the same organization. Nevertheless, even in the case of internal software development, the specification document should always be written as if it will be used as evidence in a trial.

A variety of difficulties can arise during the specification phase. One possible mistake that can be made by the specification team is that the specifications may be ambiguous—certain sentences or sections may have more than one possible valid interpretation. Consider the specification, "A part record and a plant record are read from the database. If it contains the letter A directly followed by the letter Q, then compute the cost of transporting that part to that plant." To what does the *it* in the preceding sentence refer: the part record or the plant record? In fact, the *it* could even refer to the database!

The specifications may also be incomplete, that is, some relevant fact or requirement may have been omitted. For instance, the specifications may not state what actions are to be taken if the input data contain errors. Moreover, the specifications may be contradictory. For example, in one place in the specification document for a product that controls a fermentation process, it is stated that if the pressure exceeds 35 psi, then valve M17 must immediately be shut. However, in another place it is stated that if the pressure exceeds 35 psi, then the operator must immediately be alerted; only if the operator takes no remedial action within 30 seconds should valve M17 be shut automatically. Software development cannot proceed until such problems in the specification document have been corrected.

The specification phase is described in Chapters 8 and 9; structured techniques are described in Chapter 8, whereas object-oriented analysis is the subject of Chapter 9. (The term *analysis* is sometimes used to describe activities of the specification phase, hence the phrase *object-oriented analysis*.)

2.3.1   SPECIFICATION PHASE TESTING

As pointed out in Chapter 1, a major source of faults in delivered software is faults in the specification document that are not detected until the software has gone into operations mode; that is, it is being used by the client's organization for its intended purpose. Before the specification phase can be deemed to be finished, the SQA group must carefully check the specifications, looking for contradictions, ambiguities, and any signs of incompleteness. In addition, the SQA group must ensure that the specifications are feasible, for example, that any specified hardware component is fast enough or that the client's current online disk storage capacity is adequate for handling the new product. If a specification document is to be testable, then one of the properties it must have is *traceability*. It must be possible to trace every statement in the specification document back to a statement made by the client team during the requirements phase. If the requirements have been methodically presented, properly numbered, cross-referenced, and indexed, then the SQA group should not have too much difficulty tracing through the specification document and ensuring that it is indeed a true reflection of the client's requirements. If rapid prototyping has been used in the requirements phase, then the relevant statements of the specification document should be traceable to the rapid prototype.

An excellent way of checking the specification document is by means of a review. Representatives of the specification team and of the client are present. The meeting is usually chaired by a member of the SQA group. The aim of the review is to determine whether the specifications are correct. The reviewers go through the specification document, ensuring that there are no misunderstandings about the document. Walkthroughs and inspections are two types of reviews, and they are described in Section 5.2.

2.4   PLANNING PHASE

No client will authorize a software project without knowing in advance how long the project will take and how much it will cost. From the viewpoint of the developers, these two items are just as important. If the developers underestimate the cost of a project, then the client will pay the agreed fee, which may be significantly less than the actual cost to the developers. Conversely, if the developers overestimate what the project will cost, then the client may turn the project down or have the job done by other developers whose estimate is more reasonable. Similar issues arise with regard to duration estimation. If the developers underestimate how long it will take to complete a project, then the resulting late delivery of the product will, at best, result in a loss of confidence on the part of the client. At worst, lateness penalty clauses in the contract will be invoked, causing the developers to suffer financially. Again, if the developers overestimate how long it will take for the product to be delivered, the client may well award the job to developers who promise faster delivery.

For the developers, merely estimating the duration and total cost is not enough. The developers need to assign the appropriate personnel to the various stages of the development process. For example, the coding team cannot start until the design documents have been approved by the SQA group, and the design team is not needed until the specification team has completed its task. In other words, the developers have to plan ahead. A software project management plan (SPMP) must be drawn up that reflects the separate phases of the development process and that shows which members of the development organization are involved in each task, as well as the deadlines for completing each task.

The earliest that such a detailed plan can be drawn up is when the specifications have been finalized. Before that time, the project is too amorphous for complete planning to be undertaken. Some aspects of the project can certainly be planned right from the start, but until the developers know exactly what is to be built, they cannot specify all aspects of the plan for building it.

Thus, once the specification document has been finished and checked, preparation of the software project management plan commences. Major components of the plan are the deliverables (what the client is going to get), the milestones (when the client gets them), and the budget (how much it is going to cost).

The plan describes the software process in fullest detail. It includes aspects such as the life-cycle model to be used, the organizational structure of the development organization, project responsibilities, managerial objectives and priorities, the techniques and CASE tools to be used, and detailed schedules, budgets, and resource allocations. Underlying the entire plan are the duration and cost estimates; techniques for obtaining such estimates are described in Section 10.1.

2.4.1   PLANNING PHASE TESTING

Whereas it is essential that every aspect of the SPMP be meticulously checked by the SQA group, particular attention must be paid to the plan's duration and cost estimates. One way to do this is for management to obtain two (or more) independent estimates of both duration and cost at the start of the planning phase, and then to reconcile any significant differences. With regard to the SPMP document, an excellent way to verify it is by a review similar to the review of the specification document.

If the duration and cost estimates are satisfactory, then the client will give permission for the project to proceed. The next stage is to design the product.

2.5   DESIGN PHASE

The specifications of a product spell out *what* the product is to do. The aim of the design phase is to determine *how* the product is to do it. Starting with the specification document, the design team determines the internal structure of the product. During the design phase, algorithms are selected and data structures chosen. The inputs to and outputs from the product are laid down in the specifications, as are all other external aspects of the product. During the design phase, the internal data flows are determined. The design team decomposes the product into *modules*, independent pieces of code with well-defined interfaces to the rest of the product. (An object is a specific type of module.) For each module, the designer specifies what it has to do and how it is to do it. The interface of each module, that is, the arguments passed to the module and the arguments returned by the module, must be specified in detail. For example, a module might measure the water level in a nuclear reactor and cause an alarm to sound if the level is too low. A module in an avionics product might take as input two or more sets of coordinates of an incoming enemy missile, compute its trajectory, and advise the pilot as to possible evasive action.

While this decomposition is being performed, the design team must keep a careful record of the design decisions that are made. This information is essential for two reasons. First, while the product is being designed there will be times when a dead end is reached, and the design team feels the need to backtrack and redesign certain pieces. Having a written record of why specific decisions were made will assist the team when this occurs and help them to get back on track.

The second reason for keeping the design decisions concerns maintenance. Ideally, the design of the product should be open-ended, meaning that future enhancements can be done simply by adding new modules or replacing existing modules without affecting the design as a whole. Of course, in practice this ideal product is difficult to achieve. Deadline constraints in the real world are such that designers struggle against the clock to complete a design that will satisfy the original specification document, without worrying about any later enhancements. If future enhancements (to be added after the product has gone into the operations mode) are included in the specification document, then these must be allowed for in the design, but this situation is extremely rare. In general the specification document, and hence the design, will deal with only present requirements. In addition there is no way of determining, while the product is still at the design phase, what all possible future enhancements might be. And finally, if the design has to take *all* future possibilities into account, at best it will be unwieldy; at worst it will be so complicated that implementation will be impossible. So the designers have to compromise, putting together a design that can be extended in many reasonable ways without the need for total redesign. But in a product that undergoes major enhancements, the time will come when the design simply cannot handle further changes. When this stage is reached, it is time to redesign the product. If the redesign team has a record of the reasons for all the original design decisions, its job will be easier.

The major output from the design phase is the *design* itself that has two parts: the *architectural design*, a description of the product in terms of its modules, and the *detailed design*, a description of each module. The latter descriptions are given to the programmers for implementation. Chapter 6 is devoted to the theory of design, and objects in particular. Design techniques, including object-oriented design, are described in Chapter 11, together with ways of describing the design, such as graphics and pseudocode.

2.5.1 DESIGN PHASE TESTING

As mentioned in Section 2.3.1, a critical aspect of testability is *traceability*. In the case of the design, this means that every part of the design can be linked to a statement in the specification document. A suitably cross-referenced design gives the SQA group a powerful tool for checking that the design agrees with the specification document and that every statement of the specification document is reflected in some part of the design.

Design reviews are similar to the reviews that the specifications undergo. However, in view of the technical nature of most design documents, the client is not usually present. Members of the design team and the SQA group work through the design as a whole and each separate module, ensuring that the design is correct. The types of faults to look for include: logic faults, interface faults, lack of exception handling (processing of error conditions), and, most important, nonconformance to the specifications. In addition, the review team should always be aware of the possibility that some specification faults were not detected during the previous phase. A detailed description of the review process is given in Section 5.2.

2.6 IMPLEMENTATION PHASE

During the implementation phase, the various component modules of the design are coded. Implementation is discussed in detail in Chapters 12 and 13. The major documentation associated with implementation is the source code itself, suitably commented. But the programmer should provide additional documentation to assist in maintenance, including all test cases against which the code was tested, the expected results, and the actual output. These documents will be used in regression testing, as explained in Section 2.8.

2.6.1 IMPLEMENTATION PHASE TESTING

The modules should be tested while they are being implemented (*desk checking*), and after they have been implemented they are run against test cases. This informal testing is done by the programmer. Thereafter, the quality assurance group tests the modules methodically. A variety of module testing techniques are described in Chapter 12.

In addition to running test cases, a code review is a powerful and successful technique for detecting programming faults. Here the programmer guides the members of the review team through the listing of the module. The review team must include an SQA representative. The procedure is similar to reviews of specifications and designs described previously.

2.7   INTEGRATION PHASE

The next stage is to combine the modules and determine whether the product as a whole functions correctly. The way in which the modules are integrated (all at once or one at a time) and the specific order (from top to bottom in the module interconnection diagram or bottom to top) can have a critical influence on the quality of the resulting product. For example, suppose the product is integrated bottom-up. If there is a major design fault, then it will show up late, necessitating an expensive rewrite. Conversely, if the modules are integrated top-down, then the lower-level modules usually will not receive as thorough a testing as would be the case if the product were integrated bottom-up. These and other problems are discussed in detail in Chapter 13. A careful explanation is given in that chapter as to why implementation and integration must be performed in parallel.

2.7.1   INTEGRATION PHASE TESTING

The purpose of *integration testing* is to check that the modules combine correctly to achieve a product that satisfies its specifications. During integration testing, particular care must be paid to testing the module interfaces. It is important that the number, order, and types of formal arguments match the number, order, and types of actual arguments. This strong type checking [van Wijngaarden et al., 1975] is best performed by the compiler and linker. Unlike Java, however, many languages are not strongly typed. When such a language is used, checking of interfaces must be done by members of the SQA group.

When the integration testing has been completed, the SQA group performs *product testing*. The functionality of the product as a whole is checked against the specifications. In particular, the constraints listed in the specification document must be tested. A typical example is whether the response time is short enough. Because the aim of product testing is to determine if the specifications have been correctly implemented, many of the test cases can be drawn up once the specification document is complete.

Not only must the correctness of the product be tested, but also its robustness. That is, intentionally erroneous input data are submitted to determine whether the product will crash or whether its error-handling capabilities are adequate for dealing with bad data. If the product is to be run together with the client's currently installed software, then tests must also be performed to check that the new product will not have an adverse effect on the client's existing computer operations. Finally, a check must also be made as to whether the source code and all other types of documentation are complete and internally consistent. Product testing is discussed in Section 13.4.

The final aspect of integration testing is *acceptance testing*. The software is delivered to the client, who tests the software on the actual hardware using actual data, as opposed to test data. No matter how careful the development team or the SQA group might be, there is a significant difference between test cases, which by their very nature are artificial, and actual data. A software product cannot be considered to satisfy its specifications until the product has passed its acceptance tests. More details about acceptance testing are given in Section 13.5.

In some cases, early versions of the complete product are shipped to the client for testing on site. The first such version is termed the alpha version. The corrected alpha version is called the beta version; in general the beta version is intended to be close to the final version. Alpha testing and beta testing are particularly important for so-called shrink-wrapped software. As opposed to expensive custom software, multiple copies of shrink-wrapped software, such as word processors or spreadsheets, are sold at much lower prices to a large number of buyers. That is to say, the manufacturers of shrink-wrapped software (such as Microsoft or Borland) recover the cost of developing a product by volume selling. (The term *shrink-wrapped software* comes from the fact that the box containing the diskettes, the manuals, and the license agreement is almost always shrink-wrapped.)

Faults in shrink-wrapped software usually result in poor sales of the product and huge losses for the development company. In order for as many faults as possible to come to light as early as possible, developers of shrink-wrapped software frequently give alpha or beta versions to selected companies, in the expectation that on-site tests will uncover any latent faults. In return, the alpha and beta sites are frequently promised free copies of the delivered version of the software. There are risks involved for a company participating in alpha or beta testing. In particular, alpha test versions can be fault-laden, resulting in frustration, time wasting, and possible damage to databases. However, the company gets a head start in using the new shrink-wrapped software, which can give it an advantage over its competitors.

2.8   MAINTENANCE PHASE

Once the product has been accepted by the client, any changes constitute maintenance. Maintenance is not an activity that is grudgingly carried out after the product has gone into operations mode. On the contrary, it is an integral part of the software process that must be planned for from the beginning. As explained in Section 2.5, the design should, as far as is feasible, take future enhancements into account. Coding must be performed with future maintenance constantly in mind. After all, as pointed out in Section 1.3, more money is spent on maintenance than on all other software activities combined. It is therefore almost always a vital aspect of software production. Maintenance must never be treated as an afterthought. Instead, the entire software development effort must be carried out in such a way as to minimize the impact of the inevitable future maintenance.

A common problem with maintenance is documentation, or rather a lack of it. In the course of developing software against a time deadline, the original specification and design documents are frequently not updated and are, consequently, almost useless to the maintenance team. Other documentation such as the database manual or the operating manual may never be written, because management decided that delivering the product to the client on time was more important than developing the documentation in parallel with the software. In many instances, the source code is the only documentation available to the maintainer. The high rate of personnel turnover in the software industry exacerbates the maintenance situation in that none of the original developers may be working for the organization at the time when maintenance is performed.

Maintenance is frequently the most challenging phase of software production for the reasons stated previously and for the additional reasons given in Chapter 14.

2.8.1   MAINTENANCE PHASE TESTING

There are two aspects to the testing of changes to a product in operations mode. The first is checking that the required changes have been correctly implemented. The second aspect is ensuring that, in the course of making the required changes to the product, no other inadvertent changes were made. Thus, once the programmer has determined that the desired changes have been implemented, the product must be tested against previous test cases to make certain that the functionality of the rest of the product has not been compromised. This procedure is called *regression testing*. To assist in performing regression testing, it is necessary that all previous test cases be retained, together with the results of running those test cases. Testing during the maintenance phase is discussed in greater detail in Chapter 14.

2.9   RETIREMENT

The final phase in the software life cycle is retirement. After many years of service, a stage is reached when further maintenance is not cost-effective. Sometimes the proposed changes are so drastic that the design as a whole would have to be changed. In such a case it is less expensive to redesign and recode the entire product. Or perhaps so many changes may have been made to the original design that interdependencies have inadvertently been built into the product, and there is a real danger that even a small change to one minor module might have a drastic effect on the functionality of the product as a whole. Third, the documentation may not have been adequately maintained, thus increasing the risk of a regression fault to the extent that it would be safer to recode than to maintain. A fourth possibility is that the hardware (and operating system) on which the product runs is to be replaced; it may be more economical to rewrite than to modify. In each of these instances the current version is replaced by a new version, and the software process continues.

True retirement, on the other hand, is a somewhat rare event that occurs when a product has outgrown its usefulness. The client organization no longer requires the functionality provided by the product, and it is finally removed from the computer.

After this review of the complete software process, together with some of the difficulties attendant on each phase, it is time to consider difficulties associated with software production as a whole.

2.10 PROBLEMS WITH SOFTWARE PRODUCTION: ESSENCE AND ACCIDENTS

Over the past 30 years hardware has become cheaper and faster. It was mentioned in Section 1.5 that the performance–price factor has decreased by an order of magnitude six times during the past 30 years. Furthermore, hardware has shrunk in size. In the 1950s, companies paid hundreds of thousands of preinflation dollars for a machine as large as a room that was no more powerful than today's desktop personal computer selling for under $1,000. It would seem that this trend is inexorable, and that computers will continue to become smaller, faster, and cheaper.

Unfortunately, this is not the case. There are a number of physical constraints that must eventually impose limits on the possible future size and speed of hardware. The first of these constraints is the speed of light. Electrons, or more precisely, electromagnetic waves, simply cannot travel faster than 186,300 miles per second. One way to speed up a computer is therefore to miniaturize its components. In that way, the electrons will have shorter distances to travel. Second, there are also lower limits on the size of a component. An electron travels along a path that can be as narrow as three atoms in width. But if the path along which the electron is to travel is any narrower than that, then the electron can stray onto an adjacent path. For the same reason parallel paths must not be located too close to one another. Thus the speed of light and the nonzero width of an atom impose physical limits on hardware size and speed. We are nowhere near these limits yet—computers can easily become at least two orders of magnitude faster and smaller without reaching these physical limits. But there are intrinsic laws of nature that will eventually prevent computers from becoming arbitrarily fast or arbitrarily small.

Now what about software? Software is essentially conceptual, and therefore nonphysical, although it is of course always stored on some physical medium such as paper or magnetic disk. Superficially, it might appear that with software anything is possible. But Brooks, in a landmark article entitled "No Silver Bullet" [Brooks, 1986], exploded this belief. He argued that, analogous to hardware speed and size limits that cannot physically be exceeded, there are inherent problems with current techniques of software production that can never be solved. To quote Brooks, ". . . building software will always be hard. There is inherently no silver bullet."

(An explanation of the term "silver bullet" is in the Just in Case You Wanted to Know box on this page.)

Recall that the title of Brooks's article is "*No* Silver Bullet" (author's italics). Brooks's theme is that the very nature of software makes it highly unlikely that a silver bullet will be discovered that will magically solve all the problems of software production, let alone help to achieve software breakthroughs that are comparable to those that have occurred with unfailing regularity in the hardware field. He divides the difficulties of software into two Aristotelian categories: *essence*, the difficulties inherent in the intrinsic nature of software, and *accidents*, the difficulties that are encountered today but are not inherent in software production. That is, essence constitutes those aspects of software production that probably cannot be changed, whereas accidents are amenable to research breakthroughs, or silver bullets.

What then are the aspects of software production that are inherently difficult? Brooks lists four, which he terms complexity, conformity, changeability, and invisibility. Brooks's use of the word *complexity* is somewhat unfortunate in that the term has many different meanings in computer science in general, and in software engineering in particular. In the context of his article, Brooks uses the word *complex* in the sense of complicated or intricate. In fact, the names of all four aspects are used in their nontechnical sense.

Each of the four aspects is now examined.

2.10.1 Complexity

Software is more complex than any other construct made by human beings. Even hardware is almost trivial compared to software. To see this, consider a 16-bit word w in the main memory of a computer. Because each of the 16 bits comprising the word can take on exactly two values, namely 0 and 1, word w as a whole can be in any of 2^{16} different states. If we have two words, w_1 and w_2, each 16 bits in length, then the number of possible states of words w_1 and w_2 together is 2^{16} times 2^{16}, or 2^{32}. In general, if a system consists of a number of independent pieces, then the number of possible states of that system is the product of the numbers of possible states of each component.

Now suppose the computer is to be used to run a software product p, and the 16-bit word w is to be used to store the value of an integer x. If the value of x is read in by a statement such as read (x), then, because the integer x can take on 2^{16} different values, at first sight it might seem that the number of states in which the product could be is the same as the number of states in which the word could be. If the product p consisted only of the single statement read (x), then the number of states of p would indeed be 2^{16}. But in a realistic, nontrivial software product the value of a variable that is input is later used elsewhere in the product. There is thus an interdependence between the read (x) statement and any statement that uses the value of x. The situation is more complex if the flow of control within the product depends on the value of x. For example, x may be the control variable in a **switch** statement, or there may be a **for** loop or **while** loop whose termination depends on the value of x. Thus the number of states in any nontrivial product is greater, because of this interaction, than the product of the number of states of each variable. As a consequence of this combinatorial explosion in the number of states, complexity does not grow linearly with the size of the product, but much faster.

Complexity is an inherent property of software. No matter how a nontrivial piece of software is designed, the pieces of the product will interact. For example, the states of a module will depend on the states of its arguments, and the states of global variables (variables that can be accessed by more than one module) will also affect the state of the product as a whole. Certainly, complexity can be reduced, for example by using the object-oriented paradigm. Nevertheless, it can never be totally eliminated. In other words, complexity is an essential property of software, not an accidental one.

Brooks points out that complex phenomena can be described and explained in disciplines such as mathematics and physics. Mathematicians and physicists have learned how to abstract the essential features of a complex system, to build a simple model that reflects only those essential features, to validate the simple model, and to make predictions from it. In contrast, if software is simplified the whole exercise is useless; the simplifying techniques of mathematics and physics work only because the complexities of those systems are accidents, not essence, as is the case with software products.

The consequence of this essential complexity of software is that a product becomes difficult to understand. In fact, it is often true that no one really understands a large product in its entirety. And if the product as a whole is not understood, then only the smaller, independent components can be fully understood. This leads to imperfect communication between team members that, in turn, results in the time and cost overruns that characterize the development of large-scale software products. In addition, errors in specifications are made simply because of a lack of understanding of all aspects of the product.

This essential complexity affects not only the software process itself, but also the management of the process. Unless a manager can obtain accurate information regarding the process that he or she is managing, it is difficult to determine personnel needs for the succeeding stages of the project and to budget accurately. Reports to senior management regarding both progress-to-date and future deadlines are likely to be inaccurate. Drawing up a testing schedule is difficult when neither the manager nor anyone reporting to the manager knows what loose ends still have to be tied. And if a project staffer leaves, trying to train a replacement can be a nightmare.

A further consequence of the complexity of software is that it complicates the maintenance process. As shown in Figure 1.2, about two-thirds of the total software effort is devoted to maintenance. Unless the maintainer really understands the product, there is always the danger that corrective maintenance or enhancement can damage the product in such a way that further maintenance is required to repair the damage caused by the original maintenance. The possibility of this sort of damage being caused by carelessness is always present, even when the original author makes the change, but it is exacerbated when the maintenance programmer is effectively working in the dark. Poor documentation; or worse, no documentation; or still worse, incorrect documentation, is often a major cause of incorrectly performed maintenance. But no matter how good the documentation may be, the inherent complexity of software transcends all attempts to cope with it, and this complexity will unfavorably impact maintenance. Again, the object-oriented paradigm can help to reduce complexity (and hence improve maintenance), but it cannot eliminate it completely.

2.10.2 CONFORMITY

A manually controlled gold refinery is to be computerized. Instead of the plant being operated via a series of buttons and levers, a computer will send the necessary control signals to the components of the plant. Although the plant is working perfectly, management feels that a computerized control system will increase the gold yield. The task of the software development team is to construct a product that will interface with the existing plant. That is to say, the software must conform to the plant, not the plant to the software. This is the first type of conformity identified by Brooks, where software acquires an unnecessary degree of complexity because it has to interface with an existing system.

What if a brand-new computerized gold refinery were to be constructed? It would appear that the mechanical engineers, metallurgical engineers, and software engineers could sit down together and come up with a plant design in which the machinery and the software fit together in a natural and straightforward manner. In practice, however, there is generally a perception that it is easier to make the software interface conform to the other components, rather than to change the way the other components have been configured in the past. As a result, even in a new gold refinery the other engineers will insist on designing the machinery as before, and the software will be forced to conform to the hardware interfaces. This is the second type of conformity identified by Brooks, where software acquires an unnecessary degree of complexity because of the misconception that software is the component that is the most conformable.

The problems caused by this forced conformity cannot be removed by redesigning the software, because the complexity is not due to the structure of the software

---

JUST IN CASE YOU WANTED TO KNOW

According to Section 1.4, pages 15–17 of the Technical Manual for the U.S.S. Enterprise, NCC-1701-D, much of the software development was started before the hardware development [Sternbach and Okuda, 1991]. I hope that, in this respect at least, *Star Trek* turns out to be science fact rather than science fiction!

---

itself. Instead, it is due to the structure of software caused by the interfaces, to humans or to hardware, imposed on the software designer (but see the Just in Case You Wanted to Know box on this page for details of how this may change in the future).

2.10.3 CHANGEABILITY

As pointed out in Section 1.1, it is considered unreasonable to ask a civil engineer to move a bridge 200 miles or rotate it through 90°, but it is perfectly acceptable to tell a software engineer to rewrite half an operating system over a 5-year period. Civil engineers know that redesigning half a bridge is expensive and dangerous; it is both cheaper and safer to rebuild it from scratch. Software engineers are equally well aware that, in the long run, extensive maintenance is unwise and that rewriting the product from scratch will sometimes prove to be less expensive. Nevertheless, clients frequently demand major changes to software.

Brooks points out that there will always be pressures to change software. After all, it *is* easier to change software than, say, the hardware on which it runs; that is the reason behind the terms *soft*ware and *hard*ware. In addition, the functionality of a system is embodied in its software, and changes in functionality are achieved through changing the software. It has been suggested that the problems caused by frequent and drastic maintenance are merely problems caused by ignorance, and if the public at large were better educated with regard to the nature of software, then demands for major changes would not occur. But Brooks points out that changeability is a property of the essence of software, an inherent problem that cannot be surmounted. That is to say, the very nature of software is such that, no matter how the public is educated, there will always be pressures for changes in software, and often these changes will be drastic.

There are four reasons why useful software has to undergo change. First, as pointed out in Section 1.3, software is a model of reality, and as the reality changes, so the software must adapt or die. Second, if software is found to be useful, then there are pressures, chiefly from satisfied users, to extend the functionality of the product beyond what is feasible in terms of the original design. Third, one of the greatest strengths of software is that it is so much easier to change than hardware. Fourth, successful software survives well beyond the lifetime of the hardware for which it was written. In part this is due to the fact that, after 4 or 5 years, hardware often does not function as well as it did. But more significant is the fact that technological change is so rapid that more appropriate hardware components, such as larger disks, faster CPUs, or more powerful monitors, become available while the software is still viable. In general, the software will have to be modified to some extent in order to run on the new hardware.

For all these reasons, part of the essence of software is that it has to be changed, and this inexorable and continual change has a deleterious effect on the quality of software.

2.10.4   INVISIBILITY

A major problem with the essence of software is that it is "invisible and unvisualizable" [Brooks, 1986]. Anyone who has been handed a 150-page listing and told to modify the software in some way will know exactly what Brooks is getting at. Unfortunately, there is no acceptable way to represent either a complete product or some sort of overview of the product. In contrast, architects, for example, can provide 3-dimensional models that give an idea of the overall design, as well as 2-dimensional blueprints and other detailed diagrams that, to the trained eye, will reflect every detail of the structure to be built. Chemists can build models of molecules, engineers can construct scale models, and plastic surgeons can use the computer to show potential clients exactly how their faces will look after surgery. Diagrams can be drawn to reflect the structure of silicon chips and other electronic components; the components of a computer can be represented by means of various sorts of schematics, at various levels of abstraction.

Certainly there are ways in which software engineers can represent specific views of their product. For example, a software engineer can draw one directed graph depicting flow of control, another showing flow of data, a third with patterns of dependency, and a fourth depicting time sequences. The problem is that few of these types of graphs are planar, let alone hierarchical. The many crossovers in these graphs are a distinct obstacle to understanding. Parnas [Parnas, 1979] suggests cutting the arcs of the graphs until one or more becomes hierarchical. The problem is that the resulting graph, though comprehensible, makes only a subset of the software visualizable, and the arcs that have been cut may be critical from the viewpoint of comprehending the interrelationships between the components of the software.

The result of this inability to represent software visually not only makes software difficult to comprehend, it also severely hinders communication among software professionals—there does not seem to be an alternative to handing a colleague a 150-page listing together with a list of modifications to be made.

It must be pointed out that visualizations of all kinds, such as flowcharts, data flow diagrams (Section 8.3.1), or module interconnection diagrams, are extremely useful and powerful ways of visualizing certain aspects of the product. Visual representations are an excellent means of communicating with the client, as well as with other software engineers. The problem is that such diagrams cannot embody *every* aspect of the product, nor is there a way of determining what is missing from any one visual representation of the product.

2.10.5 NO SILVER BULLET?

Brooks's article [Brooks, 1986] is by no means totally gloom-filled. He describes what he considers to be the three major breakthroughs in software technology, namely, high-level languages, time sharing, and software development environments (such as the UNIX Programmer's Workbench), but stresses that they solved only accidental, and not essential, difficulties. He evaluates various technical developments that are currently advanced as potential silver bullets, including proofs of correctness (Section 5.5), object-oriented design (Section 11.8), Ada, and artificial intelligence and expert systems. Although some of these approaches may solve remaining accidental difficulties, Brooks feels that they are irrelevant to the essential difficulties.

In order to achieve comparable future breakthroughs, Brooks suggests that we change the way that software is produced. For example, whenever possible, software products should be bought off the shelf (that is, shrink-wrapped software) rather than custom-built. For Brooks, the hard part of building software lies in the requirements, specification, and design phases, not in the implementation phase. The use of rapid prototyping (Section 7.2) is for him a major potential source of an order-of-magnitude improvement. Another suggestion that, in Brooks's opinion, may lead to a major improvement in productivity is greater use of the principle of incremental development, where instead of trying to build the product as a whole, it is constructed stepwise. This concept is described in Section 4.1.

For Brooks, the greatest hope of a major breakthrough in improving software production lies in training and encouraging great designers. As stated previously, in Brooks's opinion one of the hardest aspects of software production is the design phase, and to get great designs, we need great designers. Brooks cites UNIX, APL, Pascal, Modula-2, Smalltalk, and FORTRAN as exciting products of the past. He points out that they have all been the products of one, or a very few, great minds. On the other hand, more prosaic but useful products like COBOL, PL/I, ALGOL, MVS/360, and MS-DOS have all been products of committees. Nurturing great designers is for Brooks the most important objective if we wish to improve software production.

Parts of Brooks's paper make depressing reading. After all, from the title onwards he states that the inherent nature (or essence) of current software production makes the finding of a silver bullet a dubious possibility. Nevertheless, he concludes on a note of hope, suggesting that if we change our software production strategies by buying ready-made software wherever possible, using rapid prototyping and incremental building techniques, and attempting to nurture great designers, we may increase software productivity. However, an order of magnitude breakthrough, the "silver bullet," is most unlikely.

Brooks's pessimism must be put into perspective. Over the past 20 years there has been a steady productivity increase in the software industry of roughly 6 percent per year. This productivity increase is comparable to what has been observed in many manufacturing industries. What Brooks is looking for though is a "silver bullet," a way of rapidly obtaining an order of magnitude increase in productivity. It is difficult to disagree with his view that we cannot hope to double productivity overnight. At the same time, the compound growth rate of 6 percent means that productivity is doubling every 12 years. This improvement may not be as rapid and spectacular as we would like, but the practice of software engineering is steadily improving from year to year.

Chapter Review

The various phases of the software process, from requirements (Section 2.2) to retirement (Section 2.9), are outlined, with special attention paid to the problems associated with each phase. Testing is not considered to be a separate phase, because testing must be carried out in parallel with all software production activities. A description of testing activities during each of the life-cycle phases is also given (Section 2.2.1 through 2.8.1).

In addition to the problems associated with each separate software life-cycle phase, Brooks's views regarding the inherent difficulties of software production are presented (Section 2.10). Brooks's four aspects of essential software difficulty, namely, complexity, conformity, changeability, and invisibility, are described and discussed in Sections 2.10.1 through 2.10.4. Finally, Brooks's viewpoint is analyzed (Section 2.10.5).

For Further Reading

The review articles in the For Further Reading section of Chapter 1, namely [Brooks, 1975], [Boehm, 1976], [Goldberg, 1986], [Mathis, 1986], [Card, McGarry, and Page, 1987], [Boehm and Papaccio, 1988], [DeMarco and Lister, 1989], and [Yourdon, 1992] also highlight the problems associated with software production.

With regard to testing during each of the phases of the life cycle, a good general source is [Beizer, 1990]. More specific references are given in Chapter 5 of this book and at the end of that chapter.

No summary such as that presented here can do justice to Brooks's "No Silver Bullet"—the article must be read in the original [Brooks, 1986]. Among the many thoughtful responses to Brooks's article, Cox suggests [Cox, 1990] that there is indeed a silver bullet, namely reuse of objects (described in Chapter 9). The view expressed in [Harel, 1992], although largely agreeing with Brooks, is that as a consequence of the newer technologies, the future will be less bleak than in Brooks's opinion. [Mays, 1994] provides another interesting view on the silver bullet issue.

Problems

Describe a situation in which the client, developer, and user are one and the same person.   **2.1**

What problems can arise if the client, developer, and user are one and the same person? How can these problems be solved?   **2.2**

What are the potential advantages if the client, developer, and user are one and the same person?   **2.3**

How do your answers to Problems 2.2 and 2.3 change if the object-oriented paradigm is used?   **2.4**

Consider the requirements phase and the specification phase. Would it make more sense to combine these two activities into one phase rather than treating them separately?   **2.5**

List the documentation that should be produced during each phase of the software life cycle.   **2.6**

More testing is performed during the integration phase than in any other development phase. Would it be better to divide this phase into two separate phases, one incorporating the nontesting aspects, the other all the testing?   **2.7**

Maintenance is one of the most important phases of software production and also the most difficult to perform. Nevertheless, it is looked down on by many software professionals, and maintenance programmers are often paid less than developers. Do you think that this is reasonable? If not, how would you try to change it?   **2.8**

Why do you think that, as stated in Section 2.9, true retirement is a rare event?   **2.9**

Due to a fire at Intergalactic Software, all documentation for a product is destroyed just before it is delivered. What is the impact on maintenance of the resulting lack of documentation?   **2.10**

Brooks says that software production is inherently difficult because of complexity, conformity, changeability, and invisibility. Other areas of human endeavor, including law, medicine, theology, and engineering, are also difficult. To what extent is each of these areas affected by complexity, conformity, changeability, and invisibility?   **2.11**

Brooks considers the most important breakthroughs in software technology to be high-level languages, time sharing, and software development environments. What do *you* consider to be the major software breakthroughs? Give reasons for your answer.   **2.12**

Draw a detailed flowchart of the software distributed by your instructor. Is it easy to understand? Now make the flowchart planar by deleting all edges that cross over another edge. Is the resulting flowchart easier to understand? How much of the original functionality has been lost? Translate the resulting planar flowchart back into the original programming language and run it. Do you agree with Brooks's statement that software is "invisible and unvisualizable"?   **2.13**

(Term Project) Discuss how the four essential problems of software production (complexity, conformity, changeability, and invisibility) affect the Osbert Oglesby product described in Appendix A.   **2.14**

2.15 (Readings in Software Engineering) Your instructor will distribute copies of [Brooks, 1986] and [Cox, 1990]. Do you agree with Cox that there is a silver bullet, namely, reuse of objects?

References

[Beizer, 1990] B. BEIZER, *Software Testing Techniques*, Second Edition, Van Nostrand Reinhold, New York, NY, 1990.

[Boehm, 1976] B. W. BOEHM, "Software Engineering," *IEEE Transactions on Computers* **C-25** (December 1976), pp. 1226–1241.

[Boehm and Papaccio, 1988] B. W. BOEHM AND P. N. PAPACCIO, "Understanding and Controlling Software Costs," *IEEE Transactions on Software Engineering* **14** (October 1988), pp. 1462–1477.

[Brooks, 1975] F. P. BROOKS, JR., *The Mythical Man-Month: Essays on Software Engineering*, Addison-Wesley, Reading, MA, 1975.

[Brooks, 1986] F. P. BROOKS, JR., "No Silver Bullet," in: *Information Processing '86*, H.-J. Kugler (Editor), Elsevier North-Holland, New York, NY, 1986. Reprinted in: *IEEE Computer* **20** (April 1987), pp. 10–19.

[Card, McGarry, and Page, 1987] D. N. CARD, F. E. McGARRY, AND G. T. PAGE, "Evaluating Software Engineering Technologies," *IEEE Transactions on Software Engineering* **SE-13** (July 1987), pp. 845–851.

[Cox, 1990] B. J. COX, "There *Is* a Silver Bullet," *Byte* **15** (October 1990), pp. 209–218.

[DeMarco and Lister, 1989] T. DeMARCO AND T. LISTER, "Software Development: The State of the Art vs. State of the Practice," *Proceedings of the 11th International Conference on Software Engineering*, Pittsburgh, May 1989, pp. 271–275.

[Goldberg, 1986] R. GOLDBERG, "Software Engineering: An Emerging Discipline," *IBM Systems Journal* **25** (No. 3/4, 1986), pp. 334–353.

[Harel, 1992] D. HAREL, "Biting the Silver Bullet," *IEEE Computer* **25** (January 1992), pp. 8–24.

[Mathis, 1986] R. F. MATHIS, "The Last 10 Percent," *IEEE Transactions on Software Engineering* **SE-12** (June 1986), pp. 705–712.

[Mays, 1994] R. G. MAYS, "Forging a Silver Bullet from the Essence of Software," *IBM Systems Journal* **33** (No. 1, 1994) pp. 20–45.

[Parnas, 1979] D. L. PARNAS, "Designing Software for Ease of Extension and Contraction," *IEEE Transactions on Software Engineering* **SE-5** (March 1979), pp. 128–138.

[Sternbach and Okuda, 1991] R. STERNBACH AND M. OKUDA, *Star Trek: The Next Generation, Technical Manual*, Pocket Books, New York, 1991.

[van Wijngaarden et al., 1975] A. VAN WIJNGAARDEN, B. J. MAILLOUX, J. E. L. PECK, C. H. A. KOSTER, M. SINTZOFF, C. H. LINDSEY, L. G. L. T. MEERTENS, AND R. G. FISKER, "Revised Report on the Algorithmic Language ALGOL 68," *Acta Informatica* **5** (1975), pp. 1–236.

[Yourdon, 1992] E. YOURDON, *Decline and Fall of the American Programmer*, Yourdon Press, Englewood Cliffs, NJ, 1992.

chapter

3

SOFTWARE LIFE-CYCLE MODELS

A software product usually begins as a vague concept, such as "Wouldn't it be nice if the computer could plot our graphs of radioactivity levels," or "If this corporation doesn't have an exact picture of our cash flow on a daily basis, we will be insolvent in six months," or even "If we develop and market this new type of spreadsheet, we'll make a million dollars!" Once the need for a product has been established, the product goes through a series of developmental phases. Typically, the product is specified, designed, and then implemented. If the client is satisfied, the product is installed, and while it is operational it is maintained. When the product finally comes to the end of its useful life, it is decommissioned. The series of steps through which the product progresses is called the *life-cycle model*.

The life-cycle history of each product is different. Some products will spend years in the conceptual stage, perhaps because current hardware is just not fast enough for the product to be viable or because fundamental research has to be done before an efficient algorithm can be developed. Other products will be quickly designed and implemented, and then spend years in the maintenance phase being modified to meet the users' changing needs. Yet other products will be designed, implemented, and maintained; then after many years of radical maintenance, it will be cheaper to develop a completely new product rather than to attempt to patch the current version yet again.

In this chapter a number of different life-cycle models are described. The two most widely used models are the waterfall model and the rapid prototyping model. In addition, the spiral model is now receiving considerable attention. To help shed light on the strengths and weaknesses of these three models, other life-cycle models will also be examined, including incremental models and the highly unsatisfactory build-and-fix model.

3.1 BUILD-AND-FIX MODEL

It is unfortunate that many products are developed using what might be termed the *build-and-fix* model. The product is constructed without specifications or any attempt at design. Instead, the developers simply build a product that is reworked as many times as necessary to satisfy the client. This approach is shown in Figure 3.1. Although this approach may work well on short programming exercises 100 or 200

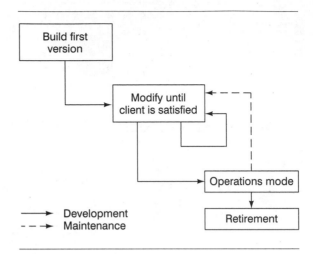

Figure 3.1 Build-and-fix model.

lines long, the build-and-fix model is totally unsatisfactory for products of any reasonable size. Figure 1.5 shows that the cost of changing a software product is relatively small if the change is made at the requirements, specification, or design phases, but grows unacceptably large if changes are made after the product has been coded, or worse, if it is already in operations mode. Thus, the cost of the build-and-fix approach is actually far greater than the cost of a properly specified and carefully designed product. In addition, maintenance of a product can be extremely difficult without specification or design documents, and the chances of a regression fault occurring are considerably greater.

Instead of the build-and-fix approach, it is essential that before development of a product begins, an overall game plan, or *life-cycle model*, be chosen. The life-cycle model (sometimes abbreviated to just "model") specifies the various phases of the software process, such as the requirements, specification, planning, design, implementation, integration, and maintenance phases, and the order in which they are to be carried out. Once the life-cycle model has been agreed to by all parties, development of the product can begin.

Until the early 1980s, the waterfall model was the only widely accepted life-cycle model. This model is now examined in some detail.

3.2 WATERFALL MODEL

The waterfall model was first put forward by Royce [Royce, 1970]. A version of the model appears as Figure 3.2. First, requirements are determined, and checked by the client and members of the SQA group. Then the specifications for the product are drawn up; that is, a document is produced stating what the product is to do. This phase is complete when the document has been checked by the SQA group and

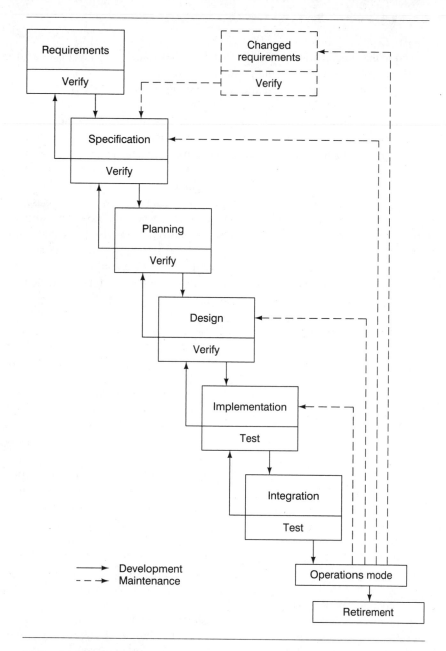

Figure 3.2 Waterfall model.

approved by the client. Once the client has signed off on the specification document, the planning phase commences and a detailed timetable for developing the software is drawn up. This plan is also checked by the SQA group. When the client has approved the developers' duration and cost estimates for the product, the design phase begins.

In contrast to the specification document that describes *what* the product is to do, the design documents describe *how* the product is to do it.

During the design phase, it sometimes becomes apparent that there is a fault in the specification document. The specifications may be incomplete (some features of the product have been omitted), contradictory (two or more statements in the specification document define the product in an incompatible way), or ambiguous (the specification document has more than one possible interpretation). The presence of incompleteness, contradictions, or ambiguities necessitates a revision of the specification document before the software development process can continue. Referring again to Figure 3.2, the arrows from the left side of the design phase box back to the planning phase box and thence to the specification phase box constitute a feedback loop. The software production process follows this loop if the developers have to revise the specification document during the design phase. With the client's permission, the necessary changes are then made to the specification document, and the planning and design documents are adjusted to incorporate these changes. When the developers are finally satisfied, the design documents are handed to the programmers for implementation.

Flaws in the design may appear during implementation. For example, the design of a real-time system may prove to be too slow when implemented. An example in FORTRAN of such a design flaw results from the fact that the elements of an array b are stored in column-major order, that is to say, in the order $b(1, 1), b(2, 1), b(3, 1),$ . . . , $b(n, 1), b(1, 2), b(2, 2), b(3, 2),$ . . . , $b(n, 2)$, and so on. Suppose a 200×200 FORTRAN array b is stored on disk with one column to a block; that is, a 200-word column is read into a buffer in main memory each time a FORTRAN read statement is executed. The complete array is to be read from disk into main memory. If the array is read column by column, then exactly 200 blocks will have to be transferred from the disk to main memory to read all 40,000 elements. The first read statement will cause the first column to be put in the buffer, and the first 200 reads will use the contents of the buffer. Only when the 201st element is required will a second block need to be transferred from disk to main memory. But if the product reads the array row by row, then a fresh block will have to be transferred for every read, because consecutive reads access different columns and, hence, different blocks. Thus 40,000 block transfers would be required, instead of 200 when the array is read in column-major order, and the input/output time for that part of the product would be 200 times longer. Design faults of this type have to be corrected before the team can continue with software development.

During the implementation phase, the waterfall model with its feedback loops permits modifications to be made to the design documents, the software project management plan, and even the specification document, if necessary. Modules are implemented, documented, and then integrated to form a complete product. (In practice, the implementation and integration phases are usually carried out in parallel. As described in Chapter 13, each module is integrated as soon as it has been implemented and tested.) During integration it may be necessary to backtrack and make modifications to the code, preceded perhaps by modifications to the specification and design documents.

A critical point regarding the waterfall model is that no phase is complete until the documentation for that phase has been completed and the products of that phase have been approved by the SQA group. This carries over into modifications; if the products of an earlier phase have to be changed as a consequence of following a feedback loop, that earlier phase is deemed to be complete only when the documentation for the phase has been modified and the modifications have been checked by the SQA group.

When the developers feel that the product has been successfully completed, it is given to the client for acceptance testing. Deliverables at this stage include the user manual and other documentation listed in the contract. When the client agrees that the product indeed satisfies its specification document, the product is handed over to the client, installed, and put into operations mode.

Once the client has accepted the product, any changes, whether to remove residual faults or to extend the product in any way, constitute maintenance. As can be seen in Figure 3.2, maintenance may require not just implementation changes, but also design and specification changes. In addition, enhancement is triggered by a change in requirements. This, in turn, is implemented via changes in the specification document, design documents, and code. The waterfall model is a dynamic model, and the feedback loops play an important role in this dynamism. Again, it is vital that the documentation be maintained as meticulously as the code itself and that the products of each phase be carefully checked before the next phase commences.

The waterfall model has been used with great success on a wide variety of products. However, there have also been failures. In order to decide whether or not to use the waterfall model for a project, it is necessary to understand both its strengths and weaknesses.

3.2.1 ANALYSIS OF THE WATERFALL MODEL

The waterfall model has many advantages, including the enforced disciplined approach, the stipulation that documentation be provided at each phase, and the requirement that all the products of each phase (including the documentation) be carefully checked by SQA. An essential aspect of the milestone terminating each phase is approval by the SQA group of all the products of that phase, including all the documentation stipulated for that phase.

Inherent in every phase of the waterfall model is testing. Testing is not a separate phase to be performed only after the product has been constructed; it is not to be performed only at the end of each phase. Instead, as stated in Chapter 2, testing should proceed continuously throughout the software process. Specifically, while the requirements are being drawn up they must be verified, as must the specification document, the design documents, and the software project management plan. The code must be tested in a variety of ways. During maintenance it is necessary to ensure not only that the modified version of the product still does what the previous version did—and still does it correctly (regression testing)—but that it totally satisfies any new requirements imposed by the client.

The specification document, design documents, code documentation, and other documentation such as the database manual, user manual, and operations manual are essential tools for maintaining the product. As stated in Chapter 1, on average 67 percent of a software budget is devoted to maintenance, and adherence to the waterfall model with its documentation stipulations will make this maintenance easier. As mentioned in the previous section, the same methodical approach to software production continues during maintenance. Every change must be reflected in the relevant documentation. Many of the successes of the waterfall model have been due to the fact that it is essentially a documentation-driven model.

However, the fact that the waterfall model is documentation-driven can also be a disadvantage. To see this, consider the following two somewhat bizarre scenarios. First, Joe and Jane Johnson decide to build a house. They consult with an architect. Instead of showing them sketches, plans, and perhaps a model, the architect gives them a 20-page single-spaced typed document describing the house in highly technical terms. Despite the fact that neither Joe nor Jane have any previous architectural experience and hardly understand the document, they enthusiastically sign it and say, "Go right ahead, build the house!"

Another scenario is as follows. Mark Marberry buys his suits by mail order. Instead of mailing him pictures of their suits and samples of available cloths, the company sends Mark a written description of the cut and the cloth of their products. Mark then orders a suit solely on the basis of a written description.

The preceding two scenarios are highly unlikely. Nevertheless, they typify precisely the way software is often constructed using the waterfall model. The process begins with the specifications. In general, specification documents are long, detailed, and, quite frankly, boring to read. The client is usually inexperienced in the reading of software specifications, and this difficulty is compounded by the fact that specification documents are usually written in a style with which the client is unfamiliar. The difficulty is even worse when the specifications are written in a formal specification language like Z [Spivey, 1992] (Section 8.8). Nevertheless, the client proceeds to sign off the specification document, whether properly understood or not. In many ways there is little difference between Joe and Jane Johnson contracting to have a house built from a written description that they only partially comprehend and clients approving a software product described in terms of a specification document that they only partially understand.

Mark Marberry and his mail-order suits may seem bizarre in the extreme, but that is precisely what happens when the waterfall model is used in software development. The first time that the client sees a working product is only after the entire product has been coded. Small wonder that software developers live in fear of the sentence "I know this is what I asked for, but it isn't really what I wanted."

What has gone wrong? There is a considerable difference between the way a client understands a product as described by the specification document and the actual product. The specifications exist only on paper; the client therefore cannot really understand what the product itself will be like. The waterfall model, depending as it does so crucially on written specifications, can lead to the construction of products that simply do not meet the clients' real needs.

In fairness it should be pointed out that, just as an architect can help a client understand what is to be built by providing models, sketches, and plans, so the software engineer can use graphical techniques, such as data flow diagrams (Section

8.3.1), to communicate with the client. The problem is that these graphical aids do not describe how the finished product will work. For example, there is a considerable difference between a flowchart (a diagrammatic description of a product) and the working product itself.

The strength of the next life-cycle model to be examined, the rapid prototyping model, is that it can help to ensure that the client's real needs are met.

3.3   RAPID PROTOTYPING MODEL

A *rapid prototype* is a working model that is functionally equivalent to a subset of the product. For example, if the target product is to handle accounts payable, accounts receivable, and warehousing, then the rapid prototype might consist of a product that performs the screen handling for data capture and prints the reports, but does no file updating or error handling. A rapid prototype for a target product that is to determine the concentration of an enzyme in a solution might perform the calculation and display the answer, but without doing any validation or reasonableness checking of the input data.

The first step in the rapid prototyping life-cycle model depicted in Figure 3.3 is to build a rapid prototype and to let the client and future users interact with the rapid prototype and experiment with it. Once the client is satisfied that the rapid prototype indeed does most of what is required, the developers can draw up the specification document with some assurance that the product meets the client's real needs.

Having constructed the rapid prototype, the software process continues as shown in Figure 3.3. A major strength of the rapid prototyping model is that the development of the product is essentially linear, proceeding from the rapid prototype to the delivered product; the feedback loops of the waterfall model (Figure 3.2) are less likely to be needed in the rapid prototyping model. There are a number of reasons for this. First, the members of the development team use the rapid prototype to construct the specification document. Because the working rapid prototype has been validated through interaction with the client, it is reasonable to expect that the resulting specification document will be correct. Second, consider the design phase. Even though the rapid prototype has (quite rightly) been hurriedly assembled, the design team can gain insights from it—at worst they will be of the "how not to do it" variety. Again the feedback loops of the waterfall model are less likely to be needed here.

Implementation comes next. In the waterfall model, implementation of the design sometimes leads to design faults coming to light. In the rapid prototyping model, the fact that a preliminary working model has already been built tends to lessen the need to repair the design during or after implementation. The prototype will give some insights to the design team, even though it may reflect only partial functionality of the complete target product.

Once the product has been accepted by the client and then installed, maintenance begins. Depending on the maintenance that has to be performed, the cycle is reentered at the requirements, specification, design, or implementation phase.

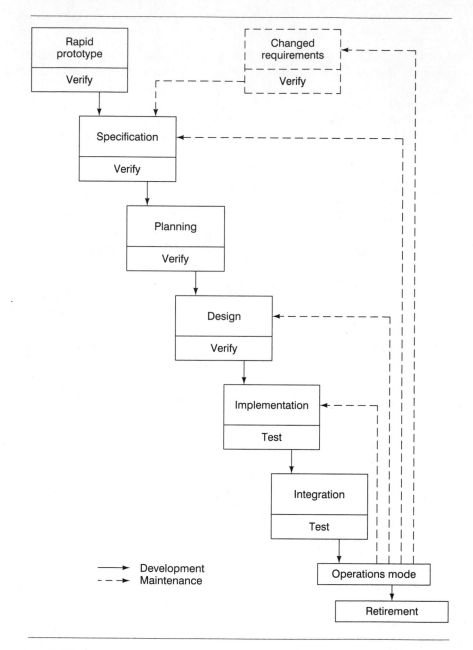

Figure 3.3 Rapid prototyping model.

An essential aspect of a rapid prototype is embodied in the word *rapid*. The developers should endeavor to construct the rapid prototype as rapidly as possible to speed up the software development process. After all, the sole use of the rapid prototype is to determine what the client's real needs are; once this has been determined, the rapid prototype is effectively discarded. For this reason, the internal structure of the rapid prototype is not relevant. What is important is that the prototype be built rapidly, and then modified rapidly to reflect the client's needs. Thus, speed is of the essence.

3.3.1 INTEGRATING THE WATERFALL AND RAPID PROTOTYPING MODELS

Despite the many successes of the waterfall model, it has a major drawback in that what is delivered to the client may not be what the client really needs. The rapid prototyping model has also had many successes. Nevertheless, as described in Chapter 7, it has not yet been proved beyond all doubt, and the model may have weaknesses of its own.

One solution is to combine the two approaches; this can be seen by comparing the phases of Figure 3.2 (waterfall model) with those of Figure 3.3 (rapid prototyping model). Rapid prototyping can be used as a requirements analysis technique; in other words, the first step is to build a rapid prototype in order to determine the client's real needs and then to use that rapid prototype as the input to the waterfall model.

This approach has a useful side effect. Some organizations are reluctant to use the rapid prototyping approach because of the risks involved in using any new technology. Introducing rapid prototyping into the organization as a front end to the waterfall model gives management the opportunity to assess the technique while minimizing the associated risk.

The rapid prototyping model is analyzed in greater detail in Chapter 7 where the requirements phase is described. A different class of life-cycle model is now examined.

3.4 INCREMENTAL MODEL

Software is built, not written. That is to say, software is constructed step by step, in the same way that a building is constructed. While a software product is in the process of being developed, each step adds to what has gone before. One day the design is extended; the next day another module is coded. The construction of the complete product proceeds incrementally in this way until completion.

Of course, it is not quite true that progress is made every day. Just as a contractor occasionally has to tear down an incorrectly positioned wall or replace a pane of glass that a careless painter has cracked, it sometimes is necessary to respecify, redesign, recode, or at worst, throw away what has already been completed and start again. But the fact that the product sometimes advances in fits and starts does not negate the basic reality that a software product is built piece by piece.

The realization that software is engineered incrementally has led to the development of a model that exploits this aspect of software development, the so-called incremental model shown in Figure 3.4. The product is designed, implemented, integrated, and tested as a series of incremental *builds*, where a build consists of code pieces from various modules interacting to provide a specific functional capability.

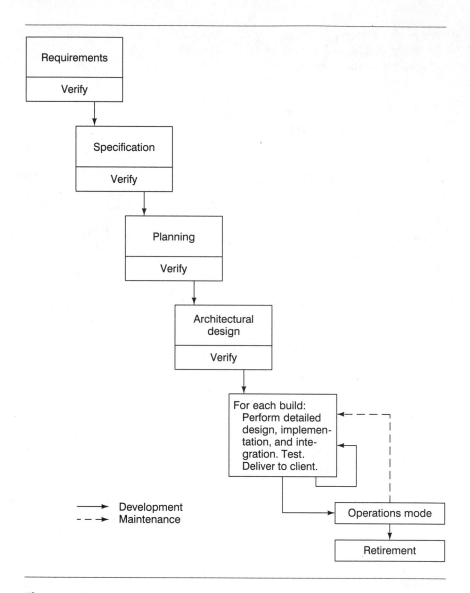

Figure 3.4 Incremental model.

For example, if the product is to control a nuclear submarine, then the navigation system could constitute a build, as could the weapons control system. In an operating system, the scheduler could be a build, and so could the file management system. At each stage of the incremental model a new build is coded and then integrated into the structure that is tested as a whole. The process stops when the product achieves target functionality, that is, when the product satisfies its specifications. The developer is free to break up the target product into builds as he or she sees fit, subject only to the constraint that as each build is integrated into the existing software, the resulting product must be testable. If the product is broken into too few builds, then the incremental model degenerates into the build-and-fix approach (Figure 3.1). Conversely, if the product consists of too many builds, then at each stage considerable time is spent in the integration testing of only a small amount of additional functionality. What constitutes an optimal decomposition into builds will vary from product to product and from developer to developer.

The incremental model has had some successes. For example, Wong has reported that she used it, together with other modern software development techniques, to deliver the software for an air defense system within budget and within 25 months [Wong, 1984].

The strengths and weaknesses of the incremental model are now presented.

3.4.1   ANALYSIS OF THE INCREMENTAL MODEL

The aim of both the waterfall and rapid prototyping models is the delivery of a complete, operational quality product. That is to say, the client is presented with a product that satisfies all requirements and is ready for use in operations mode by the client. Correct use of either the waterfall or the rapid prototyping model results in a product that will have been thoroughly tested, and the client should be confident that the product can be utilized for the purpose for which it was designed. Furthermore, the product will come with adequate documentation, so that not only can it be used in operations mode, but all three types of maintenance (adaptive, perfective, and corrective) can be performed as necessary. With both models there is a projected delivery date, and the intention is to deliver the complete product in full working order on or before that date.

In contrast, the incremental model does deliver an operational quality product at each stage, but one that satisfies only a subset of the client's requirements. The complete product is divided into builds, and the developer delivers the product build by build. A typical product will usually consist of 10 to 50 builds. At each stage the client has an operational quality product that does a portion of what is required; from delivery of the first build the client is able to do useful work. With the incremental model, portions of the total product might be available within weeks, whereas the client generally waits months or years to receive a product built using the waterfall or rapid prototyping models.

Another advantage of the incremental model is that it reduces the traumatic effect of imposing a completely new product on the client organization. The gradual introduction of the product via the incremental model provides time for the client to adjust to the new product. Change is an integral part of every growing organization; and because a software product is a model of reality, the need for change is also an integral part of delivered software. Change and adaptation are natural to the incremental model, whereas change can be a threat when products are developed and introduced in one large step.

From the client's financial viewpoint, phased delivery does not require a large capital outlay. Instead, there is an excellent cash flow, particularly if the earliest builds are chosen on the basis of delivering a high return on investment. A related advantage of the incremental model is that it is not necessary to complete the product to get a return on investment. Instead, the client can stop development of the product at any time.

A difficulty with the incremental model is that each additional build somehow has to be incorporated into the existing structure without destroying what has been built to date. Furthermore, the existing structure must lend itself to extension in this way, and the addition of each succeeding build must be simple and straightforward. Although this need for an open architecture is certainly a short-term liability, in the long term it can be a real strength. Every product undergoes development, followed by maintenance. During development it is indeed important to have clear specifications and a coherent and cohesive design. But once a product enters the maintenance phase, the requirements for that product change and radical enhancement can easily destroy a coherent and cohesive design to the extent that further maintenance becomes impossible. In such a case, the product must be rebuilt virtually from scratch. The fact that the design must be open-ended is not merely a prerequisite for development using the incremental model, but is essential for maintenance, irrespective of the model selected for the development phase. Thus, although the incremental model may require more careful design than the holistic waterfall and rapid prototyping models, the payoff comes in the maintenance phase. If a design is flexible enough to support the incremental model, then it will certainly allow virtually any sort of maintenance without falling apart. In fact, the incremental model does not distinguish between developing a product and enhancing (maintaining) it; each enhancement is merely an additional build.

It happens all too frequently that the requirements change while development is in progress; this problem is discussed in greater detail in Section 14.4.4. The flexibility of the incremental model gives it a major advantage over the waterfall and rapid prototyping models in this regard. On the negative side, the incremental model can too easily degenerate into the build-and-fix approach. Control of the process as a whole can be lost, and the resulting product, instead of being open-ended, becomes a maintainer's nightmare. In a sense, the incremental model is a contradiction in terms, requiring the developer to view the product as a whole in order to begin with a design that will support the entire product, including future enhancements, but simultaneously, to view that product as a sequence of builds, each essentially independent of the next. Unless the developer is skilled enough to be able to handle this apparent contradiction, the incremental model may lead to an unsatisfactory product.

In the incremental model of Figure 3.4, the requirements, specifications, planning, and architectural design must all be completed before implementation of the various builds commences. A more risky version of the incremental model is depicted in Figure 3.5. Once the client's requirements have been elicited, the specifications of the first build are drawn up. When this has been completed, the specifications team turns to the specifications of the second build while the design team designs the first build. Thus, the various builds are constructed in parallel, with each team making use of information gained in all the previous builds.

This approach incurs the real risk that the resulting builds will not fit together. With the incremental model of Figure 3.4, the fact that the specifications and architectural design must be completed before starting the first build means that there

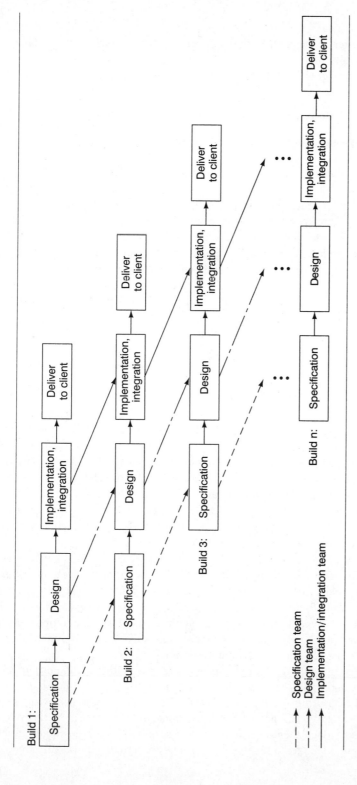

3.5 More risky incremental model.

is an overall design at the start. With the incremental model of Figure 3.5, unless the process is carefully monitored the entire project risks falling apart.

The spiral model has been left to last because it incorporates aspects of all the other models.

3.5   SPIRAL MODEL

There is almost always an element of risk involved in the development of software. For example, key personnel can resign before the product has been adequately documented. The manufacturer of hardware on which the product is critically dependent can go bankrupt. Too much, or too little, can be invested in testing and quality assurance. After spending hundreds of thousands of dollars on developing a major software product, technological breakthroughs can render the entire product worthless. An organization may research and develop a database management system, but before the product can be marketed, a lower-priced, functionally-equivalent package is announced. The components of a product built using the incremental model of Figure 3.5 may not fit together. For obvious reasons, software developers try to minimize such risks wherever possible.

One way of minimizing certain types of risk is to construct a prototype. As described in Section 3.3, an excellent way of reducing the risk that the delivered product will not satisfy the client's real needs is to construct a rapid prototype during the requirements phase. During subsequent phases, other sorts of prototypes may be appropriate. For example, a telephone company may devise a new, apparently highly effective algorithm for routing calls through a long-distance network. If the product is implemented but does not work as expected, the telephone company will have wasted the cost of developing the product. In addition, angry or inconvenienced customers may take their business elsewhere. This scenario can be avoided by constructing a prototype to handle only the routing of calls and testing it on a simulator. In this way the actual system is not disturbed, and for the cost of implementing just the routing algorithm, the telephone company can determine whether it is worthwhile to develop an entire network controller incorporating the new algorithm.

The idea of minimizing risk via the use of prototypes and other means is the concept underlying the *spiral model* [Boehm, 1988]. A simplistic way of looking at this life-cycle model is as a waterfall model with each phase preceded by risk analysis, as shown in Figure 3.6. (A portion of that figure is redrawn as Figure 3.7, to reflect the term *spiral model*.) Before commencing each phase, an attempt is made to control (or resolve) the risks. If it is impossible to resolve all the significant risks at that stage, then the project is immediately terminated.

Prototypes can be used effectively to provide information about certain classes of risk. For example, timing constraints can generally be tested by constructing a prototype and measuring whether the prototype can achieve the necessary performance. If the prototype is an accurate functional representation of the relevant features of the product, then measurements made on the prototype should give the developers a good idea as to whether the timing constraints can be achieved.

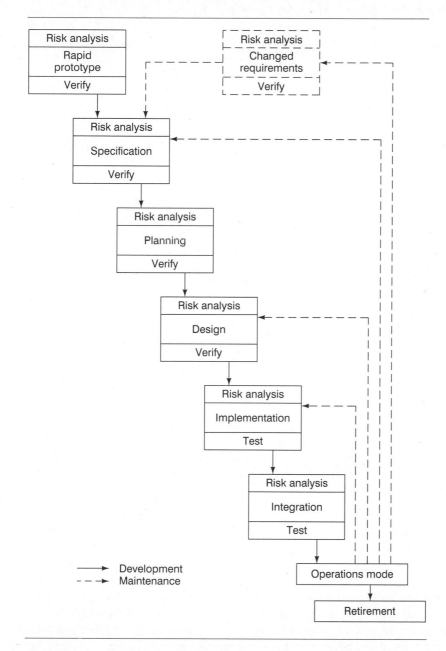

Figure 3.6 Simplistic version of spiral model.

Other areas of risk are less amenable to prototyping. For example, there is often a risk that the software professionals necessary to build the product cannot be hired or that key personnel may resign before the project is complete. Another potential risk is that a particular team may not be competent enough to develop a specific large-scale product. This risk cannot be resolved by testing their performance on a much smaller

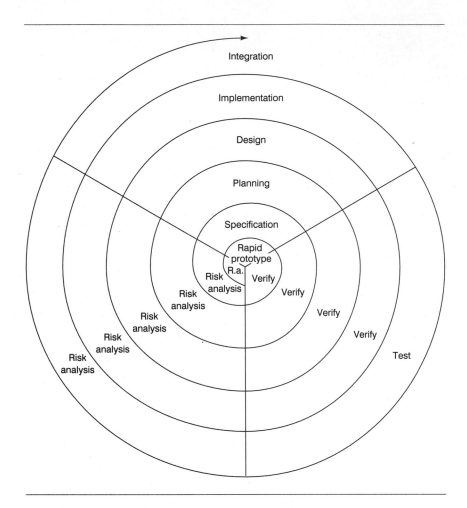

Figure 3.7   Portion of Figure 3.6 redrawn as a spiral.

prototype. There are essential differences between large-scale and small-scale software, and prototyping is thus of little use. Another area of risk for which prototyping cannot be employed is evaluating the delivery promises of a hardware supplier. A strategy the developer can adopt is to determine how well previous clients of the supplier have been treated, but past performance is by no means a certain predictor of future performance. A penalty clause in the delivery contract is one way of trying to ensure that essential hardware will be delivered on time, but what if the supplier refuses to sign an agreement that includes such a clause? Even with a penalty clause, late delivery may occur and eventually lead to legal action that can drag on for years. In the meantime, the software developer may have gone bankrupt because nondelivery of the promised hardware caused nondelivery of the promised software. In short, whereas

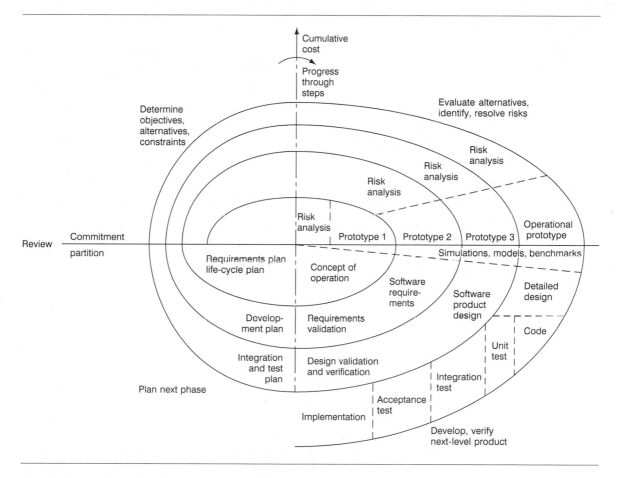

Figure 3.8 Full spiral model [Boehm, 1988]. (© 1988 IEEE.)

prototyping helps reduce risk in some areas, in other areas it is at best a partial answer, and in some areas it is no answer at all.

The full spiral model is shown in Figure 3.8. The radial dimension represents cumulative cost to date, the angular dimension represents progress through the spiral. Each cycle of the spiral corresponds to a phase. A phase begins (in the top left quadrant), by determining objectives of that phase, alternatives for achieving those objectives, and constraints imposed on those alternatives. This process results in a strategy for achieving those objectives. Next, that strategy is analyzed from the viewpoint of risk. Attempts are made to resolve every potential risk, in some cases by building a prototype. If certain risks cannot be resolved, the project may be terminated immediately; under some circumstances, however, a decision could be made to continue the project but on a significantly smaller scale. If all risks are successfully resolved, the next development step is started (bottom right quadrant).

This quadrant of the spiral model corresponds to the pure waterfall model. Finally, the results of that phase are evaluated, and the next phase is planned.

The spiral model has been used successfully to develop a wide variety of products. In one set of 25 projects in which the spiral model was used in conjunction with other means of increasing productivity, the productivity of every project increased by at least 50 percent over previous productivity levels and by 100 percent in most of the projects [Boehm, 1988]. In order to be able to decide whether the spiral model should be used for a given project, the advantages and disadvantages of the spiral model are now assessed.

3.5.1 ANALYSIS OF THE SPIRAL MODEL

The spiral model has a number of strengths. The emphasis on alternatives and constraints supports the reuse of existing software (Section 6.10) and the incorporation of software quality as a specific objective. In addition, a common problem in software development is determining when the products of a specific phase have been adequately tested. Spending too much time on testing is a waste of money, and delivery of the product may be unduly delayed. Conversely, if too little testing is performed then the delivered software may contain residual faults, resulting in unpleasant consequences for the developers. The spiral model answers this question in terms of the risks that would be incurred by not doing enough testing, or by doing too much testing. Perhaps most important, within the structure of the spiral model, maintenance is simply another cycle of the spiral; there is essentially no distinction between maintenance and development. Thus, the problem that maintenance is sometimes maligned by ignorant software professionals does not arise, because maintenance is treated the same way as development.

There are restrictions on the applicability of the spiral model. Specifically, in its present form the model is intended exclusively for internal development of large-scale software [Boehm, 1988]. Consider an internal project, that is, one where the developers and client are members of the same organization. If risk analysis leads to the conclusion that the project should be terminated, in-house software personnel can simply be reassigned to a different project. However, once a contract has been signed by a development organization and an external client, an effort by either side to terminate that contract can lead to a breach-of-contract lawsuit. Thus in the case of contract software, all risk analysis must be performed by both client and developers before the contract is signed, and not as in the spiral model.

A second restriction on the spiral model relates to the size of the project. Specifically, the spiral model is applicable to only large-scale software projects. It makes no sense to perform risk analysis if the cost of performing the risk analysis is comparable to the cost of the project as a whole, or if performing the risk analysis would significantly affect the profit potential. Instead, the developers should first decide how much is at risk and then decide how much risk analysis, if any, to perform.

A major strength of the spiral model is that it is risk-driven, but this can also be a weakness. Unless the software developers are skilled at pinpointing the possible risks and analyzing the risks accurately, there is a real danger that the team may believe that all is well at a time when the project, in fact, is headed for disaster. Only if the members of the development team are competent risk analysts should management decide to use the spiral model.

3.6 COMPARISON OF LIFE-CYCLE MODELS

Five different classes of software life-cycle models have been examined with special attention paid to some of their strengths and weaknesses. The waterfall model is a known quantity. Its strengths are understood, and so are its weaknesses. The rapid prototyping model was developed as a reaction to a specific perceived weakness in the waterfall model; namely, that the delivered product may not be what the client really needs. Less is known about the newer rapid prototyping model than the familiar waterfall model, and the rapid prototyping model may have some problems of its own. One alternative is to combine the strengths of both models, as suggested in Section 3.3.1. Another is to use a different model, namely, the incremental model. This model, notwithstanding its successes, also has some drawbacks. Yet another alternative is to use the spiral model, but only if the developers are adequately trained in risk analysis and risk resolution. A further factor that needs to be considered is that when the object-oriented paradigm is used, the life-cycle model needs to be iterative, that is, it must support feedback. In addition, incremental approaches seem to be appropriate. Object-oriented life-cycle models are discussed in Chapter 9.

Each software development organization should decide on a life-cycle model that is appropriate for that organization, its management, its employees, and its software process; and vary the model depending on the features of the specific product currently under development. Such a model will incorporate appropriate features from the various life-cycle models, minimizing their weaknesses and utilizing their strengths.

3.7 CAPABILITY MATURITY MODEL

The capability maturity model (CMM) is not a software life-cycle model. Instead, it is a strategy for improving the software process, irrespective of the actual life-cycle model used. The CMM was first put forward in 1986 by Watts Humphrey of the Software Engineering Institute (SEI) of Carnegie-Mellon University [Humphrey, 1989] (for the earlier name for the CMM, refer to the Just in Case You Wanted to Know box on page 72). Underlying the CMM is the belief that the use of new software techniques will not in itself result in increased productivity and profitability, because the cause of our problems is how we manage the software process. The CMM assists organizations in providing the infrastructure for a disciplined and mature software process. The improved process should result in better quality software and fewer software projects that suffer from time and cost overruns.

Recall that the software process encompasses the activities, techniques, and tools used to produce software. It thus incorporates both technical and managerial aspects of software production. The strategy of the CMM is to improve the management of the software process in the belief that improvements in techniques will be a natural consequence.

Bearing in mind that improvements in the software process cannot occur overnight, the CMM induces change incrementally. More specifically, five different levels of "maturity" are defined, and an organization then advances slowly in a series of small, evolutionary steps toward the higher levels of process maturity. In order to understand this approach, the five levels are now described [Paulk, Curtis, Chrissis, and Weber, 1993].

Maturity Level 1: Initial Level   At this the lowest level, there are essentially no sound software engineering management practices in place in the organization. Instead, everything is done on an ad hoc basis. If one specific project happens to be staffed by a competent manager and a good software development team, then that project may be successful. However, the usual pattern is time and cost overruns caused by a lack of sound management in general, and planning in particular. As a result, most activities are responses to crises, rather than preplanned tasks. In maturity level 1 organizations the software process is unpredictable, because it depends totally on the current staff; as the staff changes, so does the process. As a consequence, it is impossible to predict with any accuracy such important items as the time it will take to develop a product or the cost of that product.

It is an unfortunate fact that the vast majority of software organizations all over the world are level 1 organizations.

Maturity Level 2: Repeatable Level   At this level, basic software project management practices are in place. Planning and management techniques are based on experience with similar products; hence the name *repeatable*. At this level measurements are taken, an essential first step in achieving an adequate process. Typical measurements include the careful tracking of costs and schedules. Instead of functioning in crisis mode as in level 1, managers identify problems as they arise and take immediate corrective action to prevent them from becoming crises. The key point is that without measurements it is impossible to detect problems before they get out of hand. Also, measurements taken during one project can be used to draw up realistic duration and cost schedules for future projects.

Maturity Level	Characterization
1. Initial	Ad hoc process
2. Repeatable	Basic project management
3. Defined level	Process definition
4. Managed level	Process measurement
5. Optimizing level	Process control

Figure 3.9 The five levels of the capability maturity model.

Maturity Level 3: Defined Level   At level 3 the process for software production is fully documented. Both the managerial and technical aspects of the process are clearly defined, and continual efforts are made to improve the process wherever possible. Reviews (Section 5.2) are used to achieve software quality. At this level it makes sense to introduce new technology such as CASE environments (Section 4.3.1) in order to increase quality and productivity further. In contrast, "high tech" only makes the crisis-driven level 1 process even more chaotic.

Although a number of organizations have attained maturity levels 2 and 3, no organization has yet reached levels 4 and 5, although individual projects and groups have. The two highest levels are thus targets for the future.

Maturity Level 4: Managed Level   A level 4 organization sets quality and productivity goals for each project. These two quantities are continually measured, and corrective action is taken when there are unacceptable deviations from the goal. Statistical quality controls [Deming, 1986; Juran, 1988] are in place to enable management to distinguish a random deviation from a meaningful violation of quality or productivity standards. (A simple example of a statistical quality control measure is the number of faults detected per 1000 lines of code. A corresponding objective is to reduce this quantity over time.)

Maturity Level 5: Optimizing Level   The goal of a level 5 organization is continuous process improvement. Statistical quality and process control techniques are used to guide the organization. The knowledge gained from each project is utilized in future projects. The process thus incorporates a positive feedback loop, resulting in a steady improvement in productivity and quality.

These five maturity levels are summarized in Figure 3.9. In order to improve its software process, an organization first attempts to gain an understanding of its current process and then formulates the intended process. Next, actions that will result in achieving this process improvement are determined and ranked in priority order. Finally, a plan to accomplish this improvement is drawn up and executed. This series of steps is then repeated, with the organization successively improving its software process.

Experience with the capability maturity model has shown that advancing a complete maturity level usually takes from 18 months to 3 years, but moving from level 1 to level 2 sometimes takes 3 or even 5 years. This is a reflection of how difficult it is to instill a methodical approach in an organization that up to now has functioned on a purely ad hoc and reactive basis.

For each maturity level, the SEI has highlighted a series of key process areas which an organization should target in its endeavor to reach the next maturity level. Within each process area is a group of related goals that, if achieved, will result in the next maturity level being attained. For example, for maturity level 2, the key process areas include software quality assurance (Section 5.1.1), configuration management (Section 4.6), and project planning (Chapter 10). Within this last area, one of the goals is the development of a plan that appropriately and realistically covers the activities of software development. At the highest level, maturity level 5, the key practices include defect prevention, technology innovation, and process change management. Comparing the goals of the two levels, it is clear that a level 5 organization is far in advance of one that is at level 2. For example, a level 2 organization is concerned with software quality assurance, that is, with detecting and correcting faults (software quality is discussed in more detail in Chapter 5). In contrast, the process of a level 5 organization incorporates defect prevention, or trying to ensure that there are no faults in the software in the first place.

To aid an organization to reach the higher maturity levels, the SEI has developed a series of questionnaires that form the basis for an assessment by an SEI team. The purpose of the assessment is to highlight current shortcomings in an organization's software process and to indicate ways in which the organization can improve its process.

The Software Engineering Institute is largely funded by the U.S. Department of Defense (DoD). One of the original goals of the CMM program was to raise the quality of defense software by evaluating the processes of contractors who produce software for DoD and awarding contracts to those contractors who demonstrate a mature process level. However, the CMM program has moved far beyond this limited goal of improving DoD software and is being implemented by a wide variety of software organizations that wish to improve software quality and productivity.

Does implementing the CMM lead to increased profitability? Preliminary results indicate that this is indeed the case. For example, the Software Engineering Division of Hughes Aircraft in Fullerton, California, spent nearly $500,000 between 1987 and 1990 for assessments and improvement programs [Humphrey, Snider, and Willis, 1991]. During this 3-year period, Hughes Aircraft moved up from maturity level 2 to level 3, with every expectation of future improvement to level 4 and even level 5. As a consequence of improving its process, Hughes Aircraft estimates its annual savings to be of the order of $2 million. These savings have accrued in a number of ways, including decreased overtime hours, fewer crises, improved employee morale, and lower turnover of software professionals.

Comparable results have been reported at other organizations. For example, the Equipment Division at Raytheon moved from level 1 in 1988 to level 3 in 1993. A twofold increase in productivity has resulted, as well as a return of $7.70 for every dollar invested in the process improvement effort [Dion, 1993]. Shlumberger has had similar successes [Wohlwend and Rosenbaum, 1993]. As a consequence of results

CMM Level	Duration (Calendar Months)	Effort (Person Months)	Faults Detected during Development	Faults Delivered to Client and Installed	Total Cost of Development
Level 1	29.8	593.5	1,348	61	$5,440,000
Level 2	18.5	143.0	328	12	$1,311,000
Level 3	15.2	79.5	182	7	$ 728,000
Level 4	12.5	42.8	97	5	$ 392,000
Level 5	9.0	16.0	37	1	$ 146,000

Figure 3.10 Model predictions when a 200,000-line data processing product is developed by organizations at CMM levels 1 through 5. (Copyright 1993 by Master Systems, Inc.)

like these, the capability maturity model is starting to be applied widely within the software industry.

Using data from over 1300 projects, Rifkin has modeled the expected number of faults and total cost if the same 200,000-line data processing product were to be developed by organizations at levels 1 through 5 [Rifkin, 1993]. The model predictions are shown in Figure 3.10. It appears that the costs of advancing an organization from level 1 to level 5 can be more than recouped by the resulting increased software quality and drastically decreased development costs.

There is yet another reason for the growing importance of the CMM. The U.S. Air Force has stipulated that any software development organization that wishes to be an Air Force contractor must conform to CMM level 3 by 1998, and it is probable that the Department of Defense as a whole will issue a similar directive in due course. Thus, there is pressure for organizations to improve the maturity of their software processes.

3.8   ISO 9000

As explained in the previous section, the SEI Capability Maturity Model (CMM) initiative is an attempt to improve software quality by improving the process by which software is developed. The term *maturity* is essentially a measure of the goodness of the process itself. A different attempt to improve software quality is based on International Standards Organization (ISO) 9000-series standards.

ISO 9000 is a series of five related standards that are applicable to a wide variety of industrial activities, including design, development, production, installation, and servicing; ISO 9000 is certainly not just a software standard. Within the ISO 9000 series, standard ISO 9001 for quality systems [ISO 9001, 1987] is the standard that is most applicable to software development. Because of the broadness of ISO 9001, ISO has published specific guidelines to assist in applying ISO 9001 to software, namely, ISO 9000-3 [ISO 9000-3, 1991].

ISO 9000 has a number of features that distinguish it from the CMM [Dawood, 1994]. In ISO 9000 there is a stress on documenting the process in both words and pictures in order to ensure consistency and comprehensibility. Also, the ISO 9000 philosophy is that adherence to the standard does not guarantee a 100 percent quality product, but rather reduces the risk of a poor quality product. ISO 9000 is only one part of a quality system. Also required are management commitment to quality, intensive training of workers, and setting and achieving goals for continual quality improvement.

Like the CMM, ISO 9000 emphasizes measurement. Both models stress the corrective actions that need to be taken to ensure process improvement. Finally, both strongly underline the need for continuous training of software professionals, not just when introducing quality-improvement measures.

ISO 9000-series standards have been adopted by over 60 countries, including the United States, Japan, Canada, and the European Union (E.U.). This means, for example, that if a U.S. software organization wishes to do business with a European client, the U.S. organization must first be certified to be ISO 9000-compliant. A certified registrar (auditor) has to examine the company's process and certify that its process complies with the ISO standard.

Although the CMM and ISO 9000 have the same objective, namely, improved software quality, each considers different attributes when determining maturity level or compliance with ISO 9000. Thus, even though there are major areas of overlap, it has been reported that at least two level 1 organizations have been certified as compliant with ISO 9000 [Bishop, 1994]. Conversely, it is possible in principle for an organization to demonstrate a high level of maturity without complying with ISO 9000 [Bamford and Deibler, 1993a]. In general, however, there is a high probability that a mature organization will have a software process that is ISO 9000-compliant.

Following their European counterparts, more and more U.S. organizations are requiring ISO 9000 certification. For example, General Electric Plastic Division insisted that 340 vendors achieve the standard by June 1993 [Dawood, 1994]. It is unlikely that the U.S. government will follow the E.U. lead and require ISO 9000 compliance for non-U.S. companies that wish to do business with organizations in the United States. Nevertheless, there are pressures both within the United States and from its major trading partners that may ultimately result in significant worldwide ISO 9000 compliance.

Chapter Review

A number of different process models are described. The build-and-fix model (Section 3.1) should be avoided. The strength of the waterfall model (Section 3.2) is its disciplined, documentation-driven approach. The problem with the model is that the delivered product may not be what the client really needs. The rapid prototyping model (Section 3.3) was developed to solve this problem. The incremental model (Section 3.4) has advantages such as maximizing early return on investments and ease of maintenance, but has difficulties of its own, particularly the need for an open architecture. The risk-driven spiral model is applicable to large-scale internal projects (Section 3.5). It is suggested in Section 3.6 that aspects of various life-cycle models should be combined in order to come up with an appropriate life-cycle model. The form of this life-cycle model will depend on the organization, its management, its employees, and the specific product to be built. Finally, the capability maturity model is described in Section 3.7, and ISO 9000 in Section 3.8.

For Further Reading

A description of the waterfall model appears in Chapter 4 of [Boehm, 1981]. The same chapter also includes an example of an incremental model different from the one presented here in Section 3.4.

For an introduction to rapid prototyping, three suggested books are [Lantz, 1985], [Connell and Shafer, 1989], and [Gane, 1989]. The role of computer-aided prototyping is assessed in [Luqi and Royce, 1992].

A description of the evolutionary delivery model, one version of the incremental model, can be found in [Gilb, 1988]. Another type of incremental model is described in [Currit, Dyer, and Mills, 1986] and [Selby, Basili, and Baker, 1987]. The spiral model is explained in [Boehm, 1988], and its application to the TRW Software Productivity System appears in [Boehm, Penedo, Stuckle, Williams, and Pyster, 1984]. Risk analysis is described in [Charette, 1989] and [Boehm, 1991].

Many other life-cycle models have been put forward. A life-cycle model that emphasizes human factors is presented in [Mantei and Teorey, 1988]. The life-cycle model recommended by the NASA Software Engineering Laboratory is described in [Landis et al., 1992]. Object-oriented life-cycle models are described in [Henderson-Sellers and Edwards, 1990], [Booch, 1994], and [Rajlich, 1994]. A method for comparing alternative life-cycle models is presented in [Davis, Bersoff, and Comer, 1988]. The proceedings of the International Software Process Workshops are a useful source of information on life-cycle models.

A detailed description of the SEI capability maturity model (CMM) is given in [Humphrey, 1989]. A new version is described in [Paulk, Curtis, Chrissis, and Weber, 1993] and [Paulk et al., 1993]. Successes of the CMM are described in [Humphrey, Snider, and Willis, 1991] and [Hicks and Card, 1994], while criticism of the assessment process appears in [Bollinger and McGowan, 1991]. The July 1993 issue of *IEEE Software* contains a number of papers on the CMM. An assessment of SEI software process assessments between 1987 and 1991 is given in [Kitson and Masters, 1993]; its impact on the software industry is discussed in [Saiedien and Kuzara; 1995]. [Bamford and Deibler, 1993b] is a detailed comparison of ISO 9000 and the CMM; an overview appears in [Bamford and Deibler, 1993a]. [Paulk, 1995] is another comparison. The December 1993 issue of *IEEE Transactions on Software Engineering* and the July 1994 issue of *IEEE Software* contain a number of papers on process improvement. [Fuggetta and Picco, 1994] is an annotated bibliography on process improvement.

Problems

3.1   Suppose that you have to build a product to determine the square root of 73,624.9385 to four decimal places. Once the product has been implemented and tested, it will be thrown away. What life-cycle model would you use? Give reasons for your answer.

3.2   You are a software engineering consultant and have been called in by the vice-president for finance of a corporation that manufactures and sells boots. She wants your organization to build a product that will monitor the company's stock, starting with the purchasing of the leather and keeping track of the boots as they are manufactured, distributed to the individual stores, and sold to customers. What criteria would you use in selecting a life-cycle model for the project?

3.3   List the risks involved in developing the software of Problem 3.2. How would you attempt to resolve each risk?

3.4   Your development of the stock control product for the bootwear chain is so successful that your organization decides that it must be rewritten as a package to be sold to a variety of different organizations that manufacture and sell products via their own retailers. The new product must therefore be portable and easily adapted to new hardware and/or operating systems. How do the criteria you would use in selecting a life-cycle model for this project differ from those in your answer to Problem 3.2?

3.5   Describe the sort of product that would be an ideal application for the incremental model.

3.6   Now describe the type of situation where the incremental model might lead to difficulties.

3.7   Describe the sort of product that would be an ideal application for the spiral model.

3.8   Now describe the type of situation where the spiral model is inappropriate.

3.9   You have been hired by Olde Fashioned Software Developers to improve their productivity and profitability. You quickly discover that the company is undoubtedly at maturity level 1. What is the first step that you will take?

3.10   (Term Project) Which software life-cycle model would you use for the Osbert Oglesby project described in Appendix A? Give reasons for your answer.

3.11   (Readings in Software Engineering) Your instructor will distribute copies of [Boehm, 1988]. Show that the spiral model incorporates aspects of both the waterfall model and the rapid prototyping model. Which of the two models predominates?

References

[Bamford and Deibler, 1993a] R. C. BAMFORD AND W. J. DEIBLER, II, "Comparing, Contrasting ISO 9001 and the SEI Capability Maturity Model," *IEEE Computer* **26** (October 1993), pp. 68–70.

[Bamford and Deibler, 1993b] R. C. BAMFORD AND W. J. DEIBLER, II, "A Detailed Comparison of the SEI Software Maturity Levels and Technology Stages to the

Requirements for ISO 9001 Registration," Software Systems Quality Consulting, San Jose, CA, 1993.

[Bishop, 1994] M. BISHOP, Usenet posting <2p8pab$rv0@source.asset.com> on **comp.software-eng**, April 22, 1994.

[Boehm, 1981] B. W. BOEHM, *Software Engineering Economics,* Prentice-Hall, Englewood Cliffs, NJ, 1981.

[Boehm, 1988] B. W. BOEHM, "A Spiral Model of Software Development and Enhancement," *IEEE Computer* **21** (May 1988), pp. 61–72.

[Boehm, 1991] B. W. BOEHM, "Software Risk Management: Principles and Practices," *IEEE Software* **8** (January 1991), pp. 32–41.

[Boehm, Penedo, Stuckle, Williams, and Pyster, 1984] B. W. BOEHM, M. H. PENEDO, E. D. STUCKLE, R. D. WILLIAMS, AND A. B. PYSTER, "A Software Development Environment for Improving Productivity," *IEEE Computer* **17** (June 1984), pp. 30–44.

[Bollinger and McGowan, 1991] T. BOLLINGER AND C. McGOWAN, "A Critical Look at Software Capability Evaluations," *IEEE Software* **8** (July 1991), pp. 25–41.

[Booch, 1994] G. BOOCH, *Object-Oriented Analysis and Design with Applications, Second Edition,* Benjamin/Cummings, Redwood City, CA, 1994.

[Charette, 1989] R. N. CHARETTE, *Software Engineering Risk Analysis and Management,* McGraw-Hill, New York, 1989.

[Connell and Shafer, 1989] J. L. CONNELL AND L. SHAFER, *Structured Rapid Prototyping: An Evolutionary Approach to Software Development,* Yourdon Press, Englewood Cliffs, NJ, 1989.

[Currit, Dyer, and Mills, 1986] P. A. CURRIT, M. DYER, AND H. D. MILLS, "Certifying the Reliability of Software," *IEEE Transactions on Software Engineering* **SE-12** (January 1986), pp. 3–11.

[Davis, Bersoff, and Comer, 1988] A. M. DAVIS, E. H. BERSOFF, AND E. R. COMER, "A Strategy for Comparing Alternative Software Development Life-Cycle Models," *IEEE Transactions on Software Engineering* **14** (October 1988), pp. 1453–1461.

[Dawood, 1994] M. DAWOOD, "It's Time for ISO 9000," *CrossTalk* (March 1994), pp. 26–28.

[Deming, 1986] W. E. DEMING, *Out of the Crisis,* MIT Center for Advanced Engineering Study, Cambridge, MA, 1986.

[Dion, 1993] R. DION, "Process Improvement and the Corporate Balance Sheet," *IEEE Software* **10** (July 1993), pp. 28–35.

[Fuggetta and Picco, 1994] A. FUGGETTA AND G. P. PICCO, "An Annotated Bibliography on Software Process Improvement," *ACM SIGSOFT Software Engineering Notes* **19** (July 1994), pp. 66–68.

[Gane, 1989] C. GANE, *Rapid System Development: Using Structured Techniques and Relational Technology,* Prentice-Hall, Englewood Cliffs, NJ, 1989.

[Gilb, 1988] T. GILB, *Principles of Software Engineering Management,* Addison-Wesley, Wokingham, UK, 1988.

[Henderson-Sellers and Edwards, 1990] B. HENDERSON-SELLERS AND J. M. EDWARDS, "The Object-Oriented Systems Life Cycle," *Communications of the ACM* **33** (September 1990), pp. 142–159.

[Hicks and Card, 1994] M. HICKS AND D. CARD, "Tales of Process Improvement," *IEEE Software* **11** (January 1994), pp. 114–115.

[Humphrey, 1989] W. S. HUMPHREY, *Managing the Software Process,* Addison-Wesley, Reading, MA, 1989.

[Humphrey, 1995] W. S. HUMPHREY, *A Discipline for Software Engineering,* Addison-Wesley, Reading, MA, 1995.

[Humphrey, Snider, and Willis, 1991] W. S. HUMPHREY, T. R. SNIDER, AND R. R. WILLIS, "Software Process Improvement at Hughes Aircraft," *IEEE Software* **8** (July 1991), pp. 11–23.

[ISO 9000-3, 1991] "ISO 9000-3, Guidelines for the Application of ISO 9001 to the Development, Supply and Maintenance of Software," International Organization for Standardization, Geneva, 1991.

[ISO 9001, 1987] "ISO 9001, Quality Systems—Model for Quality Assurance in Design/Development, Production, Installation, and Servicing," International Organization for Standardization, Geneva, 1987.

[Juran, 1988] J. M. JURAN, *Juran on Planning for Quality,* Macmillan, New York, 1988.

[Kitson and Masters, 1993] D. H. KITSON AND S. M. MASTERS, "An Analysis of SEI Software Process Assessment Results: 1987–1991," *Proceedings of the Fifteenth International Conference on Software Engineering,* Baltimore, MD, May 1993, pp. 68–77.

[Landis et al., 1992] L. LANDIS, S. WALIGARA, F. MCGARRY, ET AL. "Recommended Approach to Software Development: Revision 3," Technical Report SEL-81-305, Software Engineering Laboratory, Greenbelt, MD, June 1992.

[Lantz, 1985] K. E. LANTZ, *The Prototyping Methodology,* Prentice-Hall, Englewood Cliffs, NJ, 1985.

[Luqi and Royce, 1992] LUQI AND W. ROYCE, "Status Report: Computer-Aided Prototyping," *IEEE Software* **9** (November 1992), pp. 77–81.

[Mantei and Teorey, 1988] M. M. MANTEI AND T. J. TEOREY, "Cost/Benefit Analysis for Incorporating Human Factors in the Software Development Lifecycle," *Communications of the ACM* **31** (April 1988), pp. 428–439.

[Paulk, 1995] M. C. PAULK, "How ISO 9001 Compares with the CMM," *IEEE Software* **12** (January 1995), pp. 74–83.

[Paulk, Curtis, Chrissis, and Weber, 1993] M. C. PAULK, B. CURTIS, M. B. CHRISSIS, AND C. V. WEBER, "Capability Maturity Model for Software, Version 1.1," Report CMU/SEI-93-TR-24, ADA263403, Software Engineering Institute, Carnegie Mellon University, Pittsburgh, February 1993.

[Paulk et al., 1993] M. C. PAULK, C. V. WEBER, S. GARCIA, M. B. CHRISSIS, AND M. BUSH, "Key Practices of the Capability Maturity Model, Version 1.1," Report CMU/SEI-93-TR-25 ADA263432, Software Engineering Institute, Carnegie Mellon University, Pittsburgh, February 1993.

[Rajlich, 1994] V. RAJLICH, "Decomposition/Generalization Methodology for Object-Oriented Programming," *Journal of Systems and Software* **24** (February 1994), pp. 181–186.

[Rifkin, 1993] S. RIFKIN, Usenet posting <1993Mar1.201334.20244@seas.gwu.edu> on comp.software-eng, March 1, 1993.

[Royce, 1970] W. W. ROYCE, "Managing the Development of Large Software Systems: Concepts and Techniques," *1970 WESCON Technical Papers, Western Electronic Show and Convention,* Los Angeles, August 1970, pp. A/1-1–A/1-9. Reprinted in: *Proceedings of the 11th International Conference on Software Engineering,* Pittsburgh, May 1989, pp. 328–338.

[Saiedien and Kuzara, 1995] H. SAIEDIEN AND R. KUZARA, "SEI Capability Maturity Model's Impact on Contractors," *IEEE Computer* **28** (January 1995), pp. 16–26.

[Selby, Basili, and Baker, 1987] R. W. SELBY, V. R. BASILI, AND F. T. BAKER, "Cleanroom Software Development: An Empirical Evaluation," *IEEE Transactions on Software Engineering* **SE-13** (September 1987), pp. 1027–1037.

[Spivey, 1992] J. M. SPIVEY, *The Z Notation: A Reference Manual,* Prentice-Hall, New York, 1992.

[Wohlwend and Rosenbaum, 1993] H. WOHLWEND AND S. ROSENBAUM, "Software Improvements in an International Company," *Proceedings of the 15th International Conference on Software Engineering,* Baltimore, MD, May 1993, pp. 212–220.

[Wong, 1984] C. WONG, "A Successful Software Development," *IEEE Transactions on Software Engineering* **SE-10** (November 1984), pp. 714–727.

4

STEPWISE REFINEMENT, CASE, AND OTHER TOOLS OF THE TRADE

A software engineer needs two classes of tools. First, there are analytical tools such as stepwise refinement and cost–benefit analysis, used in software development. And then there are software tools, that is, products that assist the software engineer in developing and maintaining software. These are usually termed *CASE* tools (CASE is an acronym that stands for computer-aided software engineering).

We begin examining an analytical tool, namely, stepwise refinement.

4.1 STEPWISE REFINEMENT

Stepwise refinement is a problem-solving technique that underlies many software engineering techniques. It can be defined as a means to "postpone decisions on details until as late as possible in order to be able to concentrate on the important issues."

As will be seen during the course of this book, stepwise refinement underlies many specification techniques, design and implementation techniques, even testing and integration techniques. The reason stepwise refinement is so important is because of Miller's law [Miller, 1956], which states that at any one time a human being can concentrate on 7 ± 2 *chunks* (quanta of information).

The problem when developing software is that we need to concentrate on many more than seven chunks at a time. For example, a module usually has considerably more than seven variables, and a client has more than seven requirements. Stepwise refinement enables the software engineer to concentrate on those seven chunks that are the most relevant at the current phase of development.

The following example illustrates how stepwise refinement can be used in the design of a product.

Transaction Type	Name	Address
3	Brown	
1	Harris	2 Oak Lane, Townsville
2	Jones	Box 345, Tarrytown
3	Jones	
1	Smith	1304 Elm Avenue, Oak City

Figure 4.1 Input transaction records for sequential master file update.

4.1.1 STEPWISE REFINEMENT EXAMPLE

The example presented in this section seems almost trivial, in that it involves updating a sequential master file, a common operation in many application areas. This choice of a familiar example is deliberate in order to enable the reader to concentrate on stepwise refinement rather than the problem in hand:

> Design a product to update the sequential master file containing name and address data for the monthly magazine, *True Life Software Disasters*. There are three types of transactions, namely insertions, modifications, and deletions, with transaction codes 1, 2, and 3 respectively. Thus the transaction types are:
>
> Type 1: INSERT (a new subscriber into the master file)
>
> Type 2: MODIFY (an existing subscriber record)
>
> Type 3: DELETE (an existing subscriber record)
>
> Transactions are sorted into alphabetical order by name of subscriber. If there is more than one transaction for a given subscriber, the transactions for that subscriber have been sorted so that insertions occur before modifications and modifications before deletions.

The first step in designing a solution is to set up a typical file of input transactions, such as that shown in Figure 4.1. The file contains five records, namely DELETE Brown, INSERT Harris, MODIFY Jones, DELETE Jones, and INSERT Smith. (It is not unusual to perform both a modification and a deletion of the same subscriber in one run.)

The problem may be represented as shown in Figure 4.2. There are two input files:

1. Old master file name and address records

2. Transaction records

and there are three output files:

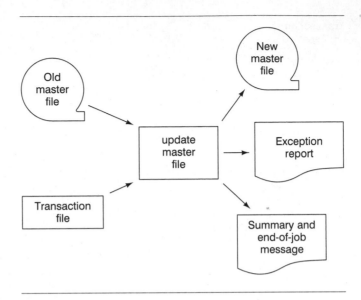

Figure 4.2 Sequential master file update.

3. New master file name and address records

4. Exception report

5. Summary and end-of-job message

To begin the design process, the starting point is the single box **update master file** shown in Figure 4.3. This box can be decomposed into three boxes, labeled **input, process,** and **output.** The assumption is that when **process** requires a record, our level of competence is such that the correct record can be produced at the right time. Similarly, we are capable of writing the correct record to the correct file at the right time. Therefore, the technique is to separate out the **input** and **output** aspects and concentrate on **process.** What is this **process**? To determine what it

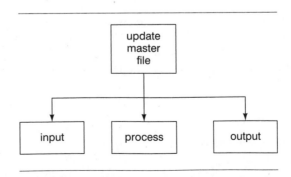

Figure 4.3 First refinement of design.

Transaction file	Old master file	New master file
3 Brown	Abel	Abel
1 Harris	Brown	Harris
2 Jones	James	James
3 Jones	Jones	Smith
1 Smith	Smith	Townsend
	Townsend	

Exception report

Smith

Figure 4.4 Transaction file, old master file, new master file, and exception report.

does, consider the example shown in Figure 4.4. The key of the first transaction record (Brown) is compared with the key of the first old master file record (Abel). Because Brown comes after Abel, the Abel record is written to the new master file, and the next old master file record (Brown) is read. In this case the key of the transaction record matches the key of the old master file record, and because the transaction type is 3 (DELETE), the Brown record must be deleted. This is implemented by not copying the Brown record onto the new master file. The next transaction record (Harris) and old master file record (James) are read, overwriting the Brown records in their respective buffers. Harris comes before James and is, therefore, inserted into the new master file; the next transaction record (Jones) is read. Because Jones comes after James, the James record is written to the new master file, and the next old master file record is read; this is Jones. As can be seen from the transaction file, the Jones record is to be modified and then deleted, so the next transaction record (Smith) and the next old master file record (also Smith) are read. Unfortunately, the transaction type is 1 (INSERT), but Smith is already in the master file. So there is an error of some sort in the data, and the Smith record is written to the exception report. To be more precise, the Smith transaction record is written to the exception report, the Smith old master file record is written to the new master file.

Now that process is understood, it may be represented as in Figure 4.5. Next, the process box of Figure 4.3 may be refined, resulting in the second refinement shown in Figure 4.6. The dashed lines to the input and output boxes denote that decisions as to how to handle input and output have been deferred until a later refinement. The remainder of the figure is the flowchart of the process, or rather, an early refinement of the flowchart. As already pointed out, input and output have been deferred. Also, there is no provision for an end-of-file condition, nor has it yet been specified what to do when an error condition is encountered. The strength of stepwise refinement is that these and similar problems can be solved in later refinements.

Transaction record key = old master file record key	1. INSERT: Print error message
	2. MODIFY: Change master file record
	3. DELETE: *Delete master file record
Transaction record key > old master file record key	Copy old master file record onto new master file
Transaction record key < old master file record key	1. INSERT: Write transaction record to new master file
	2. MODIFY: Print error message
	3. DELETE: Print error message

*Deletion of a master file record is implemented by not copying the record onto the new master file.

Figure 4.5 Diagrammatic representation of process.

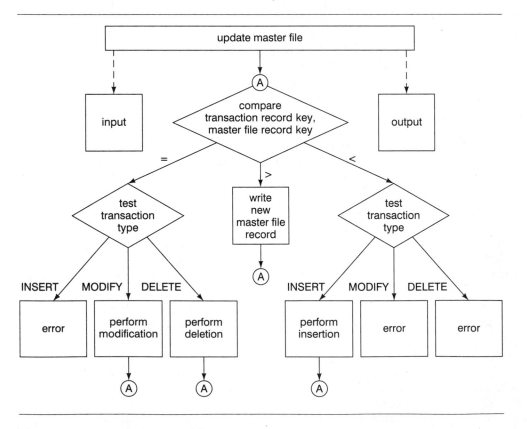

Figure 4.6 Second refinement of design.

The next step is to refine the input and output boxes of Figure 4.6, resulting in Figure 4.7. End-of-file conditions have still not been handled, nor has the writing of the end-of-job message. Again, these can be done at a later iteration. What is critical, however, is that the design of Figure 4.7 has a major fault. To see this, consider the situation with regard to the data of Figure 4.4 when the current transaction is 2 Jones, that is, modify Jones, and the current old master file record is Jones. In the design of Figure 4.7, because the key of the transaction record is the same as the key of the old master file record, the leftmost path is followed to the test transaction type decision box. Because the current transaction type is MODIFY, the old master file record is modified and written to the new master file, and the next transaction record is read. This record is 3 Jones, that is, delete Jones. But the modified Jones record has already been written to the new master file.

The reader may be wondering why an incorrect refinement has deliberately been presented. The point is that, when using stepwise refinement, it is necessary to desk-check each successive refinement before proceeding to the next. If a particular refinement turns out to be faulty, it is not necessary to restart the process from the beginning, but merely to go back to the previous refinement and proceed from there. In this instance, the second refinement (Figure 4.6) is correct, so it may be used as the basis for another attempt at a third refinement. This time, the design uses *level-1 lookahead,* that is, a transaction record is processed only after the next transaction record has been analyzed. Details are left as an exercise; see Problem 4.1.

In the fourth refinement, details that have been ignored up to now, such as opening and closing files, have to be introduced. With stepwise refinement such details are handled last, after the logic of the design has been fully developed. Obviously, it is impossible to execute the product without opening and closing files. However, what is important here is the stage in the design process at which such details as file openings and closings are handled. While the design is being developed, the seven or so chunks on which the designer can concentrate at once should not include details like opening and closing files; file openings and closings have nothing to do with the design itself, they are merely implementation details that are part of any design. However, in later refinements opening and closing files becomes vital. In other words, stepwise refinement can be considered to be a technique for prioritizing the various problems that have to be solved within a phase. Stepwise refinement ensures that every problem is solved and that each is solved at the appropriate time, but at no time need more than 7 ± 2 chunks be handled.

The term *stepwise refinement* was first introduced by Wirth [Wirth, 1971]. In the preceding example, stepwise refinement was applied to a flowchart, whereas Wirth applied the technique to pseudocode. The specific representation to which stepwise refinement is applied is not important; stepwise refinement is a general technique that can be used in every phase of software development and with almost every representation.

The power of stepwise refinement is that it helps the software engineer concentrate on the relevant aspects of the current development phase (design phase in the preceding example) and to ignore details that, though necessary in the overall scheme, need not be considered, and in fact should be ignored, until later. Miller's

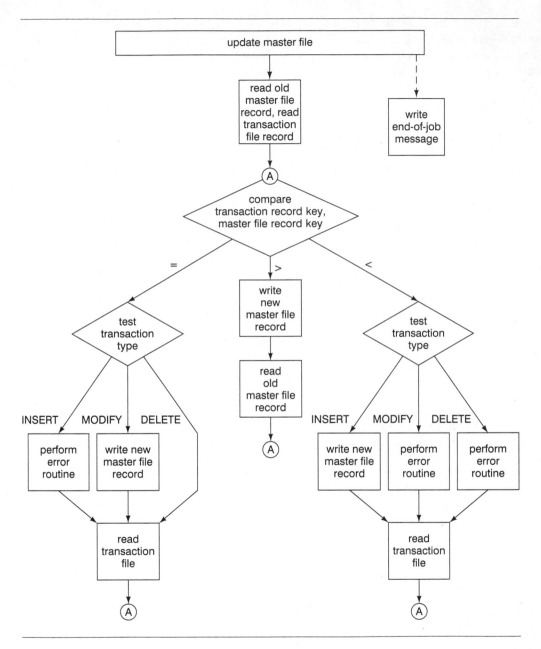

Figure 4.7 Third refinement of design (design has major fault).

law is a fundamental restriction on the mental powers of human beings. Because we cannot fight our nature, we must live with it, accepting our limitations and doing the best we can under the circumstances.

Like stepwise refinement, cost–benefit analysis is another fundamental software engineering technique that is used throughout the software life cycle. This technique is described in the next section.

4.2   C<small>OST</small>–B<small>ENEFIT</small> A<small>NALYSIS</small>

One way of determining whether a possible course of action would be profitable is to compare estimated future benefits against projected future costs. This is termed *cost–benefit analysis*. As an example of cost–benefit analysis within the computer context, consider how Krag Central Electric Company (KCEC) decided in 1965 whether or not to computerize its billing system. Billing was then being done manually by 80 clerks who mailed bills every 2 months to KCEC customers. Computerization would require KCEC to buy or lease the necessary software and hardware, including data-capture equipment for recording the input data on punch cards or magnetic tape.

One advantage of computerization would be that bills could be mailed monthly instead of every two months, thereby improving the company's cash flow considerably. Furthermore, the 80 billing clerks would be replaced by 11 data-capture clerks. Salary savings were estimated to be $1,575,000, and improved cash flow was projected to be worth $875,000. The total benefits were therefore estimated at $2,450,000. On the other hand, a complete data processing department would have to be set up and staffed by well-paid computer professionals. Over a 7-year period, costs were estimated as follows. The cost of hardware and software, including maintenance, was estimated to be $1,250,000. In the first year there would be a conversion cost of $350,000, and the cost of explaining the new system to customers was estimated at an additional $125,000. Total costs were estimated at $1,725,000, about $750,000 less than the estimated benefits. KCEC immediately decided to computerize.

Cost–benefit analysis is not always straightforward. On the one hand, salary savings can be estimated by a management consultant; cash flow can be projected by an accountant; the change in the cost of money with time can be handled in terms of net present value [Yourdon, 1989]; and the costs of hardware, software, and conversion can be estimated by a software engineering consultant. But how is the cost of dealing with customers trying to adjust to computerization to be determined? Or how can the benefits of inoculating an entire population against measles be measured?

The point is that tangible benefits are easy to measure, but intangible benefits can be hard to quantify directly. A practical way of assigning a dollar value to intangible benefits is to make *assumptions*. These assumptions must always be stated in conjunction with the resulting estimates of the benefits. After all, managers have to make decisions. If no data are available, then making assumptions from which such data can be determined is usually the best that can be done under the circumstances. This approach has the further advantage that if someone else reviewing the data and the underlying assumptions can come up with better assumptions, then better data can be produced, and the associated intangible benefits can be computed more accurately. The same technique can be used for intangible costs.

Cost–benefit analysis is a fundamental technique in deciding whether a client should computerize his or her business, and if so, in what way. The costs and benefits of various alternative strategies are compared. For example, a product for storing the results of drug trials can be implemented in a number of different ways, including flat files and various database management systems. For each possible strategy the costs and benefits are computed, and the one for which the difference between benefits and costs is the largest will then be selected as the optimal strategy.

We now turn to software tools.

4.3   CASE (COMPUTER-AIDED SOFTWARE ENGINEERING)

During the development of a software product, a number of very different operations have to be carried out. Typical activities include estimating resource requirements, drawing up the specification document, performing integration testing, and writing the user manual. Unfortunately, neither these activities, nor the others in the software process, can yet be fully automated and performed by a computer without human intervention.

However, computers can assist every step of the way. The title of this section, CASE, stands for computer-aided (or computer-assisted) software engineering. Computers can help by carrying out much of the drudge work associated with software development, including the organization of documentation of all kinds such as plans, contracts, specifications, designs, source code, and management information. Documentation is essential for software development and maintenance, but the majority of individuals involved in software development are not fond of either creating or updating documentation. Maintaining diagrams on the computer is especially useful as it allows changes to be made with ease.

But CASE is not restricted to assisting with documentation. In particular, computers can assist software engineers to cope with the complexity of software development, especially in managing all the details. It involves all aspects of computer support for software engineering. At the same time, it is important to remember that CASE stands for computer-*aided* software engineering, and not computer-*automated* software engineering—no computer can yet replace a human being with respect to development or maintenance of software. For the foreseeable future at least, the computer must remain a tool of the software professional.

4.3.1   TAXONOMY OF CASE

The simplest form of CASE is the software *tool,* a product that assists in just one aspect of the production of software. CASE tools are currently being used in every phase of the life cycle. For example, there are a variety of tools on the market, many of them for use with personal computers, that assist in the construction of graphical representations of software products, such as flowcharts (Figures 4.6 and 4.7). CASE tools that help the developer during the earlier phases of the process, namely, the requirements, specification, planning, and design phases, are sometimes termed *upperCASE* or *front-end* tools, whereas those that assist with implementation, integration, and maintenance are termed *lowerCASE* or *back-end* tools.

One important class of CASE tools is the *data dictionary*, a computerized list of all data defined within the product. In a large product there will be tens (if not hundreds) of thousands of data items, and the computer is ideal for storing information such as variable names and types and the location where each is defined. The power of a data dictionary can be enhanced by combining it with a *consistency checker*, a tool that can check that every data item in the specification document is reflected in the design, and conversely that every item in the design has been defined in the specification document.

Another use of a data dictionary is to provide the data for report generators and screen generators. A *report generator* is used to generate the code needed for producing a report. A *screen generator* is used to assist the software developer in producing the code for a data capture screen. Suppose that a screen is being designed for entering the weekly sales at each branch of a chain of book stores. The branch number, a four-digit integer in the range 1000 to 4500 or 8000 to 8999, is entered on the screen three lines from the top. This information is given to the screen generator. The screen generator then automatically generates code to display the string BRANCH NUMBER _ _ _ _ three lines from the top and to position the cursor at the first underline character. As the user enters each digit, it is displayed; and the cursor moves on to the next underline. The screen generator also generates code for checking that the user enters only digits and that the resulting four-digit integer is in the specified range. If the data entered are invalid, or if the user presses the **?** key, help information is displayed.

Use of such generators can result in rapid prototypes being quickly constructed. Furthermore, a graphical representation tool combined with a data dictionary, consistency checker, report generator, and screen generator together constitute a specification and design *workbench* that supports rapid prototyping. Examples[1] of commercial workbenches that incorporate all these features include ADW, Analyst/ Designer, Excelerator, Software through Pictures, System Architect, and Teamwork.

A CASE workbench is thus a collection of tools that together support one or two *activities,* where an activity is a related collection of tasks. For example, the coding activity includes editing, compiling, linking, testing, and debugging. An activity is not the same thing as a phase of a life-cycle model. In fact, the tasks of an activity can even cross phase boundaries. For example, a project-management workbench is used for every phase of the project, and a coding workbench can be used for rapid prototyping as well as for the implementation, integration, and maintenance phases.

Continuing the progression of CASE technology from tools to workbenches, the next item is the CASE *environment*. Unlike the workbench that supports one or two activities, an environment supports the complete software process or, at the very least, a large portion of the software process [Fuggetta, 1993]. Environments are discussed in detail in Chapter 13.

---

[1]The fact that a specific CASE tool is cited in this book in no way implies any form of endorsement of that CASE tool by the author or publisher. Each CASE tool mentioned in this book has been included because it is a typical example of the class of CASE tools of which it is an instance.

Having set up a CASE taxonomy, namely, tools, workbenches, and environments, the scope of CASE is now considered.

4.4   SCOPE OF CASE

As mentioned previously, the need to have accurate and up-to-date documentation available at all times is a primary reason for implementing CASE technology. For example, suppose that specifications are produced manually. A member of the development team has no way of telling whether a particular specification document is the current version or an older version. There is no way of knowing if the handwritten changes on that document are part of the current specification, or were merely a suggestion that was later rejected. On the other hand, if the specifications of the product are produced using a CASE tool, then at any time there is only one copy of the specifications, namely the online version accessed via the CASE tool. Then, if the specifications are changed, members of the development team can easily access the document and be sure that they are seeing the current version. In addition, the consistency checker will flag any design changes without corresponding changes to the specification document.

Programmers also need online documentation. For example, online help information must be provided for the operating system, editor, programming language, and so on. In addition, programmers have to consult manuals of many kinds, such as editor manuals and programming manuals. It is highly desirable that, wherever possible, these manuals be available online. Apart from the convenience of having everything at one's fingertips, it is generally quicker to query by computer than to try to find the appropriate manual and then plow through it to find the needed item. In addition, it is usually much easier to update an online manual than to try to find all hard-copy versions of a manual within an organization and make the necessary page changes. As a result, online documentation is likely to be more accurate than hard-copy versions of the same material—another reason for providing online documentation to programmers. An example of such online documentation is the UNIX *manual* pages [Sobell, 1995].

CASE can also assist with communication among team members. E-mail is rapidly becoming as much part of an average office as a computer or a fax machine. There are many advantages to e-mail. From the viewpoint of software production, if copies of all e-mail relevant to a specific project are stored in a particular mailbox, then there will be a written record of the decisions that were made during the project. This can be used to resolve conflicts that may arise later. Many CASE environments and some CASE workbenches now incorporate e-mail systems. Other tools that are equally essential are spreadsheets and word processors.

The term *coding tools* refers to CASE tools such as text editors, debuggers, and pretty printers designed to simplify the programmer's task, to reduce the frustration that many programmers experience in their work, and to increase programmer productivity. Before discussing such tools, three definitions are required. *Programming-in-the-small* refers to software development at the level of the code of a single module, whereas *programming-in-the-large* is software development at the module level [DeRemer and Kron, 1976]. The latter includes aspects such as architectural design and integration. *Programming-in-the-many* refers to software production by a team. At times the team will be working at the module level, at times at the code level. Thus programming-in-the-many incorporates aspects of both programming-in-the-large and programming-in-the-small.

A *structure editor* is a text editor that "understands" the implementation language. That is, a structure editor is able to detect a syntax fault as soon as it has been keyed in by the programmer, thus speeding up the implementation phase because time is not wasted on futile compilations. Structure editors exist for a wide variety of languages, operating systems, and hardware. Because a structure editor has knowledge of the programming language, it is easy to incorporate a pretty printer (or formatter) into the editor, to ensure that the code always has a good visual appearance. For example, a pretty printer for Java will ensure that each } is indented the same amount as its corresponding {. An example of a structure editor that incorporates a formatter is the Macintosh Pascal editor [Apple, 1984]. Reserved words are automatically put in boldface so that they stand out, and indentation has been carefully designed to aid readability. In fact, many Macintosh editors are totally or partially structured.

Now consider the problem of invoking a method within the code, only to discover at linkage time either that the method does not exist or that it has been wrongly specified in some way. What is needed is for the structure editor to support *online interface checking*. That is to say, just as the structure editor has information regarding the name of every variable declared by the programmer, so it must also know the name of every method defined within the product. For example, if the programmer enters a call such as

average = computeAverage (dataArray, numberOfValues);

but method computeAverage has not yet been defined, then the editor immediately responds with a message such as

Method computeAverage not known

At this point, the programmer is given two choices, either to correct the name of the method or to declare a new method named computeAverage. If the second option is chosen, the programmer must also specify the arguments of the new method. Argument types must be supplied when declaring a new method because the major reason for having online interface checking is precisely in order to be able to check full interface information, not just the names of methods. A common fault is for method p to call method q passing, say, four arguments, whereas method q has been specified with five arguments. It is more difficult to detect the fault when the call correctly uses four arguments, but two of the arguments are transposed. For example, the declaration of method q might be

void q (**float** floatVar, **int** intVar, string s1, string s2)

whereas the call is

q (intVar, floatVar, string1, string2);

The first two arguments have been transposed in the call statement. Java compilers and interpreters will detect this fault, but only when they are later invoked. In contrast, an online interface checker immediately detects this and similar faults. In addition, if the editor has a help facility, the programmer can request online information as to the precise arguments of method q, before attempting to code the call to q. Better yet, the editor should generate a template for the call, showing the type of each of the arguments. The programmer merely has to replace each formal argument by an actual argument of the correct type.

A major advantage of online interface checking is that hard-to-detect faults caused by the calling of methods with the wrong number of arguments, or with arguments of the wrong type, are immediately flagged. Online interface information is important for the efficient production of high-quality software, particularly when the software is produced by a team (programming-in-the-many). It is essential that online interface information regarding all modules be available to all programming team members at all times. Furthermore, if one programmer changes the interface of method vaporCheck, perhaps by changing the type of one argument from **int** to **float** or by adding an additional argument, then every object that calls vaporCheck must automatically be disabled until the relevant call statements have been altered to reflect the new state of affairs.

Even with a structure editor incorporating an online interface checker, the programmer still has to exit from the editor and invoke the compiler and linker. Clearly, there can be no compilation faults, but the compiler still has to be invoked to perform code generation. Then the linker has to be called. Again, the programmer can be sure that all external references will be satisfied as a consequence of the presence of the online interface checker, but the linker is still needed to link the product. The solution to this is to incorporate an *operating system front end* within the editor. That is to say, a programmer should be able to give operating system commands from within the editor. In order to cause the editor to invoke the compiler, linker, loader, and any other system software needed to cause the module to be executed, the programmer should be able to type a single command named GO or RUN, or use the mouse to choose the appropriate icon or menu selection. In UNIX, this can be achieved by using the *make* command (Section 4.7) or by invoking a shell script [Sobell, 1995]. Such front ends can also be implemented in other operating systems.

One of the most frustrating computing experiences is for a product to execute for a second or so, then terminate abruptly, printing a message such as

Overflow at 4B06

The programmer is working in a high-level language such as FORTRAN or Java, not a low-level language like assembler or machine code. But when debugging support is of the Overflow at 4B06 variety, then the programmer is forced to examine machine code core dumps, assembler listings, linker listings, and a variety of similar low-level documentation, thereby destroying the whole advantage of programming in a high-level language. A similar situation arises when the only information provided is the infamous UNIX message

Core dumped

OVERFLOW ERROR

Class: cyclotronEnergy

Method: performComputation

Line 6:   newValue = (oldValue + tempValue) / tempValue;
              oldValue = 3.9583   tempValue = 0.0000

Figure 4.8   Output from source level debugger.

or the equally uninformative

Segmentation fault

Here again, the user is forced to examine low-level information.

In the event of a failure, the message shown in Figure 4.8 is a great improvement over the earlier terse error messages. The programmer can immediately see that the method failed because of an attempt to divide by 0. Even more useful is for the operating system to enter edit mode and automatically display the line at which the failure was detected, namely line 6, together with the preceding and following four or five lines. The programmer can probably then see what caused the failure and make the necessary changes.

Another type of source level debugging is tracing. Before the advent of CASE tools, programmers had to insert appropriate print statements into their code by hand that, at execution time, would indicate the line number and the values of relevant variables. This can now be done by giving commands to a *source level debugger* that automatically causes trace output to be produced. Even better is an *interactive source level debugger*. Suppose that the value of variable escapeVelocity seems to be incorrect and that method computeTrajectory seems to be faulty. Using the interactive source level debugger, the programmer can set breakpoints in the code. When a breakpoint is reached, execution stops and debugging mode is entered. The programmer now asks the debugger to trace variable escapeVelocity and method computeTrajectory. That is to say, every time the value of escapeVelocity is subsequently either used or changed, execution again halts. The programmer then has the option of entering further debugging commands, for example, to request that the value of a specific variable be displayed. Alternatively, the programmer may choose to continue execution in debugging mode or to return to normal execution mode. The programmer can similarly interact with the debugger whenever method computeTrajectory is entered or exited. Such an interactive source level debugger offers almost every conceivable type of assistance to the programmer when the product fails. The UNIX debugger *dbx* is a good example of such a CASE tool.

As pointed out many times, it is essential that documentation of all kinds be available online. In the case of programmers, all documentation they might need should be accessible from within the editor.

What has now been described, namely, a structure editor with online interface checking capabilities, operating system front end, source level debugger, and online documentation, constitutes an adequate and effective programming workbench.

This sort of workbench is by no means new. All the preceding features were supported by the FLOW software development workbench as far back as 1980 [Dooley and Schach, 1985]. Thus, what has been put forward as a minimal, but essential, programming workbench does not require many years of research before a prototype can be tentatively produced. Quite the contrary, the necessary technology has been in place for a decade or more, and it is therefore somewhat surprising that there are programmers who still implement code "the old-fashioned way."

An essential tool, especially when software is developed by a team, is a version control tool.

4.5 SOFTWARE VERSIONS

Whenever a product is maintained, there will be at least two versions of the product, the old version and the new version. Because a product is comprised of modules, there will also be two or more versions of each of the component modules that have been changed.

Version control is first described within the context of maintenance and is then broadened to include earlier phases of the process.

4.5.1 REVISIONS

Suppose that a product is in operations mode at a number of different sites. If a fault is found in a module, then that module has to be fixed. After appropriate changes have been made, there will be two versions of the module, the old version and the new version intended to replace it. The new version is termed a *revision*. The presence of multiple versions is apparently easy to solve—any old versions should be thrown away, leaving just the correct one. But that would be most unwise. Suppose that the previous version of the module was revision n, and that the new version is revision $n + 1$. First, there is no guarantee that revision $n + 1$ will be any more correct than revision n. Even though revision $n + 1$ may have been thoroughly tested by the SQA group, both in isolation and also linked to the rest of the product, there may be disastrous consequences when the new version of the product is run by the user on actual data. Revision n must be kept for a second reason. The product may have been distributed to a variety of sites, and not all of them may replace revision n by revision $n + 1$. If a fault report is now received from a site that is still using revision n, then in order to analyze this new fault, it is necessary to configure the product in exactly the same way it is configured at the user's site, that is, incorporating revision n of the module. It is therefore necessary to retain a copy of every revision of each module.

As described in Section 1.3, perfective maintenance is performed to extend the functionality of a product. In some instances new modules are written; in other cases existing modules are changed to incorporate this additional functionality. These new versions are also revisions of existing modules. So are modules that are changed when performing adaptive maintenance, that is, changes made to the product in

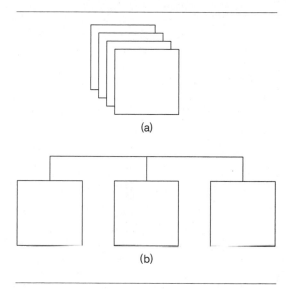

(a)

(b)

Figure 4.9 Schematic representation of multiple versions of modules, showing (a) revisions and (b) variations.

response to changes in the portion of the real world modeled by the product. As with corrective maintenance, all previous versions must be retained.

These issues arise not just during the maintenance phase, but from the implementation phase onwards. After all, once a module has been coded it continually undergoes changes as a consequence of faults being detected and corrected. As a result, there will be numerous versions of every module, and it is vital that there be some sort of control to ensure that every member of the development team always knows which version is the current version of a given module. Before we can present a solution to this problem, there is a further complication that must be taken into account.

4.5.2 VARIATIONS

Consider the following example. Most computers support more than one type of printer. For example, a personal computer may support a dot-matrix printer and a laser printer. The operating system must therefore contain two *variations* of the printer driver, one for each type of printer. Unlike revisions, each of which is specifically written to replace its predecessor, variations are designed to coexist. Another situation where variations are needed is when a product is to be ported to a variety of operating systems and/or hardware. A different variation of many of the modules may have to be produced for each operating system/hardware combination.

Versions are schematically depicted in Figure 4.9, which shows both revisions and variations. To complicate matters further, in general there will be multiple revisions of each variation. In order for a software organization to avoid drowning in a morass of multiple versions, a CASE tool is needed.

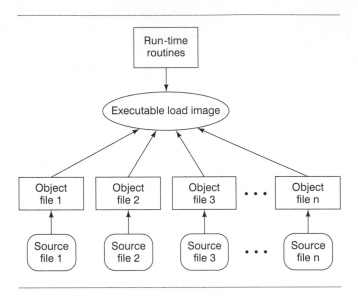

Figure 4.10   Components of executable load image.

4.6   CONFIGURATION CONTROL

The code for every module exists in three forms. First, there is the source code, nowadays generally written in a high-level language like Pascal, C++, COBOL, Java, or Ada. Then there is the object code, produced by compiling the source code. Finally, the object code for each module is combined with run-time routines to produce an executable load image. This is shown in Figure 4.10. The programmer can use various versions of each module. The specific version of each module from which a given version of the complete product is built is called the *configuration* of that version of the product.

Suppose that a programmer is given a test report from SQA stating that a module failed on a specific set of test data. One of the first things that must be done is to attempt to recreate the failure. But how can the programmer determine which revisions of which variations went into the version of the product that crashed? Unless a configuration control tool (described in the following discussion) is used, the only way to pinpoint the source of error is to look at the executable load image, in octal or hexadecimal format, and compare it to the object code, also in octal or hexadecimal. Specifically, the various versions of the source code have to be compiled and compared to the object code that went into the executable load image. Although this can be done, it can take a long time, particularly if the product has dozens (if not hundreds) of modules, each with multiple versions. There are thus two problems that must be solved when dealing with multiple versions. First, it is necessary to be able to distinguish between versions so that the correct version of

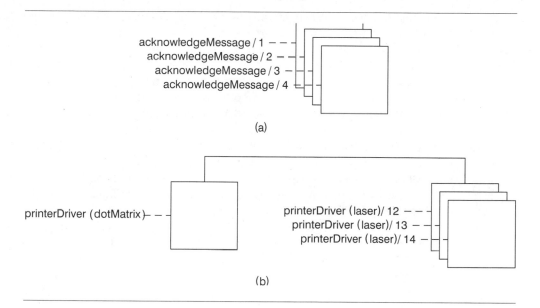

(a)

(b)

Figure 4.11 Multiple revisions and variations. (a) Four revisions of module acknowledgeMessage. (b) Two variations of module printerDriver, with three revisions of variation printerDriver (laser).

each module is compiled and linked into the product. Second, there is the inverse problem: Given an executable load image, determine which version of each of its components went into it.

The first thing that is needed to solve this problem is a version control tool. Many operating systems, particularly for mainframe computers, support version control. But many do not, in which case a separate version control tool is needed. A common technique used in version control is for the name of each file to consist of two pieces, the file name itself and the revision number. Thus a module that acknowledges receipt of a message will have revisions acknowledgeMessage / 1, acknowledgeMessage / 2, and so on, as depicted in Figure 4.11(a). A programmer can then specify exactly which revision is needed for a given task.

With regard to multiple variations (slightly changed versions that fulfill the same role in different situations), one useful notation is to have a basic file name, followed by a variation name in parentheses [Babich, 1986]. Thus two printer drivers are given the names printerDriver (dotMatrix) and printerDriver (laser). Of course, there will be multiple revisions of each variation, such as printerDriver (laser) / 12, printerDriver (laser) / 13, and printerDriver (laser) / 14. This is depicted in Figure 4.11(b).

A version control tool is the first step toward being able to manage multiple versions. Once it is in place, a detailed record (or *derivation*) of every version of the product must be kept. The derivation contains the name of each source code element, including the variation and revision, the versions of the various compilers and linkers used, the name of the person who constructed the product, and of course, the date and the time at which it was constructed.

Version control is a great help in managing multiple versions of modules and the product as a whole. But more than just version control is needed, because of additional problems associated with maintaining multiple variations.

Consider the two variations printerDriver (dotMatrix) and printerDriver (laser). Suppose that a fault is found in printerDriver (dotMatrix) and suppose that the fault occurs in a part of the module that is common to both variations. Then it is necessary to fix not only printerDriver (dotMatrix), but also printerDriver (laser). In general, if there are v variations of a module, all v of them have to be fixed. Not only that, but they have to be fixed in the exact same way.

One solution to this problem is to store just one variation, say printerDriver (dotMatrix). Then any other variation is stored in terms of the list of changes that have to be made to go from the original to that variation. The list of differences is termed a *delta*. Thus what is stored is one variation and $v - 1$ deltas. Variation printerDriver (laser) is retrieved by accessing printerDriver (dotMatrix) and applying the delta. A change made just to printerDriver (laser) is implemented by changing the appropriate delta. However, any change made to printerDriver (dotMatrix), the original variation, will automatically apply to all the other variations.

A configuration control tool can automatically manage multiple variations. But configuration control goes beyond multiple variations. A configuration control tool can also handle problems caused by development and maintenance by teams, as described in the next sections.

4.6.1 CONFIGURATION CONTROL DURING PRODUCT MAINTENANCE

All sorts of difficulties can arise when more than one programmer is simultaneously maintaining a product. For example, suppose two programmers are each assigned a different fault report on a Monday morning. By coincidence, they both localize the fault they are to fix to different parts of the same module mDual. Each programmer makes a copy of the current version of the module, namely, mDual / 16, and they start to work on the faults. The first programmer fixes the first fault, has the changes approved, and replaces the module, now called mDual / 17. A day later the second programmer fixes the second fault, has the changes approved, and installs module mDual / 18. Unfortunately, revision 17 contains the changes of only the first programmer, while revision 18 contains those of only the second programmer. Thus all the changes of the first programmer have been lost.

While the idea of each programmer making individual copies of a module is far better than both working together on the same piece of software, it is clear that it is inadequate for maintenance by a team. What is needed is some mechanism that allows only one user at a time to change a module.

4.6.2 BASELINES

The maintenance manager must set up a *baseline*, a configuration (set of versions) of all the modules in the product. When trying to find a fault, a maintenance programmer puts copies of any needed modules into his or her own *private workspace*. In this private workspace the programmer can change anything at all without having an impact on any other programmer in any way, because all changes are made to the programmer's private copy; the baseline version is left untouched.

Once it has been decided which module has to be changed to fix the fault, the programmer *freezes* the current version of the module that he or she is going to alter. No other programmer may ever make changes to any frozen version. After the maintenance programmer has made changes and they have been tested, the new version of the module is installed, thereby modifying the baseline. The previous version, now frozen, is retained because it may be needed in the future, as explained previously, but it cannot be altered. Once a new version has been installed, any other maintenance programmer can freeze the new version and make changes to it. The resulting module will, in turn, become the next baseline version. A similar procedure is followed if two or more modules have to be changed simultaneously.

This scheme solves the problem with module mDual. Both programmers make private copies of mDual / 16 and use those copies to analyze the respective faults that they have been assigned to fix. The first programmer decides what changes to make, freezes mDual / 16, and makes the changes to it to repair the first fault. After the changes have been tested, the resulting revision mDual / 17 becomes the baseline version. In the meantime, the second programmer has found the second fault by experimenting with a private copy of mDual / 16. However, changes cannot now be made to mDual / 16 because it was frozen by the first programmer. Once mDual / 17 becomes the baseline, it is frozen by the second programmer, whose changes are made to mDual / 17. The resulting module is now installed as mDual / 18, a version that will incorporate the changes of both programmers. Revisions mDual / 16 and mDual / 17 are retained for possible future reference, but they can never be altered.

4.6.3 CONFIGURATION CONTROL DURING PRODUCT DEVELOPMENT

While a module is in the process of being coded, versions are changing too rapidly for configuration control to be helpful. However, once coding of the module has been completed, it should immediately be tested informally by its programmer, as described in Section 5.6. During this informal testing, the module will again pass through numerous versions. When the programmer is satisfied, it is handed over to the SQA group for methodical testing. As soon as the module has been passed by the SQA group, it should be subject to the same configuration control procedures as those of the maintenance phase, and integrated into the product. Any change to an integrated module can impact the product as a whole in the same way as a change made during the maintenance phase. Thus configuration control is needed not only during maintenance, but also during the implementation and integration phases. Furthermore, management cannot monitor the development process adequately unless every module is subject to configuration control as soon as is reasonable, namely, after it has been passed by SQA. When configuration control is properly applied, management is aware of the status of every module and can take early corrective action if it seems that project deadlines are slipping.

The two major UNIX version control tools are *sccs* (source code control system) [Rochkind, 1975] and *rcs* (revision control system) [Tichy, 1985]. Popular commercially available configuration control tools include CCC, CVS, and Aide-de-Camp.

4.7 BUILD TOOLS

If a software organization does not wish to purchase a complete configuration control tool, then at the very least a *build* tool must be used in conjunction with a version control tool, that is, a tool that assists in selecting the correct version of each object-code module to be linked to form a specific version of the product. At any time there will be multiple variations and revisions of each module in the product library. Any version control tool will assist users in distinguishing between different versions of modules of source code. But keeping track of object code is more difficult, because some version control tools do not attach revision numbers to object versions.

To cope with this, some organizations automatically compile the latest version of each module every night, thereby ensuring that all the object code is always up to date. Although this technique works, it can be extremely wasteful of computer time because a large number of unnecessary compilations will frequently be performed. The UNIX tool *make* can solve this problem [Feldman, 1979]. For each executable load image, the programmer sets up a **Makefile** specifying the hierarchy of source and object files that go into that particular configuration; such a hierarchy is shown in Figure 4.10. More complex dependencies, such as included files in C or C++, can also be handled by *make*. When invoked by a programmer, the tool works as follows: UNIX, like virtually every other operating system, attaches a date and time stamp to each file. Suppose that the stamp on a source file is Friday, June 6 at 11:24 a.m., whereas the stamp on the corresponding object file is Friday, June 6 at 11:40 a.m. Then it is clear that the source file has not been changed since the object file was created by the compiler. On the other hand, if the date and time stamp on the source file is later than that on the object file, then *make* calls the appropriate compiler or assembler to create a version of the object file that will correspond to the current version of the source file.

Next, the date and time stamp on the executable load image is compared to those on every object file in that configuration. If the executable load image was created later than all the object files, then there is no need to relink. But if an object file has a later stamp than that of the load image, then the load image does not incorporate the latest version of that object file. In this case *make* will call the linker and construct an updated load image.

In other words, *make* checks whether the load image incorporates the current version of every module. If so, then nothing further is done, and no CPU time is wasted on needless compilations and/or linkage. But if not, then *make* calls the relevant system software to create an up-to-date version of the product.

In addition, *make* simplifies the task of building an object file. There is no need for the user to specify each time what modules are to be used and how they are to be connected, because this information is already in the Makefile. Thus, a single *make* command is all that is needed to build a product with hundreds of modules and ensure that the complete product is put together correctly.

4.8   PRODUCTIVITY GAINS WITH CASE TECHNOLOGY

Reifer (as reported in [Myers, 1992]) conducted an investigation into productivity gains as a consequence of introducing CASE technology. He collected data from 45 companies in 10 industries. Half the companies were in the field of information systems, 25 percent in scientific areas, and 25 percent in real-time aerospace. Average annual productivity gains varied from 9 percent (real-time aerospace) to 12 percent (information systems). If only productivity gains are considered, then these figures do not justify the cost of $125,000 per user of introducing CASE technology. However, the companies surveyed felt that the justification for CASE is not merely increased productivity, but also shorter development time, and improvement in software quality. In other words, the introduction of CASE environments boosts productivity, though less than some proponents of CASE technology have claimed. Nevertheless, there are other, equally important reasons for introducing CASE technology into a software organization, such as faster development, fewer faults, better usability, easier maintenance, and improved morale.

4.9   SOFTWARE METRICS

As explained in Section 3.7, without measurements (or *metrics*) it is impossible to detect problems early in the software process, before they get out of hand. Metrics can thus serve as an early warning system for potential problems. A wide variety of metrics can be used. For example, lines of code (LOC) is one way of measuring the size of a product (see Section 10.1.1). If LOC measurements are taken at regular intervals, they will provide a measure of how fast the project is progressing. In addition, metrics for defects (faults) per 1000 lines of code provide a measure of software quality. After all, it is of little use if a programmer consistently turns out 2000 lines of code a month but half of it has to be thrown away because it is of unacceptable quality. Thus, LOC in isolation is not a very meaningful metric.

When a product is in operations mode, a metric such as mean time between failures provides management with an indication of the reliability of an installed product. If a certain product fails every other day, its quality is clearly lower than that of a similar product that on average runs for 9 months without a failure.

Certain metrics can be applied throughout the software process. For example, effort in *person-months* (one person-month is the amount of work that is done by one person in one month) can be measured for each phase. Staff turnover is another important metric. High turnover will adversely affect current projects because it takes time for a new employee to learn the relevant facts about the project. In addition, new employees may have to be trained in aspects of the software process; if new employees are less educated in software engineering than the individuals they replace, then the process as a whole may suffer. Of course, cost is an essential metric that must also be monitored continually throughout the entire process.

A number of different metrics are described in this book. Some are *product metrics,* that is, they measure some aspect of the product itself, such as its size or its reliability. In contrast, others are *process metrics*; these metrics are used by the developers to deduce information about their software process. A typical metric of this kind is the efficiency of fault detection during development, that is, the ratio of the number of faults detected during development to the total number of faults detected in the product over its lifetime.

Many metrics are specific to a given phase. For example, lines of code cannot be used before implementation begins, and the number of defects detected per hour in reviewing specifications is relevant to only the specification phase. In subsequent chapters describing the various phases of the software process, metrics that are relevant to that phase are discussed.

There is a cost involved in gathering the data needed to compute the values of metrics. Even if the data gathering is fully automated, the CASE tool that accumulates the required information is not free, and interpreting the output from the tool consumes human resources. Bearing in mind that literally hundreds (if not thousands) of different metrics have been put forward, an obvious question is: What should a software organization measure? There are five essential, fundamental metrics:

1. Size (in lines of code or, better, in a more meaningful metric such as those of Section 10.1.1)

2. Cost (in dollars)

3. Duration (in months)

4. Effort (in person-months)

5. Quality (number of faults detected)

Each of these metrics must be measured by phase. On the basis of the data from these fundamental metrics, management can identify problems within the software organization, such as high fault rates during the design phase or code output that is well below industry averages. Once problem areas have been highlighted, a strategy to correct these problems can be introduced. In order to monitor the success of this strategy, more detailed metrics can be introduced. For example, it may be deemed appropriate to collect data on fault rates of each individual programmer or to conduct a survey of user satisfaction. Thus, other than the five fundamental metrics, more

JUST IN CASE YOU WANTED TO KNOW

I first published my five fundamental metrics in late 1992. The following year I was amused to read U.S. Air Force Acquisition Policy 93M–017, which states "Software metrics shall cover cost, schedule, and quality. The metrics will be further subdivided to portray the following 'core' attributes:

* Size

* Effort

* Schedule

* Software Quality

* Rework"

It really is amazing how virtually the same result can be obtained by two totally independent individuals or groups working on the problem at the same time.

The same thing happened to me in the late 1970s when I worked with Klaas van der Poel on the FFP metric (Section 10.1.1), completely unaware of the fact that Allan Albrecht was developing his similar function point theory (Section 10.1.1) at the same time.

---

detailed data gathering and analysis should be performed only toward a specific objective. (See the Just in Case You Wanted to Know box above for a different insight into the five fundamental metrics.)

Finally, one aspect of metrics is still fairly controversial. Questions have been raised as to the validity of many of the popular metrics; some of these issues are discussed in Section 12.16.2. Although it is agreed that we cannot control the software process unless we can measure it, there is some disagreement as to precisely what should be measured [Fenton, 1994].

Chapter Review

Miller's law (Section 4.1) states that at any one time human beings can concentrate on only 7 ± 2 chunks of information. Stepwise refinement is a technique that allows the software engineer to concentrate on the currently relevant seven chunks. The application of stepwise refinement to design is illustrated. Another analytical tool, namely, cost–benefit analysis, is presented in Section 4.2.

A variety of computer-aided software engineering (CASE) tools are described in Sections 4.3 and 4.4. When large products are constructed, version control, configuration control, and build tools are essential; these are presented in Sections 4.5 through 4.7. Productivity gains as a consequence of the use of CASE technology are described in Section 4.8. Finally, the area of software metrics is introduced in Section 4.9.

For Further Reading

For further information regarding Miller's law, and for his theory of how the brain operates on chunks, the reader should consult [Tracz, 1979] and [Moran, 1981], as well as Miller's original paper [Miller, 1956]. An analysis of Miller's law from the viewpoint of cognitive psychology and software science is to be found in [Coulter, 1983].

Wirth's paper on stepwise refinement is a classic of its kind and deserves careful study [Wirth, 1971]. Equally significant from the viewpoint of stepwise refinement are the books by Dijkstra [Dijkstra, 1976] and Wirth [Wirth, 1975]. Mills applies stepwise refinement to box-structured design, a technique for producing a design from a specification [Mills, Linger, and Hevner, 1987; Mills, 1988]. Rajlich extends stepwise refinement to large-scale products [Rajlich, 1985]. Stepwise design of real-time systems is described in [Kurki-Suonio, 1993].

There are articles on CASE in the April 1992 issue of *Communications of the ACM*, as well as in the May 1992 issue of *IEEE Software* where a detailed description of a number of CASE tools can also be found. CASE tools for the separate phases of the software process are described in the chapters on each phase. Details of simple programming workbenches (then called environments) appear in [Teitelbaum and Reps, 1981] and [Dooley and Schach, 1985]. Information on how to design online help systems can be found in [Houghton, 1984]. For information on CASE environments, consult the For Further Reading section of Chapter 13.

For more information on workbenches, the reader should refer to the For Further Reading section of Chapter 13.

[Whitgift, 1991] is a good introduction to configuration management. The impact of the choice of a software life-cycle model is described in [Bersoff and Davis, 1991]. The proceedings of the International Workshops on Software Configuration Management are a useful source of information.

There are many excellent books on cost–benefit analysis, including [Dasgupta and Pearce, 1972] and [Mishan, 1982]. For information on cost–benefit analysis as applied to information systems, the reader should consult [King and Schrems, 1978].

Important books on metrics include [Conte, Dunsmore, and Shen, 1986] and [Musa, Iannino, and Okumoto, 1987]. A particularly clearly written text is [Grady, 1992]. Over 120 papers on software metrics published between 1980 and 1988 are listed in [Côté, Bourque, Oligny, and Rivard, 1988]. Later articles on metrics appear in the March 1990 issue of *IEEE Software* and the September 1994 issue of *IEEE Computer*. The need for a scientific basis for measurement within the software field is discussed in [Fenton, 1994].

Problems

4.1   Consider the effect of introducing *lookahead* to the design of the corrected third refinement of the sequential master file update problem. That is to say, before processing a transaction the next transaction must be read. If both transactions apply to the same master file record, then the decision regarding the processing of the current transaction will depend on the type of the next transaction. Draw up a 3×3 table with the rows labeled by the type of the current transaction and the columns labeled by the type of the next transaction and fill in the action to be taken in each instance. For example, two successive insertions of the same record are clearly an error. But two modifications may be perfectly valid—for example, a subscriber can change address more than once in a given month. Now develop a flowchart for the third refinement that incorporates lookahead.

4.2 Check whether your solution to Problem 4.1 can correctly handle a modification transaction followed by a deletion transaction, both transactions being applied to the same master file record. If not, modify your solution.

4.3 Check whether your solution to Problem 4.1 can also correctly handle an insertion followed by a modification followed by a deletion, all applied to the same master file record. If not, modify your solution.

4.4 Check whether your solution can also correctly handle n insertions, modifications, or deletions, $n > 2$, all applied to the same master file record. If not, modify your solution.

4.5 The last transaction record does not have a successor. Check whether your flowchart for Problem 4.1 takes this into account and processes the last transaction record correctly. If not, modify your solution.

4.6 In some applications an alternative to lookahead can be achieved by careful ordering of the transactions. For example, the original problem caused by a modification followed by a deletion of the same master file record could have been solved by processing a deletion before a modification. This would have resulted in the master file being correctly written and an error message appearing in the exception report. Investigate whether there is an ordering of the transactions that can solve all of the difficulties listed in Problems 4.2, 4.3, and 4.4.

4.7 A new form of gastrointestinal disease is sweeping the country of Veloria. Like histoplasmosis, it is transmitted as an airborne fungus. Although the disease is almost never fatal, an attack is very painful, and the sufferer is unable to work for about 2 weeks. The government of Veloria wishes to determine how much money, if any, to spend on attempting to eradicate the disease. The committee charged with advising the Department of Public Health is considering four aspects of the problem, namely health care costs (Veloria provides free health care to all its citizens), loss of earnings (and hence loss of taxes), pain and discomfort, and gratitude toward the government. Explain how cost–benefit analysis can assist the committee. For each benefit or cost, suggest how a dollar estimate for that benefit or cost could be obtained.

4.8 Does a one-person software production organization need a version control tool, and if so, why?

4.9 Does a one-person software production organization need a configuration control tool, and if so, why?

4.10 You are the manager in charge of the software that controls the navigation system of a new fuel-efficient long-range aircraft. Three different user-reported faults have to be fixed, and you assign one each to Ron, Stella, and Ted. A day later you learn that in order to implement each of the three fixes, the same four modules must be changed. However, your configuration control tool is inoperative, so you will have to manage the changes yourself. How will you do it?

4.11   In Section 3.7 it was stated that it makes little sense to introduce CASE environments within organizations at maturity levels 1 or 2. Explain why this is so.

4.12   What is the effect of introducing CASE tools (as opposed to environments) within organizations with low maturity level?

4.13   (Term Project) What types of CASE tools would be appropriate for developing the Osbert Oglesby product described in Appendix A?

4.14   (Reading in Software Engineering) Your instructor will distribute copies of [Wirth, 1971]. List the differences between Wirth's approach and the approach to stepwise refinement presented in this chapter.

References

[Apple, 1984] *Macintosh Pascal User's Guide,* Apple Computer, Inc., Cupertino, CA, 1984.

[Babich, 1986] W. A. BABICH, *Software Configuration Management: Coordination for Team Productivity,* Addison-Wesley, Reading, MA, 1986.

[Bersoff and Davis, 1991] E. H. BERSOFF AND A. M. DAVIS, "Impacts of Life Cycle Models on Software Configuration Management," *Communications of the ACM* **34** (August 1991), pp. 104–118.

[Conte, Dunsmore, and Shen, 1986] S. D. CONTE, H. E. DUNSMORE, AND V. Y. SHEN, *Software Engineering Metrics and Models,* Benjamin/Cummings, Menlo Park, CA., 1986.

[Côté, Bourque, Oligny, and Rivard, 1988] V. CÔTÉ, P. BOURQUE, S. OLIGNY, AND N. RIVARD, "Software Metrics: An Overview of Recent Results," *Journal of Systems and Software* **8** (March 1988), pp. 121–131.

[Coulter, 1983] N. S. COULTER, "Software Science and Cognitive Psychology," *IEEE Transactions on Software Engineering* **SE-9** (March 1983), pp. 166–171.

[Dasgupta and Pearce, 1972] A. K. DASGUPTA AND D. W. PEARCE, *Cost–Benefit Analysis,* Macmillan, London, 1972.

[DeRemer and Kron, 1976] F. DEREMER AND H. H. KRON, "Programming-in-the-Large versus Programming-in-the-Small," *IEEE Transactions on Software Engineering* **SE-2** (June 1976), pp. 80–96.

[Dijkstra, 1976] E. W. DIJKSTRA, *A Discipline of Programming,* Prentice-Hall, Englewood Cliffs, NJ, 1976.

[Dooley and Schach, 1985] J. W. M. DOOLEY AND S. R. SCHACH, "FLOW: A Software Development Environment Using Diagrams," *Journal of Systems and Software* **5** (August 1985), pp. 203–219.

[Feldman, 1979] S. I. FELDMAN, "Make—A Program for Maintaining Computer Programs," *Software—Practice and Experience* **9** (April 1979), pp. 225–265.

[Fenton, 1994] N. FENTON, "Software Measurement: A Necessary Scientific Basis," *IEEE Transactions on Software Engineering* **20** (March 1994), pp. 199–206.

[Fuggetta, 1993] A. FUGGETTA, "A Classification of CASE Technology," *IEEE Computer* **26** (December 1993), pp. 25–38.

[Grady, 1992] R. B. GRADY, *Practical Software Metrics for Project Management and Process Improvement,* Prentice-Hall, Englewood Cliffs, NJ, 1992.

[Houghton, 1984] R. C. HOUGHTON, JR., "Online Help Systems: A Conspectus," *Communications of the ACM* **27** (February 1984), pp. 126–133.

[King and Schrems, 1978] J. L. KING AND E. L. SCHREMS, "Cost–Benefit Analysis in Information Systems Development and Operation," *ACM Computer Surveys* **10** (March 1978), pp. 19–34.

[Kurki-Suonio, 1993] R. KURKI-SUONIO, "Stepwise Design of Real-Time Systems," *IEEE Transactions on Software Engineering* **19** (January 1993), pp. 56–69.

[Miller, 1956] G. A. MILLER, "The Magical Number Seven, Plus or Minus Two: Some Limits on Our Capacity for Processing Information," *The Psychological Review* **63** (March 1956), pp. 81–97.

[Mills, 1988] H. D. MILLS, "Stepwise Refinement and Verification in Box-Structured Systems," *IEEE Computer* **21** (June 1988), pp. 23–36.

[Mills, Linger, and Hevner, 1987] H. D. MILLS, R. C. LINGER, AND A. R. HEVNER, "Box-Structured Information Systems," *IBM Systems Journal* **26** (No. 4, 1987), pp. 395–413.

[Mishan, 1982] E. J. MISHAN, *Cost–Benefit Analysis: An Informal Introduction,* Third Edition, George Allen & Unwin, London, 1982.

[Moran, 1981] T. P. MORAN (Editor), Special Issue: The Psychology of Human-Computer Interaction, *ACM Computing Surveys* **13** (March 1981).

[Musa, Iannino, and Okumoto, 1987] J. D. MUSA, A. IANNINO, AND K. OKUMOTO, *Software Reliability: Measurement, Prediction, Application,* McGraw-Hill, New York, 1987.

[Myers, 1992] W. MYERS, "Good Software Practices Pay Off—or Do They?" *IEEE Software* **9** (March 1992), pp. 96–97.

[Rajlich, 1985] V. RAJLICH, "Stepwise Refinement Revisited," *Journal of Systems and Software* **5** (February 1985), pp. 81–88.

[Rochkind, 1975] M. J. ROCHKIND, "The Source Code Control System," *IEEE Transactions on Software Engineering* **SE-1** (October 1975), pp. 255–265.

[Sobell, 1995] M. G. SOBELL, *A Practical Guide to the UNIX System,* Third Edition, Benjamin/Cummings, Menlo Park, CA, 1995.

[Teitelbaum and Reps, 1981] T. TEITELBAUM AND T. REPS, "The Cornell Program Synthesizer: A Syntax-Directed Programming Environment," *Communications of the ACM* **24** (September 1981), pp. 563–573.

[Tichy, 1985] W. F. TICHY, "RCS—A System for Version Control," *Software—Practice and Experience* **15** (July 1985), pp. 637–654.

[Tracz, 1979] W. J. TRACZ, "Compute Programming and the Human Thought Process," *Software—Practice and Experience* **9** (February 1979), pp. 127–137.

[Whitgift, 1991] D. WHITGIFT, *Methods and Tools for Software Configuration Management,* John Wiley and Sons, New York, 1991.

[Wirth, 1971] N. WIRTH, "Program Development by Stepwise Refinement," *Communications of the ACM* **14** (April 1971), pp. 221–227.

[Wirth, 1975] N. WIRTH, *Algorithms + Data Structures = Programs,* Prentice-Hall, Englewood Cliffs, NJ, 1975.

[Yourdon, 1989] E. YOURDON, *Modern Structured Analysis,* Yourdon Press, Englewood Cliffs, NJ, 1989.

chapter

5

TESTING PRINCIPLES

Software life-cycle models all too frequently include a separate testing phase, after integration and before maintenance. Nothing could be more dangerous from the viewpoint of trying to achieve high-quality software. On the contrary, testing is an integral component of the software process and an activity that must be carried out throughout the life cycle. During the requirement phase the requirements must be checked; during the specification phase the specifications must be checked; during the planning phase the software production management plan must undergo similar scrutiny. The design phase requires careful checking at every stage. During the coding phase each module must certainly be tested, and the product as a whole needs testing at the integration phase. After passing the acceptance test, the product is installed and goes into operations mode, and maintenance begins. And hand in hand with maintenance goes repeated checking of modified versions of the product.

In other words, it is not sufficient to test the end-product of a phase merely at the end of that phase. For example, consider the specification phase. The members of the specification team must consciously and conscientiously check the specifications while they develop them. It is not much use for the team to develop the complete specification document only to find, weeks or months later, that they made an error early in the process that necessitates rewriting almost all the specifications. Thus, what is needed is continual testing by the development team while they perform each phase, in addition to more methodical testing at the end of each phase.

The terms *verification* and *validation* were introduced in Chapter 2. Verification refers to the process of determining whether a phase has been correctly carried out; this takes place at the end of each phase. On the other hand, validation is the intensive evaluation process that takes place just before the product is delivered to the client. Its purpose is to determine whether the product as a whole satisfies its specifications. Despite the fact that both these terms are defined in the IEEE software engineering glossary [IEEE 610.12, 1990] in this way, and notwithstanding the common usage of the term *V & V* to denote testing, the words *verification* and *validation* are avoided as far as possible in this book (but see the Just in Case You Wanted to Know box on page 111 for a different definition). One reason is that, as explained in Section 5.5, the word *verification* has another meaning within the context of testing. A second reason is that the phrase *verification and validation* (or V & V) implies that the process of checking a phase can wait until the end of that phase. On the contrary, it is essential that checking be carried out in parallel with all software development and maintenance activities. Thus, in order to avoid the undesirable implications of the phrase *V & V,* the term *testing* is used.

JUST IN CASE YOU WANTED TO KNOW

Barry Boehm is the author of the following definitions for verification and validation [Boehm, 1984a]:

Verification: Are we building the product right?
Validation: Are we building the right product?

There are essentially two types of testing: execution-based testing and nonexecution-based testing. For example, it is impossible to execute a written specification document; the only alternatives are to review it as carefully as possible or to subject it to some form of analysis. However, once there is executable code, it becomes possible to run test cases, that is, to perform execution-based testing. Nevertheless, the existence of code does not preclude nonexecution-based testing because, as will be explained, carefully reviewing code will uncover at least as many faults as running test cases. In this chapter principles of both execution-based and nonexecution-based testing are described. These principles are applied in Chapters 7 through 14, where a description is given of each phase of the process model and the specific testing practices applicable to it.

5.1 QUALITY ISSUES

The term *quality* is frequently misunderstood when used within the software context. After all, quality implies excellence of some sort, but this unfortunately is not the meaning intended by software engineers. To put it bluntly, the state of the art in software development is such that merely getting the software to function correctly is enough—excellence is an order of magnitude more than what is generally possible with our current software technology. The *quality* of software is the extent to which the product satisfies its specifications (see the Just in Case You Wanted to Know box on page 112).

The task of every software professional is to ensure, at all times, high quality software. Notwithstanding this, the software quality assurance (SQA) group has additional responsibilities with regard to software quality.

5.1.1 SOFTWARE QUALITY ASSURANCE

One aspect of the job of the SQA group is to ensure that the product is correct. More precisely, once the developers have completed a phase, members of the SQA group have to check that that phase has been carried out correctly. Also, when the product is complete, the SQA group has to check that the product as a whole is correct. However, software quality assurance goes further than just testing (or V & V) at the end of a phase or at the end of the development process; SQA applies to the software process itself. For example, the responsibilities of SQA include the development of the various standards to which the software must conform, as well as the establishment of the monitoring procedures for assuring compliance with those standards. In brief, the role of the SQA group is to ensure the quality of the software process and thereby ensure the quality of the product.

5.1.2   MANAGERIAL INDEPENDENCE

It is important to have *managerial independence* between the development team and the SQA group. That is, development should be under one manager, SQA under a different manager, and neither manager should be able to overrule the other. The reason is that all too frequently serious faults are found in a product as the delivery deadline approaches. The software organization must choose between two unsatisfactory options. Either the product can be released on time but full of faults, leaving the client to struggle with faulty software; or the developers can fix the software but deliver it late. No matter what, the client will probably lose confidence in the software organization. The decision to deliver faulty software on time should not be made by the manager responsible for development; nor should the SQA manager be able to make the decision to perform further testing and deliver the product late. Instead, both managers should report to a more senior manager who can decide which of the two choices would be in the best interest of both the software development organization and the client.

At first sight, having a separate SQA group would appear to add considerably to the cost of software development. But this is not so. The additional cost is relatively small compared to the resulting benefit, namely, higher quality software. Without an SQA group, every member of the software development organization would have to be involved to some extent with quality assurance activities. Suppose that there are 100 software professionals in an organization and that they each devote about 30 percent of their time to quality assurance activities. Instead, the 100 individuals should be divided into two groups, with 70 individuals performing software development and the other 30 people responsible for SQA. The same amount of time is still devoted to SQA, the only additional expense being a manager to lead the SQA group. Quality assurance can now be performed by an independent group of specialists, leading to products of higher quality than when SQA activities are performed throughout the organization.

In the case of a very small software company (four employees or fewer), it may simply not be economically viable to have a separate SQA group. The best that can be done under such circumstances is to ensure that the specification document be checked by someone other than the person responsible for producing those specifications, and similarly for the design, code, and so on. The reason for this is explained in the next section.

5.2 NONEXECUTION-BASED TESTING

It is not a good idea for the person responsible for drawing up a document to be the only one responsible for reviewing it. Almost everyone has blind spots that allow faults to creep into the document, and those same blind spots will prevent the faults from being detected on review. Thus, the review task must be assigned to someone other than the original author of the document. In addition, having only one reviewer may not be adequate; we have all had the experience of reading through a document many times, but failing to detect a blatant spelling error that a second reader picks up almost immediately. This is one of the principles underlying review techniques like walkthroughs or inspections. In both types of review, a document (such as a specification document or design document) is carefully checked by a team of software professionals with a broad range of skills. The advantage of a review by a team of experts is that the different skills of the participants increase the chances of finding a fault. In addition, a team of skilled individuals working together often generates a synergistic effect.

Walkthroughs and inspections are two types of reviews. The fundamental difference between them is that walkthroughs have fewer steps and are less formal than inspections.

5.2.1 WALKTHROUGHS

A walkthrough team should consist of four to six individuals. A specification walkthrough team should include at least one representative from the team responsible for drawing up the specifications; the manager responsible for the specifications; a client representative; a representative of the team who will perform the next phase of the development (in this instance the design team, because they are the immediate users of the specification document [Dunn, 1984]); and last, but definitely not least, a representative of the software quality assurance group. For reasons that will be explained, the SQA group member should chair the walkthrough.

The members of the walkthrough team should, as far as possible, be experienced senior technical staff because they tend to find the important faults. That is, they detect the faults that would otherwise have a major negative impact on the project [New, 1992].

The material for the walkthrough must be distributed to the participants well in advance to allow for careful preparation. Each reviewer should study the material and develop two lists: a list of items the reviewer does not understand and a list of items the reviewer believes are incorrect.

5.2.2   MANAGING WALKTHROUGHS

The walkthrough should be chaired by the SQA representative, because the SQA representative has the most to lose if the walkthrough is poorly performed and faults slip through. In contrast, the representative responsible for the specification phase may be eager to have the specification document approved as quickly as possible in order to start some other task. The client representative may decide that any defects not detected at the review will probably show up during acceptance testing and will therefore be fixed at no cost to the client organization. But the SQA representative has the most at stake: The quality of the product is a direct reflection of the professional competence of the SQA group.

The person leading the walkthrough guides the other members of the walk-through team through the document in order to uncover any faults. It is not the task of the team to correct faults, but merely to record them for later correction. One reason is that a document produced by a committee (that is, the walkthrough team) within the time constraints of the walkthrough is likely to be inferior in quality to one drawn up by an individual trained in the necessary techniques. Second, a correction produced by a walkthrough team of five individuals will take at least as much time as a correction produced by one person and, therefore, costs five times as much when the salaries of the five participants are considered. A third reason is that not all items that are flagged as faults are actually incorrect. In accordance with the dictum, "If it ain't broke, don't fix it," it is better for faults to be carefully analyzed and then corrected only if there really is a problem, rather than have a team attempt to "fix" something that is completely correct. The fourth reason is that there simply is not enough time in a walkthrough both to detect and to correct faults. No walkthrough should last longer than 2 hours. The time should be spent detecting and recording faults, not correcting them.

There are two ways of conducting a walkthrough. The first is participant-driven. Participants present their lists of unclear items and items they think are incorrect. The representative of the specifications team must respond to each query, clarifying what is unclear to the reviewer and will either agree that there is indeed a fault or will explain why the reviewer is mistaken.

The second way of conducting a review is document-driven. A person responsible for the document, either individually or as part of a team, walks the participants through that document, with the reviewers interrupting either with their prepared comments or with comments triggered by the presentation. This second approach is likely to be more thorough. In addition, it generally leads to the detection of more faults because the majority of faults at a document-driven walkthrough are spontaneously detected by the presenter. Time after time the presenter will pause in the middle of a sentence, his or her face will light up, and a fault, one that has lain dormant through many readings of the document, will suddenly be obvious. A fruitful field for research by a psychologist would be to determine why verbalization so often leads to fault detection during walkthroughs of all kinds, including specification walkthroughs, design walkthroughs, plan walkthroughs, and code walkthroughs. Not surprisingly, the more thorough document-driven review is the technique prescribed in the IEEE standard for software reviews [IEEE 1028, 1988].

The primary role of the walkthrough leader is to elicit questions and facilitate discussion. A walkthrough is an interactive process; it is not supposed to be one-sided instruction by the presenter. It is also essential that the walkthrough not be used as a means of evaluating the participants. If this happens, the walkthrough will degenerate into a point-scoring session and will not detect faults, no matter how well the session leader tries to run the walkthrough. It has been suggested that the manager who is responsible for the document being reviewed should be a member of the walkthrough team. If this manager is also responsible for the annual evaluations of the members of the walkthrough team (and particularly of the presenter), the fault detection capabilities of the team will be compromised because the primary motive of the presenter will be to minimize the number of faults that show up. To prevent this conflict of interests, the person responsible for a given phase should not also be directly responsible for evaluating any member of the walkthrough team for that phase.

5.2.3 INSPECTIONS

Inspections were first proposed by Fagan for the testing of designs and code [Fagan, 1976]. For Fagan, an inspection goes far beyond a walkthrough and has five formal steps. First, an *overview* of the document is given by one of the individuals responsible for producing that document. At the end of the overview session, the document is distributed to the participants. In the second step, *preparation,* the participants try to understand the document in detail. Lists of fault types found in recent inspections, with the fault types ranked by frequency, are excellent aids. These lists will help team members concentrate on the areas where the most faults have occurred. The third step is the *inspection.* To begin, one participant walks through the document with the inspection team, ensuring that every item is covered and that every branch is taken at least once. Then fault finding commences. As with walkthroughs, the purpose is to find and document the faults, not to correct them. Within one day the leader of the inspection team (the moderator) must produce a written report of the inspection to ensure meticulous follow-through. The fourth stage is the *rework* in which the individual responsible for that document resolves all faults and problems noted in the written report. The final stage is the *follow-up.* The moderator must ensure that every single issue raised has been satisfactorily resolved, either by fixing the document or by clarifying items that were incorrectly flagged as faults. All fixes must be checked to ensure that no new faults have been introduced [Fagan, 1986]. If more than 5 percent of the material inspected has been reworked, then the team reconvenes for a 100 percent reinspection.

The inspection should be conducted by a team of four. For example, in the case of a design inspection, the team will consist of a moderator, designer, implementer, and tester. The moderator is both manager and leader of the inspection team. There must be a representative of the team responsible for the current phase, as well as a representative of the team responsible for the next phase. The designer is a member of the team that produced the design, whereas the implementer will be responsible, either individually or as part of a team, for translating the design into code. Fagan suggested that the tester be any programmer responsible for setting up test cases; it is of course preferable that the tester should be a member of the SQA group. The IEEE standard recommends a team of between three and six participants [IEEE 1028, 1988]. Special roles are played by the moderator, the reader who leads the team through the design, and the recorder who is responsible for producing a written report of the detected faults.

An essential component of an inspection is the checklist of potential faults. For example, the checklist for a design inspection should include items such as: Is each item of the specification document adequately and correctly addressed? For each interface, do the actual and formal arguments correspond? Have error-handling mechanisms been adequately identified? Is the design compatible with the hardware resources, or does it require more hardware than is actually available? Is the design compatible with the software resources—for example, does the operating system stipulated in the specification document have the functionality required by the design?

An important component of the inspection procedure is the record of fault statistics. Faults must be recorded by severity (major or minor—an example of a major fault is one that causes premature termination or damages a database) and by fault type. In the case of a design inspection, typical fault types include interface faults and logic faults. This information can be used in a number of useful ways. First, the number of faults in a given product can be compared with averages of faults detected at the same stage of development in comparable products, giving management an early warning that something is amiss and allowing timely corrective action to be taken. Second, if inspecting the design of two or three modules results in the discovery of a disproportionate number of faults of a particular type, management can begin checking other modules and take corrective action. Third, if the inspection of the design of a particular module reveals far more faults than were found in any other module in the product, then there is usually a strong case for redesigning that module from scratch. Finally, information regarding the number and types of faults detected at a design inspection will aid the team performing the code inspection of the same module at a later stage.

Fagan's first experiment was performed on a systems product [Fagan, 1976]. One hundred person-hours were devoted to inspections, at a rate of two 2-hour inspections per day by a four-person team. Of all the faults that were found during the development of the product, 67 percent were located by inspections before module testing was started. Furthermore, during the first 7 months of operations mode, 38 percent fewer faults were detected in the inspected product than in a comparable product reviewed using informal walkthroughs.

Fagan conducted another experiment on an applications product [Fagan, 1976] and found that 82 percent of all detected faults were discovered during design and code inspections. A useful side effect of the inspections was that programmer productivity rose because less time had to be spent on module testing. Using an automated estimating model, Fagan determined that as a result of the inspection process, the savings on programmer resources were 25 percent despite the fact that time had to be devoted to the inspections. In a different experiment Jones found that over 70 percent of detected faults could be detected by conducting design and code inspections [Jones, 1978].

More recent studies produced equally impressive results. In a 6000-line business data processing application, 93 percent of all detected faults were found during inspections [Fagan, 1986]. As reported in [Ackerman, Buchwald, and Lewski, 1989], the use of inspections rather than testing during the development of an operating system decreased the cost of detecting a fault by 85 percent; in a switching system product, the decrease was 90 percent [Fowler, 1986]. At the Jet Propulsion Laboratory (JPL), on average each 2-hour inspection has exposed 4 major faults and 14 minor faults [Bush, 1990]. Translated into dollar terms, this means a saving of approximately $25,000 per inspection. Another JPL study [Kelly, Sherif, and Hops, 1992] has shown that the number of faults detected decreases exponentially by phase. In other words, with the aid of inspections, faults can be detected early in the software process. The importance of this early detection is reflected in Figure 1.5.

A risk of the inspection process is that, like the walkthrough, it might be used for performance appraisal. The danger is particularly acute in the case of inspections because of the detailed fault information that is available. Fagan dismisses this fear by stating that over a period of 3 years he knew of no IBM manager who used such information against a programmer, or as he put it, no manager tried to "kill the goose that lays the golden eggs" [Fagan, 1976]. However, if inspections are not conducted properly, they may not be as wildly successful as they have been at IBM. Unless top management is aware of the potential problem, misuse of inspection information is a distinct possibility.

5.2.4 COMPARISON OF INSPECTIONS AND WALKTHROUGHS

Superficially, the difference between an inspection and a walkthrough is that the inspection team uses a checklist of queries to aid it in finding the faults. But the difference goes deeper than that. A walkthrough is a two-step process: preparation, followed by team analysis of the document. An inspection is a five-step process, namely overview, preparation, inspection, rework, and follow-up, and the procedure to be followed in each of those steps is formalized. Examples of this formalization are the careful categorization of faults and the use of that information in inspections of the documents of the succeeding phases, as well as in inspections of future products.

The inspection process takes much longer than a walkthrough. The question is then: Is inspection worth the additional time and effort? The key is that an inspection is an excellent way to detect a fault, and that faults are detected early in the software process, that is, before they become expensive to fix. For example, design faults are usually detected before implementation commences. Similarly, coding faults are found before the module is integrated into the product. The data of the previous section clearly indicate that inspections are a powerful and cost-effective tool for fault detection.

5.2.5 METRICS FOR INSPECTIONS

In order to determine the effectiveness of inspections, a number of different metrics can be used. The first is the *fault density.* When specifications and designs are inspected, faults per page inspected can be measured; for code inspections, an appropriate metric is faults per 1000 lines of code (KLOC) inspected. These metrics can be broken up into major faults per unit of material and minor faults per unit of material. Another useful metric is the *fault detection rate,* that is, the number of major/minor faults detected per hour. A third metric is the *fault detection efficiency,* that is, the number of major/minor faults detected per person-hour.

Although the purpose of these metrics is to measure the effectiveness of the inspection process, the results may instead reflect deficiencies of the development team. For example, if the fault detection rate suddenly rises from 20 defects per thousand lines of code to 30, this does not necessarily mean that the inspection team has suddenly become 50 percent more efficient. Another explanation could be that the quality of code has decreased and that there are simply more faults to be detected.

Having discussed nonexecution-based testing, the next topic is execution-based testing.

5.3 EXECUTION-BASED TESTING

It has been claimed that testing is a demonstration that faults are not present. (A *fault* is the IEEE standard terminology for what is popularly called a "bug," whereas a *failure* is the incorrect behavior of the product as a consequence of the fault [IEEE 610.12, 1990]. Finally, an *error* is the mistake made by the programmer.) Despite the fact that some organizations spend up to 50 percent of their software budget on testing, delivered "tested" software is notoriously unreliable.

The reason for this contradiction is simple. As Dijkstra put it, "Program testing can be a very effective way to show the presence of bugs, but it is hopelessly inadequate for showing their absence" [Dijkstra, 1972]. What Dijkstra is saying is that if a product is executed with test data and the output is wrong, then the product definitely contains a fault. But if the output is correct, then there still may be a fault in the product; all that particular test has shown is that the product runs correctly on that particular set of test data.

5.4 WHAT SHOULD BE TESTED?

In order to be able to describe what properties should be tested, it is first necessary to give a precise description of execution-based testing. According to Goodenough, execution-based testing is a process of inferring certain behavioral properties of a product based, in part, on the results of executing the product in a known environment with selected inputs [Goodenough, 1979].

This definition has three troubling implications. First, the definition states that testing is an inferential process. The tester takes the product, runs it with known input data, and examines the output. The tester has to infer what, if anything, is wrong with the product. From this viewpoint, testing is comparable to trying to find the proverbial black cat in a dark room, but without knowing whether or not there is a cat in the room in the first place. The tester has few clues to help find any faults: perhaps 10 or 20 sets of inputs and corresponding outputs, possibly a user fault report, and thousands of lines of code. From this the tester has to deduce if there is a fault, and if so, what it is.

A second problem with the definition arises from the phrase *in a known environment*. We can never really know our environment, either the hardware or the software. We can never be certain that the operating system is functioning correctly or that the run-time routines are correct. There may be an intermittent hardware fault in the main memory of the computer. So what is observed as the behavior of the product may in fact be a correct product interacting with a faulty compiler or faulty hardware or some other faulty component of the environment.

The third worrisome part of the definition of execution-based testing is the phrase *with selected inputs*. In the case of a real-time system, there is frequently no control over the inputs to the system. Consider avionics software. The flight control system has two types of inputs. The first type of input is what the pilot wants the aircraft to do. Thus, if the pilot pulls back on the joystick in order to climb or opens the throttle in order to increase the speed of the aircraft, these mechanical motions are transformed into digital signals that are sent to the flight control computer. The second type of input is the current physical state of the aircraft, such as its altitude, speed, and the elevations of the wing flaps. The flight control software uses the values of such quantities to compute what signals should be sent to the components of the aircraft such as the wing flaps and the engines in order to implement the pilot's directives. Whereas the pilot's inputs can easily be set to any desired values simply by setting the aircraft's controls appropriately, the inputs corresponding to the current physical state of the aircraft cannot be so easily manipulated. In fact, there is no way that one can force the aircraft to provide "selected inputs." How then can such a real-time system be tested? The answer is to use a simulator.

A *simulator* is a working model of the environment in which the product, in this case the flight control software, executes. The flight control software can be tested by causing the simulator to send selected inputs to the flight control software. The simulator has controls that allow the operator to set an input variable to any selected value. Thus, if the purpose of the test is to determine how the flight control software performs if one engine catches fire, then the controls of the simulator are set so that the inputs sent to the flight control software are indistinguishable from what the inputs would be if an engine of the actual aircraft were on fire. The output is analyzed by examining the output signals sent from the flight control software to the simulator. But a simulator can at best be a good approximation of a faithful model of some aspect of the system; it can never be the system itself. Using a simulator means that whereas there is indeed a "known environment," there is little likelihood that this known environment is in every way identical to the actual environment in which the product will be installed.

The preceding definition of testing speaks of "behavioral properties." What behavioral properties must be tested? An obvious answer is: Test whether the product functions correctly. But as will be shown, correctness is neither necessary nor sufficient. Before discussing correctness, four other behavioral properties will be considered, namely utility, reliability, robustness, and performance [Goodenough, 1979].

5.4.1 UTILITY

Utility is the extent to which a user's needs are met when a correct product is used under conditions permitted by its specifications. In other words, a product that is functioning correctly is now subjected to inputs that are valid in terms of the specifications. The user may test, for example, how easy the product is to use, whether the product performs useful functions, and whether the product is cost-effective compared to competing products. Irrespective of whether the product is correct or not, these are vital issues that have to be tested. If the product is not cost-effective, then there is no point in buying it. And unless the product is easy to use, it will not be used at all or it will be used incorrectly. Thus, when considering buying an existing product (including shrink-wrapped software), the utility of the product should be tested first, and if the product fails on that score, testing should stop.

5.4.2 RELIABILITY

Another aspect of a product that must be tested is its reliability. *Reliability* is a measure of the frequency and criticality of product failure; recall that a failure is an unacceptable effect or behavior, under permissible operating conditions, that occurs as a consequence of a fault. In other words, it is necessary to know how often the product fails *(mean time between failures)* and how bad the effects of that failure can be. When a product fails, an important issue is how long it takes, on average, to repair it *(mean time to repair)*. But often more important is how long it takes to repair the results of the failure. This last point is frequently overlooked. Suppose that the software running on a communications front end fails, on average, only once every 6 months, but when it fails it completely wipes out a database. At best the database can be reinitialized to its status when the last checkpoint dump was taken, and the audit trail can then be used to put the database into a state that is virtually up-to-date. But if this recovery process takes the better part of 2 days, during which time the database and communications front end are inoperative, then the reliability of the product is low, notwithstanding the fact that the mean time between failures is 6 months.

5.4.3 ROBUSTNESS

Another aspect of every product that requires testing is its *robustness*. Although it is difficult to come up with a precise definition, robustness is essentially a function of a number of factors such as the range of operating conditions, the possibility of unacceptable results with valid input, and the acceptability of effects when the product is given invalid input. A product with a wide range of permissible operating conditions is more robust than a product that is more restrictive. A robust product should not yield unacceptable results when the input satisfies its specifications; for example, giving a valid command should not have disastrous consequences. A robust product should not crash when the product is *not* used under permissible operating conditions. To test for this aspect of robustness, test data that do not satisfy the input specifications are deliberately input, and the tester determines how badly the product reacts. For example, when the product solicits a name, the tester may reply with a stream of unacceptable characters such as control-A escape-% ?$#@. If the computer responds with a message such as Incorrect data—Try again, or better, informs the user as to why the data do not conform to what was expected, it is more robust than a product that crashes whenever the data deviate even slightly from what is required.

5.4.4 PERFORMANCE

Performance is another aspect of the product that must be tested. For example, it is essential to know the extent to which the product meets its constraints with regard to response time or space requirements. For an embedded computer system[1] such as an on-board computer in a handheld antiaircraft missile, the space constraints of the system may be such that only 128 kilobytes (Kb) of main memory are available for the software. No matter how excellent the software may be, if it needs 256 Kb of main memory, then it cannot be used.

Real-time software is characterized by hard time constraints, that is, time constraints of such a nature that if a constraint is not met, information is lost. For example, a nuclear reactor control system may have to sample the temperature of the core and process the data every 10th of a second. If the system is not fast enough to

---

[1]An embedded computer is an integral part of a larger system whose primary purpose is not computation. Examples are a computer built into the carburetor of a car or a network of computers controlling a steel mill. The primary function of an embedded system is to control the device in which it is embedded.

Input specification:	p : array of n integers, n > 0.
Output specification:	q : array of n integers such that $q[0] \leq q[1] \leq ... \leq q[n-1]$

Figure 5.1   Incorrect specification for a sort.

be able to handle interrupts from the temperature sensor every 10th of a second, then data will be lost, and there is no way of ever recovering the data; the next time that the system receives temperature data it will be the current temperature, not the reading that was missed. If the reactor is on the point of a meltdown, then it is critical that all relevant information be both received and processed as laid down in the specifications. With all real-time systems, the performance must meet every time constraint listed in the specifications.

5.4.5   CORRECTNESS

Finally, a definition of correctness can be given. A product is *correct* if it satisfies its output specifications, independent of its use of computing resources, when operated under permitted conditions [Goodenough, 1979]. In other words, if input that satisfies the input specifications is provided and the product is given all the resources it needs, then the product is correct if the output satisfies the output specifications.

This definition of correctness, like the definition of testing itself, has worrisome implications. Suppose that a product has been successfully tested against a broad variety of test data. Does this mean that the product is acceptable? Unfortunately, it does not. If a product is correct, all that it means is that it satisfies its specifications. But what if the specifications themselves are incorrect? To illustrate this difficulty, consider the specification shown in Figure 5.1. The specification states that the input to the sort is an array p of n integers, whereas the output is another array q that is sorted in nondecreasing order. Superficially, the specification seems to be perfectly correct. But consider method trickSort shown in Figure 5.2. In that method, all n

```
void trickSort (int p[ ], int q[ ])
{
    int i;
    for (i = 0; i < n; i++)
        q[i] = 0;
}
```

Figure 5.2   Method trickSort which satisfies specification of Figure 5.1.

Input specification:	p : array of n integers, n > 0.
Output specification:	q : array of n integers such that q[0] ≤ q[1] ≤ . . . ≤ q[n − 1] The elements of array q are a permutation of the elements of array p, which are unchanged.

Figure 5.3   Corrected specification for the sort.

elements of array q are set to 0. The method satisfies the specification of Figure 5.1 and is therefore correct!

What has happened? Unfortunately, the specification of Figure 5.1 is wrong. What has been omitted is a statement that the elements of q, the output array, are a permutation (rearrangement) of the elements of the input array p. An intrinsic aspect of sorting is that it is a rearrangement process. And the method of Figure 5.2 capitalizes on this specification fault. In other words, trickSort is correct, but the specification of Figure 5.1 is wrong. A corrected specification appears in Figure 5.3.

From the preceding example, it is clear that the consequences of specification faults are nontrivial. After all, the correctness of a product is meaningless if its specifications are incorrect.

The fact that a product is correct is not sufficient, because the specifications in terms of which it was shown to be correct may themselves be wrong. But is it necessary? Consider the following example. A software organization has acquired a superb new Java compiler. The new compiler can translate twice as many lines of source code per minute as the old compiler, the object code runs nearly 45 percent faster, and the size of the object code is about 20 percent smaller. In addition, the error messages are much clearer, and the cost of annual maintenance and updates is less than half of that of the old compiler. There is one problem, however: The first time that a **for** statement appears in any class, the compiler prints a spurious error message. The compiler is therefore not correct, because the specifications for a compiler implicitly or explicitly require that error messages be printed if, and only if, there is a fault in the source code. It is certainly possible to use the compiler—in fact, in every way but one the compiler is absolutely ideal. Furthermore, it is reasonable to expect that this minor fault will be corrected in the next release. In the meantime, the programmers will learn to ignore the spurious error message. Not only can the organization live with the incorrect compiler, but if anyone were to suggest replacing it by the old correct compiler there would be an outcry. Thus the correctness of a product is neither necessary nor sufficient.

Both the preceding examples are admittedly somewhat artificial. But they do make the point that correctness simply means that the product is a correct implementation of its specifications. In other words, there is more to testing than just showing that the product is correct.

With all the difficulties associated with execution-based testing, computer scientists have tried to come up with other ways of ensuring that the product does what it is supposed to do. One such nonexecution-based alternative that has received considerable attention for more than 25 years is correctness proving.

5.5   TESTING VERSUS CORRECTNESS PROOFS

A correctness proof is a mathematical technique for showing that a product is correct, that is, that it satisfies its specifications. The technique is sometimes termed *verification*. However, as previously pointed out, the term verification is often used to denote all nonexecution-based techniques, not only correctness proving. For clarity, this mathematical procedure will be termed *correctness proving*, to remind the reader that it is a mathematical proof process.

5.5.1   EXAMPLE OF A CORRECTNESS PROOF

To see how correctness is proved, consider the code fragment shown in Figure 5.4. The flowchart equivalent to the code is given in Figure 5.5. It will now be shown that the code fragment is correct—that after the code has been executed, the variable s will contain the sum of the n elements of the array y. In Figure 5.6 an *assertion* has been placed before and after each statement, at the places labeled with the letters *A* through *H*; that is, a claim has been made at each place that a certain mathematical property holds there. The correctness of each assertion is now proved.

```
int     k, s;
int     y[ ] = new int[n];


k = 0;
s = 0;


while (k < n)
{
    s = s + y[k];
    k = k + 1;
}
```

Figure 5.4   Code fragment to be proved correct.

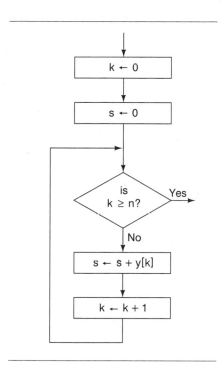

Figure 5.5   Flowchart of Figure 5.4.

The input specification, the condition that holds at A before the code is executed, is that the variable n is a natural number, that is,

$$A: \quad n \in \{1, 2, 3,...\} \tag{5.1}$$

An obvious output specification is that if control reaches point H, the value of s contains the sum of the n values stored in array y, that is,

$$H: \quad s = y[0] + y[1] + ... + y[n - 1] \tag{5.2}$$

In fact, the code fragment can be proved to be correct with respect to a stronger output specification, namely

$$H: \quad k = n \text{ and } s = y[0] + y[1] + ... + y[n - 1] \tag{5.3}$$

A natural reaction to the last sentence is to ask: From where did output specification (5.3) come? By the end of the proof, the reader will hopefully have the answer to that question; also see Problems 5.10 and 5.11.

In addition to the input and output specifications, a third aspect of the proof process is to provide an invariant for the loop. That is to say, a mathematical expression must be provided that holds at point D irrespective of whether the loop has been executed 0, 1, or many times. The loop invariant that will be proved to hold is

$$D: \quad k \le n \text{ and } s = y[0] + y[1] + ... + y[k - 1] \tag{5.4}$$

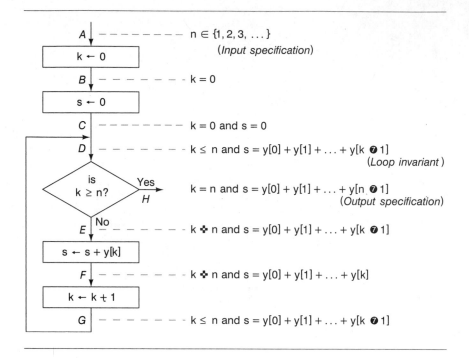

Figure 5.6   Figure 5.5 with input specification, output specification, loop invariant, and assertions.

Now it will be shown that if specification (5.1) holds at point *A*, then specification (5.3) will hold at point *H*, that is, the code fragment will be proved to be correct.

First, the assignment statement $k \leftarrow 0$ is executed. Control is now at point *B*, where the following assertion holds:

$$B: \quad k = 0 \qquad (5.5)$$

To be more precise, at point *B* the assertion should read $k = 0$ and $n \in \{1, 2, 3,...\}$. However, the input specification (5.1) holds at all points in the flowchart. For brevity, the "and $n \in \{1, 2, 3,...\}$" will therefore be omitted from now on.

At point *C*, as a consequence of the second assignment statement, namely $s \leftarrow 0$, the following assertion is true:

$$C: \quad k = 0 \text{ and } s = 0 \qquad (5.6)$$

Now the loop is entered. It will be proved by induction that the loop invariant (5.4) is indeed correct. Just before the loop is executed for the first time, assertion (5.6) holds, that is, $k = 0$ and $s = 0$. Now consider loop invariant (5.4). Because $k = 0$ by assertion (5.6), and $n \geq 1$ from input specification (5.1), it follows that $k \leq n$ as required. Furthermore, because $k = 0$ it follows that $k - 1 = -1$, so the sum in (5.4) is empty and $s = 0$ as required. Loop invariant (5.4) is therefore true just before the loop is entered for the first time.

Now the inductive hypothesis step is performed. Assume that at some stage during the execution of the code fragment the loop invariant holds. That is, for k equal to some value k_0, $0 \leq k_0 \leq n$, execution is at point D, and the assertion that holds is

$$D: \quad k_0 \leq n \text{ and } s = y[0] + y[1] + ... + y[k_0 - 1] \qquad \textbf{(5.7)}$$

Control now passes to the test box. If $k_0 \geq n$, then because $k_0 \leq n$ by hypothesis, it follows that $k_0 = n$. By inductive hypothesis (5.7), this implies that

$$H: \quad k_0 = n \text{ and } s = y[0] + y[1] + ... + y[n - 1] \qquad \textbf{(5.8)}$$

that is precisely the output specification (5.3).

On the other hand, if the test is $k_0 \geq n$? fails, then control passes from point D to point E. Because k_0 is not greater than or equal to n, $k_0 < n$, and (5.7) becomes

$$E: \quad k_0 < n \text{ and } s = y[0] + y[1] + ... + y[k_0 - 1] \qquad \textbf{(5.9)}$$

The statement $s \leftarrow s + y[k_0]$ is now executed, so from assertion (5.9), at point F the following assertion must hold:

$$F: \quad k_0 < n \text{ and } s = y[0] + y[1] + ... + y[k_0 - 1] + y[k_0]$$
$$= y[0] + y[1] + ... + y[k_0] \qquad \textbf{(5.10)}$$

The next statement to be executed is $k_0 \leftarrow k_0 + 1$. To see the effect of this statement, suppose that the value of k_0 before executing this statement is 17. Then the last term in the sum in (5.10) is $y[17]$. Now the value of k_0 is increased by 1 to 18. The sum s is unchanged, so the last term in the sum is still $y[17]$, which is now $y[k_0 - 1]$. Also, at point F, $k_0 < n$. Increasing the value of k_0 by 1 means that if the inequality is to hold at point G then $k_0 \leq n$. Thus the effect of increasing k_0 by 1 is that the following assertion holds at point G:

$$G: \quad k_0 \leq n \text{ and } s = y[0] + y[1] + ... + y[k_0 - 1] \qquad \textbf{(5.11)}$$

Assertion (5.11) that holds at point G is identical to assertion (5.7) that, by assumption, holds at point D. But point D is topologically identical to point G. In other words, if (5.7) holds at D for $k = k_0$, then it will again hold at D with $k = k_0 + 1$. It has been shown that the loop invariant holds for $k = 0$. By induction it follows that loop invariant (5.4) holds for all values of k, $0 \leq k \leq n$.

All that remains is to prove that the loop terminates. Initially, by assertion (5.6), the value of k is equal to 0. Each iteration of the loop increases the value of k by 1 when the statement $k \leftarrow k + 1$ is executed. Eventually, k must reach the value n, at which time the loop is exited, and the value of s is given by assertion (5.8), thus satisfying output specification (5.3).

To review, given the input specification (5.1), it was proved that loop invariant (5.4) holds whether the loop has been executed 0, 1, or more times. Furthermore, it was proved that after n iterations the loop terminates, and when it does so the values of k and s satisfy the output specification (5.3). In other words, the code fragment of Figure 5.4 has been mathematically proved to be correct.

5.5.2   CORRECTNESS PROOF CASE STUDY

An important aspect of correctness proofs is that they should be done in conjunction with design and coding. As Dijkstra put it, "The programmer should let the program proof and program grow hand in hand" [Dijkstra, 1972]. For example, when a loop is incorporated into the design, a loop invariant is put forward; and as the design is refined stepwise, so is the invariant. Developing a product in this way gives the programmer confidence that the product is correct and tends to reduce the number of faults. Quoting Dijkstra again, "The only effective way to raise the confidence level of a program significantly is to give a convincing proof of its correctness" [Dijkstra, 1972]. But even if a product is proved to be correct, it must be thoroughly tested as well. To illustrate the necessity for testing in conjunction with correctness proving, consider the following.

In 1969, Naur published a paper on a technique for constructing and proving a product correct [Naur, 1969]. The technique was illustrated by what Naur termed a *line-editing problem,* but today would be considered a text-processing problem. it may be stated as follows:

> Given a text consisting of words separated by blank characters or by newline (new line) characters, convert it to line-by-line form in accordance with the following rules:
>
> 1.   line breaks must be made only where the given text contains a blank or newline;
> 2.   each line is filled as far as possible, as long as
> 3.   no line will contain more than maxpos characters

Naur constructed a procedure using his technique and informally proved its correctness. The procedure consisted of approximately 25 lines of ALGOL 60. The paper was then reviewed by Leavenworth in *Computing Reviews* [Leavenworth, 1970]. The reviewer pointed out that in the output of Naur's procedure, the first word of the first line is preceded by a blank unless the word is exactly maxpos characters long. Although this may seem a trivial fault, it is a fault that would surely have been detected had the procedure been tested, that is, executed with test data, rather than only proved correct. But worse was to come. London detected three additional faults in Naur's procedure [London, 1971]. One is that the procedure does not terminate unless a word longer than maxpos characters is encountered. Again, this fault is likely to have been detected if the procedure had been tested. London then presented a corrected version of the procedure and proved formally that the resulting procedure was correct; recall that Naur had used only informal proof techniques.

The next episode in this saga is that Goodenough and Gerhart found three faults that London had not detected, despite his formal proof [Goodenough and Gerhart, 1975]. These included the fact that the last word will not be output unless it is followed by a blank or newline. Yet again, reasonable choice of test data would have detected this fault without much difficulty. In fact, of the total of seven faults collectively detected by Leavenworth, London, and Goodenough and Gerhart, four could have been detected simply by running the procedure on test data, such as the illustrations given in Naur's original paper. The lesson from this saga is clear. Even if a product has been proved to be correct, it must still be tested thoroughly.

The example in Section 5.5.1 showed that proving the correctness of even a small code fragment can be a lengthy process. Furthermore, the case study for the section showed that it is a difficult and error-prone process, even for a 25-line procedure. The following issue must therefore be put forward: Is correctness proving an interesting research idea or is it a powerful software engineering technique whose time has come? This is answered in the next section.

5.5.3 CORRECTNESS PROOFS AND SOFTWARE ENGINEERING

A number of software engineering practitioners have put forward reasons why correctness proving should not be viewed as a standard software engineering technique. First, it is claimed that software engineers do not have adequate mathematical training. Second, it is suggested that proving is too expensive to be practical, and third, that proving is too hard. Each of these reasons will be shown to be an oversimplification.

Although the proof given in Section 5.5.1 can be understood with hardly more than high school algebra, nontrivial proofs require that input specifications, output specifications, and loop invariants be expressed in first- or second-order predicate calculus, or equivalent. Not only does this make the proof process simpler for a mathematician, but it allows correctness proving to be done by a computer. To complicate matters further, predicate calculus is now somewhat outdated. To prove the correctness of concurrent products, techniques using temporal or other modal logics are required [Lamport, 1980; Manna and Pnueli, 1992]. There is no doubt that correctness proving requires training in mathematical logic. Fortunately, most computer science majors today either take courses in the requisite material or have the background to learn correctness-proving techniques on the job. Thus colleges are now turning out computer science graduates with sufficient mathematical skills for correctness proving. The claim that practicing software engineers do not have the necessary mathematical training may have been true in the past, but no longer applies in the light of the thousands of computer science majors joining the industry each year.

The claim that proving is too expensive for use in software development is also false. On the contrary, the economic viability of correctness proving can be determined on a project-by-project basis using cost–benefit analysis (Section 4.2). For example, consider the software for the NASA space station. Human lives are at stake, and if something goes wrong a space shuttle rescue mission may not arrive in time. The cost of proving life-critical space station software correct is large. But the potential cost of a software fault that might be overlooked if correctness proving is not performed is even larger.

The third claim is that correctness proving is too hard. Despite this claim, many nontrivial products have been successfully proved to be correct, including operating

```
void theoremProver ( )
{
    printf ("This product is correct");
}
```

Figure 5.7   Theorem prover.

system kernels, compilers, and communications systems [Landwehr, 1983; Berry and Wing, 1985]. Furthermore, many tools such as theorem provers exist to assist in correctness proving. A theorem prover takes as input a product, its input and output specifications, and loop invariants. The theorem prover then attempts to prove mathematically that the product, when given input data satisfying the input specifications, will produce output data satisfying the output specifications.

At the same time, there are some difficulties with correctness proving. For example, how can we be sure that a theorem prover is correct? If the theorem prover prints out **This product is correct**, can we believe it? To take an extreme case, consider the so-called theorem prover shown in Figure 5.7. No matter what code is submitted to this theorem prover, it will print out **This product is correct**. In other words, what reliability can be placed on the output of a theorem prover? One suggestion is to submit a theorem prover to itself and see whether it is correct. Apart from the philosophical implications, a simple way of seeing that this will not work is to consider what would happen if the theorem prover of Figure 5.7 were submitted to itself for proving. It will, as always, print out **This product is correct**, thereby "proving" its own correctness.

A further difficulty is finding the input and output specifications, and especially the loop invariants, or their equivalents in other logics such as modal logic. Suppose that a product is correct. Unless a suitable invariant for each loop can be found, there is no way of proving the product correct. Yes, tools do exist to assist in this task [Tamir, 1980]. But even with state-of-the-art tools, a software engineer may simply not be able to come up with a correctness proof. One solution to this problem is to develop the product and proof in parallel, as advocated in Section 5.5.2. When a loop is designed, an invariant for that loop is specified at the same time. With this approach, it is somewhat easier to prove the code modules correct.

Worse than not being able to find loop invariants, what if the specifications themselves are incorrect? An example of this is method trickSort (Figure 5.2). A good theorem prover, when given the incorrect specifications of Figure 5.1, will undoubtedly declare that the method shown in Figure 5.2 is correct.

Manna and Waldinger have stated, "We can never be sure that the specifications are correct" and, "We can never be certain that a verification system is correct" [Manna and Waldinger, 1978]. These statements from two of the leading experts in the field encapsulate the various points made previously.

Does all this mean that there is no place for correctness proofs in software engineering? Quite the contrary. Proving products correct is an important, and sometimes vital, software engineering tool. Proofs are appropriate where human lives are at stake or where otherwise indicated by cost–benefit analysis. If the cost of proving software correct is less than the probable cost if the product fails, then the product should be proved. However, as the text-processing case study shows, proving alone is not enough. Instead, correctness proving should be viewed as an important component of the set of techniques that must be utilized together to check that a product is correct. Because the aim of software engineering is the production of quality software, correctness proving is indeed an important software engineering technique.

Even when a full formal proof is not justified, the quality of software can be markedly improved through the use of informal proofs. For example, a proof similar to that of Section 5.5.1 will assist in checking that a loop will be executed the correct number of times. A second way of improving software quality is to insert assertions such as those of Figure 5.6 into the code. Then, if at execution time an assertion does not hold, the product will be halted, and the software team can investigate whether the assertion that terminated execution is incorrect or whether there is indeed a fault in the code that was detected by triggering the assertion. Languages such as Eiffel [Meyer, 1992b] support assertions directly by means of an **assert** statement. Suppose that an informal proof requires that the value of variable xxx be positive at a particular point in the code. Even though the design team may be convinced that there is no way for xxx to be negative, for additional reliability they may specify that the statement

$$\textbf{assert} \ (\text{xxx} > 0)$$

appear at that point in the code. If xxx is less than or equal to zero, execution will terminate, and the situation can then be investigated by the software team. (Unfortunately, *Assert* in C++ is a debugging statement, similar to *assert* in C; it is not part of the language itself.)

Once the users are confident that the product is working correctly, they have the option of switching off assertion checking. This will speed up execution, but if there is a fault that would have been detected by an assertion, it may not be found if assertion checking is switched off. Thus there is a trade-off between run-time efficiency and continuing assertion checking even after the product is in operations mode. (The Just in Case You Wanted to Know box on page 132 gives an interesting insight on this issue.)

A fundamental issue in execution-based testing is which members of the software development team should be responsible for carrying it out.

5.6   Who Should Perform Execution-Based Testing?

Suppose a programmer is asked to test a module that he or she has written. Testing has been described by Myers as the process of executing a product with the intention of finding faults [Myers, 1979]. Testing is thus a destructive process. On the other hand, the programmer who is doing the testing will ordinarily not wish to destroy his or her work. If the fundamental attitude of the programmer toward the code is the

JUST IN CASE YOU WANTED TO KNOW

One feature of languages such as Java and Ada (but not C or C++) is bounds checking. One example of bounds checking is examining every array index during execution to ensure that it is within its declared range. Another example is subrange checking, that is, checking during execution that when a value is assigned to a variable, that value is within a specific declared range for that variable.

Tony Hoare has suggested that using bounds checking while developing a product, but turning it off once the product is working correctly, can be likened to learning to sail on dry land wearing a life jacket and then taking the life jacket off when actually at sea. In his Turing Award lecture, Hoare described a compiler for ALGOL 60 that he developed in 1961 [Hoare, 1981]. When users were later offered the opportunity to turn off bounds checking in operations mode they unanimously refused, because they had experienced so many incidents of values out of range during earlier production runs.

Bounds checking can be viewed as a special case of a more general concept, namely assertion checking. Hoare's life jacket analogy is just as applicable to turning off assertion checking in operations mode.

usual protective one, then the chances of that programmer using test data that will highlight faults is considerably lower than if the major motivation were truly destructive.

A successful test is one that finds faults. This, too, poses a difficulty. It means that if the module passes the test, then the test has failed. Conversely, if the module does not perform according to specifications, then the test succeeds. When a programmer is asked to test a module he or she has written, the programmer is being asked to execute the module in such a way that a failure (incorrect behavior) ensues. This goes against the creative instincts of programmers.

An inescapable conclusion of this is that programmers should not test their own modules. After a programmer has been *con*structive and has built a module, testing that module requires the programmer perform a *de*structive act and to attempt to destroy the very thing that he or she has created. A second reason why execution-based testing should be done by someone else is that the programmer may have misunderstood some aspect of the design or specifications. If testing is done by someone else, such faults may be discovered. Nevertheless, the debugging (finding the cause of the failure and correcting the fault) is best done by the original programmer, the person who is most familiar with the code.

The statement that a programmer should not test his or her own code must not be taken too far. Consider the programming process. The programmer begins by reading the detailed design of the module that may be in the form of a flowchart or, more likely, pseudocode. But whatever technique is used, the programmer must certainly desk-check the module before entering it into the computer. That is to say, the programmer must try out the flowchart or pseudocode with various test cases, tracing through the detailed design to check that each test case is correctly executed. Only when the programmer is satisfied that the detailed design is correct should the text editor be invoked and the module coded.

Once the module is in machine-readable form, it undergoes a series of tests. First, the programmer attempts to compile the module. When this has been successfully achieved, the following step is to link and load it. Then the programmer attempts to execute the module. If the module executes, then test data are used to determine that the module works successfully, probably the same test data that were used to desk-check the detailed design. Next, if the module executes correctly when correct test data are used, then the programmer tries out incorrect data to test the robustness of the module. When the programmer is satisfied that the module is operating correctly, systematic testing commences. It is this *systematic testing* that should not be performed by the programmer.

If the programmer is not to perform this systematic testing, who is to do it? As stated in Section 5.1.2, independent testing must be performed by the SQA group. The key word here is *independent*. Only if the SQA group is truly independent of the development team can its members fulfill their mission of ensuring that the product indeed satisfies its specifications, without software development managers applying pressures, such as product deadlines, that might hamper their work. SQA personnel must report to their own managers and thus protect their independence.

How is systematic testing performed? An essential part of a test case is a statement of the expected output before the test is executed. It is a complete waste of time for the tester to sit at a terminal, execute the module, enter haphazard test data, and then peer at the screen and say, "I guess that looks right." Equally futile is for the tester to plan test cases with great care and then execute each test case in turn, look at the output, and say, "Yes, that certainly looks right." It is far too easy to be fooled by plausible results. If programmers are allowed to test their own code, then there is always the danger that a programmer will see what he or she wants to see. The same danger can occur even when the testing is done by someone else. The solution is for management to insist that before a test is performed, both the test data and the expected results of that test be recorded. After the test has been performed, the actual results should be recorded and compared with the expected results.

Even in small organizations and with small products, it is important that this recording be done in machine-readable form, because test cases should never be thrown away. The reason for this is maintenance. While the product is being maintained, regression testing must be performed. Stored test cases that the product has previously executed correctly must be rerun to ensure that the modifications made to add new functionality to the product have not destroyed the product's existing functionality. This is discussed further in Chapter 14.

5.7 WHEN TESTING STOPS

After a product has been successfully maintained for many years it may eventually lose its usefulness and be superseded by a totally different product, in much the same way that electronic valves were replaced by transistors. Alternatively, a product may still be useful, but the cost of porting it to new hardware or of running it under a new operating system may be larger than the cost of constructing a new product, using the old one as a prototype. Thus, finally, the software product is decommissioned and removed from service. Only at that point, when the software has been irrevocably discarded, is it time to stop testing.

Now that all the necessary background material has been covered, objects can be examined in greater detail. This is the subject of the next chapter.

Chapter Review

A key theme of this chapter is that testing must be carried out in parallel with all activities of the software process. The chapter begins with a description of quality issues (Section 5.1). Next, nonexecution-based testing is described (Section 5.2), with a careful discussion of walkthroughs and inspections. This is followed by a definition of execution-based testing (Sections 5.3 and 5.4) and a discussion of behavioral properties of a product that must be tested, including utility, reliability, robustness, performance, and correctness (Sections 5.4.1 through 5.4.5). In Section 5.5 correctness proving is introduced and an example of such a proof is given in Section 5.5.1. The role of correctness proofs in software engineering is then analyzed (Sections 5.5.2 and 5.5.3). Another important issue is that systematic execution-based testing must be performed by the independent SQA group and not by the programmer (Section 5.6). Finally, the issue of when testing can finally stop is discussed in Section 5.7.

For Further Reading

The attitude of software producers to the testing process has changed over the years, from viewing testing as a means of showing that a product runs correctly to the modern attitude that testing should be used to prevent requirements, specification, design, and implementation faults. This progression is described in [Gelperin and Hetzel, 1988].

Books on software quality assurance include [Dunn and Ullman, 1982] and [Schulmeyer and McManus, 1987]. There is also an IEEE Computer Society tutorial containing a number of useful papers on SQA [Chow, 1985]. Practical experiences with SQA are described in [Poston and Bruen, 1987].

Good introductions to proving programs correct include Chapter 3 of [Manna, 1974] and [Baber 1987]. One of the standard techniques of correctness proving is using the so-called Hoare logic, as described in [Hoare, 1969]. An alternative approach to ensuring that products satisfy their specifications is to construct the product stepwise, checking that each step preserves correctness. This is described in [Dijkstra, 1968], [Wirth, 1971], [Dahl, Dijkstra, and Hoare, 1972], and [Dijkstra, 1976]. Functional correctness is another approach. It has been developed by Mills and co-workers [Linger, Mills, and Witt, 1979; Mills, Basili, Gannon, and Hamlet,

1987] and is used in the IBM Cleanroom software development method [Dyer, 1992; Trammel, Binder, and Snyder, 1992] described in Section 12.19. A collection of research papers on correctness proving can be found in the August 1985 Special Issue of *ACM SIGSOFT Software Engineering Notes* devoted to the proceedings of the Third Formal Verification Workshop. An important article regarding acceptance of correctness proofs by the software engineering community is [DeMillo, Lipton, and Perlis, 1979].

The IEEE "Standard for Software Reviews and Audits" [IEEE 1028, 1988] is an excellent source of information on nonexecution-based testing. A paper on how to conduct inspections as well as their effectiveness is [Ackerman, Buchwald, and Lewski, 1989]. Inspection of a very large software product (2.5 million lines of code) is described in [Russell, 1991]. Other sources of information on experience with inspections are [Doolan, 1992] and [Weller, 1993]. Cost issues, such as reducing the size of a team and minimizing the time lost while waiting for reviewers to meet, are described in [Volta, 1993].

The classic work on execution-based testing is [Myers, 1979], a work that has had a significant impact on the field of testing. [DeMillo, Lipton, and Sayward, 1978] is still an excellent source of information on selection of test data. [Beizer, 1990] is a compendium on testing, a true handbook on the subject. A similar work is [Hetzel, 1988].

The May 1989 issue of *IEEE Software* has a wide variety of papers on testing issues. Both execution-based and nonexecution-based testing are covered. The proceedings of the International Symposium on Software Testing and Analysis cover a similar broad spectrum of testing issues. Turning specifically to the object-oriented paradigm, the September 1994 issue of *Communications of the ACM* contains a number of articles on testing object-oriented software.

Problems

How are the terms *correctness proving, verification,* and *validation* used in this book?

5.1

A software development organization currently employs 75 software professionals, including 13 managers, all of whom do both development, and verification and validation of software. Latest figures show that 28 percent of their time is spent on verification and validation. The average annual cost to the company of a manager is $115,000, whereas nonmanagerial professionals cost $84,000 a year on average; both figures include overheads. Use cost–benefit analysis to determine whether a separate SQA group should be set up within the organization.

5.2

5.3   Repeat the cost–benefit analysis of Problem 5.2 for a firm with only seven software professionals, including two managers. Assume that the other figures remain unchanged.

5.4   You have been testing a module for 11 days and have found two faults. What does this tell you about the existence of other faults?

5.5   What are the similarities between a walkthrough and an inspection? What are the differences?

5.6   You are a member of the SQA group at Olde Fashioned Software. You suggest to your manager that inspections be introduced. He responds that he sees no reason why four people should waste their time looking for faults when one person can run test cases on the same piece of code. How do you respond?

5.7   You are the SQA manager at Honey For My Honey, a regional chain of 426 stores selling raw-wild pure honey. Your organization is considering buying a stock-control package for use throughout the organization. Before authorizing the purchase of the package, you decide to test it thoroughly. What properties of the package do you investigate?

5.8   All 426 stores in the Honey For My Honey organization are now to be connected by a communications network. A salesman is offering you a 4-week free trial to experiment with the communications package he is trying to sell you. What sort of software tests would you perform and why?

5.9   You are the admiral in charge of developing the software for controlling a new ship-to-ship missile. The software has been delivered to you for acceptance testing. What properties of the software do you test?

5.10   What happens to the correctness proof of Section 5.5.1 if loop invariant

$$s = y[0] + y[1] + \dots + y[k - 1]$$

is used instead of (5.4)?

5.11   Assume that you have some experience with loop invariants and that you know that invariant (5.4) is the correct invariant for the loop of Figure 5.6. Show that output specification (5.3) is a natural consequence of the loop invariant.

5.12   Consider the following code fragment:

```
k = 1;
g = 2;
while (k < n)
{
    k = k + 1;
    g = g * 2;
}
```

Prove that this code fragment correctly computes $g = 2^n$ if $n \in \{1, 2, 3, \dots\}$.

5.13   Can correctness proving solve the problem that the product as delivered to the client may not be what the client really needs? Give reasons for your answer.

How should Dijkstra's statement (Section 5.3) be changed to apply to correctness proofs rather than testing? Bear in mind the case study of Section 5.5.2. **5.14**

Design and implement a solution to the Naur text-processing problem (Section 5.5.2) using the language specified by your instructor. Execute it against test data and record the number of faults that you find and also the cause of the faults (e.g., logic fault, loop counter fault). Do not correct any of the faults you detect. Now exchange products with a fellow student and see how many faults each of you finds in the other's product and whether or not they are new faults. Again record the cause of each fault, and compare the fault types found by each of you. Tabulate the results for the class as a whole. **5.15**

(Term Project) Explain how you would test the utility, reliability, robustness, performance, and correctness of the Osbert Oglesby product in Appendix A. **5.16**

(Readings in Software Engineering) Your instructor will distribute copies of [Gelperin and Hetzel, 1988]. The authors view the period since 1988 as the "prevention-oriented period." To what extent do you agree with this assertion? **5.17**

References

[Ackerman, Buchwald, and Lewski, 1989] A. F. ACKERMAN, L. S. BUCHWALD, AND F. H. LEWSKI, "Software Inspections: An Effective Verification Process," *IEEE Software* **6** (May 1989), pp. 31–36.

[Baber, 1987] R. L. BABER, *The Spine of Software: Designing Provably Correct Software: Theory and Practice,* John Wiley and Sons, New York, 1987.

[Beizer, 1990] B. BEIZER, *Software Testing Techniques,* Second Edition, Van Nostrand Reinhold, New York, 1990.

[Berry and Wing, 1985] D. M. BERRY AND J. M. WING, "Specifying and Prototyping: Some Thoughts on Why They Are Successful," in: *Formal Methods and Software Development, Proceedings of the International Joint Conference on Theory and Practice of Software Development, Volume 2,* Springer-Verlag, Berlin, 1985, pp. 117–128.

[Boehm 1984a] B.W. BOEHM, "Verifying and Validating Software Requirements and Design Specifications," *IEEE Software* **1** (January 1984), pp. 75–88.

[Bush, 1990] M. BUSH, "Improving Software Quality: The Use of Formal Inspections at the Jet Propulsion Laboratory," *Proceedings of the 12th International Conference on Software Engineering,* Nice, France, March 1990, pp. 196–199.

[Chow, 1985] T. S. CHOW (Editor) *Tutorial: Software Quality Assurance: A Practical Approach,* IEEE Computer Society Press, Washington, DC, 1985.

[Dahl, Dijkstra, and Hoare, 1972] O.-J. DAHL, E.W. DIJKSTRA, AND C.A.R. HOARE, *Structured Programming,* Academic Press, New York, 1972.

[DeMillo, Lipton, and Perlis, 1979] R. A. DeMILLO, R. J. LIPTON, AND A. J. PERLIS, "Social Processes and Proofs of Theorems and Programs," *Communications of the ACM* **22** (May 1979), pp. 271–280.

[DeMillo, Lipton, and Sayward, 1978] R. A. DeMILLO, R. J. LIPTON, AND F. G. SAYWARD, "Hints on Test Data Selection: Help for the Practicing Programmer," *IEEE Computer* **11** (April 1978), pp. 34–43.

[Dijkstra, 1968c] E. W. DIJKSTRA, "A Constructive Approach to the Problem of Program Correctness," *BIT* **8** (No. 3, 1968), pp. 174–186.

[Dijkstra, 1972] E. W. DIJKSTRA, "The Humble Programmer," *Communications of the ACM* **15** (October 1972), pp. 859–866.

[Dijkstra, 1976] E.W. DIJKSTRA, *A Discipline of Programming,* Prentice-Hall, Englewood Cliffs, NJ, 1976.

[Doolan, 1992] E. P. DOOLAN, "Experience with Fagan's Inspection Method," *Software—Practice and Experience* **22** (February 1992), pp. 173–182.

[Dunn, 1984] R. H. DUNN, *Software Defect Removal,* McGraw-Hill, New York, 1984.

[Dunn and Ullman, 1982] R. DUNN AND R. ULLMAN, *Quality Assurance for Computer Software,* McGraw-Hill, New York, 1982.

[Dyer, 1992] M. DYER, *The Cleanroom Approach to Quality Software Development,* John Wiley and Sons, New York, 1992.

[Fagan, 1976] M. E. FAGAN, "Design and Code Inspections to Reduce Errors in Program Development," *IBM Systems Journal* **15** (No. 3, 1976), pp. 182–211.

[Fagan, 1986] M. E. FAGAN, "Advances in Software Inspections," *IEEE Transactions on Software Engineering* **SE-12** (July 1986), pp. 744–751.

[Fowler, 1986] P. J. FOWLER, "In-Process Inspections of Workproducts at AT&T," *AT&T Technical Journal* **65** (March/April 1986), pp. 102–112.

[Gelperin and Hetzel, 1988] D. GELPERIN AND B. HETZEL, "The Growth of Software Testing," *Communications of the ACM* **31** (June 1988), pp. 687–695.

[Goodenough, 1979] J. B. GOODENOUGH, "A Survey of Program Testing Issues," in: *Research Directions in Software Technology,* P. Wegner (Editor), The MIT Press, Cambridge, MA, 1979, pp. 316–340.

[Goodenough and Gerhart, 1975] J. B. GOODENOUGH AND S. L. GERHART, "Toward a Theory of Test Data Selection," *Proceedings of the Third International Conference on Reliable Software,* Los Angeles, 1975, pp. 493–510. Also published in: *IEEE Transactions on Software Engineering* **SE-1** (June 1975), pp. 156–173. Revised version: J. B. Goodenough, and S. L. Gerhart, "Toward a Theory of Test Data Selection: Data Selection Criteria," in: *Current Trends in Programming Methodology, Volume 2,* R.T. Yeh (Editor), Prentice-Hall, Englewood Cliffs, NJ, 1977, pp. 44–79.

[Hetzel, 1988] W. C. HETZEL, *The Complete Guide to Software Testing,* Second Edition, QED Information Systems, Wellesley, MA, 1988.

[Hoare, 1969] C. A. R. HOARE, "An Axiomatic Basis for Computer Programming," *Communications of the ACM* **12** (October 1969), pp. 576–583.

[Hoare, 1981] C. A. R. HOARE, "The Emperor's Old Clothes," *Communications of the ACM* **24** (February 1981), pp. 75–83.

[IEEE 610.12, 1990] "A Glossary of Software Engineering Terminology," IEEE 610.12-1990, Institute of Electrical and Electronic Engineers, Inc., 1990.

[IEEE 1028, 1988] "Standard for Software Reviews and Audits," IEEE 1028, Institute of Electrical and Electronic Engineers, Inc., 1988.

[Jones, 1978] T. C. JONES, "Measuring Programming Quality and Productivity," *IBM Systems Journal* **17** (No. 1, 1978), pp. 39–63.

[Kelly, Sherif, and Hops, 1992] J. C. KELLY, J. S. SHERIF, AND J. HOPS, "An Analysis of Defect Densities Found during Software Inspections," *Journal of Systems and Software* **17** (January 1992), pp. 111–117.

[Lamport, 1980] L. LAMPORT, " 'Sometime' Is Sometimes 'Not Never': On the Temporal Logic of Programs," *Proceedings of the Seventh Annual ACM Symposium on Principles of Programming Languages,* Las Vegas, NV, 1980, pp. 174–185.

[Landwehr, 1983] C. E. LANDWEHR, "The Best Available Technologies for Computer Security," *IEEE Computer* **16** (July 1983), pp. 86–100.

[Leavenworth, 1970] B. LEAVENWORTH, Review #19420, *Computing Reviews* **11** (July 1970), pp. 396–397.

[Linger, Mills, and Witt, 1979] R. C. LINGER, H. D. MILLS, AND B. I. WITT, *Structured Programming: Theory and Practice,* Addison-Wesley, Reading, MA, 1979.

[London, 1971] R. L. LONDON, "Software Reliability through Proving Programs Correct," *Proceedings of the IEEE International Symposium on Fault-Tolerant Computing,* March 1971.

[Manna, 1974] Z. MANNA, *Mathematical Theory of Computation,* McGraw-Hill, New York, 1974.

[Manna and Pnueli, 1992] Z. MANNA AND A. PNUELI, *The Temporal Logic of Reactive and Concurrent Systems,* Springer-Verlag, New York, 1992.

[Manna and Waldinger, 1978] Z. MANNA AND R. WALDINGER, "The Logic of Computer Programming," *IEEE Transactions on Software Engineering* **SE-4** (1978), pp. 199–229.

[Meyer, 1992b] B. MEYER, *Eiffel: The Language,* Prentice-Hall, New York, 1992.

[Mills, Basili, Gannon, and Hamlet, 1987] H. D. MILLS, V. R. BASILI, J. D. GANNON, AND R. G. HAMLET, *Principles of Computer Programming: A Mathematical Approach,* Allyn and Bacon, Newton, MA, 1987.

[Myers, 1979] G. J. MYERS, *The Art of Software Testing,* John Wiley and Sons, New York, 1979.

[Naur, 1969] P. NAUR, "Programming by Action Clusters," *BIT* **9** (No. 3, 1969), pp. 250–258.

[New, 1992] R. NEW, Personal Communication, 1992.

[Poston and Bruen, 1987] R. M. POSTON AND M. W. BRUEN, "Counting Down to Zero Software Failures," *IEEE Software* **4** (September 1987), pp. 54–61.

[Russell, 1991] G. W. RUSSELL, "Experience with Inspection in Ultralarge-Scale Developments," *IEEE Software* **8** (January 1991), pp. 25–31.

[Shulmeyer and McManus, 1987] G. G. SCHULMEYER AND J. I. MCMANUS (Editors), *Handbook of Software Quality Assurance,* Van Nostrand Reinhold, New York, 1987.

[Tamir, 1980] M. TAMIR, "ADI: Automatic Derivation of Invariants," *IEEE Transactions on Software Engineering* **SE-6** (January 1980), pp. 40–48.

[Trammel, Binder, and Snyder, 1992] C. J. TRAMMEL, L. H. BINDER, AND C.E. SNYDER, "The Automated Production Control Documentation System: A Case Study in Cleanroom Software Engineering," *ACM Transactions on Software Engineering and Methodology* **1** (January 1992), pp. 81–94.

[Volta, 1993] L. G. VOLTA, JR., "Does Every Inspection Need a Meeting?" *Proceedings of the First ACM SIGSOFT Symposium on the Foundations of Software Engineering, ACM SIGSOFT Software Engineering Notes* **18** (December 1993), pp. 107–114.

[Weller, 1993] E. F. WELLER, "Lessons from Three Years of Inspection Data," *IEEE Software* **10** (September 1993), pp. 38–45.

[Wirth, 1971] N. WIRTH, "Program Development by Stepwise Refinement," *Communications of the ACM* **14** (April 1971), pp. 221–227.

6

INTRODUCTION TO OBJECTS

Some of the more lurid computer magazines seem to suggest that the object-oriented paradigm was a sudden and dramatic new discovery of the mid-1980s, a revolutionary alternative to the then popular structured paradigm. That is not the case. Instead, the theory of modularity underwent steady progress during the 1970s and the 1980s, and objects were simply a logical development within the theory of modularity (but see the Just in Case You Wanted to Know box on page 141). This chapter describes objects in the context of modularity.

This approach is taken because it is extremely difficult to use objects correctly without understanding why the object-oriented paradigm is superior to the structured paradigm. And to do that, it is necessary to appreciate that an object is merely the next step in the body of knowledge that begins with the concept of a module.

6.1 WHAT IS A MODULE?

When a large product consists of a single monolithic block of code, maintenance is a nightmare. Even for the author of such a monstrosity, attempting to debug the code is extremely difficult; for another programmer to understand it is virtually impossible. The solution is to break the product into smaller pieces, called modules. What is a module? Is the way a product is broken into modules important in itself, or is it important only to break a large product into smaller pieces of code?

An early attempt to describe modules is the work of Stevens, Myers, and Constantine. They defined a module as "A set of one or more contiguous program statements having a name by which other parts of the system can invoke it, and preferably having its own distinct set of variable names" [Stevens, Myers, and Constantine, 1974]. In other words, a module consists of a single block of code that can be invoked in the way that a procedure, function, or method is invoked. This definition seems to be extremely broad. It includes procedures and functions of all kinds, whether internal or separately compiled. It includes COBOL paragraphs and sections, even though they cannot have their own variables, because

---

JUST IN CASE YOU WANTED TO KNOW

Object-oriented concepts were introduced as early as 1966 in the simulation language Simula 67 [Dahl and Nygaard, 1966]. However, at that time the technology was too radical for practical use, so it lay dormant until the early 1980s when it was essentially reinvented within the context of the theory of modularity.

There are other examples in this chapter of the way that leading-edge technology lies dormant until the world is ready for it. For example, information hiding (Section 6.6) was first proposed by David Parnas in 1971 [Parnas, 1971], but the technology was not widely adopted until 10 years later when encapsulation and abstract data types had become part of software engineering.

It seems that we adopt new ideas only when we are ready to use them, not necessarily when they are first presented.

---

the definition states that the property of possessing a distinct set of variable names is merely "preferable." But broad as it is, the definition does not go far enough. For example, an assembler macro is not invoked and therefore, by the preceding definition, is not a module. In C and C++, a header file of declarations that is **#include**d in a product is similarly not invoked; neither is an Ada package (implementation of an abstract data type) nor an Ada generic (macro). In short, this definition is too restrictive.

Yourdon and Constantine give a broader definition, namely, "A module is a lexically contiguous sequence of program statements, bounded by boundary elements, having an aggregate identifier" [Yourdon and Constantine, 1979]. Examples of boundary elements are begin . . . end pairs in a block-structured language like Pascal or Ada, or { . . . } pairs in Java. This definition not only includes all the cases excluded by the previous definition, but is broad enough to be used throughout this book. In particular, procedures and functions of the classical paradigm are modules. In the object-oriented paradigm, an object is a module and so is a method within an object.

To understand the importance of modularization, consider the following somewhat fanciful example. John Fence is a highly incompetent computer architect. He has still not discovered that both NAND gates and NOR gates are complete, that is, every circuit can be built with only NAND gates or with only NOR gates. John therefore decides to build an ALU, shifter, and 16 registers using AND, OR, and NOT gates. The resulting computer is shown in Figure 6.1. The three components are connected together in a simple fashion. Now our architect friend decides that the circuit should be fabricated on three silicon chips, so he designs the three chips shown in Figure 6.2. One chip has all the gates of the ALU, a second contains the shifter, and the third is for the registers. At this point John vaguely recalls that someone in a bar told him that it is best to build chips so they have only one kind of gate; he redesigns his chips. On chip 1 he puts all the AND gates, on chip 2 all the OR gates, and all the NOT gates go onto chip 3. The resulting "work of art" is shown schematically in Figure 6.3.

Figure 6.2 and 6.3 are functionally equivalent, that is, they do exactly the same thing. But the two designs have markedly different properties. First, Figure 6.3 is

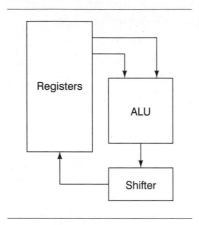

Figure 6.1   Design of computer.

considerably harder to understand than Figure 6.2. Almost anyone with a knowledge of digital logic will immediately know that the chips in Figure 6.2 comprise an ALU, a shifter, and a set of registers. However, even a leading hardware expert will have trouble understanding the function of the various AND, OR, and NOT gates in Figure 6.3.

Second, corrective maintenance of the circuits shown in Figure 6.3 is difficult. Should there be a design fault in the computer—and anyone capable of coming up with Figure 6.3 is undoubtedly going to make lots and lots of mistakes—it will be difficult to determine where the fault is located. On the other hand, if there is a fault

Figure 6.2   Computer of Figure 6.1 fabricated on three chips.

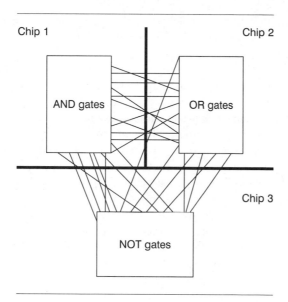

Figure 6.3 Computer of Figure 6.1 fabricated on three other chips.

in the design of the computer in Figure 6.2, the fault can be localized by determining whether it appears to be in the way the ALU works, the way the shifter works, or the way the registers work. Similarly, if the computer of Figure 6.2 breaks down, it is relatively easy to determine which chip to replace; if the computer in Figure 6.3 breaks down, it is probably best to replace all three chips.

Third, the computer of Figure 6.3 is difficult to extend or enhance; if a new type of ALU is needed or if faster registers are required, it is back to the drawing board. But the design of the computer in Figure 6.2 makes it easy to replace the appropriate chip. Perhaps worst of all, the chips of Figure 6.3 cannot be reused in any new product. There is no way that those three specific combinations of AND, OR, and NOT gates can be utilized for any product other than the one for which they were designed. In all probability the three chips of Figure 6.2 can be reused in other products that require an ALU, a shifter, or registers.

The point here is that software products have to be designed to look like Figure 6.2, where there is a maximal relationship within each chip and a minimal relationship between chips. A module can be likened to a chip in that it performs an action or series of actions and is connected to other modules. The functionality of the product as a whole is fixed; what has to be determined is how to break the product into modules. Composite/structured design [Stevens, Myers, and Constantine, 1974] provides a rationale for breaking a product into modules as a way to reduce the cost of maintenance that, as pointed out in Chapter 1, is the major component of the total software budget. The maintenance effort, whether corrective, perfective, or adaptive, is reduced when there is maximal interaction within each module and minimal interaction between modules. In other words, the aim of composite/structured design (C/SD) is to ensure that the module decomposition of the product resembles Figure 6.2 rather than Figure 6.3.

Myers quantified the ideas of *module cohesion,* the degree of interaction within a module, and *module coupling,* the degree of interaction between two modules [Myers, 1978b]. To be more precise, Myers used the term *strength* rather than *cohesion.* However, cohesion is preferable because modules can have high strength or low strength, and there is something inherently contradictory in the expression *low strength*—if something is not strong, it is weak. In order to prevent terminological inexactitude C/SD now uses the term *cohesion.* Some authors have used the term *binding* in place of *coupling.* Unfortunately, *binding* is also used in other contexts in computer science, for example, the binding of values to variables. But *coupling* does not have these overtones and is therefore preferable.

It is necessary at this point to distinguish between the action of a module, the logic of a module, and the context of a module. The *action* of a module is what it does, that is, its behavior. For example, the action of module m is to compute the square root of its argument. The *logic* of a module is how the module performs its action; in the case of module m the specific way of computing the square root is Newton's method [Young and Gregory, 1972]. The *context* of a module is the specific usage of that module. For example, module m is used to compute the square root of a double precision integer. A key point in C/SD is that the name assigned to a module is its action, and not its logic or its context. Thus, in C/SD module m should be named **compute square root**; its logic and its context are irrelevant from the viewpoint of its name.

6.2 COHESION

Myers defined seven categories or levels of cohesion [Myers, 1978b]. In the light of modern theoretical computer science, Myers's first two levels are considered to be equally good. More precisely, as will be shown, functional cohesion is optimal for the structured paradigm, whereas informational cohesion is optimal for the object-oriented paradigm. The resulting ranking is shown in Figure 6.4. This is not a linear

7. { Functional cohesion
     Informational cohesion   (Good)
5.   Communicational cohesion
4.   Procedural cohesion
3.   Temporal cohesion
2.   Logical cohesion
1.   Coincidental cohesion   (Bad)

Figure 6.4 Levels of cohesion.

scale of any sort. It is merely a relative ranking, a way of determining which types of cohesion are high (good) and which are low (bad).

In order to understand what constitutes a module with high cohesion, it is necessary to start at the other end and consider the lower cohesion levels.

6.2.1   COINCIDENTAL COHESION

A module has coincidental cohesion if it performs multiple, completely unrelated actions. An example of a module with coincidental cohesion is a module named print next line, reverse the string of characters comprising the second argument, add 7 to the fifth argument, convert the fourth argument to floating point.

An obvious question is: How can such modules possibly arise in practice? The most common cause is as a consequence of rigidly enforcing rules such as "every module will consist of between 35 and 50 executable statements." If a software organization insists that modules must neither be too big nor too small, then two undesirable things will happen. First, two or more otherwise ideal smaller modules have to be lumped together to create a larger module with coincidental cohesion. Second, pieces hacked from well-designed modules that management considers too large will be combined, again resulting in modules with coincidental cohesion.

Why is coincidental cohesion so bad? Modules with coincidental cohesion suffer from two serious drawbacks. First, such modules degrade the maintainability of the product, both corrective maintenance and enhancement. From the viewpoint of trying to understand a product, modularization with coincidental cohesion is worse than no modularization at all [Shneiderman and Mayer, 1975]. Second, these modules are not reusable. It is extremely unlikely that the module with coincidental cohesion in the first paragraph of this section could be reused in any other product.

Lack of reusability is a serious drawback. The cost of building software is so great that it is essential to try to reuse modules wherever possible. Designing, coding, documenting, and above all, testing a module are time-consuming and hence costly processes. If an existing well-designed, thoroughly tested, and properly documented module can be used in another product, then management should insist that the existing module be reused. But there is no way that a module with coincidental cohesion can be reused, and the money spent to develop it can never be recouped.

It is generally easy to rectify a module with coincidental cohesion—because it performs multiple actions, break it into modules that each perform one action.

6.2.2   LOGICAL COHESION

A module has logical cohesion when it performs a series of related actions, one of which is selected by the calling module. The following are all examples of modules with logical cohesion:

Example 1   Module new operation which is invoked as follows:

```
function code = 7;
new operation (function code, dummy 1, dummy 2, dummy 3);
// dummy 1, dummy 2, and dummy 3 are dummy variables,
// not used if function code is equal to 7
```

In this example, new operation is called with four arguments, but as stated in the pseudocode comment lines, three of them are not needed if function code is equal to 7. This degrades readability, with the usual implications for maintenance, both corrective and enhancement.

Example 2   An object whose methods perform all input and output.

Example 3   A module performing editing of insertions and deletions and modifications of master file records.

Example 4   A module with logical cohesion in an early version of OS/VS2 performed 13 different actions; its interface contained 21 pieces of data [Myers, 1978b].

There are two problems when a module has logical cohesion. First, the interface is difficult to understand, *Example 1* being a case in point, and comprehensibility of the module as a whole may suffer as a result. Second, the code for more than one action may be intertwined, leading to severe maintenance problems. For instance, a module that performs all input and output may be structured as shown in Figure 6.5. If a new tape unit is installed, it may be necessary to modify the sections numbered 1, 2, 3, 4, 6, 9, and 10. These changes may adversely affect other forms of input/output, such as laser printer output, because the laser printer will be affected by changes to sections 1 and 3. This intertwined property is characteristic of modules with logical cohesion. A further consequence of this intertwining is that it is difficult to reuse such a module in other products.

6.2.3   TEMPORAL COHESION

A module has temporal cohesion when it performs a series of actions related in time. An example of a module with temporal cohesion is one named open old master file, new master file, transaction file, and print file, initialize sales district table, read first transaction record, and first old master file record. In the bad old days before C/SD such a module would be called perform initialization.

The actions of this module are weakly related to one another, but more strongly related to actions in other modules. Consider, for example, the sales district table. It is initialized in this module, but actions such as update sales district table and print sales district table are located in other modules. Thus,

module performing all input and output
1. Code for all input and output
2. Code for input only
3. Code for output only
4. Code for disk and tape I/O
5. Code for disk I/O
6. Code for tape I/O
7. Code for disk input
8. Code for disk output
9. Code for tape input
10. Code for tape output
$\vdots$ $\vdots$ $\vdots$
37. Code for keyboard input

Figure 6.5 Module that performs all input and output.

if the structure of the **sales district table** is changed, perhaps because the organization is expanding into areas of the country where it has previously not done business, a number of modules will have to be changed. Not only is there more chance of a regression fault (a fault caused by a change being made to an apparently unrelated part of the product), but if the number of affected modules is large, there is a good chance that one or two modules will be overlooked. It is much better to have all the operations on the **sales district table** in one module; this is shown in Section 6.2.6. In addition, a module with temporal cohesion is unlikely to be reusable in a different product.

6.2.4 PROCEDURAL COHESION

A module has procedural cohesion if it performs a series of actions related by the sequence of steps to be followed by the product. An example of a module with procedural cohesion is **read part number from database and update repair record on maintenance file.**

This is clearly better than temporal cohesion—at least the actions are procedurally related to one another. But even so, the actions are still weakly connected, and again, the module is unlikely to be reusable in another product.

Figure 6.6 Module with informational cohesion.

6.2.5 COMMUNICATIONAL COHESION

A module has communicational cohesion if it performs a series of actions related by the sequence of steps to be followed by the product and if all the actions are performed on the same data. Two examples of modules with communicational cohesion are **update record in database and write *it* to the audit trail,** and **calculate new trajectory and send *it* to the printer.** This is better than procedural cohesion because the actions of the module are more closely connected, but it still has the same drawback as coincidental, logical, temporal, and procedural cohesion, namely, that the module cannot be reused.

In passing, it is interesting to note that Berry uses the term *flowchart cohesion* to refer to temporal, procedural, and communicational cohesion because the actions performed by such modules are adjacent in the product flowchart [Berry, 1978]. The actions are adjacent in the case of temporal cohesion because they are performed at the same time. They are adjacent in procedural cohesion because the algorithm requires the actions to be performed in series. They are adjacent in communicational cohesion because, in addition, the actions are performed on the same data, and it is natural that these actions should be adjacent in the flowchart.

6.2.6 INFORMATIONAL COHESION

A module has informational cohesion if it performs a number of actions, each with its own entry point, with independent code for each action, all performed on the same data structure. An example is given in Figure 6.6. This does not violate the tenets of structured programming (Section 12.3); each piece of code has exactly one entry point and one exit point. A major difference between logical cohesion and informational cohesion is that the various actions of a module with logical cohesion are intertwined, whereas in a module with informational cohesion the code for each action is completely independent.

A module with informational cohesion is essentially an implementation of an abstract data type, explained in Section 6.5, and all the advantages of using an abstract data type are gained when a module with informational cohesion is used. Because an object is essentially an instantiation (instance) of an abstract data type (Section 6.7), an object, too, is a module with informational cohesion. This is why it was stated in Section 6.2 that informational cohesion is optimal for the object-oriented paradigm.[1]

6.2.7   FUNCTIONAL COHESION

A module that performs exactly one action or achieves a single goal has functional cohesion. Examples of such modules are get temperature of furnace; compute orbital of electron; write to diskette; and calculate sales commission.

A module with functional cohesion can often be reused because the one action that it performs will often need to be performed in other products. A properly designed, thoroughly tested, and well-documented module with functional cohesion is a valuable (economic and technical) asset to any software organization and should be reused as often as possible (but see Section 6.13).

Maintenance is easier to perform on a module with functional cohesion. First, functional cohesion leads to fault isolation. If it is clear that the temperature of the furnace is not being read correctly, then the fault is almost certainly in module get temperature of furnace. Similarly, if the orbital of an electron is incorrectly computed, then the first place to look is compute orbital of electron.

Once the fault has been localized to a single module, the next step is to make the required changes. Because a module with functional cohesion performs one and only one action, such a module will generally be easier to understand than a module with lower cohesion. This ease in understanding also simplifies the maintenance task. Finally, when the change is made, the chance of that change impacting other modules is slight, especially if the coupling between modules is low (Section 6.3).

Functional cohesion is also valuable when a product has to be extended. For example, suppose that a personal computer has a diskette drive, but that the manufacturer now wishes to market a more powerful model of the computer with an internal hard disk instead. Reading through the list of modules, the maintenance programmer finds a module named write to diskette. The obvious thing to do is to throw away that module and replace it with a new one called write to hard disk.

In passing it should be pointed out that the three "modules" of Figure 6.2 have functional cohesion, and the arguments made in Section 6.1 for favoring the design of Figure 6.2 over that of Figure 6.3 are precisely those made in the preceding discussion for favoring functional cohesion.

---

[1] The discussion in this paragraph assumes that the abstract data type or object is well designed. If the methods of an object perform completely unrelated actions, then the object has coincidental cohesion.

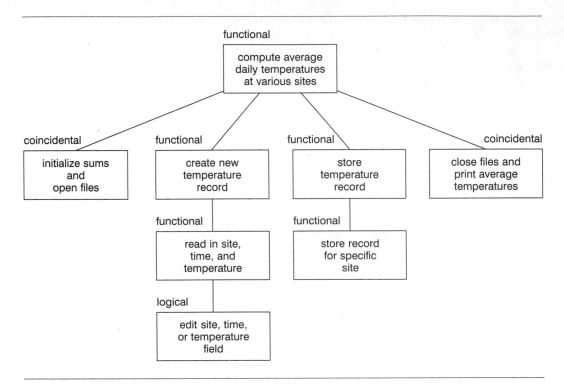

Figure 6.7 Module interconnection diagram showing cohesion of each module.

6.2.8 COHESION EXAMPLE

For further insight into cohesion, consider the example shown in Figure 6.7. Two modules in particular merit comment. The reader may be somewhat surprised that the modules initialize sums and open files and close files and print average temperatures have both been labeled as having coincidental cohesion, rather than temporal cohesion. First consider module initialize sums and open files. It performs two actions related in time in that both have to be done before any calculations can be performed, and therefore it seems that the module has temporal cohesion. Although the two actions of initialize sums and open files are indeed performed at the beginning of the calculation, there is another factor involved. Initializing the sums is related to the problem, but opening files has nothing to do with the problem itself. The rule when two or more different levels of cohesion can be assigned to a module is to assign the lowest possible level. Thus, because initialize sums and open files could have either temporal or coincidental cohesion, the lower of the two cohesions, namely coincidental, is assigned to that module. That is also the reason why close files and print average temperatures has coincidental cohesion.

5. Data coupling	(Good)
4. Stamp coupling	
3. Control coupling	
2. Common coupling	
1. Content coupling	(Bad)

Figure 6.8   Levels of coupling.

6.3   Coupling

Recall that cohesion is the degree of interaction within a module. *Coupling* is the degree of interaction between two modules. As before, a number of levels can be distinguished (shown in Figure 6.8). In order to highlight good coupling, the various levels will be described in order, from the worst to the best.

6.3.1   Content Coupling

Two modules are content-coupled if one directly references the contents of the other. The following are all examples of content coupling:

Example 1   Module p modifies a statement of module q.
   This practice is not restricted to assembly language programming. The **alter** verb, now mercifully removed from COBOL, did precisely that; it modified another statement.

Example 2   Module p refers to local data of module q in terms of some numerical displacement within q.

Example 3   Module p branches to a local label of module q.
   Suppose that module p and module q are content-coupled. One of the many dangers is that almost any change to q, even recompiling q with a new compiler or assembler, requires a change to p. Furthermore, it is impossible to reuse module p in a new product without reusing module q as well. When two modules are content-coupled, they are inextricably interlinked.

6.3.2   Common Coupling

Two modules are common-coupled if they both have access to the same global data. The situation is depicted in Figure 6.9. Instead of communicating with one another by passing arguments, modules cca and ccb can access and change the value of global variable. The most common situation in which this arises is when both

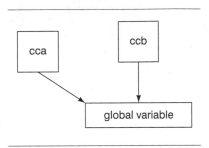

Figure 6.9 Common coupling.

cca and ccb have access to the same database and can read and write the same record. For common coupling it is necessary that both modules can read *and* write to the database; if the database access mode is read-only, then this is not common coupling. But there are other ways of implementing common coupling, including use of the **common** statement in FORTRAN, the (nonstandard) **common** statement in COBOL, the **global** statement in COBOL-80, and the Java modifier **public**.

This form of coupling is undesirable for a number of reasons. First, it contradicts the spirit of structured programming (Section 12.3) in that the resulting code is virtually unreadable. Consider the pseudocode fragment shown in Figure 6.10. If global variable is a global variable, then its value may be changed by module 3, module 4, or any module called by them. Determining under what conditions the loop terminates is then a nontrivial question; if a run-time error occurs it may be difficult to reconstruct what happened, because any one of a number of modules could have changed the value of global variable.

A second difficulty is that modules can have side effects that affect their readability. To see this, consider the call edit this transaction (record 7). If there is common coupling, this call could change not just the value of record 7, but also any global variable that can be accessed by that module. In short, the entire module must be read to find out precisely what it does.

```
while (global variable == 0)
{
    if (argument xyz > 25)
        module 3 ();
    else
        module 4 ();
}
```

Figure 6.10 Pseudocode fragment reflecting common coupling.

Third, if a maintenance change is made in one module to the declaration of a global variable, then every module that can access that global variable has to be changed. Furthermore, all changes must be consistent.

A fourth problem is that modules that are common-coupled are difficult to reuse because the identical list of global variables has to be supplied each time the module is reused.

The fifth problem is potentially the most dangerous. As a consequence of common coupling, a module may be exposed to more data than it needs. This defeats any attempts to control data access and may ultimately lead to computer crime. Many types of computer crime need some form of collusion. Properly designed software should not allow any one programmer to have access to all the data and/or modules needed to commit a crime. For example, a programmer writing the check printing part of a payroll product needs to have access to employee records, but in a well-designed product such access will be exclusively in read-only mode, thus precluding the programmer making unauthorized changes to his or her monthly salary. In order to make such changes, the programmer has to find another dishonest employee, one with access to the relevant records in update mode. But if the product has been badly designed and every module can access the payroll database in update mode, then an unscrupulous programmer acting alone can make unauthorized changes to any record in the database.

Although it is hoped that the previous arguments will dissuade all but the most daring of readers from using common coupling, there are situations where common coupling might seem to be preferable to the alternatives. Consider, for example, a product that performs computer-aided design of petroleum storage tanks [Schach and Stevens-Guille, 1979]. A tank is specified by a large number of descriptors such as height, diameter, maximum wind speed to which the tank will be subjected, and insulation thickness. The descriptors have to be initialized but do not change in value thereafter, and most of the modules in the product need to have access to the values of the descriptors. Suppose that there are 55 tank descriptors. If all these descriptors are passed as arguments to every module, then the interface to each module will consist of at least 55 arguments, and the potential for faults is huge. Even in a language like Ada, which requires strict type checking of arguments, it is still possible to interchange two arguments of the same type, a fault that would not be detected by a type checker.

One solution is to put all the tank descriptors in a database and to design the product in such a way that one module initializes the values of all the descriptors, whereas all the other modules access the database exclusively in read-only mode. However, if the database solution is impractical, perhaps because the specified implementation language cannot be interfaced with the available database management system, then the best that can be done is to use common coupling, but in a controlled way. That is to say, the product should be designed so that the 55 descriptors are initialized by one module, but none of the other modules changes the value of a descriptor. This programming style has to be enforced by management, unlike the database solution where enforcement is imposed by the software. Thus, in situations where there is no good alternative to the use of common coupling, close supervision by management can reduce some of the risks.

6.3.3   CONTROL COUPLING

Two modules are control-coupled if one passes an element of control to the other module; that is, one module explicitly controls the logic of the other. For example, control is passed when a function code is passed to a module with logical cohesion (Section 6.2.2). Another example of control coupling is when a control switch is passed as an argument.

If module p calls module q, and q passes back a flag to p that says, "I am unable to complete my task," then q is passing data. But if the flag means, "I am unable to complete my task; accordingly, write error message ABC123," then p and q are control-coupled. In other words, if q passes information back to p and p then decides what action to take as a consequence of receiving that information, then q is passing data. But if q passes back not only information but also informs module p as to what action p must take, then control coupling is present.

The major difficulty that arises as a consequence of control coupling is that the two modules are not independent; module q, the called module, has to be aware of the internal structure and logic of module p. As a result, the possibility of reuse is reduced. In addition, control coupling is generally associated with modules that have logical cohesion, and the difficulties associated with logical cohesion will then be present.

6.3.4   STAMP COUPLING

In some programming languages only simple variables such as part number, satellite altitude, or degree of multiprogramming can be passed as arguments. But many languages also support the passing of data structures, such as records or arrays, as arguments. In such languages valid arguments would include part record, satellite coordinates, or segment table. Two modules are stamp-coupled if a data structure is passed as an argument, but the called module operates on only some of the individual components of that data structure.

Consider, for example, the call calculate withholding (employee record). It is not clear, without reading the entire calculate withholding module, which fields of the employee record the module accesses or changes. Passing the employee's salary is obviously essential for computing the withholding, but it is difficult to see how the employee's home telephone number is needed for this purpose. Instead, module calculate withholding should be passed only those fields that it actually needs for computing the withholding. Not only is the resulting module, and particularly its interface, easier to understand, but it is likely to be reusable in a variety of other products that also need to compute withholding. (See the Just in Case You Wanted to Know box on page 155 for another perspective on this.)

Perhaps even more important, because the call calculate withholding (employee record) passes more data than strictly necessary, the problems of uncontrolled data access, and conceivably computer crime, once again can arise. This issue was discussed in Section 6.3.2.

There is nothing at all wrong with passing a data structure as an argument,

> ### JUST IN CASE YOU WANTED TO KNOW
>
> Passing four or five different fields to a module may be slower than passing a complete record. This situation leads to a larger issue: What should be done when optimization issues (such as response time or space constraints) clash with what is generally considered to be good software engineering practice?
>
> In my experience, this question frequently turns out to be irrelevant. The recommended approach may slow down the response time, but by only a millisecond or so, far too small to be detected by users. Thus, in accordance with Don Knuth's First Law of Optimization: *Don't!*—there is rarely a need for optimization of any kind, including for performance reasons [Knuth, 1974].
>
> But what if optimization really is required? In this case, Knuth's Second Law of Optimization applies. The Second Law (labeled "for experts only") is: *Not yet!* In other words, first complete the entire product using appropriate software engineering techniques. Then, if optimization really is required, make only the necessary changes, carefully documenting what is being changed and why. If at all possible, this optimization should be done by an experienced software engineer.

provided that *all* the components of the data structure are used by the called module. For example, calls like invert matrix (original matrix, inverted matrix) or print inventory record (warehouse record) pass a data structure as an argument, but they operate on all the components of that data structure. Stamp coupling is present when a data structure is passed as an argument, but only some of the components are used by the called module.

A subtle form of stamp coupling can occur in languages like C or C++ when a pointer to a record is passed as an argument. Consider the call check altitude (pointer to position record). At first sight, what is being passed is a simple variable. But the called module has access to all of the fields in the position record pointed to by pointer to position record. Because of the potential problems, it is a good idea to examine the coupling closely whenever a pointer is passed as an argument.

6.3.5 DATA COUPLING

Two modules are data-coupled if all arguments are homogeneous data items. That is, every argument is either a simple argument or a data structure in which all elements are used by the called module. Examples include display time of arrival (flight number), compute product (first number, second number, result), and determine job with highest priority (job queue).

Data coupling is a desirable goal. To put it in a negative way, if a product exhibits data coupling exclusively, then the difficulties of content, common, control, and stamp coupling will not be present. From a more positive viewpoint, if two modules are data-coupled, then maintenance is easier, because a change to one module is less likely to cause a regression fault in the other. The following example clarifies certain aspects of coupling.

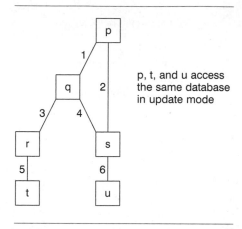

p, t, and u access
the same database
in update mode

Figure 6.11 Module interconnection diagram for coupling example.

Number	In	Out
1	aircraft type	status flag
2	—	list of aircraft parts
3	function code	—
4	—	list of aircraft parts
5	part number	part manufacturer
6	part number	part name

Figure 6.12 Interface description for Figure 6.11.

6.3.6   COUPLING EXAMPLE

Consider the example shown in Figure 6.11. The numbers on the arcs represent interfaces that are defined in greater detail in Figure 6.12. Thus, for example, when module p calls module q (interface 1), it passes one argument, namely, the type of the aircraft. When q returns control to p, it passes a status flag back. Using the information in Figures 6.11 and 6.12, the coupling between every pair of modules can be deduced. The results are shown in Figure 6.13.

Some of the entries in Figure 6.13 are obvious. For instance, the data coupling between p and q (interface 1 in Figure 6.11), between r and t (interface 5), and between s and u (interface 6) is a direct consequence of the fact that a simple variable is passed in each direction. The coupling between p and s (interface 2) would be data coupling if all the elements of the list of parts passed from s to p are used and/or updated, but it is stamp coupling if p operates on only certain elements of the list. The coupling between q and s (interface 4) is similar. Because the function of the various modules is not clear (from Figures 6.11 and 6.12), there is no way of determining

	q	r	s	t	u
p	Data	—	{ Data or Stamp	Common	Common
q		Control	{ Data or Stamp	—	—
r			—	Data	—
s				—	Data
t					Common

Figure 6.13 Coupling between pairs of modules of Figure 6.11.

whether the coupling is data or stamp. The coupling between q and r (interface 3) is control coupling, because a function code is passed from q to r.

Perhaps somewhat surprising are the three entries marked common coupling in Figure 6.13. The three module pairs that are farthest apart in Figure 6.11, namely p and t, p and u, and t and u, at first appear not to be coupled in any way. After all, there is no interface of any kind connecting them, so the very idea of coupling between them, let alone common coupling, requires some explanation. The answer lies in the annotation on the right-hand side of Figure 6.11, namely that p, t, and u all access the same database in update mode. The result is that a number of global variables can be changed by all three modules, and hence they are pairwise common-coupled.

Given that a design in which modules have high cohesion and low coupling is a good design, the obvious question is: How can such a design be achieved? Because this chapter is devoted to theoretical concepts surrounding design, the answer to the question, namely data flow analysis, is presented in Section 11.3. In the meantime, those qualities that identify a good design are further examined and refined. For convenience, the key definitions in this chapter appear in Figure 6.14, together with the section in which each definition appears.

6.4 DATA ENCAPSULATION

Consider the problem of designing an operating system for a large mainframe computer. According to the specifications, any job submitted to the computer will be classified as high priority, medium priority, or low priority. Deciding which job to load into memory next, deciding which of the jobs in memory gets the next time slice and how long that time slice should be, or deciding which of the jobs that require disk access has priority (that is, scheduling), one must consider the priority of each job: the higher the priority, the sooner that job should be assigned the resources of the

---

Abstract data type   a data type together with the actions performed on instantiations of that data type (Section 6.5)

Abstraction   a means of achieving stepwise refinement by suppressing unnecessary details and accentuating relevant details (Section 6.4.1)

Class   an abstract data type that supports inheritance (Section 6.7)

Cohesion   the degree of interaction within a module (Section 6.1)

Coupling   the degree of interaction between two modules (Section 6.1)

Data encapsulation   a data structure together with the actions performed on that data structure (Section 6.4)

Encapsulation   the gathering together into one unit of all aspects of the real-world entity modeled by that unit (Section 6.4.1)

Information hiding   structuring the design so that the resulting implementation details will be hidden from other modules (Section 6.6)

Object   an instantiation of a class (Section 6.7)

Figure 6.14   Key definitions of this chapter and the sections in which they appear.

computer. One way of achieving this is to maintain separate job queues for each job-priority level. The job queues have to be initialized, and facilities must exist for adding a job to a job queue when the job requires memory, CPU time, or disk access, as well as for removing a job from a queue when the operating system decides to allocate the required resource to that job.

To simplify matters, consider the restricted problem of batch jobs queuing up for memory access. There are three queues for incoming batch jobs, one for each priority level. When a job is submitted by a user, the job is added to the appropriate queue, and when the operating system decides that a job is ready to be run, it is removed from its queue and memory is allocated to it.

There are a number of different ways to build this portion of the product. One possible design is shown in Figure 6.15 that depicts modules for manipulating one of the three job queues. A C-like pseudocode is used to highlight some of the problems that can arise in the classical paradigm. Later in this chapter, these problems will be solved using the object-oriented paradigm.

Consider Figure 6.15. Function initialize_job_queue[2] in module m_1 is responsible for the initialization of the job queue, and functions add_job_to_queue and remove_job_from_queue in modules m_2 and m_3, respectively, are responsible for the addition and deletion of jobs. Module m_123 contains invocations of all three functions in order to manipulate the job queue. In order to concentrate on data encapsulation, issues such as underflow (trying to remove a job from an empty queue) and overflow (trying to add a job to a full queue) have been suppressed here, as well as in the remainder of this chapter.

---

[2]For added clarity, the underscore is used in function names like initialize_job_queue to highlight that the structured paradigm is being used. When the object-oriented paradigm is used, the corresponding method is named initializeJobQueue, using the Java capitalization convention.

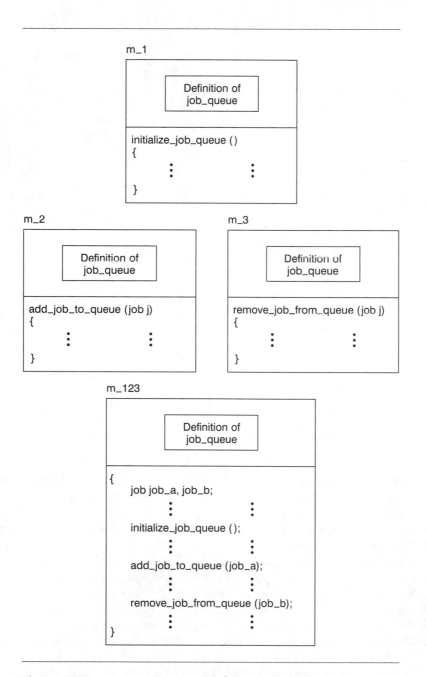

Figure 6.15   One possible design of job queue portion of operating system.

m_123   m_encapsulation

```
{                                                        ┌─────────────────────────┐
    job  job_a, job_b;                                   │   Definition of         │
              ⋮              ⋮                            │   job_queue             │
                                                         └─────────────────────────┘

    initialize_job_queue ();                              initialize_job_queue ()
              ⋮              ⋮                             {
                                                                   ⋮              ⋮
    add_job_to_queue (job_a);                             }
              ⋮              ⋮

    remove_job_from_queue (job_b);                        add_job_to_queue (job j)
              ⋮              ⋮                             {
}                                                                  ⋮              ⋮
                                                          }


                                                          remove_job_from_queue (job j)
                                                          {
                                                                   ⋮              ⋮
                                                          }
```

Figure 6.16 Design of job queue portion of operating system using data encapsulation.

The modules of the design of Figure 6.15 have low cohesion, because actions on the job queue are spread all over the product. If a decision is made to change the way job_queue is implemented (for example, as a linked list of records instead of as a linear list), then modules m_1, m_2, and m_3 have to be drastically revised and m_123 also has to be changed.

Now suppose that the design of Figure 6.16 is chosen instead. The module on the right-hand side of the figure has informational cohesion (Section 6.2.6) in that it performs a number of actions on the same data structure. Each action has its own entry point and exit point, and independent code. Module m_encapsulation in Figure 6.16 is an implementation of *data encapsulation,* that is to say, a data structure, in this case the job queue, together with the actions to be performed on that data structure.

An obvious question to ask at this point is: What is the advantage of designing a product using data encapsulation? This will be answered in two ways, from the viewpoint of development and from the viewpoint of maintenance.

6.4.1 DATA ENCAPSULATION AND PRODUCT DEVELOPMENT

Data encapsulation is an example of *abstraction*. Returning to the job queue example, a data structure, namely the job queue, has been defined, together with three associated actions: initialize the job queue, add a job to the queue, and delete a job from the queue. The developer is able to conceptualize the problem at a higher level, the level of jobs and job queues, rather than at the lower level of records or arrays.

The basic theoretical concept behind abstraction is, once again, stepwise refinement. First, a design for the product is produced in terms of high-level concepts such as jobs, job queues, and the actions that are performed on job queues. At this stage it is entirely irrelevant how the job queue is implemented. Once a complete high-level design has been obtained, the second step is to design the lower level components in terms of which the data structure and actions on the data structure will be implemented. In C, for example, the data structure, that is, the job queue, will be implemented in terms of records (structures) or arrays; the three actions, namely initialize the job queue, add a job to the queue, and remove a job from the queue, will be implemented as functions. The key point is that while this lower level is being designed, the designer totally ignores the intended use of the jobs, job queue, and actions. Thus during the first step, the existence of the lower level is assumed, even though at that stage no thought has been given to that level; during the second step (that is, the design of the lower level) the existence of the higher level is ignored. At the higher level the concern is with the behavior of the data structure, namely the job queue; at the lower level, the implementation of that behavior is the primary concern. Of course, in a larger product there will be many levels of abstraction. Examples of such multilevel products are now given.

The concept of levels of abstraction was described by Dijkstra in terms of layers of an operating system [Dijkstra, 1968b]. The highest level, level 5, is the computer operator. Level 4 is the user program level. Each of the higher levels of abstraction is then implemented using some of the functions of the levels below it. For example, level 1, the memory-segment controller, utilizes some of the functions of level 0, where clock-interrupt handling and processor allocation are implemented. Suppose that the implementation of a lower-level function is changed. Provided that the interface between that function and the rest of the machine is not altered, that is, the number and types of the arguments are not changed, the higher levels should not even be aware that the change was made.

The same concept can be applied to computer organization. A computer can be thought of as consisting of levels of abstract machines [Tanenbaum, 1990]. The highest level, level 5, is the problem-oriented language level (Figure 6.17). Level 4 is the assembly language level, level 3 is the operating system level, level 2, the machine code level. Suppose a product is written in C (level 5). It is compiled down to machine code (level 2). However, some compilers translate from C (level 5) to assembler (level 4), and then from assembler to machine code. Level 1 is the

---

Level 5: Problem-oriented language level

Level 4: Assembly language level

Level 3: Operating system level

Level 2: Machine code level

Level 1: Microprogramming level

Level 0: Digital logic level

Figure 6.17 Levels of abstraction of a computer.

microprogramming level; machine code (level 2) is interpreted by the microprogram of level 1. The microcode is directly executed by the hardware of level 0, the digital logic level. This level is implemented in terms of silicon chips. Again there is independence of the various levels. Provided that the functionality and interfaces are not changed, it is possible to replace the digital logic level by faster hardware without altering any other aspect of the computer. The microprogram can be rewritten to achieve further speed improvement, and provided again that the functionality and interfaces are not changed, this should not require any sort of change to products at level 5 or level 4, to the operating system level (level 3), or to the machine code level (level 2). By designing and implementing a computer in this way, each level of abstraction is independent. This allows a user working at level n to think conceptually at level n without having to descend to a lower level. Also, changes made at one level should not impact other levels in any way.

The description of abstraction in this section has glossed over the fact that different types of abstraction exist. Consider Figure 6.16. In that figure there are two types of abstraction. Data encapsulation, that is, a data structure together with the actions to be performed on that data structure, is an example of *data abstraction;* the C functions themselves are an example of *procedural abstraction*. Abstraction, as stated previously, is simply a means of achieving stepwise refinement by suppressing unnecessary details and accentuating relevant details. *Encapsulation* can now be defined as the gathering together into one unit of all aspects of the real-world entity modeled by that unit; this was termed conceptual independence in Section 1.6.

Data abstraction allows the designer to think at the level of the data structure and the actions performed on it, and only later be concerned with the details of how the data structure and actions are to be implemented. Turning now to procedural abstraction, consider the result of defining a C function, initialize_job_queue. The effect is to extend the language by supplying the developer with another function, one that is not part of the language as originally defined. The developer can now use initialize_job_queue in the same way as sqrt or printf.

The implications of procedural abstraction for design are as powerful as those of data abstraction. The designer can conceptualize the product in terms of high-level actions. These actions can be defined in terms of lower-level actions, until the lowest level is reached. At this level the actions are expressed in terms of the predefined

---

JUST IN CASE YOU WANTED TO KNOW

I deliberately wrote the code examples in this chapter in such a way as to highlight data abstraction issues at the cost of good programming practice. For example, the number 25 in the definition of **class** jobQueue in Figure 6.18 should certainly be coded as a parameter, that is, as a **public static final** variable.

In addition, because some readers may not be familiar with Java, language-specific features have been minimized. For instance, a Java programmer usually writes

queueLength++;

to increment the value of queueLength by 1, rather than

queueLength = queueLength + 1;

Also, for simplicity I have omitted checks for conditions such as underflow (trying to remove an item from an empty queue) or overflow (trying to add an item to a full queue). In any real product, it is absolutely essential to include such checks.

Another deliberate omission is constructors (for initializing a data structure when created) because the Java notion for constructors can be confusing to the uninitiated. Also, I have not included finalizers for explicit cleanup before deleting an object. Instead, as is usually the case, I have relied on the Java automatic garbage collector.

In summary, then, I wrote the code of Figures 6.18 through 6.25 for pedagogic purposes only. It should not be utilized for any other purpose!

---

constructs of the programming language. At each level the designer is concerned only with expressing the product in terms of actions appropriate to that level. The designer can ignore the level below, which will be handled at the next level of abstraction, that is, the next refinement step. The designer can also ignore the level above, a level that is irrelevant from the viewpoint of designing the current level.

6.4.2 DATA ENCAPSULATION AND PRODUCT MAINTENANCE

Approaching data encapsulation from the viewpoint of maintenance, a basic issue is to identify the aspects of a product that are likely to change and to design the product so as to minimize the effects of future changes. Data structures as such are unlikely to change; if a product includes job queues, for instance, then it is likely that future versions will incorporate them. At the same time, the specific way that job queues are implemented may well change, and data encapsulation provides a means of coping with that change.

Figure 6.18 depicts an implementation in Java of the job queue data structure as **class** JobQueue. (The Just in Case You Wanted to Know box on this page has comments on the programming style in this and the following seven figures). The queue is implemented as an array of up to 25 job numbers; the first element is queue[0] and the 25th is queue[24]. Each job number is represented as an integer. (The reserved word **public** allows queueLength and queue to be visible everywhere in the operating system. The resulting common coupling is extremely poor practice, and will be corrected in Section 6.6.)

```
//
// Warning:
// This code has been written in such a way so as to be accessible to readers
// who are not Java experts, as opposed to using good Java style.
// Also, vital features such as checks for overflow and underflow
// have been omitted, for simplicity.
// See the Just in Case You Wanted to Know box on page 163 for details.
//
class JobQueue
{

    // instance variables
    public int    queueLength;             // length of job queue
    public int    queue[] = new int[25];   // queue can contain up to 25 jobs
    // methods
    public void initialize.JobQueue ()
    /*
     * empty job queue has length 0
     */
    {
       queueLength = 0;
    }

    public void addJobToQueue (int jobNumber)
    /*
     * add job to end of job queue
     */
    {
       queue[queueLength] = jobNumber;
       queueLength = queueLength + 1;
    }

    public void removeJobFromQueue (int jobNumber)
    /*
     * set jobNumber equal to the number of the job stored at the head of the queue,
     * remove the job at the head of the job queue, and move up the remaining jobs
     */
    {
       jobNumber = queue[0];
       queueLength = queueLength − 1;
       for (int k = 0; k < queueLength; k++)
           queue[k] = queue[k + 1];
    }
} // class JobQueue
```

Figure 6.18 Java implementation of **class** JobQueue. (Problems caused by **public** instance variables will be solved in Section 6.6.)

```
class Scheduler
{
    . . .
    public void queueHandler ()
    {
        int                jobA, jobB;
        JobQueue           jobQueueJ = new JobQueue ();
            // various statements
        jobQueueJ.initializeJobQueue ();
            // more statements
        jobQueueJ.addJobToQueue (jobA);
            // still more statements
        jobQueueJ.removeJobFromQueue (jobB);
            // further statements
    } // queueHandler
    . . .
} // class Scheduler
```

Figure 6.19 Java implementation of queueHandler.

```
class JobRecord
{
    public int        jobNo;        // number of the job (integer)
    public JobRecord  inFront;      // reference to job record in front
    public JobRecord  inRear;       // reference to job record behind
} // class JobRecord
```

Figure 6.20 Java specification of two-way linked **class** JobRecord. (Problems caused by **public** instance variables will be solved in Section 6.6.)

Because they are **public,** the methods in **class** JobQueue may be invoked from anywhere in the operating system. In particular, Figure 6.19 shows how **class** JobQueue may be used by method queueHandler. Method queueHandler invokes methods initializeJobQueue, addJobToQueue, and removeJob-FromQueue of JobQueue without having any knowledge as to how the job queue is implemented; the only information needed to use **class** JobQueue is interface information regarding the three methods.

Now suppose that the job queue is currently implemented as a linear list of job numbers, but a decision has been made to implement it as a two-way linked list of job records. Each job record will have three components, namely, the job number as before, a reference (link) to the job record in front of it in the linked list, and a reference to the job record behind it. This is specified in Java as shown in Figure 6.20.

The question now is: What changes have to be made to the software product as a whole as a consequence of this modification to the way the job queue is implemented? In fact, only JobQueue itself has to be changed. Figure 6.21 shows the outline of a Java implementation of JobQueue using the two-way linked list of Figure 6.20. Implementation details have been suppressed to highlight the fact that the interface between JobQueue and the rest of the product (including queueHandler) has not changed in any way (but see Problem 6.10). That is, the three methods initializeJobQueue, addJobToQueue, and removeJobFromQueue are invoked in exactly the same way that they were before. Specifically, when method addJobToQueue is invoked it still passes an integer value to JobQueue, and removeJobFromQueue still returns an integer value from JobQueue, despite the fact that the job queue itself has been implemented in an entirely different way. Consequently, the source code of method queueHandler (Figure 6.19) need not be changed at all.

Thus data encapsulation supports the implementation of data abstraction in a way that simplifies product maintenance and reduces the chance of a regression fault.

6.5 ABSTRACT DATA TYPES

Figures 6.18 and 6.21 are implementation of a job queue class, that is, a data type together with the actions to be performed on instantiations of that data type. Such a construct is called an *abstract data type*. A Java implementation of the job queue abstract data type is shown in Figure 6.22, which is identical to Figure 6.18.

Figure 6.23 shows how this abstract data type may be utilized for the three job queues of the operating system. Three job queues are instantiated, namely, highPriorityQueue, mediumPriorityQueue and lowPriorityQueue. The statement highPriorityQueue.initializeJobQueue () means: apply method initializeJobQueue to data structure highPriorityQueue.

Abstract data types are a widely applicable design tool. For example, suppose that a product is to be written in which a large number of actions have to be performed on rational numbers, that is, numbers that can be represented in the form $n\,/\,d$, where n and d are integers, $d \neq 0$. Rational numbers can be represented in a variety of different ways, such as two elements of a one-dimensional array of integers or as two attributes of a class. To implement rational numbers in terms of an abstract data type, a suitable representation for the data structure is chosen. In Java it could be defined as shown in Figure 6.24, together with the various actions that are performed on rational numbers, such as constructing a rational number from two integers, adding two rational numbers, and multiplying two rational numbers. (The problems induced by **public** instance variables such as numerator and denominator in Figure 6.24 will be fixed in Section 6.6).

Abstract data types support both data abstraction and procedural abstraction (Section 6.4.1). In addition, when a product is modified, it is unlikely that the abstract data types will be changed; at worst, additional actions may have to be added to an

---

```
class JobQueue
{
    public JobRecord    frontOfQueue;        // reference to front of queue
    public JobRecord    rearOfQueue;         // reference to rear of queue

    void initialize JobQueue ()
    {
        /*
         * initialize the job queue by setting frontOfQueue and rearOfQueue to null
         */
    }

    void addJobToQueue (int jobNumber)
    {
        /*
         * Create a new job record,
         * place jobNumber in its jobNo field,
         * set its inFront field to the current rearOfQueue
         * (thereby linking the new record to the rear of the queue),
         * and set its inRear field to null.
         * Set inRear field of current rearOfQueue
         * to the new record (thereby setting up a two-way link), and
         * finally, set rearOfQueue to this new record
         */
    }

    void removeJobFromQueue (int jobNumber)
    {
        /*
        /*
         * set jobNumber equal to the jobNo field of the record at the front of the queue,
         * update frontOfQueue to the next item in the queue,
         * set the inFront field of the record that is now the head of the queue to null
         */
    }
} // class JobQueue
```

Figure 6.21 Outline of Java implementation of **class** JobQueue using a two-way linked list.

```
class JobQueue
{
    // instance variables
    public int          queueLength;            // length of job queue
    public int          queue[] = new int[25];  // queue can contain up to 25 jobs

    // methods
    public void initializeJobQueue ()
    {
      // body of method unchanged from Figure 6.18
    }

    public void addJobToQueue (int jobNumber)
    {
      // body of method unchanged from Figure 6.18
    }

    public void removeJobFromQueue (int jobNumber)
    {
      // body of method unchanged from Figure 6.18
    }
} // class JobQueue
```

Figure 6.22 Job queue implemented in Java as abstract data type. (Problems caused by **public** instance variables will be solved in Section 6.6.)

abstract data type. Thus, from both the product development and the product maintenance viewpoints, abstract data types are an attractive tool for software producers.

In addition to data abstraction and procedural abstraction, there is in fact a third type of abstraction, namely *iteration abstraction* [Liskov and Guttag, 1986]. Iteration abstraction allows a programmer to specify at a higher level that a loop is to be used, and then to describe at a lower level the exact elements over which the iteration is to be performed and the order in which the elements are to be processed.

6.6 INFORMATION HIDING

The three types of abstraction discussed in the previous section, namely, data abstraction, procedural abstraction, and iteration abstraction, are in turn instances of a more general design concept put forward by Parnas, *information hiding* [Parnas, 1971, 1972a, 1972b]. Parnas's ideas are directed toward future maintenance. Before a product is designed, a list should be made of implementation decisions likely to

```
class Scheduler
{
    . . .
    public void queueHandler ()
    {
        int                         job1, job2;
        JobQueue                    highPriorityQueue = new JobQueue ();
        JobQueue                    mediumPriorityQueue = new JobQueue ();
        JobQueue                    lowPriorityQueue = new JobQueue ();
            // some statements
        highPriorityQueue.initializeJobQueue ();
            // some more statements
        mediumPriorityQueue.addJobToQueue (job1);
            // still more statements
        lowPriorityQueue.removeJobFromQueue (job2);
            // even more statements
    } // queueHandler
    . . .
} // class Scheduler
```

Figure 6.23 Java method queueHandler using abstract data type of Figure 6.22.

change in the future. Modules should then be designed so that the implementation details of the resulting design are hidden from other modules. Thus, each future change is localized to one specific module. Because the details of the original implementation decision are not visible to other modules, changing the design clearly cannot affect any other module. (See the Just in Case You Wanted to Know box on page 170 for a further insight into information hiding.)

To see how these ideas can be used in practice, consider the abstract data type implementation of Figures 6.22 and 6.23. A primary reason for using an abstract data type is to ensure that the contents of a job queue can be changed exclusively by invoking one of the three methods in Figure 6.22. Unfortunately, the nature of that implementation is such that job queues can be changed in other ways. Instance variables queueLength and queue are both declared to be **public** in Figure 6.22 and are therefore accessible everywhere within the product. As a result, it is perfectly legal Java to use an assignment statement such as

$$\text{highPriorityQueue.queue[7]} = -5678;$$

anywhere in queueHandler to change highPriorityQueue. In other words, it is possible to change the contents of a job queue without using any of the three actions of the abstract data type. In addition to the implications this might have for lowering

---

JUST IN CASE YOU WANTED TO KNOW

The term *information hiding* is somewhat of a misnomer. A more accurate description would be "details

hiding," because what is hidden is not information, but rather implementation details.

```
class Rational
{
    public int              numerator;
    public int              denominator;

    public void sameDenominator (Rational r, Rational s)
    {
        // code to reduce r and s to the same denominator
    }

    public boolean equal (Rational t, Rational u)
    {
        Rational            v, w;
        v = t;
        w = u;
        sameDenominator (v, w);
        return (v.numerator == w.numerator);
    }

    // methods to add, subtract, multiply, and divide two rational numbers
}
```

Figure 6.24   Abstract data type definition of a rational number. (Problems caused by **public** instance variables will be solved in Section 6.6.)

cohesion and increasing coupling, management must recognize that the product may be vulnerable to computer fraud as described in Section 6.3.2.

Fortunately, there is a way out. The designer of Java provided for information hiding within a class specification. This is shown in Figure 6.25. Other than the two **private** visibility modifiers, Figure 6.25 is identical to Figure 6.22. Now the only information visible to other modules is that JobQueue is a **class** and that three actions with specified interfaces can operate on the resulting job queues. But the exact way that job queues are implemented is **private**, that is, invisible to the outside. The diagram in Figure 6.26 shows how a class with **private** instance variables enables a Java user to implement an abstract data type with full information hiding.

```
class JobQueue
{
    // instance variables
    private int         queueLength;              // length of job queue
    private int         queue[] = new int[25];    // queue can contain up to 25 jobs

    // methods
    public void initializeJobQueue ()
    {
        // body of method unchanged from Figure 6.18
    }

    public void addJobToQueue (int JobNumber)
    {
        // body of method unchanged from Figure 6.18
    }

    public void removeJobFromQueue (int JobNumber)
    {
        // body of method unchanged from Figure 6.18
    }
} // class JobQueue
```

Figure 6.25 Abstract data type implementation with information hiding, correcting the problem of Figures 6.18, 6.20, 6.22, and 6.24.

6.7 OBJECTS

As described at the beginning of this chapter, objects are simply the next step in the progression shown in Figure 6.27. There is nothing special about objects; they are as ordinary as abstract data types or modules with informational cohesion. The importance of objects is that they have all the properties possessed by their predecessors in Figure 6.27, as well as additional properties of their own.

An incomplete definition of an object is that an object is an instantiation (instance) of an abstract data type. That is, a product is designed in terms of abstract data types, and the variables (objects) of the product are then instantiations of the abstract data types. But defining an object as an instantiation of an abstract data type is too simplistic. Something more is needed, namely, *inheritance,* a concept first introduced in Simula 67 [Dahl and Nygaard, 1966; Dahl, Myrhaug, and Nygaard, 1973]. Inheritance is supported by most object-oriented programming languages, such as C++ [Stroustrup, 1991], Smalltalk [Goldberg and Robson 1989], and Java [Flanagan, 1966]. The basic idea behind inheritance is that new data types can be

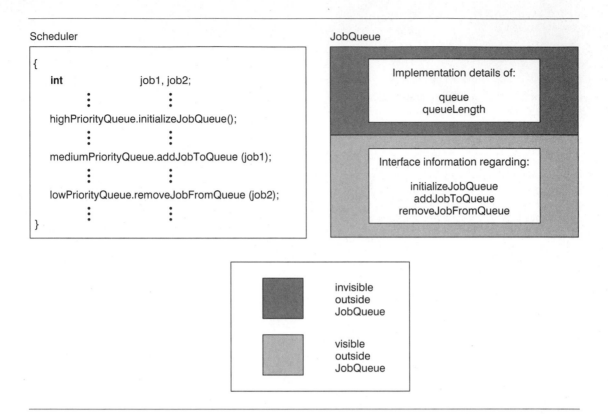

Figure 6.26 Representation of abstract data type with information hiding achieved via **class** with **private** instance variables (Figure 6.25 with Figure 6.23).

defined as extensions of previously defined types, rather than having to be defined from scratch [Meyer, 1986].

In an object-oriented language, a *class* can be defined. A class is an abstract data type that supports inheritance. An object is then an instantiation of a class. To see how classes are used, consider the following example. Define HumanBeing to be a class, and Joe to be an object, an instance of that class. Every HumanBeing has certain attributes such as age and height, and values can be assigned to those attributes when describing the object Joe. Now suppose that Parent is defined to be a *subclass* of HumanBeing. This means that a Parent has all the attributes of a HumanBeing, but in addition may have attributes of his or her own such as name of oldest child and number of children. This is depicted in Figure 6.28. In object-oriented terminology, a Parent *isA* HumanBeing. That is why the arrow in Figure 6.28 seems to be going in the wrong direction. In fact, the arrow is depicting the *isA* relation and therefore points from the derived class to the base class (but see the Just In Case You Wanted to Know box on page 173).

JUST IN CASE YOU WANTED TO KNOW

In the terminology of the object-oriented paradigm, there are two other ways of looking at the relationship between Parent and HumanBeing in Figure 6.28. We can say that Parent is a *specialization* of HumanBeing, or that HumanBeing is a *generalization* of Parent.

In addition to specialization/generalization, there are two other basic relationships between classes [Blaha, Premerlani, and Rumbaugh, 1988], namely aggregation and association. *Aggregation* refers to the components of a class. For example, **class** Per-

sonalComputer might contain components cpu, monitor, keyboard, and printer. There is nothing new about this; it occurs whenever a language supports records, such as a **struct** in C. Within the object-oriented context, however, it is used to group related items, resulting in a reusable class (Section 6.10).

Association refers to a relationship of some kind between two apparently unrelated classes. For example, there does not seem to be any connection between pigeons and semaphore flags, but both were used to transmit messages during the First World War.

Figure 6.27 Major concepts of Chapter 6.

Class Parent *inherits* all the attributes of HumanBeing, because class Parent is a subclass (or derived class) of base class HumanBeing. If Fred is an object and an instance of class Parent, then Fred has all the attributes of a Parent, but also inherits all the attributes of a HumanBeing. A Java implementation is shown in Figure 6.29.

The property of inheritance is an essential feature of object-oriented languages such as Smalltalk [Goldberg and Robson, 1989], C++ [Stroustrup, 1991], Eiffel [Meyer, 1992b], Ada 95 [ISO/IEC 8652, 1995], and Java [Flanagan, 1996]. However, neither inheritance nor the concept of a class is supported by languages such as

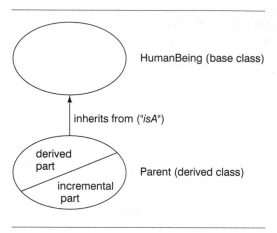

Figure 6.28 Derived types and inheritance.

```
class HumanBeing
{
    private int                 age;
    private float               height;

    // public declarations of operations on HumanBeing
}

class Parent extends HumanBeing
{
    private String              nameOfOldestChild;
    private int                 numberOfChildren;
    // public declarations of operations on Parent
}
```

Figure 6.29 Java implementation of Figure 6.28.

C or COBOL. Thus the object-oriented paradigm cannot be directly implemented in these popular languages.

In passing, one aspect of Java notation, like that of other object-oriented languages, explicitly reflects the equivalence of action and data. First, consider a classical language that supports records, C for example. Suppose that record_1 is a **struct** (record), and field_2 is a field within the class. Then, the field is referred to as record_1.field_2. That is, the period denotes membership within the record. If function_3 is a function within a C module, then function_3 () denotes the invocation of that function.

In contrast, suppose that Class_A is a class with attribute (instance variable) attributeB and method methodC. Suppose further that thatObject is an instance of ClassA. Then the field is referred to as thatObject.attributeB. Furthermore, thatObject.methodC () denotes an invocation of the method. Thus, the period is used to denote membership within an object, whether the member is an attribute or a method.

The advantages of using objects (or rather, classes) are precisely those of using abstract data types, including data abstraction and procedural abstraction. In addition, the inheritance aspects of classes provide a further layer of data abstraction, leading to easier and less fault-prone product development. Yet another strength follows from polymorphism and dynamic binding, the subject of the next section.

6.8   POLYMORPHISM AND DYNAMIC BINDING

Suppose that the operating system of a computer is called on to open a file. That file could be stored on a number of different media. For example, it could be a disk file, a tape file, or a diskette file. Using the structured paradigm, there would be three differently named functions, namely open_disk_file, open_tape_file, and open_diskette_file; this is shown in Figure 6.30(a). If my_file is declared to be a file, then at run time it is necessary to test whether it is a disk file, a tape file, or a diskette file in order to determine which of the three functions to invoke.

In contrast, when the object-oriented paradigm is used, a class named FileClass is defined, with three subclasses DiskFileClass, TapeFileClass, and DisketteFileClass. This is shown in Figure 6.30(b). Now, suppose that method open were defined in parent class FileClass and inherited by the three subclasses. Unfortunately, this would not work because different actions need to be carried out to open the three different types of files.

The solution is as follows. In parent class FileClass, a dummy method open is declared. (In Java, such a method is declared to be **abstract**). A specific implementation of the method appears in each of the three subclasses and each method is given the identical name, that is, open, as shown in Figure 6.30(b). Again, suppose that myFile is declared to be a file. At run time the message myFile.open () is sent. The object-oriented system now determines whether myFile is a disk file, a tape file, or a diskette file and invokes the appropriate version of open. That is to say, the system determines at run-time whether object myFile is an instance of class DiskFileClass, class TapeFileClass, or class DisketteFileClass and automatically invokes the correct method. Because this has to be done at run-time (dynamically), and not at compile time (statically), the act of connecting an object to the appropriate method is termed *dynamic binding*. Furthermore, because the method open can be applied to objects of different classes, it is termed *polymorphic*. The term literally means "of different shapes." Just as carbon crystals come in different shapes, including hard diamonds and soft graphite, so method open comes in three different versions. In Java, these versions are denoted DiskFileClass.open, TapeFile-

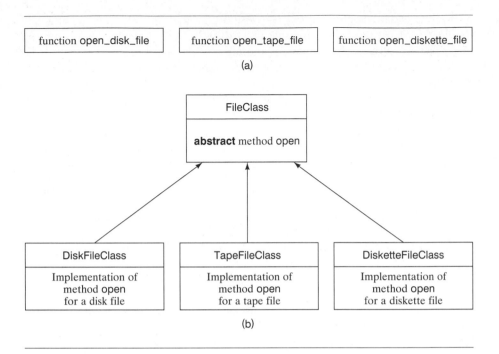

Figure 6.30 Operations needed to open files. (a) Structured implementation and (b) object-oriented file class hierarchy.

Class.open, and DisketteFileClass.open. However, because of dynamic binding, it is not necessary to determine which method to invoke to open a specific file. Instead it is only necessary to send the message myFile.open (), and the system will determine the type (class) of myFile and invoke the correct method.

These ideas are applicable to more than just **abstract** methods. Consider a hierarchy of classes, as shown in Figure 6.31. All classes are derived from the Base class. Suppose method checkOrder (b : Base) takes as argument an instance of class Base. Then, as a consequence of inheritance, polymorphism, and dynamic binding, it is valid to invoke checkOrder with an argument not just of class Base, but also of any subclass of class Base, that is, any class derived from Base. All that is needed is to invoke checkOrder, and everything will be taken care of at run time. This technique is extremely powerful in that the software professional need not be concerned about the precise type of an argument at the time that a message is sent.

However, there are also major disadvantages of polymorphism and dynamic binding. First, it is generally not possible to determine at compilation time which version of a specific polymorphic method will be invoked. Accordingly, it can be extremely difficult to determine the cause of a failure. Polymorphism and dynamic binding can also have a negative impact on maintenance. The first task of a maintenance programmer is usually to try to understand the product. (As explained in Chapter 14, the maintainer is rarely the person who developed that code.)

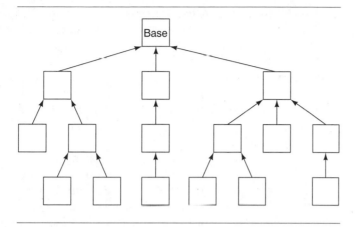

Figure 6.31   Hierarchy of classes.

However, this can be laborious if there are multiple possibilities for a specific method. The programmer has to consider all the possible methods that could be dynamically invoked at a specific place in the code; this can be a time-consuming task. Thus, polymorphism and dynamic binding add both strengths and weaknesses to the object-oriented paradigm.

The reasons for the superiority of the object-oriented paradigm given in Section 1.6 included conceptual and physical independence. To measure this independence, the concepts of cohesion and coupling must now be re-examined within the context of objects.

6.9   Cohesion and Coupling of Objects

An object is a kind of module. Consequently, the material of Sections 6.2 and 6.3 concerning modules with high cohesion and low coupling applies equally to objects. The question arises as to whether special types of cohesion and coupling occur within the object-oriented paradigm.

First consider cohesion. (Recall that, as explained in Section 6.2, the cohesion of a module is the extent to which the actions performed by that module are functionally related.) A class can include actions of two kinds, namely inherited methods and methods specific to that class. The cohesion of a class is determined from its functionality, irrespective of the source of that functionality. To see this, suppose that two classes have identical functionality. However, one class inherits all its functionality from its superclasses (its ancestors in the inheritance hierarchy); the other class inherits nothing. Because both classes have identical functionality, they have identical levels of cohesion. In other words, there can be no types of cohesion that are specific to classes; cohesion applies equally to all types of modules, including classes [Schach, 1996].

With regard to coupling, first ignore inheritance. In the absence of inheritance, the coupling between two classes can be determined as in Section 6.3. For example, if an attribute of a class is defined to be **public** (accessible to all other units within the product), then this can induce common coupling. In addition, a type of coupling can arise as a consequence of inheritance. Suppose that class B is a subclass of class A. There is clearly some sort of coupling between A and B; unless specific measures have been taken to override this, all the attributes of A will be present in B. If an attribute of A is changed in any way, this change will be reflected in B and in any objects that are instantiations of B [Schach, 1996].

This type of coupling is different than the levels of coupling described in Section 6.3. First, with those types of coupling, the ideal is to have as low a level of coupling as possible, in order to promote maintainability and reusability. In contrast, when setting up an inheritance hierarchy of classes, the aim is to maximize the extent to which elements of commonality can be extracted; the higher the level of this type of coupling, the better. Second, within Section 6.3 there is an implicit assumption that it is possible to design the modules of a product so that the coupling is minimized. However, classes and subclasses are intended to be models of real-world entities. The number of attributes that a subclass inherits from a superclass is not a design decision, but is dictated by physical realities. Thus, this coupling is not something that can be adjusted by the design team [Schach, 1996].

A number of different reasons for the superiority of the object-oriented paradigm were given in Section 1.6. A further reason is that the use of objects and classes promotes reuse.

6.10   REUSE

A product is *portable* if it is significantly easier to modify the product as a whole in order to run it on another compiler/hardware/operating system configuration than to recode it from scratch. In contrast, *reuse* refers to taking components of one product in order to facilitate the development of a different product with different functionality. A reusable component need not necessarily be a module or a code fragment—it could be a design, a part of a manual, a set of test data, or a duration and cost estimate.

There are two types of reuse, accidental reuse and deliberate reuse. If the developers of a new product realize that a component of a previously developed product can be reused in the new product, then this is *accidental reuse*. On the other hand, utilization of software components constructed specifically for the purpose of possible reuse in future products is *deliberate reuse*. One potential advantage of deliberate reuse over accidental reuse is that components specially constructed for use in future products are more likely to be easy and safe to reuse; such components are generally well documented and thoroughly tested. In addition, they will usually display a uniformity of style that makes maintenance easier. The other side of the coin is that implementing deliberate reuse within a company can be expensive. It takes time to specify, design, implement, test, and document a software component.

However, there can be no guarantee that such a component will ever be reused, and thereby recoup the money invested in developing the potentially reusable component.

When computers were first constructed, nothing was reused. Every time a product was developed, items such as multiplication routines, input/output routines, or routines for computing sines and cosines were constructed from scratch. Quite soon, however, it was realized that this was a considerable waste of effort, and subroutine libraries were constructed. Programmers could then simply invoke square root or sine functions whenever they wished. These subroutine libraries have become more and more sophisticated and have developed into run-time support routines. Thus, when a programmer calls a Java method, there is no need to write code to manage the stack or to pass the arguments explicitly; it is automatically handled by calling the appropriate run-time support routines. The concept of subroutine libraries has also been extended to large-scale statistical libraries such as SPSS [Norusis, 1982] and to numerical analysis libraries like NAG [Phillips, 1986]. Class libraries also play a major role in assisting users of object-oriented languages. The environment for the language Eiffel incorporates seven libraries of classes [Meyer, 1990]. The success of Smalltalk is at least partly due to the wide variety of items in the Smalltalk library. In both instances, the presence of a browser, a CASE tool that assists the user to scan a class library, is of enormous assistance. The Java Application Programming Interface (API) includes eight packages (libraries). With regard to C++, there are a large number of different libraries available, many in the public domain. Thus, developers can reuse both their own routines and items in class libraries.

No matter how high the quality of a software product may be, it will not sell if it takes 4 years to get it onto the market when a competitive product can be delivered in only 2 years. The length of the development process is critical in a market economy. All other criteria as to what constitutes a "good" product are irrelevant if the product cannot compete timewise. For a corporation that has repeatedly failed to get a product to market first, software reuse is a tempting technique. After all, if an existing component is reused, then there is no need to design, implement, test, and document that component. The key point is that, on average, only about 15 percent of any software product serves a truly original purpose [Jones, 1984]. The other 85 percent of the product could in theory be standardized and then reused in future products.

The figure of 85 percent is essentially a theoretical upper limit for the reuse rate; nevertheless, reuse rates of the order of 40 percent can be achieved in practice, as described in Section 6.11. This leads to an obvious question: If such reuse rates are attainable in practice and if reuse is by no means a new idea, why are so few organizations employing reuse to shorten the development process?

6.10.1 IMPEDIMENTS TO REUSE

There are a number of impediments to reuse. The first impediment is ego. All too many software professionals would rather rewrite a routine from scratch than reuse a routine written by someone else, the implication being that a routine cannot be any good unless they wrote it themselves. This is a management issue and can be solved if management is aware of the problem. A second impediment is economic. Some developers try to avoid writing routines that are too general-purpose for fear that reuse would then put them out of work. Of course, this fear is groundless as can be seen from the huge backlog of work in virtually every software organization. Again, this issue can be solved by managerial intervention. A third impediment is the retrieval problem. That is to say, a large organization may have hundreds of thousands of potentially reusable components. How should these components be stored for effective retrieval? For example, a reusable components database might consist of 20,000 items, 125 of which are sort routines. The database must be organized so that the designer of a new product can quickly determine which (if any) of those 125 sort routines are appropriate for the new product. Solving the storage/retrieval problem is a technical issue for which a wide variety of solutions have been proposed, such as [Meyer, 1987; Prieto-Díaz, 1991]. Fourth, reuse is expensive. Tracz has stated that there are three costs involved, namely the cost of making something reusable, the cost of reusing it, and the cost of defining and implementing a reuse process [Tracz, 1994]. He estimates that just making a component reusable increases its cost by at least 60 percent. Some organizations have reported cost increases of 200 percent and even up to 480 percent, but the cost of making a component reusable was only 11 percent in one Hewlett-Packard reuse project, as reported in Section 6.11.5 [Lim, 1994].

The preceding four impediments can be overcome, at least in principle. The fifth impediment is more problematic, namely, legal issues that arise with contract software. In terms of the type of contract that is usually drawn up between a client and a software development organization, the software product belongs to the client. Thus, if the software developer reuses a component of one client's product in a new product for a different client, this essentially constitutes a violation of the first client's copyright. For internal software, that is, when the developers and client are members of the same organization, this problem does not arise. Thus, other than certain legal issues, there are essentially no major impediments to implementing reuse within a software organization.

6.11   REUSE CASE STUDIES

Five case studies showing how reuse has been achieved in practice are now presented. They span the period from 1976 to 1994.

6.11.1   RAYTHEON MISSILE SYSTEMS DIVISION

In 1976 a study was undertaken at Raytheon's Missile Systems Division to determine whether deliberate reuse of designs and code was feasible [Lanergan and Grasso, 1984]. Over 5000 COBOL products in use were analyzed and classified. The researchers determined that only six basic actions are performed in a business application product. As a result between 40 percent and 60 percent of business application designs and modules could be standardized and reused. The basic actions were found to be: sort data, edit or manipulate data, combine data, explode data, update data, and report on data. For the next 6 years, a concerted attempt was made to reuse both design and code wherever possible.

The Raytheon approach employed reuse in two ways, namely, what the researchers termed functional modules and COBOL program logic structures. In Raytheon's terminology a *functional module* is a COBOL code fragment designed and coded for a specific purpose, such as an edit routine, database procedure division call, tax computation routine, or date aging routine for accounts receivable. Use of the 3200 reusable modules resulted in applications that on average consisted of 60 percent reused code. Functional modules were carefully designed, tested, and documented. Products that used these functional modules were found to be more reliable, and less testing of the product as a whole was needed.

The modules were stored in a standard copy library and were obtained with the **copy** verb. That is, the code was not physically present within the application product, but was included by the COBOL compiler at compilation time; the mechanism is similar to **#include** in C or C++. The resulting source code was, therefore, shorter than if the copied code were physically present. As a consequence, maintenance was easier.

The Raytheon researchers also used what they termed a *COBOL program logic structure*. This is essentially a template, a framework that has to be fleshed out into a complete product. One example of a logic structure is the update logic structure. This is used for performing a sequential update, such as the case study in Section 4.1.1. Error handling is built in, as is sequence checking. The logic structure is 22 paragraphs (units of a COBOL program) in length. Many of the paragraphs can be filled in by using functional modules such as get_transaction, print_page_headings, and print_control_totals.

There are many advantages to the use of templates. It makes the design and coding of a product quicker and easier because the framework of the product is already present; all that is needed is to fill in the details. Fault-prone areas such as end-of-file conditions have already been tested. In fact, testing as a whole is easier. But Raytheon believed that the major advantage occurs when the user requests modifications or enhancements. Once a maintenance programmer is familiar with the relevant logic structure, it is almost as if that maintenance programmer had been a member of the original development team.

By 1983 logic structures had been used over 5500 times in developing new products. About 60 percent of the code consisted of functional modules, that is, reusable code. This meant that design, coding, module testing, and documentation time could also be reduced by 60 percent, leading to an estimated 50 percent increase in productivity in software product development. But for Raytheon, the real benefit of the technique lay in the hope that the readability and understandability resulting from the consistent style would reduce the cost of maintenance by between 60 percent and 80 percent. (Unfortunately, Raytheon closed the division before the necessary maintenance data could be obtained.)

It might seem that reuse is applicable only to business data-processing applications. But that is not so, as is demonstrated by the second case study, the Toshiba Software Factory.

6.11.2   TOSHIBA SOFTWARE FACTORY

In 1977 the Toshiba Corporation started the Fuchu Software Factory at the Toshiba Fuchu Works in Tokyo, Japan. At the Fuchu Works, industrial process control systems are manufactured for, among other areas, electric power networks, nuclear power generators, factory automation, and traffic control; at the Software Factory, application software is developed for the process control computers for those systems [Matsumoto, 1984; 1987].

By 1985 the Software Factory employed a total of 2300 technicians and managers. About 60 percent of the code is in FORTRAN augmented by real-time routines, 20 percent in an assembler-like language, and the rest in user-specified problem-oriented languages. The Software Factory measures productivity in lines of code. Because the effort to produce 1000 lines of FORTRAN is different from that needed to produce 1000 lines of assembler, the unit of productivity used is *equivalent assembler source lines* (EASL) [Jones, 1978]; the usual conversion factor is that one line of high-level language is equivalent to four lines of assembler. Using this measure, output from the Software Factory in 1985 was 7.2 million EASL. Products ranged in size from 1 to 21 million EASL, with an average size of 4 million EASL.

Software is developed using the waterfall model, with detailed reviews and inspections at the end of each phase. Productivity, measured in EASL, is the driving force behind the Software Factory. It is monitored on both a projectwide basis and on an individual basis. Annual productivity increases for the Factory as a whole have been of the order of 8 percent to 9 percent. One of the items measured when appraising the performance of individuals is their fault rate. In the case of a programmer, for example, the number of faults per 1000 EASL is expected to decrease over time as a consequence of training and experience. Quality is an important aspect of the Factory and is achieved through a number of different mechanisms, including reviews, inspections, and quality circles (groups of workers who meet on a regular basis to find ways to improve quality).

Matsumoto attributes improvements in both productivity and quality to reuse of existing software (that is, accidental reuse) [Matsumoto, 1987]. This reusable software includes not only modules, but also documentation of all kinds, such as designs, specifications, contracts, and manuals. A committee is responsible for deciding what components should be placed in the *reusable software components database* where they are indexed by keyword for later retrieval. Careful statistics are kept on the reuse rate of every component in the database. In 1985 the documentation reuse rate, that is, the number of reused pages divided by the total number of pages of documentation, was 32 percent. In the design phase, the reuse rate was 33 percent, whereas 48 percent of code was reused during the implementation phase. In addition, statistics are kept on the sizes of reused software components; about 55 percent were 1 to 10K EASL in size, and 36 percent were in the 10K to 100K EASL range.

Corresponding statistics for 25 software products developed by NASA follow in the next section.

6.11.3   NASA SOFTWARE

Selby has characterized the accidental reuse of software in a NASA software production group that produces ground support software for unmanned spacecraft control [Selby, 1989]. Altogether 25 software products were investigated. They ranged in size from 3000 to 112,000 lines of source code. The 7188 component modules were classified into four categories. Group 1 consisted of modules that were used without any changes. Group 2 were those modules reused with slight revisions, that is, less than 25 percent of the code was changed. Modules falling into group 3 were reused with major revisions; 25 percent or more of the code was changed. Group 4 modules were developed from scratch.

A total of 2954 FORTRAN modules in the sample were studied in detail. On average, 45 percent of the modules were reused in modified or unmodified form. More specifically, 28 percent fell into group 1, 10 percent into group 2, and 7 percent into group 3. In general, the reused modules were small, well documented, with simple interfaces and little input/output processing, and tended to be terminal nodes in a module interconnection diagram (such as Figure 6.7).

These results were not really surprising. Small, well-documented modules are easier to comprehend than large modules with poor documentation, and are therefore more likely to be reused. In addition, a large module is likely to perform a number of different actions, or perhaps one rather specialized action, and is therefore less likely to be reused than its smaller counterpart. A complex interface implies a large number of arguments, which tends to reduce the reuse of a module. Input/output processing can be somewhat application-specific and, therefore, less reusable. Finally, comparing terminal modules in a module interconnection diagram with modules higher up in the diagram, a terminal module is more likely to carry out a specific task, whereas a module higher up is usually decision-oriented (this is discussed in more depth in Section 13.1.1). As a result, a terminal module is more likely to be reusable than a nonterminal one.

A more constructive way of looking at Selby's results is to utilize them to ensure that modules can be reused in future products. Management should ensure that a specific design objective should be small modules with simple interfaces. Input/output processing should be localized to a few modules. All modules must be properly documented.

There are considerable differences between the NASA group and the Fuchu Software Factory. In particular, the decision to reuse software was the personal choice of the NASA software developers; there were no managerial directives of any kind. The NASA staffers reused software simply because they believed that reuse is a worthwhile software engineering technique. In addition, there were no software tools to assist with the reuse process. This situation is in stark contrast to the reuse-oriented management of the Fuchu Works and the sophisticated software component retrieval mechanisms employed there. Despite this, surprisingly high reuse rates have been obtained at NASA.

The fourth case study highlights the effect of management commitment to reuse.

6.11.4   GTE DATA SERVICES

A successful accidental reuse scheme has been implemented at GTE Data Services [Prieto-Díaz, 1991]. Unlike the NASA case study, a key aspect of the GTE scheme was full management commitment to the reuse of source code modules. In order to promote reuse, cash incentives of between $50 and $100 were paid for a module that was accepted for possible reuse, and royalties were paid when that module was actually reused. In addition, managers' budgets were increased when projects they were managing achieved a high level of reuse. There was even a "Reuser of the Month" award.

The results of this scheme were as follows. In 1988 a reuse level of 14 percent was achieved; this saved the company an estimated $1,500,000. The following year it was estimated that the reuse level rose to 20 percent, and a 50 percent level was predicted for 1993. The overall savings by that date were predicted to be well over $10 million.

There are a number of interesting aspects of the GTE reuse program. First, the total number of modules available for reuse dropped from 190 in 1988 to 128 in 1990, despite the fact that new modules were added. It appears that, at least in organizations such as GTE Data Services, it is not necessary to build a huge inventory of reusable components. Second, the emphasis was on larger modules (10,000 lines of code or more) because of the greater payoff. In contrast to the NASA experience where smaller modules tended to be reused, GTE succeeded in reusing larger modules. This disparity emphasizes the importance of having management commitment to any reuse program.

6.11.5   HEWLETT-PACKARD

Hewlett-Packard has implemented reuse programs in many different divisions of the company [Lim, 1994]. In general, these programs have been successful from the viewpoint of improved software quality as a consequence of reuse. Two specific programs are discussed here.

The manufacturing productivity section of the software technology division has had an accidental reuse program in place since 1983. The section develops software for manufacturing resource planning. The components chosen for reuse are written in Pascal and SPL (the language for systems software on the HP 3000 computer system). The fault rate for new code is 4.1 faults per 1,000 non-comment lines of code (KLOC), but only 0.9 faults per KLOC for the reused code. As a consequence of reuse, the fault rate has dropped to only 2.0 faults per KLOC, a 51 percent reduction. Productivity has increased 57 percent to 1.1 KLOC per person-month in 1992. The program has cost $1 million, but has saved $4.1 million between 1983 and 1992. Amazingly, the project broke even in its second year.

Since 1987, there has been a planned reuse program in the San Diego Technical Graphics (STG) division of Hewlett-Packard. This division develops and maintains firmware for plotters and printers. A single product consisting of 20,000 non-comment lines of C was developed over a period of 3 years and then reused. The gross cost of the reuse program between 1987 and 1994 (1994 data estimated) was $2.6 million, and savings were $5.6 million. There was a 24 percent reduction in fault rate to 1.3 faults per KLOC. Also, productivity increased by 40 percent to 0.7 KLOC per person-month. Finally, the delivery time for a product decreased by 24 percent.

The costs of the STG reuse program are also interesting. The cost of developing the reusable firmware component was only 11 percent more than the cost of a similar nonreusable component. Integration costs were 19 percent of the cost of developing a nonreusable component. That is to say, each time the component was reused, the cost was only about one-fifth of the cost of developing that component from scratch.

The overall lesson of all five case studies is that reuse is possible in practice and can result in significant cost savings. However, the major push for reuse must come from management.

6.12 REUSE AND MAINTENANCE

The traditional reason for promoting reuse is that it can shorten the development process. For example, a number of major software organizations are trying to halve the time needed to develop a new product, and reuse is a primary strategy in these endeavors. However, as reflected in Figure 1.2, for every $1 spent on developing a product, $2 is spent on maintaining that product. Thus, a second important reason for reuse is to reduce the time and cost of maintaining a product. In fact, reuse has a greater impact on maintenance than on development.

Suppose now that 40 percent of a product consists of components reused from earlier products and that this reuse is evenly distributed across the entire product. That is, 40 percent of the specification document consists of reused components, 40 percent of the design, 40 percent of the code modules, 40 percent of the manuals, and so on. Unfortunately, this does not mean that the time to develop the product as a whole will be 40 percent less than it would have been without reuse. First, some of the components will have to be changed to tailor them to the new product. Suppose that one-quarter of the reused components are changed. If a component has to be changed, then the documentation for that component will also have to be changed. Also, the changed component will have to be verified. Second, if a code module is reused unchanged then unit testing of that module is not required. However, integration testing of that module is still needed. Thus, even if 30 percent of a product consists of components reused unchanged and a further 10 percent are reused changed, the time needed to develop the complete product will at best be only about 27 percent less [Schach, 1992]. On average, 33 percent of a software budget is devoted to development. Consequently, if reuse reduces development costs by 27 percent, then the overall cost of that product over its 12- to 15-year lifetime is reduced by only about 9 percent as a consequence of reuse; this is reflected in Figure 6.32.

Activity	Percentage of Total Cost over Product Lifetime	Percentage Savings over Product Lifetime
Development	33%	9.3%
Maintenance	67	17.9

Figure 6.32 Average percentage cost savings under the assumption that 40 percent of new product consists of reused components, three-quarters of which are reused unchanged.

Similar but lengthier arguments can be applied to the maintenance component of the software process [Schach, 1994]. Under the assumptions of the previous paragraph, the effect of reuse on maintenance is an overall cost saving of about 18 percent, as shown in Figure 6.32. It is clear that the major impact of reuse is on maintenance rather than development. The underlying reason is that reused components are generally well designed, thoroughly tested, and comprehensively documented, thereby simplifying all three types of maintenance.

If the actual reuse rates in a given product are lower (or higher) than what has been assumed in this section, then the benefits of reuse will be different. But the overall result will still be the same, namely, that reuse affects maintenance more than it does development.

The key issue now is: Is there evidence that designing a product in terms of objects encourages reuse and improves software productivity?

6.13   OBJECTS AND PRODUCTIVITY

When the theory of composite/structured design (C/SD) was first put forward, the assertion was made that an ideal module was one with functional cohesion (Section 6.2.7). That is, if a module performed one and only one action, it was thought to be an ideal candidate for reuse, and maintenance of such a module was expected to be easy. The flaw in this reasoning is that a module with functional cohesion is not self-contained and independent. Instead, it has to operate on data. If such a module is reused, then the data on which it is to operate must be reused, too. If the data in the new product are not identical to those in the original, then either the data have to be changed or the module with functional cohesion has to be changed. Similar issues arise with regard to maintenance; a module with functional cohesion is not as self-contained as was once believed.

According to C/SD the next best type of module is a module with informational cohesion (Section 6.2.6). Such a module is essentially an object, that is, an instance of a class. An object is the fundamental building block of software because it models all aspects of a particular real-world entity (conceptual independence, or encapsulation), but conceals its implementation of both its data and the actions that operate on that data (physical independence, or information hiding). This self-contained nature of an object is why use of the object-oriented paradigm can make both development and maintenance easier.

It is therefore not surprising that many organizations have reported that when they use object-oriented techniques for software development their software costs appear to decrease and overall quality improves. Team organization (Section 12.6) is frequently a major cause of problems in the development of large-scale products. The object-oriented paradigm allows a large product to be treated, in many ways, as a collection of essentially independent smaller products, and managing the development is far easier. This is one of the reasons why the object-oriented paradigm is superior to the structured paradigm for large products.

Notwithstanding the many advantages of the object-oriented paradigm, some difficulties and problems have been reported. A frequently reported problem concerns development effort and size. The first time anything new is done, it takes longer than on subsequent occasions; this initial period is sometimes referred to as the learning curve. But when the object-oriented paradigm is used for the first time by an organization, it often takes longer than anticipated, even allowing for the learning curve. This is because the size of the product is larger than when structured techniques are used. This is particularly noticeable when the product has a graphical user interface (GUI) (see Section 7.3). Thereafter, however, things improve greatly. First, maintenance costs are lower, thus reducing the overall lifetime cost of the product. Second, the next time that a new product is developed, some of the objects from the previous project can be reused, further reducing software costs. This has been especially significant when a GUI has been used for the first time; much of the effort that went into the GUI can be recouped in subsequent products.

Problems of inheritance are harder to solve. A major reason for using inheritance is that a new subclass that differs slightly from its parent class can be created without affecting the parent class or any other ancestor class in the inheritance hierarchy. Conversely, however, once a product has been implemented, any change to an existing class directly affects all its descendants in the inheritance hierarchy. At the very least, the affected units will have to be recompiled. In some cases, the methods of the relevant objects (instantiations of the affected subclasses) will have to be recoded; this can be a nontrivial task. To minimize this problem, it is important that all classes be carefully designed during the development process. This will reduce the ripple effect induced by a change to an existing class.

A second problem can result from a cavalier use of inheritance. Unless explicitly prevented, a subclass inherits all the attributes of its parent class(es). Usually, subclasses have additional attributes of their own. As a consequence, objects lower in the inheritance hierarchy can quickly get large, with resulting storage problems [Bruegge, Blythe, Jackson, and Shufelt, 1992]. One way to prevent this is to change the dictum "use inheritance wherever possible" to "use inheritance wherever appropriate." In addition, if a descendant class does not need an attribute of an ancestor, then that attribute should be explicitly excluded.

A third group of problems stems from polymorphism and dynamic binding. These were described in Section 6.8.

Despite these problems, there is no shortage of informal reports on the benefits of using object-oriented techniques. In addition, published papers such as [Capper, Colgate, Hunter, and James, 1994] describe successful projects that have been carried out using the object-oriented paradigm. A large body of evidence is accumulating that indicates that the object-oriented paradigm is now the appropriate software process. This is discussed further in Chapter 9.

Chapter Review

The chapter begins with a description of a module (Section 6.1). In the next two sections an analysis is given of what constitutes a well-designed module in terms of module cohesion and module coupling (Sections 6.2 and 6.3). Specifically, a module should have high cohesion and low coupling. Various types of abstraction are presented in Sections 6.4 through 6.7, including data abstraction and procedural abstraction. In data encapsulation (Section 6.4), a module comprises a data *structure* together with the actions performed on that data structure. An abstract data type (Section 6.5) is a data *type,* together with the actions performed on instances of that type. Information hiding (Section 6.6) consists of designing a module in such a way that implementation details are hidden from other modules. The progression of increasing abstraction culminates in the description of a class, namely, an abstract data type that supports inheritance (Section 6.7). An object is then an instance of a class. Polymorphism and dynamic binding are the subjects of Section 6.8, and cohesion and coupling of objects are described in Section 6.9. Reuse is described in Section 6.10; five case studies of successful reuse are presented in Section 6.11. The impact of reuse on maintenance is discussed in Section 6.12, and the impact of objects on productivity is analyzed in Section 6.13.

For Further Reading

Many of the ideas in this chapter were originally put forward by Parnas [Parnas, 1971; 1972a; 1972b]. Objects were first described in [Dahl and Nygaard, 1966].

The primary source on cohesion and coupling is [Stevens, Myers, and Constantine, 1974]; also important are [Myers, 1975; 1978b; Yourdon and Constantine, 1979]. The ideas of composite/structured design have subsequently been extended to objects [Schach, 1996].

The use of abstract data types in software development was put forward in [Liskov and Zilles, 1974]. Another important early paper is [Guttag, 1977]. Later papers on abstraction include [Feldman, 1981], in which a practical approach to data abstraction is presented, and [Shaw, 1984], a discussion of how abstraction is achieved in modern programming languages. A useful book on abstraction is [Liskov and Guttag, 1986]. [Berry, 1985] discusses information hiding in Ada. The application of information hiding to the U.S. Navy A-7 project appears in [Parnas, Clements, and Weiss, 1985]. In [Neumann, 1986], a description is given of the use of abstraction for designing safer software for controlling life-critical systems in areas such as air-traffic control or medical care. An account of experiences with abstraction-based software development techniques in a university environment is found in [Berzins, Gray, and Naumann, 1986].

Introductory material on objects can be found in [Cox, 1986], [Stefik and Bobrow, 1986], [Korson and McGregor, 1990] and [Snyder, 1993]. Ways in which object-oriented programming promotes reuse are put forward in [Meyer, 1987; 1990]. The proceedings of the annual Conference on Object-Oriented Programming Systems, Languages, and Applications (OOPSLA) have a wide selection of research papers; the addendum to the proceedings (published annually in *ACM SIGPLAN Notices*) contains informal reports describing successful object-oriented projects. [Shriver and Wegner, 1987] contains many worthwhile earlier papers on various aspects of object-oriented software development. The successful use of the object-oriented paradigm in three IBM projects is described in [Capper, Colgate, Hunter, and James, 1994].

The October 1992 issue of *IEEE Computer* contains a number of important articles on objects, including [Meyer, 1992a] which describes "design by contract." A variety of articles on objects can be found in the January 1993 issue of *IEEE Software;* the paper by Snyder carefully defining key terms in the field [Snyder, 1993] is particularly useful. Possible drawbacks of polymorphism are described in [Ponder and Bush, 1994].

Further information on the reuse case studies in this chapter can be found in [Lanergan and Grasso, 1984], [Matsumoto, 1984, 1987], [Selby, 1989], [Prieto-Díaz, 1991], and [Lim, 1994]. Two pilot studies at Motorola are described in [Joos, 1994]. Some warnings regarding reuse are given in [Tracz, 1988] and [Tracz, 1994]. A classification scheme for module retrieval and reuse is described in [Prieto-Díaz and Freeman, 1987]. Reuse issues regarding Ada can be found in [Nissen and Wallis, 1984] and [Gargaro and Pappas, 1987]; successful Ada reuse case studies are outlined in [Wildblood, 1990]. The cost-effectiveness of reuse is described in [Barnes and Bollinger, 1991] and ways of identifying components for future reuse in [Caldiera and Basili, 1991]. [Prieto-Díaz, 1993] is a status report on reuse. Further papers on reuse are to be found in [Freeman, 1987], [Biggerstaff and Perlis, 1989], and the September 1994 issue of *IEEE Software*.

Problems

Choose any programming language with which you are familiar. Consider the two   **6.1**
definitions of modularity given in Section 6.1. Determine which of the two defini-

tions includes what you intuitively understand to constitute a module in the language you have chosen.

6.2 Determine the cohesion of the following modules:
   read tape record and check parity bits
   edit salary and withholding record
   edit salary record and withholding record
   perform fast Fourier transform using Aksen's Algorithm
   measure pressure in tank and sound alarm if necessary

6.3 You are a software engineer involved in product development. Your manager asks you to investigate ways of ensuring that modules designed by your group will be as reusable as possible. What do you tell her?

6.4 Your manager now asks you to determine how existing modules can be reused. Your first suggestion is to break up each module with coincidental cohesion into separate modules with functional cohesion. Your manager correctly points out that the separate modules have not been tested, nor have they been documented. What do you say now?

6.5 What is the influence of cohesion on maintenance?

6.6 What is the influence of coupling on maintenance?

6.7 Carefully distinguish between data encapsulation and abstract data types.

6.8 Carefully distinguish between abstraction and information hiding.

6.9 Carefully distinguish between polymorphism and dynamic binding.

6.10 Convert the comments in Figure 6.21 to Java. Make sure that the resulting module executes correctly.

6.11 It has been suggested that Java supports implementation of abstract data types, but only at the cost of giving up information hiding. Discuss this claim.

6.12 What is the influence of cohesion on reuse?

6.13 What is the influence of coupling on reuse?

6.14 As pointed out in the "Just in Case You Wanted to Know" box at the beginning of this chapter, objects were first put forward in 1966. Only after essentially being reinvented nearly 20 years later did objects begin to receive widespread acceptance. Can you explain this phenomenon?

6.15 Your instructor will distribute a structured software product. Analyze the modules from the viewpoints of information hiding, levels of abstraction, coupling, and cohesion.

6.16 Your instructor will distribute an object-oriented software product. Analyze the modules from the viewpoints of information hiding, levels of abstraction, coupling, and cohesion. Compare your answer with that of Problem 6.15.

6.17 You are required to build a product for determining whether a bank statement is correct. The data needed include the balance at the beginning of the month; the number, date, and amount of each check; the date and amount of each deposit; and the balance at the end of the month. Explain how you would ensure that as many modules as possible of the product can be reused in future products.

Consider an automated library circulation system. Every book has a bar code, and **6.18** every borrower has a card bearing a bar code. When a borrower wishes to check out a book, the librarian scans the bar code on the book and on the borrower's card, and then enters C at the computer terminal. Similarly, when a book is returned, it is again scanned and the librarian enters R. Librarians can add books (+) to the library collection or remove them (−). Borrowers can go to a terminal and determine all the books in the library by a particular author (the borrower enters A= followed by the author's name), all the books with a specific title (T= followed by the title), or all the books in a particular subject area (S= followed by the subject area). Finally, if a borrower wants a book that is currently checked out, the librarian can place a hold on the book so that when it is returned it will be held for the borrower who requested it (H= followed by the number of the book). Explain how you would ensure a high percentage of reusable modules.

You have just joined a large software organization that has hundreds of products **6.19** comprising some 95,000 COBOL modules. You have been hired to come up with a plan for reusing as many of the modules as possible in future products. What is your proposal?

(Term Project) What parts of the Osbert Oglesby product of Appendix A could be **6.20** reused in future products?

(Readings in Software Engineering) Your instructor will distribute copies of [Meyer, **6.21** 1990]. To what extent do you agree with Meyer that the object-oriented approach promotes reuse? What experimental evidence supports his claims?

References

[Barnes and Bollinger, 1991] B. H. BARNES AND T. B. BOLLINGER, "Making Reuse Cost-Effective," *IEEE Software* **8** (January 1991), pp. 13–24.

[Berry, 1978] D. M. BERRY, Personal Communication, 1978.

[Berry, 1985] D. M. BERRY, "On the Application of Ada and Its Tools to the Information Hiding Decomposition Methodology for the Design of Software Systems," in: *Methodologies for Computer System Design*, W. K. Giloi and B. D. Shriver (Editors), Elsevier North-Holland, Amsterdam, 1985, pp. 308–321.

[Berzins, Gray, and Naumann, 1986] V. BERZINS, M. GRAY, AND D. NAUMANN, "Abstraction-Based Software Developments," *Communications of the ACM* **29** (May 1986), pp. 402–415.

[Biggerstaff and Perlis, 1989] T. J. BIGGERSTAFF AND A. J. PERLIS (Editors), *Software Reusability, Volumes I and II*, ACM Press, New York, 1989.

[Blaha, Premerlani, and Rumbaugh, 1988] M. R. BLAHA, W. J. PREMERLANI, AND J. E. RUMBAUGH, "Relational Database Design Using an Object-Oriented Methodology," *Communications of the ACM* **31** (April 1988), pp. 414–427.

[Bruegge, Blythe, Jackson, and Shufelt, 1992] B. BRUEGGE, J. BLYTHE, J. JACKSON, AND J. SHUFELT, "Object-Oriented Modeling with OMT," *Proceedings of the Conference on Object-Oriented Programming, Languages, and Systems, OOPSLA '92, ACM SIGPLAN Notices* **27** (October 1992), pp. 359–376.

[Caldiera and Basili, 1991] G. CALDIERA AND V. R. BASILI, "Identifying and Qualifying Reusable Software Components," *IEEE Computer* **24** (February 1991), pp. 61–70.

[Capper, Colgate, Hunter, and James, 1994] N. P. CAPPER, R. J. COLGATE, J. C. HUNTER, AND M. F. JAMES, "The Impact of Object-Oriented Technology on Software Quality: Three Case Histories," *IBM Systems Journal* **33** (No. 1, 1994), pp. 131–157.

[Cox, 1986] B. J. COX, *Object-Oriented Programming: An Evolutionary Approach,* Addison-Wesley, Reading, MA, 1986.

[Dahl and Nygaard, 1966] O.-J. DAHL AND K. NYGAARD, "SIMULA—An ALGOL-Based Simulation Language," *Communications of the ACM* **9** (September 1966), pp. 671–678.

[Dahl, Myrhaug, and Nygaard, 1973] O.-J. DAHL, B. MYRHAUG, AND K. NYGAARD, *SIMULA begin,* Auerbach, Philadelphia, 1973.

[Dijkstra, 1968b] E. W. DIJKSTRA, "The Structure of the 'THE' Multiprogramming System," *Communications of the ACM* **11** (May 1968), pp. 341–346.

[Feldman, 1981] M. B. FELDMAN, "Data Abstraction, Structured Programming, and the Practicing Programmer," *Software—Practice and Experience* **11** (July 1981), pp. 697–710.

[Flanagan, 1996] D. FLANAGAN, *Java in a Nutshell,* O'Reilly and Associates, Sebastopol, CA, 1996.

[Freeman, 1987] P. FREEMAN (Editor), *Tutorial: Software Reusability,* IEEE Computer Society Press, Washington, DC, 1987.

[Gargaro and Pappas, 1987] A. GARGARO AND T. L. PAPPAS, "Reusability Issues and Ada," *IEEE Software* **4** (July 1987), pp. 43–51.

[Goldberg and Robson, 1989] A. GOLDBERG AND D. ROBSON, *Smalltalk-80: The Language,* Addison-Wesley, Reading, MA, 1989.

[Guttag, 1977] J. GUTTAG, "Abstract Data Types and the Development of Data Structures," *Communications of the ACM* **20** (June 1977), pp. 396–404.

[ISO/IEC 8652, 1995] "Programming Language Ada: Language and Standard Libraries, ISO/IEC 8652, International Organization for Standardization, International Electrotechnical Commission, 1995.

[Jones, 1978] T. C. JONES, "Measuring Programming Quality and Productivity," *IBM Systems Journal* **17** (No. 1, 1978), pp. 39–63.

[Jones, 1984] T. C. JONES, "Reusability in Programming: A Survey of the State of the Art," *IEEE Transactions on Software Engineering* **SE-10** (September 1984), pp. 488–494.

[Joos, 1994] R. JOOS, "Software Reuse at Motorola," *IEEE Software* **11** (September 1994), pp. 42–47.

[Knuth, 1974] D. E. KNUTH, "Structured Programming with **go to** Statements," *ACM Computing Surveys* **6** (December 1974), pp. 261–301.

[Korson and McGregor, 1990] T. KORSON AND J. D. MCGREGOR, "Understanding Object-Oriented: A Unifying Paradigm," *Communications of the ACM* **33** (September 1990), pp. 40–60.

[Lanergan and Grasso, 1984] R. G. LANERGAN AND C. A. GRASSO, "Software Engineering with Reusable Designs and Code," *IEEE Transactions on Software Engineering* **SE-10** (September 1984), pp. 498–501.

[Lim, 1994] W. C. LIM, "Effects of Reuse on Quality, Productivity, and Economics," *IEEE Software* **11** (September 1994), pp. 23–30.

[Liskov and Guttag, 1986] B. LISKOV AND J. GUTTAG, *Abstraction and Specification in Program Development,* The MIT Press, Cambridge, MA, 1986.

[Liskov and Zilles, 1974] B. LISKOV AND S. ZILLES, "Programming with Abstract Data Types," *ACM SIGPLAN Notices* **9** (April 1974), pp. 50–59.

[Matsumoto, 1984] Y. MATSUMOTO, "Management of Industrial Software Production," *IEEE Computer* **17** (February 1984), pp. 59–72.

[Matsumoto, 1987] Y. MATSUMOTO, "A Software Factory: An Overall Approach to Software Production," in: *Tutorial: Software Reusability,* P. Freeman (Editor), Computer Society Press, Washington, DC, 1987, pp. 155–178.

[Meyer, 1986] B. MEYER, "Genericity versus Inheritance," *Proceedings of the Conference on Object-Oriented Programming Systems, Languages and Applications, ACM SIGPLAN Notices* **21** (November 1986), pp. 391–405.

[Meyer, 1987] B. MEYER, "Reusability: The Case for Object-Oriented Design," *IEEE Software* **4** (March 1987), pp. 50–64.

[Meyer, 1990] B. MEYER, "Lessons from the Design of the Eiffel Libraries," *Communications of the ACM* **33** (September 1990), pp. 68–88.

[Meyer, 1992a] B. MEYER, "Applying 'Design by Contract'," *IEEE Computer* **25** (October 1992), pp. 40–51.

[Meyer, 1992b] B. MEYER, *Eiffel: The Language,* Prentice-Hall, New York, 1992.

[Myers, 1975] G. J. MYERS, *Reliable Software through Composite Design,* Petrocelli/Charter, New York, 1975.

[Myers, 1978b] G. J. MYERS, *Composite/Structured Design,* Van Nostrand Reinhold, New York, 1978.

[Neumann, 1986] P. G. NEUMANN, "On Hierarchical Design of Computer Systems for Critical Applications," *IEEE Transactions on Software Engineering* **SE-12** (September 1986), pp. 905–920.

[Nissen and Wallis, 1984] J. NISSEN AND P. WALLIS (Editors), *Portability and Style in Ada,* Cambridge University Press, Cambridge, UK, 1984.

[Norusis, 1982] M. J. NORUSIS, *SPSS Introductory Guide: Basic Statistics and Operations,* McGraw-Hill, New York, 1982.

[Parnas, 1971] D. L. PARNAS, "Information Distribution Aspects of Design Methodology," *Proceedings of the IFIP Congress,* Ljubljana, Yugoslavia, 1971, pp. 339–344.

[Parnas, 1972a] D. L. PARNAS, "A Technique for Software Module Specification with Examples," *Communications of the ACM* **15** (May 1972), pp. 330–336.

[Parnas, 1972b] D. L. PARNAS, "On the Criteria to Be Used in Decomposing Systems into Modules," *Communications of the ACM* **15** (December 1972), pp. 1053–1058.

[Parnas, Clements, and Weiss, 1985] D. L. PARNAS, P. C. CLEMENTS, AND D. M. WEISS, "The Modular Structure of Complex Systems," *IEEE Transactions on Software Engineering* **SE-11** (March 1985), pp. 259–266.

[Phillips, 1986] J. PHILLIPS, *The NAG Library: A Beginner's Guide,* Clarendon Press, Oxford, UK, 1986.

[Ponder and Bush, 1994] C. PONDER AND B. BUSH, "Polymorphism Considered Harmful," *ACM SIGSOFT Software Engineering Notes* **19** (April, 1994), pp. 35–38.

[Prieto-Díaz, 1991] R. PRIETO-DÍAZ, "Implementing Faceted Classification for Software Reuse," *Communications of the ACM* **34** (May 1991), pp. 88–97.

[Prieto-Díaz, 1993] R. PRIETO-DÍAZ, "Status Report: Software Reusability," *IEEE Software* **10** (May 1993), pp. 61–66.

[Prieto-Díaz and Freeman, 1987] R. PRIETO-DÍAZ AND P. FREEMAN, "Classifying Software for Reusability," *IEEE Software* **4** (January 1987), pp. 6–16.

[Schach, 1992] S. R. SCHACH, *Software Reuse: Past, Present, and Future,* Videotape, 150 mins, US-VHS format. IEEE Computer Society Press, Los Alamitos, CA, November 1992.

[Schach, 1994] S. R. SCHACH, "The Economic Impact of Software Reuse on Maintenance," *Software Maintenance—Research and Practice* **6** (July/August 1994), pp. 185–196.

[Schach, 1996] S. R. SCHACH, "The Cohesion and Coupling of Objects," *Journal of Object-Oriented Programming* **8** (January 1966), pp. 48–50.

[Schach and Stevens-Guille, 1979] S. R. SCHACH AND P. D. STEVENS-GUILLE, "Two Aspects of Computer-Aided Design," *Transactions of the Royal Society of South Africa* **44** (Part 1, 1979), 123–126.

[Selby, 1989] R. W. SELBY, "Quantitative Studies of Software Reuse," in: *Software Reusability. Volume II: Applications and Experience,* T. J. Biggerstaff and A. J. Perlis (Editors), ACM Press, New York, 1989, pp. 213–233.

[Shaw, 1984] M. SHAW, "Abstraction Techniques in Modern Programming Languages," *IEEE Software* **1** (October 1984), pp. 10–26.

[Shneiderman and Mayer, 1975] B. SHNEIDERMAN AND R. MAYER, "Towards a Cognitive Model of Programmer Behavior," Technical Report TR-37, Indiana University, Bloomington, IN, 1975.

[Shriver and Wegner, 1987] B. SHRIVER AND P. WEGNER (Editors), *Research Directions in Object-Oriented Programming,* The MIT Press, Cambridge, MA, 1987.

[Snyder, 1993] A. SNYDER, "The Essence of Objects: Concepts and Terms," *IEEE Software* **10** (January 1993), pp. 31–42.

[Stefik and Bobrow, 1986] M. STEFIK AND D. G. BOBROW, "Object-Oriented Programming: Themes and Variations," *The AI Magazine* **6** (No. 4, 1986), pp. 40–62.

[Stevens, Myers, and Constantine, 1974] W. P. STEVENS, G. J. MYERS, AND L. L. CONSTANTINE, "Structured Design," *IBM Systems Journal* **13** (No. 2, 1974), pp. 115–139.

[Stroustrup, 1991] B. STROUSTRUP, *The C++ Programming Language,* Second Edition, Addison-Wesley, Reading, MA, 1991.

[Tanenbaum, 1990] A. S. TANENBAUM, *Structured Computer Organization,* Third Edition, Prentice-Hall, Englewood Cliffs, NJ, 1990.

[Tracz, 1988] W. TRACZ, "Software Reuse Myths," *ACM SIGSOFT Software Engineering Notes* **13** (January 1988), pp. 17–21.

[Tracz, 1994] W. TRACZ, "Software Reuse Myths Revisited," *Proceedings of the 16th International Conference on Software Engineering,* Sorrento, Italy, May 1994, pp. 271–272.

[Wildblood, 1990] A. WILDBLOOD, "Ada Reuse: The Promises Ring True," *Defense Science* **9** (April 1990), pp. 38–39.

[Young and Gregory, 1972] D. M. YOUNG AND R. T. GREGORY, *A Survey of Numerical Mathematics, Volume I,* Addison-Wesley, Reading, MA, 1972.

[Yourdon and Constantine, 1979] E. YOURDON AND L. L. CONSTANTINE, *Structured Design: Fundamentals of a Discipline of Computer Program and Systems Design,* Prentice-Hall, Englewood Cliffs, NJ, 1979.

2

THE PHASES OF THE SOFTWARE PROCESS

In Part Two the phases of the software process are described in depth. For each phase, the CASE tools, metrics, and testing techniques appropriate to that phase are also presented.

Chapter 7 is entitled "Requirements Phase." The aim of this phase is to determine the client's real needs. One technique for achieving this is rapid prototyping. Various types of rapid prototyping and other requirements analysis techniques are examined.

In Chapter 8, "Specification Phase," three approaches to specifications are presented, namely informal, semiformal, and formal. Instances of each approach are described. Techniques that are described in depth and illustrated by case studies include structured systems analysis, finite state machines, Petri nets, and Z. All of the techniques in this chapter are from the structured paradigm. The chapter concludes with a comparison of the various techniques.

"Object-Oriented Analysis Phase" is the title of Chapter 9. This specification technique is presented in detail and is contrasted with the structured approaches of the previous chapter. Strengths and weaknesses of the object-oriented paradigm are examined.

Chapter 10 is entitled "Planning Phase." Before starting a software project, it is essential to plan the entire operation in detail. Once the project begins, management must closely monitor progress, noting deviations from the plan and taking corrective action where necessary. Metrics for estimating project cost and duration are carefully analyzed. A detailed description of a software project management plan is given.

In Chapter 11, "Design Phase," three classes of design techniques are presented, namely data oriented, action oriented, and object oriented. Instances of each are described in detail, including data flow analysis, transaction analysis, Jackson system development, and object-oriented design; case studies are presented. Again, the emphasis is on comparison and contrast.

Implementation issues are discussed in Chapters 12 and 13. Chapter 12 is entitled "Implementation Phase." Areas covered include the choice of programming language, fourth-generation languages, good programming practice, and programming standards. The issue of programming team organization is handled in depth. An analysis is made of the advantages and disadvantages of democratic teams, chief programmer teams, and hybrid teams. The chapter concludes with a detailed discussion of portability, and a description of testing techniques and CASE tools for the implementation phase.

The implementation phase and integration phase should be performed in parallel. This is the subject of Chapter 13, "Implementation and Integration Phase." There is a description of how this combined phase is carried out. Finally, there is a discussion of CASE environments that support the complete software process.

Part Two concludes with Chapter 14, "Maintenance Phase." Topics covered in this chapter include the importance of maintenance and the challenge of maintenance. The management of maintenance is considered in some detail.

By the end of Part Two, the reader should have a clear understanding of all the phases of the software process, the difficulties associated with each phase, and how to solve those difficulties.

A detailed case study is presented in Part Two. At the end of each chapter, the appropriate phase of the case study is presented. Thus, requirements are presented in Chapter 7, specifications in Chapter 8 and 9, and so on.

Exercises have been set on the case study. Some of those exercises require access to the source code. This can be obtained by anonymous ftp from ftp.vuse.vanderbilt.edu (129.59.100.10) in directory /pub/Software_Eng/ Java. It is also available on diskette from Richard D. Irwin, 1333 Burr Ridge Parkway, Burr Ridge, Illinois 60521.

7

REQUIREMENTS PHASE

The chances of a product being developed on time and within budget are somewhat slim unless the members of the software development team agree on what the software product will do. The first step in achieving this unanimity is to analyze the client's current situation as precisely as possible. For example, it is inadequate to say: "They need a computer-aided design system because they claim their manual design system is lousy." Unless the development team knows exactly what is wrong with the current manual system, there is a high probability that aspects of the new computerized system will be equally "lousy." Similarly, if a personal computer manufacturer is contemplating development of a new operating system, the first step is to evaluate their current operating system and analyze exactly why it is unsatisfactory. To take an extreme example, it is vital to know whether the problem exists only in the mind of the sales manager who is attempting to blame the operating system for poor sales or whether users of the operating system are thoroughly disenchanted with its functionality and reliability. Only after a clear picture of the present situation has been gained can the team attempt to answer the critical question: What must the new product be able to do? The process of answering this question is carried out during the requirements phase.

A commonly held misconception is that during the requirements phase the developers must determine what software the client *wants*. On the contrary, the real objective of the requirements phase is to determine what software the client *needs*. The problem is that many clients do not know what they need. Furthermore, even if the client has a good idea of what is needed, he or she may have difficulty in accurately conveying these ideas to the developers, because most clients are less computer-literate than the members of the development team.

During the 1960s a U.S. presidential candidate put his foot into his mouth one time too many. Calling a press conference, he proceeded to announce: "I know you believe you understood what you think I said, but I am not sure you realize that what you heard is not what I meant!" This excuse applies equally well to the issue of requirements analysis. The developers hear their client's requests, but what they hear is not what the client should be saying.

In Chapter 3 it was pointed out that this communication-based problem can be solved by building a rapid prototype. In this chapter the requirements phase is described in greater detail, and the strengths and weaknesses of various requirements analysis techniques are described.

7.1   REQUIREMENTS ANALYSIS TECHNIQUES

Requirements analysis begins with members of the requirements team meeting with members of the client organization to determine what is needed in the target product. The client usually sets up the initial interviews. Additional interviews may be scheduled during the interview process. Interviews continue until the requirements team is convinced that it has elicited all relevant information from the client and future users of the product.

There are two basic types of interview, namely structured and unstructured. In a structured interview, specific preplanned close-ended questions are posed. For example, the client might be asked how many salespeople the company employs or how fast a response time is required. In an unstructured interview, open-ended questions are asked to encourage the person being interviewed to speak out. For instance, asking the client why the current product is unsatisfactory may explain many aspects of the client's approach to business. Some of these facts might not have come to light had the interview been more structured.

The interviewer prepares a written report outlining the results of the interview. It is a good idea to give a copy of the report to the people who were interviewed; they may want to clarify statements or add overlooked items.

Another way of eliciting needs is to send a questionnaire to the relevant members of the client organization. This technique is useful when the opinions of, say, hundreds of individuals need to be determined. Furthermore, a carefully thought-out written answer may be more accurate than an immediate verbal response to a question posed by an interviewer. However, an unstructured interview conducted by a methodical interviewer who listens carefully and poses questions that expand on initial responses will usually yield far better information than a thoughtfully worded questionnaire. Because questionnaires are preplanned, there is no way that a question can be posed in response to an answer.

A different way of obtaining information, particularly in a business environment, is to examine the various forms used by the client. For example, a form in a print shop might reflect press number, paper roll size, humidity, ink temperature, paper tension, and so on. The various fields in this form shed light on the flow of print jobs and the relative importance of various phases. Other documents, such as operating procedures and job descriptions, can also be powerful tools for finding out exactly what is done and how. Comprehensive information regarding how the client currently does business can be extraordinarily helpful in determining the client's needs.

A newer way of obtaining such information is to set up video cameras within the workplace to record exactly what is being done. This technique has been known to backfire badly because employees may view the cameras as an unwarranted invasion of privacy. It is important that the requirements analysis team have the full cooperation of all employees; if people feel threatened or harassed, it can be extremely difficult to obtain necessary information. The possible risks should be carefully considered before introducing video cameras or, for that matter, taking any other action that has the potential to anger employees.

Scenarios are another technique for requirements analysis. A scenario is a possible way a user can utilize the target product to accomplish some objective. For example, suppose the target product is a weight-loss planner. One possible scenario describes what happens when the dietitian enters the age, gender, height, and other personal data of an obese patient. The product then prints out sample menus for that patient. When this scenario is shown to a future user of the target product, the dietitian quickly points out that the menus would be unsuitable for a patient with special food requirements, such as a diabetic, a vegetarian, or someone who is lactose intolerant. The developers modify the scenario so that the user is asked about special dietary needs before any menus are printed. The use of scenarios enables users to communicate their needs to the requirements analysts.

A scenario can be depicted in a number of ways. One technique is a story board, a series of diagrams depicting the sequence of events. A story board can be considered to be a paper prototype [Rettig, 1994], that is, a series of sheets of paper each depicting the relevant screen and the user's response.

Sometimes scenarios are best represented by a tree. The nodes of the tree correspond to specific screens, and the branches represent the possible actions that the user can take at that point in the scenario. Scenarios are also used in object-oriented analysis (Section 9.3.2) to help determine all the actions performed by or to each class.

Scenarios are useful in a number of different ways. First, they can demonstrate the behavior of the product in a way that is comprehensible to the user. This can result in additional requirements coming to light, as in the weight-loss planner example. Second, because scenarios can be understood by users, the utilization of scenarios can ensure that the client and users play an active role throughout the requirements analysis process. After all, the aim of the requirements analysis phase is to elicit the real needs of the client, and the only source of this information is the client and the users.

The most accurate and powerful requirements analysis technique is rapid prototyping, described in the next section.

7.2 RAPID PROTOTYPING

A rapid prototype is hastily built software that exhibits the key functionality of the target product. For example, a product that helps to manage an apartment complex must incorporate an input screen that allows the user to enter details of a new tenant and print an occupancy report for each month. These aspects will be incorporated in the rapid prototype. However, error-checking capabilities, file-updating routines, and complex tax computations will probably not be included. The key point is that a rapid prototype reflects the functionality that the client sees, such as input screens and reports, but omits "hidden" aspects such as file updating. (For a different way of looking at rapid prototypes, see the Just in Case You Wanted to Know box on page 200.)

JUST IN CASE YOU WANTED TO KNOW

The idea of constructing models to show key aspects of a product goes back a long time. For example, a 1618 painting by Domenico Cresti (known as "Il Passignano") shows Michelangelo presenting a wooden model of his design for St. Peter's (in Rome) to Pope Paul IV. Architectural models could be huge; a model of an earlier design proposal for St. Peter's by the architect Bramante is more than 20 feet long on each side.

Architectural models were used for a number of different purposes. First, as depicted in the Cresti painting (now hanging in Casa Buonarroti in Florence), models were used to try to interest a client in funding a project. This is analogous to the use of a rapid prototype to determine the client's real needs.

Second, in an age before architectural drawings, the model showed the builder the structure of the building and indicated to the stone masons how the building was to be decorated. This is similar to the way we now build a rapid prototype of the user interface, as described in Section 7.3.

It is not a good idea, however, to draw too close a parallel between such architectural models and software rapid prototypes. Rapid prototypes are used during the requirements phase to elicit the client's needs. Unlike architectural models, they are not used to represent either the architectural design or the detailed design; the design is produced three phases later, that is, during the design phase.

The client and intended users of the product now experiment with the rapid prototype, with members of the development team watching and taking notes. Based on hands-on experience, users tell the developers how the rapid prototype satisfies their needs and, more importantly, identify the areas that need improvement. The developers change the rapid prototype until both sides are convinced that the needs of the client are accurately encapsulated in the rapid prototype. The rapid prototype is then used as the basis for drawing up the specifications.

An important aspect of the rapid prototyping model is embodied in the word *rapid*. The whole idea is to build the rapid prototype as quickly as possible. After all, the purpose of the rapid prototype is to provide the client with an understanding of the product, and the sooner, the better. It does not matter if the rapid prototype hardly works, if it crashes every few minutes, or if the screen layouts are less than perfect. The purpose of the rapid prototype is to enable the client and the developers to agree as quickly as possible on what the product is to do. Thus any imperfections in the rapid prototype may be ignored, provided that they do not seriously impair the functionality of the rapid prototype and thereby give a misleading impression of how the product will behave.

A second major aspect of the rapid prototyping model is that the rapid prototype must be built for change. If the first version of the rapid prototype is not what the client needs, then the prototype must be transformed rapidly into a second version that, it is hoped, will better satisfy the client's requirements. In order to achieve rapid development throughout the rapid prototyping process, fourth-generation languages (4GL) and interpreted languages, such as Smalltalk, Prolog, Lisp, and Java, are used for rapid prototyping purposes. The UNIX shell programming language is being used more and more for constructing rapid prototypes because it is an interpreted language that is supported by the UNIX Programmer's Workbench, a powerful and comprehensive set of CASE tools. Another popular technique is to use hypertext. Concerns have been expressed about the maintainability of certain interpreted languages, but from the viewpoint of classic rapid prototyping this is irrelevant. All that counts is: Can a given language be used to produce a rapid prototype quickly? And can the rapid prototype be changed quickly? If the answer to both questions is yes, then the language is probably a good candidate for rapid prototyping.

Turning now to the use of rapid prototyping in conjunction with the object-oriented paradigm, three very different object-oriented projects carried out by IBM showed significant improvements compared to projects using the structured paradigm [Capper, Colgate, Hunter, and James, 1994]. One of the recommendations that resulted from these projects is that it is important to build a rapid prototype as early as possible in the object-oriented life cycle.

Rapid prototyping is also particularly effective when developing the user interface to a product. This use is discussed in the next section.

7.3   HUMAN FACTORS

It is important that both the client and the future users of the product interact with the rapid prototype of the user interface. Encouraging users to experiment with the human–computer interface (HCI) greatly reduces the risk that the finished product will have to be altered. In particular, this experimentation will help achieve user friendliness, a vital objective for all software products.

The term *user friendliness* refers to the ease with which human beings can communicate with the software product. If users have difficulty in learning how to use a product or find the screens confusing or irritating, then they will either not use the product or use it incorrectly. To try to eliminate this problem, menu-driven products were introduced. Instead of having to enter a command such as **Perform computation** or **Print service rate report**, the user merely has to select from a set of possible responses, such as

1.   Perform computation

2.   Print service rate report

3.   Select view to be graphed

In this example, the user enters 1, 2, or 3 in order to invoke the corresponding command.

Nowadays, instead of simply displaying lines of text, HCIs employ graphics. Windows, icons, and pull-down menus are components of a graphical user interface (GUI). Because of the plethora of windowing systems, standards such as X Windows are evolving. Also, "point and click" selection is becoming the norm. The user moves a mouse (that is, a hand-held pointing device), to move the screen cursor to the desired response ("point") and pushes a mouse button ("click") to select that response.

However, even when the target product employs modern technology, the designers must never forget that the product is to be used by human beings. In other words, the HCI designers must consider *human factors* such as size of letters, capitalization, color, line length, and the number of lines on the screen.

Another example of human factors applies to the above menu. If the user chooses option **3. Select view to be graphed,** then another menu will appear with another list of choices. Unless a menu-driven system is thoughtfully designed, there is the danger that users will encounter a lengthy sequence of menus, even to achieve a relatively simple operation. This delay can anger users, sometimes causing them to make inappropriate menu selections. Also, the HCI must allow the user to change a previous selection without having to return to the first menu level. This problem can exist even when a GUI is used because many graphical user interfaces are essentially a series of menus displayed in an attractive screen format.

Sometimes it is impossible for a single user interface to cater to all users. For example, if a product is to be used by both computer professionals and high-school dropouts with no previous computer experience, then it is preferable that two different sets of HCIs be designed, each carefully tailored to the skill level and psychological profile of its intended users. This technique can be extended by incorporating sets of user interfaces requiring varied levels of sophistication [Schach and Wood, 1986]. If the product deduces that the user would be more comfortable with a less sophisticated user interface, perhaps because the user is making frequent mistakes or is continually invoking help facilities, then the user is automatically shown screens that are more appropriate to his or her current skill level. But as the user becomes more familiar with the product, streamlined screens that provide less information are displayed, leading to speedier completion. This automated approach reduces user frustration and increases productivity.

Many benefits can accrue when human factors are taken into account during the design of an HCI, including reduced learning times and lower error rates. Although help facilities must always be provided, they will be utilized less with a carefully designed HCI. This, too, will increase productivity. Uniformity of HCI appearance across a product or group of products can result in users intuitively knowing how to use a screen they have never seen before because it is similar to other screens with which they are familiar. Designers of Macintosh software have taken this principle into account; this is one of the many reasons that software for the Macintosh is generally so user friendly.

It has been suggested that simple common sense is all that is needed to design a user friendly HCI. Whether or not this charge is true, it is essential that a rapid prototype of the HCI of every product be constructed. Intended users of the product can experiment with the rapid prototype of the HCI and inform the designers whether the target product will indeed be user friendly, that is, whether the designers have taken the necessary human factors into account.

In the next two sections, superficially attractive but dangerous variants of the rapid prototyping model are discussed.

7.4   RAPID PROTOTYPING AS A SPECIFICATION TECHNIQUE

The conventional form of the rapid prototyping model, as described in Section 3.3 and depicted in Figure 3.3, is reproduced here as Figure 7.1. (Again, the implementation and integration steps will generally be performed in parallel.) The rapid prototype is used solely to determine the client's needs accurately and is discarded after the client signs off on the specifications. That is, rapid prototyping is used as a requirements analysis technique. A second approach is to dispense with specifications as such and to use the rapid prototype itself either as the specifications or as a significant part of the specifications. This second type of rapid prototyping model is shown in Figure 7.2. This approach offers both speed and accuracy. No time is wasted drawing up written specifications; and the difficulties associated with specifications, such as ambiguities, omissions, and contradictions, cannot arise. Instead, because the rapid prototype constitutes the specifications, all that needs to be done is to state that the product will do what the rapid prototype does and to list any additional features that the product must support, such as file updating, security, and error handling.

This version of the rapid prototyping model can have a major drawback. If there is a disagreement as to whether the developers have satisfactorily discharged their obligations, it is unlikely that a rapid prototype will stand as a legal statement of a contract between developer and client. For this reason, using the rapid prototype as the sole specification should never be done, not even if the software is developed internally (that is, when the client and developers are members of the same organization). After all, it is unlikely that the head of the investment management division of a bank will take the data-processing division to court. Nevertheless, disagreements between client and developers can arise just as easily within an organization. Thus, in order to protect themselves, software developers should not use the rapid prototype as the specifications even when software is developed internally. The only exception is when the client and developer are one and the same person.

A second reason that the rapid prototype should not take the place of written specifications is potential problems with maintenance. Because there are no written specifications, during the maintenance phase the current specifications are simply the current version of the product, and changes to the specifications must be made in terms of the functionality of the current version of the product. As described in Chapter 14, maintenance is challenging even when all the documentation is available and up-to-date. If there are no specifications, maintenance can rapidly become a nightmare. The problem is particularly acute in the case of enhancement, where changes in requirements have to be implemented. It can be exceedingly difficult to change the design documents to reflect the new specifications because, in the absence

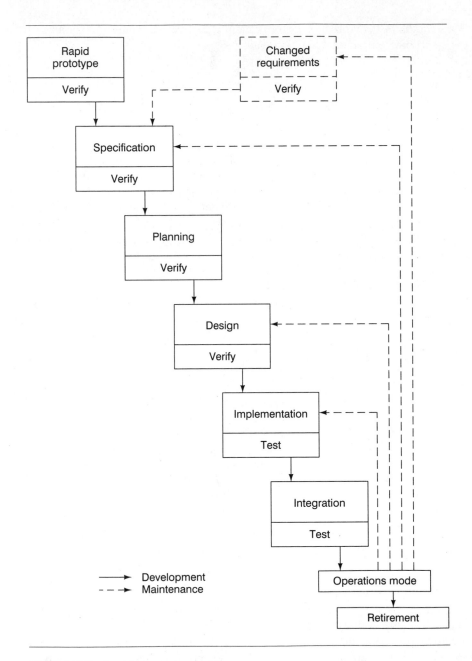

Figure 7.1   Rapid prototyping model.

of written specifications, the maintenance team will not have a clear statement of the current specifications.

For both these reasons, the rapid prototype should simply be used as a requirements analysis technique, that is, as a means of determining the client's real needs.

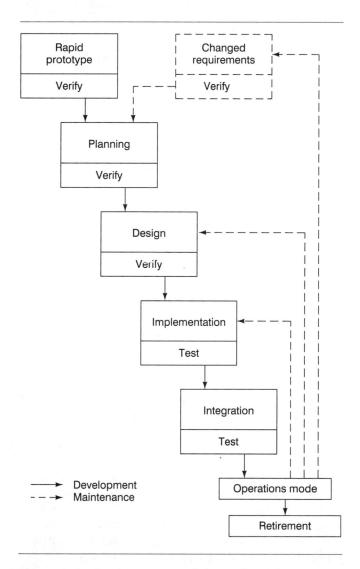

Figure 7.2 Rapid prototyping with the rapid prototype serving as specifications.

Thereafter, written specification documents should be produced using the rapid prototype as a basis.

7.5 REUSING THE RAPID PROTOTYPE

In both versions of the rapid prototyping model discussed previously, the rapid prototype is discarded early in the software process. An alternate, but generally unwise, way of proceeding is to develop and refine the rapid prototype until it

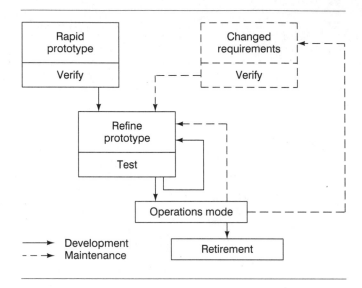

Figure 7.3   Unwise version of rapid prototyping model.

becomes the product. This is shown in Figure 7.3. In theory, this approach should lead to fast software development; after all, instead of throwing away the code constituting the rapid prototype, as well as the knowledge built into it, the rapid prototype is converted into the final product. However, in practice the process is very similar to the build-and-fix approach of Figure 3.1. Thus, as with the build-and-fix model, the first problem with this form of the rapid prototyping model follows from the fact that, in the course of refining the rapid prototype, changes have to be made to a working product. This is an expensive way to proceed, as shown in Figure 1.5. A different problem is that a primary objective when constructing a rapid prototype is speed of building. A rapid prototype is (correctly) hurriedly put together, rather than carefully specified, designed, and then implemented. In the absence of specification and design documents, the resulting code is difficult and expensive to maintain. It might seem wasteful to construct a rapid prototype and then to throw it away and design the product from scratch, but it is far cheaper in both the short term and the long term to do this rather than to try to convert a rapid prototype into production quality software [Brooks, 1975].

Another reason for discarding the rapid prototype is the issue of performance, particularly of real-time systems. In order to ensure that time constraints are met, it is necessary to design the product carefully. In contrast, a rapid prototype is constructed so as to display key functionality to the client; performance issues are not handled. As a result, if an attempt is made to refine a rapid prototype into a delivered product, it is unlikely that response times and other timing constraints will be met.

One way of ensuring that the rapid prototype is thrown away and that the product is properly designed and implemented is to build the rapid prototype in a different language from that of the product. For example, the client may specify that the product must be written in Java. If the rapid prototype is implemented in hypertext, for example, it will have to be discarded. First, the rapid prototype is implemented in hypertext and refined until the client is satisfied that it does everything, or almost everything, that the target product is to do. Next the product is designed, relying on the knowledge and skills acquired in constructing the rapid prototype. Finally, the design is implemented in Java, and the tested product handed over to the client in the usual way.

Nevertheless, there is one instance when it is permissible to refine a rapid prototype or, more specifically, portions of the rapid prototype. When portions of the rapid prototype are computer-generated, then those portions may be used in the final product. For example, user interfaces are often a key aspect of a rapid prototype (Section 7.3). When CASE tools such as screen generators and report generators (Section 4.3.1) have been utilized to generate the user interfaces, then those portions of the rapid prototype may indeed be used as part of production quality software.

The desire not to "waste" the rapid prototype has resulted in a modified version of the rapid prototyping model being adopted by some organizations. Here, management decides *before* the rapid prototype is built that portions may be utilized in the final product, provided that those portions pass the same quality assurance tests as other software components. Thus, after the rapid prototype is complete, those sections that the developers wish to continue to use must pass design and code inspections. This approach goes beyond rapid prototyping. For example, components that are of sufficiently high quality to pass design and code inspections are not usually found in a rapid prototype. Furthermore, design documents are not part of classic rapid prototyping. Nevertheless, this hybrid approach is attractive to some organizations, hoping to recover some of the time and money invested in the rapid prototype. However, in order to ensure that the quality of its code is sufficiently high, the rapid prototype will have to be built somewhat more slowly than is customary for a "rapid" prototype.

7.6 OTHER USES OF RAPID PROTOTYPING

A different use of rapid prototyping is as a means of arriving at consensus where there is disagreement as to the client's requirements. The author was once called in to advise a committee of six top executives of a major corporation with regard to the development of a management information system (MIS) [Blair, Murphy, Schach, and McDonald, 1988]. A requirement of the product was that one-page reports had to be printed incorporating month-by-month information for a full year. Each member of the committee then insisted that every one-page report had to incorporate data from his or her specific area of responsibility. Because there were six areas in all, this was clearly impossible. The solution was to construct a rapid prototype. Within 4 person-days, a working product was constructed; it computed the relevant quantities and printed a one-page report incorporating what the author felt was the most important management information. The rapid prototype was partially acceptable to the management team, the necessary changes were made rapidly, and within 4 weeks the complete operational quality product was in place. Without rapid prototyping, consensus would not have been reached as quickly and as amicably. In fact, it is possible that no consensus at all could have been achieved, and the product would never have then been developed.

Management implications of the rapid prototyping model are now considered.

7.7   MANAGEMENT IMPLICATIONS OF THE RAPID PROTOTYPING MODEL

One difficulty with rapid prototyping is that the ease with which changes can generally be made to a rapid prototype may encourage the client to request all sorts of major changes to the delivered operational quality version of the product. Furthermore, the client may expect the changes to be implemented as rapidly as were changes to the rapid prototype. This was the author's experience with the MIS described previously. A related problem is having to explain to the client that the rapid prototype is not of operational quality and that the client will have to wait for the operational quality version, despite the fact that the rapid prototype appears to do everything needed. Before rapid prototyping is used, it is essential that the managers responsible for developing the product discuss these and related issues with the client.

As with the introduction of any new technology, before an organization introduces the rapid prototyping model it is vital that management be aware of the advantages and disadvantages of rapid prototyping. In all fairness, while the case for rapid prototyping is a strong one, it has not yet been proved beyond all doubt. For example, a frequently quoted experiment is that of Boehm, Gray, and Seewaldt who compared seven different versions of a product [Boehm, Gray, and Seewaldt, 1984]. Four versions were specified and three were prototyped with the rapid prototype serving as the specifications. The results were that rapid prototyping and specifying yielded products with roughly equivalent performance, but the prototyped versions contained about 40 percent less code and required about 45 percent less effort. The reason was that the specification teams had no compunctions about adding bells and whistles to the specification document. On the other hand, the rapid prototypers realized that they would have to build every feature into the rapid prototype and were, therefore, reluctant to incorporate any functionality that did not seem to be essential. With on average 40 percent less code, it is not surprising that the prototyped versions were rated somewhat lower on functionality and robustness. But interestingly enough, they were rated higher on ease of use and ease of learning. Finally, specifying produced more coherent designs and software that was easier to integrate.

One important point about this experiment was that it was conducted on seven teams of graduate students, three two-member teams and four three-member teams. The project was only 10 weeks in duration, and no maintenance of the product was performed. In other words, the experiment is not typical of real products with respect to number of participants, team size, project size, or software process. It is therefore perhaps unwise to accept Boehm's results as a blanket endorsement for rapid prototyping. Instead, they should be taken as indications of the comparative strengths and weaknesses of rapid prototyping when compared to specifying. In addition to the weaknesses pointed out previously, Boehm and his collaborators found that prototyped products are harder to integrate than specified products. Ease of integration is important for large-scale products, especially C^4I (command, control, communications, computers, and intelligence) software. This is a further reason to use the rapid prototyping model depicted in Figure 7.1 where rapid prototyping is employed as a requirements analysis technique and not to use the model of Figure 7.2 where rapid prototyping replaces specifying.

Two aspects of rapid prototyping must be taken into account by any manager. In Section 7.4 it was pointed out that it is short-sighted to turn a rapid prototype into the final product; the rapid prototype should be used solely as a means of accurately determining the client's requirements. A second important issue is that under some circumstances rapid prototyping can take the place of the specifications phase; it can *never* replace the design phase. A team can certainly use the information and experience gained from the rapid prototype as a guide to fashioning a good design; however, because the rapid prototype is rapidly thrown together, it is unlikely that a good rapid prototype will have a good design.

A more fundamental issue is that managing the rapid prototyping model requires a major change in outlook for a manager who is accustomed to managing only the waterfall model. The concept underlying the waterfall model is to do things correctly the first time. Certainly the waterfall model incorporates a number of feedback loops if the team does not accomplish this goal (and the goal is seldom, if ever, reached). However, the ideal for the waterfall model team is to perform each phase of the development process one time only. In contrast, a rapid prototype is specifically built to be changed frequently and then thrown away. This concept is diametrically opposed to the approach to which the average manager is accustomed. The rapid prototyping approach of taking several iterations to get it right is probably a more realistic approach than the first-time-right waterfall model expectation, and this logic may help convince a manager to change to the rapid prototyping model.

Another aspect of the rapid prototyping model that requires a different approach on the part of the manager is the increased interaction between the client and the developers, particularly the rapid prototyping team. In the waterfall model, interaction between client and developers is essentially restricted to a series of interviews between the requirements team and the client and his or her employees. When rapid prototyping is used, there is almost continual interaction between the rapid prototyping team and the client's team until the rapid prototype has been accepted.

7.8 EXPERIENCES WITH RAPID PROTOTYPING

Gordon and Bieman have analyzed 39 published and unpublished case studies that use rapid prototyping [Gordon and Bieman, 1995]. Of these 33 were considered successes, 3 were considered failures, and 3 were not rated. Gordon and Bieman have pointed out that studies of unsuccessful cases are rarely published. Consequently, they do not claim that their analysis reflects a high success rate as a consequence of rapid prototyping. Their work is rather a report on a number of commercial software projects in which rapid prototyping was used with some success.

Not all the case studies, as published, reflected every issue of interest. For example, comments on ease of use appeared in only 17 of the case studies. In all 17 instances, improved ease of use of the delivered product as a consequence of rapid prototyping was reported; none of the other 22 case studies claimed that the product was harder to use. Thus, although the data are incomplete and specific topics may not be explicitly mentioned, it is possible to draw some conclusions.

All the case studies that commented on user participation reported enthusiastic user participation early in the process. It was also found that rapid prototyping meets client needs. There was less unanimity in other issues. For example, four sources reported that rapid prototyping resulted in smaller delivered products, while one reported increased code size. Many case studies mentioned that fewer unnecessary features were implemented with rapid prototyping, but two reported an increase in such features.

Choice of language for rapid prototyping does not appear to be of critical importance. A total of 26 different languages were used in the 39 case studies. The most popular languages were Lisp (4 instances) and Smalltalk (3 instances).

The most controversial part of the results relates to whether or not the rapid prototype should be discarded. It is difficult to reach definite conclusions on this issue, because of the wide variety of software processes that were used. In some cases the rapid prototype as a whole was successfully refined until it became the final product. In others only part of the rapid prototype was retained, and the rest was discarded. In one instance a design phase was required for each iteration of the rapid prototype. For some of the case studies, management specified in advance that the rapid prototype would be retained and refined. Twenty-two of the cases specifically recommended retaining and refining all or part of the rapid prototype, and eight insisted that it be discarded. It has been suggested that retaining the rapid prototype is particularly important for large products. Of the 39 case studies, 7 were considered large (over 100,000 lines of code), and all 7 recommended retaining all or part of the rapid prototype. In view of the generally held belief that rapid prototypes for large products should be discarded, further research needs to be conducted in this area. In particular, it is important to know whether the modified rapid prototyping model described at the end of Section 7.5 was followed, that is, whether management decided *before* the rapid prototypes were built that portions might be utilized in the final product and if the parts that the developers wished to retain passed design and code inspections.

A number of tentative conclusions can be drawn from this work. The first is that rapid prototyping is a viable technique that can lead to successful software development. At the same time, there are a number of possible risks. If the rapid prototype is retained, there is a danger that the resulting product will be poorly designed, hard to maintain, and perform poorly; these risks appear to grow in proportion to the size of the product. However, the risks can be reduced. One way is to use the modified version of rapid prototyping described in Section 7.4.

There is a difference between reporting on case studies and conducting controlled experiments. But bearing in mind that controlled experimentation in software engineering can be extremely difficult, one alternative is to learn from the experiences of others.

7.9 JOINT APPLICATION DESIGN

When rapid prototyping is used for the requirements phase, the role of the members of the client organization is largely restricted to responding to actions of the developers. In contrast, joint application design (JAD) is an extended form of rapid prototyping in which the client organization plays a more active role. Notwithstanding the name joint application *design,* JAD is a technique for the requirements and specification phases in which members of the development and client organizations work as a team and take joint responsibility for the result.

A joint team, consisting of representatives of both the development organization and the client organization, discusses the needs of the client. The team designs the screens and reports, builds the rapid prototype, and draws up the specification document. The client organization takes an active, rather than reactive, role in the first two phases of the software process.

As a consequence of team synergy, productivity increases of between 20 percent and 60 percent have been reported [Gibson and Jackson, 1987]. An important proviso for the success of this technique is that the JAD team leader should not have a vested interest in the success of the project. The aim of the team leader should be to obtain consensus without having a specific interest in the decisions [Gane, 1989]; the leader must therefore be a skilled facilitator.

7.10 COMPARISON OF REQUIREMENTS ANALYSIS TECHNIQUES

The primary requirements analysis technique is interviewing (Section 7.1). To illustrate, suppose that the requirements analysis team decides at the start of the project to build a rapid prototype. Before the first iteration of the rapid prototype can be built, however, it is necessary for the team to interview the relevant client personnel. The more thorough these interviews, the greater is the probability that this first iteration will accurately reflect the client's needs. On the other hand, simply throwing together a rapid prototype and then going through a lengthy refinement process will not be time- or cost-effective.

Interviewing is also required if the forms technique is used (Section 7.1). Careful perusal of forms, reports, and job descriptions can be extremely useful. However, the only way to be sure of the accuracy of the information gleaned from this process is to interview the relevant members of the client organization. Finally, if JAD is used (Section 7.9), the developers on the joint client-developer team have to interview the client members in order to start the process, just as when rapid prototyping is used.

Consequently, as claimed at the beginning of this section, interviewing is indeed the primary requirements analysis technique. On the other hand, it was pointed out in Section 7.1 that rapid prototyping is the most accurate requirements analysis technique. Rapid prototyping results in the construction of a working model of the product and is more likely to meet the client's real needs than other techniques.

It is appropriate that any combination of requirements techniques must include interviewing. In addition, unless rapid prototyping or a related technique such as JAD is utilized, there is a significant risk that the requirements analysis phase will not be adequately performed and that the target product will not completely meet the client's needs.

7.11   T ESTING   DURING   THE   R EQUIREMENTS   P HASE

Although the aim of the requirements phase is to establish the client's real needs, usually the client will not be the primary user of the target product. It is therefore essential to give the users the opportunity to experiment with the rapid prototype and to suggest changes that, when approved by the client, will be implemented in the delivered version of the software product.

Thus the role of the software quality assurance (SQA) group during the rapid prototyping phase is to ensure that the relevant individuals in the client organization have the opportunity to interact with the rapid prototype and to make sure that their suggestions actually reach the client or, perhaps, a committee of client managers responsible for analyzing the suggestions of the users.

7.12   CASE   T OOLS   FOR   THE   R EQUIREMENTS   P HASE

Interpreted languages generally serve as good media for rapid prototyping. Because interpreted languages do not need to be compiled or linked, the development of the rapid prototype is faster. Interpreted languages are, in general, less efficient to execute than compiled languages, and difficulties with maintenance have been associated with some interpreted languages. However, neither of these issues is relevant within the context of rapid prototyping. The key point is that a rapid prototype is rapidly put together and then discarded, and most interpreted languages are ideal for this purpose.

Further efficiency can be gained by using CASE tools associated with the rapid prototyping language. For example, Smalltalk has an environment that assists the user with a variety of tools and speeds up the rapid prototyping process. The Interlisp environment is a similar product that assists Lisp programmers. As previously mentioned, the UNIX shell programming language is being used more and more for constructing rapid prototypes. Hypertext is another important and widely used rapid prototyping language. If it has been decided that the rapid prototype will be discarded (as described in Section 7.8), then hypertext has a further advantage. It is almost inconceivable that the delivered product will be written in hypertext, so use of hypertext virtually guarantees that the rapid prototype will be discarded.

With regard to rapid prototyping of user interfaces, two popular CASE tools are Demo II and Guide. Hypertext is especially useful for rapid prototyping of user interfaces. Examples of hypertext CASE tools are Hypercard and Hypertalk.

A recent trend is the widespread use of fourth-generation languages (4GL) such as Focus, Informix, Natural, Nomad, and Powerhouse for rapid prototyping. There are a number of reasons for this. First, a design goal of every 4GL is that fewer statements are needed to achieve the same functionality than with a third-generation language like COBOL, Ada, or C++. Thus the rapid prototype is likely to be delivered more rapidly when a 4GL is used. Second, many 4GLs are interpreted. This speeds up rapid prototyping, as explained at the beginning of this section. Third, many 4GLs are supported by powerful CASE tools, thus speeding up the rapid prototyping process even more.

On the other hand, the use of a 4GL for rapid prototyping can have an inherent disadvantage. The CASE environment in which a 4GL is embedded is frequently part of a larger set of tools to be used for the complete software process. The software process that is usually recommended by a 4GL supplier is to build the rapid prototype and then to refine it successively until it becomes the final product. After all, the supplier frequently does not care if the software process degenerates into the build-and-fix model; unfortunately, the sole aim of many 4GL suppliers is to ensure that development organizations purchase their product, a single CASE environment which can handle all aspects of a project.

Suppose that a software development manager has just paid tens if not hundreds of thousands of dollars for a CASE environment that will support every phase of the software process. It is certainly not easy to convince that manager to spend still more money on a workbench for a different language to be used for rapid prototyping in order to ensure that rapid prototypes can be discarded. The manager may well retort that he or she has purchased a perfectly good rapid prototyping tool as part of the new environment and is now being asked to throw away money buying an unnecessary additional rapid prototyping tool so that rapid prototypes can be thrown away! The manager must be shown that the cost of a rapid prototyping tool or workbench is small compared to the potentially huge expense of trying to convert a rapid prototype into production quality software and then attempting to maintain that product.

7.13   METRICS FOR THE REQUIREMENTS PHASE

Bearing in mind that software quality and reliability are not important when building a rapid prototype, measures such as defect rates or mean time between failures are less meaningful within the context of rapid prototyping than in later phases. What is important is how rapidly the rapid prototyping team determines the client's real needs. So a useful metric during this phase is a measure of requirements volatility. Keeping a record of how frequently the requirements change during the requirements phase gives management a way of determining the rate at which the rapid prototyping team converges on the actual requirements of the product. This metric has the further advantage that it can be applied to any requirements analysis technique, such as interviews or scenarios.

Another measure of how well the requirements team is doing its job is the number of requirements that change during the rest of the software development process. If a large number of requirements have to be changed during the specification, design, and subsequent phases, then it is clear that the way that the team carries out the requirements phase should be thoroughly analyzed. Again, this metric is applicable not just to rapid prototyping, but also to all the other techniques described in section 7.1.

A useful metric when rapid prototyping is used is the number of times each feature of the rapid prototype is tried when the client and users experiment with the rapid prototype. For example, if every user selects Screen J from the menu at least once but no one ever chooses Screen B, then the development team should ask the client about those two screens. Specifically, the developers need to know whether Screen J is so important that the design should minimize execution time for that screen and whether Screen B even needs to be included in the product. If so, then at least one user should experiment with Screen B; it is vital that all screens meet the user's needs.

7.14   MSG CASE STUDY: REQUIREMENTS PHASE

When Martha Stockton Greengage died at the age of 87, she left her entire $2 billion fortune to charity. Specifically, her will set up the Martha Stockton Greengage Foundation (MSG) to assist young couples in purchasing their own homes.

In order to reduce operating expenses, the trustees of MSG are investigating computerization. Because none of the trustees has any experience with computers, they decide to commission a small software organization to implement a pilot project, namely, using a computer to perform the calculation to determine how much money is available each week to purchase homes. Members of the development organization interview various MSG managers and staffers and discover the way the foundation works. MSG grants a 100 percent mortgage to buy a home under the following conditions.

1.   The couple has been legally married for at least 1 year but not more than 10 years.

2.   Both man and woman are gainfully employed. Specifically, proof must be provided that both were employed full-time for at least 48 weeks of the preceding year.

3. The price of the home must be below the published median price for homes in that area for the past 12 months.

4. The installments on a fixed-rate 30-year 90 percent mortgage would exceed 28 percent of their combined gross income and/or they do not have sufficient savings to pay 10 percent of the cost of the home plus $7,000. (The $7,000 is an estimate of the additional costs involved, such as closing costs, points, and so on.)

5. The foundation has sufficient funds to purchase the home; this is described below in more detail.

If the applicant is approved, then the amount that the couple must pay MSG every week for the next 30 years is computed as follows:

1. The capital repayment is 1/1560th of the purchase price of the home.

2. The interest payment is 1/52 of 4 percent of the current mortgage balance.

3. The escrow payment is 1/52nd of the sum of the annual property tax and the annual homeowner's insurance premium.

4. The total amount to be paid that week to MSG is the sum of (1), (2), and (3).

5. If (4) is greater than 28 percent of the couple's gross weekly income, then MSG will pay the difference in the form of a grant. Thus the mortgage is paid in full each week, but the couple will never have to pay more than 28 percent of their combined gross income.

The couple must provide a copy of their income tax return each year so that MSG has proof of the previous year's income. In addition, the couple may file copies of pay slips as proof of current gross income. The amount the couple has to pay for their mortgage may therefore vary from week to week.

MSG determines whether it has the funds to approve a mortgage application as follows:

1. At the beginning of each week, the expected annual income from its investments is computed and divided by 52.

2. The expected annual MSG operating expenses are divided by 52.

3. The total of the expected mortgage payments for that week is computed.

4. The total of the expected grants for that week is computed.

5. The amount available is then (1) − (2) + (3) − (4).

6. If the cost of the home is no more than (5), then MSG deems that it has the funds needed to purchase the home.

7. At the end of the week, any unspent funds are invested by MSG investment advisors.

To keep the cost of the pilot project as low as possible, the developers are told that only those data items needed for the weekly funds computation should be incorporated into the product. The rest can be added later if MSG decides to computerize all aspects of its operation. Therefore, only three types of data are needed, namely investment data, operating expenses data, and mortgage data. There is no need to incorporate the action MSG takes if mortgagees fail to make their weekly payment, as the records show that this is infrequent.

With regard to investments, the following data are required:

Item number (12 digits)

Item name

Expected annual return (up to $999,999,999.99)

> (This figure is updated whenever new information becomes available. On average, this occurs about four time a year.)

Date expected annual return was updated

With regard to operating expenses, the following data are required:

Expected annual operating expenses (up to $999,999,999.99)

> (This figure is currently computed four times a year.)

For each mortgage, the following data are required:

Account number (12 digits)

Last name of mortgagees

> (If husband and wife have different last names, then this field contains the last name of the husband, followed by a hyphen, followed by the last name of the wife

Original purchase price of home (up to $999,999.99)

Date mortgage was issued

Current combined gross weekly income (up to $999,999.99)

Date combined gross weekly income was updated

Annual property tax (up to $99,999.99)

Annual homeowner's insurance premium (up to $99,999.99)

Mortgage balance (up to $999,999.99)

Routines are required to add, modify, and delete investment and mortgage data; to adjust the value of the annual operating expenses; and to perform the weekly computation regarding availability of funds to purchase homes. Three types of reports are needed, namely a listing of all investments, a listing of all mortgages (both to be printed on demand), and the results of the weekly computation.

7.15 MSG CASE STUDY: RAPID PROTOTYPE

Notwithstanding the care taken when interviewing MSG staff and managers to determine their requirements accurately, the only way to be sure that the final product will indeed meet the real needs of both clients and users is to build a rapid prototype.

Unfortunately, the only language available to the developers is Java. Thus, both the rapid prototype and the production-quality version will have to be written in that language. Java is a good language for rapid prototyping because it is interpreted. Nevertheless, a better choice would have been an interpreted language other than Java; this would guarantee that the rapid prototype would be discarded once the users' requirements have been determined.

The rapid prototype is shown in Appendix C. The code is straightforward. Nevertheless, three aspects need to be discussed. First, the investments are stored in an array **portfolio** of **InvestmentRecord**. In the delivered product, a data structure that allows for a variable number of investments is needed. For example, a file or a dynamic data structure could be used. In the rapid prototype, however, an array is used because it is easy and quick to implement, and the rapid prototype will be run with only a small number of investments.

The second important aspect of the rapid prototype is that it is unfinished. For example, only the investments report can be printed. Similarly, it contains complete routines to add, modify, and delete investments. However, methods **addMortgage**, **modifyMortgage**, and **deleteMortgage** are stubs, that is, dummy methods consisting of an interface but with no body; they just display a message when invoked. Omitting these three methods speeds up development of the rapid prototype without significantly detracting from its functionality. After all, the actions performed on investments and mortgages are remarkably similar. (In fact, in Section 9.6 **Investment** and **Mortgage** are identified as subclasses of the more general class **Financial Instrument**.) Thus, if the complete functionality for investments is implemented in the rapid prototype, there is probably no need to do the same for mortgages.

Finally, the user interface of the rapid prototype is menu-driven. This is certainly not as elegant as a graphical user interface (GUI). However, it does have two advantages. First, the emphasis in rapid prototyping is on speed. Unless a powerful GUI generator is available, it is usually far quicker to code a menu-driven user interface. Second, a GUI is often hardware/operating system dependent. If the delivered product is implemented on a hardware/operating system platform that is significantly different from that on which the rapid prototype was run, then the GUI may have to be reimplemented from scratch, consuming additional cost and additional time. For both these reasons, it is often better to build a rapid prototype with a simple user interface. Later in the process, decisions regarding more elaborate user interfaces can be made.

Chapter Review

The chapter begins with a description of requirements analysis techniques (Section 7.1). A careful definition is given of rapid prototyping (Section 7.2). The importance of taking human factors into account when designing user interfaces is discussed in Section 7.3. The use of rapid prototyping as a specification technique is discouraged in Section 7.4. The issue of reusing a rapid prototype is discussed in Section 7.5. In Section 7.6 other uses of rapid prototyping are discussed. Management implications of the rapid prototyping model appear in Section 7.7. Experiences with rapid prototyping are discussed in Section 7.8. In Section 7.9 joint application design (JAD) is described. Other techniques of requirements analysis are compared in Section 7.10. Next are presented ways of checking the rapid prototype (Section 7.11), CASE tools for the requirements phase (Section 7.12), and metrics for the requirements phase (Section 7.13). The chapter concludes with the MSG Case Study (Sections 7.14 and 7.15).

For Further Reading

Books on requirements analysis include [Gause and Weinberg, 1990] and [Davis, 1993]. The current state of the art is described in [Hsia, Davis, and Kung, 1993]. [Thayer and Dorfman, 1990] is a collection of papers on requirements analysis. The strengths of paper prototypes are discussed in [Rettig, 1994]. Articles on the requirements phase appear in the March 1994 issue of *IEEE Software*.

For an introduction to rapid prototyping, suggested books include [Lantz, 1985], [Connell and Shafer, 1989], and [Gane, 1989]. The application of rapid prototyping to interactive information systems is described in [Mason and Carey, 1983]. A graphical tool for rapid prototyping of real-time systems appears in [Coomber and Childs, 1990]. Articles on rapid prototyping include [Luqi, 1989]. The role of computer-aided prototyping is assessed in [Luqi and Royce, 1992]. In addition to the experiment on prototyping by Boehm and his co-workers [Boehm, Gray, and Seewaldt, 1984], another experiment on rapid prototyping is described in [Alavi, 1984].

The May 1989 issue of *IEEE Computer* contains a number of different articles on rapid prototyping. Sources of information on joint application design (JAD) include [Gane, 1989] and [August, 1991]. The report on the use of rapid prototyping in 39 commercial products is an extremely useful source of information [Gordon and Bieman, 1995].

Human factors are discussed in [Dix, Finlay, Abowd, and Beale, 1993], [Browne, 1994], and [Preece, 1994]. [Nielsen, 1993] describes how user interaction with a user interface can significantly improve usability. [Myers and Rosson, 1992] point out that up to half of the total software effort can be devoted to portions of the product that are related to the user interface.

Articles on interface design can be found in the November 1992 issue of *IEEE Software* and the April 1993 issue of *Communications of the ACM*. The proceedings of the Annual Conference on Human Factors in Computer Systems (sponsored by

ACM SIGCHI) are a valuable source of information on wide-ranging aspects of human factors.

Problems

7.1 You have just joined Texas Taxes as a software manager. Texas Taxes has been developing tax preparation software for years using the waterfall model, usually with some success. On the basis of your experience, you think that the rapid prototyping model is a far superior way of developing software. Write a report addressed to the vice-president for software development explaining why you believe that the organization should switch to the rapid prototyping model. Remember that vice-presidents do not like reports that are more than one page in length.

7.2 You are the vice-president for software development of Texas Taxes. Reply to the memo of Problem 7.1.

7.3 Of the programming languages available to you, which should not be used for rapid prototyping? Give reasons for your answer.

7.4 Describe a project in which rapid prototyping is unlikely to be of much assistance to the development team.

7.5 In Section 7.3 it is stated that rapid prototyping is particularly effective when developing the user interface. Is there an equally effective alternative way to determine the client's needs in this regard?

7.6 Under what circumstances does it make sense to refine a rapid prototype?

7.7 What is the result if a rapid prototype is not constructed rapidly?

7.8 Should rapid prototyping be used if the product is to be developed using the object-oriented paradigm?

7.9 (Term Project) Construct a rapid prototype for the Osbert Oglesby project in Appendix A. Use the software and hardware specified by your instructor.

7.10 (Case Study) Starting with the requirements of Section 7.14, construct a rapid prototype in an interpreted language such as Lisp, Smalltalk, or UNIX shell language.

7.11 (Case Study) The rapid prototype of Appendix C is written in Java and the production-quality version is also to be written in Java. How would you prevent the rapid prototype from being refined into the delivered version of the product?

7.12 (Case Study) If you have access to a screen generator and/or report generator, improve the user interface of the rapid prototype.

7.13 (Case Study) In the rapid prototype, an array of records is used for storing the investments. The code includes a comment to the effect that, in the actual implementation, a dynamic data structure is needed because the number of investments is not known. Was this a good decision on the part of the rapid prototyping team? To support your answer, recode the rapid prototype using a dynamic data structure.

(Case Study) A significant number of the routines of the rapid prototype are empty.   **7.14**
For example, the routines to add, modify, or delete a mortgage have not been coded.
Also, only one report can be printed. Was this a good decision on the part of the rapid
prototyping team? To support your answer, complete the bodies of the empty
routines.

7.15   (Readings in Software Engineering) Your instructor will distribute copies of [Gordon
and Bieman, 1995]. To what extent do you believe that the case for rapid prototyping
has been adequately proved?

References

[Alavi, 1984] M. ALAVI, "An Assessment of the Prototyping Approach to Information
    Systems Development," *Communications of the ACM* **27** (June 1984), pp. 556–563.

[August, 1991] J. H. AUGUST, *Joint Application Design: The Group Session Approach to
    System Design,* Yourdon Press, Englewood Cliffs, NJ, 1991.

[Blair, Murphy, Schach, and McDonald, 1988] J. A. BLAIR, L. C. MURPHY, S. R. SCHACH,
    AND C. W. McDONALD, "Rapid Prototyping, Bottom-Up Design, and Reusable
    Modules: A Case Study," *ACM Mid-Southeast Summer Meeting,* Nashville, TN, May
    1988.

[Boehm, Gray, and Seewaldt, 1984] B. W. BOEHM, T. E. GRAY, AND T. SEEWALDT,
    "Prototyping versus Specifying: A Multi-Project Experiment," *IEEE Transactions on
    Software Engineering* **SE-10** (May 1984), pp. 290–303.

[Brooks, 1975] F. P. BROOKS, JR., *The Mythical Man-Month: Essays on Software
    Engineering,* Addison-Wesley, Reading, MA, 1975.

[Browne, 1994] D. BROWNE, *STUDIO: STructured User-interface Design for Interaction
    Optimization,* Prentice-Hall, Englewood Cliffs, NJ, 1994.

[Capper, Colgate, Hunter, and James, 1994] N. P. CAPPER, R. J. COLGATE, J. C. HUNTER,
    AND M. F. JAMES, "The Impact of Object-Oriented Technology on Software Quality:
    Three Case Histories," *IBM Systems Journal* **33** (No. 1, 1994), pp. 131–157.

[Connell and Shafer, 1989] J. L. CONNELL AND L. SHAFER, *Structured Rapid Prototyping:
    An Evolutionary Approach to Software Development,* Yourdon Press, Englewood
    Cliffs, NJ, 1989.

[Coomber and Childs, 1990] C. J. COOMBER AND R. E. CHILDS, "A Graphical Tool for the
    Prototyping of Real-Time Systems," *ACM SIGSOFT Software Engineering Notes* **15**
    (April 1990), pp. 70–82.

[Davis, 1993] A. M. DAVIS, "Software Requirements: Objects, Functions, and States,"
    Revised Edition, Prentice-Hall, Englewood Cliffs, NJ, 1993.

[Dix, Finlay, Abowd, and Beale, 1993] A. DIX, J. FINLAY, G. ABOWD, AND R. BEALE,
    Human-Computer Interaction, Prentice-Hall, Englewood Cliffs, NJ, 1993.

[Gane, 1989] C. GANE, *Rapid System Development: Using Structured Techniques and
    Relational Technology,* Prentice-Hall, Englewood Cliffs, NJ, 1989.

[Gause and Weinberg, 1990] D. GAUSE AND G. WEINBERG, *Are Your Lights On? How to
    Figure Out What the Problem Really Is,* Dorset House, New York, 1990.

[Gibson and Jackson, 1987] C. F. GIBSON AND B. B. JACKSON, *The Information Imperative:
    Managing the Impact of Information Technology on Business and People,* Lexington
    Books, Lexington, MA, 1987.

[Gordon and Bieman, 1995] V. S. GORDON AND J. M. BIEMAN, "Rapid Prototyping Lessons Learned," *IEEE Software* **12** (January 1995), pp. 85–95.

[Hsia, Davis, and Kung, 1993] P. HSIA, A. DAVIS, AND D. KUNG, "Status Report: Requirements Engineering," *IEEE Software* **10** (November 1993), pp. 75–79.

[Lantz, 1985] K. E. LANTZ, *The Prototyping Methodology,* Prentice-Hall, Englewood Cliffs, NJ, 1985.

[Luqi, 1989] LUQI, "Software Evolution through Rapid Prototyping," *IEEE Computer* **22** (May 1989), pp. 13–25.

[Luqi and Royce, 1992] LUQI AND W. ROYCE, "Status Report: Computer-Aided Prototyping," *IEEE Software* **9** (November 1992), pp. 77–81.

[Mason and Carey, 1983] R. E. A. MASON AND T. T. CAREY, "Prototyping Interactive Information Systems," *Communications of the ACM* **26** (May 1983), pp. 347–354.

[Myers and Rosson, 1992] B. A. MYERS AND M. B. ROSSON, "Survey on User Interface Programming," *Proceedings of ACM SIGCHI Conference on Human Factors in Computing Systems,* Monterey, CA, May 1992, pp. 195–202.

[Nielsen, 1993] J. NIELSEN, "Iterative User-Interface Design," *IEEE Computer* **26** (November 1993), pp. 32–41.

[Preece, 1994] J. PREECE, *Human-Computer Interaction,* Addison-Wesley, Reading, MA, 1994.

[Rettig, 1994] M. RETTIG, "Prototyping for Tiny Fingers," *Communications of the ACM* **37** (April 1994), pp. 21–27.

[Schach and Wood, 1986] S. R. SCHACH AND P. T. WOOD, "An Almost Path-Free Very High-Level Interactive Data Manipulation Language for a Microcomputer-Based Database System," *Software—Practice and Experience* **16** (March 1986), pp. 243–268.

[Thayer and Dorfman, 1990] R. THAYER AND M. DORFMAN, *Tutorial: System and Software Requirements Engineering,* IEEE Computer Society Press, Los Alamitos, CA, 1990.

8

SPECIFICATION PHASE

A specification document must satisfy two mutually contradictory requirements. On the one hand, it is important that this document be clear and intelligible to the client, who is probably not a computer expert. After all, the client is paying for the product, and unless the client believes that he or she really understands what the new product will be like, there is a good chance that the client will either decide not to authorize the development of the product or will ask some other development organization to build it.

On the other hand, the specification document must be complete and detailed because it is virtually the sole source of information available to the design team for drawing up the design. Even if the client agrees that all needs have been accurately determined during the requirements phase, if the specification document contains faults such as omissions, contradictions, and ambiguities, the inevitable result will be faults in the design that will be carried over into the implementation. What is needed, therefore, are techniques for representing the target product in a format that is sufficiently nontechnical to be intelligible to the client, yet at the same time precise enough to result in a fault-free product being delivered to the client at the end of the development cycle. These specification techniques are the subjects of this and the next chapter. The emphasis in this chapter is on structured specification techniques, whereas Chapter 9 is devoted to object-oriented analysis.

8.1 THE SPECIFICATION DOCUMENT

Virtually every specification document incorporates constraints that the product has to satisfy. There is almost always a deadline specified for delivering the product. Another common stipulation is "The product shall be installed in such a way that it can run in parallel with the existing product" until the client is satisfied that the new product indeed satisfies every aspect of the specification document. Other constraints might include portability, namely, that the product be constructed to run on other hardware under the same operating system or perhaps run under a variety of different operating systems. Reliability may be another constraint. If the product has to monitor patients in an intensive care unit, then it is of paramount importance that it should be fully operational 24 hours a day. Rapid response time may be another requirement; a typical constraint in this category might be "95 percent of all queries of Type 4 shall be answered within 0.25 seconds." Many response-time constraints have to be expressed in probabilistic terms because the response time depends on the current load on the computer. In contrast, so-called hard real-time constraints are expressed in absolute terms. For instance, it is useless to develop software that informs a warplane pilot of an incoming missile within 0.25 seconds only 95 percent of the time—the product must meet the constraint 100 percent of the time.

A vital component of the specification document is the set of acceptance criteria. It is important from the viewpoint of both the client and the developer to spell out a series of tests to prove that the product does indeed satisfy its specifications and that the developer's job is done. Some of the acceptance criteria may be restatements of the constraints, whereas others will address different issues. For example, the client might supply the developer with a description of the data that the product will handle. Appropriate acceptance criteria would be that the product correctly process data of this type and filter out nonconforming (that is, erroneous) data.

The specification document is a contract between client and developer. It specifies precisely what the product must do and the constraints on the product. Once the development team fully understands the problem, possible solution strategies can be suggested. A *solution strategy* is a general approach to building the product. For example, one possible solution strategy for a product would be to use an online database; another would be to use conventional flat files and to extract the required information using overnight batch runs. When determining solution strategies it is often a good idea to come up with strategies without worrying about the constraints in the specification document. Then the various solution strategies can be evaluated in the light of the constraints and necessary modifications can be made. There are a number of ways of determining whether a specific solution strategy will satisfy the client's constraints. An obvious one is prototyping, which can be a good technique for resolving issues relating to user interfaces and timing constraints, as previously discussed in Section 3.5. Other techniques for determining whether constraints will be satisfied include simulation [Bratley, Fox, and Schrage, 1987] and analytic network modeling [Jain, 1991].

During this process a number of solution strategies will be put forward and then discarded. It is important that a written record be kept of all discarded strategies and the reasons they were rejected. This will assist the development team if they are ever called upon to justify their chosen strategy. But more importantly, there is an ever-present danger during the maintenance phase that the process of enhancement will be accompanied by an attempt to come up with a new and unwise solution strategy. Having a record of why certain strategies were rejected during development can be extremely helpful during maintenance.

By this point the development team will have determined one or more possible solution strategies that satisfy the constraints. A two-stage decision now has to be made. First, whether the client should be advised to computerize, and if so, which of the viable solution strategies should be adopted. The answer to the first question can best be decided on the basis of cost–benefit analysis (Section 4.2). Second, if the client decides to proceed with the project, then the client must inform the development team as to the optimization criterion to be used, such as minimizing the total cost to the client or maximizing the return on investment. The developers will then advise the client as to which of the viable solution strategies will best satisfy the optimization criterion.

8.2 INFORMAL SPECIFICATIONS

In many development projects, the specification document consists of page after page of English, or some other natural language such as French or Xhosa. A typical paragraph of such a specification document reads:

> BV.4.2.5. If the sales for the current month are below the target sales, then a report is to be printed, unless the difference between target sales and actual sales is less than half of the difference between target sales and actual sales in the previous month or if the difference between target sales and actual sales for the current month is under 5 percent.

The background leading up to that paragraph is as follows. The management of a retail chain sets a target sales figure for each shop for each month, and if a shop does not meet this target, then a report is to be printed. Consider the following scenario: Suppose that the January sales target for one particular shop is $100,000, but actual sales are only $64,000, that is, 36 percent below target. In this case, a report must be printed. Now suppose further that the February target figure is $120,000 and that actual sales are only $100,000, 16.7 percent below target. Although sales are below the target figure, the percentage difference for February, namely, 16.7 percent, is less than half of the previous month's percentage difference, namely, 36 percent; management believes that an improvement has been made, and no report is to be printed. Now suppose that in March the target is again $100,000 but the shop makes $98,000, only 2 percent below target. Because the percentage difference is small, less than 5 percent, no report should be printed.

Careful rereading of the preceding specification paragraph shows some divergence from what the retail chain's management actually requested. Paragraph BV.4.2.5 speaks of the "difference between target sales and actual sales"; percentage difference is not mentioned. The difference in January was $36,000 and in February it was $20,000. The percentage difference, which is what management wanted, dropped from 36 percent in January to 16.7 percent in February, less than half of the January percentage difference. However, the actual difference dropped from $36,000 to $20,000, which is greater than half of $36,000. So if the development team had faithfully implemented the specification document, the report would have been printed, which is not what management wanted. Then the last clause speaks of a "difference . . . [of] 5 percent." What is meant, of course, is a percentage difference of 5 percent, only the word *percentage* does not occur anywhere in the paragraph.

There are thus a number of faults in the specification document. First, the wishes of the client have been ignored. Second, there is ambiguity—should the last clause read "percentage difference . . . [of] 5 percent," or "difference . . . [of] $5,000," or something else entirely? In addition, the style is poor. What the paragraph says is "If something happens, print a report. However, if something else happens, don't print it. And if a third thing happens, don't print it either." It would have been much clearer if the specifications had simply stated when the report is to be printed. All in all, paragraph BV.4.2.5 is not a very good example of how to write a specification document.

In fact, paragraph BV.4.2.5 is fictitious, but it is, unfortunately, typical of too many specification documents. The reader may think that the example is unfair and that this sort of problem cannot arise if specifications are written with care by professional specification writers. To refute this charge, the case study of Chapter 5 is resumed below.

8.2.1 CASE STUDY: TEXT PROCESSING

Recall from Section 5.5.2 that in 1969 Naur published a paper on correctness proving [Naur, 1969]. He illustrated his technique by means of a text-processing problem. Using his technique, Naur constructed an ALGOL procedure to solve the problem and informally proved the correctness of his procedure. A reviewer of Naur's paper pointed out one fault in the procedure [Leavenworth, 1970]. London then detected three additional faults in Naur's procedure and presented a corrected version of the procedure and formally proved its correctness [London, 1971]. Goodenough and Gerhart then found three further faults that London had not detected [Goodenough and Gerhart, 1975]. Of the total of seven faults collectively detected by the reviewer London, and Goodenough and Gerhart, two can be considered as specification faults. For example, Naur's specifications do not state what happens if the input includes two successive adjacent breaks (**blank** or **newline** characters). For this reason, Goodenough and Gerhart then produced a new set of specifications. Their specifications were about four times longer than Naur's, which are given in Section 5.5.2.

In 1985 Meyer wrote an article on formal specification techniques [Meyer, 1985]. The main thrust of his article is that specifications written in a natural language such as English tend to have contradictions, ambiguities, and omissions. He recommends using mathematical terminology to express specifications formally. Meyer detected some 12 faults in Goodenough and Gerhart's specifications and then developed a set of mathematical specifications to correct all the problems. Meyer then paraphrased his mathematical specifications and constructed English specifications. In the author's opinion, Meyer's English specifications contain a fault. Meyer points out in his paper that if the maximum number of characters per line is, say, 10, and the input is, for instance, WHO WHAT WHEN, then in terms of both Naur's and Goodenough and Gerhart's specifications, there are two equally valid outputs, namely WHO WHAT on the first line and WHEN on the second, or WHO on the first line and WHAT WHEN on the second. In fact, Meyer's paraphrased English specifications also contain this ambiguity.

The key point is that Goodenough and Gerhart's specifications were constructed with the greatest of care. After all, the reason they were constructed was to correct

Naur's specifications. Furthermore, Goodenough and Gerhart's paper went through two versions, the first of which was published in the proceedings of a refereed conference and the second in a refereed journal [Goodenough and Gerhart, 1975]. Finally, both Goodenough and Gerhart are experts in software engineering in general, and specifications in particular. Thus, if two experts with as much time as they needed carefully produced specifications in which Meyer detected 12 faults, what chance does an ordinary computer professional working under time pressure have of producing a fault-free specification document? Worse still, the text-processing problem can be coded in 25 or 30 lines, whereas real-world products can consist of hundreds of thousands or even millions of lines of source code.

It is clear that natural language is not a good way of specifying a product. In this chapter better alternatives are described. The order in which the specification techniques are presented is from the informal to the more formal.

8.3 STRUCTURED SYSTEMS ANALYSIS

The use of graphics to specify software was an important technique of the 1970s. Three techniques making uses of graphics became particularly popular, namely those of DeMarco [DeMarco, 1978], Gane and Sarsen [Gane and Sarsen, 1979], and Yourdon and Constantine [Yourdon and Constantine, 1979]. The three techniques are all equally good and are essentially equivalent. Gane and Sarsen's approach is presented here because their notation is used in object-oriented analysis (Section 9.3.3).

As an aid to understanding the technique, consider the following example.

8.3.1 SALLY'S SOFTWARE SHOP

Sally's Software Shop buys software from various suppliers and sells it to the public. Sally stocks popular software packages and orders others as required. Sally extends credit to institutions, corporations, and some individuals. Sally's Software Shop is doing well, with a monthly turnover of 300 packages at an average retail cost of $250 each. Despite her business success, Sally has been advised to computerize. Should she?

The question, as stated, is inadequate. It should read: Which, if any, business functions, namely accounts payable, accounts receivable, and inventory, should be computerized? Even this is not enough—is the system to be batch or online? Is there to be an in-house computer or is outsourcing to be used? But even if the question is refined further, it still misses the fundamental issue: What is Sally's objective in computerizing her business?

Only when Sally's objectives are known can the analysis continue. For example, if she wishes to computerize simply because she sells software, then she needs an in-house system with a variety of sound and light effects that ostentatiously shows off the possibilities of a computer. On the other hand, if she uses her business to launder "hot" money, then she needs a product that keeps four or five different sets of books and does not have an audit trail.

This example assumes that Sally wishes to computerize "in order to make more money." This does not help very much, but it is clear that cost–benefit analysis can determine whether or not to computerize each (or any) of the three sections of her business.

The main danger of many standard approaches is that one is tempted to come up with the solution first, for example, a Lime III computer with a 380-megabyte hard disk and a laser printer, and find out what the problem is later! In contrast, Gane and Sarsen use a nine-step technique to analyze the client's needs [Gane and Sarsen, 1979]. An important point is that stepwise refinement is used in many of those nine steps; this will be indicated as the technique is demonstrated.

Having determined Sally's requirements, the first step in the structured systems analysis is to determine the *logical data flow*, as opposed to the *physical data flow* (that is, *what* happens, as opposed to *how* it happens). This is done by drawing a data flow diagram (DFD). The DFD uses the four basic symbols shown in Figure 8.1. (The notation of Gane and Sarsen is similar, but not identical, to that of DeMarco [DeMarco, 1978] and that of Yourdon and Constantine [Yourdon and Constantine, 1979].)

Step 1. Draw the DFD   The DFD is a pictorial representation of all aspects of the logical data flow and as such is guaranteed to contain considerably more than 7 ± 2 elements, that is, the DFD for any nontrivial product is likely to be large. For this reason, the DFD must be developed by stepwise refinement (Section 4.1). Returning to the example, the first refinement is shown in Figure 8.2.

This diagram of *logical data flow* can have many interpretations. Two possible implementations are as follows:

Implementation 1. Data store PACKAGE DATA consists of some 900 boxes containing diskettes displayed on shelves as well as a number of catalogs in a desk drawer. Data store CUSTOMER DATA is a collection of 5×7 cards held together by a rubber band plus a list of customers whose payments are overdue. Process (action) *process orders* is Sally looking for the appropriate package on the shelves, if necessary looking it up in a catalog, then finding the correct 5×7 card and checking that the customer's name is not on the list of defaulters. This implementation is totally manual and corresponds to the way Sally currently conducts her business.

Implementation 2. Data stores PACKAGE DATA and CUSTOMER DATA are computer files and *process orders* is Sally entering the customer's name and the name of the package at a terminal. This implementation corresponds to a fully computerized solution with all information available online.

The DFD of Figure 8.2 represents not only the preceding two implementations, but also literally an infinity of other possibilities. The key point is that the DFD represents a flow of information—the actual package that Sally's customer wants is not important to the flow.

Figure 8.1   Symbols of Gane and Sarsen's structured systems analysis.

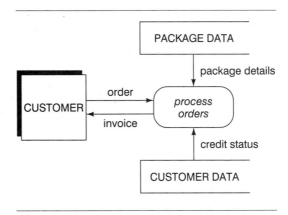

Figure 8.2   Data flow diagram: first refinement.

The DFD is now refined stepwise. The second refinement is depicted in Figure 8.3. Now when the customer requests a package that Sally does not have on hand, details of that package are placed in the data store PENDING ORDERS, which might be a computer file, but at this stage could equally well be a manila folder. Data store PENDING ORDERS is scanned daily by the computer or by Sally, and if there are sufficient orders for one supplier, then a batched order is placed. Also, if an order has been waiting for 5 working days, it is ordered, regardless of how many packages are waiting to be ordered from the relevant supplier. This DFD does not

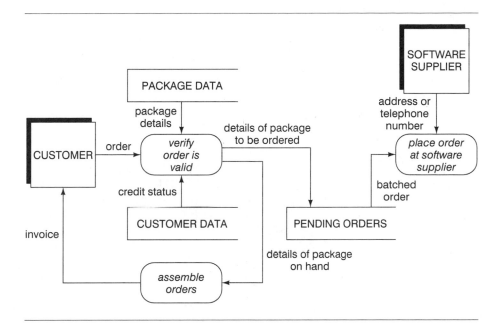

Figure 8.3 Data flow diagram: second refinement.

show the logical flow of data when the software package arrives from the supplier, nor does it show financial functions such as accounts payable and accounts receivable. These will be added in the third refinement.

Only a portion of the third refinement is shown in Figure 8.4 because the DFD is starting to become large. The rest of the DFD relates to accounts payable and to the software suppliers. The final DFD will be larger still, stretching over perhaps six pages. But it will be easily understood by Sally who will sign it off, confirming that it is an accurate representation of the logical flow of data in her business.

Of course, for a larger product the DFD will be larger. After a certain point it becomes impractical to have just one DFD, and a hierarchy of DFDs is needed. A single box at one level is expanded into a complete DFD at a lower level. A difficulty with this approach frequently arises as a consequence of the positioning of sources and destinations of data. For instance, a particular process p may be reflected at level L and expanded at level $L + 1$. The correct place for the sources and destinations of data for process p is level $L + 1$, because that is where they are used. But a client, even one who is experienced in reading a DFD, frequently cannot understand the DFD at level L because the sources and destinations of data relating to process p appear to be missing. In order to prevent this confusion, it is sometimes advisable to draw the correct DFD and then modify it by moving sources and destinations of data one or more levels up so that the client will not be confused.

Step 2. Decide What Sections to Computerize and How (Batch or Online) The choice of what to automate often depends on how much the client is prepared to

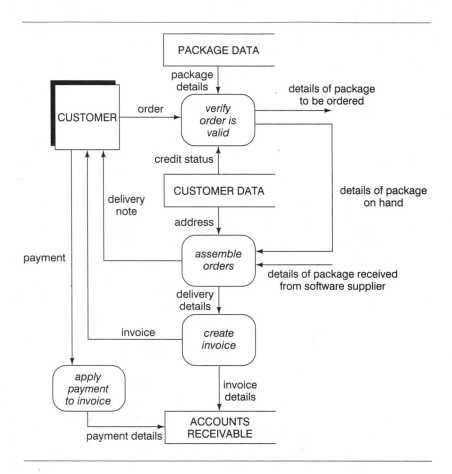

Figure 8.4 Data flow diagram: part of third refinement.

spend. Obviously, it would be nice to automate the entire operation, but the cost of this may be prohibitive. In order to determine which sections to automate, cost–benefit analysis is applied to the various possible strategies for computerizing each section. For example, for each section of the DFD a decision has to be made as to whether that group of operations should be performed in batch or online. With large volumes to process and tight controls required, batch processing is often the answer, but with small volumes and an in-house microcomputer, online processing appears to be better. Returning to the example, one alternative is to automate accounts payable in batch and to perform validation of orders online. A second alternative is to automate everything, with the editing of the software supplier consignment notes against orders being done online or batch, the rest of the operations online. A key point is that the DFD corresponds to all the preceding possibilities. This is consistent with not making a commitment as to how to solve the problem during the specification phase, but rather waiting until the design phase.

give educational discount

Figure 8.5 Decision tree depicting Sally's Software Shop educational discount policy.

The next three stages of Gane and Sarsen's technique are the stepwise refinement of the flows of data (arrows), processes (rounded rectangles), and data stores (open rectangles).

Step 3. Put in the Details of the Data Flows First, decide what data items must go into the various data flows. Then, refine each flow stepwise.

In the example, there is a data flow **order**. This can be refined as follows:

> order:
>   order identification
>   customer details
>   package details

Now, each of the preceding components of **order** is refined further. In the case of a larger product, a data dictionary (Section 4.3.1) keeps track of all the data elements.

Step 4. Define the Logic of the Processes Now that the data elements within the product have been determined, it is time to investigate what happens within each process. Suppose that the example has a process *give educational discount.* Sally must provide the software developers with details about the discount she gives to educational institutions, for example, 10 percent on up to four packages, 15 percent on five or more. In order to cope with the difficulties of natural language specification documents, this should be translated from English into a decision tree. Such a tree is shown in Figure 8.5.

A decision tree makes it easy to check that all possibilities have been taken into account, especially in more complex cases. An example is shown in Figure 8.6. From Figure 8.6 it is immediately obvious that the cost to an alumnus of a seat behind the end zone has not been specified. Another good way of representing processes is with decision tables [Pollack, Hicks, and Harrison, 1971]. Decision tables have an advantage over decision trees in that CASE tools exist that allow the contents of a

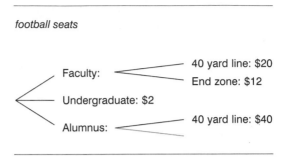

Figure 8.6 Decision tree describing seating prices for college football games.

decision table to be entered automatically into a computer, thereby obviating the need to code that part of the product.

Step 5. Define the Data Stores   At this stage it is necessary to define the exact contents of each store and its representation (format). Thus, if the product is to be implemented in COBOL, this information must be provided down to the **pic** level; if Ada is to be used, the **digits** or **delta** must be specified. In addition, it is necessary to specify where immediate access is required.

The issue of immediate access depends on what queries are going to be put to the product. For example, suppose that in the example it is decided to validate orders online. A customer may order a package by name ("Do you have Lotus 1-2-3 in stock?"), by function ("What accounting packages do you have?"), or by machine ("Do you have anything new for the 686?"), but rarely by price ("What do you have for $149.50?"). Thus immediate access to PACKAGE DATA is required by name, function, and machine. This is depicted in the data immediate-access diagram (DIAD) of Figure 8.7.

Step 6. Define the Physical Resources   Now that the developers know what is required online and the representation (format) of each element, a decision can be made regarding blocking factors. In addition, for each file the following can be specified: file name; organization (sequential, indexed, etc.); storage medium; and records, down to the field level. If a database management system (DBMS) is to be used, then the relevant information for each table is specified here.

Step 7. Determine the Input/Output Specifications   The input forms must be specified, at least with respect to components, if not detailed layout. Input screens must similarly be determined. The printed output must also be specified, where possible in detail; otherwise just estimated length is given.

Step 8. Perform Sizing   Now it is necessary to compute the numerical data that will be used in step 9 to determine the hardware requirements. This includes the volume of input (daily or hourly), the frequency of each printed report and its deadline, the

Figure 8.7 Data immediate-access diagram (DIAD) for PACKAGE DATA.

size and number of records of each type that are to pass between the CPU and mass storage, and the size of each file.

Step 9. Determine the Hardware Requirements   From the sizing information on the disk files determined in step 8, mass storage requirements can be computed. In addition, mass storage requirements for back-up purposes can also be determined. From knowledge of input volumes, the needs in this area can be found. Because the number of lines and frequency of printed reports is known, output devices can be specified. If the client already has hardware, it can be determined whether this hardware will be adequate or if additional hardware will have to be purchased. On the other hand, if the client does not have suitable hardware, a recommendation can be made as to what should be acquired, and whether it should be purchased or leased.

Determining the hardware requirements is the ninth and final step of Gane and Sarsen's specification technique, and the example is therefore concluded. After approval by the client, the resulting specification document is handed to the design team, and the software process continues.

Despite its many strengths, Gane and Sarsen's technique does not provide the answer to every question. For example, it cannot be used to determine response times. The number of input/output channels can at best be roughly gauged. Also, CPU size and timing cannot be estimated with any degree of accuracy. These are distinct drawbacks of Gane and Sarsen's technique and, to be fair, virtually every other technique for either specification or design. Nonetheless, at the end of the specification phase, hardware decisions have to be made, whether or not accurate information is available. The situation is considerably better than what was done before methodical approaches to specifying were put forward, when decisions regarding hardware were made right at the beginning of the software development process. Gane and Sarsen's technique has led to major improvements in the ways that products are specified, and the fact that Gane and Sarsen and the authors of most competing techniques essentially ignore time as a variable should not detract from the advantages that these techniques have brought to the software industry.

8.4   OTHER SEMIFORMAL TECHNIQUES

Gane and Sarsen's technique is clearly more formal than writing a specification in a natural language. At the same time, it is less formal than many of the techniques presented in the following discussion such as Petri nets (Section 8.7) and Z (Section 8.8). Dart and her co-workers classify specification and design techniques as informal, semiformal, or formal [Dart, Ellison, Feiler, and Habermann, 1987]. In terms of this classification Gane and Sarsen's structured systems analysis is a semiformal technique, while the other two techniques mentioned in this paragraph are formal techniques.

Structured systems analysis has been included in this book for two reasons. First, it is widely used; there is a good chance that the reader may be employed by an organization that uses structured systems analysis or some variant of it. Second, data flow diagrams are used in object-oriented analysis (Chapter 9). However, there are many other good semiformal techniques; see, for example, the proceedings of the various International Workshops on Software Specification and Design. Because of space limitations, all that will be given here is a brief description of a few well-known techniques.

PSL/PSA [Teichroew and Hershey, 1977] is a computer-aided technique for specifying information processing products. The name comes from the two components of the technique, namely the problem statement language (PSL) that is used to describe the product, and the problem statement analyzer (PSA) that enters the PSL description into a database and produces reports on request. PSL/PSA is widely used, particularly for documenting products.

SADT [Ross, 1985] consists of two interrelated components, a box-and-arrow diagramming language termed *structural analysis* (SA) and a design technique (DT)—hence the name SADT. Stepwise refinement underlies SADT to a greater extent than with Gane and Sarsen's technique; a conscious effort has been made to adhere to Miller's law. As Ross puts it, "Everything worth saying, about anything worth saying something about, must be expressed in six or fewer pieces" [Ross, 1985]. SADT has been used successfully in specifying a wide variety of products, especially complex, large-scale projects. Like many other similar semiformal techniques, its applicability to real-time systems is less clear.

On the other hand, SREM (software requirements engineering method, pronounced "shrem") was explicitly designed for specifying the conditions under which specific actions are to occur [Alford, 1985]. For this reason SREM has been particularly useful for specifying real-time systems and has been extended to distributed systems. SREM consists of a number of components. RSL is a specification language. REVS is a set of tools which perform a variety of specification-related tasks such as translating the RSL specifications into an automated database, automatically checking for data flow consistency (ensuring that no data item is used before it has been assigned a value), and generating simulators from the specifications that can be used to ensure that the specifications are correct. In addition, SREM has a design technique named DCDS, distributed computing design system.

The power of SREM comes from the fact that the model underlying the whole technique is a finite state machine (FSM), described in Section 8.6. As a result of this formal model underlying SREM, it is possible to perform the consistency checking mentioned previously and also to verify that performance constraints on the product as a whole can be met, given the performance of individual components. SREM has been used by the U.S. Air Force to specify two C³I (command, control, communications, and intelligence) systems [Scheffer, Stone, and Rzepka, 1985]. Although SREM proved to be of great use in the specification phase, it appears that the REVS tools employed later in the development cycle were considered to be less useful.

8.5   ENTITY-RELATIONSHIP MODELING

The emphasis in structured systems analysis is on the actions, rather than the data, of the product to be built. It is certainly true that the data of the product are also modeled, but the data are secondary to the actions. In contrast, entity-relationship modeling (ERM) is a semiformal data-oriented technique for specifying a product. It is widely used for specifying databases. In that application area, the emphasis is on the data. Of course, actions are needed to access the data, and the database must be organized in such a way as to minimize access times. Nevertheless, the actions that are performed on the data are less significant.

Entity-relationship modeling is not a new technique; it is has been widely used since 1976 [Chen, 1976; 1983]. Now it is undergoing a new lease on life, because entity-relationship modeling is one element of object-oriented analysis, described in detail in Chapter 9.

A simple entity-relationship diagram is shown in Figure 8.8. This diagram models the relationships between authors, autobiographies, and readers. There are three entities, namely **Author**, **Autobiography**, and **Reader**. The top relationship, namely writes, reflects the fact that an author writes an autobiography. This is a one-to-many relationship, because one author can write more than one autobiography; this is reflected by the 1 next to **Author** and the n next to **Autobiography**. The entity-relationship diagram also shows two relationships between **Autobiography** and **Reader**. Both are one-to-many relationships. The relationship on the left models the fact that a reader may have read many autobiographies. Similarly, as shown on the right, a reader may own many autobiographies. Two separate relationships are shown because a reader can read an autobiography without owning it, and a reader can buy an autobiography but not read it.

The next example is taken from the domain of suppliers and the parts they supply. Figure 8.9 shows a many-to-many relationship between parts and suppliers. That is to say, one supplier supplies many parts and, conversely, a specific part can be

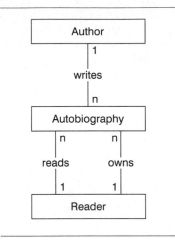

Figure 8.8 Simple entity-relationship diagram.

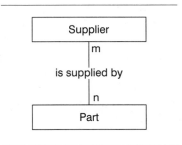

Figure 8.9 Many-to-many entity-relationship diagram.

obtained from many suppliers. This many-to-many relationship is reflected by the m next to entity Supplier and the n next to entity Part.

More complex relationships are also possible. For example, as shown in Figure 8.10, a Part may in turn be viewed as consisting of a number of component Parts. Also, many-to-many-to-many relationships are possible. Consider the three entities Supplier, Part, and Project shown in that figure. A particular part may be supplied by several suppliers, depending on the project. Also, the various parts supplied for a specific project may come from different suppliers. A many-to-many-to-many relationship is necessary to model such a situation accurately.

Entity-relationship modeling is discussed further in the following chapter, which describes object-oriented analysis, another semiformal technique. The next topic of

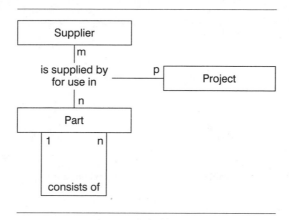

Figure 8.10 More complex entity-relationship diagram.

this chapter is formal techniques. The underlying theme of the next four sections is that employing formal techniques can lead to more precise specifications than are possible with semiformal or informal techniques. However, the use of formal techniques in general requires lengthy training, and software engineers using formal techniques need exposure to the relevant mathematics. The following sections have been written with the mathematical content kept to a minimum. Furthermore, wherever possible, mathematical formulations are preceded by informal presentations of the same material. Nevertheless, the level of Sections 8.6 through 8.9 is higher than that of the rest of the book.

8.6 FINITE STATE MACHINES

Consider the following example, originally formulated by the M202 team at the Open University, U.K. [Brady, 1977]. A safe has a combination lock that can be in one of three positions, labeled 1, 2, and 3. The dial can be turned left or right (L or R). Thus at any time there are six possible dial movements, namely 1L, 1R, 2L, 2R, 3L, and 3R. The combination to the safe is 1L, 3R, 2L; any other dial movement will cause the alarm to go off. The situation is depicted in Figure 8.11. There is one initial state, namely Safe Locked. If the input is 1L, then the next state is A, but if any other dial movement, 1R, say, or 3L, is made, then the next state is Sound Alarm, one of the two final states. If the correct combination is chosen, then the sequence of transitions is from Safe Locked to A to B to Safe Unlocked, the other final state. What is shown in Figure 8.11 is a state transition diagram (STD) of a finite state machine (FSM). It is not necessary to depict a STD graphically; the same information is shown in tabular form in Figure 8.12. For each state other than the two

Figure 8.11 State transition diagram for combination safe.

Dial movement	Table of Next States Current state Safe locked	A	B
1L	A	Sound Alarm	Sound Alarm
1R	Sound Alarm	Sound Alarm	Sound Alarm
2L	Sound Alarm	Sound Alarm	Safe Unlocked
2R	Sound Alarm	Sound Alarm	Sound Alarm
3L	Sound Alarm	Sound Alarm	Sound Alarm
3R	Sound Alarm	B	Sound Alarm

Figure 8.12 Transition table for finite state machine.

final states, the transition to the next state is indicated, depending on the way the dial is moved.

A finite state machine consists of five parts: a set of states J, a set of inputs K, the transition function T that specifies the next state given the current state and the current input, the initial state S, and the set of final states F. In the case of the combination lock on the safe:

The set of states J is {Safe Locked, A, B, Safe Unlocked, Sound Alarm}.

The set of inputs K is {1L, 1R, 2L, 2R, 3L, 3R}.

The transition function T is depicted in tabular form in Figure 8.12.

The initial state S is Safe Locked.

The set of final states F is {Safe Unlocked, Sound Alarm}.

In more formal terms, a finite state machine is a 5-tuple (J, K, T, S, F), where

J is a finite, nonempty set of states.

K is a finite, nonempty set of inputs.

T is a function from $(J \sim F) \times K$ into J called the transition function.

$S \in J$ is the initial state.

F is the set of final states, $F \subseteq J$.

Use of the finite state machine approach is widespread in computing applications. For example, every menu-driven user interface is an implementation of a finite state machine. The display of a menu corresponds to a state, and entering an input at the keyboard or selecting an icon with the mouse is an event that causes the product to go into some other state. For example, entering V when the main menu appears on the screen might cause a volumetric analysis to be performed on the current data set. A new menu then appears, and the user may enter G, P, or R. Selecting G causes the results of the calculation to be graphed, P causes them to be printed, and R causes a return to the main menu. Each transition has the form

current state [menu] and **event** [option selected] $\Rightarrow$ **next state (8.1)**

For the purposes of specifying a product, a useful extension of FSMs is to add a sixth component to the preceding 5-tuple, namely a set of predicates P, where each predicate is a function of the global state Y of the product [Kampen, 1987]. More formally, the transition function T is now a function from $(J \sim F) \times K \times P$ into J. Transition rules now have the form

current state and **event** and **predicate** $\Rightarrow$ **next state** **(8.2)**

To see how this formalism works in practice, the technique will now be applied to a modified version of the so-called elevator problem; see the Just in Case You Wanted to Know box on page 240 for background information on the problem.

8.6.1 ELEVATOR PROBLEM: FINITE STATE MACHINES

The problem concerns the logic required to move n elevators between floors according to the following constraints:

C_1. Each elevator has a set of m buttons, one for each floor. These illuminate when pressed and cause the elevator to visit the corresponding floor. The illumination is canceled when the corresponding floor is visited by the elevator.

C_2. Each floor, except the first floor and top floor, has two buttons, one to request an up-elevator and one to request a down-elevator. These buttons illuminate when pressed. The illumination is canceled when an elevator visits the floor and then moves in the desired direction.

C_3. When an elevator has no requests, it remains at its current floor with its doors closed.

JUST IN CASE YOU WANTED TO KNOW

The elevator problem is a truly classic problem of software engineering. It first appeared in print in 1968 in Don Knuth's landmark book, *The Art of Computer Programming, Volume I, Fundamental Algorithms*, pages 280–295 [Knuth, 1968]. It is based on the single elevator in the mathematics building at the California Institute of Technology. The example was used to illustrate coroutines in the mythical language MIX.

By the mid 1980s, the elevator problem was generalized to n elevators; in addition, specific properties of the solution had to be proved, for example, that an elevator would eventually arrive within a finite time. It was now *the* problem for researchers working in the area of formal specification languages, and any proposed formal specification language had to work for the elevator problem.

The problem attained broader prominence in 1986 when it was published in *ACM SIGSOFT Soft-*

ware Engineering Notes in the Call for Papers for the Fourth International Workshop on Software Specification and Design [IWSSD, 1986]. The elevator problem was one of five problems that were to be used as examples by researchers in their submissions to the conference, held in Monterey, California, in May 1987. In the form in which it appeared in the Call for Papers, it was termed the *lift problem* and was attributed to N. [Neil] Davis of STC-IDEC [a division of Standard Telecommunications and Cable, in Stevenage, United Kingdom].

Since then, the problem has attained even wider prominence and has been used to demonstrate an extensive variety of techniques within software engineering in general, not just formal specification languages. It is used in this book to illustrate every technique because, as the reader will soon discover, the problem is by no means as simple as it looks!

Figure 8.13   STD for elevator button [Kampen, 1987].
(© 1987 IEEE)

The product will now be specified using an extended finite state machine [Kampen, 1987]. There are two sets of buttons in the problem. In each of the n elevators there is a set of m buttons, one for each floor. Because these n × m buttons are inside the elevators, they will be referred to as *elevator buttons*. Then, on each floor there are two buttons, one to request an up-elevator, one to request a down-elevator. These will be referred to as *floor buttons*.

The state transition diagram (STD) for an elevator button is shown in Figure 8.13. Let $EB(e, f)$ denote the button in elevator e that is pressed to request floor f. $EB(e, f)$ can be in two states, namely, with the button on (illuminated) or off. More precisely, the states are

$$EBON(e, f): \quad \underline{E}levator \ \underline{B}utton \ (e, f) \ \underline{ON} \qquad (8.3)$$
$$EBOFF(e, f): \quad \underline{E}levator \ \underline{B}utton \ (e, f) \ \underline{OFF}$$

Figure 8.14 STD for floor button [Kampen, 1987].
| (© 1987 IEEE)

If the button is on and the elevator arrives at floor f, then the button is turned off. Conversely, if the button is off and it is pressed, then the button comes on. There are thus two events involved, namely

EBP(e, f):   Elevator Button (e, f) Pressed   **(8.4)**
EAF(e, f):   Elevator e Arrives at Floor f

In order to define the state transition rules connecting these events and states, a predicate $V(e, f)$ is needed. (A predicate is a condition that is either true or false.)

V(e, f):   Elevator e is Visiting (stopped at) floor f   **(8.5)**

Now the formal transition rules can be stated. If elevator button (e, f) is off [current state] and elevator button (e, f) is pressed [event] and elevator e is not visiting floor f [predicate], then the button is turned on. In the format of transition rule (8.2) this becomes

EBOFF(e, f) and EBP(e, f) and not V(e, f) $\Rightarrow$ EBON(e, f)   **(8.6)**

If the elevator is currently visiting floor f, nothing happens. In Kampen's formalism, events that do not trigger a transition may indeed occur, but if they do then they are ignored.

Conversely, if the elevator arrives at floor f and the button is on, then it is turned off. This is expressed as

EBON(e, f) and EAF(e, f) $\Rightarrow$ EBOFF(e, f)   **(8.7)**

Now the floor buttons are considered. $FB(d, f)$ denotes the button on floor f that requests an elevator traveling in direction d. The STD for floor button $FB(d, f)$ is shown in Figure 8.14. More precisely, the states are

FBON(d, f):   Floor Button (d, f) ON   **(8.8)**
FBOFF(d, f):   Floor Button (d, f) OFF

If the button is on and an elevator arrives at floor f traveling in the correct direction d, then the button is turned off. Conversely, if the button is off and it is pressed, then the button comes on. Again there are two events involved, namely

FBP(d, f):   Floor Button (d, f) Pressed   **(8.9)**
EAF(1..n, f): Elevator 1 or ... or n Arrives at Floor f

Note the use of 1..n to denote disjunction. Throughout this section an expression such as P(a, 1..n, b) denotes

$$\text{P(a, 1, b) or P(a, 2, b) or ... or P(a, n, b)} \qquad \textbf{(8.10)}$$

In order to define the state transition rules connecting these events and states, a predicate is again needed. In this case it is S(d, e, f), which is defined as follows:

S(d, e, f):   Elevator e is visiting floor f and the direction in   **(8.11)**
               which it is about to move is either up (d = U), down
               (d = D), or no requests are pending (d = N)

This predicate is actually a state. In fact, the formalism allows both events and states to be treated as predicates.

Using S(d, e, f) the formal transition rules are then

$$\text{FBOFF(d, f) and FBP(d, f) and not S(d, 1..n, f)} \qquad \textbf{(8.12)}$$
$$\Rightarrow \text{FBON(d, f),}$$

$$\text{FBON(d, f) and EAF(1..n, f) and S(d, 1..n, f)}$$
$$\Rightarrow \text{FBOFF(d, f), d = U or D.}$$

That is to say, if the floor button at floor f for motion in direction d is off and the button is pushed and none of the elevators are currently visiting floor f and about to move in direction d, then the floor button is turned on. Conversely, if the button is on and at least one of the elevators arrives at floor f and the elevator is about to move in direction d, then the button is turned off. The notation 1..n in S(d, 1..n, f) and EAF(1..n, f) was defined in definition (8.10). The predicate V(e, f) of definition (8.5) can be defined in terms of S(d, e, f) as follows:

$$\text{V(e, f) = S(U, e, f) or S(D, e, f) or S(N, e, f)} \qquad \textbf{(8.13)}$$

The states of the elevator button and floor button were straightforward to define. Turning now to the elevators, complications arise. The state of an elevator essentially consists of a number of component substates. Kampen identifies several, such as the elevator slowing and stopping, the door opening, the door open with a timer running, or the door closing after a timeout [Kampen, 1987]. He makes the reasonable assumption that the elevator controller (the mechanism that directs the motion of the elevator) initiates a state such as S(d, e, f) and that the controller then moves the elevator through the substates. Three elevator states can now be defined, one of which S(d, e, f) was defined in definition (8.11), but is included here for completeness.

M(d, e, f):   Elevator e is Moving in direction d (floor f is next)   **(8.14)**
S(d, e, f):   Elevator e is Stopped (d-bound) at floor f
W(e, f):   Elevator e is Waiting at floor f (door closed)

These states are shown in Figure 8.15. Note that the three stopped states S(U, e, f), S(N, e, f), and S(D, e, f) have been grouped into one larger state in order to simplify the diagram and to reduce the overall number of states.

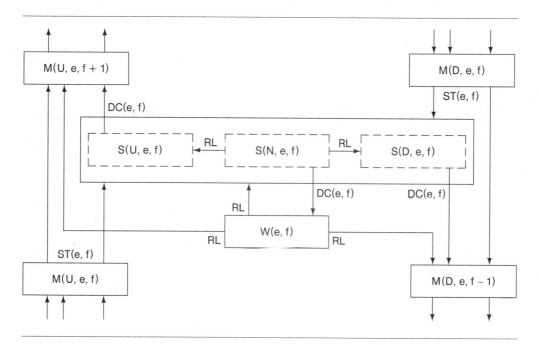

Figure 8.15 STD for elevator [Kampen, 1987].
(© 1987 IEEE)

The events that can trigger state transitions are: $DC(e, f)$, the closing of the door of elevator e at floor f; $ST(e, f)$, which occurs when the sensor on the elevator is triggered as it nears floor f and the elevator controller must decide whether or not to stop the elevator at that floor; and RL, which occurs whenever an elevator button or a floor button is pressed, and enters its ON state.

$DC(e, f)$:	Door Closed for elevator e, at floor f	**(8.15)**
$ST(e, f)$:	Sensor Triggered as elevator e nears floor f	
RL:	Request Logged (button pressed)	

These events are indicated in Figure 8.15.

Finally, the state transition rules for an elevator can be presented. They can be deduced from Figure 8.15, but in some cases additional predicates are necessary. To be more precise, Figure 8.15 is nondeterministic; among other reasons the predicates are necessary to make the STD deterministic. The interested reader should consult [Kampen, 1987] for the complete set of rules; for the sake of brevity, the only rules presented here are those which declare what happens when the door closes. The elevator moves up, down, or enters a wait state, depending on the current state.

$$S(U, e, f) \text{ and } DC(e, f) \Rightarrow M(U, e, f + 1) \qquad \textbf{(8.16)}$$
$$S(D, e, f) \text{ and } DC(e, f) \Rightarrow M(D, e, f - 1)$$
$$S(N, e, f) \text{ and } DC(e, f) \Rightarrow W(e, f)$$

The first rule states that if elevator e is in state S(U, e, f), that is, stopped at floor f about to go up and the doors close, then the elevator will move up toward the next floor. The second and third rules correspond to the cases of the elevator about to go down or with no requests pending.

The format of these rules reflects the power of finite state machines for specifying complex products. Instead of having to list a complex set of preconditions that have to hold the product to do something and then having to list all the conditions that hold after the product has done it, the specifications take the simple form

current state and **event** and **predicate** ⇒ **next state**

This type of specification is easy to write down, easy to validate, and easy to convert into a design and into code. In fact it is straightforward to construct a CASE tool that will translate a finite state machine (FSM) specification directly into source code. Maintenance is then achieved by replay. That is, if new states and/or events are needed, the specifications are modified and a new version of the product generated directly from the new specifications.

The FSM approach is more precise than the graphical technique of Gane and Sarsen presented in Section 8.3, but it is almost as easy to understand. It has a drawback in that for large systems the number of (state, event, predicate) triples can grow rapidly. Also, like Gane and Sarsen's technique, timing considerations are not handled in Kampen's formalism.

These problems can be solved using statecharts, an extension of FSMs [Harel et al., 1990]. Statecharts are extremely powerful and are supported by a CASE workbench, Statemate. The approach has been successfully used for a number of large real-time systems.

Another formal technique that can handle timing issues is Petri nets.

8.7   PETRI NETS

A major difficulty with specifying concurrent systems is coping with timing. This difficulty can manifest itself in many different ways, such as synchronization problems, race conditions, and deadlock [Silberschatz and Galvin, 1994]. While it is true that timing problems can arise as a consequence of a poor design or a faulty implementation, such designs and implementations are often the consequence of poor specifications. If the specifications are not properly drawn up, there is a very real risk that the corresponding design and implementation will be inadequate. One powerful technique for specifying systems with potential timing problems is Petri nets. A further advantage of this technique is that it can be used for the design as well.

Petri nets were invented by Carl Adam Petri [Petri, 1962]. Originally of interest only to automata theorists, Petri nets have found wide applicability in computer science, being used in such fields as performance evaluation, operating systems, and

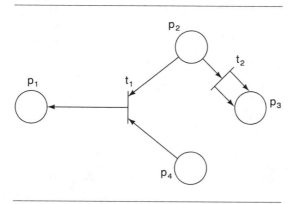

Figure 8.16 Petri net.

software engineering. In particular, Petri nets have proved to be useful for describing concurrent interrelated activities. But before the use of Petri nets for specifications can be demonstrated, a brief introduction to Petri nets is given for those readers who may be unfamiliar with them.

A Petri net consists of four parts: a set of places P, a set of transitions T, an input function I, and an output function O. Consider the Petri net shown in Figure 8.16.

The set of places P is $\{p_1, p_2, p_3, p_4\}$.

The set of transitions T is $\{t_1, t_2\}$.

The input functions for the two transitions, represented by the arrows from places to transitions, are

$$I(t_1) = \{p_2, p_4\}$$
$$I(t_2) = \{p_2\}$$

The output functions for the two transitions, represented by the arrows from transitions to places, are

$$O(t_1) = \{p_1\}$$
$$O(t_2) = \{p_3, p_3\}$$

Note the duplication of p_3; there are two arrows from t_2 to p_3.

More formally [Peterson, 1981], a Petri net structure is a 4-tuple $C = (P, T, I, O)$.

$P = \{p_1, p_2, ..., p_n\}$ is a finite set of *places*, $n \geq 0$.

$T = \{t_1, t_2, ..., t_m\}$ is a finite set of transitions, $m \geq 0$, with P and T disjoint.

$I : T \rightarrow P^\infty$ is the *input* function, a mapping from transitions to bags of places.

$O : T \rightarrow P^\infty$ is the *output* function, a mapping from transitions to bags of places. (A *bag*, or *multiset*, is a generalization of a set that allows for multiple instances of an element.)

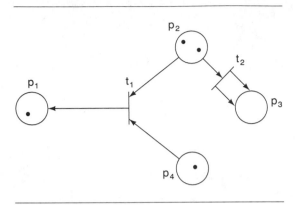

Figure 8.17 Marked Petri net.

A *marking* of a Petri net is an assignment of *tokens* to that Petri net. In Figure 8.17 there are four tokens, one in p_1, two in p_2, none in p_3, and one in p_4. The marking can be represented by the vector $(1, 2, 0, 1)$. Transition t_1 is enabled (ready to fire), because there are tokens in p_2 and in p_4; in general, a transition is enabled if each of its input places has as many tokens in it as there are arcs from the place to that transition. If t_1 were to fire, one token would be removed from p_2 and one from p_4, and one new token would be placed in p_1. The number of tokens is not conserved— two tokens are removed, but only one new one is placed in p_1. In Figure 8.17 transition t_2 is also enabled because there are tokens in p_2. If t_2 were to fire, one token would be removed from p_2 and two new tokens would be placed in p_3.

Petri nets are nondeterministic; that is, if more than one transition is able to fire, then any one of them may be fired. Figure 8.17 has marking $(1, 2, 0, 1)$; both t_1 and t_2 are enabled. Suppose that t_1 fires. The resulting marking $(2, 1, 0, 0)$ is shown in Figure 8.18 where only t_2 is enabled. It fires, the enabling token is removed from p_2, and two new tokens are placed in p_3. The marking is now $(2, 0, 2, 0)$ as shown in Figure 8.19.

More formally [Peterson, 1981], a marking M of a Petri net $C = (P, T, I, O)$ is a function from the set of places P to the set of nonnegative integers.

$$M : P \rightarrow \{0, 1, 2, ... \}$$

A marked Petri net is then a 5-tuple (P, T, I, O, M).

An important extension to a Petri net is an inhibitor arc. Referring to Figure 8.20, the inhibitor arc is marked by a small circle rather than an arrowhead. Transition t_1 is enabled because there is a token in p_3 but no token in p_2. In general a transition is enabled if there is at least one token on each of its (normal) input arcs and no tokens on any of its inhibitor input arcs. This extension will be used in a Petri net specification of the elevator problem presented in Section 8.6.1 [Guha, Lang, and Bassiouni, 1987].

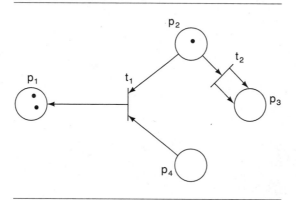

Figure 8.18 Petri net of Figure 8.17 after firing transition t_1.

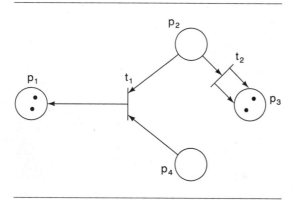

Figure 8.19 Petri net of Figure 8.18 after firing transition t_2.

8.7.1 ELEVATOR PROBLEM: PETRI NETS

Recall that an n elevator system is to be installed in a building with m floors. In this Petri net specification each floor in the building will be represented by a place F_f, $1 \leq f \leq m$, in the Petri net; an elevator is represented by a token. A token in F_f denotes that an elevator is at floor f.

First constraint Each elevator has a set of m buttons, one for each floor. These illuminate when pressed and cause the elevator to visit the corresponding floor. The illumination is canceled when the corresponding floor is visited by the elevator.

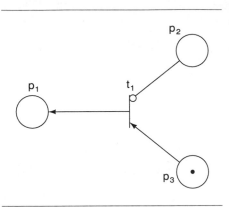

Figure 8.20   Petri net with inhibitor arc.

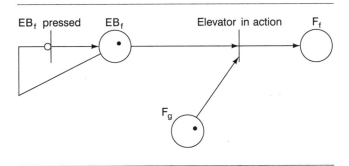

Figure 8.21   Petri net representation of an elevator button
[Guha, Lang, and Bassiouni, 1987].
(© 1987 IEEE)

To incorporate this into the specification, additional places are needed. The elevator button for floor f is represented in the Petri net by place EB_f, $1 \leq f \leq m$. More precisely, because there are n elevators, the place should be denoted $EB_{f,e}$ with $1 \leq f \leq m$, $1 \leq e \leq n$. But for the sake of simplicity of notation, the subscript e representing the elevator will be suppressed. A token in EB_f denotes that the elevator button for floor f is illuminated. Because the button must be illuminated the first time the button is pressed and subsequent button presses must be ignored, this is specified using a Petri net as shown in Figure 8.21. First, suppose that button EB_f is not illuminated. There is accordingly no token in place and hence, because of the presence of the inhibitor arc, transition EB_f pressed is enabled. The button is now pressed. The transition fires and a new token is placed in EB_f, shown in Figure 8.21. Now, no matter how many times the button is pressed, the combination of the inhibitor arc and the presence of the token means that transition EB_f pressed cannot be enabled. Therefore, there can never be more than one token in place EB_f. Suppose

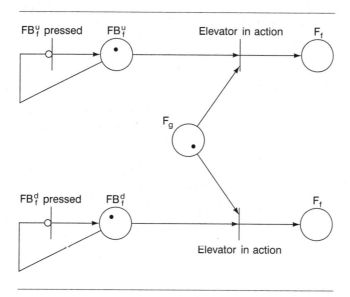

Figure 8.22 Petri net representation of floor buttons [Guha, Lang, and Bassiouni, 1987].
| (© 1987 IEEE)

that the elevator is to travel from floor g to floor f. Because the elevator is at floor g, a token is in place F_g, as shown in Figure 8.21. Transition **Elevator in action** is enabled and then fires. The tokens in EB_f and F_g are removed, thereby turning off button EB_f, and a new token appears in F_f; the firing of this transition brings the elevator from floor g to floor f.

This motion from floor g to floor f cannot take place instantaneously. To handle this and similar issues, such as the fact that it is physically impossible for a button to illuminate at the very instant it is pressed, timing must be added to the Petri net model. That is to say, in classical Petri net theory transitions are instantaneous. In practical situations such as the elevator problem, timed Petri nets [Coolahan and Roussopoulos, 1983] are needed in order to be able to associate a nonzero time with a transition.

Second constraint Each floor, except the first floor and top floor, has two buttons, one to request an up-elevator and one to request a down-elevator. These buttons illuminate when pressed. The illumination is canceled when an elevator visits the floor and then moves in the desired direction.

The floor buttons are represented by places FB_f^u and FB_f^d representing the buttons for requesting up- and down-elevators, respectively. More precisely, floor 1 has a button FB_1^u, floor m has a button FB_m^d, and the intermediate floors each have two buttons, FB_f^u and FB_f^d, $1 < f < m$. The situation when an elevator reaches floor f from floor g with one or both buttons illuminated is shown in Figure 8.22. If both the

---

JUST IN CASE YOU WANTED TO KNOW

The name *Z* was given to the formal specification language by its inventor Jean-Raymond Abrial in honor of the great set theorist Ernst Friedrich Ferdinand Zermelo (1871–1953). Because it was developed at Oxford University [Abrial, 1980], the name *Z* is properly pronounced "zed" because that is the way that the British pronounce the 26th letter of the alphabet.

Lately, however, there are moves afoot to acknowledge that Z is named after a German mathematician, and to pronounce it the German way, namely, "tzet." In response, Francophiles and Francophones point out that Abrial is a Frenchman, and that the letter Z is pronounced "zed" in French, too.

The one pronunciation that is totally unacceptable is American-style, that is, "zee." The reason is that Z (pronounced "zee") is an American fourth-generation language (see Section 12.2). More precisely, System Z is a workbench for the fourth-generation language Z. The name *System Z* is a trademark of Zortec International, Inc. However, we cannot trademark a single letter of the alphabet. Furthermore, we are all free to pronounce the letter Z the way we wish. Nevertheless, within the programming language context, the pronunciation "zee" refers to the 4GL, not the formal specification language.

Watch this space for the next round in the Z pronunciation wars!

---

buttons are illuminated, only one is turned off. To ensure that the correct button is turned off requires a more complex Petri net model; see, for example, [Ghezzi and Mandrioli, 1987].

Third constraint   When an elevator has no requests, it remains at its current floor with its doors closed.

This is easily achieved: If there are no requests, no **Elevator in action** transition is enabled.

Not only can Petri nets be used to represent the specifications, they can be used for the design as well [Guha, Lang, and Bassiouni, 1987]. Even at this stage of the development of the product, it is clear that Petri nets possess the expressive power necessary for specifying the synchronization aspects of concurrent systems.

8.8   Z

A formal specifications language that is gaining widely in popularity is Z [Spivey, 1992]. (For the correct pronunciation of the name Z, see the Just in Case You Wanted to Know box on this page.) Use of Z requires knowledge of set theory, functions, and discrete mathematics, including first-order logic. Even for users with the necessary background (and this includes most computer science majors), Z is initially difficult to learn because, in addition to the usual set theoretic and logic symbols like $\exists$, $\supset$, and $\Rightarrow$, it also uses many unusual special symbols, such as $\oplus$, $\lhd$, $\mapsto$, and $\twoheadrightarrow$.

For insight into how Z is used to specify a product, the elevator problem of Section 8.6.1 is now considered again.

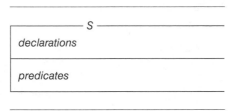

Figure 8.23   Format of Z schema *S*.

8.8.1 Elevator Problem: Z

In its simplest form, a Z specification consists of four sections, namely:

1. Given sets, data types, and constants
2. State definition
3. Initial state
4. Operations

Each of these sections is now examined in turn.

1. Given Sets   A Z specification begins with a list of *given sets*, that is, sets that need not be defined in detail. The names of any such sets appear in brackets. For the elevator problem, the given set will be called Button, the set of all buttons. The Z specification therefore begins:

[Button]

2. State Definition   A Z specification consists of a number of schemata. Each schema consists of a group of variable declarations together with a list of predicates that constrain the possible values of the variables. The format of a schema *S* is shown in Figure 8.23.

In the case of the elevator problem, there are four subsets of Button, namely the floor buttons, the elevator buttons, buttons (the set of all buttons in the elevator problem), and pushed, the set of those buttons that have been pushed (and are therefore on). Figure 8.24 depicts schema *Button_State*. The symbol P denotes the power set (the set of all subsets of a given set). The constraints, that is, the statements below the horizontal line, state that the set of floor_buttons and elevator_buttons are disjoint, and that together they constitute the set of buttons. (The sets floor_buttons and elevator_buttons are not needed in what follows; they are included in Figure 8.24 only to demonstrate the power of Z.)

3. Initial State   The *abstract initial state* describes the state when the system is first turned on. The abstract initial state for the elevator problem is

$$Button\_Init \triangleq [Button\_State' \mid pushed' = \emptyset\ ]$$

```
┌──────── Button_State ────────────────────────
│ floor_buttons, elevator_buttons: P Button
│ buttons                        : P Button
│ pushed                         : P Button
│ ─────────────────────────────────────────────
│ floor_buttons ∩ elevator_buttons = ∅
│
│ floor_buttons ∪ elevator_buttons = buttons
│
└───────────────────────────────────────────────
```

Figure 8.24 Z schema *Button_State*.

```
┌──────── Push_Button ─────────────────────────
│ Δ Button_State
│
│ button?: Button
│ ─────────────────────────────────────────────
│ (button? ∈ buttons) ∧
│ (((button? ∉ pushed) ∧ (pushed' = pushed ∪ { button? })) ∨
│   ((button? ∈ pushed) ∧ (pushed' = pushed)))
│
└───────────────────────────────────────────────
```

Figure 8.25 Z specification of operation *Push_Button*.

This is a *vertical schema definition*, as opposed to a *horizontal schema definition*, such as Figure 8.24. The vertical schema states that when the elevator system is first turned on, the set pushed is initially empty, that is, all the buttons are off.

4. Operations If a button is pushed for the first time, then that button is turned on. The button is added to the set pushed. This is depicted in the schema of Figure 8.25 in which operation *Push_Button* is defined. The Δ in the first line of the schema denotes that this operation changes the state of **Button_State**. The operation has one input variable, namely button?. As in various other languages (such as CSP), the question mark ? denotes an input variable, whereas an exclamation mark ! denotes an output variable.

The predicate part of an operation consists of a group of preconditions that must hold before the operation is invoked and postconditions that must hold after the operation has completed execution. Provided the preconditions are met, the postconditions will hold after completing execution. However, if the operation is invoked without the preconditions being satisfied, unspecified (and therefore unpredictable) results can occur.

```
┌─────────────── Floor_Arrival ──────────────────────┐
│ ΔButton_State                                       │
│                                                     │
│ button?: Button                                     │
├─────────────────────────────────────────────────────┤
│ (button? ∈ buttons) ∧                               │
│ (((button? ∈ pushed) ∧ (pushed' = pushed \ {button?}))∨│
│  ((button? ∉ pushed) ∧ (pushed' = pushed)))         │
└─────────────────────────────────────────────────────┘
```

Figure 8.26   Z specification of operation *Floor_Arrival*.

The first precondition of Figure 8.25 states that **button?** must be a member of **buttons**, the set of all buttons in this elevator system. If the second precondition, namely **button?** $\notin$ **pushed**, is met (that is, if the button is not on), then the set of **pushed** buttons is updated to include **button?**. In Z the new value of a variable is denoted by a prime ('). Thus, the postcondition says that after operation *Push_ Button* has been performed, **button?** must be added to the set **pushed**. There is no need to turn on the button explicitly; it is sufficient that **button?** is now an element of **pushed**.

The other possibility is that a button that has already been pushed is pushed again. Because **button?** $\in$ **pushed**, the third precondition holds[1] and, as required, nothing happens. This is indicated by the statement **pushed' = pushed**; the new state of **pushed** is the same as the old state.

Now suppose an elevator arrives at a floor. If the corresponding floor button is on, then it must be turned off, and similarly for the corresponding elevator button. That is, if **button?** is an element of **pushed**, then it must be removed from the set, as shown in Figure 8.26. (The symbol \ denotes set difference.) However, if a button is not on, then set **pushed** is unchanged.

The solution presented in this section is an oversimplification in that it does not distinguish between up and down floor buttons. Nevertheless, it gives an indication how Z can be used to specify the behavior of the buttons in the elevator problem.

8.8.2   ANALYSIS OF Z

Z has been used successfully in a wide variety of projects, including CASE tools [Hall, 1990], a real-time kernel [Spivey, 1990], and an oscilloscope [Delisle and Garlan, 1990]. Z has also been used to specify large portions of a new release of CICS, the IBM transaction-processing system [Nix and Collins, 1988].

---

[1]Without the third precondition, the specification would not state what is to happen if a button that has already been pushed is pushed again. The results would then be unspecified.

These successes are perhaps somewhat surprising in view of the fact that, even for the simplified version of the elevator problem, it is clear that Z is not straightforward to use. First, there is the problem caused by the notation; a new user has to learn the set of symbols and their meanings before being able to read Z specifications, let alone write them. Second, not every software engineer necessarily has the required training in mathematics to be able to use Z (although recent graduates of almost all computer science programs either know enough mathematics to use Z, or could learn what they still need to know without much difficulty).

Z is perhaps the most widely used formal language of its type. Why is this, and why has Z been so successful, especially on large-scale projects? A number of different reasons have been put forward.

First, it is easy to find faults in specifications written in Z, especially during inspections of the specifications themselves and inspections of designs or code against the formal specifications [Nix and Collins, 1988; Hall, 1990].

Second, writing Z specifications requires the specifier to be extremely precise; as a result of this need for exactness, there appear to be fewer ambiguities, contradictions, and omissions than with informal specifications.

Third, the fact that Z is a formal language allows developers to prove specifications correct when necessary. Thus, although some organizations rarely do any correctness proving of Z, such proofs have been done, even for such practical specifications as the CICS storage manager [Woodcock, 1989].

Fourth, it has been suggested that software professionals with only high-school mathematics can be taught in a relatively short period of time to write Z specifications [Hall, 1990]. Clearly such individuals cannot prove the resulting specifications to be correct, but then formal specifications do not necessarily always have to be proved to be correct.

Fifth, the use of Z has decreased the cost of software development. There is no doubt that more time has to be spent on the specifications themselves than when informal techniques are used, but the overall time for the complete development process is decreased.

Sixth, the problem that the client cannot understand specifications written in Z has been solved in a number of ways, including rewriting the specifications in natural language. It has been found that the resulting natural language specifications are clearer than informal specifications constructed from scratch. (This was also the experience with Meyer's English paraphrase of his formal specification for Naur's text-processing problem, described in Section 8.2.1.)

The bottom line is that, notwithstanding arguments to the contrary, Z has been successfully used in the software industry for a number of large-scale projects. Although it is true that the vast majority of specifications continue to be written in languages considerably less formal than Z, there is a growing global trend toward the use of formal specifications. The use of such formal specifications has traditionally been largely a European practice. However, more and more organizations in the United States are employing formal specifications of one sort or another. The extent to which Z and similar languages will be used in the future remains to be seen.

8.9   OTHER FORMAL TECHNIQUES

Many other formal techniques have been proposed. These techniques are extremely varied. For example, Anna [Luckham and von Henke, 1985] is a formal specification language for Ada. Some formal techniques are knowledge-based such as Refine [Smith, Kotik, and Westfold, 1985] and Gist [Balzer, 1985]. Gist was designed so that users can describe processes in a way that is as close as possible to the way that we think about processes. This was to be achieved by formalizing the constructs used in natural languages. In practice, Gist specifications are as hard to read as most other formal specifications, so much so that a paraphraser from Gist to English has had to be written.

Vienna definition method (VDM) [Jones, 1986b; Bjørner, 1987] is a technique based on denotational semantics [Gordon, 1979]. VDM can be applied not just to the specifications, but also to the design and implementation. VDM has been successfully used in a number of projects, most spectacularly in the Dansk Datamatik Center development of the DDC Ada Compiler System [Oest, 1986].

A different way of looking at specifications is to view them in terms of sequences of events, where an event is either a simple action or a communication that transfers data into or out of the system. For example, in the elevator problem, one event consists of pushing the elevator button for floor f on elevator e and its resulting illumination. Another event is elevator e leaving floor f in the downward direction and the canceling of the illumination of the corresponding floor button. The language Communicating Sequential Processes (CSP) invented by Hoare is based on the idea of describing the behavior of a system in terms of such events [Hoare, 1985]. In CSP, a process is described in terms of the sequences of events in which the process will engage with its environment. Processes interact with each other by sending messages to one another. CSP allows processes to be combined in a wide variety of ways, such as sequentially, in parallel, or interleaved nondeterministically.

The power of CSP lies in the fact that CSP specifications are executable [Delisle and Schwartz, 1987] and, as a result, can be checked for internal consistency. In addition, CSP provides a framework for going from specifications to design to implementation by a sequence of steps that preserve validity. In other words, if the specifications are correct and if the transformations are correctly performed, then the design and implementation will be correct as well. Going from design to implementation is particularly straightforward if the implementation language is Ada.

However, CSP also has its disadvantages. In particular, like Z it is not an easy language to learn. An attempt was made to include a CSP specification for the elevator problem in this book [Schwartz and Delisle, 1987]. But the quantity of essential preliminary material and the level of detail of explanation needed to describe each CSP statement adequately were simply too great to permit inclusion in a book as general as this one. The relationship between the power of a specification language and its degree of difficulty of use is expanded in the next section.

8.10 COMPARISON OF SPECIFICATION TECHNIQUES

The main lesson of this chapter is that every development organization has to decide what type of specification language is appropriate for the product about to be developed. An informal technique is easy to learn, but does not have the power of a semiformal or formal technique. Conversely, each formal technique supports a variety of features that may include executability, correctness proving, or transformability to design and implementation through a series of correctness-preserving steps. But while it is generally true that the more formal the technique the greater its power, it is also generally true that formal techniques can be difficult to learn and use. Also, a formal specification can be difficult for the client to understand. In other words, there is a trade-off between ease of use and the power of a specification language.

In some circumstances, the choice of specification language type is easy. For example, if the vast majority of the members of the development team do not have any training in computer science, then it is virtually impossible to use anything other than an informal or semiformal specification technique. Conversely, where a mission-critical real-time system is being built in a research laboratory, the power of a formal specification technique will almost certainly be required.

An additional complicating factor is that many of the newer formal techniques have not been tested under practical conditions. There is a considerable risk involved in using such a technique. Large sums of money will be needed to pay for training the relevant members of the development team, and more money will be spent while the team adjusts from using the language in the classroom to using it on the actual project. It may well happen that the language's supporting software tools do not work properly, as happened with SREM [Scheffer, Stone, and Rzepka, 1985], with the resulting additional expense and time slippage. But if everything works, and if the software project management plan takes into account the additional time and money needed when a new technology is used on a nontrivial project for the first time, huge gains are possible.

What specification technique should be used for a specific project? It depends on the project, the development team, the management team, and on myriad other factors, such as the client insisting that a specific method be used (or not be used). As with so many other aspects of software engineering, trade-offs have to be made. Unfortunately, there is no simple rule for deciding which specification technique to use.

8.11 TESTING DURING THE SPECIFICATION PHASE

During the specification phase the functionality of the proposed product is precisely expressed in the specification document. It is vital to verify that the specification document is correct. One way to do this is by means of a walkthrough of the specification document (Section 5.2.1).

A more powerful mechanism for detecting faults in a specification document is an inspection (Section 5.2.3). A team of inspectors reviews the specifications against a checklist. Typical items on a specification inspection checklist include: Have the required hardware resources been specified? Have the acceptance criteria been specified?

Inspections were first suggested by Fagan in the context of testing the design and the code [Fagan, 1976]. Fagan's work is described in detail in Section 5.2.3. However, inspections have also proved to be of considerable use in the testing of specifications. For example, Doolan used inspections to validate the specifications of a product that, when built, consisted of over 2 million lines of FORTRAN [Doolan, 1992]. From data on the cost of fixing faults in the product, he was able to deduce that each hour invested in inspections saved 30 hours of execution-based fault detection and correction.

When a specification has been drawn up using a formal technique, other testing techniques can be applied. For example, correctness proving methods (Section 5.5) can be employed. Even if formal proofs are not performed, informal proof techniques such as those used in Section 5.5.1 can be an extremely useful way of highlighting specification faults. In fact, the product and its proof should be developed in parallel. In this way, faults will be quickly detected.

8.12   CASE Tools for the Specification Phase

Two classes of CASE tools are particularly helpful during the specification phase. The first is a graphical tool. Whether a product is represented using data flow diagrams (DFD), Petri nets, entity-relationship diagrams, or any of the many other representations omitted from this book simply for reasons of space, drawing the entire product by hand is a lengthy process. In addition, making substantial changes can result in having to redraw everything from scratch. Having a drawing tool is therefore a great time-saver. Tools of this type exist for the specification techniques described in this chapter, as well as for many other graphical representations for specifications. A second tool that is needed during this phase is a data dictionary. As mentioned in Section 4.3.1, this is a tool that stores the name and representation (format) of every component of every data item in the product, including data flows and their components, data stores and their components, and processes and their internal variables. Again, there is a wide selection of data dictionaries running on a variety of hardware.

What really is needed is not a separate graphical tool and a separate data dictionary. Instead, the two tools should be integrated, so that any change made to a data component is automatically reflected in the corresponding part of the specification. There are many examples of this type of tool; some of the more popular are ADW, Analyst/Designer, Excelerator, Software through Pictures, System Architect, and Teamwork. Furthermore, many such tools also incorporate an automatic consistency checker that ensures consistency between the specification document and the corresponding design document. For example, it is possible to check that every item in the specification document is carried forward to the design document and that everything mentioned in the design has been declared in the data dictionary.

A specification technique is unlikely to receive widespread acceptance unless there is a tool-rich CASE environment supporting that technique. For example, SREM (Section 8.4) would probably be used far more widely today had REVS, its associated CASE tool set, performed better in the U.S. Air Force tests [Scheffer, Stone, and Rzepka, 1985]. It is not easy to specify a system correctly, even for experienced software professionals. It is only reasonable to provide specifiers with a set of state-of-the-art CASE tools to assist them in every way possible.

8.13   METRICS FOR THE SPECIFICATION PHASE

As with all other phases, during the specification phase it is necessary to measure the five fundamental metrics, namely size, cost, duration, effort, and quality. One measure of the size of a specification is the number of pages in the specification document. If the same technique is used for specifying a number of products, then differences in specification size may be significant predictors of the effort that will be needed to build the various products.

Turning to quality, a vital aspect of specification inspections is the record of fault statistics. Noting the number of faults of each type found during an inspection is thus an integral part of the inspection process. Also, the rate at which faults are detected can give a measure of the efficiency of the inspection process.

Metrics for predicting the size of the target product include the number of items in the data dictionary. Several different counts should be taken, including the number of files, data items, processes, and so on. This information can give management a preliminary estimate regarding the effort that will be required to build the product. It is important to note that this information will be tentative at best. After all, during the design phase a process in a DFD may be broken down into a number of different modules. Conversely, a number of processes may together constitute a single module. Nevertheless, metrics derived from the data dictionary can give management an early clue as to the eventual size of the target product.

8.14   MSG CASE STUDY: STRUCTURED SYSTEMS ANALYSIS

As a consequence of the careful interviews followed by the building of a rapid prototype in the requirements analysis phase, the Gane and Sarsen structured systems analysis process is straightforward. The data flow diagram is shown in Figure 8.27. The remainder of the structured systems analysis appears in Appendix D.

One aspect of the specifications requires comment. In the data flow diagram (Figure 8.27), two of the stores of data are INCOME DATA and GRANT DATA.

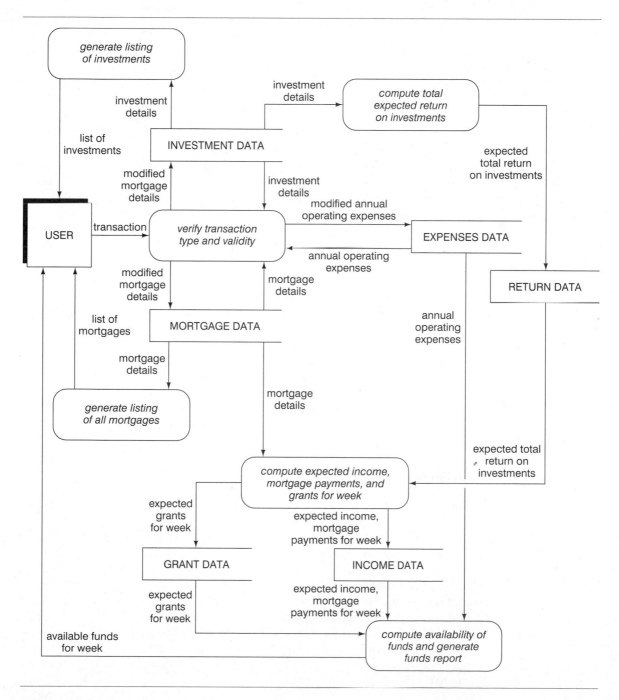

Figure 8.27 Data flow diagram for MSG Case Study.

These two stores of data are then refined in Step 5, and their physical structure specified in Step 6. In fact, neither INCOME DATA nor GRANT DATA need be implemented as files. INCOME DATA consists of two amounts, namely, the expected income and the expected mortgage payments for the coming week, and GRANT DATA is the expected amount that is available for grants in the coming week. These three quantities are computed by process *compute expected income, mortgage payments, and grants for week*. They could in theory be stored as global variables or passed as parameters from process *compute expected income, mortgage payments, and grants for week* to process *compute availability of funds and generate funds report*. However, that design is not a good idea for two reasons. First, the standard for specification documents in many organizations does not allow two processes to be directly linked in a data flow diagram. Thus, data stores INCOME DATA and GRANT DATA are needed in Figure 8.27 in order to conform to that standard. Second, having the two data stores reduces the coupling between processes *compute expected income, mortgage payments, and grants for week* and *compute availability of funds and generate funds report*. As depicted in Figure 8.27, once the expected income, mortgage, and grants data have been computed and stored, a separate program to determine the available funds for the week can be run at any time. In short, having the two "unnecessary" files is in fact good software engineering practice and increases the maintainability of the resulting product by reducing the coupling of the two processes. Data store RETURN DATA is needed for similar reasons.

The organization and presentation of the material in Appendix D is such that the client can rapidly understand exactly what is going to be built. However, a major factor in achieving that understanding is the fact that the client was able to experiment with the rapid prototype during the requirements phase.

Chapter Review

Specifications (Section 8.1) can be expressed informally (Section 8.2), semiformally (Sections 8.3 through 8.5), or formally (Sections 8.6 through 8.9). The major theme of this chapter is that informal techniques are easy to use, but imprecise; this is demonstrated by means of an example (Section 8.2.1). Conversely, formal techniques are powerful, but require a nontrivial investment in training time (Section 8.10). One semiformal technique, namely Gane and Sarsen's structured systems analysis, is described in some detail (Section 8.3). Formal techniques that are described include finite state machines (Section 8.6), Petri nets (Section 8.7), and Z (Section 8.8). Material on specification reviews appears in Section 8.11. Next follows a description of CASE tools (Section 8.12) and metrics (Section 8.13) for the specification phase. The chapter ends with the specification phase of the MSG Case Study (Section 8.14).

For Further Reading

The classic texts on specific semiformal techniques are the books by DeMarco [DeMarco, 1978], Gane and Sarsen [Gane and Sarsen, 1979], and Yourdon and Constantine [Yourdon and Constantine, 1979]. These ideas have been updated in [Martin and McClure, 1985] and also in [Yourdon, 1989]. Data-oriented design, described in Section 11.5, is a design technique that is integrated with a different class of semiformal specification techniques; details are found in [Orr, 1981], [Warnier, 1981], and [Jackson, 1983]. SADT is described in [Ross, 1985], and PSL/PSA is described in [Teichroew and Hershey, 1977]. Two sources of information on SREM are [Alford, 1985] and [Scheffer, Stone, and Rzepka, 1985].

An outstanding collection of papers on formal techniques can be found in the September 1990 issues of *IEEE Transactions on Software Engineering, IEEE Computer, IEEE Software*, and *ACM SIGSOFT Software Engineering Notes*. Of particular interest is [Hall, 1990] that should be read in its entirety. Six formal techniques are described in [Wing, 1990].

An early reference to the finite state machine approach is [Naur, 1964] where it is unfortunately referred to as the Turing machine approach. The finite state machine approach is described in [Ferrentino and Mills, 1977] and [Linger, 1980]. An FSM model for real-time systems is given in [Chandrasekharan, Dasarathy, and Kishimoto, 1985]. A graphical tool for FSMs is described in [Jacob, 1985], and the use of FSMs in specifying the interaction between humans and computers is found in [Wasserman, 1985]. Statecharts are a powerful extension of FSMs; they are described in [Harel, 1987] and [Harel et al., 1990]. An object-oriented extension of statecharts appears in [Coleman, Hayes, and Bear, 1992].

[Peterson, 1981] is an excellent introduction to Petri nets and their applications. The use of Petri nets in prototyping is described in [Bruno and Marchetto, 1986]. Timed Petri nets are described in [Coolahan and Roussopoulos, 1983].

With regard to Z, [Spivey, 1988] and [Diller, 1990] are good introductory texts. For the reference manual with full details about the specification language, see [Spivey, 1992].

Specification of real-time systems is discussed in the September 1992 issue of *IEEE Transactions on Software Engineering*. The specification of distributed systems is described in [Kramer, 1994]. The proceedings of the International Workshops on Software Specification and Design are a preeminent source for research ideas regarding specifications.

Problems

8.1 Why should the following constraints not appear in a specification document:

(i) The product must significantly improve data collection rates on a national basis.

(ii) The graphical display unit must be set up at a reasonable cost.

8.2 Consider the following recipe for grilled pockwester.

Ingredients

1 large onion

1 can of frozen orange juice

Freshly squeezed juice of 1 lemon

½ cup bread crumbs

Flour

Milk

3 medium-sized shallots

2 medium-sized eggplants

1 fresh pockwester

½ cup Pouilly Fuissé

1 garlic

Parmesan cheese

4 free-range eggs

The night before, take one lemon, squeeze it, strain the juice, and freeze it. Take one large onion and three shallots, dice them, and grill them in a skillet. When clouds of black smoke start to come off, add 2 cups of fresh orange juice. Stir vigorously. Slice the lemon into paper-thin slices and add to the mixture. In the meantime, coat the mushrooms in flour, dip them in milk, and then shake them up in a paper bag with the bread crumbs. In a saucepan heat ½ cup of Pouilly Fuissé. When it reaches 170° add the sugar and continue to heat. When the sugar has caramelized, add the mushrooms. Blend the mixture for 10 minutes or until all lumps have been removed. Add the eggs. Now take the pockwester and kill it by sprinkling it with frobs. Skin the pockwester, break it into bite-sized chunks, and add it to the mixture. Bring to a boil and simmer uncovered. The eggs should previously have been vigorously stirred with a wire whisk for 5 minutes. When the pockwester is soft to the touch, place it on a serving platter, sprinkle with Parmesan cheese, and broil for not more than 4 minutes.

Determine the ambiguities, omissions, and contradictions in the preceding specification. (For the record, a pockwester is an imaginary sort of fish and "frobs" is slang for generic hors d'oeuvres.)

Correct the specification paragraph of Section 8.2 to reflect the client's wishes more accurately. **8.3**

Use mathematical formulas to represent the specification paragraph of Section 8.2. **8.4** Compare your answer with your answer to Problem 8.3.

Write a precise English specification for the product to determine whether a bank **8.5** statement is correct (Problem 6.17).

Draw a data flow diagram for the specification you drew up for Problem 8.5. Ensure **8.6** that your DFD simply reflects the flow of data and that no assumptions regarding computerization have been made.

Consider the automated library circulation system of Problem 6.18. Write down **8.7** precise specifications for the library circulation system.

Draw a data flow diagram showing the operation of the library circulation system of **8.8** Problem 6.18.

Complete the specification document for the library circulation system of Problem **8.9** 6.18 using Gane and Sarsen's technique. Where data have not been specified (for example, the total number of books checked in/out each day), make your own assumptions, but make sure that they are clearly indicated.

A floating-point binary number consists of an optional sign followed by one or more **8.10** bits, followed by the letter E, followed by another optional sign, followed by one or more bits. Examples of floating-point binary numbers include 11010E−1010, −100101E11101, and +1E0.
　　More formally, this can be expressed as:

```
<floating-point binary>  ::=  [<sign>] <bitstring> E [<sign>] <bitstring>
<sign>                   ::=  + | −
<bitstring>              ::=  <bit> [<bitstring>]
<bit>                    ::=  0 | 1
```

(The notation [...] denotes an optional item, and a | b denotes a or b).
　　Specify a finite state machine that will take as input a string of characters and determine whether or not that string constitutes a valid floating-point binary number.

Use the finite state machine approach to specify the library circulation system of **8.11** Problem 6.18.

Show how your solution to Problem 8.11 can be used to design and implement a **8.12** menu-driven product for the library circulation system.

Use a Petri net to specify the circulation of a single book through the library of **8.13** Problem 6.18. Include operations H, C, and R in your specification.

You are a software engineer working for a large company that specializes in **8.14** computerizing library systems. Your manager asks you to specify the complete library circulation system of Problem 6.18 using Z. What is your reaction?

(Term Project) Using the technique specified by your instructor, draw up a specifica- **8.15** tion document for the Osbert Oglesby product described in Appendix A.

8.16 (Case Study) Draw up the requirements of the MSG product using the finite state machine approach.

8.17 (Case Study) Use the Petri net technique to specify the states through which a single investment in the MSG product passes.

8.18 (Case Study) Specify a portion of the MSG product using the Z constructs of Section 8.8.

8.19 (Reading in Software Engineering) Your instructor will distribute copies of [Hall, 1990]. Do you agree with Hall's position, or do you feel that some of the "seven myths" are at least partially true? Justify your answer.

References

[Abrial, 1980] J.-R. ABRIAL, "The Specification Language Z: Syntax and Semantics," Oxford University Computing Laboratory, Programming Research Group, Oxford, UK, April 1980.

[Alford, 1985] M. ALFORD, "SREM at the Age of Eight: The Distributed Computing Design System," *IEEE Computer* **18** (April 1985), pp. 36–46.

[Balzer, 1985] R. BALZER, "A 15 Year Perspective on Automatic Programming," *IEEE Transactions on Software Engineering* **SE-11** (November 1985), pp. 1257–1268.

[Bjørner, 1987] D. BJØRNER, "On the Use of Formal Methods in Software Development," *Proceedings of the Ninth International Conference on Software Engineering,* Monterey, CA, March 1987, pp. 17–29.

[Brady, 1977] J. M. BRADY, *The Theory of Computer Science,* Chapman and Hall, London, 1977.

[Bratley, Fox, and Schrage, 1987] P. BRATLEY, B. L. FOX, AND L. E. SCHRAGE, *Guide to Simulation,* Second Edition, Springer-Verlag, New York, 1987.

[Bruno and Marchetto, 1986] G. BRUNO AND G. MARCHETTO, "Process-Translatable Petri Nets for the Rapid Prototyping of Process Control Systems," *IEEE Transactions on Software Engineering* **SE-12** (February 1986), pp. 346–357.

[Chandrasekharan, Dasarathy, and Kishimoto, 1985] M. CHANDRASEKHARAN, B. DASARATHY, AND Z. KISHIMOTO, "Requirements-Based Testing of Real-Time Systems: Modeling for Testability," *IEEE Computer* **18** (April 1985), pp. 71–80.

[Chen, 1976] P. CHEN, "The Entity-Relationship Model—Towards a Unified View of Data," *ACM Transactions on Database Systems* **1** (March 1976), pp. 9–36.

[Chen, 1983] P. P.-S. CHEN, "ER—A Historical Perspective and Future Directions," in: *Entity Relationship Approach to Software Engineering,* C. G. Davis (Editor), North-Holland, Amsterdam, 1983.

[Coleman, Hayes, and Bear, 1992] D. COLEMAN, F. HAYES, AND S. BEAR, "Introducing Objectcharts or How to Use Statecharts in Object-Oriented Design," *IEEE Transactions on Software Engineering* **18** (January 1992), pp. 9–18.

[Coolahan and Roussopoulos, 1983] J. E. COOLAHAN, JR., AND N. ROUSSOPOULOS, "Timing Requirements for Time-Driven Systems Using Augmented Petri Nets," *IEEE Transactions on Software Engineering* **SE-9** (September 1983), pp. 603–616.

[Dart, Ellison, Feiler, and Habermann, 1987] S. A. DART, R. J. ELLISON, P. H. FEILER, AND A. N. HABERMANN, "Software Development Environments," *IEEE Computer* **20** (November 1987), pp. 18–28.

[Delisle and Garlan, 1990] N. DELISLE AND D. GARLAN, "A Formal Description of an Oscilloscope," *IEEE Software* **7** (September 1990), pp. 29–36.

[Delisle and Schwartz, 1987] N. DELISLE AND M. SCHWARTZ, "A Programming Environment for CSP," *Proceedings of the Second ACM SIGSOFT/SIGPLAN Software Engineering Symposium on Practical Software Development Environments, ACM SIGPLAN Notices* **22** (January 1987), pp. 34–41.

[DeMarco, 1978] T. DEMARCO, *Structured Analysis and System Specification,* Yourdon Press, New York, 1978.

[Diller, 1990] A. DILLER, *Z: An Introduction to Formal Methods,* John Wiley and Sons, Chichester, UK, 1990.

[Doolan, 1992] E. P. DOOLAN, "Experience with Fagan's Inspection Method," *Software— Practice and Experience* **22** (February 1992), pp. 173–182.

[Fagan, 1976] M. E. FAGAN, "Design and Code Inspections to Reduce Errors in Program Development," *IBM Systems Journal* **15** (No. 3, 1976), pp. 182–211.

[Ferrentino and Mills, 1977] A. B. FERRENTINO AND H. D. MILLS, "State Machines and Their Semantics in Software Engineering," *Proceedings of the First International Computer Software and Applications Conference, COMPSAC '77,* Chicago, 1977, pp. 242–251.

[Gane and Sarsen, 1979] C. GANE AND T. SARSEN, *Structured Systems Analysis: Tools and Techniques,* Prentice-Hall, Englewood Cliffs, NJ, 1979.

[Ghezzi and Mandrioli, 1987] C. GHEZZI AND D. MANDRIOLI, "On Eclecticism in Specifications: A Case Study Centered around Petri Nets," *Proceedings of the Fourth International Workshop on Software Specification and Design,* Monterey, CA, 1987, pp. 216–224.

[Goodenough and Gerhart, 1975] J. B. GOODENOUGH AND S. L. GERHART, "Toward a Theory of Test Data Selection," *Proceedings of the Third International Conference on Reliable Software,* Los Angeles, 1975, pp. 493–510. Also published in: *IEEE Transactions on Software Engineering* **SE-1** (June 1975), pp. 156–173. Revised version: J. B. Goodenough, and S. L. Gerhart, "Toward a Theory of Test Data Selection: Data Selection Criteria," in: *Current Trends in Programming Methodology, Volume 2,* R. T. Yeh (Editor), Prentice-Hall, Englewood Cliffs, NJ, 1977, pp. 44–79.

[Gordon, 1979] M. J. C. GORDON, *The Denotational Description of Programming Languages: An Introduction,* Springer-Verlag, New York, 1979.

[Guha, Lang, and Bassiouni, 1987] R. K. GUHA, S. D. LANG, AND M. BASSIOUNI, "Software Specification and Design Using Petri Nets," *Proceedings of the Fourth International Workshop on Software Specification and Design,* Monterey, CA, April 1987, pp. 225–230.

[Hall, 1990] A. HALL, "Seven Myths of Formal Methods," *IEEE Software* **7** (September 1990), pp. 11–19.

[Harel, 1987] D. HAREL, "Statecharts: A Visual Formalism for Complex Systems," *Science of Computer Programming* **8** (June 1987), pp. 231–274.

[Harel et al., 1990] D. HAREL, H. LACHOVER, A. NAAMAD, A. PNUELI, M. POLITI, R. SHERMAN, A. SHTULL-TRAURING, AND M. TRAKHTENBROT, "STATEMATE: A Working Environment for the Development of Complex Reactive Systems," *IEEE Transactions on Software Engineering* **16** (April 1990), pp. 403–414.

[Hoare, 1985] C. A. R. HOARE, *Communicating Sequential Processes,* Prentice-Hall International, Englewood Cliffs, NJ, 1985.

[IWSSD, 1986] Call for Papers, Fourth International Workshop on Software Specification and Design, *ACM SIGSOFT Software Engineering Notes* **11** (April 1986), pp. 94–96.

[Jackson, 1983] M. A. JACKSON, *System Development,* Prentice-Hall, Englewood Cliffs, NJ, 1983.

[Jacob, 1985] R. J. K. JACOB, "A State Transition Diagram Language for Visual Programming," *IEEE Computer* **18** (August 1985), pp. 51–59.

[Jain, 1991] R. JAIN, *The Art of Computer Systems Performance Analysis: Techniques for Experimental Design, Measurement, Simulation, and Modeling,* John Wiley and Sons, New York, 1991.

[Jones, 1986b] C. B. JONES, *Systematic Software Development Using VDM,* Prentice-Hall, Englewood Cliffs, NJ, 1986.

[Kampen, 1987] G. R. KAMPEN, "An Eclectic Approach to Specification," *Proceedings of the Fourth International Workshop on Software Specification and Design,* Monterey, CA, April 1987, pp. 178–182.

[Knuth, 1968] D. E. KNUTH, *The Art of Computer Programming, Volume I, Fundamental Algorithms,* Addison-Wesley, Reading, MA, 1968.

[Kramer, 1994] J. KRAMER, "Distributed Software Engineering," *Proceedings of the 16th International Conference on Software Engineering,* Sorrento, Italy, May 1994, pp. 253–263.

[Leavenworth, 1970] B. LEAVENWORTH, Review #19420, *Computing Reviews* **11** (July 1970), pp. 396–397.

[Linger, 1980] R. C. LINGER, "The Management of Software Engineering. Part III. Software Design Practices," *IBM Systems Journal* **19** (No. 4, 1980), pp. 432–450.

[London, 1971] R. L. LONDON, "Software Reliability through Proving Programs Correct," *Proceedings of the IEEE International Symposium on Fault-Tolerant Computing,* March 1971.

[Luckham and von Henke, 1985] D. C. LUCKHAM AND F. W. VON HENKE, "An Overview of Anna, a Specification Language for Ada," *IEEE Software* **2** (March 1985), pp. 9–22.

[Martin and McClure, 1985] J. P. MARTIN AND C. MCCLURE, *Diagramming Techniques for Analysts and Programmers,* Prentice-Hall, Englewood Cliffs, NJ, 1985.

[Meyer, 1985] B. MEYER, "On Formalism in Specifications, " *IEEE Software* **2** (January 1985), pp. 6–26.

[Naur, 1964] P. NAUR, "The Design of the GIER ALGOL Compiler," in: *Annual Review in Automatic Programming, Volume 4,* Pergamon Press, Oxford, UK, 1964, pp. 49–85.

[Naur, 1969] P. NAUR, "Programming by Action Clusters," *BIT* **9** (No. 3, 1969), pp. 250–258.

[Nix and Collins, 1988] C. J. NIX AND B. P. COLLINS, "The Use of Software Engineering, Including the Z Notation, in the Development of CICS," *Quality Assurance* **14** (September 1988), pp. 103–110.

[Oest, 1986] O. N. OEST, "VDM from Research to Practice," *Proceedings of the IFIP Congress, Information Processing '86,* 1986, pp. 527–533.

[Orr, 1981] K. ORR, *Structured Requirements Definition,* Ken Orr and Associates, Inc., Topeka, KS, 1981.

[Peterson, 1981] J. L. PETERSON, *Petri Net Theory and the Modeling of Systems,* Prentice-Hall, Englewood Cliffs, NJ, 1981.

[Petri, 1962] C. A. PETRI, "Kommunikation mit Automaten," Ph.D. Dissertation, University of Bonn, Germany, 1962. (In German)

[Pollack, Hicks, and Harrison, 1971] S. L. POLLACK, H. T. HICKS, JR., AND W. J. HARRISON, *Decision Tables: Theory and Practice,* Wiley-Interscience, New York, 1971.

[Ross, 1985] D. T. Ross, "Applications and Extensions of SADT," *IEEE Computer* **18** (April 1985), pp. 25–34.

[Scheffer, Stone, and Rzepka, 1985] P. A. Scheffer, A. H. Stone, III, and W. E. Rzepka, "A Case Study of SREM," *IEEE Computer* **18** (April 1985), pp. 47–54.

[Schwartz and Delisle, 1987] M. D. Schwartz and N. M. Delisle, "Specifying a Lift Control System with CSP," *Proceedings of the Fourth International Workshop on Software Specification and Design,* Monterey, CA, April 1987, pp. 21–27.

[Silberschatz and Galvin, 1994] A. Silberschatz and P. B. Galvin, *Operating System Concepts,* Fourth Edition, Addison-Wesley, Reading, MA, 1994.

[Smith, Kotik, and Westfold, 1985] D. R. Smith, G. B. Kotik, and S. J. Westfold, "Research on Knowledge-Based Software Environments at the Kestrel Institute," *IEEE Transactions on Software Engineering* **SE-11** (November 1985), pp. 1278–1295.

[Spivey, 1988] J. M. Spivey, *Understanding Z: A Specification Language and Its Informal Semantics,* Cambridge University Press, Cambridge, UK, 1988.

[Spivey, 1990] J. M. Spivey, "Specifying a Real-Time Kernel," *IEEE Software* **7** (September 1990), pp. 21–28.

[Spivey, 1992] J. M. Spivey, *The Z Notation: A Reference Manual,* Prentice-Hall, New York, 1992.

[Teichroew and Hershey, 1977] D. Teichroew and E. A. Hershey, III, "PSL/PSA: A Computer-Aided Technique for Structured Documentation and Analysis of Information Processing Systems," *IEEE Transactions on Software Engineering* **SE-3** (January 1977), pp. 41–48.

[Warnier, 1981] J. D. Warnier, *Logical Construction of Systems,* Van Nostrand Reinhold, New York, 1981.

[Wasserman, 1985] A. I. Wasserman, "Extending State Transition Diagrams for the Specification of Human-Computer Interaction," *IEEE Transactions on Software Engineering* **SE-11** (August, 1985), pp. 699–713.

[Wing, 1990] J. Wing, "A Specifier's Introduction to Formal Methods," *IEEE Computer* **23** (September 1990), pp. 8–24.

[Woodcock, 1989] J. Woodcock, "Calculating Properties of Z Specifications," *ACM SIGSOFT Software Engineering Notes* **14** (July 1989), pp. 43–54.

[Yourdon, 1989] E. Yourdon, *Modern Structured Analysis,* Yourdon Press, Englewood Cliffs, NJ, 1989.

[Yourdon and Constantine, 1979] E. Yourdon and L. L. Constantine, *Structured Design: Fundamentals of a Discipline of Computer Program and Systems Design,* Prentice-Hall, Englewood Cliffs, NJ, 1979.

9

OBJECT-ORIENTED ANALYSIS PHASE

As mentioned in Chapter 1, the object-oriented paradigm was introduced in reaction to perceived short-comings in the structured paradigm. Many small- and medium-scale software projects made use of the structured paradigm with great success. However, the structured paradigm seemed to be less successful when applied to the larger software products that were starting to become more common towards the end of the 1980s.

9.1 OBJECT-ORIENTED VERSUS STRUCTURED PARADIGM

There are two ways of looking at every structured software product. One way is to consider just the data, including local and global variables, parameters, dynamic data structures, files, and so on. Another way of viewing a product is to consider just the actions performed on the data, that is, the procedures and the functions. Using this division of software into data and actions, the structured techniques essentially fall into two groups. The action-oriented techniques primarily consider the actions of the product. The data are then of secondary importance and are considered only after the actions of the product have been analyzed in depth. Conversely, the data-oriented techniques stress the data of the product; the actions are examined only within the framework of the data.

An example of an action-oriented structured technique is the finite state machine (Section 8.6). Here the emphasis is on the actions; data are considerably less important to a FSM. Structured systems analysis (Section 8.3) is another example of an action-oriented technique. It is true that a data flow diagram shows both data and actions. But the purpose of a data flow diagram is to show all the various actions that are performed by the product; the data are secondary to the actions. There are also data-oriented structured techniques. One example that will be examined in detail in Chapter 11 is Jackson system development in which the structure of the data is determined first and then used to determine the structure of the actions that operate on that data. In other words, the structure of the actions conforms to the structure of the data. Another example of a data-oriented structured technique is entity-relationship modeling, described in Section 8.5.

A fundamental weakness of both data- and action-oriented approaches is that data and action are two sides of the same coin. After all, a data item cannot change unless an action is performed on it, and actions without associated data are equally meaningless. Therefore, techniques that give equal weight to data and to actions are needed. It should not come as a surprise that the object-oriented techniques do this. After all, an object comprises both data and actions. Recall from Chapter 6 that an object is an instance of an abstract data type (or more precisely, of a class). It therefore incorporates both data and the actions that are performed on those data. The data of an object are variously called *attributes, state variables, instance variables, fields,* or *data members.* The actions are called *methods* or *member functions.* But irrespective of the terminology used for data and actions, both are present in objects as equal partners. Similarly, in all the object-oriented techniques, data and actions are considered to be of the same importance, and neither takes precedence.

It is false to say that data and actions are considered simultaneously in the techniques of the object-oriented paradigm. From the material on stepwise refinement (Section 4.1), it is clear that there are times when data have to be stressed and times when actions are more critical. Overall, however, data and actions are given equal importance during the phases of the object-oriented paradigm.

Many reasons are given in Chapters 1 and 6 as to why the object-oriented paradigm is superior to the structured paradigm. Underlying all these reasons is the fact that a well-designed object, that is, an object with high cohesion and low coupling, models all aspects of one physical entity. The details of how this is implemented are hidden; the only communication with an object is via messages. As a result, objects are essentially independent units with a well-defined interface. Consequently, they are easily and safely maintainable; the chance of a regression fault is reduced. Furthermore, objects are reusable, and this reusability is enhanced by the property of inheritance. Turning now to development using objects, these fundamental building blocks of software can be safely combined to construct a larger-scale product than is possible with the structured paradigm. Because objects are essentially independent components of a product, development of the product, as well as management of that development, is easier and hence less likely to induce faults.

All these aspects of the superiority of the object-oriented paradigm raise a question: If the structured paradigm is so inferior to the object-oriented paradigm, why has the structured paradigm had so many successes? This can be explained by realizing that the structured paradigm was adopted at a time when software engineering was not widely practiced. Instead, software was simply "written." For managers, the most important thing was for programmers to churn out lines of code. Little more than lip-service was paid to the requirements and specification (*systems analysis*) of a product, and design was almost never performed. The build-and-fix model (Section 3.1) was typical of the techniques of the 1970s. Thus, use of the structured paradigm exposed the majority of software developers to methodical techniques for the first time. Small wonder, then, that the structured techniques led to major improvements in the software industry worldwide. However, as software products grew in size, inadequacies of the structured techniques started to become apparent, and the object-oriented paradigm was proposed as a better alternative.

This, in turn, leads to another question: How do we know for certain that the object-oriented paradigm is superior to all other present-day techniques? There are no data available that prove beyond all doubt that object-oriented technology is the best that is currently available, and it is hard to imagine how such data could be obtained. The best that we can do is to rely on the experiences of organizations that have adopted the object-oriented paradigm. Although not all reports are favorable, the majority (if not the overwhelming majority) attest that using the object-oriented paradigm was a wise decision.

For example, IBM has reported on three totally different projects that were developed using object-oriented technology [Capper, Colgate, Hunter, and James, 1994]. In almost every respect, the object-oriented paradigm greatly outperformed the structured paradigm. Specifically, there were major decreases in the number of faults detected, there were far fewer change requests during both development and maintenance that were not the result of unforeseeable business changes, and both adaptive and perfective maintainability increased significantly. There was also an improvement in usability, though not as large as the previous four improvements, and no meaningful difference in performance.

One final question: Is it not possible that someday there will be something better than the object-oriented paradigm? Even its strongest proponents do not claim that the object-oriented paradigm is the ultimate answer to all software engineering problems. Furthermore, today's software engineers are looking beyond objects to the next major breakthrough. After all, there are few fields of human endeavor in which the techniques of the past are superior to anything that is being put forward today. Present-day techniques, such as the object-oriented paradigm, are equally likely to be superseded by the techniques of the future. The important lesson is that, based on today's knowledge, the object-oriented techniques appear to be the best.

9.2 OBJECT-ORIENTED ANALYSIS

Object-oriented analysis (OOA) is a semiformal specification technique for the object-oriented paradigm. In Chapter 8 it was pointed out that there are a number of different techniques for structured systems analysis, all essentially equivalent. Similarly, there are currently more than 40 different techniques for performing object-oriented analysis, and new techniques are put forward on a regular basis. Again, all the techniques are largely equivalent. The "For Further Reading" section of this chapter includes references to a wide variety of techniques, as well as to published comparisons of different techniques.

Currently, the most popular techniques are OMT [Rumbaugh et al., 1991] and Booch's technique [Booch, 1994]. The technique presented here is based on OMT, but somewhat generalized in order to capture the essential features of most OOA techniques.

OOA consists of three steps:

1. Class modeling   Determine the classes and their attributes. Then, determine the interrelationships between the classes. Present this information in the form of a diagram somewhat similar to an entity-relationship diagram (Section 8.5), termed the *class model*. (Some authors refer to this diagram as the *object model*.) This step is purely data oriented.

2. Dynamic modeling   Determine the actions performed by or to each class or subclass. Present this information in the form of a diagram somewhat similar to a finite state machine (Section 8.6), termed the *dynamic model*. This step is purely action oriented.

3. Functional modeling   Determine how the various results are computed by the product (without regard to sequencing). Present this information in the form of a diagram similar to a data flow diagram (Section 8.3), termed the *functional model*. This step is largely action oriented.

In practice, the three steps are not performed purely sequentially. It is always advisable to start with Step 1, because the entire development is based on the classes determined in this step. However, during succeeding steps, the members of the specification team frequently have to modify the class model. These changes can, in turn, trigger changes in the dynamic model and the functional model. In other words, the three steps of OOA are effectively performed in parallel. This makes sense in view of the fact that, in the object-oriented paradigm, neither data (Step 1) nor actions (Steps 2 and 3) take precedence over the other.

OOA should certainly not be viewed as a combination of the three structured specification techniques of the previous chapter, namely entity-relationship modeling, finite state machines, and structured systems analysis. On the contrary, OOA is a modeling technique that makes use of diagrams for specifying the results of the three modeling steps. Instead of inventing totally new ways of displaying this information, it makes sense to employ notations based on widely-used structured techniques.

Another way of looking at this is to appreciate that the aim of OOA, like that of all other specification techniques, is to specify the target product to be built. Two critical aspects of that product are its data and its actions. OOA uses three different modeling techniques in order to understand the data, the actions, and the interplay between data and actions. During the course of the analysis, the knowledge gained about the product is represented in three different ways, each reflecting a different aspect of the target product. The diagrams are continually updated as a more thorough perception of the system being modeled is achieved. By the end of the OOA phase, the three views together reflect an overall understanding of the product that would be difficult to achieve if only one modeling technique were employed.

9.3   ELEVATOR PROBLEM: OBJECT-ORIENTED ANALYSIS

The steps of OOA are described by means of an example, namely the elevator problem first described in Chapter 8. For ease of reference, the problem is repeated here.

A product is to be installed to control n elevators in a building with m floors. The problem concerns the logic required to move elevators between floors according to the following constraints:

C_1. Each elevator has a set of m buttons, one for each floor. These illuminate when pressed and cause the elevator to visit the corresponding floor. The illumination is canceled when the corresponding floor is visited by the elevator.

C_2. Each floor, except the first floor and top floor, has two buttons, one to request an up-elevator and one to request a down-elevator. These buttons illuminate when pressed. The illumination is canceled when an elevator visits the floor and then moves in the desired direction.

C_3. When an elevator has no requests, it remains at its current floor with its doors closed.

The first step in OOA is to model the objects or, more correctly, the classes.

9.3.1   CLASS MODELING

In this step, the classes and their attributes are extracted and represented using an entity-relationship diagram. Only the attributes of a class are determined at this time, not the methods; the latter are assigned to the classes during the object-oriented design (OOD) phase.

A characteristic of the whole object-oriented paradigm is that the various steps are rarely easy to carry out. Fortunately, the resulting benefits of using objects make the effort worthwhile. So it should not come as a surprise that the very first part of class modeling, namely extracting classes and their attributes, is usually difficult to get right the first time. A good way to proceed is to use the following three-stage process to get candidate classes and then to refine the solution.

Stage 1. Concise Problem Definition   Define the product as briefly and concisely as possible, preferably in a single sentence. In the case of the elevator problem, one possible way of doing this is

Buttons in elevators and on the floors are to be used to control the motion of n elevators in a building with m floors.

Stage 2. Informal Strategy   In order to come up with an informal strategy for solving the problem, the constraints must be determined. The three constraints of the elevator problem appear at the end of the previous section. Now the informal strategy can be expressed, preferably in a single paragraph. One possible paragraph for the elevator problem is

> Buttons in elevators and on the floors control the movement of n elevators in a building with m floors. Buttons illuminate when pressed to request an elevator to stop at a specific floor; the illumination is canceled when the request has been satisfied. When an elevator has no requests, it remains at its current floor with its doors closed.

Stage 3. Formalize the Strategy   Identify the nouns in the informal strategy (excluding those that lie outside the problem boundary) and then use these nouns as candidate classes. The informal strategy is now reproduced, but this time the nouns are identified by being printed in a different typeface.

> Buttons in elevators and on the floors control the movement of n elevators in a building with m floors. Buttons illuminate when pressed to request the elevator to stop at a specific floor; the illumination is canceled when the request has been satisfied. When an elevator has no requests, it remains at its current floor with its doors closed.

There are eight different nouns, namely button, elevator, floor, movement, building, illumination, request, and door. Three of these nouns, namely floor, building, and door, lie outside the problem boundary and may therefore be ignored. Three of the remaining nouns, namely movement, illumination, and request, are abstract nouns. That is to say, they "identify ideas or quantities that have no physical existence" [World Book Encyclopedia, 1992]. A useful rule of thumb is that abstract nouns rarely end up corresponding to classes. Instead, they frequently are attributes of classes. For example, illumination turns out to be an attribute of button. Other abstract nouns (for example, request) turn out to be extraneous to the problem description. This leaves two candidate classes, namely Elevator and Button (the convention used in this book is to capitalize the initial letter of the name of a class).

The problem specifies two types of button, so two subclasses of Button will be defined, namely Elevator Button and Floor Button. The resulting class model is shown in Figure 9.1. There are two base classes, namely Elevator, with attribute doors open, and Button, with attribute illuminated. There are two subclasses, namely Elevator Button and Floor Button; the triangle denotes inheritance.

This is not a good beginning. In a real elevator, the buttons do not directly communicate with the elevators; there must be some sort of elevator controller, if only to decide which elevator to dispatch in response to a particular request. However, the problem statement makes no mention of a controller, so it was not selected as a class. In other words, the technique for finding candidate classes provides a starting point, but certainly should not be relied upon to do more than that.

Adding the controller yields Figure 9.2. This certainly makes more sense. In addition, the fact that all relationships are now one-to-many may make the design and implementation easier. It seems reasonable to go on to Step 2 at this point, bearing in mind that it is possible to return to class modeling at any time.

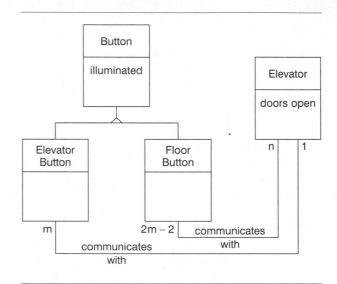

Figure 9.1 First iteration of class model.

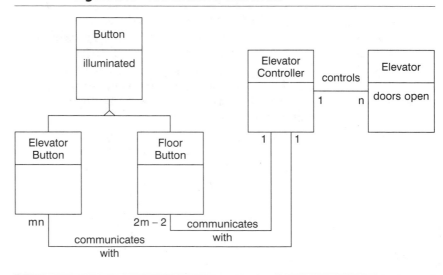

Figure 9.2 Second iteration of class model.

User A presses Up floor button at floor 3 to request elevator. User A wishes to go to floor 7.

Up floor button is turned on.

An elevator arrives at floor 3. It contains User B who has pressed elevator button for floor 9.

Up floor button is turned off.

Elevator doors open.

User A enters elevator.

User A presses elevator button for floor 7.

Floor 7 elevator button is turned on.

Elevator doors close.

Elevator travels to floor 7.

Floor 7 elevator button is turned off.

Elevator doors open to allow User A to exit elevator.

User A exits.

Elevator doors close after timeout.

Elevator proceeds to floor 9 with User B.

Figure 9.3 A normal scenario.

9.3.2 Dynamic Modeling

The aim of this step is to determine all the actions performed by or to each class. A good way to do this is to list typical scenarios (Section 7.1) of the interaction between users and the system, both normal and exceptional. A normal scenario is given in Figure 9.3, and an abnormal scenario is given in Figure 9.4.

Sufficient scenarios should be studied to give the specification team a comprehensive insight into the behavior of the system being modeled. Then the dynamic model, a description of the target product similar to a finite state model, is constructed. First consider class Elevator Controller. For simplicity, only one elevator is considered. The relevant dynamic model for the Elevator Controller is shown in Figure 9.5. The notation is somewhat similar to that of the finite state machines of Section 8.6, but there is a significant difference. A FSM as presented in Chapter 8 is an example of a formal technique. The state transition diagrams (STD) themselves are not a complete representation of the product to be built. Instead, the model consists of a set of transition rules of the form given in Equation (8.2), namely

current state and **event** and **predicate** ⇒ **next state**

Formality is achieved by presenting the model in the form of a set of mathematical rules.

In contrast, the representation of the dynamic model is somewhat less formal. The clear delineation of a finite state machine into its three aspects of state, event, and predicate is missing. For example, when state Process next request in Figure

User A presses Up floor button at floor 3 to request elevator. User A wishes to go to floor 1.

Up floor button is turned on.

An elevator arrives at floor 3. It contains User B who has pressed elevator button for floor 9.

Up floor button is turned off.

Elevator doors open

User A enters elevator.

User A presses elevator button for floor 1.

Floor 1 elevator button is turned on.

Elevator doors close after timeout.

Elevator travels to floor 9.

Floor 9 elevator button is turned off.

Elevator doors open to allow User B to exit elevator.

User B exits.

Elevator doors close after timeout.

Elevator proceeds to floor 1 with User A.

Figure 9.4 An abnormal scenario.

9.5 is entered, three actions have to be carried out, including the action *If lit, turn off floor button.* That is to say, if the elevator is about to move in direction d and the button for an elevator moving in that direction is on, then the button is to be turned off. This action incorporates elements of state, event, and global predicate. Current versions of OOA are semiformal techniques, and the intrinsic lack of formality of the dynamic model is accordingly not a problem. However, when the object-oriented paradigm matures, it is likely that more formal versions will be developed and that the corresponding dynamic models will be somewhat closer to finite state machines.

To see the equivalence of the dynamic model of Figure 9.5 on the one hand, and the STDs of Figures 8.13 through 8.15 on the other, consider various scenarios. For example, consider the first part of the scenario of Figure 9.3. First, User A presses the Up floor button at floor 3. If the floor button is not on, then, according to both Figure 8.14 and the leftmost path of Figure 9.5, the button comes on as required. In the case of the dynamic model, the next state is **Elevator controller loop**.

Next, the elevator nears floor 3. In Figure 8.15, the elevator goes into state S(U, 3), that is, it stops at floor 3, about to go up. (Because the simplifying assumption has been made that there is only one elevator, the argument e in Figure 8.15 is suppressed here). From Figure 8.14, when the elevator arrives, the floor button is turned off. Now (Figure 8.15) the doors close, and the elevator starts to move towards floor 4.

Returning to the dynamic model of Figure 9.5, consider what happens when the elevator nears floor 3. Because the elevator is in motion, the next state entered is **Determine if stop requested**. The requests are checked and, because User A has

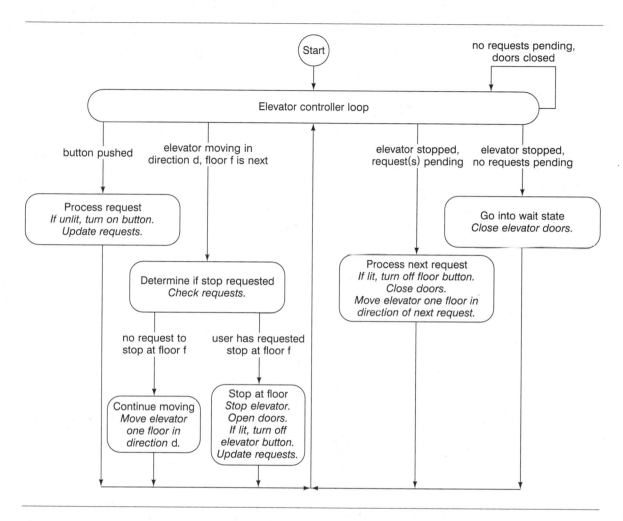

Figure 9.5 Dynamic model for Elevator Controller class.

requested the elevator to stop there, it stops at floor 3 (state Stop at floor). The doors open. The elevator button for floor 3 has not been pressed, so it is not turned off. The requests are updated to reflect that a stop has been made at floor 3. State Elevator controller loop is next. The elevator has stopped and there are requests pending, so state Process next request is next. When this latter state is entered, the floor button is turned off. Now the doors close, and the elevator starts to move towards floor 4. The relevant aspects of the corresponding diagrams are clearly equivalent with respect to this scenario; the reader may wish to consider other possible scenarios as well.

The dynamic models for the other classes are relatively straightforward and are left as an exercise (Problem 9.1). Once the dynamic model as a whole has been

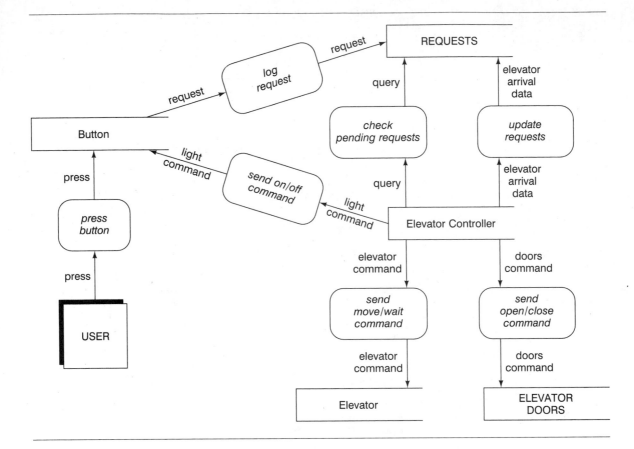

Figure 9.6 First iteration of functional model.

completed, it is advisable to reconsider the class model (Figure 9.2) in the light of the information gained during the dynamic modeling step. Everything still seems satisfactory. The third step, functional modeling, can now be started.

9.3.3   FUNCTIONAL MODELING

The third step in OOA is to determine how the product performs the various actions without considering the order in which they are performed. This information is presented in the form of a diagram similar to a data flow diagram (Section 8.3) and is termed the *functional model* because it shows the functional dependencies within the product.

The functional model for the elevator problem is shown in Figure 9.6. As required, it shows the various actions, reflecting how the data move through the product, but it does not reflect the order of the actions.

A problem that is sometimes encountered is how to decide whether an item in the functional model is a source or destination of data (such as USER), or a store of data (such as Elevator or Elevator Controller). The key to this decision is the notion of *state*. The attributes of a class are sometimes termed *state variables*. The reason for this terminology is that in most object-oriented implementations the state of the product is determined by the values of the attributes of the various component objects. The dynamic model has many features in common with a finite state machine. Accordingly, it is not surprising that the concept of state plays an important role in the object-oriented paradigm. This concept can be used to help determine whether an item should be modeled as a source or destination of data, or as a store of data. If the item in question possesses a state that will be changed during execution of the implementation, then it should be modeled as a store of data. It is clear from Figure 9.6 that the elevator controller, requests, elevator, and doors are all characterized by states that change dynamically. However, a user simply presses buttons; the state of a user does not change.

The difference between a DFD for the structured paradigm and a functional model relates to data stores. Specifically, in the structured paradigm a store of data will almost certainly be implemented as some sort of file. However, as explained in the previous paragraph, the state variables of a class are also stores of data. Thus the functional model can contain two types of stores of data, namely, classes and stores of data that do not correspond to classes.

With regard to notation, every store of data in a functional model is represented by an open rectangle, as in Figure 8.1. If the store of data has been identified as a class then, as explained in Section 9.3.1, the initial letter of its name is capitalized; Elevator and Button are two examples of this in Figure 9.6. If it is not a class, then the name of that store of data appears in uppercase letters. The two examples of this in Figure 9.6 are REQUESTS and ELEVATOR DOORS. During the object-oriented analysis phase, further classes may be extracted and existing classes may be modified or even rejected. Hence, the nature of a store of data in a functional model may change.

It is now advisable to reconsider both the class model (Figure 9.2) and the dynamic model (Figure 9.5) in light of the information gained during the functional modeling step. Referring to Figure 9.6, ELEVATOR DOORS should have been identified as a class Elevator Doors, rather than attaching attribute doors open to class Elevator. The reason is that the object-oriented paradigm allows state to be hidden within an object and, hence, protected from unauthorized change. Once there is an Elevator Doors object, the only way that the doors of the elevator can be opened or shut is by sending a message to that Elevator Doors object. Serious accidents can be caused by opening or closing the doors of an elevator at the wrong time; see the Just in Case You Wanted to Know box on page 280. Thus, for certain types of products, safety considerations should be added to the other advantages of objects listed in Chapter 6.

It is clear that the data stored in REQUESTS in Figure 9.6 must be hidden for the same reason that the state of the Elevator Doors must not be changed without authorization. Making these two changes, that is, adding classes Elevator Doors

---

JUST IN CASE YOU WANTED TO KNOW

Some years ago, I was on the 10th floor of a tall building, waiting impatiently for an elevator. The doors opened, I started to step forward—only there was no elevator there. What saved me was the total blackness that I saw as I was about to step into the

elevator shaft, and I instinctively realized that something was wrong.

Perhaps if that elevator control system had been developed using the object-oriented paradigm, the inappropriate opening of the doors on the 10th floor might have been avoided.

---

and **Requests**, leads to the third refinement of the class model. This appears as Figure 9.7. The figure shows two additional classes. Class **Elevator Application** will be required for method *main.* Also, during the detailed design, various utility routines will almost certainly be needed; these will be assigned to class **Elevator Utilities**. (Recall that Java is a pure object-oriented language and hence there are no procedures or functions. Instead, all data and actions have to be fields of classes.)

Having modified the class model, the dynamic and functional models must now be reexamined to see if they, too, need further refinement. As previously noted, the functional model must be changed to indicate that **Requests** and **Elevator_Doors** are classes; this change is shown in Figure 9.8. Careful inspection leads to the conclusion that the dynamic model is still adequate. However, during the object-oriented design phase, it may be necessary to return to the object-oriented analysis and to revise one or more of the models.

9.4   OBJECT-ORIENTED LIFE-CYCLE MODELS

Experience with the object-oriented paradigm has shown that the need for iteration between phases or portions of phases of the process appears to be more common with the object-oriented paradigm than with the structured paradigm. Object-oriented life-cycle models have been proposed that explicitly reflect the need for refinement. One such model is the fountain model [Henderson-Sellers and Edwards, 1990] shown in Figure 9.9. The circles representing the various phases overlap, explicitly reflecting an overlap between activities. The arrows within a phase represent iteration (refinement) within that phase. The maintenance circle is smaller, to symbolize reduced maintenance effort when the object-oriented paradigm is used.

In addition to the fountain model, other object-oriented life-cycle models have been put forward, including the recursive/parallel life cycle [Berard, 1993], and round-trip gestalt design [Booch, 1994]. All these models are iterative, incorporate some form of parallelism (overlap of activities), and support incremental development (Section 3.4). The danger of such life-cycle models is that they may be misinterpreted as simply attempts to make a virtue out of necessity, and thereby lead to a totally undisciplined form of software development in which team members move almost

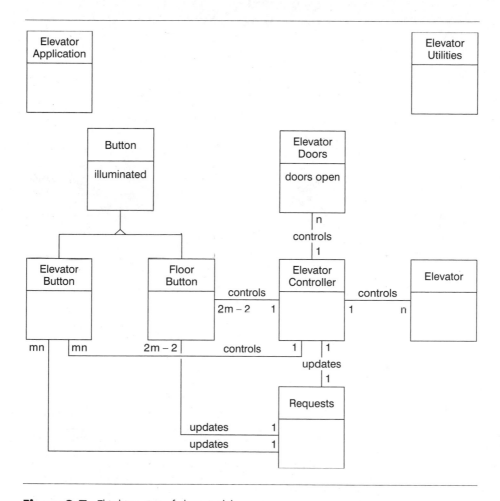

Figure 9.7   Third iteration of class model.

randomly between phases, first designing one piece of the product, next analyzing another piece, and then implementing a third piece that has been neither analyzed nor designed; the Just in Case You Wanted to Know box on page 284 gives more on this undesirable approach. A better way to proceed is to have as an overall objective a linear process (such as the rapid prototyping model of Section 3.3 or the central vertical line in Figure 9.9), but to appreciate that the realities of the object-oriented paradigm are such that frequent iterations and refinements will certainly be needed.

It might be suggested that this problem is simply a consequence of the relative newness of the object-oriented paradigm. As software professionals acquire more experience with OOA and OOD, the argument goes, and as the whole discipline matures, the need for repeated review and revision will decrease. To see that this argument is fallacious, consider the various life-cycle models for the structured paradigm described in Chapter 3. First came the waterfall model (Section 3.2) with its explicit feedback loops. The next major development was the rapid prototyping

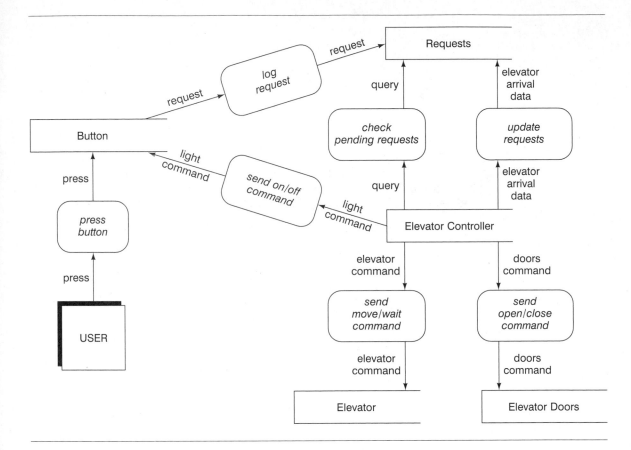

Figure 9.8 Second iteration of functional model.

model (Section 3.3); one of its major aims was to reduce the need for iteration. However, this was followed by the spiral model (Section 3.5) that explicitly reflects an iterative approach to software development and maintenance. In addition, it has been shown [Honiden, Kotaka, and Kishimoto, 1993] that backtracking is an intrinsic aspect of the Coad-Yourdon technique for object-oriented design [Coad and Yourdon, 1991a, 1991b], and it is likely that similar results can be obtained for other OOA techniques. In other words, it appears that iteration is an intrinsic property of software production in general and the object-oriented paradigm in particular.

9.5   CASE TOOLS FOR THE OBJECT-ORIENTED ANALYSIS PHASE

Bearing in mind the role played by diagrams in object-oriented analysis, it is not surprising that a number of different CASE tools have been developed for supporting

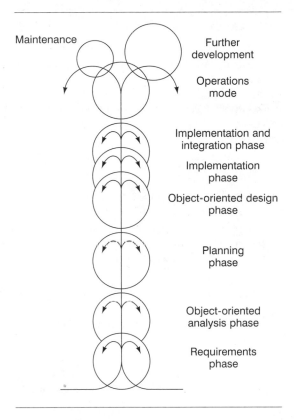

Maintenance

Further
development

Operations
mode

Implementation and
integration phase

Implementation
phase

Object-oriented design
phase

Planning
phase

Object-oriented
analysis phase

Requirements
phase

Figure 9.9   Fountain model.

object-oriented analysis. In its basic form, such a tool is essentially a drawing tool that makes it easy to perform each of the modeling steps. More importantly, it is far simpler to modify a diagram that has been constructed with a drawing tool than to attempt to change a hand-drawn figure. Thus, a CASE tool of this type supports the graphical aspects of object-oriented analysis.

On the other hand, some CASE tools support not just object-oriented analysis, but a considerable portion of the rest of the object-oriented life cycle as well. Examples of such tools include Software through Pictures, OMTool (which supports OMT [Rumbaugh et al., 1991]), and Rose (which supports Booch's technique [Booch, 1994]).

9.6   MSG Case Study: Object-Oriented Analysis

OOA consists of three steps, namely class modeling, dynamic modeling, and functional modeling. These steps are usually carried out iteratively, starting with the

---

JUST IN CASE YOU WANTED TO KNOW

When the members of the development team move in essentially haphazard fashion from one task to another, this is sometimes referred to as CABTAB (code a bit, test a bit). The acronym was initially used in a positive sense to refer to the successful iterative models, such as those which have been used in conjunction with the object-oriented paradigm. However, just as the word *hacker* now has a pejorative context in addition to its original meaning, so CABTAB is now also used in a derogatory sense to refer to this undisciplined approach to software development.

---

first step, *class modeling*. The aim of this step is to extract the classes, find their attributes, and determine their interrelationships.

Extracting the classes is usually done in three stages. Stage 1 of class modeling is to define the product as briefly and concisely as possible, preferably in a single sentence. In the case of MSG, one possible way of doing this is

Determine how much money is available each week for mortgages.

In Stage 2, an informal strategy is drawn up, preferably in a single paragraph. One possible such paragraph is

Weekly reports are to be printed showing how much money is available for mortgages. In addition, lists of investments and mortgages must be printed on demand.

In Stage 3 the nouns are extracted from this paragraph, yielding report, money, mortgage, list, and investment. Nouns report and list are part of the solution, and money is an abstract noun. This leaves two candidate classes, namely investment and mortgage. These are both financial instruments, and it appears that records of both types will have a number of actions in common, such as inserting a new record, deleting a record, and displaying a record. It therefore seems logical to define a superclass, namely Financial Instrument, with subclasses Investment and Mortgage. A minimal set of attributes of these classes can be obtained from the requirements of Section 7.14. Two other classes are needed, namely, MSG Applications for method *main* and MSG Utilities for the utility methods; during the design phase the need for utility methods arises in almost every product. Also, global constants will be declared as **public static final** variables of MSG Applications. Figure 9.10 shows the resulting class model.

The second step in object-oriented analysis is *dynamic modeling*. In order to develop the dynamic model, scenarios must first be drawn up. In the MSG model, the possible scenarios correspond to the possible actions that can be performed. These are add, modify, or delete a financial instrument (investment or mortgage object);

Figure 9.10 Class model for MSG product.

update the operational expenses; list financial instruments; and determine availability of funds. These operations are reflected in the dynamic model of Figure 9.11.

The third and final step in object-oriented analysis is functional modeling. The functional model of Figure 9.12 is similar to the data flow diagram of Figure 8.27, except for the six data stores. Two of them have been identified as classes, namely **Investment** and **Mortgage**. With regard to the other four stores of data, namely **GRANT DATA, EXPENSES DATA, RETURN DATA,** and **INCOME DATA,** the question arises whether they, too, should be classes. At this stage there is no reason to make more classes (but see Problem 9.11). It therefore seems appropriate not to return to step 1 to modify the class model of Figure 9.10, but rather to wait for the object-oriented design phase to determine whether additional classes are in fact needed.

The client will not usually be willing to consider the three models as an adequate specification document. Instead, a more conventional document will have to be drawn up. Because that document would be so similar to the material of Appendix D, it is omitted here for brevity.

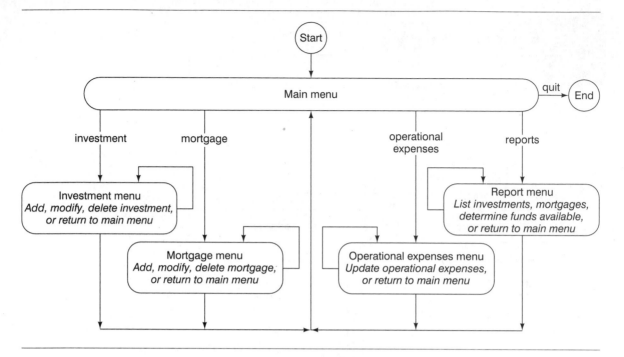

Figure 9.11 Dynamic model for Financial Instrument class of MSG product.

Chapter Review

The object-oriented and structured paradigms are compared (Section 9.1). Then, object-oriented analysis is described (Section 9.2) and demonstrated by means of a case study (Section 9.3). Next, object-oriented life-cycle models are compared (Section 9.4). CASE tools for object-oriented analysis are discussed in Section 9.5. The chapter concludes with the MSG Case Study (Section 9.6).

For Further Reading

Books describing different versions of object-oriented analysis include [Coad and Yourdon, 1991a], [Rumbaugh et al., 1991], [Jacobson, Christerson, Jonsson, and Overgaard, 1992], [Martin and Odell, 1992], [Shlaer and Mellor, 1988, 1992], and [Booch, 1994]. As mentioned in the chapter, these techniques (and others not listed here) are basically similar. In addition to object-oriented analysis techniques of this type, Fusion [Coleman et al., 1994] is a second-generation OOA technique. That is, Fusion is a combination (or fusion) of a number of first generation techniques, including OMT [Rumbaugh et al., 1991], and Objectory [Jacobson, Christerson, Jonsson, and Overgaard, 1992].

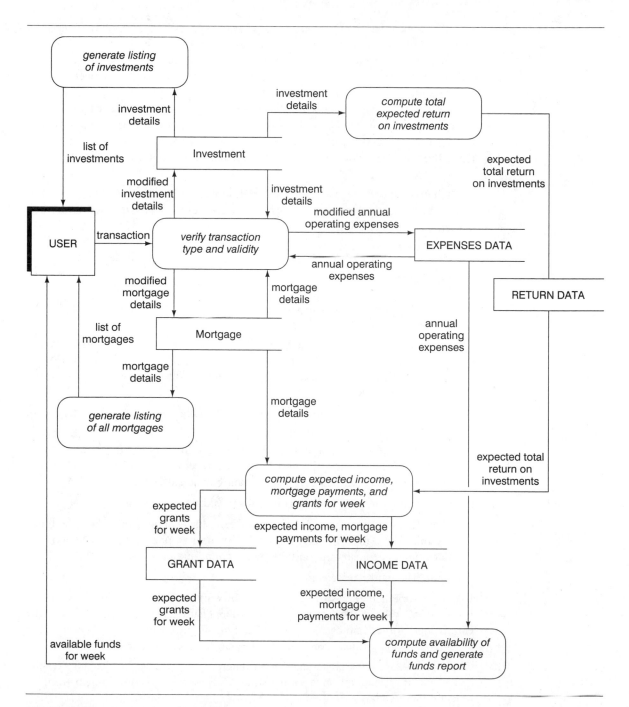

Figure 9.12 Functional model for MSG product.

The September 1992 issue of the *Communications of the ACM* contains a number of articles on object-oriented analysis. A number of comparisons of object-oriented analysis techniques have been published, including [de Champeaux and Faure, 1992] and [Monarchi and Puhr, 1992]. A comparison of both object-oriented and structured analysis techniques appears in [Fichman and Kemerer, 1992]. [Capper, Colgate, Hunter, and James, 1994] describes three projects that use the object-oriented paradigm and explains the ways that the object-oriented paradigm proved to be superior to the structured approach. Statecharts (Section 8.6.1) have been extended to the object-oriented paradigm [Coleman, Hayes, and Bear, 1992].

Object-oriented life-cycle models are described in [Henderson-Sellers and Edwards, 1990], as well as in the books on object-oriented analysis listed in the first paragraph of this section.

Problems

9.1 Complete the elevator problem case study by developing dynamic models for the other classes shown in Figure 9.7.

9.2 Consider an automated teller machine (ATM). The user puts a card into a slot and enters a four-digit personal identification number (PIN). If the PIN is incorrect, the card is ejected. Otherwise, the user may perform the following operations on up to four different bank accounts:

(i)   Deposit any amount. A receipt is printed showing the date, amount deposited, and account number.

(ii) Withdraw up to $200 in units of $20 (the account may not be overdrawn). In addition to the money, the user is given a receipt showing the date, amount withdrawn, account number, and account balance after the withdrawal.

(iii) Determine account balance. This is displayed on the screen.

(iv) Transfer funds between two accounts. Again, the account from which the funds are transferred must not be overdrawn. The user is given a receipt showing the date, amount transferred, and the two account numbers.

(v)   Quit. The card is ejected.

Use object-oriented analysis to specify the software for controlling the ATM. There is no need to consider the details of the constituent hardware components, such as the card reader, printer, and cash dispenser. Instead, simply assume that when the ATM sends commands to those components, they are correctly executed.

9.3 Object-oriented analysis uses data flow diagrams exactly as in Chapter 8. Why cannot the finite state machine formalism of Chapter 8 also be used (unchanged) in object-oriented analysis?

9.4 Use object-oriented analysis to specify the automated library circulation system of Problem 6.18.

What is the latest point in the object-oriented analysis process in which classes can **9.5** be introduced without adversely affecting the project?

What is the earliest point in the object-oriented paradigm in which classes can **9.6** meaningfully be introduced?

Is it possible to represent the dynamic model using a formalism other than the finite **9.7** state machine described in this chapter? Explain your answer.

What do waterfalls and fountains have in common? What do the waterfall model and **9.8** fountain model have in common? How do they differ?

Why do you think that the attributes of the classes, but not the methods, are **9.9** determined during object-oriented analysis?

(Term Project) Use object-oriented analysis to specify the Osbert Oglesby product **9.10** described in Appendix A.

(Case Study) Add classes Expense, Grant, Return, and Income to the object- **9.11** oriented analysis. Is this an improvement or an unnecessary complication?

(Case Study) Determine what happens when object-oriented analysis starts with the **9.12** functional modeling step. Start with the data flow diagram of Figure 8.27 and complete the object-oriented analysis process.

(Case Study) Compare and contrast the structured systems analysis of Appendix D **9.13** with the object-oriented analysis of Section 9.6.

(Readings in Software Engineering) Your instructor will distribute copies of **9.14** [Honiken, Kotaka, and Kishimoto, 1993]. Do you agree with the statement at the end of Section 9.4 of this book that it is likely that similar results can be obtained for other OOA techniques?

References

[Berard, 1993] E. V. BERARD, *Essays on Object-Oriented Software Engineering, Volume I*, Prentice-Hall, Englewood Cliffs, NJ, 1993.

[Booch, 1994] G. BOOCH, *Object-Oriented Analysis and Design with Applications, Second Edition*, Benjamin/Cummings, Redwood City, CA, 1994.

[Capper, Colgate, Hunter, and James, 1994] N. P. CAPPER, R. J. COLGATE, J. C. HUNTER, AND M. F. JAMES, "The Impact of Object-Oriented Technology on Software Quality: Three Case Histories," *IBM Systems Journal* **33** (No. 1, 1994), pp. 131–157.

[Coad and Yourdon, 1991a] P. COAD AND E. YOURDON, *Object-Oriented Analysis, Second Edition*, Yourdon Press, Englewood Cliffs, NJ, 1991.

[Coad and Yourdon, 1991b] P. COAD AND E. YOURDON, *Object-Oriented Design*, Yourdon Press, Englewood Cliffs, NJ, 1991.

[Coleman et al., 1994] D. COLEMAN, P. ARNOLD, S. BODOFF, C. DOLLIN, H. GILCHRIST, F. HAYES, AND P. JEREMAES, *Object-Oriented Development: The Fusion Method*, Prentice-Hall, Englewood Cliffs, NJ, 1994.

[Coleman, Hayes, and Bear, 1992] D. COLEMAN, F. HAYES, AND S. BEAR, "Introducing Objectcharts or How to Use Statecharts in Object-Oriented Design," *IEEE Transactions on Software Engineering* **18** (January, 1992), pp. 9–18.

[de Champeaux and Faure, 1992] D. DE CHAMPEAUX AND P. FAURE, "A Comparative Study of Object-Oriented Analysis Methods," *Journal of Object-Oriented Programming* **5** (March/April 1992), pp. 21–33.

[Fichman and Kemerer, 1992] R. G. FICHMAN AND C. F. KEMERER, "Object-Oriented and Conventional Analysis and Design Methodologies: Comparison and Critique," *IEEE Computer* **25** (October 1992), pp. 22–39.

[Henderson-Sellers and Edwards, 1990] B. HENDERSON-SELLERS AND J. M. EDWARDS, "The Object-Oriented Systems Life Cycle," *Communications of the ACM* **33** (September 1990), pp. 142–159.

[Honiden, Kotaka, and Kishimoto, 1993] S. HONIDEN, N. KOTAKA, AND Y. KISHIMOTO, "Formalizing Specification Modeling in OOA," *IEEE Software* **10** (January 1993), pp. 54–66.

[Jacobson, Christerson, Jonsson, and Overgaard, 1992] I. JACOBSON, M. CHRISTERSON, P. JONSSON, AND G. OVERGAARD, *Object-Oriented Software Engineering: A Use Case Driven Approach*, ACM Press, New York, 1992.

[Martin and Odell, 1992] J. MARTIN AND J. J. ODELL, *Object-Oriented Analysis and Design,* Prentice-Hall, Englewood Cliffs, NJ, 1992.

[Monarchi and Puhr, 1992] D. E. MONARCHI AND G. I. PUHR, "A Research Typology for Object-Oriented Analysis and Design," *Communications of the ACM* **35** (September 1992), pp. 35–47.

[Rumbaugh et al., 1991] J. RUMBAUGH, M. BLAHA, W. PREMERLANI, F. EDDY, AND W. LORENSEN, *Object-Oriented Modeling and Design,* Prentice-Hall, Englewood Cliffs, NJ, 1991.

[Shlaer and Mellor, 1988] S. SHLAER AND S. MELLOR, *Object-Oriented Systems Analysis: Modeling the World in Data,* Yourdon Press, Englewood Cliffs, NJ, 1988.

[Shlaer and Mellor, 1992] S. SHLAER AND S. MELLOR, *Object Lifecycles: Modeling the World in States,* Yourdon Press, Englewood Cliffs, NJ, 1992.

[World Book Encyclopedia, 1992] *World Book Encyclopedia,* World Book-Childcraft International, Inc., Chicago, 1992, Volume N–O, pp. 558–559.

10

PLANNING PHASE

There is no panacea for the difficulties of constructing a software product. A large software product takes time and resources to put together. And like any other large construction project, careful planning at the beginning of the project is perhaps the single most important factor that distinguishes success from failure.

Software is constructed in order to satisfy a need. For example, a corporation wishes to automate its personnel records, an air force wants to modernize by implementing electronic warfare systems on its tactical aircraft, or a programmer in an organization that builds software packages for personal computers has a wonderful idea for a new type of video game that will make millions of dollars. But before coding starts on any of these projects, it is necessary to plan in detail the entire software development effort.

This initial planning, however, is by no means enough. Planning, like testing, must continue throughout the software development and maintenance processes. Notwithstanding the need for continual planning, these activities reach a peak after the specifications have been drawn up but before design activities commence, so much so that they constitute a separate software process phase, the planning phase. During this phase the software project management plan (SPMP) is drawn up, a comprehensive blueprint for the remainder of the software process. The reason that the SPMP is drawn up at this time is that, until the specification document has been finalized, there is little point in attempting to plan for more than just the current phase; there simply is not enough accurate information regarding the target product. Thus the SPMP is drawn up at the earliest possible point in the software process.

A major aspect of the SPMP is estimating the duration of the project and how much it will cost.

10.1 ESTIMATING DURATION AND COST

The budget is an integral part of any software project management plan. Before development commences, the client will want to know how much he or she will have to pay for the product. If the development team underestimates the actual cost, the development organization can lose money on the project. On the other hand, if the development team overestimates, then the client may decide that on the basis of cost–benefit analysis or return on investment there is no point in having the product built. Alternatively, the client may give the job to another development organization whose estimate is more reasonable. Either way, it is clear that accurate cost estimation is critical.

In fact, there are two types of costs associated with software development. The first is the *internal cost,* the cost to the developers; the second is the *external cost,* the cost to the client. The internal cost includes the salaries of the development teams, managers, and support personnel involved in the project; the cost of the hardware and software for developing the product; and the cost of overheads such as rent, utilities, and salaries of senior management. Although the external cost is generally based on the internal cost plus a profit margin, in some cases economic and psychological factors are important. For example, if the developers desperately need the work, they may be prepared to charge the client the internal cost or less. A different situation arises when a contract is to be awarded on the basis of bids. The client may reject a bid that is significantly lower than all the other bids on the grounds that the quality of the resulting product would probably also be significantly lower. A development team may therefore try to come up with a bid that will be slightly, but not significantly, lower than what they believe their competitors' bids will be.

Another important part of any plan is estimating the duration of the project. The client will certainly want to know when the finished project will be delivered. If the development organization is unable to keep to its schedule, then at best the organization loses credibility; at worst penalty clauses will be invoked. In all cases, the managers responsible for the software project management plan have a lot of explaining to do. Conversely, if the development organization overestimates the time that will be needed to build the product, then there is a good chance that the client will go elsewhere.

Unfortunately, it is by no means easy to estimate cost and duration requirements accurately. There are just too many variables to be able to get an accurate handle on either cost or duration. One big difficulty is the human factor. Over 25 years ago Sackman and co-workers showed differences of up to 28 to 1 between pairs of programmers [Sackman, Erikson, and Grant, 1968]. It is easy to try to brush off Sackman's results by saying that experienced programmers will always outperform beginners, but Sackman and his colleagues compared matched pairs of programmers. They observed, for example, two programmers with 10 years of experience on similar types of projects and measured the time it took them to perform tasks like coding and debugging. Then they observed two beginners who had been in the profession for the same short length of time and who had similar educational backgrounds. Comparing worst and best performances, they observed differences of 6 to 1 in product size, 8 to 1 in product execution time, 9 to 1 in development time, 18 to 1 in coding time, and 28 to 1 in debugging time. A particularly alarming observation is that the best and worst performances on one product were by two programmers, each of whom had 11 years of experience. Even when the best and worst cases were removed from Sackman's sample, observed differences were still of the order of 5 to 1. On the basis of these results, it is clear that we cannot hope to estimate software cost or duration with any degree of accuracy (unless we have detailed information regarding all the skills of our employees, which is unusual). It has been argued that, in a large project, differences between individuals will tend to cancel out, but this is perhaps wishful thinking; the presence of one or two very good (or very bad) team members will cause marked deviations from planned milestones and significantly impact the budget.

Another human factor that can affect estimation is that in a free country there is no way of ensuring that a critical staff member will not resign during the project. Time and money are then spent attempting to fill the vacated position and integrate the replacement into the team, or in reorganizing the remaining team members to compensate for the loss. Either way schedules slip and estimates come unstuck.

Underlying the cost estimation problem is another issue: How is the size of a product to be measured?

10.1.1 METRICS FOR THE SIZE OF A PRODUCT

The most common metric for the size of a product is the number of lines of code. Two different units are commonly used, namely lines of code (LOC) and thousand delivered source instructions (KDSI). Many problems are associated with the use of lines of code [van der Poel and Schach, 1983].

First, creation of source code is only a small part of the total software development effort. It seems somewhat farfetched that the time required for specifying, planning, designing, implementing, integrating, and testing can be expressed solely as a function of the number of lines of code of the final product.

Second, implementing the same product in two different languages will result in versions with different numbers of lines of code. Also, with languages such as Lisp or with many nonprocedural 4GLs, the concept of lines of code is not defined.

Third, it is often not clear exactly how to count lines of code. Should only executable lines of code be counted, or data definitions as well? And should comments be counted? If not, there is a danger that programmers will be reluctant to spend time on what they perceive to be "nonproductive" commenting, but if comments are counted, then there is the opposite danger that programmers will write reams of comments in an attempt to boost their apparent productivity. Also, what about counting job control language statements? Another problem is how changed lines or deleted lines are counted—in the course of enhancing a product to improve its performance, it sometimes happens that the number of lines of code is decreased. Reuse of code (Section 6.10) also complicates line counting; if reused code is modified, how is it counted? In short, the apparently straightforward metric of lines of code is anything but straightforward to count.

Fourth, not all the code written is delivered to the client. It is not uncommon for half the code to consist of tools needed to support the development effort.

Fifth, the number of lines of code in the final product can be determined only when the product is completely finished. Thus, basing cost estimation on lines of code is doubly dangerous. To start the estimation process, the number of lines of code in the finished product must be estimated. Then, this estimate is used to estimate the cost of the product. Not only is there uncertainty in every costing technique, but if the input to an uncertain cost estimator is itself uncertain, namely, the number of lines of code in a product that has not yet been built, then the reliability of the resulting cost estimate is unlikely to be too high.

Because the number of lines of code is so unreliable, other metrics must be considered. So-called software science [Halstead, 1977; Shen, Conte, and Dunsmore, 1983] proposes a variety of measures of product size. These are derived from the fundamental metrics of software science, namely, the number of operands and operators in the software product and the number of unique operands and unique operators. As with lines of code, these numbers can be determined only after the product has been completed, thus severely reducing the predictive power of the metrics. Also, many studies have cast doubt on the validity of software science [Hamer and Frewin, 1982; Coulter, 1983; Shen, Conte, and Dunsmore, 1983; Shepperd, 1988a; Weyuker, 1988b; Shepperd and Ince, 1994].

An alternative approach to estimating the size of a product is the use of metrics based on measurable quantities that can be determined early in the software process. For example, van der Poel and Schach put forward the FFP metric for cost estimation of medium-scale data-processing products, that is, products that take between 2 and 10 person-years to complete [van der Poel and Schach, 1983]. The three basic structural elements of a data-processing product are its files, flows, and processes; the name FFP is an acronym formed from the initial letters of those three elements. A *file* is defined as a collection of logically or physically related records that is permanently resident in the product; transaction and temporary files are excluded. A *flow* is a data interface between the product and the environment such as a screen or a report. A *process* is a functionally defined logical or arithmetic manipulation of data. Examples include sorting, validating, or updating. Given the number of files Fi, flows Fl, and processes Pr in a product, its size S and cost C are given by

$$S = Fi + Fl + Pr \qquad\qquad \textbf{(10.1)}$$

$$C = b \times S \qquad\qquad \textbf{(10.2)}$$

where b is a constant that will vary from organization to organization. Constant b is a measure of the efficiency (productivity) of the software development process within that organization. The size of a product is simply the sum of the number of files, flows, and processes, a quantity that can be determined once the architectural design is complete. The cost is then proportional to the size, the constant of proportionality b being determined by a least-squares fit to cost data relating to products previously developed by that organization. Unlike metrics based on the number of lines of code, the cost can be estimated during the planning phase.

The validity and reliability of the FFP metric were demonstrated using a purposive sample that covered a range of medium-scale data-processing applications. Unfortunately, the metric was never extended to include databases, an essential component of many data-processing products.

A similar, but independently developed, metric for the size of a product is one developed by Albrecht based on function points [Albrecht 1979; Albrecht and

	Level of Complexity		
Component	**Simple**	**Average**	**Complex**
Input item	3	4	6
Output item	4	5	7
Inquiry	3	4	6
Master file	7	10	15
Interface	5	7	10

Figure 10.1   Table of function point values.

Gaffney, 1983]. Albrecht's metric is based on the number of input items *Inp,* output items *Out,* inquiries *Inq,* master files *Maf,* and interfaces *Inf.* In its simplest form the number of function points *FP* is given by the equation

$$FP = 4 \times Inp + 5 \times Out + 4 \times Inq + 10 \times Maf + 7 \times Inf \qquad \textbf{(10.3)}$$

Because this is a measure of the product's size, it can be used for cost estimation and productivity estimation.

Equation 10.3 is an oversimplification of a three-step calculation. First, each of the components of a product, namely *Inp, Out, Inq, Maf,* and *Inf,* must be classified as simple, average, or complex (see Figure 10.1). Each component is assigned a number of function points depending on its level. For example, an average input is assigned 4 function points, as reflected in equation 10.3, but a simple input is assigned only 3, whereas a complex input is assigned 6 function points. The data needed for this computation appear in Figure 10.1. The function points assigned to each component are then summed, yielding the unadjusted function points *(UFP).*

Second, the technical complexity factor *(TCF)* is computed. This is a measure of the effect of 14 technical factors such as high transaction rates, performance criteria (for example, throughput or response time), and online updating; the complete set of factors is shown in Figure 10.2. Each of these 14 factors is assigned a value from 0 ("not present or no influence") to 5 ("strong influence throughout"). The resulting 14 numbers are summed, yielding the total degree of influence *(DI).* The *TCF* is then given by

$$TCF = 0.65 + 0.01 \times DI \qquad \textbf{(10.4)}$$

Because *DI* can vary from 0 to 70, *TCF* will vary from 0.65 to 1.35.

Finally, *FP,* the number of function points, is given by

$$FP = UFP \times TCF \qquad \textbf{(10.5)}$$

Experiments by Albrecht and others [Albrecht, 1979; Albrecht and Gaffney, 1983; Bchrens, 1983; Jones, 1987] to measure software productivity rates have shown a better fit using function points than using KDSI. Jones states that he has observed errors in excess of 800 percent counting KDSI, but *only* [author's italics] 200 percent in counting function points [Jones, 1987], a most revealing remark.

1. Data communications
2. Distributed data processing
3. Performance criteria
4. Heavily utilized hardware
5. High transaction rates
6. Online data entry
7. End-user efficiency
8. Online updating
9. Complex computations
10. Reusability
11. Ease of installation
12. Ease of operation
13. Portability
14. Maintainability

Figure 10.2 Technical factors for function point computation.

	Assembler version	Ada version
Source code size	70 KDSI	25 KDSI
Development costs	$1,043,000	$590,000
KDSI per person-month	0.335	0.211
Cost per source statement	$14.90	$23.60
Function points per person-month	1.65	2.92
Cost per function point	$3,023	$1,170

Figure 10.3 Comparison of assembler and Ada products [Jones, 1987].
(© 1987 IEEE)

To show the superiority of function points over lines of code, Jones cites the example shown in Figure 10.3 [Jones, 1987]. The same product was coded both in assembler and in Ada and the results compared. First, consider KDSI per person-month. This metric tells us that coding in assembler is apparently 60 percent more efficient than coding in Ada, a fact that is patently false. Third-generation languages like Ada have superseded assembler simply because it is much more efficient to code in a third-generation language. Now consider the second metric, cost per source statement. Note that one Ada statement in this product is equivalent to 2.8 assembler statements. Use of cost per source statement as a measure of efficiency again implies that it is more efficient to code in assembler than in Ada, the statement rejected previously as being nonsense. However, when function points per person-month are taken as the metric of programming efficiency, the superiority of Ada over assembler is clearly reflected.

On the other hand, both function points and the FFP metric of equations (10.1) and (10.2) suffer from the same disadvantage: Product maintenance is often inaccurately measured. When a product is maintained, major changes to the product can be made without changing the number of files, flows, and processes or the number of inputs, outputs, inquiries, master files, and interfaces. Lines of code is no better in this respect. To take an extreme case, it is possible to replace every line of a product by a completely different line without changing the total number of lines of code.

10.1.2 TECHNIQUES OF COST ESTIMATION

Notwithstanding the difficulties with estimating size, it is essential that software developers simply do the best they can to obtain accurate estimates of both project duration and project cost, while taking into account as many as possible of the factors that can affect their estimates. These include the skill levels of the personnel, the complexity of the project, the size of the project (cost increases with size, but much faster than linearly), familiarity of the development team with the application area, the hardware on which the product is to run, and availability of CASE tools. Another factor is the deadline effect. If a project has to be completed within a certain time, the effort in person-months is greater than if there is no constraint on completion time.

From the preceding list, which is by no means comprehensive, it is clear that estimation is a difficult problem. There are a number of approaches that have been used, with greater or lesser success.

1. Expert Judgment by Analogy   In this technique a number of experts are consulted. An expert arrives at an estimate by comparing the target product to completed products with which the expert was actively involved and noting the similarities and differences. For example, an expert may compare the target product to a similar product developed 2 years ago for which the data were input in batch mode, whereas the target product is to have online data capture. Because the organization is familiar with the type of product to be developed, the expert reduces development time and effort by 15 percent. However, the graphical user interface (GUI) is somewhat complex; this will increase time and effort by 25 percent. Finally, the target product has to be developed in a language with which most of the team members are unfamiliar, thus increasing time by 15 percent and effort by 20 percent. Combining these three figures, the expert decides that the target product will take 25 percent more time and 30 percent more effort than the previous one. Thus, because the previous product took 12 months to complete and required 100 person-months, the target product will take 15 months and consume 130 person-months.

Two other experts within the organization compare the same two products. One concludes that the target product will take 13.5 months and 140 person-months. The other comes up with the figures of 16 months and 95 person-months. How can the predictions of these three experts be reconciled? One technique is the Delphi technique; it allows experts to arrive at a consensus without having group meetings, which can have the undesirable side effect of one persuasive member swaying the group. In this technique [Helmer-Hirschberg, 1966] the experts work independently. Each produces an estimate and a rationale for that estimate. These estimates and rationales are then distributed to all the experts, who now produce a second estimate. This process of estimation and distribution continues until the experts can agree within an accepted tolerance. No group meetings take place during the iteration process.

Valuation of real estate is frequently done on the basis of expert judgment by analogy. An appraiser will arrive at a valuation by comparing a house with similar houses that have recently been sold. Suppose that house A is to be valued, house B next door has just been sold for $150,000, and house C on the next street was sold 3 months ago for $165,000. The appraiser may reason as follows: House A has one more bathroom than house B, and the yard is 5,000 square feet larger. House C is approximately the same size as house A, but its roof is in poor condition. On the other hand, house C has a jacuzzi. After careful thought, the appraiser may arrive at a figure of $168,000 for house A.

In the case of software products, expert judgment by analogy is less precise than real estate valuation. Recall that our first software expert claimed that using an unfamiliar language would increase time by 15 percent and effort by 20 percent. Unless the expert has some validated data from which the effect of each and every difference can be determined (a highly unlikely possibility), errors induced by what can only be described as guesses will result in hopelessly incorrect cost estimates. In addition, unless the experts are blessed with total recall (or have kept detailed records), their recollections of completed products may be sufficiently inaccurate as to invalidate their predictions. Finally, experts are human and, therefore, have biases that may affect their predictions. At the same time, the results of estimation by a group of experts should reflect their collective experience; if this is broad enough, the results may well be accurate.

2. Bottom-Up Approach   One way of trying to reduce the errors resulting from evaluating a product as a whole is to break the product into smaller components. Estimates of duration and cost are made for each component separately and then combined to provide an overall figure. This approach has the advantage that estimating costs for several smaller components is generally quicker and more accurate than for one large one. In addition, the estimation process is likely to be more detailed than with one large, monolithic product. The disadvantage of this approach is that a product is more than the sum of its components.

With the object-oriented paradigm, the independence of the various classes helps the bottom-up approach. Nevertheless, interactions among the various objects in the product complicate the estimate.

3. Algorithmic Cost Estimation Models   In this approach, a metric such as function points or the FFP metric is used as input to a model for determining product cost. The estimator computes the value of the metric; duration and cost estimates can then be

---

Just in Case You Wanted to Know

COCOMO is an acronym formed from the first two letters of each word in COnstructive COst MOdel. Any connection with Kokomo, Indiana, is purely homophonic.

The term *COCOMO model* should not be used. After all, the "MO" in COCOMO already stands for "model."

---

computed using the model. On the surface an algorithmic cost estimation model is superior to expert opinion, because a human expert is, as pointed out previously, subject to biases and may overlook certain aspects of both the completed and target products. In contrast, an algorithmic cost estimation model is unbiased; every product is treated the same way. The danger with such a model is that its estimates are only as good as the underlying assumptions. For example, underlying the function-point metric is the assumption that every aspect of a product is embodied in the five quantities on the right-hand side of Equation (10.3) and the 14 technical factors. A further problem is that a significant amount of subjective judgment is often needed in deciding what values to assign to the parameters of the model. For example, it is frequently unclear whether a specific technical factor of the function-point metric should be rated a 3 or a 4.

Many algorithmic cost estimation models have been proposed. Some are based on mathematical theories as to how software is developed. For example, underlying the SLIM model [Putnam, 1978] is the assumption that resource consumption during software development obeys a specific distribution; this is described in Section 10.2. Other models are statistically based; large numbers of projects are studied and empirical rules determined from the data. Then there are hybrid models incorporating mathematical equations, statistical modeling, and expert judgment. One hybrid model is the RCA Price S model [Freiman and Park, 1979]. The most important hybrid model is Boehm's COCOMO, which is described in detail in the next section. (See the Just in Case You Wanted to Know box on this page for a discussion of the acronym COCOMO.)

10.1.3 Intermediate COCOMO

COCOMO is actually a series of three models, ranging from a macroestimation model that treats the product as a whole to a microestimation model that treats the product in detail. In this section a description is given of Intermediate COCOMO, which has a middle level of complexity and detail. COCOMO is described in detail in [Boehm, 1981]; an overview is presented in [Boehm, 1984b].

Computing the development time using Intermediate COCOMO is done in two stages. First, a rough estimate of the development effort is provided. Two parameters have to be estimated: the length of the product in KDSI (thousands of delivered source instructions) and the product's development mode, a measure of the intrinsic level of difficulty of developing that product. There are three modes, namely *organic* (small and straightforward), *semidetached* (medium-sized), and *embedded* (complex).

From these two parameters the *nominal effort* can be computed. For example, if the project is judged to be essentially straightforward (organic), then the nominal effort (in person-months) is given by the equation

$$\text{Nominal effort} = 3.2 \times (\text{KDSI})^{1.05} \text{ person-months} \qquad \textbf{(10.6)}$$

The constants 3.2 and 1.05 are the values that best fitted the data on the organic mode products used by Boehm to develop Intermediate COCOMO.

For example, if the product to be built is organic and is estimated to be 12,000 delivered source statements (12 KDSI), then the nominal effort is

$$3.2 \times (12)^{1.05} = 43 \text{ person-months}$$

Next, this nominal value must be multiplied by 15 *software development effort multipliers*. These multipliers and their values are given in Figure 10.4. Each of these multipliers can have up to six values. For example, the product complexity multiplier is assigned the values 0.70, 0.85, 1.00, 1.15, 1.30, or 1.65 according to whether the developers rate the project complexity as very low, low, nominal (average), high, very high, or extra high. As can be seen from Figure 10.4, all 15 multipliers take on the value 1.00 when the corresponding parameter is nominal.

Boehm has provided guidelines to help the developer determine whether the parameter should indeed be rated nominal or whether the rating is lower or higher. For example, consider again the module complexity multiplier. If the control operations of the module essentially consist of a sequence of the constructs of structured programming (such as if-then-else, do-while, case), then the complexity is rated *very low*. If these operators are nested, then the rating is *low*. Adding intermodule control and decision tables increases the rating to *nominal*. If the operators are highly nested, with compound predicates, and if there are queues and stacks, then the rating is *high*. The presence of reentrant and recursive coding and fixed-priority interrupt handling pushes the rating to *very high*. Finally, multiple resource scheduling with dynamically changing priorities and microcode-level control ensures that the rating is *extra high*. These ratings apply to control operations. A module also has to be evaluated from the viewpoint of computational operations, device-dependent operations, and data management operations. For details of the criteria for computing each of the 15 multipliers, the reader should refer to [Boehm, 1981].

To see how this works, [Boehm, 1984b] gives the example of microprocessor-based communications processing software for a highly reliable electronic funds transfer network, with performance, development schedule, and interface requirements. This product fits the description of embedded mode and is estimated to be 10,000 delivered source instructions (10 KDSI) in length, so the nominal development effort is given by

$$\text{Nominal effort} = 2.8 \times (\text{KDSI})^{1.20} \qquad \textbf{(10.7)}$$

Cost Drivers	Rating					
	Very Low	Low	Nominal	High	Very High	Extra High
Product Attributes						
Required software reliability	0.75	0.88	1.00	1.15	1.40	
Database size		0.94	1.00	1.08	1.16	
Product complexity	0.70	0.85	1.00	1.15	1.30	1.65
Computer Attributes						
Execution time constraint			1.00	1.11	1.30	1.66
Main storage constraint			1.00	1.06	1.21	1.56
Virtual machine volatility*		0.87	1.00	1.15	1.30	
Computer turnaround time		0.87	1.00	1.07	1.15	
Personnel Attributes						
Analyst capabilities	1.46	1.19	1.00	0.86	0.71	
Applications experience	1.29	1.13	1.00	0.91	0.82	
Programmer capability	1.42	1.17	1.00	0.86	0.70	
Virtual machine experience*	1.21	1.10	1.00	0.90		
Programming language experience	1.14	1.07	1.00	0.95		
Project Attributes						
Use of modern programming practices	1.24	1.10	1.00	0.91	0.82	
Use of software tools	1.24	1.10	1.00	0.91	0.83	
Required development schedule	1.23	1.08	1.00	1.04	1.10	

Figure 10.4 Intermediate COCOMO software development effort multipliers [Boehm, 1984b]. (© 1984 IEEE)

*For a given software product, the underlying virtual machine is the complex of hardware and software (operating system, database management system) it calls on to accomplish its task.

(Again, the constants 2.8 and 1.20 are the values that best fitted the data on embedded products.) Because the project is estimated to be 10 KDSI in length, the nominal effort is

$$2.8 \times (10)^{1.20} = 44 \text{ person-months}$$

The estimated development effort is obtained by multiplying the nominal effort by the 15 multipliers. The ratings of these multipliers and their values are given in Figure 10.5. Using these values, the product of the multipliers is found to be 1.35, so the estimated effort for the project is

$$1.35 \times 44 = 59 \text{ person-months}$$

This number is then used in additional formulas to determine dollar costs, development schedules, phase and activity distributions, computer costs, annual

Cost Drivers	Situation	Rating	Effort Multiplier
Required software reliability	Serious financial consequences of software fault	High	1.15
Data base size	20,000 bytes	Low	0.94
Product complexity	Communications processing	Very high	1.30
Execution time constraint	Will use 70% of available time	High	1.11
Main storage constraint	45K of 64K store (70%)	High	1.06
Virtual machine volatility	Based on commercial microprocessor hardware	Nominal	1.00
Computer turnaround time	Two hour average turnaround time	Nominal	1.00
Analyst capabilities	Good senior analysts	High	0.86
Applications experience	Three years	Nominal	1.00
Programmer capability	Good senior programmers	High	0.86
Virtual machine experience	Six months	Low	1.10
Programming language experience	Twelve months	Nominal	1.00
Use of modern programming practices	Most techniques in use over one year	High	0.91
Use of software tools	At basic minicomputer tool level	Low	1.10
Required development schedule	Nine months	Nominal	1.00

Figure 10.5 Intermediate COCOMO effort multiplier ratings for microprocessor communications software [Boehm, 1984b].
| (© 1984 IEEE)

maintenance costs, and other related items; for details, see [Boehm, 1981]. Intermediate COCOMO is a complete algorithmic cost estimation model, giving the user virtually every conceivable assistance in project planning.

Intermediate COCOMO has been validated with respect to a broad sample of 63 projects covering a wide variety of application areas. The results of applying Intermediate COCOMO to this sample are that the actual values come within 20 percent of the predicted values about 68 percent of the time. Attempts to improve this accuracy make little sense because in most organizations the input data for Intermediate COCOMO are generally accurate to within only 20 percent. Nevertheless, the accuracy obtained by experienced estimators places Intermediate COCOMO at the cutting edge of cost estimation research; no other technique is consistently as accurate.

The major problem with Intermediate COCOMO is that its most important input is the number of lines of code in the target product. If this estimate is incorrect, then every single prediction of the model may be incorrect. Because of the possibility that the predictions of Intermediate COCOMO or any other estimation technique may be inaccurate, management must monitor all predictions throughout software development.

10.1.4 Tracking Duration and Cost Estimates

While the product is being developed, actual development effort must be constantly compared against predictions. For example, suppose that the estimation metric used by the software developers predicted that the specification phase would last 3 months and require 7 person-months of effort. However, 4 months have gone by and 10 person-months of effort have been expended, but the specification document is by no means complete. Deviations of this kind can serve as an early warning that something has gone wrong and that corrective action must be taken. The problem could be that the size of the product was seriously underestimated or that the development team is not as competent as it was thought to be. Whatever the reason, there are going to be serious duration and cost overruns, and management must take appropriate action to minimize the effects.

Careful tracking of predictions must be done throughout the development process, irrespective of the techniques by which the predictions were made. Deviations could be due to metrics that are poor predictors, inefficient software development, a combination of both, or some other reason. The important thing is to detect deviations early and to take immediate corrective action.

Now that metrics for estimating duration and cost have been discussed, the components of the software project management plan are described.

10.2 Components of a Software Project Management Plan

A software project management plan has three main components: the work to be done, the resources with which to do it, and the money to pay for it all. In this section these three ingredients of the plan are discussed. The terminology is taken from [IEEE 1058.1, 1987], which is discussed in greater detail in Section 10.4.

Software development requires *resources*. The major resources required are the people who will develop the software, the hardware on which the software will be run, and the support software such as operating systems, text editors, and version control software (Section 4.5).

Use of resources such as personnel varies with time. Norden has shown [Norden, 1958] that for large projects, the Rayleigh distribution is a good approximation of the way that resource consumption R_c varies with time t, that is,

$$R_c = \frac{t}{k^2} e^{-t^2/2k^2} \qquad 0 \le t < \infty \qquad \textbf{(10.8)}$$

Parameter k is a constant, the time at which consumption is at its peak, and $e = 2.71828 \ldots$, the base of Naperian logarithms. A typical Rayleigh curve is shown in Figure 10.6. Resource consumption starts small, climbs rapidly to a peak, then decreases at a slower rate. Putnam investigated the applicability of Norden's results to software development and found that personnel and other resource consumption was modeled with some degree of accuracy by the Rayleigh distribution [Putnam, 1978].

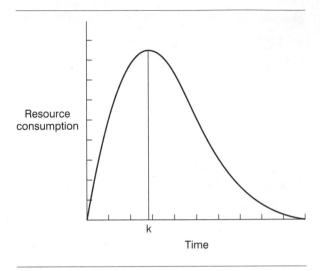

Resource consumption

k

Time

Figure 10.6 Rayleigh curve showing how resource consumption varies with time.

It is therefore insufficient in a software plan merely to state that three senior programmers with at least 5 years of experience are required. What is needed is something like the following:

> Three senior programmers with at least 5 years of experience in real-time programming are needed, two to start 3 months after the project commences, the third to start 6 months after that. Two will be phased out when product testing commences, the third when maintenance begins.

The fact that resource needs depend on time applies not only to personnel but also to computer time, support software, computer hardware, office facilities, and even travel. Thus the software project management plan will be a function of time.

The work falls into two categories. First, there is work that continues throughout the project and does not relate to any specific phase of software development. Such work is termed a *project function*. Examples are project management and quality control. Second there is work that relates to a specific phase in the development of the product; such work is termed an activity or a task. An *activity* is a major unit of work that has precise beginning and ending dates; consumes *resources* such as computer time or person-days; and results in *work products* such as a budget, design documents, schedules, source code, or user's manual. An activity, in turn, comprises a set of *tasks,* a task being the smallest unit of work subject to management accountability. There are thus three kinds of work in a software project management plan: project functions that are carried on throughout the project, activities (major units of work), and tasks (minor units of work).

A critical aspect of the plan concerns completion of work products. The date on which a work product is deemed to be completed is termed a *milestone*. In order to determine whether a work product has indeed reached a milestone, it must first pass a series of *reviews* performed by fellow team members, management, and/or the client. A typical milestone is the date on which the design is completed and passes review. Once a work product has been reviewed and agreed upon, it becomes a *baseline* and can be changed only through formal procedures as described in Section 4.6.2.

In reality, there is more to a work product than merely the product itself. A *work package* defines not just the work product, but also the staffing requirements, duration, resources, name of the responsible individuals, and acceptance criteria for the work product. Money is of course a vital component of the plan. A detailed budget must be worked out and the money allocated, as a function of time, to the project functions and activities.

The issue of how to draw up a plan for software production is now addressed.

10.3 SOFTWARE PROJECT MANAGEMENT PLAN FRAMEWORK

Figure 10.7 shows the section headings of the software project management plan (SPMP) prescribed in IEEE Standard 1058.1 [IEEE 1058.1, 1987]. Although there are many other ways of drawing up a SPMP, there are distinct advantages to following the IEEE standard. First, it is a standard drawn up by representatives of many major organizations involved in software. There was input from both industry and universities, and the members of the working group and reviewing teams had many years of experience in drawing up project management plans. The standard incorporates this experience. A second advantage is that the IEEE SPMP is designed for use with all types of software products, irrespective of size. It does not impose a specific process model or prescribe specific techniques. The plan is essentially a framework, the contents of which will be tailored by each organization for a particular application area, development team, or technique. By adhering to this framework on an industrywide basis, the advantages of standardization will accrue. Eventually, all software personnel will become familiar with the IEEE Software Project Management Plan format, and companies will be saved the expense of training new hires.

10.4 IEEE SOFTWARE PROJECT MANAGEMENT PLAN

The plan framework itself is now described in detail. The numbers and headings in the text correspond to the entries in Figure 10.7. The various terms used have been defined in Section 10.2.

1. Introduction. The five subsections of this section of the SPMP provide an overview of the project and of the product to be developed.

1.1. Project Overview. A brief description is given of the project objectives, the product to be delivered, the activities, and their resulting work products. In addition,

---

1. Introduction

    1.1 Project Overview

    1.2 Project Deliverables

    1.3 Evolution of the Software Project Management Plan

    1.4 Reference Materials

    1.5 Definitions and Acronyms

2. Project Organization

    2.1 Process Model

    2.2 Organizational Structure

    2.3 Organizational Boundaries and Interfaces

    2.4 Project Responsibilities

3. Managerial Process

    3.1 Management Objectives and Priorities

    3.2 Assumptions, Dependencies, and Constraints

    3.3 Risk Management

    3.4 Monitoring and Controlling Mechanisms

    3.5 Staffing Plan

4. Technical Process

    4.1 Methods, Tools, and Techniques

    4.2 Software Documentation

    4.3 Project Support Functions

5. Work Packages, Schedule, and Budget

    5.1 Work Packages

    5.2 Dependencies

    5.3 Resource Requirements

    5.4 Budget and Resource Allocation

    5.5 Schedule

Additional Components

Figure 10.7 Components of IEEE software project
management plan [IEEE 1058.1, 1987].
| (© 1987 IEEE.)

the milestones are listed, as are the required resources, the master schedule, and master budget.

1.2. Project Deliverables. All the items to be delivered to the client are listed here, together with the delivery dates.

1.3. Evolution of the Software Project Management Plan. No plan can be cast in concrete. The SPMP, like any other plan, requires continual updating in the light of experience and of change within both the client organization and the software development organization. In this section the formal procedures and mechanisms for changing the plan are described.

1.4. Reference Materials. All documents referenced in the SPMP are listed here.

1.5. Definitions and Acronyms. This information ensures that the SPMP will be understood the same way by everyone.

2. Project Organization. The four subsections of the project organization section specify how the product is to be developed, both from the viewpoint of the software process and the organizational structure of the developers.

2.1. Process Model. The process model is specified in terms of the activities, such as designing the product or performing product testing, and the project functions, such as project management or configuration management. Key aspects here include specification of milestones, baselines, reviews, work products, and deliverables.

2.2. Organizational Structure. The management structure of the development organization is described. It is important to demarcate the lines of authority and responsibility within the organization.

2.3. Organizational Boundaries and Interfaces. No project is constructed in a vacuum. The project members have to interact with the client organization and with other members of their own organization. In addition, subcontractors may be involved in a large project. Administrative and managerial boundaries between the project itself and these other entities must be laid down. In addition, many software development organizations are divided into two types of groups, namely, development groups who work on a single project and support groups who provide support functions, such as configuration management and SQA, on an organization-wide basis. Administrative and managerial boundaries between the project group and the support groups must also be clearly defined.

2.4. Project Responsibilities. For each project function, such as SQA, and for each activity, such as product testing, the responsible individual must be identified.

3. Managerial Process. The five subsections of this section describe how the project is to be managed.

3.1. Management Objectives and Priorities. The philosophy, goals, and priorities for management are described. The types of items that appear in this subsection of the plan may include frequency and mechanism of reporting; the relative priorities among requirements; schedule and budget for the project; and risk management procedures.

3.2. Assumptions, Dependencies, and Constraints. Any assumptions and constraints in the specification document appear here.

3.3. Risk Management. The various risk factors associated with the project are listed in this subsection, as well as the mechanisms used for tracking these risk factors.

3.4. Monitoring and Controlling Mechanisms. Reporting mechanisms for the project are described in detail, including review and audit mechanisms.

3.5. Staffing Plan. The personnel who will be staffing the project constitute an important resource. The numbers and types of personnel required are listed, together with the durations for which they will be needed.

4. Technical Process. Technical aspects of the project are specified in the three subsections of this section.

4.1. Methods, Tools, and Techniques. Technical aspects of hardware and software are described in detail in this subsection. Items that should be covered include the computing systems (hardware, operating systems, and software) to be used for developing the product, as well as the target systems on which the product will be run. Other necessary aspects include development techniques, testing techniques, team structure, programming language(s), and CASE tools to be employed. In addition, technical standards such as documentation standards and coding standards are included, perhaps by reference to other documents, as well as procedures for developing and modifying work products.

4.2. Software Documentation. This subsection contains the documentation requirements, namely the milestones, baselines, and reviews for software documentation.

4.3. Project Support Functions. This subsection details plans for the supporting functions such as configuration management and quality assurance, including test plans.

5. Work Packages, Schedule, and Budget. The five subsections of this section emphasize the work packages, their interdependencies, resource requirements, and associated budgeting allocations.

5.1. Work Packages. In this subsection the work packages are specified, with their associated work products broken down into activities and tasks.

5.2. Dependencies. Module coding follows design and precedes integration testing. In general, there will be interdependencies among the work packages and dependencies on external events. In this subsection these dependencies are specified.

5.3. Resource Requirements. To complete the project, a wide variety of resources will be required. Total resources are presented as a function of time.

5.4. Budget and Resource Allocation. The various resources previously listed cost money. Just as the resource needs vary with time, so does the allocation of the budget to the various component resources. The allocation of resources and budget to the various project functions, activities, and tasks is presented.

5.5. Schedule. A detailed schedule is given for each component of the project. This master plan will then be followed; it is hoped that the project will be completed on time and within budget.

Additional Components. For certain projects, additional components may need to appear in the plan. In terms of the IEEE framework, they appear at the end of the plan. Additional components may include subcontractor management plans, security plans, test plans, training plans, hardware procurement plans, installation plans, and the product maintenance plan.

10.5 PLANNING OF TESTING

One component of the SPMP that frequently is overlooked is test planning. Like every other activity of software development, testing must be planned. The SPMP must include resources for testing, and the detailed schedule must explicitly indicate the testing that is to be done during each phase.

Without a test plan, a project can go awry in a number of ways. For example, during product testing (Section 2.7.1), the SQA group must check that every aspect of the specification document, as signed off by the client, has been implemented in the completed product. A good way of assisting the SQA group in this task is to require that the development be traceable. That is, it must be possible to connect each statement in the specification document to a part of the design, and each part of the design must be explicitly reflected in the code. One technique of achieving this is to number each statement in the specification document and ensure that these numbers are reflected in both the design and the resulting code. However, if the test plan does not specify that this is to be done, it is highly unlikely that the design and the code will be labeled appropriately. Consequently, when the product testing is finally performed, it will be extremely difficult for the SQA team to determine that the product is a complete implementation of the specifications. In fact, traceability should start with the requirements phase; each statement in the requirements document (or each portion of the rapid prototype) must be connected to part of the specification document.

One powerful aspect of inspections is the detailed list of faults detected during an inspection. Suppose that a team is inspecting the specifications of a product. As explained in Section 5.2.3, the list of faults is used in two ways. First, the fault statistics from this inspection must be compared with accumulated averages of fault statistics from previous specification inspections. Deviations from previous norms indicate that there are problems within the project. Second, the fault statistics from the current specification inspection must be carried forward to the design and code inspections of the product. After all, if there are large number of faults of a particular type, it is possible that not all of them were detected during the inspection of the specifications, and the design and code inspections provide an additional opportunity for locating any remaining faults of this type. However, unless the test plan states that details of all faults have to be carefully recorded, it is unlikely that this task will be done.

One important way of testing code modules is so-called black-box testing (Section 12.15) in which the code is executed with test cases based on the specifications. Members of the SQA team read through the specifications and draw up test cases to check whether the code obeys the specification document. The best time to draw up black-box test cases is at the end of the specification phase, when the details of the specification document are still fresh in the minds of the members of the SQA team that inspected them. However, unless the test plan explicitly states that the black-box test cases are to be selected at this time, in all probability what will happen is that a few black-box test cases will hurriedly be thrown together later. That is to say, a limited number of test cases will be rapidly assembled only when the pressure starts mounting from the programming team for the SQA group to approve their modules so that they can be integrated into the product as whole. As a result, the quality of the product as a whole will suffer.

Thus, every test plan must specify what testing is to be performed, when it is to be performed, and how it is to be performed. Such a test plan is an essential part of

Section 4.3 of the SPMP. Without it, the quality of the overall product will undoubtedly suffer.

10.6   PLANNING OF OBJECT-ORIENTED PROJECTS

Suppose the structured paradigm is used. From a conceptual viewpoint the resulting product is generally one large unit, even though it is composed of separate modules. In contrast, use of the object-oriented paradigm results in a product consisting of a number of relatively independent smaller components, namely, the classes at the analysis and architectural design levels of abstraction or the objects at the detailed design and implementation levels. This makes planning considerably easier, in that cost and duration estimates can be computed more easily and more accurately on smaller units. Of course, the estimates must take into account that a product is more than just the sum of its parts. The separate components are not totally independent; they can invoke one another, and these effects must not be overlooked.

Are the techniques described in this chapter for estimating cost and duration, such as function points (Section 10.1.1) and Intermediate COCOMO (Section 10.1.3), applicable to the object-oriented paradigm? In the case of COCOMO, minor changes to some of the cost multipliers are required [Pittman, 1993]. Other than that, the estimation tools of the structured paradigm appear to work reasonably well on object-oriented projects—provided that there is no reuse. Reuse enters the object-oriented paradigm in two ways, namely, reuse of existing components during development, and the deliberate production (during the current project) of components to be reused in future products. Both these forms of reuse affect the planning phase. Reuse during development clearly reduces the cost and duration. Formulas have been published showing the savings as a function of this reuse [Schach, 1994], but these results relate to the structured paradigm. At present, no information is available as to how the cost and duration change when reuse is utilized in the development of an object-oriented product.

Turning now to the goal of reusing parts of the current project, it can take about three times as long to design, implement, test, and document a reusable component compared to a similar nonreusable component [Pittman, 1993]. Cost and duration estimates must be modified to incorporate this additional labor, and the SPMP as a whole must be adjusted to incorporate the effect of the reuse endeavor. Thus, the two reuse activities work in opposite directions. Reuse of existing components reduces the overall effort in developing an object-oriented product, whereas designing components for reuse increases the effort. It is anticipated that, in the long term, the savings due to reuse of classes will outweigh the costs, and there is already some evidence to support this [Lim, 1994].

10.7   TRAINING REQUIREMENTS

When the subject of training is raised during the planning phase, a common response is "We don't need to worry about training until the product is finished, and then we can train the users." This is a somewhat unfortunate remark, implying as it does that only users require training. In fact, training may also be needed by members of the development team, starting with training in software planning. When new software development techniques, such as new design techniques or testing procedures, are used, training must be provided to every member of the team involved in using the new technique.

Introduction of the object-oriented paradigm has major training consequences. The introduction of hardware or software tools such as workstations or an integrated environment (see Section 13.11) also requires training. Programmers may need training in the operating system of the machine to be used for product development, as well as in the implementation language. Documentation preparation training is frequently overlooked, as evidenced by the poor quality of so much documentation. Computer operators will certainly require some sort of training in order to be able to run the new product; they may also require additional training if new hardware is utilized.

The required training can be obtained in a number of ways. The easiest and least disruptive is in-house training, either by fellow employees or by consultants. Many companies offer a variety of training courses, and colleges often offer training courses in the evenings. Videotape-based courses for self-instruction are another alternative.

Once the training needs have been determined and the training plan drawn up, the plan must be incorporated into the SPMP.

10.8 DOCUMENTATION STANDARDS

The development of a software product is accompanied by a wide variety of documentation. Jones has found that 28 pages of documentation were generated per 1000 instructions (KDSI) for an IBM internal commercial product around 50 KDSI in size and about 66 pages per KDSI for a commercial software product of the same size. Operating system IMS/360 Version 2.3 was about 166 KDSI in size, and 157 pages of documentation per KDSI were produced. The documentation was of various types, including planning, control, financial, and technical [Jones, 1986a]. In addition to these types of documentation, the source code itself is a form of documentation; comments within the code constitute further documentation.

A considerable portion of the software development effort is absorbed by documentation. A survey of 63 development projects and 25 maintenance projects showed that for every 100 hours spent on activities related to code, 150 hours were spent on activities related to documentation [Boehm, 1981]. For large TRW products, the proportion of time that was devoted to documentation-related activities rose to 200 hours per 100 code-related hours [Boehm, Penedo, Stuckle, Williams, and Pyster, 1984].

Standards are needed for every type of documentation. For instance, uniformity in design documentation reduces misunderstandings between team members and aids the SQA group. Although new employees have to be trained in the documentation standards, no further training will be needed when existing employees move from project to project within the organization. From the viewpoint of product maintenance, uniform coding standards assist maintenance programmers in understanding source code. Standardization is even more important for user manuals, because these have to be read by a wide of variety of users, few of whom are computer experts. The IEEE has developed a standard for user manuals (IEEE Standard 1063 for Software User Documentation).

As part of the planning process, standards must be established for all documentation to be produced during software production. These standards are incorporated in the SPMP. Where an existing standard is to be used, such as the IEEE Standard for Software Test Documentation [ANSI/IEEE 829, 1983], the standard is listed in section 1.4 of the SPMP (Reference Materials). If a standard is specially written for the development effort, then it appears in section 4.1 (Methods, Tools, and Techniques).

Documentation is an essential aspect of the software production effort; in a very real sense the product *is* the documentation. Planning the documentation effort in every detail, and then ensuring that the plan is adhered to, is a critical component of successful software production.

10.9   CASE TOOLS FOR THE PLANNING PHASE

A number of tools are available that automate Intermediate COCOMO. For speed of computation when the value of a parameter is modified, several implementations of Intermediate COCOMO have been written in spreadsheet languages such as Lotus 1-2-3 or Excel. For developing and updating the plan itself, a word processor is essential.

Management information tools are also useful during the planning phase. For example, suppose that a large software organization has 150 programmers. A scheduling tool can help planners keep track of programmers that have already been assigned to specific tasks and who is available for the current project.

More general types of management information are also needed. An example of this is critical path management (CPM), otherwise known as program evaluation review techniques (PERT) [Moder, Phillips, and Davis, 1983]. For background information on PERT, see the Just in Case You Wanted to Know box on page 313.

Many hundreds of activities have to be performed in the course of building a product, such as projecting cash flow or checking that the database manual is an accurate reflection of the structure of the database. Some activities have to precede others; for instance, a module cannot be coded until it has been designed. Other activities can be carried on in parallel. For example, implementation of the various modules can be assigned to different members of the programming team.

Suppose that two activities are started at the same time and can be performed in parallel, but that both have to be completed before proceeding with the project as a whole. If the first takes 12 days, while the second needs only 3 days, then the first activity is *critical*. Any delay in the first activity will cause the project as a whole to be delayed. However, the second activity can be delayed up to 9 days without adversely

---

JUST IN CASE YOU WANTED TO KNOW

PERT was developed in 1957 by the U.S. Navy to plan and schedule the development of the Polaris missiles. When applied to the missile program, the technique was found to yield overly optimistic results, and the missiles were delivered late. Afterwards it was discovered that the PERT network had many paths that were almost critical. When some of the activities on the almost-critical paths had actual durations that were longer than predicted, those paths then became critical. The project managers had concentrated their efforts on ensuring that the original critical activities would be completed on time. The project as a whole was then slowed by the newly critical activities that had not received the same managerial monitoring as the original critical activities.

The solution to this problem is to replace the single value for a predicted duration by an appropriate statistical distribution. Then the PERT network is simulated. For each simulation run, the value of the duration will be a random value selected from the distribution, rather than a fixed value as before. The critical activities flagged in each simulation run are recorded. Any activity that is flagged as critical in a large percentage of the runs is then closely monitored by management; such an activity has a high probability of turning out to be critical in the actual project. This statistical technique yields more accurate predictions than deciding which activities are critical on the basis of a single estimated duration. For details of this approach, see [Deo, 1983].

---

impacting the project; there is a *slack* of 9 days associated with the second activity. When using PERT/CPM, the manager inputs the activities, their estimated durations, and any precedence relations, that is, the activities that have to be completed before a specific activity can be started. The PERT/CPM package will then determine which of the hundreds of activities are critical, and it will also compute the slack for each of the noncritical activities. Most packages also print out a PERT chart showing the precedence relationships between the activities and highlighting the *critical path,* the path through the chart that consists of critical activities only. If any activity on the critical path is delayed, then so is the project as a whole.

A simple PERT chart is shown in Figure 10.8. There are 12 activities and 9 milestones. Starting with milestone A, activities AB, AC, and AD can be started in parallel. Activity FJ cannot be started until both BF and CF are finished. The project as a whole is complete when activities HJ, FJ, and GJ are all complete. Completing the whole project will take at least 25 days. The critical path is ACGJ; if any one of the critical activities, namely AC, CG, or GJ, is delayed in any way, the project as a whole will be delayed. On the other hand, if activity AD is delayed by up to 15 days, the project as a whole will not be delayed, because there is a slack of 15 days associated with activity AD.

Now suppose that activity AD is in fact delayed by 15 days. The situation at day 17 is shown in Figure 10.9. Actual durations of completed activities are italicized; activities that have been completed cannot be critical. There are now two critical paths, and activity DG has become critical. In other words, simply printing out a PERT chart showing the expected duration of each activity is in itself of little use. Data regarding actual durations must be input continually, and the PERT chart updated.

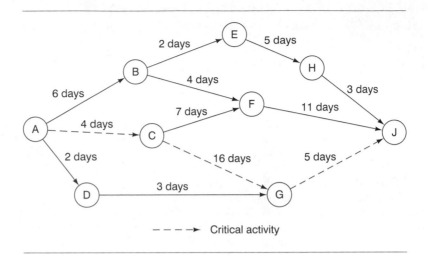

Figure 10.8 PERT chart showing estimated durations of activities and critical path.

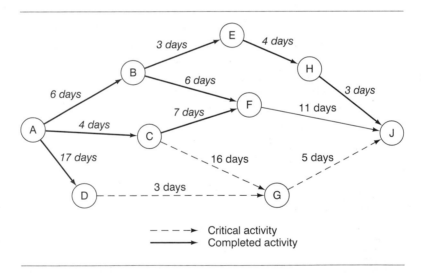

Figure 10.9 Updated PERT chart at day 17. Actual durations of completed activities are italicized.

An important issue is: Who is responsible for the continual updating of the PERT data? After all, unless the information for the PERT chart is up to the minute, management will be unable to determine which activities are currently critical and take appropriate action. What is needed is for all the software development tools to be integrated, and for information of all kinds, including source code, designs, documentation, contracts, and management information, to be stored in a product development database. The CASE tool that generates the PERT chart can then obtain its information from the database. In other words, what is needed is an integrated environment. This concept is discussed in detail in Chapter 13.

A number of commercially available management tools can be used both to assist with the planning phase and to monitor the development process as a whole. These include MacProject, Method/1, Teamwork Access, and CA-Tellaplan.

10.10   TESTING DURING THE PLANNING PHASE

As pointed out at the beginning of this chapter, a fault in the software project management plan can have serious financial implications for the developers. It is critical that the development organization neither overestimate nor underestimate the cost of the project or its duration. For this reason, the entire SPMP must be checked by the SQA group before estimates are given to the client. The best way to test the plan is by means of a plan inspection, similar to the specification inspection described in Section 8.11.

The plan inspection team must review the SPMP in detail, paying particular attention to the cost and duration estimates. To reduce risks even further, irrespective of the metrics used, the duration and cost estimates should be independently computed by a member of the SQA group as soon as the members of the planning team have delivered their estimates.

10.11   MSG CASE STUDY: PLANNING PHASE

Appendix F contains a software project management plan (SPMP) for development of the MSG product by a small (three person) software organization. The Instructor's Manual for the First Edition of *Software Engineering* (available from Irwin) contains a SPMP for a project developed by a large software organization. Both types of plan fit the IEEE SPMP format equally well, further evidence of its broad range of applicability.

Chapter Review

The main theme of this chapter is the importance of planning in the software process. A vital component of any software project management plan is estimating the duration and the cost (Section 10.1). Several metrics are put forward for estimating the size of a product, including function points (Section 10.1.1). Various metrics for cost estimation are then described, especially Intermediate COCOMO (Section 10.1.3). The three major components of a software project management plan, namely the work to be done, the resources with which to do it, and the money to pay for it, are explained in Section 10.2. One particular SPMP, namely the IEEE standard, is outlined in Section 10.3 and described in detail in Section 10.4. Next follow sections on planning of testing (Section 10.5); planning of object-oriented projects (Section 10.6); and training requirements and documentation standards, and their implications for the planning process (Sections 10.7 and 10.8). CASE tools for the planning phase are described in Section 10.9. Material on testing during the planning phase appears in Section 10.10. The chapter concludes with an SPMP for the MSG Case Study (Section 10.11).

For Further Reading

An introduction to software management can be found in [DeMarco, 1986]. A somewhat more advanced text is [Jones, 1986a]. Two IEEE Computer Society tutorials, namely [Reifer, 1986] and [Thayer, 1988], consist of papers that are good sources for more information on software management in general, as well as planning in particular. For management of the object-oriented paradigm, [Pittman, 1993] should be consulted.

For further information on IEEE Standard 1058.1 for Software Project Management Plans, the standard itself should be carefully read [IEEE 1058.1, 1987].

Sackman's work is described in [Sackman, Erikson, and Grant, 1968]. A more detailed source is [Sackman, 1970].

Many critical reviews of software science have been published, including [Hamer and Frewin, 1982], [Coulter, 1983], and [Shen, Conte, and Dunsmore, 1983]. A further source of information on software science is [Conte, Dunsmore, and Shen, 1986]; the book also contains analyses of many other metrics, including lines of code, Putnam's SLIM model, Intermediate COCOMO, and function points. Information on function points can also be found in [Albrecht and Gaffney, 1983], [Jones, 1987], and [Low and Jeffrey, 1990]. A careful analysis of function points, as well as suggested improvements, appears in [Symons, 1991]. Other analyses are given in [Jeffrey, Low, and Barnes, 1993] and [Kitchenham and Känsälä, 1993]. [Dreger, 1989] is a detailed description of the use of function points. Suggestions for improving the cost estimation process are found in [Lederer and Prasad, 1992]. The reliability of function points is discussed in [Kemerer and Porter, 1992] and [Kemerer, 1993].

The theoretical justification for Intermediate COCOMO, together with full details for implementing it, appears in [Boehm, 1981]; a shorter version is found in [Boehm, 1984b]. Extensions of Intermediate COCOMO that consider reuse (Section 6.10) and rapid prototyping (Section 3.3) appear in [Balda and Gustafson, 1990]. REVIC (Revised Intermediate COCOMO) is intended for use in Department of Defense projects. For example, it estimates the size of the documentation required by a project that conforms to MIL-STD-2167A, the standard for military software development.

Data on the validity of certain metrics, including function points, can be found in [Kemerer, 1987]. [Myers, 1989] provides information on metrics for estimating development time for very large software projects.

An introduction to PERT/CPM can be found in [Wiest and Levy, 1977] and [Moder, Phillips, and Davis, 1983].

Standards of various types are described in [Branstad and Powell, 1984]. A complete listing of IEEE standards can be obtained from IEEE, 345 East 47th Street, New York, NY 10017.

Problems

10.1 Why do you think that some cynical software organizations refer to *milestones* as *millstones?* (Hint: Look up the figurative meaning of "millstone" in a dictionary.)

10.2 You are a software engineer at OGO Software Developers. A year ago your manager announced that your next product would comprise 17 files, 61 flows, and 89 processes.

  (i) Using the FFP metric, determine its size.

 (ii) For OGO Software Developers, the constant b in Equation (10.2) has been determined to be $793. What cost estimate did the FFP metric predict?

(iii) The product was recently completed at a cost of $127,000. What does this tell you about the productivity of your development team?

10.3 A target product has 6 simple inputs, 7 average inputs, and 10 complex inputs. There are 7 average outputs, 41 simple inquiries, 11 average master files, and 21 complex interfaces. Determine the unadjusted function points (UFP).

10.4 If the total degree of influence for the product of Problem 10.3 is 57, determine the number of function points.

10.5 Why do you think that, despite its drawbacks, lines of code (LOC or KDSI) is so widely used as a metric of product size?

10.6 You are in charge of developing a 75-KDSI embedded product that is nominal except that the database size is rated very high and the use of software tools is low. Using Intermediate COCOMO, what is the estimated effort in person-months?

10.7 You are in charge of developing two 35-KDSI organic-mode products. Both are nominal in every respect except that product P_1 has extra-high complexity and product P_2 has extra-low complexity. To develop the product, you have two teams at your disposal. Team A has very high analyst capability, applications experience, and programmer capability; and high virtual machine experience and programming language experience. Team B is rated very low on all five attributes.

  (i) What is the total effort (in person-months) if team A develops product P_1 and team B develops product P_2?

(ii) What is the total effort (in person-months) if team B develops product P_1 and team A develops product P_2?

(iii) Which of the two preceding staffing assignments makes more sense? Is your intuition backed by the predictions of Intermediate COCOMO?

10.8 You are in charge of developing a 42-KDSI organic-mode product that is nominal in every respect.

(i) Assuming a cost of $8,200 per person-month, how much is the project estimated to cost?

(ii) Your entire development team resigns at the start of the project. You are fortunate enough to be able to replace the nominal team with a very highly experienced and capable team, but the cost per person-month will rise to $10,800. How much money do you expect to gain (or lose) as a result of the personnel change?

10.9 You are in charge of developing the software for a product that monitors pollution levels. Using Intermediate COCOMO, you determine that the cost of the product will be $235,000. However, as a check, you ask a member of your team to estimate the effort using function points. She reports that the function point metric predicts a cost of $495,000, more than twice as large as your COCOMO prediction. What do you do now?

10.10 Show that the Rayleigh distribution (equation 10.8) attains its maximum value when $t = k$. Find the corresponding resource consumption.

10.11 A product maintenance plan is considered an ''additional component'' of an IEEE SPMP. Bearing in mind that every nontrivial product is maintained and that the cost of maintenance is, on average, about twice the cost of developing the product, how can this be justified?

10.12 (Term Project) Draw up a software project management plan for the Osbert Oglesby product described in Appendix A.

10.13 (Case Study) The SPMP of Appendix F is for a small software engineering organization consisting of 3 software engineers. Modify the plan so that it is appropriate for a medium-sized organization with between 50 and 100 software engineers.

10.14 (Case Study) Now modify the SPMP so that it is appropriate for a large organization with over 1000 software engineers.

10.15 (Case Study) In what way would the SPMP of Appendix F have to be modified if the project had to be completed in only 8 weeks?

10.16 (Readings in Software Engineering) Your instructor will distribute copies of [Pittman, 1993]. Do you agree with Pittman's approach to the estimation of the cost and effort of object-oriented projects? If not, what additional research is necessary?

References

[Albrecht, 1979] A. J. ALBRECHT, ''Measuring Application Development Productivity,'' *Proceedings of the IBM SHARE/GUIDE Applications Development Symposium,* Monterey, CA, October 1979, pp. 83–92.

[Albrecht and Gaffney, 1983] A. J. ALBRECHT AND J. E. GAFFNEY, JR., "Software Function, Source Lines of Code, and Development Effort Prediction: A Software Science Validation," *IEEE Transactions on Software Engineering* **SE-9** (November 1983), pp. 639–648.

[ANSI/IEEE 829, 1983] "Software Test Documentation," ANSI/IEEE 829-1983, American National Standards Institute, Inc., Institute of Electrical and Electronic Engineers, Inc., 1983.

[Balda and Gustafson, 1990] D. M. BALDA AND D. A. GUSTAFSON, "Cost Estimation Models for the Reuse and Prototype Software Development Life Cycles," *ACM SIGSOFT Software Engineering Notes* **15** (July 1990), pp. 42–50.

[Behrens, 1983] C. A. BEHRENS, "Measuring the Productivity of Computer Systems Development Activities with Function Points," *IEEE Transactions on Software Engineering* **SE-9** (November 1983), pp. 648–652.

[Boehm, 1981] B. W. BOEHM, *Software Engineering Economics,* Prenctice-Hall, Englewood Cliffs, NJ, 1981.

[Boehm, 1984b] B. W. BOEHM, "Software Engineering Economics," *IEEE Transactions on Software Engineering* **SE-10** (January 1984), pp. 4–21.

[Boehm, Penedo, Stuckle, Williams, and Pyster, 1984] B. W. BOEHM, M. H. PENEDO, E. D. STUCKLE, R. D. WILLIAMS, AND A. B. PYSTER, "A Software Development Environment for Improving Productivity," *IEEE Computer* **17** (June 1984), pp. 30–44.

[Branstad and Powell, 1984] M. BRANSTAD AND P. B. POWELL, "Software Engineering Project Standards," *IEEE Transactions on Software Engineering* **SE-10** (January 1984), pp. 73–78.

[Conte, Dunsmore, and Shen, 1986] S. D. CONTE, H. E. DUNSMORE, AND V. Y. SHEN, *Software Engineering Metrics and Models,* Benjamin/Cummings, Menlo Park, CA, 1986.

[Coulter, 1983] N. S. COULTER, "Software Science and Cognitive Psychology," *IEEE Transactions on Software Engineering* **SE-9** (March 1983), pp. 166–171.

[DeMarco, 1986] T. DEMARCO, *Controlling Software Projects: Management, Measurement, and Estimation,* Second Edition, Yourdon Press, Englewood Cliffs, NJ, 1986.

[Deo, 1983] N. DEO, *System Simulation with Digital Computer,* Prentice-Hall, Englewood Cliffs, NJ, 1983.

[Dreger, 1989] J. B. DREGER, *Function Point Analysis,* Prentice-Hall, Englewood Cliffs, NJ, 1989.

[Freiman and Park, 1979] F. R. FREIMAN AND R. E. PARK, "PRICE Software Model— Version 3: An Overview," *Proceedings of the IEEE-PINY Workshop on Quantitative Software Models,* October 1979, pp. 32–41.

[Halstead, 1977] M. H. HALSTEAD, *Elements of Software Science,* Elsevier North-Holland, New York, 1977.

[Hamer and Frewin, 1982] P. G. HAMER AND G. D. FREWIN, "M. H. Halstead's Software Science–A Critical Examination," *Proceedings of the Sixth International Conference on Software Engineering,* Tokyo, 1982, pp. 197–205.

[Helmer-Hirschberg, 1966] O. HELMER-HIRSCHBERG, *Social Technology,* Basic Books, New York, 1966.

[IEEE 1058.1, 1987] "Standard for Software Project Management Plans," IEEE 1058.1, Institute of Electrical and Electronic Engineers, Inc., 1987.

[Jeffrey, Low, and Barnes, 1993] D. R. JEFFREY, G. C. LOW, AND M. BARNES, "A Comparison of Function Point Counting Techniques," *IEEE Transactions on Software Engineering* **19** (May 1993), pp. 529–532.

[Jones, 1986a] C. Jones, *Programming Productivity,* McGraw-Hill, New York, 1986.

[Jones, 1987] C. Jones, Letter to the Editor, *IEEE Computer* **20** (December 1987), p. 4.

[Kemerer, 1987] C. F. Kemerer, "An Empirical Validation of Software Cost Estimation Models," *Communications of the ACM* **30** (May 1987), pp. 416–429.

[Kemerer, 1993] C. F. Kemerer, "Reliability of Function Points Measurement: A Field Experiment," *Communications of the ACM* **36** (February 1993), pp. 85–97.

[Kemerer and Porter, 1992] C. F. Kemerer and B. S. Porter, "Improving the Reliability of Function Point Measurement: An Empirical Study," *IEEE Transactions on Software Engineering* **18** (November 1992), pp. 1011–1024.

[Kitchenham and Känsälä, 1993] B. Kitchenham and K. Känsälä, "Inter-Item Correlations among Function Points," *Proceedings of the Fifteenth International Conference on Software Engineering,* Baltimore, MD, May 1993, pp. 477–480.

[Lederer and Prasad, 1992] A. L. Lederer and J. Prasad, "Nine Management Guidelines for Better Cost Estimating," *Communications of the ACM* **35** (February 1992), pp. 51–59.

[Lim, 1994] W. C. Lim, "Effects of Reuse on Quality, Productivity, and Economics," *IEEE Software* **11** (September 1994), pp. 23–30.

[Low and Jeffrey, 1990] G. C. Low and D. R. Jeffrey, "Function Points in the Estimation and Evaluation of the Software Process," *IEEE Transactions on Software Engineering* **16** (January 1990), pp. 64–71.

[Moder, Phillips, and Davis, 1983] J. J. Moder, C. R. Phillips, and E. W. Davis, *Project Management with CPM, PERT, and Precedence Diagramming,* Third Edition, Van Nostrand Reinhold, New York, 1983.

[Myers, 1989] W. Myers, "Allow Plenty of Time for Large-Scale Software," *IEEE Software* **6** (July 1989), pp. 92–99.

[Norden, 1958] P. V. Norden, "Curve Fitting for a Model of Applied Research and Development Scheduling," *IBM Journal of Research and Development* **2** (July 1958), pp. 232–248.

[Pittman, 1993] M. Pittman, "Lessons Learned in Managing Object-Oriented Development," *IEEE Software* **10** (January 1993), pp. 43–53.

[Putnam, 1978] L. H. Putnam, "A General Empirical Solution to the Macro Software Sizing and Estimating Problem," *IEEE Transactions on Software Engineering* **SE-4** (July 1978), pp. 345–361.

[Reifer, 1986] D. J. Reifer (Editor), *Tutorial: Software Management,* Third Edition, IEEE Computer Society Press, Washington, DC, 1986.

[Sackman, 1970] H. Sackman, *Man–Computer Problem Solving: Experimental Evaluation of Time-Sharing and Batch Processing,* Auerbach, Princeton, NJ, 1970.

[Sackman, Erikson, and Grant, 1968] H. Sackman, W. J. Erikson, and E. E. Grant, "Exploratory Experimental Studies Comparing Online and Offline Programming Performance," *Communications of the ACM* **11** (January 1968), pp. 3–11.

[Schach, 1994] S. R. Schach, "The Economic Impact of Software Reuse on Maintenance," *Journal of Software Maintenance: Research and Practice* **6** (July/ August 1994), pp. 185–196.

[Shen, Conte, and Dunsmore, 1983] V. Y. Shen, S. D. Conte, and H. E. Dunsmore, "Software Science Revisited: A Critical Analysis of the Theory and Its Empirical Support," *IEEE Transactions on Software Engineering* **SE-9** (March 1983), pp. 155–165.

[Shepperd, 1988a] M. J. Shepperd, "An Evaluation of Software Product Metrics," *Information and Software Technology* **30** (No. 3, 1988), pp. 177–188.

[Shepperd and Ince, 1994] M. SHEPPERD and D. C. INCE, "A Critique of Three Metrics," *Journal of Systems and Software* **26** (September 1994), pp. 197–210.

[Symons, 1991] C. R. SYMONS, *Software Sizing and Estimating: Mk II FPA,* John Wiley and Sons, Chichester, UK, 1991.

[Thayer, 1988] R. H. THAYER (Editor), *Tutorial: Software Engineering Management,* IEEE Computer Society Press, Washington, DC, 1988.

[van der Poel and Schach, 1983] K. G. VAN DER POEL AND S. R. SCHACH, "A Software Metric for Cost Estimation and Efficiency Measurement in Data Processing System Development," *Journal of Systems and Software* **3** (September 1983), pp. 187–191.

[Weyuker, 1988b] E. J. WEYUKER, "Evaluating Software Complexity Measures," *IEEE Trans. on Software Engineering* **14** (September 1988), pp. 1357–1365.

[Wiest and Levy, 1977] J. D. WIEST AND F. K. LEVY, *A Management Guide to PERT/ CPM: With GERT/PDM/DCPM and Other Networks,* Second Edition, Prentice-Hall, Englewood Cliffs, NJ, 1977.

11

DESIGN PHASE

Over the past 30 or so years, literally hundreds of design techniques have been put forward. Some are variations of existing techniques, others are radically different from anything previously proposed. A few design techniques have been used by tens of thousands of software engineers, many have been used only by their authors. Some design strategies, particularly those developed by academics, have a firm theoretical basis. Others, including many drawn up by academics, are more pragmatic in nature; they were put forward because their authors found that they worked well in practice. Most design techniques are manual, but automation is increasingly becoming an important aspect of design, if only to assist in management of documentation.

Notwithstanding this plethora of design techniques, there is a certain underlying pattern. A major theme of this book is that two essential aspects of a product are its actions and the data on which the actions operate. Thus, the two basic ways of designing a product are action-oriented design and data-oriented design. In *action-oriented design*, the emphasis is on the actions. An example is data flow analysis (DFA), where the objective is to design modules with high cohesion (Section 6.2). In *data-oriented design,* the data come first. For example, in Jackson's technique (Section 11.6) the structure of the data is determined first. Then the procedures are designed to conform to the structure of the data.

A weakness of action-oriented design techniques is that they concentrate on the actions; the data are only of secondary importance. Data-oriented design similarly emphasizes the data, to the detriment of the actions. The solution is to use object-oriented techniques, which give equal weight to actions and data. In this chapter action- and data-oriented designs are described first, and then object-oriented design is described. Just as an object incorporates both action and data, so object-oriented design combines features of action-oriented and data-oriented designs. Thus, a basic understanding of action- and data-oriented designs is needed to get a full understanding of object-oriented design.

Before specific design techniques are examined, some general remarks must be made regarding the design phase.

11.1 DESIGN AND ABSTRACTION

The software design phase consists of three activities: architectural design, detailed design, and design testing. The input to the design process is the specification

---

JUST IN CASE YOU WANTED TO KNOW

The term *architectural design* should not be confused with an important emerging concept in software engineering, namely *software architecture*. The architectural style of a cathedral could be described as Romanesque, Gothic, or Baroque. Similarly, the architectural style of a software product could be described as object-oriented, pipes and filters (UNIX components), or client-server (with a central server providing computing facilities for a network of client computers). This informal type of description, usually accompanied by a rough sketch showing the components, would be more useful if we could make it more rigorous and precise. Research is currently being undertaken in this direction; for example, see [Abowd, Allen, and Garlan, 1993].

---

document, a description of *what* the product is to do. The output is the design document, a description of *how* the product is to achieve this.

During *architectural design* (also known as *general design, logical design,* or *high-level design*), a modular decomposition of the product is developed. That is, the specifications are carefully analyzed, and a module structure that has the desired functionality is produced. The output from this activity is a list of the modules and a description of how they are to be interconnected. From the viewpoint of abstraction, what is going on during architectural design is that the existence of certain modules is assumed; the design is then developed in terms of those modules. (See the Just in Case You Wanted to Know box above to clarify the difference between architectural design and software architecture.)

When the object-oriented paradigm is used, as explained in Section 1.6, part of the architectural design is performed during the object-oriented analysis phase (Chapter 9). This is because the first step in OOA is to determine the classes, and hence the objects. Because an object is a type of module, some of the modular decomposition has been performed during the analysis phase.

The next activity is *detailed design,* also known as *modular design, physical design*, or *low-level design*, during which each module is designed in detail. For example, specific algorithms are selected and data structures are chosen. Again from the viewpoint of abstraction, during this activity the fact that the modules are to be interconnected to form a complete product is ignored.

This two-stage process is typical of abstraction as described in Chapter 6. First, the top level (the overall product) is designed in terms of modules that do not yet exist. Then each module is designed without regard to its being a component of the complete product.

It was stated previously that the design phase has three activities and that the third activity is testing. The word *activity* was used, rather than *stage* or *step* to emphasize that testing is an integral part of design, just as it is an integral part of the entire software development and maintenance process. Testing is not something that is performed only after the architectural design and detailed design have been completed.

A variety of different design techniques are now presented, first action-oriented techniques, then data-oriented techniques, and finally object-oriented techniques.

11.2   ACTION-ORIENTED DESIGN

In Sections 6.2 and 6.3 a theoretical case was made for decomposing a product into modules with high cohesion and low coupling. A description is now given of two practical techniques, namely data flow analysis (Section 11.3) and transaction analysis (Section 11.4), for achieving this design objective. In theory, data flow analysis can be applied whenever the specifications can be represented by a data flow diagram (DFD), and because (in theory) every product can be represented by a DFD, data flow analysis is accordingly universally applicable. In practice, however, there are a number of situations where there are more appropriate design techniques, specifically for designing products where the flow of data is secondary to other considerations. Examples where other design techniques are indicated include rule-based systems (expert systems), databases, and transaction processing products. (Transaction analysis (Section 11.4) is a good way of decomposing transaction processing products into modules.)

11.3   DATA FLOW ANALYSIS

Data flow analysis (DFA) is a design technique for achieving modules with high cohesion. It can be used in conjunction with most specification techniques. Here DFA will be presented in conjunction with structured systems analysis (Section 8.3). The input to the technique is a data flow diagram (DFD). A key point is that once the DFD has been completed, the software designer has precise and complete information regarding the input to and output from every module.

Consider the flow of data in the product represented by the DFD of Figure 11.1. The product is somehow transforming input into output. At some point in the DFD the input ceases to be input and becomes some sort of internal data. Then, at some further point, these internal data take on the quality of output. This is shown in more detail in Figure 11.2. The point at which the input loses the quality of being input and simply becomes internal data operated on by the product is termed the *point of highest abstraction of input*. The *point of highest abstraction of output* is similarly the first point in the flow of data at which the output can be identified as such, rather than as some sort of internal data.

Using the points of highest abstraction of input and output, the product is decomposed into three modules, namely the *input module, transform module*, and *output module*. Now each module is taken in turn, its points of highest abstraction found, and the module is decomposed again. This procedure is continued stepwise until each module performs a single action, that is, the design consists of modules with high cohesion. Thus stepwise refinement, the foundation of so many other software engineering techniques, also underlies data flow analysis.

In fairness it should be pointed out that minor modifications might have to be made to the decomposition in order to achieve the lowest possible coupling. Data flow analysis is a way of achieving high cohesion. The aim of composite/structured design

Figure 11.1 Data flow diagram showing flow of data and actions of product.

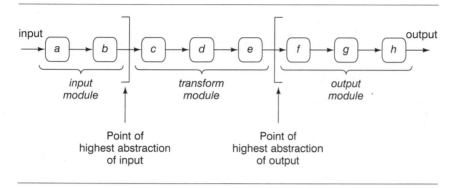

Figure 11.2 Points of highest abstraction of input and output.

is high cohesion but also low coupling. In order to achieve the latter it is sometimes necessary to make minor modifications to the design. For example, because DFA does not take coupling into account, control coupling may inadvertently arise in a design constructed using DFA. In such a case, all that is needed is to modify the two modules involved so that data, and not control, are passed between them.

11.3.1 DATA FLOW ANALYSIS EXAMPLE

Consider the problem of designing a product which will take as input a file name and return the number of words in that file, similarly to the UNIX *wc* utility.

Figure 11.3 depicts the data flow diagram. There are five modules. Module *read file name* reads the name of the file that is validated by *validate file name*. The validated name is passed to *count number of words*, which does precisely that. The word count is passed on to *format word count*, and the formatted word count is finally passed to *display word count* for output.

Examining the data flow, the initial input is file name. When this becomes validated file name it is still a file name, and therefore has not lost its quality of being input data. But consider module *count number of words*. Its input is validated file name and its output is word count. The output from this module is totally different in quality from the input to the product as a whole. It is clear that the point of highest abstraction of input is as indicated on Figure 11.3. Similarly, even though the output from *count number of words* undergoes some sort of formatting, it is essentially

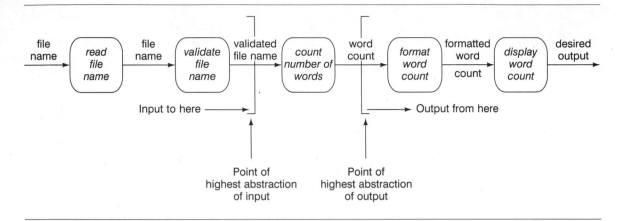

Figure 11.3 Data flow diagram: first refinement.

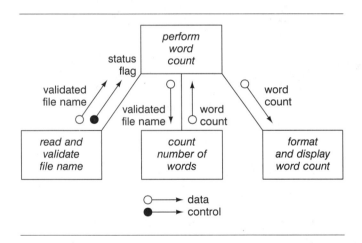

Figure 11.4 Structure chart; first refinement.

output from the time it emerges from module *count number of words*. The point of highest abstraction of output is therefore as shown in Figure 11.3.

The result of decomposing the product using these two points of highest abstraction is shown in the structure chart of Figure 11.4. Figure 11.4 also reveals that the data flow diagram of Figure 11.3 is somewhat too simplistic. The DFD does not show the logical flow corresponding to what happens if the file specified by the user does not exist. Module *read and validate file name* must return a status flag to *perform word count*. If the name is invalid, then it is ignored by *perform word count* and an error message of some sort is printed. But if the name is valid it is passed on to *count number of words*.

In Figure 11.4 there are two modules with communicational cohesion, namely *read and validate file name* and *format and display word count*. These must

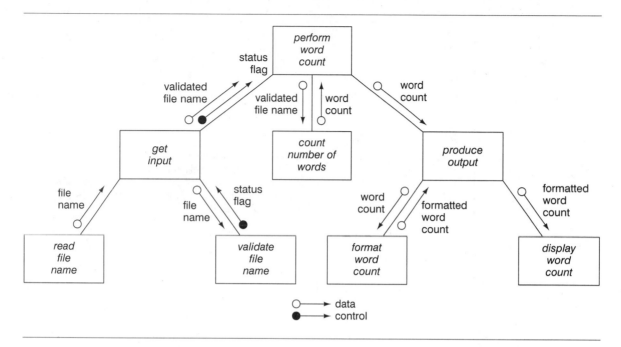

Figure 11.5 Structure chart: second refinement.

be decomposed further. The final result is shown in Figure 11.5. All eight modules have functional cohesion, and there is either data coupling or no coupling between them.

Now that the architectural design has been completed, the next step is the detailed design. Here data structures are chosen and algorithms selected. The detailed design of each module is then handed to the programmers for implementation. Just as with virtually every other phase of software production, time constraints usually require that the implementation be done by a team, rather than having a single programmer responsible for coding all the modules. For this reason, the detailed design of each module must be presented so it can be understood without reference to any other module. The detailed design of four of the eight modules appears in Figure 11.6; the other four modules will be presented in a different format.

The design of Figure 11.6 is language independent. However, if management has decided on an implementation language before the detailed design is started, then the use of pseudocode for representing the detailed design is an attractive alternative. Pseudocode essentially consists of comments connected by the control statements of the chosen implementation language. Figure 11.7 shows a detailed design for the remaining four modules of the product written in a pseudocode with the flavor of Java. Pseudocode has the advantage that it is generally clear and concise, and the implementation step usually consists merely of translating the comments into the relevant programming language. The disadvantage is that there is sometimes a

Module name	*read file name*
Module returns	string
Input arguments	none
Output arguments	none
Error messages	none
Files accessed	none
Files changed	none
Modules called	none
Narrative	The product is invoked by the user by means of the command string *wordcount* \<file name\> Using an operating system call, this module accesses the contents of the command string that was input by the user, extracts \<file name\> and returns it as the value of the module.

Module name	*validate file name*
Module returns	boolean
Input arguments	file name : string
Output arguments	none
Error messages	none
Files accessed	none
Files changed	none
Modules called	none
Narrative	This module makes an operating system call to determine whether file file name exists. The module returns true if the file exists and false otherwise.

Module name	*count number of words*
Module returns	integer
Input arguments	validated file name : string
Output arguments	none
Error messages	none
Files accessed	none
Files changed	none
Modules called	none
Narrative	This module determines whether validated file name is a text file, that is, divided into lines of characters. If so, the module returns the number of words in the text file. Otherwise, the module returns −1.

Figure 11.6 Detailed design of four modules of example.

tendency for the designers to go into too much detail and to produce a complete code implementation of a module rather than a pseudocode detailed design.

After it has been fully documented and successfully tested, the detailed design is handed over to the implementation team for coding. The product then proceeds through the remaining phases of the software process.

Module name	*produce output*
Module returns	**void**
Input arguments	word count : integer
Output arguments	none
Error messages	none
Files accessed	none
Files changed	none
Modules called	*format word count*

	arguments:	word count : integer
		formatted word count : string
	display word count	
	arguments:	formatted word count : string

Narrative	This module takes the integer word count passed to it by the calling module and calls *format word count* to have that integer formatted according to the specifications. Then it calls *display word count* to have the line printed.

Figure 11.6   (continued)

11.3.2 EXTENSIONS

The reader may well feel that this example is somewhat artificial in that the data flow diagram (Figure 11.3) has but one input stream and one output stream. To see what happens in more complex situations, consider Figure 11.8. Now there are four input streams and five output streams, a situation that corresponds more closely to reality.

When there are multiple input and output streams, the way to proceed is to find the point of highest abstraction of input for each input stream and the point of highest abstraction of output for each output stream. Use these points to decompose the given data flow diagram into modules with fewer input/output streams than the original. Continue in this way until each resulting module has high cohesion. Finally, determine the coupling between each pair of modules and make any necessary adjustments.

11.4 TRANSACTION ANALYSIS

Data flow analysis is inappropriate for the transaction-processing type of product in which a number of related actions, similar in outline but differing in detail, must be performed. A typical example is the software controlling an automated teller machine (ATM). The customer inserts a magnetized card into a slot, keys in a password, and then performs an action such as deposit to a checking, savings, or credit card account; withdraw from an account; or determine the balance in an account. This type of product is depicted in Figure 11.9. A good way to design such a product is to break it up into two pieces, the analyzer and the dispatcher. The analyzer determines the transaction type and passes this information to the dispatcher which then performs the transaction.

```
void perform word count ()
{
    String          validated file name;
    int             word count;
    if (get input (validated file name) is false)
        print "error 1: file does not exist";
    else
    {
        set word count equal to count number of words (validated file name);
        if (word count is equal to −1)
            print "error 2: file is not a text file";
        else
            produce output (word count);
    }
}


boolean get input (String validated file name)
{
    String          file name;
    file name = read file name ();
    if (validate file name (file name) is true)
    {
        set validated file name equal to file name;
        return true;
    }
    else
        return false;
}


void display word count (String formatted word count)
{
    print formatted word count, left justified;
}


String format word count (int word count);
{
    return "File contains" word count "words";
}
```

Figure 11.7 Pseudocode representation of detailed design of four methods of example.

A poor design of this type is shown in Figure 11.10, which has two modules with logical cohesion, namely *edit any transaction* and *update any file*. On the other hand, it seems a waste of effort to have five very similar edit modules and five very similar update modules. The solution is software reuse (Section 6.10): A basic edit module should be designed, coded, documented, and tested and then instantiated five times. Each version will be slightly different, but the differences will be small enough to

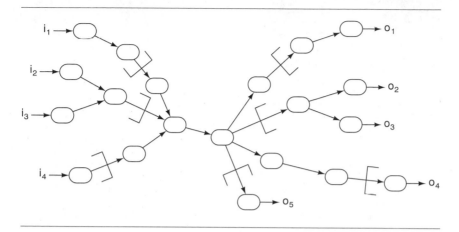

Figure 11.8 Data flow diagram with multiple input and output streams.

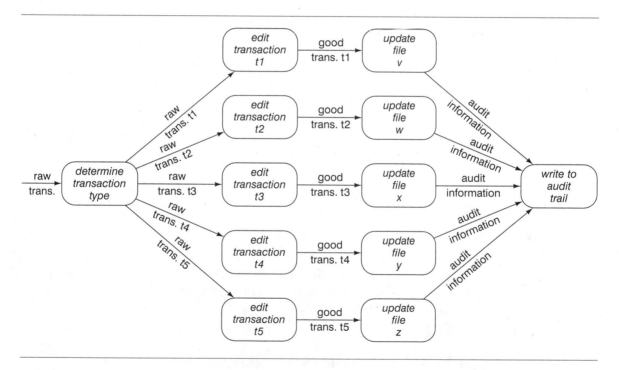

Figure 11.9 Typical transaction-processing system.

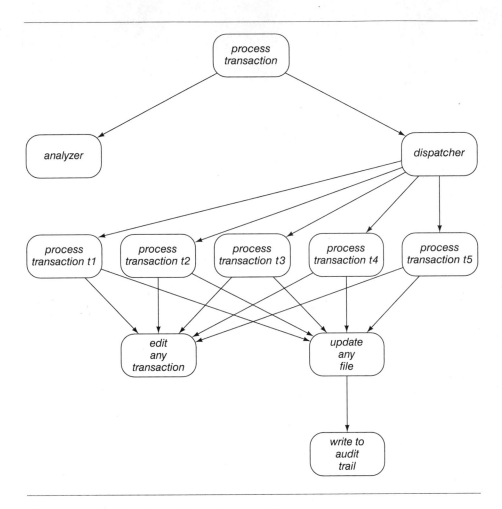

Figure 11.10   Poor design of transaction-processing system.

make this approach worthwhile. Similarly, a basic update module can be instantiated five times and slightly modified to cater to the five different update types. The resulting design has high cohesion and low coupling.

11.5   DATA-ORIENTED DESIGN

The basic principle behind data-oriented design is to design the product according to the structure of the data on which it is to operate. There are a number of data-oriented design techniques, including those of Warnier [Warnier, 1976; 1981] and Orr [Orr, 1981]. Michael Jackson, too, has developed a systematic data-oriented approach that addresses a large portion of the software life cycle, from specifications to design and implementation [Jackson, 1975; 1983]. The three techniques share many similarities.

For reasons of space, Jackson's technique is presented in detail, followed by a brief description of the other two techniques.

11.6 Jackson System Development

Before describing Jackson's technique [Jackson, 1983], some preliminary concepts are needed. Jackson is not concerned with functional decomposition, that is, Jackson system development (JSD) does not begin with some sort of functional requirement in which it is stated what the product must do and in which the inputs and the outputs of the product are laid down. Instead, the basis of JSD is real-world modeling. The developer builds a *model* of the real world, or rather, of the subset of the real world that is relevant to the product to be built, and then implements that model in software. The model of the real world is described in terms of two concepts, namely *entities* and the *actions* performed by or on them. Jackson does not use the term *entity* in quite the same way as it is used in the entity-relationship model (Section 8.5); for Jackson, an entity must have a real-world action performed by it or performed on it. For example, if the product is to control a bank of elevators, entities include **button** and **elevator**. With regard to actions, a passenger must **press** a button to summon an elevator or to request an elevator to travel to a specific floor. An elevator will **arrive** at a floor or **depart** from a floor. The actions of a design must correspond to actions that take place in the portion of the real world being modeled; aspects specific to the product that have no real-world counterparts, such as "display menu" or "print list of unmatched tokens" are not actions in JSD.

11.6.1 Overview of Jackson System Development

Jackson has developed his own notation for describing software [Jackson, 1975]. There are two types of notation, graphical and textual. Figure 11.11 shows the three different control structures for actions, using both notations. Diagram (a) in Figure 11.11 shows sequencing; action a_seq consists of action a_1 followed by action a_2. The small circles in diagram (b) denote selection; action a_sel consists of action a_3 or of action a_4 or of action a_5. The asterisk in diagram (c) in Figure 11 stands for iteration zero or more times; action a_itr consists of zero or more repetitions of action a_6. Note that the symbols are placed one level lower than might be expected. Thus, although action a_itr consists of zero or more repetitions of a_6, the asterisk is placed in a_6, rather than in a_itr.

   In JSD, a product is built out of actions. Actions can be connected in only two ways, with a data stream connection or with a state vector connection. Figure 11.12(a) shows a data stream connection. Action ds_0 sends a stream of data to action ds_1. An example of this type of situation is where action ds_0 writes a stream of records, and action ds_1 reads those records. With such a data stream connection, the elements written by ds_0 are read by ds_1 in the order in which they are sent. In contrast, in Figure 11.12(b) action sv_1 inspects the state vector of action sv_0. This type of connection frequently occurs in real-time systems, where action sv_1 continually monitors action sv_0. Action sv_1 inspects the state of

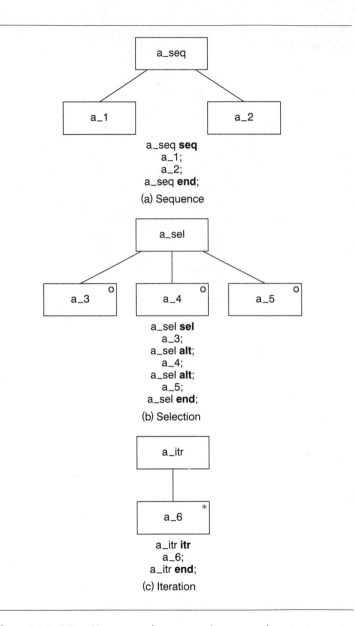

Figure 11.11 JSD structure diagrams and corresponding structure text.

sv_0 whenever it wishes; with this sort of connection there is no sequence of data written from sv_0 to sv_1.

The JSD convention is that the suffix 0 represents a real-world action and the suffix 1 represents a product action. Figure 11.12 is an example of a JSD structure diagram.

Jackson's technique consists of six steps.

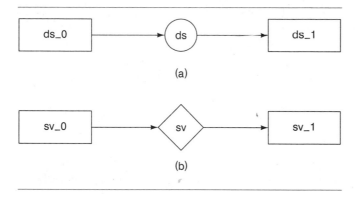

Figure 11.12 JSD structure diagram depicting the two ways of interconnecting JSD actions.

1. *Entity action step.* The real-world area of interest is delimited. The entities and actions of the proposed product are listed.

2. *Entity structure step.* The actions performed by or on the entities are displayed using Jackson's notation. The time ordering of the actions is taken into account.

3. *Initial model step.* The entities and actions are represented by an action model. Correspondences are established between the model and the real world.

4. *Function step.* Functions are specified that will result in the required outputs from the product.

5. *Product timing step.* Scheduling aspects are examined.

6. *Implementation step.* Decisions are made as to how the actions will be mapped to the available processors (hardware).

11.6.2 Why Jackson System Development Is Presented in This Chapter

Looking through the six steps of JSD, steps 1 through 5 are essentially specification steps, and the product is implemented at step 6. What has happened to design? Working through the example presented in Section 11.6.3, the reader will appreciate that steps 1 through 5 are not pure specification steps. Instead, each step also has a design component, and the proportion of design component increases with increasing step number. Thus steps 4 and 5 have a large design component, even though the product is not fully specified until the end of step 5.

At first sight it would seem that because JSD covers both specification and design, the specification aspects should be presented in Chapter 8 (Specification Phase), and the design aspects in this chapter (Design Phase). But because the specification and design components are so closely intertwined, this is not possible; JSD has to be presented as a whole. Because design concepts have not been introduced by Chapter 8, Chapter 11 is the correct place for JSD.

JUST IN CASE YOU WANTED TO KNOW

It is amusing to note that Jackson begins his treatment of the elevator problem (on which this example is based) by stating the problem in terms of two elevators, but rapidly simplifies the problem to the case of

only one elevator [Jackson, 1983]. The general case of n elevators is, therefore, "obvious" and "left as an exercise to the reader"!

But JSD does not really fit in anywhere. The technique is unique. To highlight some of the features of JSD, it is now applied to the now familiar elevator problem.

11.6.3 ELEVATOR PROBLEM: JACKSON SYSTEM DEVELOPMENT

A product is to be installed to control n elevators in a building with m floors. The problem concerns the logic required to move elevators between floors according to the following constraints:

C_1. Each elevator has a set of m buttons, one for each floor. These illuminate when pressed and cause the elevator to visit the corresponding floor. The illumination is canceled when the corresponding floor is visited by the elevator.

C_2. Each floor, except the first floor and top floor, has two buttons, one to request an up-elevator and one to request a down-elevator. These buttons illuminate when pressed. The illumination is canceled when an elevator visits the floor and then moves in the desired direction.

C_3. When an elevator has no service requests, it remains at its current floor with its doors closed.

For the sake of simplicity, the discussion in this section is restricted to one elevator (but see the Just in Case You Wanted to Know box above).

Step 1. Entity Action Step   A candidate list of entities is obtained by reading through the description and listing the nouns. At this point the reader may be somewhat confused, and understandably so. After all, the technique of identifying nouns was used in object-oriented analysis to identify candidate classes (Section 9.3.1), and now the same technique is being recommended for finding the entities of JSD. The reason for this duplication is that in both JSD and OOA the designer has to identify the data of the product. In every natural language, be it English, Czech, or North Sotho, data are represented by nouns (and actions by verbs), so this similarity is therefore not unexpected. At the same time, it is important to realize that the similarities begin and end with the identification of nouns—JSD and OOA are markedly different both before and after this identification step.

Extracting the nouns in the description gives the following list: elevator, building, floor, button, illumination, request, and door. From this list, building, floor, and door can be deleted, because they lie outside the model boundary. The model is concerned with the control of the elevator—the physical surroundings in which the elevator operates must be excluded. Also, request corresponds to the pressing of a button, as does illumination, so these two may also be deleted. This leaves only two entities, namely elevator and button. Note that user, which is not a noun that occurs in the description, is not an entity. If it were, its actions would include enter_elevator, leave_elevator, and press_button. Without some sort of photoelectric cell there is no way to detect that a user has entered or left an elevator, and without a surveillance system there is no way to determine which user pressed a particular button. Undetectable entities and events have to be excluded from a JSD model. Selecting candidate entities from the nouns in the description sometimes has the useful side effect of automatically excluding such undetectable entities.

Turning now to the actions, a candidate list of actions is similarly drawn up from the verbs in the description and results in the following list: illuminate, press, visit, cancel, request, move_up, move_down, service, and remain. Verbs visit and remain relate to floor, which has already been excluded as an entity because it lies outside the model boundaries. Verbs illuminate, cancel, request, and service are incorporated in the functionality of button. This leaves the entity button with action press and the entity elevator with actions move_up and move_down. But the problem of undetectability again arises. In most elevators, all that can be detected is that the elevator has arrived at a floor or has left a floor; there is no way of measuring its direction of motion. Making the necessary changes leaves the following entities and actions:

Entity: button

    Action: press (the button is depressed and released once)

Entity: elevator

    Action: arrive[f] (the elevator arrives at floor f, from above or from below)

    Action: depart[f] (the elevator departs from floor f, about to move up or move down)

Having identified the entities and their actions, step 1 is complete.

Step 2. Entity structure step   Using the notation of Figure 11.11, the actions performed by or on the entities are shown in Figure 11.13(a) and (b). Each button, whether in an elevator or at a floor, can be pressed zero or more times. The elevator must depart from floor one and then alternately arrives at and departs from floor f. Note that there are constraints on the value of f. Such constraints do not appear in a JSD diagram, but are added in the form of a note. In this instance, the constraints are:

1. $1 \leq f \leq m$.
2. For the first instance of floor[f], $f = 1$ or 2.
3. For any two successive instances of floor[f], the values of f must either be identical or must differ by 1.

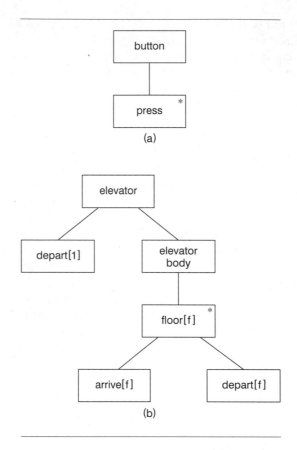

Figure 11.13 JSD structure diagrams for elevator problem.

The point is that when an elevator is installed in a building it is at the first floor. When put into service it departs from the first floor and thereafter cannot skip floors. If it is currently at, say, the sixth floor, then it can now travel to the fifth floor or to the seventh floor, and it can also return to the sixth floor, but it cannot now travel to, say, the third floor. It does not have to stop at every floor, but it certainly must pass through every floor.

Step 3. Initial Model Step   At this step the entities and actions are represented by an action model. Figure 11.14(a) shows the data stream mapping between the real-world button action button_0 and the model button action button_1. The latter must read the value of button_ds, that is to say, register the pulses sent each time the button is pressed. This is represented graphically in Figure 11.14(a), but for many purposes a textual version of the corresponding JSD structure diagram is more useful and is given in Figure 11.15. The action consists of an initial read of the button data

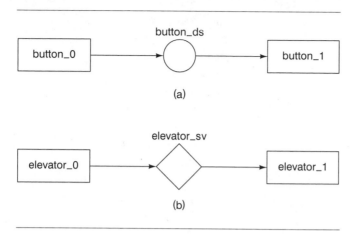

Figure 11.14   JSD structure diagrams showing connection between real-world actions and model actions.

---

button_1 **seq**
   read button_ds;
   button_body **itr**
      press;
      read button_ds;
   button_body **end;**
button_1 **end;**

Figure 11.15   Structure text for button_1.

stream, then a repetition of button pressing, followed by reading the data stream. The *read* button_ds commands in Figure 11.15 are the way that the model button action inspects the real-world button action. In other words, the *read* connects the real world to the model.

The state vector mapping between the real-world elevator action and the model elevator action is shown in Figure 11.14(b). The textual version of the structure diagram is shown in Figure 11.16. In this case, the *getsv* (get state vector) commands sense a change of state in the real world. The elevator action consists of an initial sensing of the elevator state vector followed by departure from the first floor. Next comes a repetition of arriving at floor f and departing, detected by sensing the elevator state vector at the appropriate times.

Up to now, the presentation in this section has been somewhat oversimplified. For instance, an elevator does not move continuously from floor to floor. Instead, it halts at a floor and waits for passengers to get in or get out, and only then does the elevator move up or down. To implement this, state vectors at_floor[1], at_

---

elevator_1 **seq**

    getsv elevator_sv;

    depart[1];

    elevator_body **itr**

        floor[f] **seq**

            getsv elevator_sv;

            arrive[f];

            getsv elevator_sv;

            depart[f];

        floor[f] **end;**

    elevator_body **end;**

elevator_1 **end;**

Figure 11.16 Structure text for elevator_1.

floor[2], ... , at_floor[m] are needed to denote that the elevator is at floor 1, 2 ..., m, respectively. A further state vector, moving, denotes that the elevator is in motion between floors. A refined version of the structure diagram of Figure 11.13(b) is shown in Figure 11.17, and the corresponding structure text in Figure 11.18.

Step 4. Function Step   In this step, the developer specifies the functions of the product. A JSD function specifies what outputs are produced by the product when a certain set of conditions occurs in the real world. Jackson distinguishes a number of different types of functions. The most elementary type is an *embedded function*, which simply produces a report when a specified set of circumstances holds. This is achieved by attaching the relevant operation to the structure diagram at the appropriate place. In the elevator problem, for example, a button is illuminated whenever it is pressed. The modified structure diagram is shown in Figure 11.19(a). Similarly, the elevator action elevator_1 must issue commands to the elevator motor as shown in Figure 11.19(b).

If there is to be a display at each floor showing the current position of the elevator, two additional sets of commands must be added. Command button_on[f] causes the button corresponding to floor f in each display to be illuminated, $1 \leq f \leq$ m, and similarly for button_off[f]. The structure text of Figure 11.18 must be modified so that button_on[f] is inserted immediately after arrive[f], and button_off[f] must appear immediately before depart[f]. Details of this, and of inserting button_on[1] and button_off[1], are left as an exercise (Problem 11.8).

Step 5. Product Timing Step   During this step, timing constraints on the product are specified. In the case of the elevator problem, suppose that sensors are placed at each floor so that when the elevator comes within 6 inches of floor f the state of the elevator changes from moving to at_floor[f]. Suppose further that the elevator

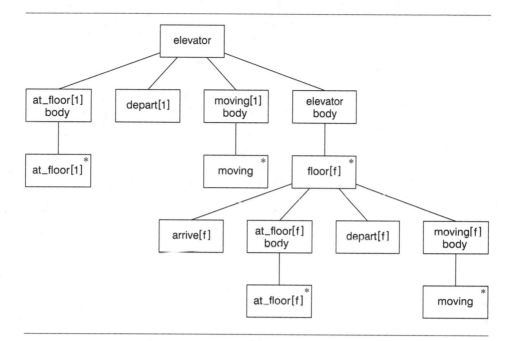

Figure 11.17 Refined structure diagram for elevator.

travels at a speed of 2 feet per second. At that speed, it would cover the 6 inches in one-quarter of a second. Within that time, action **elevator_1** (Figure 11.18) must detect that the elevator has arrived and must send a stop command to the elevator motor. Also within that time, the motor must receive the stop command and take the appropriate action to ensure that the elevator stops at the correct place. During step 6, the implementation step, the developer checks that these timing constraints are satisfied.

It was previously remarked that the specifications are not complete until the end of step 5. As an example of this, the requirement that buttons light up when pressed was not incorporated until step 4. Furthermore, timing constraints were not even mentioned until step 5. But while the specifications were being produced, the design was being developed in parallel with the specifications.

Step 6. Implementation Step   A strength of Jackson's technique is that, once the detailed design is complete, implementation is virtually automatic.

Throughout this book, a consistent effort has been made to avoid drowning the reader in a wealth of detail. The elevator problem is entirely appropriate for illustrating the first five steps of Jackson's technique. However, the implementation of a complete solution to the elevator problem is lengthy, and as a result, key aspects of the implementation step are lost. The reader who wishes to see a complete implementation is urged to consult [Jackson, 1983]; in this book, the implementation step will be illustrated by means of the following simpler problem.

```
elevator_1 seq
    getsv elevator_sv;
    at_floor[1]_body itr while (at_floor[1])
        getsv elevator_sv;
    at_floor[1]_body end;
    depart[1];
    moving[1]_body itr while (moving)
        getsv elevator_sv;
    moving[1]_body end;
    elevator_body itr
        floor[f] seq
            getsv elevator_sv;
            arrive[f];
            at_floor[f]_body itr while (at_floor[f])
                getsv elevator_sv;
            at_floor[f]_body end;
            getsv elevator_sv;
            depart[f];
            moving[f]_body itr while (moving)
                getsv elevator_sv;
            moving[f]_body end;
        floor[f] end;
    elevator_body end;
elevator_1 end;
```

Figure 11.18   Refined structure text for elevator.

A file contains pressure records and volume records. A pressure record consists of the letter p followed by an integer denoting a pressure in pounds per square inch. A volume record consists of the letter v followed by an integer denoting a volume in cubic feet. The first record is a header record consisting of the letter h. The last record is a trailer record consisting of the letter t. Determine the lowest pressure and the highest volume.

The structure of the input file is shown in Figure 11.20. The first record is of type h. It is followed by zero or more records of type p or type v. Finally, the last record is of type t. The structure text of a product to process this file is shown in Figure 11.21. Note the almost one-to-one correspondence between the structure of the data in Figure 11.20, and the actions shown in Figure 11.21. Except for the addition of the prefix process_, the names of the actions are identical to those of the data on which they operate. It is a fundamental tenet of Jackson's technique that the structure of the module must reflect the structure of the data on which that module operates.

Implementation of this structure text is now straightforward. The **procedure**

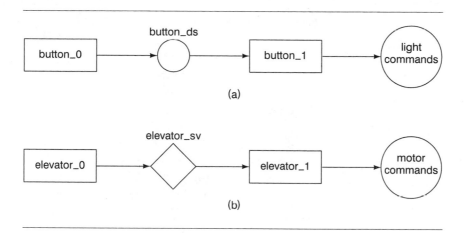

(a)

(b)

Figure 11.19 JSD structure diagrams with embedded functions added.

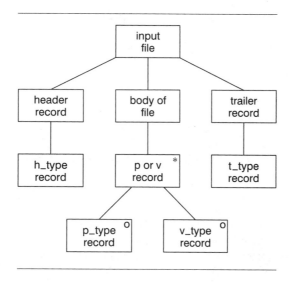

Figure 11.20 Structure of file containing pressure and volume records.

division of a COBOL implementation is shown in Figure 11.22. For the sake of brevity, details of **error-routine** have been omitted. (The unexpected **read** input-record sentence in paragraph **process-trailer-record** is necessary; in COBOL, the end-of-file condition is set to true only after an attempt has been made to read a record beyond the last record.)

There is a close correspondence between the structure text of Figure 11.21 and the code of Figure 11.22. When a design has been produced using JSD, the process of translating the design into a programming language is almost automatic.

```
process_input_file seq
    process_header_record;
    process_body_of_file itr
        process_p_or_v_record sel
            process_p_type_record;
        process_p_or_v_record alt
            process_v_type_record;
        process_p_or_v_record end;
    process_body_of_file end;
    process_trailer_record;
process_input_file end;
```

Figure 11.21 Structure text for pressure and volume problem.

11.6.4 ANALYSIS OF JACKSON SYSTEM DEVELOPMENT

Notwithstanding its many strengths as a product development technique, there are some difficulties associated with JSD. Consider, for example, paragraph **process-terminate** in Figure 11.22. It consists of three sentences, namely

> **display** minimum-pressure, maximum-volume.
> **close** input-record-file.
> **stop run**.

Even the reader who is totally unfamiliar with COBOL will quickly realize that the paragraph is a module with coincidental cohesion. It is not that JSD is incompatible with composite/structured design, but rather that the aims of JSD bear no relation to those of C/SD. As a result, it frequently happens that the module structure resulting from a JSD design is unacceptable from the viewpoint of C/SD.

The major advantages of C/SD are that the resulting product should be easily and safely maintainable and that many of the component modules should be reusable. In [Jackson, 1983] there is no mention of product maintenance or of reusability. Does this mean that JSD is unacceptable as a development technique? Not at all. There are two reasons why Jackson's technique is important. First, JSD, as well as the two related techniques, LCS [Warnier, 1981] and DSSD [Orr, 1981], has had a number of successes. These successes have not been restricted just to development, but have extended to maintenance. This means that although the techniques of C/SD are sufficient for product maintenance, they are by no means necessary. Second, many of Jackson's ideas on the nature of data and actions have proved to be important within the broader context of software engineering. Even if JSD itself never achieves universal acceptance, many of the ideas underlying JSD have already taken hold.

The related techniques of Warnier and of Orr have been mentioned a number of times. For the sake of completeness, a brief description of each is now given.

```
procedure division.
process-input-file.
    perform process-preliminary.
    perform process-header-record.
    perform process-body-of-file until (not (type-p or type-v)).
    perform process-trailer-record.
    perform process-terminate.
process-preliminary.
    open input input-record-file.
    move 10000 to minimum-pressure.
    move -10000 to maximum-volume.
    read input-record at end move "yes" to file-eof.
process-header-record.
    if (not type-h) perform error-routine.
    read input-record at end move "yes" to file-eof.
process-body-of-file.
    if type-p perform process-p-type-record
    else if type-v perform process-v-type-record
    else perform error-routine.
process-trailer-record.
    if (not type-t) perform error-routine.
    read input-record at end move "yes" to file-eof.
process-terminate.
    display minimum-pressure, maximum-volume.
    close input-record-file.
    stop run.
process-p-type-record.
    if pressure is less than minimum-pressure move pressure to minimum-pressure.
    read input-record at end move "yes" to file-eof.
process-v-type-record.
    if volume is greater than maximum-volume move volume to maximum-volume.
    read input-record at end move "yes" to file-eof.
```

Figure 11.22   Portion of COBOL implementation of pressure and volume problem.

11.7   Techniques of Jackson, Warnier, and Orr

Logical construction of systems (LCS) [Warnier, 1981] is an extension of Warnier's logical construction of programs (LCP) [Warnier, 1976]. Independently of Jackson, Warnier put forward the idea that the structure of the action should be the same as that of the data on which the action operates. In order to implement this idea he also needed a notation. Figure 11.23 depicts the Warnier diagram corresponding to Figure 11.20, the file of pressure and volume records represented in Jackson's notation. The symbol ⊕ in Figure 11.23 denotes selection, corresponding to **sel ... alt** in Jackson's textual notation.

Warnier's diagrams, like Jackson's, are hierarchical, but they differ in that the number of times an item is repeated may be explicitly stated. For example, if an item occurs between 1 and n times, then the notation used is item (1,n). If an item may or may not occur, then the notation is item (0,1).

Figure 11.23 Warnier diagram corresponding to Figure 11.20.

In Jackson's technique, the structure of a module reflects the structure of the data processed by that module. It may happen that the module has to process two or more types of incompatible data. For example, suppose that the input to a module is an array and the output is the transpose of the same array. In this case there is a *structure clash*. Jackson has developed a powerful technique for dealing with this type of situation, namely *program inversion* [Jackson, 1975]. In contrast, in Warnier's technique the structure of a module is the structure of the input data; as a result, structure clashes do not occur.

As shown in Section 11.6.3, the implementation step of JSD is virtually a straightforward translation of the structure text into the chosen programming language. Similarly, LCP supports the development of the code from the Warnier diagram; this technique is termed *detailed organization*. For more information regarding this and other aspects of Warnier's techniques, the reader should consult [Warnier, 1976] and [Warnier, 1981].

Jackson structured programming (JSP) [Jackson, 1975] is a technique for detailed design and implementation. Jackson first developed JSP, then extended his technique to the complete software development process; the resulting technique is termed JSD [Jackson, 1983]. In the same way, Orr's data structured systems development (DSSD) can be viewed as an extension of the applicability of Warnier's LCP from just detailed design and implementation to all phases of software development. The product is described using Warnier's notation, an example of which was given in Figure 11.23. In fact, such diagrams are frequently termed Warnier-Orr diagrams to reflect the role played by Orr in extending Warnier's technique. For full details of Orr's technique, the reader should refer to [Orr, 1981] or [Hansen, 1983].

11.8 OBJECT-ORIENTED DESIGN

The aim of object-oriented design (OOD) is to design the product in terms of objects, instantiations of the classes and subclasses that were extracted during object-oriented analysis. Popular languages such as C, COBOL, FORTRAN, and Pascal do not support objects as such. This might seem to imply that OOD is accessible only to users of object-oriented languages like C++ [Stroustrup, 1991], Eiffel [Meyer, 1992b], Smalltalk [Goldberg and Robson, 1989], Ada 95 [ISO/IEC, 1995], and Java [Flanagan, 1996].

That is not the case. Although it is true that OOD as such is not supported by the majority of popular languages, a large subset of OOD can be used. As explained in Section 6.7, a class is an abstract data type with inheritance, and an object is an instance of a class. When using an implementation language that does not support inheritance, the solution is to utilize those aspects of OOD that can be achieved in the programming language used in the project, that is to say, to use *abstract data type design*. Abstract data types can be implemented in virtually any language that supports **type** statements. Even in languages like FORTRAN and COBOL that do not support type statements as such, and hence cannot support abstract data types, it may still be possible to implement data encapsulation. Figure 6.27 depicts a hierarchy of design concepts starting with modules and ending with objects. In those cases where full OOD is not possible, the developers should endeavor to ensure that their design uses the highest possible concepts in the hierarchy of Figure 6.27 that their implementation language supports.

OOD consists of the following three steps:

1. Determine the actions ("methods") of the classes.

2. Design the product in terms of clients of objects.

3. Proceed to the detailed design.

(The *client* of an object is a module that makes use of that object. For example, a client may send a message to an object. A client may itself be an object, or it could be a function.)

OOD is now illustrated by means of an example. As before, the elevator problem will be presented, with just one elevator for simplicity. By using the same example, the reader is able to compare different approaches without having to worry about the ramifications of the problem itself.

11.8.1   Elevator Problem: Object-Oriented Design

Step 1. Determine the Actions (Methods) of the Classes   The class model of Figure 9.7 reflects 7 different classses, namely Button, Elevator, Elevator Button, Elevator Doors, Elevator Controller, Floor Button, and Requests. The functional model of Figure 9.8, reproduced here as Figure 11.24, shows the various actions that have to be included in the design. An action can be assigned either to an object or to a client that sends a message to that object. One way to decide how to assign an action is on the basis of information hiding. That is to say, the state variables of a class should be declared to be **private** (accessible only within an object of that class) or **private protected** (accessible only within an object of that class or of a subclass of that class). Accordingly, actions performed on those state variables must be local to that object. Even if no information hiding is required, if a particular action is invoked by a number of different clients, then it makes sense to have a single copy of that action implemented as a method of the object, rather than have a copy in each of the clients of that object. A third way to decide where to locate an action is to use responsibility-driven design.

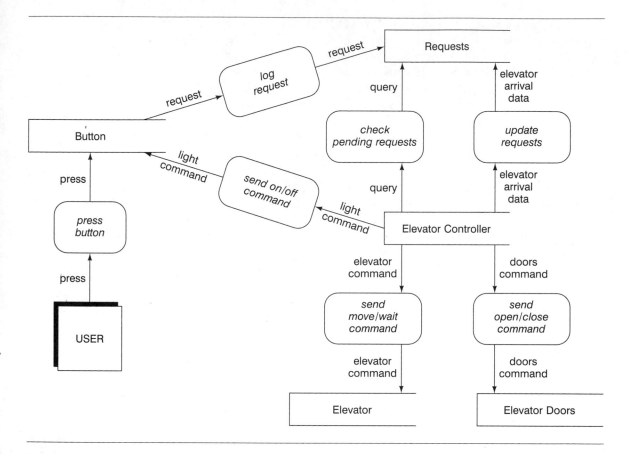

Figure 11.24   Functional model.

As explained in Section 1.6, a key aspect of the object-oriented paradigm is the principle of responsibility-driven design. If a client sends a message to an object, then that object is responsible for carrying out the request of the client. The client does not know how the request will be carried out and is not permitted to know. Once the request has been carried out, control returns to the client. At this point, all that the client knows is that the request has been carried out; it still has no idea how this was achieved.

These criteria are now applied to the example. The actions (methods) are assigned to the various classes as shown in Figure 11.25. The **Elevator Doors** class has two methods, namely *close doors* and *open doors*. That is to say, a client of **Elevator Doors** (in this instance, an instance of class **Elevator Controller**) sends a message to **Elevator Doors** to close or open the doors of the elevator, and that request is then carried out by the relevant method. Every aspect of those two methods is encapsulated within **Elevator Doors**. Information hiding results in a truly independent **Elevator Doors** class, instances of which can

Class	Attributes	Methods
Button	illuminated	*turn button off* (**abstract**) *turn button on* (**abstract**)
Elevator		*move one floor down* *move one floor up*
Elevator Application		*main*
Elevator Button	illuminated	*turn button off* *turn button on*
Elevator Controller		
Elevator Doors	doors open	*close doors* *open doors*
Elevator Utilities	(To be added later)	(To be added later)
Floor Button	illuminated	*turn button off* *turn button on*
Requests	request data	*determine if requests are pending* *log request* *update requests*

Figure 11.25 Class table. (A method will be added later to Elevator Controller.)

undergo detailed design and implementation independently and can be reused later in some other product.

Class **Elevator** also has two methods, namely *move one floor down* and *move one floor up.* There is no need to instruct an elevator to stop. If neither of its two methods is invoked, then the elevator cannot move; there is no other way to change the state of an elevator other than by invoking one of its methods.

Elevator Button and **Floor Button** both have two methods, namely *turn button off* and *turn button on.* The reasoning here is similar to that in the case of **Elevator Doors.** First, the principle of responsibility-driven design requires that the buttons themselves have full control over whether they are on or off. Second, the principle of information hiding requires the internal state of a button to be hidden. The actions that turn an elevator button on or off must therefore be local to class **Elevator Button,** and similarly for class **Floor Button.** Methods *turn button on* and *turn button off* must be declared to be **abstract** in base class **Button** for the reasons stated in Section 6.8.

Class **Requests** similarly has three methods, namely *determine if requests are pending, log request,* and *update requests.* Finally, class **Elevator Controller** does not have any methods at all. This implies that there is no way to invoke an instance of an **Elevator Controller.** This will be corrected during the next step.

Step 2. Design the Product in Terms of Clients of Objects One way to design the product in terms of objects and their clients is to find those objects that are not clients of other objects. The objects of the product are instantiations of the various classes that have been determined. Using the class model (Figure 9.7) and the class table (Figure

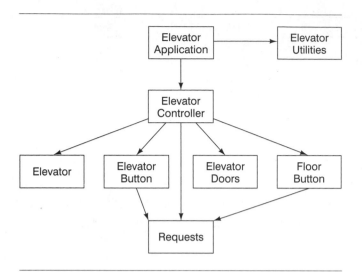

Figure 11.26 Client-object relations.

11.25), a diagram is drawn showing the clients of each object (Figure 11.26). A message that could be sent from client C to object O is represented by an arrow from C to O. Any object that is not a client of some other object then needs to be initiated, usually by method *main.* In the example, object ElevatorController sends messages to the other five objects. Thus, in order to start the product, *main* must invoke object Elevator Controller. This form of architecture is not uncommon when the object-oriented paradigm is used, namely, a simple main program that essentially starts things off; the objects themselves take over from then on.

Now that the overall architectural design is clear, it is necessary to check that each object has all the methods it needs. That is to say, it is necessary to verify that all required methods have been assigned to each object so that it can respond to each of the possible messages that could be sent to it. Now it becomes apparent that Elevator Controller requires a method so that *main* can invoke it. Thus, Figure 11.25 is amended, and method *elevator controller loop* is added to object Elevator Controller. This method can then be invoked by *main.*

Step 3. Proceed to the Detailed Design   A detailed design is now developed for *main* and the various objects. Any suitable technique may be used, such as stepwise refinement described in Chapter 4. The detailed design of method *elevator controller loop* is shown in Figure 11.27.

11.9   Detailed Design

Two techniques for detailed design have already been presented. In Chapter 4 a description of stepwise refinement was given. It was then applied to detailed design

```
void elevator control loop ()
{
    while (true)
    {
        if (a button has been pressed)
            if (button is not on)
            {
                turn button on ();
                log request ();
            }
        else if (elevator is moving up)
        {
            if (there is no request to stop at floor f)
                move one floor up ();
            else
            {
                stop elevator by not sending a message to move;
                open doors ();
                if (button is on)
                    turn button off ();
                update requests ();
            }
        }
        else if (elevator is moving down)
            [similar to up case]
        else if (request is pending ())
        {
            if (button is on)
                turn button off ();
            close doors ();
            determine direction of next request;
            move one floor up/down ();
        }
        else if (elevator is at rest and not (request is pending ()))
            close doors ();
        else
            there are no requests, elevator is stopped with doors closed, so do nothing;
    }
}
```

Figure 11.27   Pseudocode detailed design of method *elevator control loop*.

using flowcharts. Also, step 6 of JSD comprises detailed design plus implementation; this was illustrated at the end of Section 11.6.3 by means of an example, namely, the file of pressure and volume data.

In addition to stepwise refinement and Jackson's technique, formal techniques can also be used to advantage in detailed design. In Chapter 5 it was suggested that implementing a complete product and then proving it correct could be counterproductive. However, developing the proof and the detailed design in parallel, and carefully testing the code as well, is quite a different matter. Formal techniques at the detailed design phase can greatly assist in three ways. First, the state of the art in correctness proving is such that, although it cannot generally be applied to a product as a whole, it can be applied to module-sized pieces of a product. Second, developing a proof together with the detailed design should lead to a design with fewer faults than if correctness proofs were not used. Third, if the same programmer is responsible for both the detailed design and the implementation, as is often the case, then that programmer will feel confident that the detailed design is correct. This positive attitude towards the design should lead to fewer faults in the code.

11.10   COMPARISON OF ACTION-, DATA-, AND OBJECT-ORIENTED DESIGN

Examples of each of the three basic approaches to design have been presented. First, an action-oriented technique, namely data flow analysis, was described. This was followed by Jackson system development, a data-oriented approach. The third approach was object-oriented design. These three techniques are now compared.

Data flow analysis is a top-down, decompositional technique. That is, the product as a whole is decomposed stepwise into smaller parts until each part is a module with functional cohesion. In contrast, JSD is a bottom-up, compositional technique. The designer starts with nothing and adds pieces incrementally until the design is complete. Cameron, the co-inventor of JSD with Jackson, suggests that any decompositional technique is critically dependent on the initial decomposition [Cameron, 1986]. As Cameron puts it," . . . the first decomposition is a commitment to a system structure; the commitment has to be made from a position of ignorance." In other words, at the beginning of the decomposition process a decision has to be made at a stage when the designer as yet knows little about the target product. Ironically, that decision will critically affect the final product, because by decomposing the product in that way at the beginning, the designer may be precluding the possibility of decomposing the product in a different way at a later stage. Cameron suggests that techniques based on decomposition work well only when the designer really understands the product.

The first step of object-oriented design, namely, determining the actions (methods) of the classes, is a bottom-up process. However, the second step, namely, designing the product as a whole in terms of clients of objects, is a top-down technique.

Thus there is a fundamental difference between DFA, JSD, and OOD. DFA seems appropriate when the design team is familiar with the application area. But when the application area is new to the software developers, and this applies particularly when the product is of a research-oriented nature, then JSD appears to be a better choice. As for OOD, the first step (completing the design of the classes) is a bottom-up technique. By the time this is complete, the designers will probably have enough familiarity with the application area to proceed successfully with the second, top-down step. Thus OOD appears to be appropriate for both familiar and new application areas.

A second way of comparing design techniques is to consider maintenance issues. As mentioned previously, JSD is not really maintenance-oriented; however, the aim of DFA is to arrive at modules with high cohesion, and hence the attendant advantages with regard to maintenance. OOD is often strongly recommended from the viewpoint of maintainability of the resulting product.

A third way of comparing techniques is from the viewpoint of reuse. Again, DFA and OOD seem to have the edge over JSD. Nothing in Jackson's technique indicates that using it will result in reusable modules. On the contrary, the fact that JSD, as shown in Section 11.6.4, can lead to modules with coincidental cohesion implies that JSD may in fact be counterproductive from the viewpoint of reuse.

All three criteria indicate that OOD is a good design technique. Considering the apparent overall superiority of the object-oriented paradigm, it is difficult to justify not using OOD in the design of a new system. The problem arises with *legacy systems*, that is, existing systems that need to be maintained. Legacy systems usually predate the object-oriented era. When extending a product that has been designed using one technique, it is usually hard to employ a different technique for the new modules. This is especially true when a totally different paradigm is to be employed for the new technique. Thus, although OOD is usually a good choice for building a new product, it can be difficult to introduce into an existing product unless the new portion constitutes a conceptually distinct component of the product, such as a graphical user interface (GUI).

We now consider the issue of designing real-time systems.

11.11   DIFFICULTIES ASSOCIATED WITH REAL-TIME SYSTEMS

A real-time system is characterized by the fact that its inputs come from the real world and that the software has no control over the timing of those inputs. Furthermore, each input must be processed before the next input arrives. An example of such a system is a computer-controlled nuclear reactor. Inputs such as the temperature of the core and the level of the water in the reactor chamber are continually being sent to the computer that reads the value of each input and performs the necessary processing before the next input arrives. Another example is a computer-controlled intensive care unit. There are two types of patient data: routine information such as heart rate, temperature, and blood pressure of each patient, and emergency information when the system deduces that the condition of a patient has become critical. When such emergencies occur, the software must be able to process both the routine inputs as well as the emergency-related inputs from one or more patients.

A characteristic of many real-time systems is that they are implemented on distributed hardware. For example, software controlling a fighter aircraft may be implemented on five computers, one to handle navigation, another the weapons system, a third for electronic countermeasures, a fourth to control the flight hardware such as wing flaps and engines, and the fifth to propose tactics in combat. Because hardware is not totally reliable, there may be additional back-up computers that automatically replace a malfunctioning unit. Not only does the design of such a system have major communications implications, but timing issues, over and above those of the type described in the previous paragraph, arise as a consequence of the distributed nature of the system. For example, under combat conditions the tactical computer might suggest that the pilot should climb, whereas the weapons computer recommends that the pilot go into a dive so that a particular weapon may be launched under optimal conditions. However, the human pilot decides to move the stick to the right, thereby sending a signal to the flight hardware computer to make the necessary adjustments so that the plane banks in the indicated direction. All this information must be carefully managed in such a way that the actual motion of the plane takes precedence in every way over suggested maneuvers. Furthermore, the actual motion must be relayed to the tactical and weapons computers so that new suggestions can be formulated in the light of actual, rather than suggested, conditions.

A further difficulty with real-time systems is the problem of synchronization. Suppose that a real-time system is to be implemented on distributed hardware. Situations such as deadlock (or deadly embrace) can arise when two actions each have exclusive use of a data item and each then requests exclusive use of the other's data item in addition. Of course, deadlock does not occur only in real-time systems implemented on distributed hardware. But it is particularly troublesome in real-time systems where there is no control over the order or timing of the inputs, and the situation can be complicated by the distributed nature of the hardware. In addition to deadlock, other synchronization problems are also possible, including race conditions; for details, the reader may refer to [Silberschatz and Galvin, 1994] or other operating systems textbooks.

From these examples it is clear that the major difficulty with regard to the design of real-time systems is ensuring that the timing constraints are met by the design. That is to say, the design technique should provide a mechanism for checking that, when implemented, the design will be able to read and process incoming data at the required rate. Furthermore, it should be possible to show that synchronization issues in the design have also been correctly addressed. In brief, what characterizes real-time systems is timing; the difficulties that are encountered with real-time systems are essentially difficulties that arise as a direct consequence of the fact that time is a major component of the real-world system that is controlled by the real-time software.

11.12   REAL-TIME DESIGN TECHNIQUES

Since the beginning of the computer age, advances in hardware technology have outstripped, in almost every respect, advances in software technology. Thus, although the hardware exists to handle every aspect of the real-time systems described previously, software design technology has lagged considerably behind. In some areas of real-time software engineering major progress has been made. For instance, many of the specification techniques of Chapters 8 and 9 can be used to specify real-time systems. Unfortunately, software design has not reached the same level of sophistication. Great strides are indeed being made, but the state of the art is not yet comparable to what has been achieved with regard to specification techniques. Because almost any design technique for real-time systems is preferable to no technique at all, a number of real-time design techniques are being used in practice. But there is still a long way to go before it will be possible to design real-time systems such as those described previously and to be certain that, before the system has been implemented, every real-time constraint will be met and that synchronization problems cannot arise.

Most real-time design techniques are extensions of nonreal-time techniques to the real-time domain. For example, structured development for real-time systems (SDRTS) [Ward and Mellor, 1985] is essentially an extension of structured systems analysis (Section 8.3), data flow analysis (Section 11.3), and transaction analysis (Section 11.4) to real-time software. The development technique includes a component for real-time design. Another extension of the same group of techniques to the real-time domain is design approach for real-time systems (DARTS) [Gomaa, 1986]. Software cost reduction (SCR) [Kmielcik et al., 1984] is a real-time design technique based on the concept of information hiding [Parnas, 1971, 1972a, 1972b]. Other techniques in this class are described in [Hatley and Pirbhai, 1987] and [Levi and Agrawala, 1990].

As stated previously, it is unfortunate that the state-of-the-art of real-time design is not as advanced as one would wish. Nevertheless, strenuous efforts are underway to improve the situation, such as the work of Anger and Rodriguez; see [Anger, Munson, and Rodriguez, 1994].

11.13 TESTING DURING THE DESIGN PHASE

The goal of testing at the design phase is to verify that the specifications have been accurately and completely incorporated into the design, as well as to ensure the correctness of the design itself. For example, the design must not have any logic faults, and all interfaces must be correctly defined. It is important that any faults in the design be detected before coding commences, otherwise the cost of fixing the faults will be considerably higher, as reflected in Figure 1.5. Detection of design faults can be achieved by means of design inspections, as well as design walkthroughs. Design inspections are discussed in the remainder of this section, but the remarks are equally applicable to design walkthroughs.

A design inspection is similar to the inspection at the specification phase except that representatives of the client organization are not usually present at a design inspection. This is a consequence of the fact that nontechnical individuals generally find design documents harder to understand than specification documents.

When the product is transaction-oriented, the design inspection should reflect this fact [Beizer, 1990]. (Recall that a *transaction* is an operation from the viewpoint of the user of the product, such as "process a request" or "print a list of today's orders.") Inspections that will include all possible transaction types should be scheduled. The reviewer should relate each transaction in the design to the specification, showing how the transaction arises from the specification document. For example, if the application is an automated teller machine (ATM) product, a transaction will correspond to each operation that the customer performs, such as deposit to or withdraw from a credit card account. In other instances, the correspondence between specifications and transactions will not necessarily be one-to-one. In a traffic-light control system, for example, if an automobile driving over a sensor pad results in the system deciding to change a particular light from red to green in 15 seconds then further impulses from that sensor pad may be ignored. Conversely, in order to speed traffic flow, a single impulse may cause a whole series of lights to be changed from red to green.

Restricting reviews to transaction-driven inspections will not detect cases where the designers have overlooked instances of transactions required by the specifications. To take an extreme example, the specifications for the traffic-light controller may stipulate that between 11:00 p.m. and 6:00 a.m. all lights are to flash orange in one direction and red in the other direction. If the designers overlooked this stipulation, then clock-generated transactions at 11:00 p.m. and 6:00 a.m. would not be included in the design, and if these transactions were overlooked, they could not be tested in a design inspection based on transactions. Thus, it is not adequate just to schedule design inspections that are transaction-driven; specification-driven inspections are also essential to ensure that no statement in the specification document has been either overlooked or misinterpreted.

11.14 CASE TOOLS FOR THE DESIGN PHASE

As stated in the previous section, a critical aspect of the design phase is testing that the design document accurately incorporates all aspects of the specification document. What therefore is needed is a CASE tool that can be used both for the specification document and the design document, a so-called *front-end* or *upper-CASE* tool (as opposed to a *back-end* or *lowerCASE* tool, which assists with the implementation, integration, and maintenance phases).

There are a number of upperCASE tools on the market. Some of the more popular ones include Analyst/Designer, Excelerator, and Teamwork. UpperCASE tools are generally built around a data dictionary. The CASE tool can check that every field of every record in the dictionary is mentioned somewhere in the design document or that every item in the design document is reflected in the data flow diagram. In addition, many upperCASE tools incorporate a consistency checker that uses the data dictionary to determine that every item in the design has been declared in the specifications and conversely that every item in the specifications appears in the design.

Furthermore, many upperCASE tools also incorporate screen and report generators. That is, the client can specify what items are to appear in a report or on an input screen and where and how each item is to appear. Because full details regarding every item are in the dictionary, the CASE tool can then easily generate the code for printing the report or displaying the input screen according to the client's wishes. Some upperCASE products also incorporate management tools for estimating and planning.

With regard to object-oriented design, OMTool, Rose, and Software through Pictures provide support for this phase within the context of the complete object-oriented life cycle.

11.15 METRICS FOR THE DESIGN PHASE

A variety of metrics can be used to describe aspects of the design. For example, the number of modules is a crude measure of the size of the target product. Module cohesion and coupling are measures of the quality of the design, as are fault statistics. As with all other types of inspection, it is vital to keep a record of the number and type of design faults detected during a design inspection. This information is used during code inspections of the product, and also in design inspections of subsequent products.

The cyclomatic complexity M of a detailed design is the number of binary decisions (predicates) plus 1 [McCabe, 1976] or equivalently, the number of branches in the module. It has been suggested that cyclomatic complexity is a metric of design quality, the lower the value of M, the better. An advantage of this metric is that it is easy to compute. However, it has an inherent problem. Cyclomatic complexity is a measure purely of the control complexity; the data complexity is ignored. That is, M does not measure the complexity of a module that is data-driven, such as by the values in a table. For example, suppose that a designer is unaware of library method *java.lang.character.digit* and designs a module from scratch that reads a character input by the user and returns the corresponding ASCII code (an integer between 0 and 127). One way of designing this is by means of a 128-way branch to be implemented by means of a **switch** statement. A second way is to have an array containing the 128 characters in ASCII code order, utilizing a loop to compare the character input by the user with each element of the array of characters; the loop is exited when a match is obtained. The current value of the loop variable is then the corresponding ASCII code. The two designs are equivalent in functionality but have cyclomatic complexities of 128 and 1, respectively.

When the structured paradigm is used, a related class of metrics for the design phase is based on representing the architectural design as a directed graph with the modules represented by nodes and the flows between modules (procedure and function calls) represented by arcs. The *fan-in* of a module can then be defined as the number of flows into the module plus the number of global data structures accessed by the module. The *fan out* is similarly the number of flows out of the module plus the number of global data structures updated by the module. A measure of complexity of the module is then given by *length* $\times$ *(fan-in* $\times$ *fan-out)^2* [Henry and Kafura,

1981], where *length* is a measure of the size of the module (Section 10.1.1). The fact that the definitions of *fan-in* and *fan-out* incorporate global data means that this metric has a data-dependent component. Nevertheless, experiments have shown that this metric is no better a measure of complexity than simpler metrics such as cyclomatic complexity [Kitchenham, Pickard, and Linkman, 1990; Shepperd, 1990]. The issue of metrics for the design phase, other than the five fundamental metrics (Section 4.9), still remains to be resolved.

The issue of design metrics is even more complicated when the object-oriented paradigm is used. For example, the cyclomatic complexity of a class is usually low, because many classes typically include a large number of small, straightforward methods. Furthermore, as previously pointed out, cyclomatic complexity ignores data complexity. Because data and actions are equal partners within the object-oriented paradigm, cyclomatic complexity overlooks a major component that could contribute towards the complexity of an object. Thus, metrics for classes that incorporate cyclomatic complexity are generally of little use.

A number of object-oriented design metrics have been put forward. For example, the number of ancestors of a class C has been suggested as a measure of the degree of difficulty in understanding that class. After all, many of the attributes and techniques of C may not have been defined within C itself, but rather within the inheritance hierarchy in which C is a descendant. Starting at the root of that inheritance hierarchy and working downwards towards the class in question, attributes and techniques can be defined, redefined, renamed, or suppressed. For this reason, the number of ancestors (or the height of the inheritance tree) has been proposed as a metric for the difficulty in comprehending a class. The problem with this is that tools exist that "flatten out" the definition of a class. For example, this is a standard feature of Eiffel [Meyer, 1990]; command **flat** causes the text of the class to be printed out, incorporating all the inherited features. Use of such tools renders this metric effectively useless. Other object-oriented design metrics are discussed in Section 6.9.

Not much is known about the effectiveness of object-oriented design metrics because they are too new and have not yet been widely used in the industry. More experience with the object-oriented paradigm as a whole is needed to obtain definitive results regarding object-oriented design metrics.

11.16   MSG CASE STUDY: OBJECT-ORIENTED DESIGN

As described in Section 11.8, object-oriented design consists of three steps. First, the actions ("methods") of the classes are determined. Second, the product is designed in terms of objects and their clients. Third, the detailed design is produced.

The process is best performed iteratively. In the case of the MSG Case Study, by studying the class model (Figure 9.10) and functional model (Figure 9.12) an initial set of methods is extracted. Methods that will be used identically by instances of both class **Investment** and class **Mortgage** are declared to be methods of **Financial**

Instrument (refer to Figure 11.28, which shows the final version of the class table). Examples of such methods are *delete record* and *input new record.* Methods (such as *read record* and *write record*) that will be used by instances of both classes but with different implementations are declared to be **abstract** methods (Section 6.8) of Financial Instrument. Finally, a method that is specific to one or the other class, such as *change investment field* or *read mortgage data,* is declared to be a method of the relevant class. The resulting methods are then inserted into the class table. This process continues until the design team is confident that all necessary methods have been determined and assigned to the appropriate class (Figure 11.28).

Now the initial iteration of the second step (designing the product in terms of objects and their clients) is performed, followed by the initial iteration of the detailed design, the third step. When these latter two steps are performed, changes will be made to the class table. Such changes will in turn trigger changes to the design (in terms of objects and their clients) and to the detailed design. The object-oriented design phase is complete when the process is stable and the resulting design has been approved by SQA.

With regard to the design of the product in terms of objects and their clients, the rapid prototype (Appendix C) indicates that a design in terms of a hierarchy of menus would be feasible. The main menu allows the user to select whether to print a report or to perform some operation on an investment, a mortgage, or operating expenses. The methods in this menu hierarchy then invoke ("send messages to") the relevant objects. The menu methods are fields of class MSG Utilities. The final version of the client-object relations is shown in Figure 11.29.

Because of the nature of the process, a number of iterations are needed. For the sake of brevity, only the final results of the process are shown here, namely the class table (Figure 11.28), client-object relations (Figure 11.29), and a small portion of the detailed design (Figure 11.30); the complete detailed design appears in Appendix G. The use of the phrase "final results" in the previous sentence is perhaps a display of hubris. After all, when the MSG product is implemented and integrated it is quite likely that the design will change again, perhaps radically. It would have been more appropriate to have described the material as the final version of the design at this stage of the object-oriented life cycle.

Chapter Review

The design phase consists of architectural design, followed by detailed design (Section 11.1). Three approaches to design are described, namely action-oriented design (Section 11.2), data-oriented design (Section 11.5), and object-oriented design (Section 11.8). Examples of each approach are given, and case studies are presented to illustrate the techniques. Two instances of action-oriented design are described, namely data flow analysis (Section 11.3) and transaction analysis (Section 11.4). The techniques of Jackson, Warnier, and Orr (Section 11.7) are all data-

Class	Attributes	Methods
Financial Investment		**abstract** methods
		display record
		find record
		get new data
		perform deletion
		put record
		read record
		update record
		write record
		Other methods
		delete record
		input new record
Investment	expected annual return	*change investment field*
	expected annual return updated	*produce investment report*
	investment ID	*read investment data*
	investment name	*total weekly return on investment*
Mortgage	annual insurance premium	*change mortgage field*
	annual property tax	*produce mortgage report*
	current weekly income	*read mortgage data*
	date mortgage issued	*total weekly net payments*
	mortgage balance	
	mortgage ID	
	mortgage name	
	price	
	weekly income updated	
MSG Application	INTEREST_RATE	*initialize application*
	MAXIMUM_PERC_OF_ INCOME	*main*
	NUMBER_OF_MORTGAGE_ PAYMENTS	*set annual operating expenses*
	WEEKS_IN_YEAR	
MSG Utilities		*clear screen*
		display main menu
		display investment menu
		display mortgage menu
		display report menu
		funds available
		parse date
		update annual operating expenses

Figure 11.28 Class table for MSG Case Study.

Figure 11.29   Client-object relations for MSG Case Study.

oriented; Jackson's technique is described in some detail in Section 11.6. Techniques for detailed design are put forward in Section 11.9. A comparison of specific instances of the three approaches is given in Section 11.10. Aspects of real-time systems are described in Section 11.11. The lack of an all-encompassing real-time design technique is pointed out in Section 11.12. In Section 11.13, design inspections are discussed. CASE tools and metrics for the design phase are presented in Sections 11.14 and 11.15, respectively. The chapter concludes with the object-oriented design of the MSG Case Study (Section 11.16).

For Further Reading

A useful overall source on design techniques is [Freeman and Wasserman, 1983]. The tutorial covers a wide variety of techniques, including many of those described in this chapter. [Yau and Tsai, 1986] is a survey of design techniques that cites over 80 references to a broad variety of approaches to design. A wide variety of design techniques can also be found in the February 1986 issue of *IEEE Transactions on Software Engineering*.

Data flow analysis and transaction analysis are described in books such as [Gane and Sarsen, 1979] and [Yourdon and Constantine, 1979]. Related techniques are found in [Martin and McClure, 1985]. Jackson's technique is described in [Jackson, 1975] and [Jackson, 1983]; other excellent sources are the work of Cameron, Jackson's associate [Cameron, 1986; 1988], and [King, 1988]. For readers interested in Warnier's work, the original sources are [Warnier, 1976] and [Warnier, 1981]. Orr's approach can be found in [Orr, 1981] and [Hansen, 1983].

Turning now to object-oriented design, information can be obtained from [Wirfs-Brock, Wilkerson, and Wiener, 1990], [Coad and Yourdon, 1991b], [Jacobson, Christerson, Jonsson, and Overgaard, 1992], [Martin and Odell, 1992], [Rumbaugh et al., 1991], [Shlaer and Mellor, 1992], and [Booch, 1994]. A comparison of a variety of techniques for object-oriented design appears in [Monarchi and Puhr, 1992] and [Walker, 1992]. A comparison of both object-oriented and structured design techniques appears in [Fichman and Kemerer, 1992].

Class name	*Financial Instrument*
Method name	*delete record*
Modifiers, type	**public void**
Arguments	none
Error messages	If record to be deleted does not exist
Files accessed	none
Files changed	none
Methods called	*find record, perform deletion*
Narrative	Prompts user to enter ID of record to be deleted. Calls *find record* to find the specified record, then calls *perform deletion* to delete record. Finally, reports that record has been deleted.

Class name	*Investment*
Method name	*produce investment report*
Modifiers, type	**public void**
Arguments	none
Error messages	If no investments exist.
Files accessed	investment.dat
Files changed	investment.dat
Methods called	*read record, display record*
Narrative	*Reads record from* **investment.dat** *by calling* **read record** *and then displays them by calling* **display record.**

Class name	*MSG Application*
Method name	*set annual operating expenses*
Modifiers, type	**public static void**
Arguments	**float**
Error messages	none
Files accessed	opexp.dat
Files changed	opexp.dat
Methods called	none
Narrative	Validates new annual operating epenses, writes data to **opexp.dat** for use in the current execution.

Figure 11.30   Portion of detailed design of MSG Case Study.

Formal design techniques are described in [Hoare, 1987].

With regard to reviews during the design process, useful checklists for inspections can be found in [Fagan, 1976], [Perry, 1983], and [Dunn, 1984]. The original paper on design inspections is [Fagan, 1976]; detailed information can be obtained from that paper. Later advances in review techniques are described in [Fagan, 1986]. A newer approach to design reviews is presented in [Parnas and Weiss, 1987]. The use of walkthroughs to test user interface design is described in [Bias, 1991].

With regard to real-time design, specific techniques are to be found in [Kmielcik et al., 1984], [Ward and Mellor, 1985], [Gomaa, 1986], [Faulk and Parnas, 1988], and [Levi and Agrawala, 1990]. A comparison of four real-time design techniques is found in [Kelly and Sherif, 1992]. The September 1992 issue of *IEEE Software* contains a number of articles on real-time systems. The design of distributed systems is described in [Kramer, 1994].

Metrics for the design phase are described in [Henry and Kafura, 1981], [Brandl, 1990], [Henry and Selig, 1990], and [Zage and Zage, 1993]. Metrics for object-oriented design are discussed in [Chidamber and Kemerer, 1994].

The proceedings of the International Workshops on Software Specification and Design are a comprehensive source for information on design techniques.

Problems

Starting with the DFD for Problem 8.6, use data flow analysis to design a product for determining whether a bank statement is correct. **11.1**

Use transaction analysis to design the software to control an ATM (Problem 9.2). At this stage omit error-handling capabilities. **11.2**

Now take your design for Problem 11.2 and add modules to perform error handling. Carefully examine the resulting design and determine the cohesion and coupling of the modules. Be on the lookout for situations such as that depicted in Figure 11.10. **11.3**

Two different techniques for depicting a detailed design are presented in Section 11.3.1 (Figures 11.6 and 11.7). Compare and contrast the two techniques. **11.4**

Starting with your data flow diagram for the automated library circulation system (Problem 8.8), design the circulation system using data flow analysis. **11.5**

Repeat Problem 11.5 using transaction analysis. Which of the two techniques did you find to be more appropriate? **11.6**

A file contains the results of three types of medical tests: radiological tests, blood chemistry tests, and bacteriological tests. Each record includes the date and time the test was performed and the name of the patient. The records are sorted by name, by date within name, and by time within date. Use JSD notation to specify the structure of the file. **11.7**

Modify Figure 11.18 by inserting button_on and button_off commands at the appropriate places for the purposes of a display at each floor showing the current position of the elevator. **11.8**

Starting with your specifications for the automated library circulation system (Problem 8.8), design the library system using Jackson's technique. **11.9**

Design the ATM software (Problem 9.2) using Jackson's technique. **11.10**

Repeat Problem 11.7 using Warnier's notation. **11.11**

11.12   Repeat Problem 11.9 using object-oriented design.

11.13   Design the ATM software (Problem 9.2) using object-oriented design.

11.14   (Term Project) Starting with your specifications of Problem 8.15 or 9.10, design the Osbert Oglesby product (Appendix A). Use the design technique specified by your instructor.

11.15   (Case Study) Design the MSG product using data flow analysis.

11.16   (Case Study) Design the MSG product using Jackson's technique.

11.17   (Case Study) The detailed design of Figure 11.30 is represented in tabular form. Represent the design using a pseudocode of your choice. Which representation is superior? Give reasons for your answer.

11.18   (Readings in Software Engineering) Your instructor will distribute copies of [Fichman and Kemerer, 1992]. Do you agree with the authors' analysis of design methodologies?

References

[Abowd, Allen, and Garlan, 1993] G. Abowd, R. Allen, and D. Garlan, "Using Style to Understand Descriptions of Software Architecture," *Proceedings of the First ACM SIGSOFT Symposium on the Foundations of Software Engineering, ACM SIGSOFT Software Engineering Notes* **18** (December 1993), pp. 9–20.

[Anger, Munson, and Rodriguez, 1994] F. D. Anger, J. C. Munson, and R. V. Rodriguez, "Temporal Complexity and Software Faults," *Proceedings of the 5th International Symposium on Software Reliability Engineering,* Monterey, CA, November 1994, pp. 115–125.

[Beizer, 1990] B. Beizer, *Software Testing Techniques,* Second Edition, Van Nostrand Reinhold, New York, 1990.

[Bias, 1991] R. Bias, "Walkthroughs: Efficient Collaborative Testing," *IEEE Software* **8** (September 1991), pp. 94–95.

[Booch, 1994] G. Booch, *Object-Oriented Analysis and Design with Applications, Second Edition,* Benjamin/Cummings, Redwood City, CA, 1994.

[Brandl, 1990] D. L. Brandl, "Quality Measures in Design: Finding Problems before Coding," *ACM SIGSOFT Software Engineering Notes* **15** (January 1990), pp. 68–72.

[Cameron, 1986] J. R. Cameron, "An Overview of JSD," *IEEE Transactions on Software Engineering* **SE-12** (February 1986), pp. 222–240.

[Cameron, 1988] J. Cameron, *JSP & JSD—The Jackson Approach to Software Development*, Second Edition, IEEE Computer Society Press, Washington, DC, 1988.

[Chidamber and Kemerer, 1994] S. R. Chidamber and C. F. Kemerer, "A Metrics Suite for Object Oriented Design," *IEEE Transactions on Software Engineering* **20** (June 1994), pp. 476–493.

[Coad and Yourdon, 1991b] P. Coad and E. Yourdon, *Object-Oriented Design,* Yourdon Press, Englewood Cliffs, NJ, 1991.

[Dunn, 1984] R. H. Dunn, *Software Defect Removal,* McGraw-Hill, New York, 1984.

[Fagan, 1976] M. E. Fagan, "Design and Code Inspections to Reduce Errors in Program Development," *IBM Systems Journal* **15** (No. 3, 1976), pp. 182–211.

[Fagan, 1986] M. E. FAGAN, "Advances in Software Inspections," *IEEE Transactions on Software Engineering* **SE-12** (July 1986), pp. 744–751.

[Faulk and Parnas, 1988] S. R. FAULK AND D. L. PARNAS, "On Synchronization in Hard-Real-Time Systems," *Communications of the ACM* **31** (March 1988), pp. 274–287.

[Fichman and Kemerer, 1992] R. G. FICHMAN AND C. F. KEMERER, "Object-Oriented and Conventional Analysis and Design Methodologies: Comparison and Critique," *IEEE Computer* **25** (October 1992), pp. 22–39.

[Flanagan, 1996] D. FLANAGAN, *Java in a Nutshell,* O'Reilly and Associates, Sebastopol, CA, 1996.

[Freeman and Wasserman, 1983] P. FREEMAN AND A. J. WASSERMAN (Editors), *Tutorial: Software Design Techniques,* Fourth Edition, IEEE Computer Society Press, Washington, DC, 1983.

[Gane and Sarsen, 1979] C. GANE AND T. SARSEN, *Structured Systems Analysis: Tools and Techniques*, Prentice-Hall, Englewood Cliffs, NJ, 1979.

[Goldberg and Robson, 1989] A. GOLDBERG AND D. ROBSON, *Smalltalk-80: The Language*, Addison-Wesley, Reading, MA 1989.

[Gomaa, 1986] H. GOMAA, "Software Development of Real-Time Systems," *Communications of the ACM* **29** (July 1986), pp. 657–668.

[Hansen, 1983] K. HANSEN, *Data Structured Program Design,* Ken Orr and Associates, Topeka, KS, 1983.

[Hatley and Pirbhai, 1987] D. J. HATLEY AND I. A. PIRBHAI, *Strategies for Real-Time System Specification*, Dorset House, New York, 1987.

[Henry and Kafura, 1981] S. M. HENRY AND D. KAFURA, "Software Structure Metrics Based on Information Flow," *IEEE Transactions on Software Engineering* **SE-7** (September 1981), pp. 510–518.

[Henry and Selig, 1990] S. HENRY AND C. SELIG, "Predicting Source-Code Complexity at the Design Stage," *IEEE Software* **7** (March 1990), pp. 36–44.

[Hoare, 1987] C. A. R. HOARE, "An Overview of Some Formal Methods for Program Design," *IEEE Computer* **20** (September 1987), pp. 85–91.

[ISO/IEC 8652, 1995] "Programming Language Ada: Language and Standard Libraries," ISO/IEC 8652, International Organization for Standardization, International Electrotechnical Commission, 1995.

[Jackson, 1975] M. A. JACKSON, *Principles of Program Design*, Academic Press, New York, 1975.

[Jackson, 1983] M. A. JACKSON, *System Development*, Prentice-Hall, Englewood Cliffs, NJ, 1983.

[Jacobson, Christerson, Jonsson, and Overgaard, 1992] I. JACOBSON, M. CHRISTERSON, P. JONSSON, AND G. OVERGAARD, *Object-Oriented Software Engineering: A Use Case Driven Approach*, ACM Press, New York, 1992.

[Kelly and Sherif, 1992] J. C. KELLY AND J. S. SHERIF, "A Comparison of Four Design Methods for Real-Time Software Development," *Information and Software Technology* **34** (February 1992,) pp. 74–82.

[King, 1988] D. KING, *Creating Effective Software: Computer Program Design Using the Jackson Methodology*, Prentice-Hall, Englewood Cliffs, NJ, 1988.

[Kitchenham, Pickard, and Linkman, 1990] B. A. KITCHENHAM, L. M. PICKARD, AND S. J. LINKMAN, "An Evaluation of Some Design Metrics," *Software Engineering Journal* **5** (January 1990), pp. 50–58.

[Kmielcik et al., 1984] J. KMIELCIK ET AL., "SCR Methodology User's Manual," Grumman Aerospace Corporation, Report SRSR-A6-84-002, 1984.

[Kramer, 1994] J. KRAMER, "Distributed Software Engineering," *Proceedings of the 16th International Conference on Software Engineering,* Sorrento, Italy, May, 1994, pp. 253–263.

[Levi and Agrawala, 1990] S.-T. LEVI AND A. K. AGRAWALA, *Real Time System Design,* McGraw-Hill, New York, 1990.

[Martin and McClure, 1985] J. P. MARTIN AND C. MCCLURE, *Diagramming Techniques for Analysts and Programmers,* Prentice-Hall, Englewood Cliffs, NJ, 1985.

[Martin and Odell, 1992] J. MARTIN AND J. J. ODELL, *Object-Oriented Analysis and Design,* Prentice-Hall, Englewood Cliffs, NJ, 1992.

[McCabe, 1976] T. J. MCCABE, "A Complexity Measure," *IEEE Transactions on Software Engineering* **SE-2** (December 1976), pp. 308–320.

[Meyer, 1990] B. MEYER, "Lessons from the Design of the Eiffel Libraries," *Communications of the ACM* **33** (September 1990), pp. 68–88.

[Meyer, 1992b] B. MEYER, *Eiffel: The Language,* Prentice-Hall, Englewood Cliffs, NJ, 1992.

[Monarchi and Puhr, 1992] D. E. MONARCHI AND G. I. PUHR, "A Research Typology for Object-Oriented Analysis and Design," *Communications of the ACM* **35** (September 1992), pp. 35–47.

[Orr, 1981] K. ORR, *Structured Requirements Definition,* Ken Orr and Associates, Inc., Topeka, KS, 1981.

[Parnas, 1971] D. L. PARNAS, "Information Distribution Aspects of Design Methodology," *Proceedings of the IFIP Congress,* Ljubljana, Yugoslavia, 1971, pp. 339–344.

[Parnas, 1972a] D. L. PARNAS, "A Technique for Software Module Specification with Examples," *Communications of the ACM* **15** (May 1972), pp. 330–336.

[Parnas, 1972b] D. L. PARNAS, "On the Criteria to Be Used in Decomposing Systems into Modules," *Communications of the ACM* **15** (December 1972), pp. 1053–1058.

[Parnas and Weiss, 1987] D. L. PARNAS AND D. M. WEISS, "Active Design Reviews: Principles and Practices," *Journal of Systems and Software* **7** (December 1987), pp. 259–265.

[Perry, 1983] W. E. PERRY, *A Structured Approach to Systems Testing,* Prentice-Hall, Englewood Cliffs, NJ, 1983.

[Rumbaugh et al., 1991] J. RUMBAUGH, M. BLAHA, W. PREMERLANI, F. EDDY, AND W. LORENSEN, *Object-Oriented Modeling and Design,* Prentice-Hall, Englewood Cliffs, NJ, 1991.

[Shepperd, 1990] M. SHEPPERD, "Design Metrics: An Empirical Analysis," *Software Engineering Journal* **5** (January 1990), pp. 3–10.

[Shlaer and Mellor, 1992] S. SHLAER AND S. MELLOR, *Object Lifecycles: Modeling the World in States,* Yourdon Press, Englewood Cliffs, NJ, 1992.

[Silberschatz and Galvin, 1994] A. SILBERSCHATZ AND P. B. GALVIN, *Operating System Concepts,* Fourth Edition, Addison-Wesley, Reading, MA, 1994.

[Stroustrup, 1991] B. STROUSTRUP, *The C++ Programming Language,* Second Edition, Addison-Wesley, Reading, MA, 1991.

[Walker, 1992] I. J. WALKER, "Requirements of an Object-Oriented Design Method," *Software Engineering Journal* **7** (March 1992), pp. 102–113.

[Ward and Mellor, 1985] P. T. WARD AND S. MELLOR, *Structured Development for Real-Time Systems, Volumes 1, 2 and 3,* Yourdon Press, New York, 1985.

[Warnier, 1976] J. D. WARNIER, *Logical Construction of Programs,* Van Nostrand Reinhold, New York, 1976.

[Warnier, 1981] J. D. WARNIER, *Logical Construction of Systems,* Van Nostrand Reinhold, New York, 1981.

[Wirfs-Brock, Wilkerson, and Wiener, 1990] R. WIRFS-BROCK, B. WILKERSON, AND L. WIENER, *Designing Object-Oriented Software*, Prentice-Hall, Englewood Cliffs, NJ, 1990.

[Yau and Tsai, 1986], S. S. YAU AND J. J.-P. TSAI, "A Survey of Software Design Techniques," *IEEE Transactions on Software Engineering* **SE-12** (June 1986), pp. 713–721.

[Yourdon and Constantine, 1979] E. YOURDON AND L. L. CONSTANTINE, *Structured Design: Fundamentals of a Discipline of Computer Program and Systems Design,* Prentice-Hall, Englewood Cliffs, NJ, 1979.

[Zage and Zage, 1993] W. M. ZAGE AND D. M. ZAGE, "Evaluating Design Metrics on Large-Scale Software," *IEEE Software* **10** (July 1993), pp. 75–81.

chapter

12

IMPLEMENTATION PHASE

Implementation is the process of translating the detailed design into code. When this is done by a single individual, the process is relatively well understood. But most real-life products today are too large to be implemented by one programmer within the given time constraints. Instead, the product is implemented by a team, all working at the same time on different components of the product. This is termed *programming-in-the-many*. Although the objective of the programmers is to implement the design, this goal can be marred by poor cooperation and communication between the members of the development team. Issues associated with programming-in-the-many are examined in this chapter.

12.1 CHOICE OF PROGRAMMING LANGUAGE

In most cases, the issue of which programming language to choose for the implementation simply does not arise. Suppose the client wants a product to be written in BASIC. It may be the case that, in the opinion of the development team, BASIC is entirely unsuitable for the product. Such an opinion is irrelevant to the client. Management of the development organization has only two choices: Implement the product in BASIC or turn down the job.

Similarly, if the product has to be implemented on a specific computer, and the only language available on that computer is assembler, then again there is no choice. If no other language is available, either because no compiler has yet been written for any high-level language on that computer or because management is not prepared to pay for a new Java compiler for the stipulated computer, then it is again clear that the issue of choice of programming language is not relevant.

A more interesting question is: A contract specifies that the product is to be implemented in "the most suitable" programming language. What language should be chosen? In order to answer this question, consider the following scenario. QQQ Corporation has been writing COBOL products for over 25 years. The entire 200-member software staff of QQQ from the most junior programmer to the vice-president

368

for software, have COBOL expertise. Why on earth should the most suitable programming language be anything but COBOL? The introduction of a new language, Java for example, would mean having to hire new programmers, or, at the very least, existing staff would have to be intensively retrained. Having invested all that money and effort in Java training, management might well decide that future products should also be written in Java. Nevertheless, all the existing COBOL products would still have to be maintained. There would then be two classes of programmers, COBOL maintenance programmers and Java programmers writing the new applications. Quite undeservedly, maintenance is almost always considered to be an inferior activity to developing new applications, so there would be distinct unhappiness among the ranks of the COBOL programmers. This unhappiness would be compounded by the fact that Java programmers are usually paid more than COBOL programmers because Java programmers are in short supply. Although QQQ has excellent development tools for COBOL, a Java compiler would have to be purchased, as well as appropriate Java CASE tools. Additional hardware may have to be purchased or leased to run this new software. Perhaps most serious of all, QQQ has accumulated hundreds of person-years of COBOL expertise, the kind of expertise that can be gained only through hands-on experience, such as what to do when a certain cryptic error message appears on the screen, or how to handle the quirks of the compiler. In brief, it would seem that "the most suitable" programming language could only be COBOL—any other choice would be financially suicidal, either from the viewpoint of the costs involved or as a consequence of plummeting staff morale to poor quality code.

And yet, the most suitable programming language for QQQ Corporation's latest project may indeed be some language other than COBOL. Notwithstanding its position as the world's most widely used programming language (see the Just in Case You Wanted to Know box on page 370), COBOL is suited for only one class of software products—essentially, data-processing applications. But if QQQ Corporation has software needs outside this class, then COBOL rapidly loses its attractiveness. For example, if QQQ wishes to construct a knowledge-based product using artificial intelligence (AI) techniques, then an AI language such as Lisp is a prerequisite; COBOL is totally unsuitable for AI applications. If large-scale communications software is to be built, perhaps because QQQ requires satellite links to hundreds of branch offices all over the world, then a language such as Java would prove to be far more suitable than COBOL. If QQQ is to go into the business of writing systems software such as operating systems, compilers, and linkers, then COBOL is very definitely unsuitable. And if QQQ Corporation has decided to go into defense contracting, the U.S. Department of Defense directive mandating the use of Ada for embedded, real-time systems totally precludes the use of COBOL in this area (in the unlikely event of a misguided QQQ manager actually thinking that COBOL can be used for real-time embedded software).

The issue of which programming language to use can almost always be decided by cost-benefit analysis (Section 4.2). That is to say, management must compute a dollar cost of an implementation in COBOL as well as the dollar benefits, present and future, of using COBOL. This computation must be repeated for every language under consideration. The language with the largest expected gain, that is, the

JUST IN CASE YOU WANTED TO KNOW

Far more code has been written in COBOL than in all other programming languages put together. The major reason COBOL is the most widely used language stems from the fact that COBOL is a product of the U.S. Department of Defense (DoD). Developed under the direction of the late Rear-Admiral Grace Murray Hopper, COBOL was approved by DoD in 1960. Thereafter, DoD would not buy hardware for running data-processing applications unless that hardware had a COBOL compiler [Sammet, 1978]. DoD was, and still is, the world's largest purchaser of computer hardware, and in the 1960s a considerable proportion of DoD software was written for data-processing purposes. As a result, COBOL compilers were written as a matter of urgency for virtually every computer. This widespread availability of COBOL, at a time when the only alternative language was usually assembler, resulted in COBOL becoming the world's most popular programming language.

Languages such as C, C++, Java, and 4GLs are undoubtedly growing in popularity for new applications. Nevertheless, maintenance is still the major software activity, and this maintenance is being performed on existing COBOL software. In short, DoD put its stamp onto the world's software via its first major programming language, COBOL.

Another reason for the popularity of COBOL is that COBOL is frequently the best language for implementing a data-processing product. In particular, COBOL is generally the language of choice when money is involved. Financial books have to balance, so rounding errors cannot be allowed to creep in. Thus, all computations have to be performed using integer arithmetic. COBOL supports integer arithmetic on very large numbers (that is, billions of dollars). In addition, COBOL can also handle very small numbers, namely, fractions of a cent. Banking regulations require interest computations to be calculated to at least four decimal places of a cent, and COBOL can do this arithmetic with ease as well. Finally, COBOL probably has the best formatting, sorting, and report generation facilities of any third-generation language (Section 12.2). All these reasons have made COBOL an excellent choice for implementing a data-processing product.

As mentioned in Section 12.10.4, it is likely that the new COBOL Language Standard will be for an object-oriented language. This standard would further boost the popularity of COBOL.

difference between estimated benefits and estimated costs, is then the appropriate implementation language.

For example, QQQ Corporation management may decide that its COBOL expertise is worth $450,000, while the cost of trying to write a communications package in COBOL would be $400,000. Thus, the benefits of using COBOL exceed the cost by $50,000; the expected gain is therefore $50,000. On the other hand, the cost of training existing programmers in Java is estimated at $300,000, the lowering of morale among COBOL programmers appears to cost $75,000, but the benefits of writing the communications package in Java are estimated at $500,000. This latter figure is high because management realizes that, as a consequence of the wide availability of Java compilers, the resulting portable code can be run on any number of different computers within the communications network. Thus management estimates that the benefits of using Java will exceed the costs by $125,000. The expected gain is therefore $125,000. Thus Java is more attractive than COBOL for the project; the value $125,000 minus $50,000, or $75,000, can be attached to its attractiveness over COBOL. The reader who is gripped by a sense of growing amazement as to the source of the dollar amounts in this paragraph—for instance, how on earth can management claim that the cost of lowering morale among COBOL programmers is $75,000—should read the explanation of cost–benefit analysis in Section 4.2.

Another way of deciding which programming language to select is to use risk analysis. For each language under consideration a list is made of the potential risks and ways of resolving them. The language for which the overall risk is the smallest is then selected.

Currently, there is pressure on software organizations to develop new software in an object-oriented language—any object-oriented language! The question that arises is: Which is the appropriate object-oriented language? Ten years ago, there was really only one choice, namely Smalltalk. Today, however, the majority of object-oriented software is being written in C++. There are a number of reasons for this. One is the widespread availability of C++ compilers. In fact, most C++ compilers simply translate the source code from C++ into C and then invoke the C compiler. Thus, any computer with a C compiler can essentially handle C++.

But the real explanation for the popularity of C++ is its apparent similarity to C. This is unfortunate in that a number of managers view C++ simply as a superset of C and, therefore, conclude that any programmer who knows C can quickly pick up the additional pieces. It is indeed true that, from just a syntactical viewpoint, C++ is essentially a superset of C. After all, virtually any C program can be compiled using a C++ compiler. Conceptually, however, C++ is totally different from C. C is a product of the structured paradigm, whereas C++ is for the object-oriented paradigm. Using C++ makes sense only if object-oriented techniques have been used and if the product is organized around objects and classes, not modules.

Thus, before an organization adopts C++, it is essential that the relevant software professionals be trained in the object-oriented paradigm. It is particularly important that the information of Chapter 6 be taught. Unless it is clear to all involved, and particularly to management, that the object-oriented paradigm is a different way of developing software and what the precise differences are, then all that will happen is that the structured paradigm will continue to be used, but with the code written in C++ rather than C. When organizations are disappointed with the results of switching from C to C++, a major contributory factor is a lack of education in the object-oriented paradigm.

Now suppose that an organization decides to adopt Java. In that case it is not possible to move gradually from the structured paradigm to the object-oriented paradigm. Java is a pure object-oriented programming language; it does not support the functions and procedures of the structured paradigm. Unlike a hybrid object-oriented language such as C++, Java programmers have to use the object-oriented paradigm (and only the object-oriented paradigm) from the very beginning. Because of the necessity of an abrupt transition from the one paradigm to the other, education and training is even more important when adopting Java (or another pure object-oriented language such as Smalltalk) than if the organization were to switch to a hybrid object-oriented language like C++ or OO-COBOL.

What about implementation in a non-procedural fourth-generation language? This issue is addressed in the next section.

JUST IN CASE YOU WANTED TO KNOW

Some years ago I hailed a cab outside Grand Central Station in New York City and said to the driver, "Please take me to Lincoln Center." This was a *non-procedural* request because I expressed the desired result, but I left it to the driver to decide how to achieve that result. It turned out that the driver was an immigrant from Central Europe who had been in America less than two days and knew virtually nothing about the geography of New York City or the English language. As a result, I quickly replaced my non-procedural request by a *procedural* request of the form, "Straight, straight. Take a right at the next light. I said right. Right, here, yes, right! Now straight. Slow down, please. I said slow down. For heaven's sake, slow down!" and so on, until we finally reached Lincoln Center.

12.2 FOURTH GENERATION LANGUAGES

The first computers had neither interpreters nor compilers. They were programmed in binary, either hard-wired with plug boards or by setting switches. Such a binary machine code was a *first-generation language*. The *second-generation languages* were assemblers, developed in the late 1940s and early 1950s. Instead of having to program in binary, instructions could be expressed in symbolic notation such as

```
mov     $17, next
```

In general, each assembler instruction is translated into one machine code instruction. Thus, although assembler was easier to write than machine code and easier for maintenance programmers to comprehend, the assembler source code was still the same length as the machine code.

The idea behind a *third-generation language* (or high-level language) such as FORTRAN, ALGOL 60, or COBOL is that one statement of a high-level language is compiled to as many as 5 or 10 machine code instructions (this is another example of abstraction; see Section 6.4.1). High-level language code is thus considerably shorter than the equivalent assembler code. It is also simpler to understand and, therefore, easier to maintain than assembler code. The fact that the high-level language code may not be quite as efficient as the equivalent assembler code is generally a small price to pay for ease in maintenance.

This concept was taken further in the late 1970s. A major objective in the design of a *fourth-generation language* (4GL) is that each 4GL statement should be equivalent to 30, or even 50, machine code instructions. Products written in a 4GL such as Focus or Natural would then be shorter, and hence quicker to develop, and easier to maintain.

It is difficult to program in machine code. It is somewhat easier to program in assembler, and easier still to use a high-level language. A second major design objective of a 4GL is ease in programming. In particular, many 4GLs are *non-procedural* (see the Just in Case You Wanted to Know box on this page for an insight

---

for every surveyor
if rating **is** excellent
add 6500 **to** salary

Figure 12.1 Nonprocedural fourth-generation language.

into this term). For example, consider the command shown in Figure 12.1. It is up to the compiler of the 4GL to translate this nonprocedural instruction into a sequence of machine code instructions that can be executed procedurally.

There is a price to pay for the ease of use gained through nonprocedurality. The compiler or interpreter of a 4GL is generally large and slow, and it must be as fault-free as possible. Many 4GLs are more suited to management information systems than to data-processing applications. In a management information system, the objective is to extract information and present it to the manager in the desired format. However, in data processing, large volumes of data have to be handled and extensive computations performed, and many 4GLs are simply too slow for this purpose. This is one example of trade-offs in the design of a 4GL, the ease of use of a nonprocedural language as opposed to the computing power of a procedural language.

It is too soon to know all the answers regarding the benefits of 4GLs. Some organizations that previously have used COBOL have reported a 10-fold increase in productivity through use of a 4GL. Other organizations have tried a 4GL and have been bitterly disappointed with the results. The reason for this inconsistency is that no one 4GL is appropriate for all situations. On the contrary, it is important to select the correct 4GL for the specific product. For example, Playtex used IBM's Application Development Facility (ADF) and reported an 80 to 1 productivity increase over COBOL. Notwithstanding this impressive result, Playtex has subsequently used COBOL for products that were deemed by management to be less well suited to ADF [Martin, 1985].

The attitudes of 43 organizations to 4GLs is reported in [Guimaraes, 1985]. It was found that use of a 4GL reduced user frustration because the data-processing department was able to respond more quickly when a user needed information to be extracted from the organization's database. However, there were also a number of problems. 4GLs proved, on average, to be slow and inefficient, with long response times. One product consumed 60 percent of the CPU cycles on an IBM 4331, while supporting at most 12 concurrent users. Overall, the 28 organizations that had been using a 4GL for over 3 years felt that the benefits outweighed the costs.

No one 4GL dominates the software market. Instead, there are literally hundreds of 4GLs; dozens of them, including Focus, Informix, Nomad, PowerHouse, RAMIS-II, SQL, and Natural, have sizable user groups. This widespread proliferation of 4GLs is further evidence that care has to be taken in selecting the correct 4GL. Of course, few organizations can afford to support more than one 4GL. Once a 4GL has been chosen and used, the organization must either use that 4GL for subsequent products or fall back on the language that was used before the 4GL was introduced.

Notwithstanding the potential productivity gain, there is also the potential danger of using a 4GL the wrong way. In many organizations there is currently a large backlog of products to be developed and a long list of maintenance tasks to be performed. A design objective of many 4GLs is *end-user programming*, that is to say, programming by the person who will use the product. For example, before the advent of 4GLs the investment manager of an insurance company would ask the data-processing manager for a product that would display certain information regarding the bond portfolio. The investment manager would then wait a year or so for the data-processing group to find the time to develop the product. It was intended that a 4GL would be so simple to use that the investment manager, previously untrained in programming, would be able to write the desired product. End-user programming was intended to help reduce the development backlog, leaving the professionals to maintain existing products.

In practice, end-user programming can be dangerous. First, consider the situation when all product development is performed by computer professionals. Computer professionals are trained to mistrust computer output. After all, probably less than 1 percent of all output during product development is correct. On the other hand, the user is told to trust all computer output, because a product should not be delivered to the user until it is fault free. Now consider the situation when end-user programming is encouraged. When a user who is inexperienced in programming writes code with a user-friendly, nonprocedural 4GL, the natural tendency is for that user to believe the output. After all, for years the user has been instructed to trust computer output. As a result, many business decisions have been based on data generated by hopelessly incorrect end-user code. In some cases the user-friendliness of certain 4GLs has led to financial catastrophes.

Another source of problems is 4GL compiler faults; end users are rarely trained to check that a correct product does not give wrong answers because of a compiler fault. Yet another danger lies in the fact that in some organizations, end users have been allowed to write 4GL products that update the organization's database. A fault in such a product may eventually result in the corruption of the entire database. The lesson is clear: Programming by inexperienced or inadequately trained end users can be exceedingly dangerous, if not fatal, to the financial health of a corporation.

The ultimate choice of a 4GL will be made by management. In making such a decision, management should be guided by the many success stories resulting from the use of a 4GL. At the same time, management should also carefully analyze the failures caused by using an inappropriate 4GL or by poor management of the development process. For example, a common cause of failure is neglecting to train the development team thoroughly in all aspects of the 4GL, including relational database theory [Date, 1990] where appropriate. Management should study both the successes and failures in the specific application area and learn from past mistakes. Choosing the correct 4GL can make the difference between a major success and dismal failure.

Having decided on the implementation language, the next issue is how software engineering principles can lead to better quality code.

12.3 Structured Programming

Structured programming has been credited with everything from preventing tooth decay to curing athlete's foot. When structured programming was first put forward, it was seen as the panacea for all ills. Although structured programming has not fulfilled every aspect of its early promise, it has certainly led to improved code quality.

What is structured programming? Is it merely programming without **goto** statements, or is there something more? To help answer these questions, a historical perspective on structured programming must first be given.

12.3.1 History of Structured Programming

The development of structured programming took place between 1966 and 1974. Three major events can be highlighted during this period:

1. The mathematical theory of 1966
2. Dijkstra's 1968 letter
3. Knuth's landmark article of 1974

Mathematical Theory   In 1966, Böhm and Jacopini published an article that essentially showed that any software product that can be represented by a flowchart can be rewritten using only three types of control structures, namely sequence, selection, and iteration [Böhm and Jacopini, 1966]. These three control structures are depicted in Figure 12.2.

The reaction of the computer science community to this result was—so what? The fact that a product could be put together using only f **followed by** g (sequence), **if** p **then** f **else** g (selection), and **while** p **do** f (iteration) was of interest to hardly anybody at the time. In 1966 the popular and important languages were COBOL II, FORTRAN IV, and assembler, and in all three of those languages the **goto** statement was the major control structure. The fact that, in principle, it was *possible* to program without the **goto** was just not relevant. Why on earth would anyone want to?

Dijkstra's Letter   In 1968, Dijkstra published a letter in the *Communications of the ACM* entitled "**goto** Statement Considered Harmful" [Dijkstra, 1968a]. The letter caused a major furor. Many disagreed that the **goto** is harmful in any way; letters of this type still appear from time to time. Others said—so what? Even if the **goto** should in fact be avoided, nothing could be done about it. In the popular languages of 1968, it was impossible to program without the **goto**. After all, there is no alternative to using the **goto** in assembler. Because structured programming had not yet been invented, structured FORTRAN and structured COBOL had not yet been developed; there was thus no alternative to the **goto** statement in either of those languages as well. And because few people had read Böhm and Jacopini's article, and fewer still had appreciated its full significance,

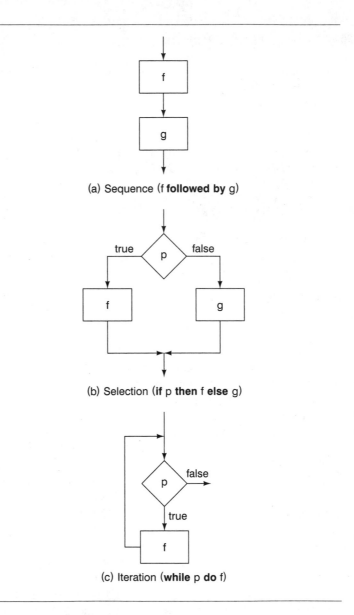

(a) Sequence (f **followed by** g)

(b) Selection (**if** p **then** f **else** g)

(c) Iteration (**while** p **do** f)

Figure 12.2 The three control structures of structured programming.

there was a third school of thought that averred that it was impossible to program without the **goto** statement.

Knuth's Article The arguments raged back and forth. It is surprising that no duels were fought over the issue, such were the passions that structured programming evoked. Finally, in 1974, Knuth published a 40-page article entitled "Struc-

```
print-paragraph.
    move 15 to switch-1.
    . . .
    . . .
dangerous-entry.
    . . .
    . . .
end-print-paragraph.
```

Figure 12.3 COBOL print paragraph with initialization condition that can be bypassed by a **goto** statement.

tured Programming with **go to** Statements" [Knuth, 1974]. The title appears to be a contradiction in terms. But the point of the article is that structured programming is *not* **goto**-less programming. Instead, it is a way of making products more readable. In some cases, a module that contains a **goto** is easier to understand than its **goto**-less counterpart.

This article ended the major controversy, but the embers are still glowing and flare up occasionally. Nevertheless, the overwhelming preponderance of the software world is united in the view that **goto** statements are almost always harmful and should be avoided.

12.3.2 W<small>HY THE</small> **goto** S<small>TATEMENT</small> I<small>S</small> C<small>ONSIDERED</small> H<small>ARMFUL</small>

After placing structured programming in its historical perspective, the question still remains: Why is the **goto** considered harmful? There are three reasons. First, a **goto** can decrease readability, and hence, maintainability. Even worse is a conditional **goto** **(if—goto)**, because the flow of control depends on the values of the variables at execution time. Depending on whether or not the condition is satisfied, execution of the module can follow two very different paths, both of which must be considered.

Second, the presence of a **goto** can mar the validity of procedures. For example, consider the COBOL paragraph shown in Figure 12.3. The print-paragraph requires the variable switch-1 to be set to 15 before the rest of the paragraph is executed. Provided that the paragraph is invoked via a call such as **perform** print-paragraph **thru** end-print-paragraph, then all will be well. However, if the product contains **goto** dangerous-entry, then the initialization statement will be bypassed, possibly with dangerous results.

Third, a backward **goto** is nothing more or less than a loop statement, and readability is considerably enhanced by coding a loop using the appropriate language construct, rather than disguising it with a **goto**. From this viewpoint, a forward **goto** (that is, a jump to a point in the code ahead of the **goto** statement) can be less harmful than a backward **goto**, particularly in the context of error handling.

To see the connection with error handling, consider the following analogy. It is customary to enter and leave a room by the door, not the window. But if the room is on fire, etiquette is irrelevant. If the safest and quickest way to exit from a burning room is via the window, then the window should be used. In the same way, the use of a **goto** is generally deleterious to readability and hence to maintainability. But if an error condition arises, then the important thing is to exit from the current routine to an error-handling routine as quickly as possible before the database is corrupted or the stack can overflow. Under error conditions the primary duty is survival, and this can often be best achieved by means of a forward **goto**.

In the light of these observations, structured programming can now be defined.

Structured programming is the writing of code with **goto** statements kept to a minimum, preferably only when an error is detected, and always in the forward direction.

Contrast this definition with the classical definition.

A product is structured if the code blocks are connected by sequence, selection, and iteration only and every block has exactly one entry and one exit.

Sequence, selection, and iteration are shown in Figure 12.2.

This classical definition has been widened to include a fourth type of control statement, namely the **call**. But even with this addition, the definition is still too narrow. Structured programming is not **goto**-less programming, but rather the writing of readable code. In most instances readable code is indeed **goto**-less code. Nevertheless, the objective of readability sometimes requires the use of a **goto** statement.

Languages such as Ada support the **exception** statement. Suppose an error of some kind is detected, such as floating-point overflow or an attempt to read past an end of file. The appropriate **exception** statement causes control to be transferred to the corresponding exception handler, a piece of code which takes remedial action, and attempts to restart execution at the point at which the error was detected, if that is possible.

Java exception handling is supported by the **try . . . catch** statement. If an exception is raised within a **try** block, control is transferred to the **catch** block following that **try** block. More precisely, it is permitted to **throw** a number of different exceptions within a **try** block, and control is then transferred to the **catch** block that corresponds to that exception. In essence, the **throw** statement is a disguised **goto.** That is, the effect of the **throw** statement is to transfer control in the event of an error being detected, just as a forward **goto** does. However, the resulting code is far more readable, which is, after all, the aim of structured programming.

12.4 GOOD PROGRAMMING PRACTICE

Many recommendations on good coding style are language specific. For example, suggestions regarding use of COBOL 88-level entries or parentheses in Lisp, are of little interest to programmers implementing a product in Pascal. The reader who is actively involved in implementation is urged to read one of the many books, such as those by Henry Ledgard, on good programming practice for the specific language in which the product is being implemented. Some recommendations regarding language-independent good programming practice are now given.

Use of Consistent and Meaningful Variable Names   As stated in Chapter 1, on average two-thirds of a software budget is devoted to maintenance. This implies that the programmer developing a module is merely the first of many other programmers who will work on that module. It is counterproductive for a programmer to give names to variables that are meaningful to only that programmer; within the context of software engineering, the term *meaningful* means "meaningful from the viewpoint of future maintenance programmers."

This point is illustrated by events at a small software production organization in Johannesburg, South Africa, in the late 1970s. The organization consisted of two programming teams. Team A was made up of émigrés from Mozambique. They were of Portuguese extraction, and their native language was Portuguese. Their code was well written. Variable names were meaningful, but unfortunately only to a speaker of Portuguese. Team B comprised Israeli immigrants whose native language was Hebrew. Their code was equally well written, and the names they chose for their variables were equally meaningful—but only to a speaker of Hebrew. One fine day, team A resigned en masse, together with the team leader. Team B was totally unable to maintain any of the excellent code that team A had written, because they could not speak a word of Portuguese. The variable names, meaningful as they were to Portuguese speakers, were incomprehensible to the Israelis whose linguistic abilities were restricted to Hebrew and English. The owner of the software organization was unable to hire enough Portuguese-speaking programmers to replace team A, and the company soon went into bankruptcy, under the weight of numerous lawsuits from disgruntled customers whose code was now essentially unmaintainable. The situation could so easily have been avoided. The head of the company should have insisted from the start that all variable names be in English, the language understood by every South African computer professional. Variable names would then have been meaningful to any maintenance programmer.

In addition to the use of meaningful variable names, it is equally essential that variable names be consistent. For example, the following four variables are declared in a module: averageFreq, frequencyMaximum, minFr, and frqncyTotl. A maintenance programmer who is trying to understand the code has to know if freq, frequency, fr, and frqncy all refer to the same thing. If yes, then the identical word should be used, preferably frequency, although freq or frqncy are marginally acceptable; fr is not. But if one or more variable names refer to a different quantity, then a totally different name, such as rate, should be used. A second aspect of consistency is the ordering of the components of variable names. For example, if one variable is named frequencyMaximum, then the name minimumFrequency would be confusing; it should be frequencyMinimum. Thus, in order to make the code clear and unambiguous for future maintenance programmers, the four variables listed previously should be named frequencyAverage, frequencyMaximum, frequencyMinimum, and frequencyTotal, respectively. Alternatively, the frequency component can appear at the end of all four variable names, yielding the variable names averageFrequency, maximumFrequency, minimumFrequency, and totalFrequency. It clearly does not matter which of the two sets is chosen; what is important is that all the names be from the one set or from the other.

A number of different naming conventions have been put forward that are intended to make it easier to understand the code. The idea is that the name of a variable should incorporate type information. For example, chPtrTmp might denote a temporary variable (Tmp) of type pointer (Ptr) to a character (ch). The best known of such schemes are the Hungarian Naming Conventions [Klunder, 1988]. (If you want to know why they are called Hungarian, see the Just in Case You Wanted to Know box above.)

The Issue of Self-Documenting Code   When asked why their code contains no comments whatsoever, programmers often reply, "I write self-documenting code." The implication is that their variable names are so carefully chosen and their code so exquisitely crafted that there is no need for any comments. Self-documenting code does exist, but it is exceedingly rare. Instead, the usual scenario is that the programmer appreciates every nuance of the code at the time the module is written. It is conceivable that the programmer uses the same style for every module, and that in 5 years' time the code will still be crystal clear in every respect to the original programmer. Unfortunately, this is irrelevant. The important point is whether the module can be understood easily and unambiguously by all the other programmers who have to read the code, starting with the SQA group and including a number of different maintenance programmers. The problem becomes more acute in the light of the unfortunate practice of assigning maintenance tasks to inexperienced programmers and not supervising them closely. The undocumented code of the module may be only partially comprehensible to an experienced programmer. How much worse, then, is the situation when the maintenance programmer is inexperienced.

To see the sort of problems that can arise, consider the variable xCoordinateOfPositionOfRobotArm. Such a variable name is undoubtedly self-documenting in every sense of the word, but few programmers are prepared to use a 31-character variable name, especially if that name is used frequently. Instead, a shorter name is used, xCoord, for example. The reasoning behind this is that if the entire module deals with the movement of the arm of a robot, xCoord can refer only to the x-coordinate of the position of the arm of the robot. Although that argument holds within the context of the development process, it is not necessarily true for maintenance. The maintenance programmer may not have sufficient knowledge of the product as a whole to realize that, within this module, xCoord refers to the arm of the robot, or may not have the necessary documentation to understand the workings of the module. The way to avoid this sort of problem is to insist that every variable name be explained at the beginning of the module, in the *prologue comments*. If this rule is followed, the maintenance programmer will quickly understand that the variable xCoord is used for the x-coordinate of the position of the robot arm.

Prologue comments are mandatory in every single module. The minimum information that must be provided at the top of every module is: module name; a brief description of what the module does; programmer's name; date module was coded; date module was approved, and by whom; module arguments; list of variable names, preferably in alphabetical order, and their uses; names of files accessed by this module, if any; names of files changed by this module, if any; module input/output, if any; error-handling capabilities; name of file containing test data, to be used later for regression testing; list of modifications made, their dates, and who approved them; and known faults, if any.

Even if a module is clearly written, it is unreasonable to expect someone to have to read every line in order to understand what the module does and how it does it. Prologue comments make it easy for others to understand the key points. Only a member of the SQA group or a maintenance programmer who is modifying a specific module should be expected to have to read every line of that module.

In addition to prologue comments, inline comments should be inserted into the code to assist maintenance programmers in understanding that code. It has been suggested that inline comments should be used only when the code is written in a nonobvious way or makes use of some subtle aspect of the language. On the contrary, confusing code should be rewritten in a clearer way. Inline comments are a means of helping maintenance programmers and should not be used to promote or excuse poor programming practice.

Use of Parameters   There are very few genuine constants, that is, variables whose values will *never* change. For instance, satellite photographs have caused changes to be made in submarine navigation systems incorporating the latitude and longitude of Pearl Harbor, Hawaii, in order to reflect more accurate geographic data regarding the exact location of Pearl Harbor. To take another example, sales tax is not a genuine constant; legislators tend to change the sales tax rate from time to time. Suppose that the sales tax rate is currently 6.0 percent. If the value 6.0 has been hard coded in a number of modules of a product, then changing the product is a major exercise, with the likely outcome of one or two instances of the "constant" 6.0 being overlooked and perhaps changing an unrelated 6.0 by mistake. A better solution is a declaration such as

public static final float salesTaxRate = **(float)** 6.0;

Then, wherever the value of the sales tax rate is needed, the constant salesTaxRate should be used and not the number 6.0. If the sales tax rate changes, then only the line containing the value of salesTaxRate need be altered using an editor. Better still, the value of the sales tax rate should be read in from a parameter file at the beginning of the run. All such apparent constants should be treated as parameters. If a value should change for any reason, this change can then be implemented quickly and effectively.

Code Layout for Increased Readability   It is relatively simple to make a module easy to read. For example, no more than one statement should appear on a line, even though many programming languages permit more than one. Indentation is perhaps the most important technique for increasing readability. Just imagine how difficult it would be to read the code examples in Chapter 6 if indentation had not been used to assist in understanding the code. In Java, indentation can be used to connect corresponding { . . . } pairs. It also shows which statements belong in a given block. In fact, correct indentation is too important to be left to human beings. Instead, as described in Section 4.4, CASE tools should be used to ensure that indentation is done correctly.

Another useful aid is blank lines. Methods should be separated by blank lines; in nontrivial compilation units, it is often helpful to break up large blocks of code with blank lines. The extra "white space" makes the code easier to read and, hence, comprehend.

Nested if Statements   Consider the following example. A map consists of two squares, as shown in Figure 12.4. It is required to write code to determine whether a point on the earth's surface lies in map square 1 or map square 2, or is not on the map at all. The solution of Figure 12.5 is so badly formatted that it is incomprehensible. A properly formatted version appears in Figure 12.6. Notwithstanding this, the combination of **if-if** and **if-else-if** constructs is so complex that it is difficult to check whether the code fragment is correct. This is fixed in Figure 12.7.

When faced with complex code containing the **if-if** construct, one way to simplify it is to make use of the fact that the **if-if** combination

$$\textbf{if} <condition\ 1>$$

$$\textbf{if} <condition\ 2>$$

is equivalent to the single condition

$$\textbf{if} <condition\ 1> \textbf{ and } <condition\ 2>$$

provided that <condition 2> is defined even if <condition 1> does not hold. For example, <condition 1> might check that a pointer is not null and, if so, then <condition 2> can use that pointer. (This problem does not arise in Java or C++. The **&&** operator is defined such that if <condition 1> is false, then <condition 2> is not evaluated.)

Another problem with the **if-if** construct is that nesting **if** statements too deeply leads to code that can be difficult to read. As a rule of thumb, **if** statements nested to a depth greater than three is poor programming practice and should be avoided.

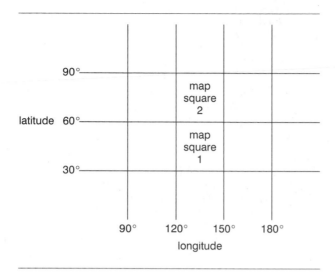

Figure 12.4 Coordinates for map.

---

if (latitude > 30 && longitude > 120) {**if** (latitude <= 60 && longitude <= 150)
mapSquareNo = 1; **else if** (latitude <= 90 && longitude <= 150) mapSquareNo
= 2 **else** System.out.println ("Not on the map");} **else** System.out.println ("Not on the map");

Figure 12.5 Badly formatted nested **if** statements.

12.5 CODING STANDARDS

Coding standards can be both a blessing and a curse. It was pointed out in Section 6.2.1 that modules with coincidental cohesion generally arise as a consequence of rules such as: Every module will consist of between 35 and 50 executable statements. Instead of stating a rule in such a dogmatic fashion, a better formulation is: Programmers should consult their managers before constructing a module with fewer than 35 or more than 50 executable statements. The point is that no coding standard can ever be applicable under all possible circumstances.

Coding standards imposed from above tend to be ignored. As mentioned previously, a useful rule of thumb is that **if** statements should not be nested to a depth greater than three. If programmers are shown examples of unreadable code resulting from nesting **if** statements too deeply, then it is likely that they will conform to such a regulation. But they are unlikely to adhere to a list of coding rules imposed on them without discussion or explanation. Furthermore, such standards are likely to lead to friction between programmers and their managers.

In addition, unless a coding standard can be checked by machine, it is either going to waste a lot of the SQA group's time, or it will simply be ignored by the programmers and SQA group alike. On the other hand, consider the following rules:

```
                    if (latitude > 30 && longitude > 120)
                    {
                      if (latitude <= 60 && longitude <= 150)
                         mapSquareNo = 1;
                      else if (latitude <= 90 && longitude <= 150)
                           mapSquareNo = 2;
                        else
                           System.out.println ("Not on the map");
                    }
                    else
                       System.out.println ("Not on the map");
```

Figure 12.6 Well formatted, but badly constructed, nested **if** statements.

```
if (longitude>120 && longitude <= 150 && latitude > 30 && latitude <= 60)
    mapSquareNo = 1;
else if (longitude>120 && longitude <= 150 && latitude > 60 && latitude <= 90)
    mapSquareNo = 2;
  else
    System.out.println ("Not on the map");
```

Figure 12.7 Acceptably nested **if** statements.

- Nesting of **if** statements should not exceed a depth of three, except with prior approval from the team leader.

- Modules should consist of between 35 and 50 statements, except with prior approval from the team leader.

- The use of **goto** statements should be avoided. However, with prior approval from the team leader, a forward **goto** may be used for error handling.

Such rules may be checked by machine, provided that some mechanism is set up for capturing the data relating to permission to deviate from the standard.

Some organizations have strict standards regarding names of modules and variables. One COBOL software organization has laid down highly restrictive coding standards. For example, if a subprogram is named sub-23, then its sections are numbered a01-sub-23 through a99-sub-23 and paragraphs within section a34-sub-23 are named b01-a34-sub-23 through b99-a34-sub-23. There are special naming conventions for error-handling paragraphs, paragraphs that perform input, paragraphs that perform output, and the exit-program paragraph. In addition, there are even more complex rules for naming variables. Such artificial names are meaningful only to someone who has been forced to learn the standard.

The aim of coding standards is to make maintenance easier. However, if the effect of a standard is to make the life of software developers difficult, then such a standard should be modified, even in the middle of a project. Overly restrictive coding standards are counterproductive in that the quality of software production must inevitably suffer if programmers have to develop software within such a framework. On the other hand, standards such as those listed previously regarding **goto** statements, nesting of **if** statements, and module size, coupled with a mechanism for deviating from those standards, can lead to improved software quality, which is, after all, a major goal of software engineering.

12.6 TEAM ORGANIZATION

Most products are too large to be completed by a single software professional within the given time constraints. As a result, the product must be assigned to a group of professionals organized as a team. For example, consider the specification phase. In order to specify the target product within two months, it may be necessary to assign the task to three specification specialists organized as a team under the direction of the specification manager. Similarly, the design task may be shared between members of the design team.

Suppose now that a product has to be coded within 3 months, even though there is 1 person-year of coding involved (a person-year is the amount of work that can be done by one person in 1 year). The solution is apparently simple: If one programmer can code the product in 1 year, four programmers can do it in 3 months.

This, of course, is nonsense. In practice, the four programmers may take nearly a year, and the quality of the resulting product may well be lower than if one programmer had coded the entire product. The reason is that some tasks can be shared; others must be done individually. For instance, if one farm hand can pick a strawberry field in 10 days, the same strawberry field can be picked by 10 farm hands in 1 day. On the other hand, one champion swimmer can cross the English Channel in 8 hours, but this feat cannot possibly be accomplished in 1 hour by eight champion swimmers!

In other words, tasks like strawberry picking can be fully shared; others, like swimming across the English Channel, cannot be shared. Unlike crossing the Channel, it is possible to share implementation tasks between members of a team by distributing the coding among the team members. However, team programming is also unlike strawberry picking in that team members have to interact with one another in a meaningful and effective way. For example, suppose Jane and Ned have to code two modules, mA and mB. A number of things can go wrong. For instance, both Jane and Ned may code mA and ignore mB. Or Jane may code mA, and Ned may code mB. But when mA calls mB it passes four arguments; Ned has coded mB in such a way that it requires five arguments. Or the order of the arguments in mA and mB may be different. Or the order may be the same, but the data types may be slightly different. Such problems are usually caused by a decision made during the

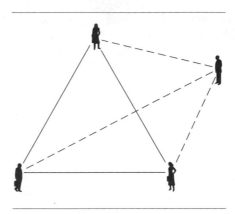

Figure 12.8 Communication paths between three computer professionals (solid lines), and when a fourth professional joins them (dashed lines).

design phase that is not propagated throughout the development organization. The issue has nothing whatsoever to do with the technical competency of the programmers. Team organization is a managerial issue; management must organize the programming teams so that each team is highly productive.

A different type of difficulty that arises from team development of software is shown in Figure 12.8. There are three channels of communication between the three computer professionals working on the project. Now suppose that the work is slipping, a deadline is rapidly approaching, but the task is not nearly complete. The obvious thing to do is to add a fourth professional to the team. But the first thing that must happen when the fourth professional joins the team is for the other three to explain in detail what has been accomplished to date, and what is still incomplete. In other words, adding personnel to a late software project makes it even later. This principle is now known as "Brooks's Law" after Fred Brooks who observed it while managing the development of OS/360 [Brooks, 1975].

In a large organization, teams are used in every phase of software production, but especially the implementation phase during which programmers work independently on separate modules. Accordingly, the implementation phase is a prime candidate for sharing the task among several computer professionals. In some smaller organizations, one individual may be responsible for the requirements, specifications, planning, and design, while the implementation is done by a team of two or three programmers. Because teams are most heavily used during the implementation phase, the problems of team organization are most acutely felt during implementation. In this book, team organization is therefore presented within the context of implementation, even though the problems and their solution are also applicable to all the other phases.

There are two extreme approaches to programming-team organization, namely democratic teams and chief programmer teams. The approach taken in this chapter is to describe each of the two approaches, highlight their strengths and weaknesses, and then suggest other ways of organizing a programming team that incorporate the best features of the two extremes.

12.7 DEMOCRATIC TEAM APPROACH

The democratic team organization was first described by Weinberg in 1971 [Weinberg, 1971]. The basic concept underlying the democratic team is *egoless programming*. Weinberg points out that programmers can be highly attached to their code. Sometimes they even name their modules after themselves; they therefore see their modules as an extension of themselves. The difficulty with this is that if a programmer sees a module as an extension of his or her ego, that programmer is certainly not going to try to find all the faults in "his" code or "her" code. And if there is a fault, it is termed a *bug,* like some insect that has crept unasked into the code and could have been prevented if only the code had been guarded more zealously against invasion. Some years ago, when software was still input on punched cards, that attitude was amusingly lampooned by the marketing of an aerosol spray named Shoo-Bug. The instructions on the label solemnly explained that spraying one's card deck with Shoo-Bug would ensure that no bugs could possibly infest the code.

Weinberg's solution to the problem of programmers being too closely attached to their own code is egoless programming. The social environment must be restructured and so must programmer values. Every programmer must encourage the other members of the team to find faults in his or her code. The presence of a fault must not be considered something bad, but rather a normal and accepted event; the attitude of the reviewer should be appreciation at being asked for advice, rather than ridicule of the programmer for making coding errors. The team as a whole will develop an ethos, a group identity, and modules will belong to the team as a whole rather than to any one individual.

A group of up to 10 egoless programmers constitutes a *democratic team.* Weinberg warns that management may have difficulty working with such a team. After all, consider the managerial career path. When a manager is promoted to a higher level, his or her fellow managers at the previous level are not promoted and must strive to attain the higher level at the next round of promotions. In contrast, a democratic team is a group working for a common cause with no single leader, with no programmers trying to get promoted to the next level. What is important is team identity and mutual respect.

Weinberg tells of a democratic team that developed an outstanding product. Management decided to give a cash award to the team's nominal manager (by definition, a democratic team has no leader). He refused to accept it personally, saying that it had to be shared equally among all members of the team. Management thought that he was angling for more money and that the team (and especially its nominal manager) had some rather unorthodox ideas. Management forced the nominal manager to accept the money, which he then divided equally among the team. Next, the entire team resigned and joined another company as a team.

The advantages and disadvantages of democratic teams are now presented.

12.7.1   ANALYSIS OF THE DEMOCRATIC TEAM APPROACH

A major advantage of the democratic team approach is the positive attitude toward the finding of faults. The more that are found, the happier are the members of a democratic team. This positive attitude leads to more rapid detection of faults, and hence to high-quality code. But there are some major problems. As pointed out previously, managers may have difficulty accepting egoless programming. In addition, a programmer with, say, 15 years of experience is likely to resent having his or her code appraised by fellow programmers, especially beginners.

Weinberg feels that egoless teams spring up spontaneously and cannot be imposed from outside. Little experimental research has been done on democratic programming teams, but the experience of Weinberg is that democratic teams are enormously productive. Mantei has analyzed the democratic team organization using arguments based on theories of and experiments on group organization in general, rather than specifically on programming teams [Mantei, 1981]. She points out that decentralized groups work best when the problem is difficult, and suggests that democratic teams should function well in a research environment. It has been the author's experience that a democratic team also works well in an industrial setting when there is a hard problem to solve. On a number of occasions he has been a member of democratic teams that have sprung up spontaneously among computer professionals with research experience. But once the task has been reduced to the implementation of a hard-won solution, the team must then be reorganized in a more hierarchical fashion, such as the chief programmer team approach described in the next section.

12.8   CLASSICAL CHIEF PROGRAMMER TEAM APPROACH

Consider the six-person team shown in Figure 12.9. There are 15 two-person communication channels. In fact, the total number of two-, three-, four-, five-, and six-person groups is 57. This multiplicity of communication channels is the major reason a six-person team structured as in Figure 12.9 is unlikely to be able to perform 36 person-months of work in 6 months; many hours are wasted in meetings involving two or more team members at a time.

Now consider the six-person team shown in Figure 12.10. Again there are six programmers, but now there are only five lines of communication. This is the basic concept behind what is now termed the *chief programmer* team. A related idea was put forward by Brooks, who drew the analogy of a chief surgeon directing an operation [Brooks, 1975]. The surgeon is assisted by other surgeons, the anesthesiologist, and a variety of nurses. In addition, when necessary the team makes use of experts in other areas such as cardiologists or nephrologists. This analogy highlights

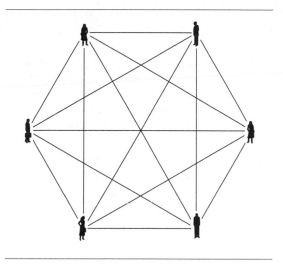

Figure 12.9 Communication paths between six computer professionals.

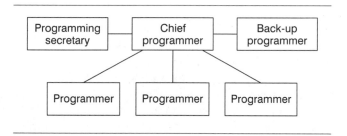

Figure 12.10 Structure of classical chief programmer team.

two key aspects of a chief programmer team. The first is *specialization*; each member of the team carries out only those tasks for which he or she has been trained. The second aspect is *hierarchy*. The chief surgeon directs the actions of all the other members of the team and is responsible for every aspect of the operation.

The chief programmer team concept was formalized by Mills [Baker, 1972]. A classical chief programmer team, as described by Baker, is shown in Figure 12.10. It consists of the chief programmer, who is assisted by the back-up programmer, the programming secretary, and from one to three programmers. When necessary, the team is assisted by specialists in other areas, such as job control language (JCL) or legal or financial matters. The *chief programmer* is both a successful manager and a highly skilled programmer who does the architectural design and any critical or complex sections of the code. The other team members work on the detailed design and the coding, under the direction of the chief programmer. As shown in Figure 12.10, there are no lines of communication between the programmers; all interfacing issues are handled by the chief programmer. Finally, the chief programmer reviews the work of the other team members, because the chief programmer is personally responsible for every line of code.

The position of *back-up programmer* is necessary only because the chief programmer is human and may therefore become ill, fall under a bus, or change jobs. Thus the back-up programmer must be as competent as the chief programmer in every respect and must know as much about the project as the chief programmer. In addition, in order to free the chief programmer to concentrate on the architectural design, the back-up programmer does black-box test case planning (Chapter 12.15) and other tasks that are independent of the design process.

The word *secretary* has a number of meanings. On the one hand, a secretary assists a busy executive by answering the telephone, typing correspondence, and so on. But when we talk about the American Secretary of State or the British Foreign Secretary, we are referring to one of the most senior members of the Cabinet. The *programming secretary* is not a part-time clerical assistant, but a highly skilled, well-paid, central member of a chief programmer team. The programming secretary is responsible for maintaining the project production library, the documentation of the project. This includes source code listings, JCL, and test data. The programmers hand their source code to the secretary who is responsible for the conversion to machine-readable form, compilation, linking, loading, execution, and running test cases. *Programmers* therefore do nothing but program. All other aspects of their work are handled by the programming secretary. (Because the programming secretary maintained the project production library, some organizations used the title "librarian.")

Recall that what is described here are Mills's and Baker's original ideas, dating back to 1971, when keypunches were still widely used. Coding is no longer done that way. Programmers now have their own terminals or workstations in which they enter their code, edit it, test it, and so on. A modern version of the classical chief programmer team is described in Section 12.9.

12.8.1 THE *NEW YORK TIMES* PROJECT

The chief programmer team concept was first used in 1971 by IBM to automate the clipping file ("morgue") of the *New York Times*. The clipping file contains abstracts and full articles from the *New York Times* and other publications. Reporters and other members of the editorial staff use this information bank as a reference source.

The facts of the project are astounding. For example, 83,000 lines of code (LOC) were written in 22 calendar months, an effort of 11 person-years. After the first year, only the file maintenance system consisting of 12,000 LOC had been written. Most of the code was written in the last 6 months. Only 21 faults were detected in the first 5 weeks of acceptance testing; only 25 further faults were detected in the first year of operation. Principal programmers averaged one detected fault and 10,000 LOC per person-year. The file maintenance system, delivered 1 week after coding was completed, operated 20 months before a single fault was detected. Almost half the subprograms, usually 200 to 400 lines of PL/I, were correct on the first compilation [Baker 1972].

Nevertheless, after this fantastic success, no comparable claims for the chief programmer team concept have been made. Yes, many successful projects have been carried out using chief programmer teams, but the figures reported, although satisfactory, are not as impressive as those obtained for the *New York Times* project. Why was the *New York Times* project such a success, and why have similar results not been obtained on other projects?

One possible explanation is that this was a prestige project for IBM. It was the first real trial for PL/I, a language developed by IBM. An organization known for its superb software experts, IBM set up a team comprising what can only be described as their crème de la crème from one division. Second, technical back-up was extremely strong. PL/I compiler writers were on hand to assist the programmers in every way they could and JCL experts assisted with the job control language. A third possible explanation was the expertise of the chief programmer, F. Terry Baker. He is what is now called a *superprogrammer,* a programmer whose output is four or five times that of an average good programmer. In addition, Baker is a superb manager and leader, and it could be that his skills, enthusiasm, and personality were the reasons underlying the success of the project.

If the chief programmer is competent, then the chief programmer team organization works well. Although the remarkable success of the *New York Times* project has not been repeated, many successful projects have employed variants of the chief programmer team approach. The reason for the phrase *variants of the approach* is that the classical chief programmer team, as described by Baker, is impractical in many ways.

12.8.2 IMPRACTICALITY OF THE CLASSICAL CHIEF PROGRAMMER TEAM APPROACH

Consider the chief programmer, a combination of a highly skilled programmer and successful manager. Such individuals are difficult to find; there is a shortage of highly skilled programmers, as well as a shortage of successful managers, and the job description of a chief programmer requires both abilities. It has also been suggested that the qualities needed to be a highly skilled programmer are different from those needed to be a successful manager; therefore, the chances of finding a chief programmer are small.

But if chief programmers are hard to find, back-up programmers are as rare as hen's teeth. After all, the back-up programmer is expected to be as good as the chief programmer, but has to take a back seat and a lower salary while waiting for something to happen to the chief programmer. Few top programmers or top managers would accept this role.

A programming secretary is also difficult to find. Software professionals are notorious for their aversion to paperwork, but the programming secretary is expected to do nothing but paperwork all day.

Thus chief programmer teams, at least as proposed by Baker, are impractical to implement. Democratic teams were also shown to be impractical, but for different reasons. Furthermore, neither technique seems to be able to handle products which require 20 or even 120 programmers for the implementation phase. What is needed is a way of organizing programming teams that makes use of the strengths of democratic teams and chief programmer teams and that can be extended to the implementation of larger products.

12.9   BEYOND CHIEF PROGRAMMER AND DEMOCRATIC TEAMS

Democratic teams have a major strength, namely a positive attitude toward the finding of faults. A number of organizations use chief programmer teams in conjunction with code walkthroughs or inspections (Section 5.2), creating a potential pitfall. The chief programmer is personally responsible for every line of code and must, therefore, be present during all walkthroughs or inspections. However, a chief programmer is also a manager, and as it was pointed out in Chapter 5, neither walkthroughs nor inspections should be used for any sort of performance appraisal. Thus, because the chief programmer is also the manager responsible for the primary evaluation of the team members, it is strongly inadvisable for that individual to be present at either a walkthrough or an inspection.

The way out of this contradiction is to remove much of the managerial role from the chief programmer. After all, the difficulty of finding one individual who is both a highly skilled programmer and successful manager has been pointed out previously. Instead, the chief programmer should be replaced by two individuals: a *team leader* who is in charge of the technical aspects of the team's activities and a *team manager* who is responsible for all nontechnical managerial decisions. The structure of the resulting team is shown in Figure 12.11. It is important to realize that this organizational structure does not violate the fundamental managerial principle that no employee should report to more than one manager. The areas of responsibility are clearly delineated. The team leader is responsible for only technical management. Thus budgetary and legal issues are not handled by the team leader, nor are performance appraisals. On the other hand, the team leader has sole responsibility on technical issues. The team manager therefore has no right to promise, say, that the product will be delivered within four weeks; promises of that sort have to be made by the team leader. The team leader naturally participates in all walkthroughs and inspections; after all, he or she is personally responsible for every aspect of the code. At the same time, the team manager is not permitted at a walkthrough or inspection, because programmer performance appraisal is a function of the team manager. Instead, the team manager acquires knowledge of the technical skills of each programmer in the team during regularly scheduled team meetings.

Before implementation begins, it is important to demarcate clearly areas that appear to be the responsibility of both the team manager and the team leader. For

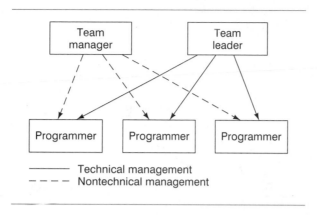

Figure 12.11 Structure of modern programming team.

example, consider the issue of annual leave. The situation can arise that the team manager approves a leave application because leave is a nontechnical issue, only to find the application vetoed by the team leader because a deadline is approaching. The solution to this and related issues is for higher management to draw up a policy regarding areas that both the team manager and the team leader consider to be their responsibility.

What about larger projects? This approach can be scaled up as shown in Figure 12.12, which shows the technical managerial organizational structure; the nontechnical side is similarly organized. Implementation of the product as a whole is under the direction of the project leader. The programmers report to their team leaders, and the team leaders report to the project leader. For even larger products, additional levels can be added to the hierarchy.

Another way of drawing on the best features of both democratic and chief programmer teams is to decentralize the decision-making process where appropriate. The resulting channels of communication are shown in Figure 12.13. This scheme is useful for the sorts of problems for which the democratic approach is good, that is to say, in a research environment or whenever there is a hard problem that requires the synergistic effect of group interaction for its solution. Notwithstanding the decentralization, the arrows from level to level still point downwards; allowing programmers to dictate to the project leader can lead only to chaos.

Unfortunately, there is no one solution to the problem of programming team organization and, by extension, to the problem of organizing teams for all the other phases. The optimal way of organizing a team depends on the product to be built, on previous experience with various team structures, and on the outlook of the heads of the organization. For example, if senior management is uncomfortable with decentralized decision making, then it will not be implemented. Unfortunately, not much research has been done on software development team organization, and many of the generally accepted principles are based on research on group dynamics in general, and not on software development teams. Until experimental results on team organization

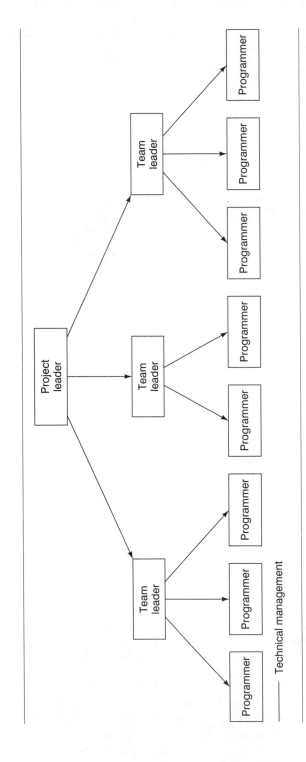

Figure 12.12 Technical managerial organizational structure for larger projects.

394

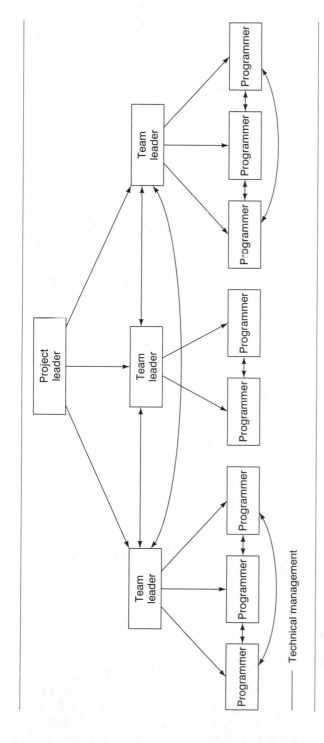

Figure 12.13 Decentralized decision-making version of team organization of Figure 12.12 showing communication channels of technical management.

―――― Technical management

have been obtained within the software industry, it will not be easy to determine the optimal team organization for a specific product.

12.10   PORTABILITY

The ever-rising cost of software makes it imperative that some means be found for containing costs. One way is to ensure that the product as a whole can easily be adapted to run on a variety of hardware/operating system combinations. Some of the costs of writing the product may then be recouped by selling versions that will run on other computers. Another reason for writing software that can easily be implemented on other computers is that the client organization may purchase new hardware, and all its software will then have to be converted to run on the new hardware. A product is considered to be *portable* if it is significantly less expensive to adapt the product to run on the new computer than to write a new product from scratch.

More precisely, portability may be defined as follows: Suppose a product P is compiled by compiler C and then runs on the *source* computer, namely hardware configuration H under operating system O. A product P' is needed that functionally is equivalent to P, but must be compiled by compiler C' and run on the *target* computer, namely, hardware configuration H' under operating system O'. If the cost of converting P into P' is significantly less than the cost of coding P' from scratch, then P is said to be *portable*.

For example, a numerical integration package has been implemented on a VAX 10000 running under the VAX/VMS operating system. It is written in FORTRAN and compiled by the VAX FORTRAN compiler. The package is to be ported to a SPARCstation 20 workstation running under the UNIX operating system. The compiler to be used will be the Sun FORTRAN compiler.

Offhand, this would seem to be a trivial task. After all, the package is written in a high-level language. But if the package contains any operating system calls, such as to determine the CPU time used so far, then these require conversion. In addition, VAX FORTRAN and Sun FORTRAN are not identical languages; there are some features that are supported by one and not the other. Overall, the problem of porting software is nontrivial, because of incompatibilities between different hardware configurations, operating systems, and compilers. Each of these aspects is now examined in turn.

12.10.1   HARDWARE INCOMPATIBILITIES

Suppose that product P currently running on hardware configuration H is to be installed on hardware configuration H'. If H and H' are both personal computers, the obvious thing to do is to use H to copy P onto a disk and then to insert the disk in the disk drive of H' and start computing. This step simply may not be physically possible, because disks come in different diameters, namely 5¼-inch floppy disks and 3½-inch diskettes. In addition, a disk drive equipped to read only single-sided disks cannot read a double-sided disk. The format of the disk is also critical; issues such as the density (number of bits per inch) also affect readability.

For larger computers, magnetic tape would seem to be the way to port products or data from one computer to another. But seven-track tape and nine-track tape are incompatible. Information (that is, products and data) can be written at a number of different tape densities including 800 bpi (bytes per inch), 1600 bpi, and 6250 bpi. These densities are incompatible. The issue of odd or even parity can be a further complication. Furthermore, newer technologies such as video and DAT tape are increasingly being used in place of magnetic tape.

Suppose now that the problem of physically copying the source code of product P to computer H' has been solved. There is no guarantee that H' can interpret the bit patterns created by H. A number of different character codes exist, the most popular of which are Extended Binary Coded Decimal Interchange Code (EBCDIC) and American Standard Code for Information Interchange (ASCII), the American version of the 7-bit ISO code [Mackenzie, 1980]. If H uses EBCDIC but H' uses ASCII, then H' will treat P as so much garbage.

Although the original reason for these differences is historical, namely that researchers working independently for different manufacturers developed different ways of doing the same thing, there are definite economic reasons for perpetuating them. To see this, consider the following imaginary situation. MCM Computer Manufacturers has sold thousands of its MCM-1 computer. MCM now wishes to design, manufacture, and market a new computer, the MCM-2, that will be more powerful in every way than the MCM-1, but will cost considerably less. Suppose further that the MCM-1 uses ASCII code, has 36-bit words consisting of four 9-bit bytes, uses seven-track tape at a density of 1600 bpi, and even parity. Now the chief computer architect of MCM decides that the MCM-2 should employ EBCDIC, have 16-bit words consisting of two 8-bit bytes, use nine-track tape at a density of 6250 bpi, and odd parity. The sales force will then have to tell current MCM-1 owners that the MCM-2 is going to cost them $35,000 less than any competitor's equivalent machine, but that it will cost them up to $200,000 to convert existing software and data from MCM-1 format to MCM-2 format. No matter how good the scientific reasons for redesigning the MCM-2, marketing considerations will ensure that the new computer will be compatible with the old one. A salesperson can then point out to an existing MCM-1 owner that not only is the MCM-2 computer $35,000 less expensive than any competitor's machine, but that any customer ill-advised enough to buy from a different manufacturer will be spending $35,000 too much and will also have to pay some $200,000 to convert existing software and data to the format of the non-MCM machine.

Moving from the preceding imaginary situation to the real world, the most successful line of computers to date has been the IBM System/360-370 series [Gifford and Spector, 1987]. The success of this line of computers is due largely to full compatibility between machines; a product that runs on an IBM System/360 Model 30 built in 1964 will run unchanged on an IBM 9021 Model 9X2 built in 1996. However, that same product that runs on the IBM System/360 Model 30 under OS/360 may require considerable modification before it can run on a more modern machine such as a VAX 10000 under VMS. Part of the difficulty may be due to hardware incompatibilities. But part may be caused by operating system incompatibilities.

12.10.2   OPERATING SYSTEM INCOMPATIBILITIES

The job control languages (JCL) of any two computers are usually vastly different. Some of the difference is syntactic—the command for executing an executable load image might be @xeq on one computer, //xqt on another, and .exc on a third. When porting a product to a different operating system, syntactic differences are relatively straightforward to handle by simply translating commands from the one JCL into the other. But other differences can be more serious. For example, some operating systems support virtual memory. Suppose that a certain operating system allows products to be up to 128 megabytes in size, but the actual area of main memory allocated to a particular product may be only 8 megabytes. What happens is that the user's product is partitioned into pages 256 kilobytes in size, and only 32 of these pages can be in main memory at any one time. The rest of the pages are stored on disk and swapped in and out as needed by the virtual memory operating system. As a result, products can be written without any effective constraints as to size. But if a product that has been successfully implemented under a virtual memory operating system is to be ported to an operating system with physical constraints on product size, the entire product may have to be rewritten and then linked using overlay techniques to ensure that the size limit is not exceeded.

12.10.3   NUMERICAL SOFTWARE INCOMPATIBILITIES

When a product is ported from one machine to another, or even compiled using a different compiler, the results of performing arithmetic may differ. On a 16-bit machine, that is, a computer with a word size of 16 bits, an integer will ordinarily be represented by one word (16 bits), and a double-precision integer by two adjacent words (32 bits). Unfortunately, some language implementations do not include double-precision integers. For example, standard Pascal does not include double-precision integers, and as a result, few Pascal implementations support that data type. Thus a product that functions perfectly on a compiler/hardware/operating system configuration in which Pascal integers are represented using 32 bits may fail to work correctly when ported to a computer in which integers are represented by only 16 bits. The obvious solution, namely, representing integers larger than 2^{16} by floating-point numbers (**type** real), does not work because integers are represented exactly whereas floating-point numbers are in general only approximated using a mantissa (fraction) and exponent.

   This problem can be solved in Ada, because in Ada it is possible to specify the range of an integer type and the precision (number of significant digits) of a floating-point type. The Ada–Europe Portability Working Group has produced a list of further recommendations for ensuring portability. These recommendations are specific to Ada and generally require a detailed understanding of the Ada 83 Reference Manual

JUST IN CASE YOU WANTED TO KNOW

In order to understand why Gosling designed Java, it is necessary to appreciate the source of the weaknesses that he perceived in C++. And to do that, we have to go back to C, the parent language of C++.

In 1972 the programming language C was developed by Dennis Ritchie at AT&T Bell Laboratories (now Lucent Technologies) for use in systems software. The language was designed to be extremely flexible. For example, it permits arithmetic on pointer variables, that is, on variables used to store memory addresses. From the viewpoint of the average programmer, this poses a distinct danger; the resulting programs can be extremely insecure because control can be passed to anywhere in the computer. Also, C does not embody arrays as such. Instead, a pointer to the address of the beginning of the array is used. As a result, the concept of an out-of-range array subscript is not intrinsic to C. This is a further source of possible insecurity.

These and other insecurities were not a problem at Bell Labs. After all, C was designed by an experienced software engineer for use by other experienced software engineers at Bell Labs. These professionals could be relied upon to use the powerful and flexible features of C in a secure way. A basic philosophy in the design of C was that the person using C would know exactly what he or she was doing. Programming catastrophes that have occurred when C is used by less competent or inexperienced programmers should not be blamed on AT&T; there was never any intent that C should be widely employed as a general-purpose programming language as it is today.

With the rise of the object-oriented paradigm, a number of object-oriented programming languages based on C were developed, including Object C, Objective-C, and C++. The idea behind these languages was to embed object-oriented constructs within C, by

then a popular programming language. It was argued that it would be easier for programmers to learn a language that was based on a familiar language than to learn a totally new syntax. However, only one of the many C-based object-oriented languages became widely accepted and that was C++, developed by Bjarne Stroustrup also of AT&T Bell Laboratories.

It has been suggested that the reason bnehind the success of C++ is the enormous financial clout of AT&T. However, if corporate size and financial strength were relevant features in promoting a programming language then today we would all be using PL/I, a language developed and strongly promoted by IBM. The reality is that PL/I, notwithstanding the prestige of IBM, has retreated into obscurity.

The real reason for the success of C++ is that it is a true superset of C. That is, unlike any of the other C-based object-oriented programming languages, virtually any C program is also valid C++. Thus, organizations realized that they could switch from C to C++ without changing any of their existing C software. They could advance from the structured paradigm to the object-oriented paradigm without disruption.

A remark that is frequently encountered in the Java literature is "Java is what C++ should have been." The implication is that, if only Stroustrup had been as smart as Gosling, C++ would have turned out to be Java. On the contrary, if C++ had not been a true superset of C, it would have gone the way of all other C-based object-oriented programming languages, that is, it would essentially have disappeared. It was only after C++ had taken hold as a popular language that Java was designed in reaction to perceived weaknesses in C++. Java is not a superset of C; for example, Java has no pointer variables. Thus, it would be more accurate to say that "Java is what C++ could not possibly have been."

[ANSI/MIL-STD-1815A, 1983]; the interested reader is referred to [Nissen and Wallis, 1984].

With regard to Java, each of the eight primitive data types has been carefully specified. For example, type **Int** is always implemented as a signed 32-bit two's complement integer, and type **float** always occupies 32 bits and satisfies IEEE Standard 754 for floating point numbers [ANSI/IEEE 754, 1985]. The problem of ensuring that a numerical computation will be correctly performed on every target hardware/operating system therefore cannot arise in Java. (For more insights into the design of Java, see the Just in Case You Wanted to Know box on page 399.)

However, where a numerical computation is performed in a language other than Ada or Java, it is important, but often difficult, to ensure that numerical computations will be correctly performed on the target hardware/operating system.

12.10.4 COMPILER INCOMPATIBILITIES

Portability is difficult to achieve if a product is implemented in a language for which few compilers exist. If the product has been implemented in a specialized language such as CLU [Liskov, Snyder, Atkinson, and Schaffert, 1977], it may be necessary to rewrite it in a different language if the target computer does not have a compiler for that language. On the other hand, if a product is implemented in a popular language such as COBOL, FORTRAN, Lisp, Pascal, C, or Java, the chances are good that a compiler or interpreter for that language can be found for a target computer.

Suppose that a product is written in a popular high-level language such as standard FORTRAN. In theory, there should be no problem in porting the product from one machine to another—after all, standard FORTRAN is standard FORTRAN. Regrettably, that is not the case; in practice, there is no such thing as standard FORTRAN. Even though there is an ANSI FORTRAN standard, colloquially known as FORTRAN 77 [ANSI X3.9, 1977], there is no reason for a compiler writer to adhere to it. For example, a decision may be taken to support additional features not usually found in FORTRAN so that the marketing division can then tout a "new, extended FORTRAN compiler." Conversely, a microcomputer compiler may not be a full FORTRAN implementation. Also, if there is a deadline to produce a compiler, management may decide to bring out a less-than-complete implementation, intending to support the full standard in a later revision. Suppose that the compiler on the source computer supports a superset of ANSI FORTRAN. Suppose further that the target compiler is an implementation of standard ANSI FORTRAN. When a product implemented on that source computer is ported to the target, any portions of the product that make use of nonstandard ANSI FORTRAN constructs from the superset have to be recoded. Thus, to ensure portability, programmers should use only standard FORTRAN language features.

There are several different Pascal standards. First came Jensen and Wirth's definition of the language [Jensen and Wirth, 1975]. Then there is the ANSI standard [ANSI/IEEE 770X3.97, 1983] and the ISO standard [ISO-7185, 1980]. Notwithstanding this plethora of standards, subsets and supersets of Pascal abound. For instance, all Pascal standards specify that procedure and function names may be passed as arguments. However, that feature is by no means universally supported by Pascal compilers. Conversely, many supersets of Pascal have been implemented. For example, some implementations of Pascal incorporate nonstandard bit manipulation operations such as bitwise **and** and **or**, perhaps to compete with C.

COBOL standards were developed by the Conference on Data Systems Languages (CODASYL), a committee of American computer manufacturers and government and private users. Unfortunately, COBOL standards do not promote portability. A COBOL standard has an official life of five years, but each successive standard is not necessarily a superset of its predecessor. It is equally worrisome that many features are left to the individual implementer, subsets may be termed *standard COBOL,* and there is no restriction on extending the language to form a superset [Wallis, 1982].

The X3J4.1 Object-Oriented COBOL Task Group has approved a technical report with the recommendation that it should be included in the next full COBOL Language Standard by ANSI Committee X3J4 in 1997. Thus, it is likely that COBOL will be an object-oriented language as of 1997.

ANSI has approved a standard for the programming language C [ANSI X3.159, 1989]. The standard was approved by ISO in 1990. Most C compilers adhere quite closely to the original language specification [Kernighan and Ritchie, 1978]. The reason for this is that almost all C compiler writers use the standard front end of the portable C compiler, *pcc* [Johnson, 1979], and as a result the language accepted by the vast majority of compilers is identical. C products are, in general, easily ported from one implementation to another. An aid to C portability is the *lint* processor that can be used to determine implementation-dependent features, as well as constructs that may lead to difficulties when the product is ported to a target computer. Unfortunately, *lint* checks only the syntax and the static semantics, and therefore is not foolproof. However, it can be of considerable help in reducing future problems. For example, in C it is legal to assign an integer value to a pointer and vice versa, but this is forbidden by *lint.* In some implementations, the size (number of bits) of an integer and a pointer will be the same, but the sizes may be different on other implementations; this sort of potential future portability problem can be flagged by *lint* and obviated by recoding the offending portions.

With regard to C++, at the time of writing, standardization committees are examining the language. A standard should therefore be expected soon.

The only truly successful language standard so far has been the Ada 83 standard, embodied in the Ada Reference Manual [ANSI/MIL-STD-1815A, 1983]. (For background information on Ada, see the Just in Case You Wanted to Know box on page 402.) Until the end of 1987, the name "Ada" was a registered trademark of the U.S. Government, Ada Joint Program Office (AJPO). As owner of the trademark, AJPO stipulated that the name Ada could legally be used only for language implementations that complied exactly with the standard; subsets and supersets were expressly forbidden. A mechanism was set up for validating Ada compilers, and only a compiler that successfully passed the validation process could be called an Ada compiler. Thus the trademark was used as a means of enforcing standards, and hence portability. It is likely that the Ada 95 standard [ISO/IEC 8652, 1995] will be equally successful.

Now that the name Ada is no longer a trademark, enforcement of the standard is being achieved via a different mechanism. There is little or no market for an Ada compiler that has not been validated. Thus there are strong economic forces encouraging Ada compiler developers to have their compilers validated and hence certified as conforming to the Ada standard. This has applied to compilers for both Ada 83 [ANSI/MIL-STD-1815A, 1983] and Ada 95 [ISO/IEC 8652, 1995].

A validation certificate is for a specific compiler running on specific hardware under a specific operating system; if an organization that has developed an Ada

JUST IN CASE YOU WANTED TO KNOW

During the early 1970s, the U.S. Department of Defense (DoD) became acutely aware of problems with its software. One of the more worrisome issues was that at least 450 different languages were being used in DoD products. A major implication of this proliferation was that maintenance, difficult enough under normal circumstances, was made all but impossible by the need to find competent maintenance programmers for this babel of languages. In addition, tools to support software development and maintenance were rudimentary, mainly because of the enormous cost of buying or building an adequate CASE toolkit for each of those languages.

The situation with regard to embedded software (the software in an embedded computer–see Section 5.4.4) was particularly bad. Each branch of the Armed Forces had its own favorite real-time language; the Army supported TACPOL, the Navy promoted CMS-2, while the choice of the Air Force was JOVIAL. In short, the situation regarding embedded software was bad and, bearing the maintenance implications in mind, could only get worse.

Embedded DoD software tends to be large, namely on the order of hundreds of thousands or millions of lines of code, to have a lifetime of 10 to 15 years, and to change frequently over that period as requirements change [Fisher, 1976]. In addition, embedded software is almost always subject to space constraints in that the size of the computer embedded within military hardware, such as a tank, a drone, or a helicopter, is generally restricted. Furthermore, the time constraints of real-time software are ever present. Finally, embedded software must be highly reliable. To put it bluntly, once a ballistic missile has been launched from a nuclear submarine, it is too late to make any changes to its software in the event of a failure of any sort being detected.

In 1975, DoD initiated a worldwide competition to find a common high-order language for all the armed services. Seventeen submissions were received from teams that included academics, industry profes-

sionals, and military experts in their ranks; four of those submissions were chosen for further development. To ensure that reviewers would not know the identities of the competing organizations, the language proposals were given the code names Blue, Green, Red, and Yellow. The overall winner was Green, a mainly European team led by Jean Ichbiah of Honeywell Bull, France. That is why the Ada Reference Manual [ANSI/MIL-STD-1815A, 1983] is bound with a green cover, as are issues of *Ada Letters,* a major Ada journal published by the Special Interest Group on Ada of the Association for Computing Machinery (ACM SIGAda).

But DoD was as unhappy with the name Green as it had been with the earlier name DoD-1. Jack Cooper of the U.S. Navy suggested the name Ada, after Ada, Countess of Lovelace, daughter of the poet Lord Byron. She had programmed Babbage's Analytic Engine, the first computer, in the first half of the nineteenth century. Although Babbage's design was correct, the Analytic Engine could not be constructed because of the limitations of nineteenth-century technology. The Deputy Secretary of Defense obtained permission from the Countess of Lovelace's heir, the Earl of Lytton, to use the name Ada [Carlson, Druffel, Fisher, and Whitaker, 1980]. That is why the name of the language is written Ada, and not ADA. It is not an acronym; it is named after Ada, Countess of Lovelace, the world's first programmer.

The language was approved by DoD in 1980 and assigned military standard MIL-STD-1815. The number 1815 is significant, being the year of birth of Ada Lovelace. In 1994 a revised version of Ada was approved by the International Organization for Standardization (ISO) and the International Electrotechnical Commission (IEC). Because the standard [ISO/IEC 8652, 1995] was published in 1995, the language is called Ada 95. A number of new features were added to the original version (Ada 83), especially object orientation.

compiler wishes to port the compiler to another hardware and/or operating system configuration, revalidation is necessary. The reference manual for every Ada compiler must incorporate an appendix, namely Appendix F, in which the implementation-dependent characteristics of that Ada implementation are described. For example, it is possible to suppress type conversion and to treat an argument simply as a bit pattern; an implementation may impose restrictions on the size of such an item. Technically, then, Ada products can be made fully portable, except with regard to features mentioned in Appendix F.

In order for Java to be a totally portable language, it is essential for the language to be standardized and to ensure that the standard is strictly obeyed. Sun Microsystems, like the Ada Joint Projects Office, is using the legal system to achieve standardization. As mentioned in the Just in Case You Wanted to Know Box on page 25, Sun chose a name for their new language that could be copyrighted. It seems likely that Sun will enforce their copyright and bring legal action against alleged violators. After all, portability is one of the most powerful features of Java. If multiple versions of Java are permitted, then the portability of Java will suffer; Java can be truly portable only if every Java program is handled identically by every Java compiler.

At the time of writing, Version 1.0 of Java has been released. In due course, a revised version of the language will be released in response to comments and criticisms of the first version. This process of stepwise refinement of Java will then continue. When the language eventually stabilizes, it is likely that a standards organization such as the American National Standards Institute (ANSI) or the International Standards Organization (ISO) will publish a draft standard and elicit comments from all over the world. These comments will then be used to put together the official Java standard.

12.11   WHY PORTABILITY?

In the light of the many barriers to porting software, the reader might well wonder if it is worthwhile to port software at all. One argument in favor of portability stated in Section 12.10 is that the cost of software can perhaps be partially recouped by porting the product to a different hardware/operating system configuration. However, selling multiple variants of the software may not be possible. The application may be highly specialized, and no other client may need the software. For instance, a management information system written for one major car rental corporation may simply be inapplicable to the operations of other car rental corporations. Alternatively, the software itself may give the client a competitive advantage, and selling copies of the product would then be tantamount to economic suicide. In the light of all this, is it not a waste of time and money to engineer portability into a product when it is designed?

The answer to this question is an emphatic NO. One major reason why portability is essential is that the life of a software product is generally longer than the life of the hardware for which it was first written. Good software products can have a life of 15 years, whereas hardware is frequently changed at least every 5 years. Thus good software can be implemented, over its lifetime, on three or more different hardware configurations.

One way to solve this problem is to buy upwardly compatible hardware. The only expense is the cost of the hardware; the software will not need to be changed. Nevertheless, in some cases it may be economically more sound to port the product to different hardware entirely. For example, the first version of a product may have been implemented 7 years ago on a mainframe. Although it may be possible to buy a new mainframe on which the product can run without any changes, it may be considerably less expensive to implement multiple copies of the product on a network of personal computers, one on the desk of each user. In this instance, if the software has been written to promote portability, then porting the product to the personal computer network makes good financial sense.

But there are other kinds of software. For example, many software organizations that write software for personal computers make their money by selling multiple copies of "shrink-wrapped software." For instance, the profit on a spreadsheet package is small and cannot possibly cover the cost of development. In order to break even, 1,000 (or perhaps 10,000) copies have to be sold. After this point, additional sales are pure profit. So if the product can be ported to additional types of hardware with ease, even more money can be made.

Of course, as with all software, the product is not just the code; there is also documentation, including the manuals. Porting the spreadsheet package to other hardware means changing the documentation as well. Thus portability also means being able to change the documentation easily to reflect the target configuration, instead of having to write new documentation from scratch. Considerably less training is needed if the familiar, existing product is ported to a new computer, than if a completely new product were to be written. For this reason, too, portability is to be encouraged; techniques to facilitate portability are now described.

12.12 TECHNIQUES FOR ACHIEVING PORTABILITY

One way to achieve portability is to forbid programmers to use constructs that might cause problems when ported to another computer. For example, an obvious principle would seem to be: Write all software in a standard version of a high-level programming language. But how then is a portable operating system to be written? After all, it is inconceivable that an operating system could be written without at least some assembler code. Similarly, a compiler has to generate object code for a specific computer. Here, too, it is impossible to avoid all implementation-dependent components.

12.12.1 PORTABLE SYSTEM SOFTWARE

Instead of forbidding all implementation-dependent aspects, which would have the consequence of preventing almost all system software from being written, a better technique is to isolate any necessary implementation-dependent pieces. An example of this technique is the way the UNIX operating system is constructed [Johnson and Ritchie, 1978]. About 9000 lines of the operating system are written in C. The remaining 1000 lines constitute the kernel. The kernel is written in assembler and must be rewritten for each implementation. About 1000 lines of the C code consist of device drivers; this code, too, must be rewritten each time. However, the remaining 8000 lines of C code remain largely unchanged from implementation to implementation.

Another useful technique for increasing the portability of system software is to use levels of abstraction (Section 6.4.1). Consider, for example, graphical display routines for a workstation. A user inserts a command such as drawLine into his or her source code. The source code is compiled and then linked together with graphical display routines. At run time, drawLine causes the workstation to draw a line on the screen as specified by the user. This can be implemented using two levels of abstraction. The upper level, written in a high-level language, interprets the user's command and calls the appropriate lower-level module to execute that command. If the graphical display routines are ported to a new type of workstation, then no changes need be made to the user's code or to the upper level of the graphical display routines. However, the lower-level modules of the routines will have to be rewritten because they interface with the actual hardware, and the hardware of the new workstation is different from that of the workstation on which the package was previously implemented. This technique has also been successfully used for porting communications software that conforms to the seven levels of abstraction of the ISO-OSI model [Tanenbaum, 1981].

12.12.2 PORTABLE APPLICATION SOFTWARE

With regard to application software, rather than system software such as operating systems and compilers, it is generally possible to write the product in a high-level language. In Section 12.1 it was pointed out that there is frequently no choice with regard to implementation language, but that where it is possible to select a language the choice should be made on the basis of cost–benefit analysis (Section 4.2). One of the factors that must enter into the cost–benefit analysis is the impact on portability.

At every stage in the development of a product, decisions can be made that will result in a more portable product. One potential problem can arise as a consequence of the fact that not all characters are supported by every computer. For example, comments in Pascal can be delimited by { . . . } pairs or by (* . . . *) pairs. Because some computers do not support brace brackets, it is preferable to use (* . . . *) pairs. Also, some compilers distinguish between uppercase and lowercase letters. For such a compiler, variables This_Is_A_Name and this_is_a_name are two different variables. But other compilers treat the two names the same. A product that relies on differences between uppercase letters and lowercase letters can lead to hard-to-discover faults when the product is ported.

Just as there frequently is no choice of programming language, there may also be no choice of operating system. However, if at all possible the operating system under which the product runs should be a popular one. This is an argument in favor of the

UNIX operating system. UNIX has been implemented on a wide range of hardware. In addition, UNIX, or more precisely, UNIX-like operating systems, have been implemented on top of mainframe operating systems such as IBM VM/370 and VAX/VMS. For personal computers, the most widely used operating system is MS-DOS, although Windows 95 may overtake MS-DOS in the future. Just as use of a widely implemented programming language will promote portability, so too will use of a widely implemented operating system.

In order to facilitate the moving of software from one UNIX-based system to another, the Portable Operating System Interface for Computer Environments (POSIX) was developed [NIST 151, 1988]. POSIX standardizes the interface between an application program and a UNIX operating system. POSIX has now been implemented on a number of non-UNIX operating systems as well, thus broadening the number of computers to which application software can be ported with little or no problem.

Language standards can play their part in achieving portability. If the coding standards of a development organization stipulate that only standard constructs may be used, then the resulting product is more likely to be portable. To this end, programmers must be provided with a list of nonstandard features supported by the compiler, but whose use is forbidden without prior managerial approval. Like other sensible coding standards, this one can be checked by machine.

Graphical user interfaces (GUI) are similarly becoming portable via the introduction of standard GUI languages. Examples of these include Motif and X11. The standardization of GUI languages is in reaction to the growing importance of GUIs as described in Section 7.3, and the resulting need for portability of human–computer interfaces.

Planning should also be done for potential future numerical incompatibilities. For example, if a product is being developed on 32-bit hardware but there is a possibility that in the future it may have to be ported to an older 16-bit machine, then integers should be kept within the range $\pm 32,767$ and the modulus of real numbers should be within the range $\pm 10^{68}$. In addition, no more than six decimal digits of precision should be assumed [Wallis, 1982]. As explained in Section 12.10.3, these problems cannot arise in Ada or Java.

It is also necessary to plan for potential lack of compatibility between the operating system under which the product is being constructed and any future operating systems to which the product may be ported. If at all possible, operating system calls should be localized to one or two modules. In any event, every operating system call must be carefully documented. The documentation standard for operating system calls should assume that the next programmer to read the code will have no familiarity whatsoever with the current operating system, often a reasonable assumption.

Documentation in the form of an installation manual should also be provided to assist with future porting. That manual will point out what parts of the product will have to be changed when porting the product, and what parts may have to be changed. In both instances, a careful explanation of what has to be done, and how to do it, must be provided. Finally, lists of changes that will have to be made in other manuals, such as the user manual or the operator manual, must also appear in the installation manual.

12.12.3   Portable Data

The problem of portability of data can be a vexing one. Problems of hardware incompatibilities were pointed out in Section 12.10.1. But even after such problems have been solved, software incompatibilities remain. Suppose that a data file is used by a Pascal or COBOL product on the source computer. If that same product is now ported to another compiler/hardware/operating system configuration, it is unlikely that the data file can be read by the ported product; the format required for Pascal or COBOL data files in the new system will probably be totally different from that in the old system. For instance, the format of an indexed-sequential file is determined by the operating system; a different operating system generally implies a different format. Many files require headers containing information such as the format of the data in that file. The format of a header is almost always unique to the specific compiler and operating system under which that file was created. But bad as the situation is with regard to porting data files used by popular programming languages, the situation is far worse when database management systems are used.

The safest way of porting data is to construct an unstructured (sequential) file, which can then be ported with minimal difficulty to the target machine. From this unstructured file, the desired structured file, be it a Pascal file, a COBOL file, or a database, can be reconstructed. Two special conversion routines have to be written, one running on the source machine to convert the original structured file into sequential form and one running on the target machine to reconstruct the structured file from the ported sequential file. Although this solution seems simple enough, the two routines will be nontrivial when conversions between complex database models have to be performed.

12.13   Module Reuse

Reuse was presented in detail in Chapter 6 (Sections 6.10 through 6.12) because of the close connection between reuse and objects, the major topic of that chapter. In fact, the material on reuse could have appeared virtually anywhere in this book, because components from all phases of the software process are reused, including portions of specifications, contracts, plans, designs, and modules. That is why the material on reuse was put into the first part of the book, rather than tying it to one or other specific phase. In particular, it was important that the material on reuse not be presented in this chapter to underline the fact that, even though reuse of modules is by far the most common form of reuse, more than just modules can be reused.

Testing during the implementation phase is examined next.

12.14   Module Test Case Selection

As explained in Chapter 6, an object is a specific type of module. Thus in this chapter, as in the rest of the book, whatever holds for a module in general also applies to objects in particular. In addition, however, there are issues that are specific to objects. In this and the following sections, testing issues that are specific to objects are highlighted within the context of the testing of modules in general.

As pointed out in Section 5.6, modules undergo two types of testing, namely informal testing performed by the programmer while developing the module and *methodical testing* carried out by the SQA group after the programmer is satisfied that the module appears to function correctly. It is this methodical testing that is described in the following discussion. There are in turn two basic types of methodical testing, namely nonexecution-based testing in which the module is reviewed by a team and execution-based testing in which the module is run against test cases. Techniques for selecting these test cases are now described.

The worst way to test a module is to use haphazard test data. The tester sits in front of the keyboard, and whenever the module requests input, the tester responds with arbitrary data. As will be shown, there is never time to test more than the tiniest fraction of all possible tests cases, which can easily number many more than 10^{100}. The few test cases that can be run, perhaps of the order of 1000, are too valuable to waste on haphazard data. Worse, there is a tendency when the machine solicits input to respond more than once with the same data, thus wasting even more test cases. It is clear that test cases must be constructed systematically.

12.14.1   TESTING TO SPECIFICATIONS VERSUS TESTING TO CODE

There are two basic ways of systematically constructing test data to test a module. The first is to *test to specifications*. This technique is also called *black-box, data-driven, functional,* or *input/output-driven* testing. In this approach, the code itself is ignored; the only information used in drawing up test cases is the specification document. The other extreme is to *test to code* and to ignore the specification document when selecting test cases. Other names for this technique are *glass-box, white-box, logic-driven,* or *path-oriented* testing (for an explanation of why there are so many different terms, see the Just in Case You Wanted to Know box on page 409).

First, the feasibility of each approach will be considered separately.

12.14.2   FEASIBILITY OF TESTING TO SPECIFICATIONS

Consider the following example. Suppose that the specifications for a certain data processing product state that five types of commission and seven types of discount must be incorporated. Testing every possible combination of just commission and discount requires 35 test cases. It is no use saying that commission and discount are computed in two entirely separate modules, and hence may be tested independently—in black-box testing the product is treated as a black box, and its internal structure is therefore completely irrelevant.

In this example, there are only two factors, namely commission and discount, taking on five and seven different values, respectively. In any realistic product there will be hundreds, if not thousands, of different factors. Even if there are only 20

JUST IN CASE YOU WANTED TO KNOW

It is reasonable to ask why there are so many different names for the same testing concept. The reason is that, as so often happens in software engineering, the same concept was discovered, independently, by a number of different researchers, each of whom invented his or her own terminology. By the time the software engineering community realized that these were different names for the identical concept it was too late—the diverse names had crept into our software engineering vocabulary.

In this book, I use the terminology *black-box testing* and *glass-box testing*. These terms are particularly descriptive. When we test to specifications, we treat the code as a totally opaque black box. Conversely, when we test to code, we need to be able to see inside the box; hence the term *glass-box testing*. I avoid the term *white-box testing* because it is somewhat confusing. After all, a box that has been painted white is just as opaque as one that is painted black!

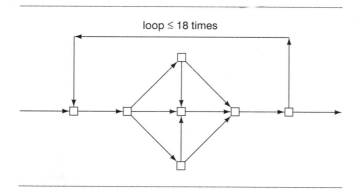

loop ≤ 18 times

Figure 12.14   Flowchart with over 10^{12} possible paths.

factors, each taking on only 4 different values, then a total of 4^{20} or 1.1×10^{12} different test cases have to be examined.

To see the implications of over a trillion test cases, consider how long it would take to test them all. If a team of programmers could be found who could generate, run, and examine test cases at an average rate of one every 30 seconds, then it would take more than a million years to test the product exhaustively.

Thus, exhaustive testing to specifications is impossible in practice because of the combinatorial explosion. There are simply too many test cases to consider. Testing to code is therefore now examined.

12.14.3   FEASIBILITY OF TESTING TO CODE

The most common form of testing to code requires that each path through the module must be executed at least once. To see the infeasibility of this, consider the flowchart depicted in Figure 12.14. Despite the fact that the flowchart appears to be almost

---

```
if ((x + y + z) / 3 == x)
    System.out.println ("x, y, z are equal in value");
else
    System.out.println ("x, y, z are unequal");



Test case 1: x = 1, y = 2, z = 3
Test case 2: x = y = z = 2
```

Figure 12.15   Incorrect code fragment for determining if three integers are equal, together with two test cases.

trivial, there are over 10^{12} different paths through the flowchart. There are five possible paths through the diamond in the center, and the total number of possible paths through the flowchart is therefore

$$5^1 + 5^2 + 5^3 + \ldots + 5^{18} = 4.77 \times 10^{12} \qquad \textbf{(12.1)}$$

If there can be this many paths through a simple flowchart containing a single loop, it is not difficult to imagine the total number of different paths in a module of reasonable size and complexity, let alone in a large module with many loops. In short, the huge number of possible paths renders exhaustive testing to code as infeasible as exhaustive testing to specifications.

There are additional reasons why testing to code is problematic. Testing to code requires the tester to exercise every path. It is possible to exercise every path without detecting every fault in the product, that is to say, testing to code is not reliable. To see this, consider the code fragment shown in Figure 12.15 [Myers, 1976]. The fragment was written to test the equality of three integers, x, y, and z, using the totally fallacious assumption that if the average of three numbers is equal to the first number then the three numbers are equal. Two test cases are also shown in Figure 12.15. In the first test case the value of the average of the three numbers is 6 / 3 or 2, which is not equal to 1. The product therefore correctly informs the tester that x, y, and z are unequal. The integers x, y, and z are all equal to 2 in the second test case, so the product computes their average as 2, which is equal to the value of x, and the product correctly concludes that the three numbers are equal. Thus both paths through the product have been exercised without the fault being detected. Of course, the fault would come to light if test data such as x = 2, y = 1, z = 3 are used.

A third difficulty with path testing is that a path can be tested only if it is present. Consider the code fragment shown in Figure 12.16(a). It is clear that there are two paths to be tested, corresponding to the cases d = 0 and d ≠ 0. Next, consider the single statement of Figure 12.16(b). Now there is only one path, and this path can be tested without the fault being detected. In fact, if a programmer omits checking whether d = 0 in his or her code, it is likely that the programmer is unaware of the potential danger and that the case d = 0 will not be included in the programmer's test

```
if (d == 0)
    zeroDivisionRoutine ();
else
    x = n / d;
```

(a)

```
x = n / d;
```

(b)

Figure 12.16 Two code fragments for computing a quotient.

data. This problem is an additional argument for having an independent software quality assurance group whose job includes detecting faults of this type.

These examples show conclusively that the criterion "exercise all paths in the product" is not *reliable,* as there exist products for which some data exercising a given path will detect a fault and different data exercising the same path will not. However, path-oriented testing is *valid,* because it does not inherently preclude selecting test data that might reveal the fault.

Because of the combinatorial explosion, neither exhaustive testing to specifications nor exhaustive testing to code is feasible. A compromise is needed, using techniques that will highlight as many faults as possible, while accepting that there is no way to guarantee that all faults have been detected. A reasonable way to proceed is to use black-box test cases first (testing to specifications) and then develop additional test cases using glass-box techniques (testing to code).

12.15 BLACK-BOX MODULE-TESTING TECHNIQUES

Exhaustive black-box testing generally requires literally billions and billions of test cases. The art of testing is to devise a small, manageable set of test cases so as to maximize the chances of detecting a fault while minimizing the chances of wasting a test case by having the same fault detected by more than one test case. Every test case must be chosen to detect a previously undetected fault. One such black-box technique is equivalence testing combined with boundary value analysis.

12.15.1 EQUIVALENCE TESTING AND BOUNDARY VALUE ANALYSIS

Suppose the specifications for a database product state that the product must be able to handle any number of records from 1 through 16,383 ($2^{14} - 1$). If the product can handle 34 records and 14,870 records, then the chances are good that it will work fine for, say, 8252 records. In fact, the chances of detecting a fault, if present, are likely to be equally good if any test case from 1 through 16,383 records is selected. Conversely, if the product works correctly for any one test case in the range from 1 through 16,383, then it will probably work for any other test case in the range. The range from 1 through 16,383 constitutes an *equivalence class,* that is to say, a set of test cases such that any one member of the class is as good a test case as any other member of the class. To be more precise, the specified range of numbers of records that the product must be able to handle defines three equivalence classes:

Equivalence class 1: Less than 1 record.

Equivalence class 2: From 1 through 16,383 records.

Equivalence class 3: More than 16,383 records.

Testing the database product using the technique of equivalence classes then requires that one test case from each equivalence class be selected. The test case from equivalence class 2 should be handled correctly, while error messages should be printed for the test cases from class 1 and class 3.

A successful test case is one that detects a previously undetected fault. In order to maximize the chances of finding such a fault, a high-payoff technique is *boundary value analysis.* Experience has shown that when a test case that is on or just to one side of the boundary of an equivalence class is selected, the probability of detecting a fault increases. Thus, when testing the database product, seven test cases should be selected:

Test Case 1:	0 records	Member of equivalence class 1 and adjacent to boundary value
Test Case 2:	1 record	Boundary value
Test Case 3:	2 records	Adjacent to boundary value
Test Case 4:	723 records	Member of equivalence class 2
Test Case 5:	16,382 records	Adjacent to boundary value
Test Case 6:	16,383 records	Boundary value
Test Case 7:	16,384 records	Member of equivalence class 3 and adjacent to boundary value

The preceding example applies to the input specifications. An equally powerful technique is to examine the output specifications. For example, in 1995 the minimum Social Security (OASDI) deduction from any one paycheck permitted by the tax code was $0.00, and the maximum was $3794.40, the latter corresponding to gross earnings of $61,200. Thus, when testing a payroll product, the test cases for the Social Security deduction from paychecks should include input data that are expected to result in deductions of exactly $0.00 and $3794.40. In addition, test data should be set up that might result in deductions of less than $0.00 or more than $3794.40.

In general, for each range (R_1, R_2) listed in either the input or the output specifications, five test cases should be selected, corresponding to values less than R_1, equal to R_1, greater than R_1 but less than R_2, equal to R_2, and greater than R_2. Where it is specified that an item has to be a member of a certain set (for example, the input must be a letter), two equivalence classes must be tested, namely a member of the specified set and a nonmember of the set. Where the specifications lay down a precise value (for example, the response must be followed by a # sign), then there are again two equivalence classes, namely the specified value and anything else.

The use of equivalence classes, together with boundary value analysis, to test both the input specifications and the output specifications is a valuable technique for generating a relatively small set of test data with the potential of uncovering a number of faults that might well remain hidden if less powerful techniques for test data selection were used.

12.15.2 FUNCTIONAL TESTING

An alternative form of black-box testing is to base the test data on the functionality of the module. In *functional testing* [Howden, 1987], each item of functionality or *function* implemented in the module is identified. Typical functions in a module for a computerized warehouse product might be: *get next database record* or *determine whether quantity on hand is below the reorder point.* In a weapons control system, a module might include the function *compute trajectory.* In a module of an operating system, one function might be *determine whether file is empty.*

After determining all the functions of the module, test data are devised to test each function separately. Now the functional testing is taken a step further. If the module consists of a hierarchy of lower-level functions, connected together by the control structures of structured programming (Section 12.3), then functional testing proceeds recursively. For example, if a higher-level function is of the form

$$\textit{<higher-level function>} \quad ::= \quad \textbf{if } \textit{<conditional expression>} \qquad \textbf{(12.2)}$$
$$\textit{<lower-level function 1>};$$
$$\textbf{else}$$
$$\textit{<lower-level function 2>};$$

then, because *<conditional expression>*, *<lower-level function 1>*, and *<lower-level function 2>* have been subjected to functional testing, *<higher-level function>* can be tested using branch coverage, a glass-box technique described in Section 12.16.1. Note that this form of structural testing is a hybrid technique—the lower-level functions are tested using a black-box technique, but the higher-level functions are tested using a glass-box technique.

In practice, however, higher-level functions are not constructed in such a structured fashion from lower-level functions. Instead, the lower-level functions are usually intertwined in some way. To determine faults in this situation, *functional analysis* is required, a somewhat complex procedure; for details, see [Howden, 1987]. A further complicating factor is that functionality frequently does not coincide with module boundaries. Thus the distinction between module testing and integration testing becomes blurred; one module cannot be tested without, at the same time, testing the other modules whose functionality it uses. This problem also arises in the object-oriented paradigm when a method of one object sends a message to invoke a method of a different object.

---

if (s > 1 && t == 0)

  x = 9;

Test case: s = 2, t = 0.

Figure 12.17   Code fragment with test data.

The random interrelationships between modules from the viewpoint of functional testing may have unacceptable consequences for management. For example, milestones and deadlines can become somewhat ill-defined, making it difficult to determine the status of the product with respect to the software project management plan.

12.16   GLASS-BOX MODULE-TESTING TECHNIQUES

In glass-box techniques, test cases are selected on the basis of examination of the code, rather than the specifications. There are a number of different forms of glass-box testing, including statement, branch, and path coverage.

12.16.1   STRUCTURAL TESTING: STATEMENT, BRANCH, AND PATH COVERAGE

The simplest form of glass box testing is *statement coverage,* that is, running a series of test cases during which every statement is executed at least once. To keep track of which statements are still to be executed, a CASE tool keeps a record of how many times each statement has been executed over the series of tests. A weakness of this approach is that there is no guarantee that all outcomes of branches are properly tested. To see this, consider the code fragment of Figure 12.17. The programmer has made a mistake; the compound conditional s > 1 && t == 0 should have read s > 1 || t == 0. The test data shown in the figure allow the statement x = 9 to be executed without the fault being highlighted.

An improvement over statement coverage is *branch coverage,* that is, running a series of tests to ensure that all branches are tested at least once. Again, a tool is usually needed to help the tester keep track of which branches have or have not been tested; *btool* and General Coverage Tool (GCT) are examples of branch coverage tools for C programs. Techniques such as statement or branch coverage are termed *structural tests.*

The most powerful form of structural testing is *path coverage,* that is, testing all paths. As shown previously, in a product with loops the number of paths can be very large indeed. As a result, researchers have been investigating ways of reducing the number of paths to be examined while still being able to uncover more faults than would be possible using branch coverage. One criterion for selecting paths is to restrict test cases to linear code sequences [Woodward, Hedley, and Hennell, 1980]. To do this, first identify the set of points L from which control flow may jump. The set L includes entry and exit points, and branch statements such as an **if** statement or a **goto** statement. Then linear code sequences are those paths that begin at an element of L and end at an element of L. The technique has been successful in that it has uncovered many faults without having to test every path.

Another way of reducing the number of paths to test is *all-definition-use-path coverage* [Rapps and Weyuker, 1985]. In this technique, each occurrence of a variable **qqq**, say, in the source code is labeled either as a *definition* of the variable, such as **qqq = 1** or **read (qqq)**, or as a *use* of the variable, such as **y = qqq + 3** or **if (qqq < 9) errorB ()**. All paths between the definition of a variable and the use of that definition are now identified, nowadays by means of an automatic tool. Finally, a test case is set up for each such path. All-definition-use-path coverage is an excellent test technique in that large numbers of faults are frequently detected by relatively few test cases. However, all-definition-use-path coverage does have the disadvantage that the upper bound on the number of paths is 2^d, where d is the number of decision statements (branches) in the product. Examples can be constructed exhibiting the upper bound. However, it has been shown that for real products, as opposed to artificial examples, this upper bound is not reached, and the actual number of paths is proportional to d [Weyuker, 1988a]. In other words, the number of test cases needed for all-definition-use-path coverage is generally much smaller than the theoretical upper bound. Thus all-definition-use-path coverage is a practical test case selection technique.

When using structural testing, the situation can arise in which the tester simply cannot come up with a test case that will exercise a specific statement, branch, or path. What may have happened is that there is an infeasible path ("dead code") in the module, that is, a path that cannot possibly be executed for any input data. Figure 12.18 shows two examples of infeasible paths. In Figure 12.18(a) the programmer has omitted a minus sign. If **k** is less than **2**, then **k** cannot possibly be greater than **3**, so the statement **x = x * k** cannot be reached. Similarly, in Figure 12.18(b), **j** is never less than **0**, so the statement **total = total + value[j]** can never be reached; the programmer had intended the test to be **j < 10**, but made a typing error. A tester using statement coverage would soon realize that neither statement could be reached, and the faults would be found.

12.16.2 COMPLEXITY METRICS

The quality assurance viewpoint provides another approach to glass-box testing. Suppose that a manager is told that module **m1** is more complex than module **m2**. Irrespective of the precise way in which the term *complex* is defined, the manager will intuitively believe that **m1** is likely to have more faults than **m2**. Following this idea, computer scientists have developed a number of metrics of software complexity to aid in determining which modules are most likely to have faults. If the

```
if (k < 2)
{
    if (k > 3)                      [should be: k > –3]
          ↑

        x = x * k;
}
```
(a)

```
for (j = 0; j < 0; j++)              [should be: j < 10]
          ↑

    total = total + value[j];
```
(b)

Figure 12.18   Two examples of infeasible paths.

complexity of a module is found to be unreasonably high, a manager may direct that the module be redesigned and reimplemented on the grounds that it will probably be less costly and faster to start from scratch than to attempt to debug a fault-prone module.

A simple metric for predicting numbers of faults is lines of code. The underlying assumption is that there is a constant probability p that a line of code contains a fault. Thus, if a tester believes that, on average, a line of code has a 2 percent chance of containing a fault, and the module under test is 100 lines long, then this implies that the module is expected to contain two faults, whereas a module that is twice as long is likely to have four faults. Basili and Hutchens as well as Takahashi and Kamayachi showed that the number of faults is indeed related to the size of the product as a whole [Basili and Hutchens, 1983; Takahashi and Kamayachi, 1985].

Attempts have been made to find more sophisticated predictors of faults based on measures of product complexity. A typical contender is McCabe's measure of cyclomatic complexity, namely the number of binary decisions (predicates) plus 1 [McCabe, 1976]. As described in Section 11.15, the cyclomatic complexity is essentially the number of branches in the module. Accordingly, cyclomatic complexity can be used as a metric for the number of test cases needed for branch coverage of a module. This is the basis for so-called structured testing [McCabe, 1983].

McCabe's metric can be computed almost as easily as lines of code. In some cases it has been shown to be a good metric for predicting faults; the higher the value of M, the greater the chance that a module contains a fault. For example, Walsh analyzed 276 modules in the Aegis system, a shipboard combat system [Walsh, 1979]. Walsh measured the cyclomatic complexity M and found that 23 percent of the modules with M greater than or equal to 10 had 53 percent of the faults detected.

```
if (k < 2)
{
    if (k > 3)
        x = x * k;
}
```

Distinct operators:

    if (<) { > = * ; }

Distinct operands:

    k 2 3 ×

Number of distinct operators $n_1 = 10$
Number of distinct operands $n_2 = 4$
Total number of operators $N_1 = 13$
Total number of operands $N_2 = 7$

Figure 12.19 Software science metrics applied to code fragment of Figure 12.18(a).

In addition, the modules with M greater than or equal to 10 had 21 percent more faults per line of code than the modules with smaller M values. However, the validity of McCabe's metric has been seriously questioned both on theoretical grounds and on the basis of the many different experiments cited in [Shepperd, 1988b] and [Shepperd and Ince, 1994].

Halstead's software science metrics [Halstead, 1977] have also been used for fault prediction. Two of the four basic elements of software science are n_1, the number of distinct operators in the module and n_2, the number of distinct operands. Typical operators include +, *, **if, goto**; operands are user-defined variables or constants. The other two basic elements are N_1, the total number of operators and N_2, the total number of operands. The code fragment of Figure 12.18(a) is reproduced in Figure 12.19. From the latter figure it can be seen that the code fragment has 10 distinct operators and 4 distinct operands. The total number of operators and operands are 13 and 7, respectively. These four basic elements then serve as input for fault prediction metrics [Ottenstein, 1979].

Musa, Iannino, and Okumoto have analyzed the data available on fault densities [Musa, Iannino, and Okumoto, 1987]. They concluded that most complexity metrics, including Halstead's and McCabe's, show a high correlation with the number of lines of code, or more precisely, the number of deliverable, executable source instructions. In other words, when researchers measure what they believe to be the complexity of a module or product, the result they obtain may largely be a reflection of the number of lines of code, a measure that correlates strongly with the number of faults. In addition, complexity metrics provide little improvement over lines of code for predicting fault rates. These conclusions are supported by Basili and Hutchens and also by Gremillion and by Shepperd [Basili and Hutchens, 1983; Gremillion, 1984; Shepperd, 1988b]. Other problems with complexity are discussed in [Shepperd, 1988a; Weyuker, 1988b; Shepperd and Ince, 1994]. In addition, there are problems when applying Halstead's metrics to modern languages such as Java or C++; for example, is a constructor an operator or an operand?

Using lines of code to predict fault rates seems to contradict the many arguments and experimental results negating the validity of that metric [van der Poel and Schach, 1983; Jones, 1986a] as described in Section 10.1.1. In fact, there is no contradiction. The work of Jones and others is within the context of software productivity, and in that area there is no question that lines of code is a poor metric. The results of Basili and others referenced in the previous paragraph relate specifically to fault rates and have nothing to do with productivity. Thus, when performing module testing, the larger modules should indeed be given special attention, whether from the viewpoint of test cases or walkthroughs and inspections.

12.17   CODE WALKTHROUGHS AND INSPECTIONS

In Section 5.2 a strong case was made for the use of walkthroughs and inspections. The same arguments hold equally well for code walkthroughs and code inspections. In brief, the fault-detecting power of these two nonexecution-based techniques leads to rapid and thorough fault detection. The additional time required for code walkthroughs or code inspections is more than repaid by increased productivity due to the presence of fewer faults at the integration-testing phase. Furthermore, code inspections have led to a reduction of up to 95 percent in corrective maintenance costs [Crossman, 1982]. Further arguments in favor of walkthroughs and inspections are given in the next section.

12.18   COMPARISON OF MODULE-TESTING TECHNIQUES

A number of studies have compared strategies for module testing. Myers compared black-box testing, a combination of black-box and glass-box testing, and three-person code walkthroughs [Myers, 1978a]. The experiment was performed using 59 highly experienced programmers testing the same product. All three techniques were equally effective in finding faults, but code walkthroughs proved to be less cost-effective than the other two techniques. Hwang compared black-box testing, glass-box testing, and code reading by one person [Hwang, 1981]. All three techniques were found to be equally effective, with each technique having its own strengths and weaknesses.

A major experiment was conducted by Basili and Selby [Basili and Selby, 1987]. The techniques compared were the same as in Hwang's experiment, namely black-box testing, glass-box testing, and one-person code reading. The subjects were 32 professional programmers and 42 advanced students. Each tested three products, using each testing technique once. Fractional factorial design [Basili and Weiss, 1984] was used to compensate for the fact that the products were tested in different ways by different participants; no participant tested the same product in more than one way. Different results were obtained from the two groups of participants. The professional programmers detected more faults with code reading than with the other two techniques, and the fault detection rate was faster. Two groups of advanced students participated. In one group there was no significant difference among the three techniques; in the other, code reading and black-box testing were equally good, and both outperformed glass-box testing. However, the rate at which students detected faults was the same for all techniques. Overall, code reading led to the detection of more interface faults than did the other two techniques, while black-box testing was most successful at finding control faults. The main conclusion that can be drawn from this experiment is that code inspection is at least as successful at detecting faults as glass-box and black-box testing.

A development technique that makes good use of this conclusion is Cleanroom.

12.19 CLEANROOM

The Cleanroom software development technique [Cobb and Mills, 1990; Dyer, 1992; Linger, 1994] incorporates a number of different techniques, including an incremental life-cycle model (Section 3.4), formal techniques for specification and design, and nonexecution-based module-testing techniques such as code reading [Mills, Dyer, and Linger, 1987; Selby, Basili, and Baker 1987] and code walkthroughs and inspections (Section 12.17). A critical aspect of the technique is that a module is not compiled until it has passed an inspection. That is, a module should be compiled only after nonexecution-based testing has been successfully accomplished.

The technique has had a number of great successes. For example, a prototype automated documentation system was developed for the U.S. Naval Underwater Systems Center using Cleanroom [Trammel, Binder, and Snyder, 1992]. Altogether 18 faults were detected while the design underwent "functional verification," a review process in which correctness-proving techniques are employed (Section 5.5). Informal proofs such as the one presented in Section 5.5.1 were used as much as possible; full mathematical proofs were developed only when participants were unsure of the correctness of the portion of the design being inspected. Another 19 faults were detected during walkthroughs of the 1820 lines of FoxBASE code; when the code was then compiled, there were no compilation errors. Furthermore, there were no failures at execution time. This is an additional indication of the power of nonexecution-based testing techniques.

This is certainly an impressive result. However, as has been pointed out, results that apply to small-scale software products cannot necessarily be scaled up to large-scale software. In the case of Cleanroom, however, results for larger products are also impressive. The relevant metric is the *testing fault rate*, that is, the total number of faults detected per KLOC (thousand lines of code). This is a relatively common metric in the software industry. However, there is a critical difference in the way this metric is computed when Cleanroom is used as opposed to traditional development techniques.

As pointed out in Section 5.6, when traditional development techniques are used, a module is tested informally by its programmer while it is being developed and thereafter it is tested methodically by the SQA group. Faults detected by the programmer while developing the code are not recorded. However, from the time the module leaves the private workspace of the programmer and is handed over to the SQA group for execution-based and nonexecution-based testing, a tally is kept of the number of faults detected. In contrast, when Cleanroom is used, "testing faults" are counted from the time of compilation. Fault counting then continues through execution-based testing. In other words, when traditional development techniques are used, faults detected informally by the programmer do not count towards the testing fault rate. When Cleanroom is used, faults detected during the inspections and other nonexecution-based testing procedures that precede compilation are certainly recorded, but they do not count towards the testing fault rate.

A report on 17 Cleanroom products appears in [Linger, 1994]. For example, Cleanroom was used to develop the 350,000-line Ericsson Telecom OS32 operating system. The product was developed in 18 months by a team of 70. The testing fault rate was only 1.0 faults per KLOC. Another product was the prototype automated documentation system described above; the testing fault rate was 0.0 faults per KLOC for the 1820-line program. The 17 products together totaled nearly 1 million lines of code. The weighted average testing fault rate was 2.3 faults per KLOC, which Linger describes as a remarkable quality achievement. That praise is certainly not an exaggeration.

12.20 TESTING OBJECTS

One of the many reasons put forward for using the object-oriented paradigm is that it reduces the need for testing. Reuse via inheritance is a major strength of the paradigm; once a class has been tested, the argument goes, there is no need to retest it. Furthermore, new methods defined within a subclass of such a tested class have to be tested, but inherited methods need no further testing.

In fact, both these claims are only partially true. In addition, the testing of objects poses certain problems that are specific to object orientation. These issues are discussed in detail in this section.

To begin, it is necessary to clarify an issue regarding the testing of classes and of objects. As explained in Section 6.7, a class is an abstract data type that supports inheritance, and an object is an instance of a class. That is to say, a class has no concrete realization, whereas an object is a physical piece of code executing within a specific environment. Thus it is impossible to perform execution-based testing on a class; only nonexecution-based testing, such as an inspection, can be done.

Information hiding and the fact that many methods consist of relatively few lines of code can have significant impact on testing. First consider a product developed using the structured paradigm. Nowadays, such a product generally consists of modules of roughly 50 executable instructions. The interface between a module and the rest of the product is the argument list. There are arguments of two kinds, namely, input arguments that are supplied to the module when it is invoked and output arguments that are returned by the module when it returns control to the calling module. Testing a module consists of supplying values to the input arguments, invoking the module, and then comparing the values of the output arguments to the predicted results of the test.

In contrast, a "typical" object will contain perhaps 30 methods, many of which are relatively small, frequently just two or three executable statements [Wilde, Matthews, and Huitt, 1993]. These methods do not return a value to the caller, but rather they change the state of the object. That is to say, these methods modify attributes (state variables) of the object. The difficulty here is that, in order to test that the change of state has in fact been correctly performed, it is necessary to send additional messages to the object. For example, consider the bank account object described in Section 1.6. The effect of method deposit is to increase the value of state variable account balance. However, as a consequence of information hiding, the only way to test whether a particular deposit action has been correctly executed is to invoke method determine balance both before and after invoking method deposit and to see how the bank balance changes.

The situation is worse if the object does not include methods that can be invoked to determine the values of all the state variables. One alternative is to include additional methods for this purpose and then use conditional compilation to ensure that they are not available other than for testing purposes. The test plan (Section 10.5) should stipulate that the value of every state variable should be accessible during testing. In order to satisfy this requirement, additional methods that return the values of the state values may have to be added to the relevant classes during the design phase. As a result, it will be possible to test the effect of invoking a specific method of an object by querying the value of the applicable state variable.

Surprisingly enough, an inherited method may still have to be tested. That is to say, even if a method has been adequately tested, the same method may still require thorough testing when inherited, unchanged, by a subclass. To see this latter point, consider the class hierarchy shown in Figure 12.20. Two methods are defined in base class RootedTree, namely, displayNodeContents and printRoutine, where method displayNodeContents uses method printRoutine.

Next consider subclass BinaryTree. This subclass inherits method printRoutine from its base class RootedTree. In addition, a new method displayNodeContents is defined that overrides the method defined in RootedTree. This new method still uses printRoutine. In Java notation, BinaryTree.displayNodeContents uses RootedTree.printRoutine.

Now consider subclass BalancedBinaryTree. This subclass inherits method displayNodeContents from its superclass BinaryTree. However, a new method printRoutine is defined that overrides the one defined in RootedTree. When

```
class RootedTree
{
   . . .
   void displayNodeContents (Node a);
   void printRoutine (Node b);
//
// method displayNodeContents uses method printRoutine
//
   . . .
}

class BinaryTree extends RootedTree
{
   . . .
   void displayNodeContents (Node a);
//
// method displayNodeContents defined in this class uses
// method printRoutine inherited from class RootedTree
//
   . . .
}

class BalancedBinaryTree extends BinaryTree
{
   . . .
   void printRoutine (Node b);
//
// method displayNodeContents (inherited from BinaryTree) uses this
// local version of printRoutine within class BalancedBinaryTree
//
   . . .
}
```

Figure 12.20   Tree hierarchy.

displayNodeContents uses printRoutine within the context of Balanced-BinaryTree, the scope rules of Java specify that the local version of printRoutine is to be used. Again in Java notation, when method BinaryTree.displayNode-Contents is invoked within the lexical scope of BalancedBinaryTree, it uses method BalancedBinaryTree.printRoutine.

Thus, the actual code (method printRoutine) that is executed when display-

NodeContents is invoked within instantiations of BinaryTree is different from what is executed when displayNodeContents is invoked within instantiations of BalancedBinaryTree. This holds notwithstanding the fact that method display-NodeContents itself is inherited, unchanged, by BalancedBinaryTree from BinaryTree. Thus, even if method displayNodeContents has been thoroughly tested within a BinaryTree object, the method has to be retested from scratch when reused within a BalancedBinaryTree environment. To make matters even more complex, there are theoretical reasons why it needs to be retested with different test cases [Perry and Kaiser, 1990].

It must immediately be pointed out that these complications are not a reason to abandon the object-oriented paradigm. First, these problems arise only through the interaction of methods (displayNodeContents and printRoutine in the example). Second, it is possible to determine when this retesting is needed [Harrold, McGregor, and Fitzpatrick, 1992]. Thus, suppose an instantiation of a class has been thoroughly tested. Any new or redefined methods of a subclass then need to be tested, together with methods that are flagged for retesting because of their interaction with other methods. In short, then, the claim that use of the object-oriented paradigm reduces the need for testing is largely true.

Some management implications of module testing are now considered.

12.21   MANAGEMENT ASPECTS OF MODULE-TESTING

An important decision that must be made during the development of every module is how much time, and therefore money, to spend on testing that module. As with so many other economic issues in software engineering, cost–benefit analysis (Section 4.2) can play a useful role. For example, the decision as to whether or not the cost of correctness proving exceeds the benefit of the assurance that a specific product satisfies its specifications can be decided on the basis of cost–benefit analysis. Cost–benefit analysis can also be used to compare the cost of running additional test cases against the cost of failure of the delivered product caused by inadequate testing.

There is another approach for determining whether testing of a specific module should continue or whether it is likely that virtually all the faults have been removed. The techniques of reliability analysis can be used to provide statistical estimates of how many faults are still remaining. A variety of different techniques have been proposed for determining statistical estimates of the number of remaining faults. The basic idea underlying these techniques is the following. Suppose that a module is tested for 1 week. On Monday 23 faults are found, and 7 more on Tuesday. On Wednesday 5 more faults are found, 2 on Thursday, and 0 on Friday. Because the rate of fault detection is steadily decreasing from 23 faults per day to none, it seems likely that most faults have been found, and testing of that module could well be halted. Determining the probability that there are no more faults in the code requires a level of mathematical statistics beyond that required for readers of this book. Details are therefore not given here; the reader who is interested in reliability analysis should

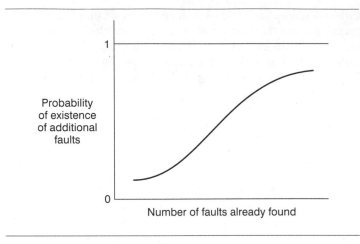

Figure 12.21 Graph showing that probability that there are faults still to be found is proportional to number of faults already detected.

consult [Shooman, 1983] or [Grady, 1992]. An example of how statistical-based testing can be used is given in Section 13.15.

12.21.1 WHEN TO REWRITE RATHER THAN DEBUG A MODULE

When a member of the SQA group detects a failure (erroneous output), the module must, as stated previously, be returned to the original programmer for debugging, that is, detection of the fault and correction of the code. There will be occasions when it is preferable for the module to be thrown away and redesigned and recoded from scratch, either by the original programmer or by another, possibly more senior, member of the development team. To see why this may be necessary, consider Figure 12.21. The graph shows the apparently nonsensical fact that the probability of the existence of more faults in a module is proportional to the number of faults already found in that module [Myers, 1979]. To see why this should be so, consider two modules, mA and mB. Suppose that both modules are approximately the same length and that both have been tested for the same number of hours. Suppose further that only 2 faults were detected in mA, but that 47 faults were detected in mB. It is likely that more faults remain to be rooted out of mB than out of mA. Furthermore, additional testing and debugging of mB is likely to be a lengthy process, and there will always be the suspicion that mB is still not perfect. In both the short run and the long run, it is preferable to discard mB, redesign it, and then recode it.

The distribution of faults in modules is certainly not uniform. Myers cites the example of faults found by users in OS/370 [Myers, 1979]. It was found that 47 percent of the faults were associated with only 4 percent of the modules. An earlier study by Endres regarding internal tests of DOS/VS (Release 28) at IBM Laboratories, Böblingen, Germany, showed similar nonuniformity [Endres, 1975]. Of the total of 512 faults detected in 202 modules, only 1 fault was detected in each of 112 of the modules. On the other hand, there were modules with 14, 15, 19, and 28 faults, respectively. Endres points out that the latter three modules were three of the largest modules in the product, each comprising over 3000 lines of DOS macro assembler language. But the module with 14 faults was a relatively small module that was previously known to be very unstable. This type of module is a prime candidate for being discarded and recoded.

The way for management to cope with this sort of situation is to predetermine the maximum number of faults that will be permitted during development of a given module; when that maximum is reached, the module must be thrown away, then redesigned and recoded, preferably by an experienced software professional. This maximum will vary from application area to application area and from module to module. After all, the maximum permitted number of faults detected in a module that reads in a record from a database and checks the validity of the part number should be far smaller than the number of faults in a complex module from a tank weapons control system that must coordinate data from a variety of sensors and direct the aim of the main gun toward the intended target. One way to decide on the maximum fault figure for a specific module is to examine fault data on similar modules that have required corrective maintenance. But whatever estimation technique is used, management must ensure that the module is scrapped if that figure is exceeded (but see the Just in Case You Wanted to Know box on page 426).

In the next two sections the testing of two somewhat specialized types of software is discussed, namely distributed software and real-time software.

12.22   TESTING DISTRIBUTED SOFTWARE

The difficulties of testing are considerably exacerbated when the product under test is implemented as a distributed product running on two or more different pieces of hardware. Examples of distributed computer systems are a hypercube [Seitz, 1985] and a network of computers connected by Ethernet [Silberschatz and Galvin, 1994]. In these systems the various component computers are loosely coupled, with the individual CPUs each having its own memory and communicating with one another by message passing.

The process of testing a product running on a uniprocessor is well understood. A vast literature exists on the subject, and tools have been constructed to aid the tester. Implicit in this uniprocessor testing process are a number of assumptions. It is assumed, for instance, that there is a global environment and that the execution of the product within that environment is deterministic. Furthermore, it is assumed that the instructions of the product are executed sequentially and that inserting debugging statements between source code statements will not modify the execution of the product in any way.

When attempting to test a product running on a distributed system, the familiar techniques of testing on a uniprocessor frequently are not very effective because the previous assumptions simply do not hold. In a distributed system there is no global

---

JUST IN CASE YOU WANTED TO KNOW

The discussion regarding the maximum permitted number of faults detected during development of a module means precisely that: the maximum number permitted *during development*. The maximum permit- ted number of faults detected after the product has been delivered to the client should be *zero* for all modules of all products!

---

environment. Instead, the instructions are executed in parallel on different processors. Furthermore, as a consequence of timing considerations, product execution behavior may not be reproducible from one execution to the next. Finally, adding debugging statements to one process could affect the behavior of other processes executing in parallel, resulting in timing-dependent faults, or so-called Heisenbugs. For example, suppose that process s is running on processor P_s, and process t is running on processor P_t. At some point process s sends a message to process t, that is to say, somewhere in process s there is a **transmit** command and a corresponding **receive** command in process t. Now suppose that the programmer has coded t incorrectly, so that if t reaches the **receive** instruction and the message from s is not waiting in the buffer, then process t fails. On the other hand, if the message from s is waiting, then process t works correctly. The programmer tests the product and it fails because process t is faster than process s, and the message is not waiting for t at the appropriate time. So the programmer attempts to debug process t by inserting a few output statements that will indicate to the programmer how much of process t has been executed before the failure. However, the additional output statements slow down process t, and process s has a chance to transmit the message before process t needs it. As a result, the product works perfectly. However, the moment the programmer removes the debugging statements from process t, it runs at its normal speed and reaches the **receive** before s can **transmit**; t therefore fails as it did before. Thus debugging causes the fault to disappear and to reappear when the process has apparently been successfully debugged.

Testing distributed software requires special tools for locating faults, especially distributed debuggers [Wahl and Schach, 1988]. Timing problems that arise when a distributed product is run on distributed hardware cannot be sorted out if the software is run on a uniprocessor. The distributed debugger must maintain history files, that is, a chronological record of events such as data inputs or messages transmitted from one process to another. The need for history files is a consequence of timing considerations. Suppose a distributed product is tested and fails. The programmer analyzes the output from the test run and concludes that a particular statement is in error. Once the statement has been changed, the test case must be rerun to determine that the fault has in fact been correctly fixed. Because the modified product is now different from the original, if only slightly so, the processes will run at different relative rates, and the messages between processors may be sent in a different order. As a result, the execution sequence of the test case after the product has been modified may not be the same as the one in which the fault was detected, and the programmer may therefore not be able to determine if the fault has in fact been fixed. History files solve this problem in that the execution record they contain can be used by a distributed debugger to reproduce the exact sequence of events that caused the failure.

12.23 TESTING REAL-TIME SOFTWARE

There are a number of difficulties specific to the testing of real-time software. It is a characteristic of real-time systems that they are critically dependent on the timing of inputs and the order of inputs, two factors over which the developer has no control. The reason for this is that inputs to a real-time system, such as the temperature of a computer-controlled nuclear reactor, the arrival of an aircraft within the ambit of an air-traffic control system, or the heart rate of a patient in a computer-controlled intensive-care unit, come from the real world. From the testing viewpoint, a relatively large number of test cases are therefore needed to be reasonably sure that the real-time software is functioning correctly. Another difficulty is that inputs to the system may well occur in parallel, and many real-time systems are therefore implemented as parallel systems running on a number of processors, with the attendant problems of testing distributed software described in the previous section.

Real-time software, and especially embedded real-time software (Section 5.4.4), frequently must run without the supervision of computer operators. For example, the computers in a deep space probe or an orbiting satellite must run untended for the entire duration of the mission. The software must be able to cope with a wide variety of emergencies and exceptional conditions. If the worst happens and the software fails, it must be able to reinitialize itself and restart its actions. Embedded real-time systems on earth must be equally robust. Consider, for example, the software for a computer controlling the engine of an automobile; if it cannot recover by itself from an unexpected event, then the engine would be immobilized until a mechanic trained in computers can restart the computer system.

This robustness requirement implies that real-time embedded software must incorporate a great number of exception-handling routines to enable the software to recover without human intervention from a wide variety of ordinarily unexpected circumstances. This means that real-time software has to be far more complicated than would be the case if a human operator were available to restart the product and perform the necessary recovery routines in the event of a failure. Testing real-time software is consequently also far more complicated.

Yet another difficulty with testing real-time software arises in setting up test cases. The inputs to most real-time systems come from the real world. The timing and sequence of inputs constitute a major aspect of real-time software that must be tested, but it is often impossible to organize a specific set of inputs occurring in a specific order at a specific time. For example, it is impossible to arrange for all the patients in a 10-bed intensive care unit to develop cardiac failure at the same time or for a set of medical emergencies to occur in a given order during a certain time interval. In other instances, the test cases may theoretically be possible to arrange, but are too hazardous to risk. For example, it is difficult to determine whether the software controlling a nuclear power plant can successfully prevent accidents of the types that occurred at Three Mile Island and at Chernobyl or whether a missile detection system would function correctly if an unfriendly power were to launch thousands of intercontinental ballistic missiles and submarine-launched ballistic missiles all at the same time.

Real-time software is frequently more complex than most people, even its developers, realize. As a result, there are sometimes subtle interactions among components that even the most skilled tester would not usually detect. As a result, an apparently minor change can have major consequences. A famous example of this is the fault that delayed the first space shuttle orbital flight in April 1981 [Garman, 1981]. The space shuttle avionics are controlled by four identical synchronized computers. There is also an independent fifth computer for back-up in case the set of four computers fails. A change had been made 2 years earlier to the module that performs bus initialization before the avionics computers are synchronized. An unfortunate side effect of this change was that a record containing a time just slightly later than the current time was erroneously sent to the data area used for synchronization of the avionics computers. The time that was sent was sufficiently close to the actual time for this fault not to be detected. About 1 year later the time difference was slightly increased, just enough to cause a 1 in 67 chance of synchronization failure. Then on the day of the first space shuttle launch the synchronization failure occurred, and three of the four identical avionics computers were synchronized one cycle late relative to the first computer. A fail-safe device that prevents the independent fifth computer from receiving information from the other four computers unless they are in agreement had the unanticipated consequence of preventing initialization of the fifth computer, and the launch had to be postponed. An all too familiar aspect of this incident was that the fault was in the bus initialization module, a module that apparently had no connection whatsoever with the synchronization routines.

There are five main approaches to testing real-time software, namely structure analysis, correctness proofs, systematic testing, statistical testing, and simulation [Quirk, 1985]. The first two approaches are nonexecution-based, the other three execution-based. *Structure analysis techniques* can be used to investigate control flow and data flow without executing the product. These techniques can then be used to prove that all parts of the product can be reached, that there is a path leading to termination from every node in the data flow graph, that all variables are assigned a value before they are used, and that all variables are referenced. These techniques are not perfect, however; for example, it is impossible to check that all elements of an array are assigned a value before they are used because the indices of array elements may be determined only at run time. Structure analysis can also assist in deadlock detection and can also be used for certain classes of timing checks [Quirk, 1983].

Correctness proofs have been discussed in Section 5.5. Real-time systems were mentioned as one of the areas where correctness proving may be an economically viable technique. A number of theorem provers have been constructed to prove real-time systems correct. *Systematic testing* is carried out by running sets of test cases consisting of the same input data arranged in all possible orderings, thereby detecting faults caused by overlooking certain orderings of the inputs. Thus, if five possible inputs are being tested, these inputs can be arranged in 5! different ways, yielding 120 different test cases. Clearly, the combinatorial explosion makes this technique infeasible when the number of different inputs is even moderately large. As a result, *statistical techniques* are employed to select a manageable sample from the huge number of possible test cases so that probabilistic statements can be made about the reliability of the product, for example, that the probability of software failure is below 0.0001%.

The most important testing technique for real-time software is *simulation*. A simulator is "a device which calculates, emulates or predicts the behavior of another device, or some aspect of the behavior of the world" [Bologna, Quirk, and Taylor, 1985]. A simulator can be considered as a test-bed on which the product can be run. The SQA group arranges for the simulator to provide selected inputs to the product, and then the simulator assists the SQA group in analyzing the outputs from the product to determine whether the product is functioning correctly.

Simulation is particularly important when it is impossible or too dangerous to test a product against suitable sets of test cases. Simulation can be used to check that a product can adequately handle situations like an aircraft stalling and about to crash, or a nuclear reactor about to go critical and explode. Another major use for a simulator is in the training environment. Perhaps the most common instance of this is a flight simulator used to train pilots. But a flight simulator can also be used to test avionics software without putting a human pilot at risk, as would be the case if an actual aircraft were flown with new and untested flight-control software.

12.24 CASE Tools for the Implementation Phase

CASE tools for the implementation phase were discussed in some detail in Section 4.4. For reason of space, that material is not repeated here.

12.25 MSG Case Study: Black-Box Test Cases

Figure 12.22 contains sample black-box test cases for the MSG case study; the complete set appears in Appendix H. The test cases are of two types, namely, those based on equivalence classes and boundary value analysis and those based on functional testing. Turning initially to equivalence classes and boundary value analysis, the first set of cases is to test whether the product will detect that an item number of an Investment should consist of up to 12 digits. This generates four test cases, corresponding to the presence of a nondigit (should be flagged as an input error), an item number less than 12 digits long (acceptable), an item number

---

Equivalence Classes and Boundary Value Analysis:

Investment information:

Equivalence classes for item number.

1. Character instead of integer	Error (not a number)
2. < 12 digits	Acceptable
3. 12 digits	Acceptable
4. > 12 digits	Error (too many digits)

Equivalence classes for item name.

1. First character not alphabetic	Error
2. < 1 character	Error
3. ≥ 1 character	Acceptable

Functional Analysis:

The functions outlined in the specification document are used to create test cases.

1. Add a mortgage
2. Add an investment
3. Modify a mortgage
4. Modify an investment
5. Delete a mortgage
6. Delete an investment
7. Update operating expenses
8. Compute funds to purchase houses
9. Print list of mortgages
10. Print list of investments

In addition to these direct tests, it is necessary to perform the following tests:

11. Attempt to add a mortgage that is already on file.
12. Attempt to add an investment that is already on file.
13. Attempt to delete a mortgage that is not on file.
14. Attempt to delete an investment that is not on file.
15. Attempt to modify a mortgage that is not on file.
16. Attempt to modify an investment that is not on file.
17. Attempt to delete twice a mortgage that is already on file.
18. Attempt to delete twice an investment that is already on file.
19. Attempt to update each field of a mortgage twice and check that the second version is stored.
20. Attempt to update each field of an investment twice and check that the second version is stored.
21. Attempt to update operating expenses twice and check that second version is stored.

Figure 12.22   Sample black-box test cases for MSG product.

exactly 12 digits long (acceptable), and an item number consisting of more than 12 digits (should be flagged as an input error).

The next set of three test cases checks that an item name of an Investment begins with a letter. Similar test cases check other statements in the specifications, as shown in Appendix H.

Turning now to functional testing, 10 functions are listed in the specification document, as reflected in Figure 12.22. An additional 11 test cases correspond to misuses of these functions.

It is important to be aware that these test cases could have been developed as soon as the specifications were complete; the only reason that they appear here is that test case selection is a topic of this chapter, rather than an earlier chapter. A major component of every test plan should be a stipulation that black-box test cases be drawn up as soon as possible (Section 10.5). If a contract has been signed for the project as a whole, then this will be as soon as the specification document has been approved. Otherwise, the contract for completing the product is signed once the client has agreed to the duration and cost estimates, that is, at the end of the planning phase. The black-box test cases can then be drawn up, for use by the SQA group during the implementation and integration phases.

Chapter Review

In this chapter various issues relating to the implementation of a product by a team are presented. These include choice of programming language (Section 12.1). The issue of fourth-generation languages is discussed in some detail in Section 12.2. Structured programming is the writing of readable, but not necessarily **goto**-less, code (Section 12.3). Good programming practice is described in Section 12.4, and the need for practical coding standards is presented in Section 12.5. The issue of team organization (Section 12.6) is approached by first considering the democratic team (Section 12.7) and the classical chief programmer team (Section 12.8) and then suggesting a team organization that makes use of the strengths of both approaches (Section 12.9). Next, portability is discussed (Section 12.10). Portability can be hampered by incompatibilities caused by hardware (Section 12.10.1), operating systems (Section 12.10.2), numerical software (Section 12.10.3), or compilers (Section 12.10.4). Nevertheless, it is important to try to make all products as portable as possible (Section 12.11). Ways of facilitating portability include using popular high-level languages, isolating the nonportable pieces of a product (Section 12.12.1), and adhering to language standards (Section 12.12.2). Then, comments are made regarding reuse of modules (Section 12.13). Test cases must be selected systematically (Section 12.14). Various black-box, glass-box, and nonexecution-based testing techniques are described (Sections 12.15, 12.16, and 12.17, respectively) and then compared (Section 12.18). The Cleanroom technique is described in Section 12.19. The testing of objects is presented in Section 12.20. This is followed by a discussion of the managerial implications of module testing (Section 12.21). Then the problems of testing distributed software and real-time software are presented (Sections 12.22 and 12.23). CASE tools for the implementation phase are mentioned next (Section 12.24). Finally (Section 12.25), black-box test cases for the MSG Case Study are presented.

For Further Reading

A wide-ranging source of information on 4GLs is [Martin, 1985]. Two opposing views on 4GLs can be found in [Cobb, 1985] and [Grant, 1985]. Contrasting productivity results with specific 4GLs are reported in [Misra and Jalics, 1988] and [Verner and Tate, 1988]. The attitudes of 43 organizations to 4GLs are reported in [Guimaraes, 1985].

For a detailed perspective on structured programming, the three landmark articles mentioned in the text, namely [Böhm and Jacopini, 1966], [Dijkstra, 1968a], and [Knuth, 1974], should be read in their entirety. *ACM SIGPLAN Notices* between 1968 and 1974 reflect the furor of the period regarding structured programming and especially the nature of the **goto** statement.

Excellent books on good programming practice include [Kernighan and Plauger, 1974], [Ledgard, 1975], [Bentley, 1986], and [McConnell, 1993]. With regard to programming team organization, the classical sources are [Weinberg, 1971], [Baker, 1972] and [Brooks, 1975]. Newer works on the subject include [Mantei, 1981], [Metzger, 1981], [Aron, 1983], [Licker, 1985], and [DeMarco and Lister, 1987].

Articles on team organization and management can be found in the October 1993 issue of the *Communications of the ACM*.

Three introductory texts on portability are [Wallis, 1982], [Wolberg, 1983], and [Lecarme and Gart, 1986]. Strategies for achieving portability can be found in [Mooney, 1990]. Portability of C and UNIX is discussed in [Johnson and Ritchie, 1978]. With regard to portability of Ada products, the reader should consult [Nissen and Wallis, 1984].

Probably the most important early work on execution-based testing is [Myers, 1979]. A comprehensive source of information on testing in general is [Beizer, 1990]. Issues in test case selection are discussed in [Petschenik, 1985]. Functional testing is described in [Howden, 1987]; structural techniques are compared in [Clarke, Podgurski, Richardson, and Zeil, 1989]. Cleanroom is described in [Cobb and Mills, 1990], [Dyer, 1992], and [Linger, 1994]. Statistical techniques are described in [Shooman, 1983] and also in [Goel, 1985]. A good introduction to software reliability is [Musa and Everett, 1990]. In addition, the proceedings of the annual International Symposium on Software Reliability Engineering contain a wide variety of articles on software reliability. The proceedings of the International Symposia on Software Testing and Analysis cover a particularly broad range of testing issues.

A survey of different approaches to the testing of objects can be found in [Turner, 1994]. Two important papers on the subject are [Perry and Kaiser, 1990] and [Harrold, McGregor, and Fitzpatrick, 1992]. The September 1994 issue of the *Communications of the ACM* contains a number of articles on the testing of object-oriented software.

With regard to metrics for the implementation phase, further information regarding the validity of software science can be found in [Coulter, 1983], [Conte, Dunsmore, and

Shen, 1986], [Musa, Iannino, and Okumoto, 1987], [Shepperd, 1988b], [Weyuker, 1988b], and [Shepperd and Ince, 1994]. McCabe's cyclomatic complexity was first presented in [McCabe, 1976]. Extensions of the metric to the design phase appear in [McCabe and Butler, 1989]. Criticisms of this metric can be found in [Shepperd, 1988a], [Weyuker, 1988b], and [Shepperd and Ince, 1994]. Metrics for managing code inspections are described in [Barnard and Price, 1994].

Approaches to testing distributed software are presented in [Garcia-Molina, Germano, and Kohler, 1984] and [Wahl and Schach, 1988]. A wide-ranging source of material on testing real-time systems is [Quirk, 1985]. Glass has written a number of works on real-time systems, including [Glass, 1982] and [Glass, 1983]. Checking that real-time constraints have been satisfied is described in [Dasarathy, 1985].

Problems

Your instructor has asked you to implement the Osbert Oglesby product (Appendix A). Which language would you choose for implementing the product, and why? Of the various languages available to you, list their benefits and their costs. Do not attempt to attach dollar values to your answers. **12.1**

Repeat Problem 12.1 for the elevator problem (Section 8.6.1). **12.2**

Repeat Problem 12.1 for the automated library circulation system (Problem 6.18). **12.3**

Repeat Problem 12.1 for the automated teller machine (Problem 9.2). **12.4**

Repeat Problem 12.1 for the product that determines whether a bank statement is correct (Problem 6.17). **12.5**

Show that if blocks are connected only by sequence, selection, and iteration, and labels are forbidden, then every block will have exactly one entry and one exit. **12.6**

Add prologue comments to a module that you have recently written. **12.7**

How do coding standards for a one-person software production company differ from those in organizations with 300 software professionals? **12.8**

How do coding standards for a software company that develops and maintains software for intensive-care units differ from those in an organization that develops and maintains accounting products? **12.9**

How would you organize a team to develop a payroll project? How would you organize a team to develop state-of-the-art military avionics software? Explain your answers. **12.10**

You have just started a new software company. All your employees are recent college graduates; this is their first programming job. Is it possible to implement democratic teams in your organization, and if so, how? **12.11**

Explain how you would ensure that the product that checks whether a bank statement is correct (Problem 6.17) is as portable as possible. **12.12**

Explain how you would ensure that the automated library circulation system (Problem 6.18) is as portable as possible. **12.13**

12.14   Explain how you would ensure that the software for the automated teller machine (ATM) of Problem 9.2 is as portable as possible.

12.15   Your organization is developing a real-time control system for a new type of laser that will be used in cancer therapy. You are in charge of writing two assembler modules. How will you instruct your team to ensure that the resulting code will be as portable as possible?

12.16   You are responsible for porting a 750,000-line FORTRAN product to your company's new computer. You manage to copy the source code to the new machine, but discover when you try to compile it that every one of the over 15,000 input/output statements has been written in a nonstandard FORTRAN syntax that the new compiler rejects. What do you do now?

12.17   Set up black-box test cases for Naur's text-processing problem (Section 5.5.2). For each test case, state what is being tested and the expected outcome of that test case.

12.18   Using your product for Problem 5.15 (or code distributed by your instructor), set up statement coverage test cases. For each test case, state what is being tested and the expected outcome of that test case.

12.19   Repeat Problem 12.18 for branch coverage.

12.20   Repeat Problem 12.18 for all-definition-use-path coverage.

12.21   Repeat Problem 12.18 for path coverage.

12.22   Repeat Problem 12.18 for linear code sequences.

12.23   Draw a flowchart of your product for Problem 5.15 (or code distributed by your instructor). Determine its cyclomatic complexity. If you are unable to determine the number of branches, consider the flowchart as a directed graph. Determine the number of edges e, nodes n, and connected components c. (Each method constitutes a connected component.) The cyclomatic complexity V is then given by [McCabe, 1976]

$$V = e - n + 2c$$

12.24   Determine Halstead's four basic metrics for the code fragment of Figure 12.18(b).

12.25   You are the owner and sole employee of One-Person Software Company. You have bought the programming environment described in Section 4.4. List its five capabilities in order of importance to you, giving reasons.

12.26   You are now the vice-president for software technology of Very Big Software Company; there are 17,500 employees in your organization. How do you rank the capabilities of the programming environment described in Section 4.4? Explain any differences between your answer to this problem and the previous one.

12.27   (Term Project) Draw up black-box test cases for the product you specified in Problem 8.15 or 9.10. For each test case, state what is being tested and the expected outcome of that test case.

12.28   (Case Study) Appendix I contains a Java implementation of the MSG Case Study. Draw up statement coverage test cases for the product. For each test case, state what is being tested and the expected outcome of that test case.

(Case Study) Repeat Problem 12.28 for branch coverage.   **12.29**

(Case Study) Repeat Problem 12.28 for all-definition-use-path coverage.   **12.30**

(Case Study) Repeat Problem 12.28 for path coverage.   **12.31**

(Case Study) Repeat Problem 12.28 for linear code sequences.   **12.32**

(Readings in Software Engineering) Your instructor will distribute copies of [Perry   **12.33**
and Kaiser, 1990] and [Harrold, McGregor, and Fitzpatrick, 1992]. Reconcile the
results of the two papers regarding the need to retest instances of a reused class even
though the class has already been thoroughly tested.

References

[ANSI X3.159, 1989] "The Programming Language C," ANSI X3.159-1989, American
National Standards Institute, Inc., 1989.

[ANSI X3.9, 1977] "Programming Language FORTRAN," ANSI X3.9-1977, American
National Standards Institute, Inc., 1977.

[ANSI/IEEE 754, 1985] "Standard for Binary Floating Point Arithmetic," ANSI/IEEE
754, American National Standards Institute, Inc., Institute of Electrical and Electronic
Engineers, Inc., 1985.

[ANSI/IEEE 770X3.97, 1983] "Pascal Computer Programming Language," ANSI/IEEE
770X3.97-1983, American National Standards Institute, Inc., Institute of Electrical
and Electronic Engineers, Inc., 1983.

[ANSI/MIL-STD-1815A, 1983] "Reference Manual for the Ada Programming Language,"
ANSI/MIL-STD-1815A, American National Standards Institute, Inc., United States
Department of Defense, 1983.

[Aron, 1983] J. D. ARON, *The Program Development Process. Part II. The Programming
Team*, Addison-Wesley, Reading, MA, 1983.

[Baker, 1972] F. T. BAKER, "Chief Programmer Team Management of Production
Programming," *IBM Systems Journal* **11** (No. 1, 1972), pp. 56–73.

[Barnard and Price, 1994] J. BARNARD AND A. PRICE, "Managing Code Inspection
Information," *IEEE Software* **11** (March 1994), pp. 59–69.

[Basili and Hutchens, 1983] V. R. BASILI AND D. H. HUTCHENS, "An Empirical Study of a
Syntactic Complexity Family," *IEEE Transactions on Software Engineering* **SE-9**
(November 1983), pp. 664–672.

[Basili and Selby, 1987] V. R. BASILI AND R. W. SELBY, "Comparing the Effectiveness of
Software Testing Strategies," *IEEE Transactions on Software Engineering* **SE-13**
(December 1987), pp. 1278–1296.

[Basili and Weiss, 1984] V. R. BASILI AND D. M. WEISS, "A Methodology for Collecting
Valid Software Engineering Data," *IEEE Transactions on Software Engineering*
SE-10 (November 1984), pp. 728–738.

[Beizer, 1990] B. BEIZER, *Software Testing Techniques,* Second Edition, Van Nostrand
Reinhold, New York, 1990.

[Bentley, 1986] J. BENTLEY, *Programming Pearls*, Addison-Wesley, Reading, MA, 1986.

[Böhm and Jacopini, 1966] C. BÖHM AND G. JACOPINI, "Flow Diagrams, Turing Machines,
and Languages with Only Two Formation Rules," *Communications of the ACM* **9**
(May 1966), pp. 366–371.

[Bologna, Quirk, and Taylor, 1985] S. BOLOGNA, W. J. QUIRK, AND J. R. TAYLOR, "Simulation and System Validation," in: *Verification and Validation of Real-Time Software*, W. J. Quirk (Editor), Springer-Verlag, Berlin, 1985, pp. 179–201.

[Brooks, 1975] F. P. BROOKS, JR., *The Mythical Man-Month: Essays in Software Engineering*, Addison-Wesley, Reading, MA, 1975.

[Carlson, Druffel, Fisher, and Whitaker, 1980] W. E. CARLSON, L. E. DRUFFEL, D. A. FISHER, AND W. A. WHITAKER, "Introducing Ada," *Proceedings of the ACM Annual Conference, ACM 80*, Nashville, TN, 1980, pp. 263–271.

[Clarke, Podgurski, Richardson, and Zeil, 1989] L. A. CLARKE, A. PODGURSKI, D. J. RICHARDSON, AND S. J. ZEIL, "A Formal Evaluation of Data Flow Path Selection Criteria," *IEEE Transactions on Software Engineering* **15** (November 1989), pp. 1318–1332.

[Cobb, 1985] R. H. COBB, "In Praise of 4GLs," *Datamation* **31** (July 15, 1985), pp. 90–96.

[Cobb and Mills, 1990] R. H. COBB AND H. D. MILLS, "Engineering Software under Statistical Quality Control," *IEEE Software* **7** (November 1990), pp. 44–54.

[Conte, Dunsmore, and Shen, 1986] S. D. CONTE, H. E. DUNSMORE, AND V. Y. SHEN, *Software Engineering Metrics and Models,"* Benjamin/Cummings, Menlo Park, CA, 1986.

[Coulter, 1983] N. S. COULTER, "Software Science and Cognitive Psychology," *IEEE Transactions on Software Engineering* **SE-9** (March 1983), pp. 166–171.

[Crossman, 1982] T. D. CROSSMAN, "Inspection Teams, Are They Worth It?" *Proceedings of the Second National Symposium on EDP Quality Assurance*, Chicago, November 1982.

[Dasarathy, 1985] B. DASARATHY, "Timing Constraints of Real-Time Systems: Constructs for Expressing Them, Methods of Validating Them," *IEEE Transactions on Software Engineering* **SE-11** (January 1985), pp. 80–86.

[Date, 1990] C. J. DATE, *An Introduction to Database Systems,* Fifth Edition, Addison-Wesley, Reading MA, 1990.

[DeMarco and Lister, 1987] T. DEMARCO, AND T. LISTER, *Peopleware: Productive Projects and Teams,* Dorset House, New York, 1987.

[Dijkstra, 1968a] E. W. DIJKSTRA, "Go To Statement Considered Harmful," *Communications of the ACM* **11** (March 1968), pp. 147–148.

[Dyer, 1992] M. DYER, *The Cleanroom Approach to Quality Software Development,* John Wiley and Sons, New York, 1992.

[Endres, 1975] A. ENDRES, "An Analysis of Errors and Their Causes in System Programs," *IEEE Transactions on Software Engineering* **SE-1** (June 1975), pp.140–149.

[Fisher, 1976] D. A. FISHER, "A Common Programming Language for the Department of Defense—Background and Technical Requirements," Report P-1191, Institute for Defense Analyses, Alexandria, VA, 1976.

[Garcia-Molina, Germano, and Kohler, 1984] H. GARCIA-MOLINA, F. GERMANO, JR., AND W. H. KOHLER, "Debugging a Distributed Computer System," *IEEE Transactions on Software Engineering"* **SE-10** (March 1984), pp. 210–219.

[Garman, 1981] J. R. GARMAN, "The 'Bug' Heard 'Round the World," *ACM SIGSOFT Software Engineering Notes* **6** (October 1981), pp. 3–10.

[Gifford and Spector, 1987] D. GIFFORD AND A. SPECTOR, "Case Study: IBM's System/360-370 Architecture," *Communications of the ACM* **30** (April 1987), pp. 292–307.

[Glass, 1982] R. L. GLASS, "Real-Time Checkout: The 'Source Error First' Approach," *Software—Practice and Experience* **12** (January 1982), pp. 77–83.

[Glass, 1983] R. L. GLASS (Editor), *Real-Time Software*, Prentice-Hall, Englewood Cliffs, NJ, 1983.

[Goel, 1985] A. L. GOEL, "Software Reliability Models: Assumptions, Limitations, and Applicability," *IEEE Transactions on Software Engineering* **SE-11** (December 1985), pp. 1411–1423.

[Grady, 1992] R. B. GRADY, *Practical Software Metrics for Project Management and Process Improvement*, Prentice-Hall, Englewood Cliffs, NJ, 1992.

[Grant, 1985] F. J. GRANT, "The Downside of 4GLs," *Datamation* **31** (July 15, 1985), pp. 99–104.

[Gremillion, 1984] L. L. GREMILLION, "Determinants of Program Repair Maintenance Requirements," *Communications of the ACM* **27** (August 1984), pp. 826–832.

[Guimaraes, 1985] T. GUIMARAES, "A Study of Application Program Development Techniques," *Communications of the ACM* **28** (May 1985), pp. 494–499.

[Halstead, 1977] M. H. HALSTEAD, *Elements of Software Science*, Elsevier North-Holland, New York, 1977.

[Harrold, McGregor, and Fitzpatrick, 1992] M. J. HARROLD, J. D. MCGREGOR, AND K. J. FITZPATRICK, "Incremental Testing of Object-Oriented Class Structures," *Proceedings of the 14th International Conference on Software Engineering*, Melbourne, Australia, May 1992, pp. 68–80.

[Howden, 1987] W. E. HOWDEN, *Functional Program Testing and Analysis*, McGraw-Hill, New York, 1987.

[Hwang, 1981] S.-S. V. HWANG, "An Empirical Study in Functional Testing, Structural Testing, and Code Reading Inspection," Scholarly Paper 362, Department of Computer Science, University of Maryland, College Park, MD, 1981.

[ISO-7185, 1980] "Specification for the Computer Programming Language Pascal," ISO-7185, International Standards Organization, 1980.

[ISO/IEC 8652, 1995] "Programming Language Ada: Language and Standard Libraries," ISO/IEC 8652, International Organization for Standardization, International Electrotechnical Commission, 1995.

[Jensen, and Wirth, 1975] K. JENSEN AND N. WIRTH, *Pascal User Manual and Report*, Second Edition, Springer-Verlag, New York, 1975.

[Johnson, 1979] S. C. JOHNSON, "A Tour through the Portable C Compiler," Seventh Edition, UNIX Programmer's Manual, Bell Laboratories, Murray Hill, NJ, January 1979.

[Johnson and Ritchie, 1978] S. C. JOHNSON AND D. M. RITCHIE, "Portability of C Programs and the UNIX System," *Bell System Technical Journal* **57** (No. 6, Part 2, 1978), pp. 2021–2048.

[Jones, 1986a] C. JONES, *Programming Productivity*, McGraw-Hill, New York, 1986.

[Kernighan and Plauger, 1974] B. W. KERNIGHAN AND P. J. PLAUGER, *The Elements of Programming Style*, McGraw-Hill, New York, 1974.

[Kernighan and Ritchie, 1978] B. W. KERNIGHAN AND D. M. RITCHIE, *The C Programming Language*, Prentice-Hall, Englewood Cliffs, NJ, 1978.

[Klunder, 1988] D. KLUNDER, "Hungarian Naming Conventions," Technical Report, Microsoft Corporation, Redmond, WA, January 1988.

[Knuth, 1974] D. E. KNUTH, "Structured Programming with **go to** Statements," *ACM Computing Surveys* **6** (December 1974), pp. 261–301.

[Lecarme and Gart, 1986] O. LECARME AND M. P. GART, *Software Portability,* McGraw-Hill, New York, 1986.

[Ledgard, 1975] H. LEDGARD, *Programming Proverbs*, Hayden Books, Rochelle Park, NJ, 1975.

[Licker, 1985] P. S. LICKER, *The Art of Managing Software Development People*, John Wiley and Sons, New York, 1985.

[Linger, 1994] R. C. LINGER, "Cleanroom Process Model," *IEEE Software* **11** (March 1994), pp. 50–58.

[Liskov, Snyder, Atkinson, and Schaffert, 1977] B. LISKOV, A. SNYDER, R. ATKINSON, AND C. SCHAFFERT, "Abstraction Mechanisms in CLU," *Communications of the ACM* **20** (August 1977), pp. 564–576.

[Mackenzie, 1980] C. E. MACKENZIE, *Coded Character Sets: History and Development*, Addison-Wesley, Reading, MA, 1980.

[Mantei, 1981] M. MANTEI, "The Effect of Programming Team Structures on Programming Tasks," *Communications of the ACM* **24** (March 1981), pp. 106–113.

[Martin, 1985] J. MARTIN, *Fourth-Generation Languages, Volumes I, II, and III*, Prentice-Hall, Englewood Cliffs, NJ, 1985.

[McCabe, 1976] T. J. MCCABE, "A Complexity Measure," *IEEE Transactions on Software Engineering* **SE-2** (December 1976), pp. 308–320.

[McCabe, 1983] T. J. MCCABE, *Structural Testing*, IEEE Computer Society Press, Los Angeles, 1983.

[McCabe and Butler, 1989] T. J. MCCABE AND C. W. BUTLER, "Design Complexity Measurement and Testing," *Communications of the ACM* **32** (December 1989), pp. 1415–1425.

[McConnell, 1993] S. MCCONNELL, *Code Complete: A Practical Handbook of Software Construction*, Microsoft Press, Redmond, WA, 1993.

[Metzger, 1981] P. W. METZGER, *Managing a Programming Project*, Second Edition, Prentice-Hall, Englewood Cliffs, NJ, 1981.

[Mills, Dyer, and Linger, 1987] H. D. MILLS, M. DYER, AND R. C. LINGER, "Cleanroom Software Engineering," *IEEE Software* **4** (September 1987), pp. 19–25.

[Misra and Jalics, 1988] S. K. MISRA AND P. J. JALICS, "Third-Generation versus Fourth-Generation Software Development," *IEEE Software* **5** (July 1988), pp. 8–14.

[Mooney, 1990] J. D. MOONEY, "Strategies for Supporting Application Portability," *IEEE Computer* **23** (November 1990), pp. 59–70.

[Musa and Everett, 1990] J. D. MUSA AND W. W. EVERETT, "Software-Reliability Engineering: Technology for the 1990s," *IEEE Software* **7** (November 1990), pp. 36–43.

[Musa, Iannino, and Okumoto, 1987] J. D. MUSA, A. IANNINO AND K. OKUMOTO, *Software Reliability: Measurement, Prediction, Application*, McGraw-Hill, New York, 1987.

[Myers, 1976] G. J. MYERS, *Software Reliability: Principles and Practices,* Wiley-Interscience, New York, 1976.

[Myers, 1978a] G. J. MYERS, "A Controlled Experiment in Program Testing and Code Walkthroughs/Inspections," *Communications of the ACM* **21** (September 1978), pp. 760–768.

[Myers, 1979] G. J. MYERS, *The Art of Software Testing,* John Wiley and Sons, New York, 1979.

[Nissen and Wallis, 1984] J. NISSEN AND P. WALLIS (Editors), *Portability and Style in Ada,* Cambridge University Press, Cambridge, UK, 1984.

[NIST 151, 1988] "POSIX: Portable Operating System Interface for Computer Environments," *Federal Information Processing Standard 151,* National Institute of Standards and Technology, Washington, DC, 1988.

[Ottenstein, 1979] L. M. OTTENSTEIN, "Quantitative Estimates of Debugging Requirements," *IEEE Transactions on Software Engineering* **SE-5** (September 1979), pp. 504–514.

[Perry and Kaiser, 1990] D. E. PERRY AND G. E. KAISER, "Adequate Testing and Object-Oriented Programming," *Journal of Object-Oriented Programming* **2** (January/ February 1990), pp. 13–19.

[Petschenik, 1985] N. H. PETSCHENIK, "Practical Priorities in System Testing," *IEEE Software* **2** (September 1985), pp. 18–23.

[Quirk, 1983] W. J. QUIRK, "Recent Developments in the SPECK Specification System," Report CSS.146, Harwell, UK, 1983.

[Quirk, 1985] W. J. QUIRK (Editor), *Verification and Validation of Real-Time Software,* Springer-Verlag, Berlin, 1985.

[Rapps and Weyuker, 1985] S. RAPPS AND E. J. WEYUKER, "Selecting Software Test Data Using Data Flow Information," *IEEE Transactions on Software Engineering* **SE-11** (April 1985), pp. 367–375.

[Sammet, 1978] J. E. SAMMET, "The Early History of COBOL," *Proceedings of the History of Programming Languages Conference,* Los Angeles, 1978, pp. 199–276.

[Seitz, 1985] C. L. SEITZ, "The Cosmic Cube," *Communications of the ACM* **28** (January 1985), pp. 22–33.

[Selby, Basili, and Baker, 1987] R. W. SELBY, V. R. BASILI, AND F. T. BAKER, "Cleanroom Software Development: An Empirical Evaluation," *IEEE Transactions on Software Engineering* **SE-13** (September 1987), pp. 1027–1037.

[Shepperd, 1988a] M. J. SHEPPERD, "An Evaluation of Software Product Metrics," *Information and Software Technology* **30** (No. 3, 1988), pp. 177–188.

[Shepperd, 1988b] M. SHEPPERD, "A Critique of Cyclomatic Complexity as a Software Metric," *Software Engineering Journal* **3** (March 1988), pp. 30–36.

[Shepperd and Ince, 1994] M. SHEPPERD AND D. C. INCE, "A Critique of Three Metrics,"*Journal of Systems and Software* **26** (September 1994), pp. 197–210.

[Shooman, 1983] M. L. SHOOMAN, *Software Engineering: Design, Reliability, and Management,* McGraw-Hill, New York, 1983.

[Silberschatz and Galvin, 1994] A. SILBERSCHATZ AND P. B. GALVIN, *Operating System Concepts,* Fourth Edition, Addison-Wesley, Reading, MA, 1994.

[Stroustrup, 1991] B. STROUSTRUP, *The C++ Programming Language,* Second Edition, Addison-Wesley, Reading, MA, 1991.

[Takahashi and Kamayachi, 1985] M. TAKAHASHI AND Y. KAMAYACHI, "An Empirical Study of a Model for Program Error Prediction," *Proceedings of the Eighth International Conference on Software Engineering,* London, 1985, pp. 330–336.

[Tanenbaum, 1981] A. S. TANENBAUM, "Network Protocols," *ACM Computing Surveys* **13** (December 1981), pp. 453–489.

[Trammel, Binder, and Snyder, 1992] C. J. TRAMMEL, L. H. BINDER, AND C. E. SNYDER, "The Automated Production Control Documentation System: A Case Study in Cleanroom Software Engineering," *ACM Transactions on Software Engineering and Methodology* **1** (January 1992), pp. 81–94.

[Turner, 1994] C. D. TURNER, "State-Based Testing: A New Method for the Testing of Object-Oriented Programs," Ph.D. Thesis, Computer Science Division, University of Durham, Durham, UK, November 1994.

[van der Poel and Schach, 1983] K. G. VAN DER POEL AND S. R. SCHACH, "A Software Metric for Cost Estimation and Efficiency Measurement in Data Processing System Development," *Journal of Systems and Software* **3** (September 1983), pp. 187–191.

[Verner and Tate, 1988] J. VERNER AND G. TATE, "Estimating Size and Effort in Fourth-Generation Development," *IEEE Software* **5** (July 1988), pp. 15–22.

[Wahl and Schach, 1988] N. J. WAHL AND S. R. SCHACH, "A Methodology and Distributed Tool for Debugging Dataflow Programs," *Proceedings of the Second Workshop on Software Testing, Verification, and Analysis,* Banff, Canada, July 1988, pp. 98–105.

[Wallis, 1982] P. J. L. WALLIS, *Portable Programming,* John Wiley and Sons, New York, 1982.

[Walsh, 1979] T. J. WALSH, "A Software Reliability Study Using a Complexity Measure," *Proceedings of the AFIPS National Computer Conference,* New York, 1979, pp. 761–768.

[Weinberg, 1971] G. M. WEINBERG, *The Psychology of Computer Programming,* Van Nostrand Reinhold, New York, 1971.

[Weyuker, 1988a] E. J. WEYUKER, "An Empirical Study of the Complexity of Data Flow Testing," *Proceedings of the Second Workshop on Software Testing, Verification, and Analysis,* Banff, Canada, July 1988, pp. 188–195.

[Weyuker, 1988b] E. J. WEYUKER, "Evaluating Software Complexity Measures," *IEEE Trans. on Software Engineering* **14** (September 1988), pp. 1357–1365.

[Wilde, Matthews, and Huitt, 1993] N. WILDE, P. MATTHEWS, AND R. HUITT, "Maintaining Object-Oriented Software," *IEEE Software* **10** (January 1993), pp. 75–80.

[Wolberg, 1983] J. R. WOLBERG, *Conversion of Computer Software,* Prentice-Hall, Englewood Cliffs, NJ, 1983.

[Woodward, Hedley, and Hennell, 1980] M. R. WOODWARD, D. HEDLEY, AND M. A. HENNELL, "Experience with Path Analysis and Testing of Programs," *IEEE Transactions on Software Engineering* **SE-6** (May 1980), pp. 278–286.

13

IMPLEMENTATION AND INTEGRATION PHASE

Up to now, implementation and integration have been treated as two separate and independent phases. In the approach that has been presented, each module (or object) is implemented by a member of the programming team and tested by SQA. Then, during the integration phase the modules are put together and tested as a whole. In fact, this is not a good way to develop software. Instead, the implementation and integration phases should be carried out in parallel. This parallel approach is the subject of this chapter.

In both the title and the body of this chapter we refer to the "implementation and integration phase." Strictly speaking, there is no such thing. Implementation and integration are two different activities, as distinct as design and planning. Nevertheless, from now on we use the term *implementation and integration phase* to describe the activities that are performed when the implementation phase and the integration phase are carried out in parallel.

First, products developed using the structured paradigm are considered, and then object-oriented products.

13.1   IMPLEMENTATION AND INTEGRATION

Consider the product depicted in Figure 13.1. One approach in developing the product is to code and test each module separately, then link all 13 modules together, and test the product as a whole. There are two difficulties with this approach. First, consider module a. It cannot be tested on its own, because it calls modules b, c, and d. Thus in order to test module a, modules b, c, and d must be coded as *stubs*. In its simplest form, a stub is an empty module. A more effective stub prints a message such as module displayRadarPattern called. Best of all, a stub should return values corresponding to preplanned test cases.

Now consider module h. To test it on its own requires a driver, a module that calls it one or more times, if possible checking the values returned by the module under test. Similarly, testing module d requires a driver and two stubs. Thus one problem that arises with separate implementation and integration is that effort has to

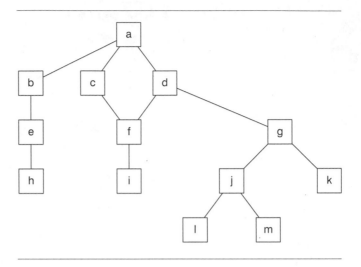

Figure 13.1 Typical module interconnection diagram.

be put into constructing stubs and drivers, all of which are thrown away after module testing is completed.

The second, and much more important, difficulty that arises when the implementation phase is completed before integration starts is lack of fault isolation. If the product as a whole is tested against a specific test case and the product fails, then the fault could lie in any of the 13 modules or 13 interfaces. In a large product with, say, 103 modules and 108 interfaces, there are no fewer than 211 places where the fault might lie.

The solution to both these difficulties is to combine module and integration testing.

13.1.1   TOP-DOWN IMPLEMENTATION AND INTEGRATION

In top-down implementation and integration, if module mAbove calls module mBelow, then mAbove is implemented and integrated before mBelow. Suppose that the product shown in Figure 13.1 is implemented and integrated top-down. One possible top-down ordering is a, b, c, d, e, f, g, h, i, j, k, l, and m. First, module a is coded and tested with b, c, and d implemented as stubs. Now stub b is expanded into module b, linked to module a, and tested with module e implemented as a stub. Implementation and integration proceeds in this way until all the modules have been integrated into the product. Another possible top-down ordering is a, b, e, h, c, d, f, i, g, j, k, l, and m. With this latter ordering, portions of the implementation and integration can proceed in parallel in the following way. After a has been coded and tested, one programmer can use module a to implement and integrate b, e, and h, while another programmer can use a to work in parallel on c, d, f, and i. Once d and f are completed, a third programmer can start work on g, j, k, l, and m.

Suppose that module a by itself executes correctly on a specific test case. However, when the same test data are submitted after b has been coded and integrated into the product, now consisting of modules a and b linked together, the test fails. The fault can be in one of two places, namely, in module b or the interface between modules a and b. In general, whenever a module mNew is added to what has been tested so far and a previously successful test case fails, the fault almost certainly will lie either in mNew or in the interface(s) between mNew and the rest of the product. Thus top-down implementation and integration supports fault isolation. A further advantage of this scheme is that little extra work is involved in writing stubs. Each stub is simply expanded into the corresponding complete module at the appropriate step in the development of the product.

A big advantage of top-down implementation and integration is that major design flaws show up early. The modules of a product can be divided in two groups, *logic modules* and *operational modules*. Logic modules essentially incorporate the decision-making flow of control aspects of the product. The logic modules are generally those situated close to the root in the module interconnection diagram. For example, in Figure 13.1 it is reasonable to expect modules a, b, c, d, and perhaps g and j to be logic modules. The operational modules, on the other hand, perform the actual operations of the product. For example, an operational module may be named getLineFromTerminal or measureTemperatureOfReactorCore. The operational modules are generally found in the lower levels, close to the leaves, of the module interconnection diagram. In Figure 13.1 modules e, f, h, i, k, l, and m turn out to be operational modules.

It is always important to code and test the logic modules before coding and testing the operational modules. This will ensure that any major design faults will show up early. Suppose that the whole product is completed before a major fault is detected. Large parts of the product will have to be rewritten, especially the logic modules that embody the flow of control. Many of the operational modules will probably be reusable in the rebuilt product; for example, a module like getLineFromTerminal or measureTemperatureOfReactorCore will be needed no matter how the product is restructured. However, the way the operational modules will be interconnected to the other modules in the product may have to be changed, resulting in unnecessary work. Thus the earlier a design fault is detected, the quicker and less costly it will be to correct the product and get back on the development schedule. The order in which modules are implemented and integrated using the top-down strategy essentially ensures that logic modules are indeed implemented and integrated before operational modules, because logic modules are almost always the ancestors of operational modules in the module interconnection diagram. This is a major strength of top-down implementation and integration.

Nevertheless, top-down implementation and integration has a disadvantage, namely, potentially reusable modules may not be adequately tested. Reuse of a module that is thought, incorrectly, to have been thoroughly tested is likely to be less cost-effective than writing that module from scratch, because the assumption that a module is correct can lead to wrong conclusions when the product fails. Instead of suspecting the insufficiently tested module, the tester may think that the fault lies elsewhere, resulting in a waste of effort.

Logic modules are likely to be somewhat problem-specific, and hence unusable in another context. However, operational modules, particularly if they have informational or functional cohesion (Section 6.2), are probably reusable in future products and, therefore, require thorough testing. Unfortunately, the operational modules are generally the lower-level modules in the module interconnection diagram and hence are not tested as frequently as the upper-level modules. For example, if there are 184 modules, the root module will be tested 184 times, whereas the last module to be integrated into the product will be tested only once. Top-down implementation and integration makes reuse a risky undertaking as a consequence of inadequate testing of operational modules.

The situation is exacerbated if the product is well designed; in fact, the better the design, the less thoroughly the modules are likely to be tested. To see this, consider a module computeSquareRoot. This module takes two arguments, a floating-point number x whose square root is to be determined and an errorFlag that is set to true if x is negative. Suppose further that computeSquareRoot is called by module m3 and that m3 contains the statement

$$\textbf{if } (x >= 0)$$
$$y = \text{computeSquareRoot } (x, \text{errorFlag});$$

In other words, computeSquareRoot is never called unless the value of x is nonnegative, and therefore the module can never be tested with negative values of x to see if it functions correctly. The type of design where the calling module includes a safety check of this kind is referred to as *defensive programming*. As a result of defensive programming, subordinate operational modules are unlikely to be thoroughly tested if implemented and integrated top-down. Despite that, defensive programming is generally considered to be good programming practice within the context of the structured paradigm (but see [Meyer, 1992a] on how an object-oriented language like Eiffel can render defensive programming unnecessary).

13.1.2   BOTTOM-UP IMPLEMENTATION AND INTEGRATION

In bottom-up implementation and integration, if module mAbove calls module mBelow, then mBelow is implemented and integrated before mAbove. Returning to Figure 13.1, one possible bottom-up ordering is l, m, h, i, j, k, e, f, g, b, c, d, and a. In order to have the product coded by a team, a better bottom-up ordering is as follows: h, e, and b are given to one programmer and i, f, and c to another. The third programmer starts with l, m, j, k, and g, then implements d and integrates his or her work with the work of the second programmer. Finally, when b, c, and d have been successfully integrated, a can be implemented and integrated.

The operational modules are thus thoroughly tested when a bottom-up strategy is used. In addition, the testing is done with the aid of drivers, rather than by fault shielding, defensively programmed calling modules. Although bottom-up implementation and integration solves the major difficulty of top-down implementation

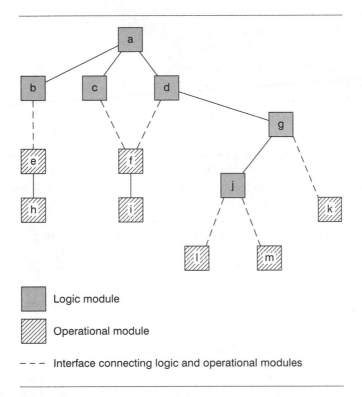

Figure 13.2 Product of Figure 13.1 developed using sandwich implementation and integration.

and integration and shares with top-down implementation and integration the advantage of fault isolation, it unfortunately has a difficulty of its own. Specifically, major design faults will be detected late in the integration phase. The logic modules are integrated last, and hence if there is a major design fault, it will be picked up at the end of the integration process with the resulting huge cost of redesigning and recoding large portions of the product.

Thus both top-down and bottom-up implementation and integration have their strengths and their weaknesses. The solution for product development is to combine the two strategies in such a way as to make use of their strengths and to minimize their weaknesses. This leads to the idea of sandwich implementation and integration.

13.1.3 SANDWICH IMPLEMENTATION AND INTEGRATION

Consider the module interconnection diagram shown in Figure 13.2. Six of the modules, namely a, b, c, d, g, and j, are logic modules, and therefore should be implemented and integrated top-down. Seven are operational modules, namely e, f, h, i, k, l, and m, and should be implemented and integrated bottom-up. That is to say, because neither top-down nor bottom-up implementation and integration is suitable

---

JUST IN CASE YOU WANTED TO KNOW

The term *sandwich implementation and integration* [Myers, 1979] comes from viewing the logic modules and the operational modules as the top and the bottom of a sandwich, and the interfaces that connect them as the sandwich filling. This can be seen (sort of!) in Figure 13.2.

---

for all the modules, the solution is to partition them. The six logic modules are implemented and integrated top-down, and any major design faults are caught early. The seven operational modules are implemented and integrated bottom-up. They thus receive a thorough testing, unshielded by defensively programmed calling modules, and can therefore be reused with confidence in other products. When all modules have been appropriately integrated, the interfaces between the two groups of modules are tested one by one. There is fault isolation at all times during this process, called *sandwich implementation and integration* (see the Just in Case You Wanted to Know box on this page).

13.1.4   IMPLEMENTATION AND INTEGRATION OF OBJECT-ORIENTED PRODUCTS

In general, objects are implemented and integrated in a bottom-up fashion. First, the objects that do not send any messages to other objects are implemented and integrated. Then, the objects that send messages to those objects are implemented and integrated, and so on, until all the objects in the product are implemented and integrated. (This process must be modified if there is recursion.)

If the product is implemented in a hybrid object-oriented language like C++, the modules that are not objects are now implemented and integrated. This is performed in a top-down manner. Finally, the nonobject modules are integrated with the objects. Even when the product is implemented using a pure object-oriented language like Java, class methods (sometimes referred to as "static methods") such as main and the utility methods are usually similar in structure to logic modules of the structured paradigm. Thus, class methods are also implemented top-down and then integrated with the other objects. In other words, when performing implementation and integration of an object-oriented product, a variant of sandwich implementation and integration is used.

13.1.5   MANAGEMENT ISSUES DURING THE IMPLEMENTATION AND INTEGRATION PHASE

A problem for management is discovering, at integration time, that pieces of the modules simply do not fit together. For example, suppose that programmer 1 coded object o1, and programmer 2 coded object o2. In the version of the design documentation used by programmer 1, object o1 sends a message to object o2 passing four arguments, but the version of the design documentation used by programmer 2 states clearly that only three arguments are passed to o2. A problem like this can arise when a change is made to only one copy of the design document, without informing all members of the development group. Both programmers know that they are in the right, and neither is prepared to compromise, because the programmer that gives in will have to recode large portions of the product.

In order to solve these and similar problems of incompatibility, the entire integration process should be run by the SQA group. Furthermore, as with testing during other phases, the SQA group has the most to lose if the integration testing is improperly performed. The SQA group is therefore the most likely to ensure that the testing is performed thoroughly. Thus the manager of the SQA group should have responsibility for all aspects of integration testing. He or she must decide which modules will be implemented and integrated top-down and which will be implemented and integrated bottom-up and will assign the integration-testing tasks to the appropriate individuals. The SQA group, which will have drawn up the integration test plan in the SPMP, is responsible for implementing that plan.

At the end of the integration phase all the modules will have been tested and combined into a single product.

13.2 TESTING DURING THE IMPLEMENTATION AND INTEGRATION PHASE

There are a number of different types of testing that have to be performed during the implementation and integration phase. First, each new module must be tested when it is added to what has already been integrated. The key points here are to test the new module as described in Chapter 12 and to check that the rest of the partial product continues to behave as it did before the new module was integrated into it.

When the product has a graphical user interface (GUI), special issues can arise with regard to integration testing. These are described in the next section.

13.3 INTEGRATION TESTING OF GRAPHICAL USER INTERFACES

Testing a product can usually be simplified by storing the input data for a test case in a file. The product is then executed, and the relevant data submitted to it. With the aid of a relatively rudimentary CASE tool, the whole process can be automated. That is to say, a set of test cases is set up, together with the expected outcome of each case. The CASE tool runs each test case in turn, compares the actual results with the expected results, and reports to the user on each case. The test cases are then stored, so that they can be used for regression testing whenever the product is modified.

However, when a product incorporates a graphical user interface (GUI), this approach does not work. Specifically, test data for pulling down a menu or clicking on a mouse button cannot be stored in a file in the same way as conventional test data. At the same time, it is both time-consuming and boring to test a GUI manually. The solution to this problem is to use a special CASE tool. Test cases are written in the form of scripts, using a special script language. A script is a machine-readable version of a manual GUI test case. Once the required scripts have been set up, automated testing proceeds as if there were no GUI. There are a number of CASE tools available that support the testing of GUIs, including QAPartner and XRunner.

When the integration process is complete, the product as a whole is tested; this is termed *product testing*. When the developers are confident about the correctness of every aspect of the product, it is handed over to the client for *acceptance testing*. These latter two forms of testing are now described in more detail.

13.4   PRODUCT TESTING

The fact that the last module has been successfully integrated into the product does not mean that the task of the developers is complete. The SQA group must still perform a number of testing tasks to be certain that the product will not fail its acceptance test, the final hurdle that the development team must overcome. The failure of a product to pass its acceptance test is almost always a poor reflection of the management capabilities of the development organization. The client may conclude that the developers are incompetent, which all but guarantees that the client will do everything in his or her power to avoid employing those developers again. Worse, the client may believe that the developers are dishonest and deliberately handed over substandard software in order to finish the contract and be paid as quickly as possible. If the client genuinely believes this and tells other potential clients, then the developers have a major public relations problem on their hands. It is up to the SQA group to make sure that the product passes the acceptance test with flying colors.

To ensure a successful acceptance test, the SQA group must perform product testing. This essentially consists of tests that the SQA group believes will closely approximate the forthcoming acceptance tests. First, black-box test cases for the product as a whole must be run. Up to now, test cases have been set up on a module-by-module or object-by-object basis, ensuring that each module or object individually satisfies its specifications. Second, the robustness of the product as a whole must be tested. Again, the robustness of individual modules and objects was tested during integration, but now product-wide robustness is the issue for which test cases must be set up and run. In addition, the product must be subjected to *stress testing*, that is, making sure that it behaves correctly when operating under a peak load, such as all terminals trying to log on at the same time or customers operating all the automated teller machines simultaneously. The product must also undergo *volume testing*, for example, making sure that it can handle large input files. Third, the SQA group must check that the product satisfies all its constraints. For example, if the specifications state that the response time for 95 percent of queries when the product is working under full load must be under 3 seconds, then it is the responsibility of the SQA group to verify that this is indeed the case. There is no question that the client will check these constraints during acceptance testing, and if the product fails to meet a major constraint, then the development organization will lose a considerable amount of credibility. Similarly, storage constraints and security constraints must be checked. Fourth, the SQA group must review all documentation that is to be handed over to the client, together with the code. The SQA group must check that the documentation conforms to the standards laid down in the SPMP. In addition, the documentation must be verified against the product. For instance, the SQA group has to determine that the user manual indeed reflects the correct way of using the product and that the product will function as specified in the user manual.

Scenarios (Section 9.3.2) can be useful in the product testing of object-oriented software. The product as a whole is inspected on a scenario-by-scenario basis to ensure that the behavior of the product is precisely as specified. It is true that scenario checking is also possible during design inspections, as well as inspections of individual modules and objects. However, many scenarios, especially the critical ones, cross module and object boundaries, so it is only during product testing that scenario checking achieves its full potential.

Once the SQA group assures management that the product can handle anything the acceptance testers can throw at it, the product (that is, the code plus all the documentation) is handed over to the client organization for acceptance testing.

13.5 ACCEPTANCE TESTING

The purpose of acceptance testing is for the client to determine whether the product indeed satisfies its specifications as claimed by the developer. Acceptance testing is done either by the client organization, by the SQA group in the presence of client representatives, or by an independent SQA group hired by the client for this purpose. Acceptance testing naturally includes correctness testing, but in addition it is necessary to test performance and robustness. The four major components of acceptance testing, namely testing correctness, robustness, performance, and documentation, are exactly what is done by the developer during product testing; this is not surprising, because product testing is a rehearsal for the acceptance test.

A key aspect of acceptance testing is that it must be performed on actual data, rather than test data. No matter how well test cases are set up, by their very nature they are artificial. More importantly, test data should be a true reflection of the corresponding actual data, but in practice this is not always the case. For example, the member of the specification team responsible for characterizing the actual data may perform this task incorrectly. Alternatively, even if the data are correctly specified, the SQA group member who uses that data specification may misunderstand it or misinterpret it. The resulting test cases will not be a true reflection of the actual data, leading to an inadequately tested product. For these reasons, acceptance testing must be performed on actual data. Furthermore, because the development team endeavors to ensure that the product testing will duplicate every aspect of the acceptance testing, as much of the product testing as possible should also be performed on actual data.

When a new product is to replace an existing product, the specification document will almost always include a clause to the effect that the new product must be installed to run in parallel with the existing product. The reason is that there is a very real possibility that the new product may be faulty in some way. The existing product works correctly, but is inadequate in some respects. If the existing product is replaced by a new product that works incorrectly, then the client is in trouble. Therefore, both products must run in parallel until the client is satisfied that the new product can take over the functions of the existing product. Successful parallel running concludes acceptance testing, and the existing product can be retired.

When the product has passed its acceptance test, the task of the developers is complete. Any changes now made to that product constitute maintenance.

13.6   CASE TOOLS FOR THE IMPLEMENTATION AND INTEGRATION PHASE

CASE tools to support implementation were described in some detail in Chapter 4. For the integration component of the implementation and integration phase, version control tools, build tools, and configuration management tools are needed (Chapter 4). The reason is that modules under test are continually changing as a consequence of faults being detected and corrected, and these CASE tools are essential to be sure that the appropriate version of each module is compiled and linked. As previously mentioned, the two major UNIX version control tools are SCCS (source code control system) [Rochkind, 1975] and rcs (revision control system) [Tichy, 1985]. Commercially available configuration control workbenches include CCC, CVS, and Aide-de-Camp.

In each chapter so far, CASE tools and workbenches specific to that phase have been described. Now that all phases of the development process have been described, it is appropriate to consider CASE tools for the process as a whole.

13.7   CASE TOOLS FOR THE COMPLETE SOFTWARE PROCESS

There is a natural progression within CASE. As described in Section 4.3.1, the simplest CASE device is a single *tool*, such as an online interface checker or a build tool. Next, tools can be combined, leading to a *workbench* that can support one or two activities within the software process, such as configuration control or coding. However, such a workbench will not necessarily provide management information even for the limited portion of the software process to which it is applicable, let alone for the project as a whole. Finally, an *environment* provides computer-aided support for most, if not all, of the process.

Ideally, every software development organization should utilize an environment. But the cost of an environment can be large, not just the package itself but also the hardware on which to run it. For a smaller organization, a workbench, or perhaps just a set of tools, may suffice. But if at all possible, an environment should be utilized to support the development and maintenance effort.

There are a number of different ways of classifying CASE environments. A crude way is to describe the environment either as upperCASE or as lowerCASE (Section 4.3.1). A more precise approach is to specify exactly which phase or phases are supported by the environment. Still better is to choose a classification that describes in what way the environment assists the software team. A number of different classification schemes have been put forward. The presentation below draws on the schemes presented in [Dart, Ellison, Feiler, and Habermann, 1987; Brown and McDermid, 1992; and Fuggetta, 1993].

First, language-centered environments are described.

13.8 LANGUAGE-CENTERED ENVIRONMENTS

Language-centered environments are built around a single language. Examples of such environments are Interlisp [Teitelman and Masinter, 1981] for Lisp and the Smalltalk environment [Goldberg, 1984] for Smalltalk. Language-centered environments are generally designed for rapid development, using tools such as incremental interpreters and compilers. When using an incremental compiler, if a small change is made to the source code then it is not necessary to reprocess the whole module; instead, the object code is modified to take the change into account.

Language-centered environments can be extended to programming-in-the-many (implementation by a team) by incorporating features needed to support multiple users. But such environments can have drawbacks. Because they are so closely bound up with a programming language, they generally support only the implementation phase and are difficult to extend to the other phases of the software process. Furthermore, current language-centered environments do not usually support project management information, such as the status of each module or object or the time that has been devoted to each activity. These environments are good for rapid prototyping, where their strength, namely, rapid development of software, outweighs their weakness, a general lack of support for programming-in-the-large.

A different sort of language-centered environment is the Ada programming support environment (APSE) [DoD, 1980]. The DoD requirements for the APSE stipulate that such environments must incorporate features for programming-in-the-large as well as programming-in-the-many. The problem of lack of support for the design phase is solved by using Ada Design Language (ADL) for the design [ANSI/ IEEE 990, 1987]. ADL can be crudely described as "Ada + comments." Implementation then consists of translating the comments into valid Ada code. Although there is as yet no complete Ada APSE implementation, a number of powerful Ada environments are commercially available, including the Rational environment.

13.9   STRUCTURE-ORIENTED ENVIRONMENTS

A second category of environment is the structure-oriented environment. Here the environment is constructed around a structure editor (Section 4.4). Such an environment is therefore tied to the specific language whose structure is built into the editor. This class of environment is not at present much used in the industry, which generally considers structure-oriented environments applicable only to the implementation phase and a tool for programming-in-the-small. One exception is the FLOW environment, which has been successfully used in industry for programming-in-the-many. It is built around a graphical design language and can therefore be used in the design phase and for implementation and maintenance. FLOW incorporates a limited management information database, as well as code generators for COBOL, FORTRAN, and Pascal [Dooley and Schach, 1985].

13.10   TOOLKIT ENVIRONMENTS

The next category is the toolkit environment. It consists of a collection of tools put together to support a variety of activities (as opposed to a workbench that supports just one or two activities). The difference between environments of this category and a structure-oriented environment is that a toolkit is designed to handle any implementation language. Thus an editor in a toolkit environment cannot be structure-based. Probably the best-known example of a toolkit environment is the UNIX Programmer's Workbench [Dolotta, Haight, and Mashey, 1984].

   The strength of a toolkit environment is that any required tool can usually be added. For example, configuration control tools can be incorporated into a toolkit to help support programming-in-the-many. The weakness of a toolkit environment is that, although the tools may share a common user interface, the tools are usually not integrated. Thus it is difficult to ensure that the tools are used correctly, or even used at all.

13.11   INTEGRATED ENVIRONMENTS

The most common meaning of the word *integrated* within the CASE context is in terms of *user interface integration*. That is to say, all the tools in the environment share a common user interface. The idea behind this is that if all the tools have the same visual appearance, the user of one tool should have little difficulty in learning and using another tool in the environment. This has been successfully achieved on

---

JUST IN CASE YOU WANTED TO KNOW

In the literature, technique-based environments are usually called "method-based environments." The rise of the object-oriented paradigm gave the word *method* a second meaning (in the software engineering context). The original meaning was a technique or an approach; this is how the word is used in the phrase "method-based environment." The object-oriented meaning, as explained in Section 6.7, is an action within an object or class. Unfortunately, it is some-

times not totally clear from the context which of the two meanings is intended!

Accordingly, I have used the word *method* exclusively in the object-oriented sense. Otherwise, I have employed the terms *technique* or *approach*. For example, that is why the term *formal method* never appears in Chapter 8. Instead, I have used the term *formal technique*. Similarly, in this chapter, I have used the term *technique-based environments*.

---

the Macintosh, where most applications have a similar "look and feel." Although this is the usual meaning, there are other types of integration as well.

13.11.1 PROCESS INTEGRATION

Process integration refers to the fact that the environment supports one specific software process. A subset of this class of environment is the *technique-based environment* (but see the Just in Case You Wanted to Know box on this page). An environment of this type supports a specific technique for developing software. Environments exist for a variety of the techniques discussed in this book, such as Gane and Sarsen's structured systems analysis (Section 8.3), Jackson system development (Section 11.6), and Petri nets (Section 8.7). The majority of these environments provide graphical support for the specification and design phases, and incorporate a data dictionary. Some consistency checking is usually provided. Support for managing the development process is frequently incorporated into the environment. There are many commercially available environments of this type, including Analyst/Designer, Statemate, and IEW. Analyst/Designer is specific to Yourdon's methodology [Yourdon, 1989], and Statemate supports Statecharts [Harel et al., 1990]. IEW implements Information Engineering [Martin, 1990]. With regard to object-oriented methodologies, OMTool is a technique-based CASE environment for OMT [Rumbaugh et al., 1991], and Rose supports Booch's methodology [Booch, 1994]. In addition, some older environments have been extended to support the object-oriented paradigm; Software through Pictures is an example of this type.

The emphasis in most technique-based environments is on the support and formalization of the manual processes for software development laid down by the technique. That is to say, these environments force users to utilize the technique step by step in the way intended by its author, while assisting the user by providing graphical tools, a data dictionary, and consistency checking. This computerized framework is a strength of technique-based environments in that users are forced to use a specific technique and to use it correctly. But it can also be a weakness. Unless the software process of the organization incorporates this specific technique, use of a technique-based environment can be counterproductive.

13.11.2 TOOL INTEGRATION

The term *tool integration* means that all the tools communicate via the same data format. For example, in the UNIX Programmer's Workbench, the UNIX pipe formalism assumes that all data are in the form of an ASCII stream. It is thus easy to combine two tools by directing the output stream from one tool to the input stream of the other tool.

There are a number of different ways of achieving tool integration, and each results in a different type of environment. The simplest is data stream tool integration.

Data Stream Tool Integration   Consider the UNIX Programmer's Workbench. The input to and output from each individual tool is an ASCII stream, and integration is effected by passing a data stream from one tool to another. As a consequence of the looseness of the coupling between the tools, the Workbench is a toolkit environment. Data stream integration is schematically depicted in Figure 13.3(a).

Front-End Tool Integration   A second form of tool integration is via a common front end into which all the tools are embedded, as shown in Figure 13.3(b). A commercially available environment of this type of front end is SoftBench [Riehle, 1991]. Communication between tools is now more than just a data stream; with SoftBench, a tool may send a message to another tool when it wants that tool to perform an action. For example, SoftBench may cause electronic mail to be sent to a specific manager if a test fails. More precisely, if a test fails then the testing tool sends a message to the mail tool telling it to inform the manager as to which test failed. It is possible to impose a wide variety of processes by specifying the messages to be sent when particular events occur. SoftBench is essentially a metaCASE tool, that is, a CASE tool that operates on CASE tools.

With front-end tool integration, each tool continues to store information the way that it does in stand-alone fashion, that is, if it were not integrated into the front end. In order to achieve integration, the front end may have to transform the way data are stored by one tool so that information can be used by a different tool. This is a possible drawback of front-end integration.

Historically computer manufacturers have built their products so that their customers are essentially "married" to that company. It has not been uncommon for company A to design its operating system for total incompatibility with software made by company B. In contrast, Hewlett-Packard, a major hardware and software manufacturer, designed SoftBench to accept a wide variety of other manufacturers' tools. Even more surprising, SoftBench is available on hardware platforms from a number of different manufacturers.

There are several reasons why many software manufacturers are now building products that can interface with competitors' products. The first is that if a software

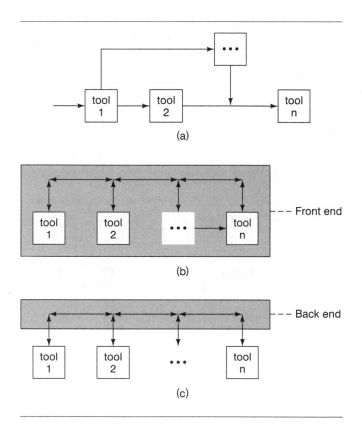

Figure 13.3 Representation of (a) stream, (b) front-end, and (c) back-end tool integration.

organization is successfully using CASE tool CT, say, with great success, then that organization will want to continue to use CT. A product like SoftBench will allow the software developer to use CT in conjunction with other tools that, up to now, have not been accessible because of interfacing problems. The software developer may therefore purchase SoftBench and boost productivity even further by using CT together with new tools. A second reason is that some clients do not like to be tied to one manufacturer, and a framework such as SoftBench allows a client to use CASE tools from a variety of different manufacturers. In addition, if a CASE tool from one manufacturer proves to be disappointing, there may well be a better tool from another manufacturer that can be substituted for it within the SoftBench framework. The third reason is that software manufacturers have realized that building an environment is a major undertaking. The cost of developing an environment can be literally tens of millions of dollars. Furthermore, there is a considerable risk involved in developing an environment. For example, after perhaps $25 million has been spent, a competing product may be marketed 6 months before the environment is due to be completed. Thus, from the viewpoint of risk management, it may make more sense for a computer manufacturer to develop a CASE framework that runs on that manufacturer's hardware, and that allows a wide variety of competitors' CASE tools to be integrated. Another example of this approach is described below.

Back-End Tool Integration   A third type of tool integration is achieved by using a common back-end, the software project database. This is depicted in Figure 13.3(c). All tools are then interfaced with this database, which is sometimes called a repository or encyclopedia. Integrated CASE tools then modify the common data stored in the repository. The key to the success of such a scheme is that the manufacturer of the repository must carefully define the interface between the repository and the tools that are to be integrated into it.

An important example of this class of tool integration is AD/Cycle [Mercurio, Meyers, Nisbet, and Radin, 1990], which is both a software development process (AD stands for application development) and the associated repository. AD/Cycle is a product of IBM, in conjunction with a large number of IBM business partners, that is, CASE tool manufacturers who will ensure that their products are compatible in every way with the AD/Cycle repository. This is another example of a major computer manufacturer deliberately building a CASE product in a way that encourages its erstwhile competitors to become collaborators in constructing an environment.

13.11.3   OTHER FORMS OF INTEGRATION

Team integration refers to the fact that the CASE environment promotes effective team coordination and communication. Another objective is *management integration*. Here, the environment supports management of the process. In particular, reports are generated directly from the software project database; management information, including all versions of all modules, classes, contracts, plans, test cases, and the myriad other components of a software project, are stored in that database. In other words, reports are generated from objective data, rather than synthesized subjectively by project managers.

In practice, not all these laudable objectives have been achieved. In most commercially available environments, tool integration is all that is available; user interface integration is becoming more widespread. Nevertheless, team integration, management integration, and especially process integration are important future goals toward which environment designers are striving.

13.12   ENVIRONMENTS FOR BUSINESS APPLICATIONS

An important class of environments are used for building business-oriented products. The emphasis is on ease of use. This is achieved in a number of ways. In particular, a number of standard forms for input and output are provided, and these can be endlessly modified via a user-friendly GUI. One popular feature of such environments is a code generator. The lowest level of abstraction of a product is then the detailed design. The detailed design is the input to a code generator that automatically generates code in a language such as COBOL or C. This automatically generated code is then compiled; no "programming" of any kind is performed on it.

Languages for specifying the detailed design could well be the programming languages of the future. The level of abstraction of programming languages rose from the physical machine level of first- and second-generation languages to the abstract machine level of third- and fourth-generation languages. Today, the level of abstraction of environments of this type is the detailed design level, a truly portable level; machine complexities devolve on the code generator for the specific target machine. In Section 12.2 it was stated that one of the objectives in using a fourth-generation language (4GL) is shorter code, and hence quicker development and easier maintenance. The use of code generators takes these goals even further, in that the programmer has to provide fewer details to a code generator than to an interpreter or compiler for a 4GL. Thus, it is expected that use of business-oriented environments that support code generators will increase productivity.

There are a number of environments of this type currently available, including ADW, Foundation, and the Bachman Product Set. Bearing in mind the size of the market for business-oriented CASE environments, it is likely that many more environments of this type will be developed in future years.

13.13 PUBLIC TOOL INFRASTRUCTURES

The European Strategic Programme for Research in Information Technology (ESPRIT) has developed an infrastructure for supporting CASE tools. Despite its name, the Portable Common Tool Environment (PCTE) [Thomas, 1989] is *not* an environment. Instead, it is an infrastructure that provides the services needed by CASE tools, in much the same way that UNIX provides the operating system services needed by user products. (The word *Common* in PCTE is in the sense of "public" or "not copyrighted.")

PCTE is starting to gain widespread acceptance. For example, in 1990 the European Computer Manufacturers Association (ECMA) adopted PCTE as ECMA Standard 149. Subsequently, the C and Ada interfaces to PCTE have also been adopted as ECMA standards. In addition, PCTE has been submitted for international standardization. Implementations of PCTE include those of Emeraude and IBM.

The hope is that, in the future, many CASE tools will conform to the PCTE standard and that PCTE itself will be implemented on a wide variety of computers. A tool that conforms to PCTE will be able to run on any computer that supports PCTE. Accordingly, this should result in the widespread availability of a broad range of CASE tools. This, in turn, should lead to better software processes and hence to better quality software.

With regard to object-oriented technology, the Object Management Group (OMG) has been set up with the aim of developing a common environment for object-oriented systems. Specifically, the Common Object Request Broker Architecture (CORBA) supports the portability of software applications between different machines within a distributed environment. Thus, if a distributed application runs on one machine under a given operating system with a specific network protocol, it should run on any other machine that supports CORBA. In particular, CORBA should provide a common environment for object-oriented CASE tools. Hewlett-Packard ORB Plus is one of a number of CORBA implementations currently available.

13.14   COMPARISON OF ENVIRONMENT TYPES

No one environment is ideal for all products and all organizations, any more than one programming language can be considered to be "the best." Each of the various categories of environment described in this chapter has its strengths and its weaknesses, and choosing an inappropriate environment can be worse than using no environment at all. For example, as explained in Section 13.11.1, a technique-based environment essentially automates a manual process. If an organization chooses to use an environment that enforces a technique that is inappropriate for that organization as a whole, or for a current software product under development, then use of that CASE environment will be counterproductive.

A worse scenario occurs when an organization chooses to ignore the advice of Section 3.7, namely that the use of a CASE environment should be firmly eschewed until the organization has attained CMM level 3. Of course, every organization should use CASE tools, and there is generally little harm in using a workbench. However, an environment imposes an automated software process on an organization that uses it. If there is a good process being used, that is, the organization is at maturity level 3 or higher, then use of the environment will assist in all aspects of software production by automating that process. But if the organization is at the crisis-driven level 1, or even at level 2, then there is no process as such in place. Automation of this nonexistent process, that is, the introduction of a CASE environment (as opposed to a CASE tool or CASE workbench), can lead only to chaos.

13.15   METRICS FOR THE IMPLEMENTATION AND INTEGRATION PHASE

A number of different complexity metrics for the implementation and integration phase are discussed in Section 12.16.2, including lines of code, McCabe's cyclomatic complexity, and the metrics of software science.

From a testing viewpoint, relevant metrics include the total number of test cases and the number of test cases that resulted in a failure. The usual fault statistics must be maintained for code inspections. The total number of faults is important, because if the number of faults detected in a module or object exceeds a predetermined maximum, then that module or object must be redesigned and recoded, as discussed in Section 12.21.1. But in addition, detailed statistics need to be kept regarding the types of faults detected. Typical fault types include misunderstanding the design, lack of initialization, and inconsistent use of variables. The fault data can then be incorporated into the checklists used during code inspections of future products.

A powerful set of metrics for the implementation and integration phase is associated with statistical-based testing (Section 12.21). To see how these metrics work, we consider one, namely the zero-failure technique. This is a technique for determining how long to continue testing a product. The underlying idea is that the longer a product is tested without a single failure being observed, the greater the likelihood that the product is free of faults. The technique specifies how long the product must be tested without a single failure in order for the developers to be confident that the product is fault-free. Under the reasonable assumption that the chance of a failure occurring decreases exponentially as testing proceeds, the number of test hours required without a single failure occurring is given by the formula [Brettschneider, 1989]

$$\frac{\ln\left(\dfrac{f_{target}}{0.5 + f_{target}}\right)}{\ln\left(\dfrac{0.5 + f_{target}}{f_{total} + f_{target}}\right)} \times t_h \qquad\qquad \textbf{[13.1]}$$

where f_{target} is the target projected number of failures, f_{total} is the total number of failures detected so far, t_h denotes the total number of test hours up to the last failure, and ln denotes logarithm to base e.

For example, suppose that a product is 50,000 lines of code in length, and the contract stipulates not more than 0.02 failures per thousand lines of delivered code. This implies 1 delivered failure, so $f_{target} = 1$. Suppose further that the product has so far been tested for 400 hours. During this time, a total of 20 failures has been detected, and the product has run for 50 hours since the last failure occurred. This means that $f_{total} = 20$, and $t_h = 400 - 50 = 350$ hours. Substituting these figures into Equation (13.1) yields

$$\frac{\ln\left(\dfrac{1}{0.5 + 1}\right)}{\ln\left(\dfrac{0.5 + 1}{20 + 1}\right)} \times 350 = 54 \text{ hours}$$

The product has already run failure-free for 50 hours, so a further 4 hours of testing are required. Of course, if a failure is detected during these last 4 hours, additional failure-free execution is required for a time that is again determined from Equation (13.1).

13.16   MSG CASE STUDY: IMPLEMENTATION AND INTEGRATION PHASE

A complete Java implementation of the MSG Case Study is presented in Appendix I. To aid the reader, it is preceded by an alphabetical list of the various classes and their methods.

The implementation can be considered to be a direct translation of the detailed design (Appendix G) into code. That is to say, the designers presented the programming team with a well-thought out design that merely required implementation in Java. The programmers have included a variety of comments to aid the maintenance programmers. The next chapter describes the many difficulties of maintenance and suggests ways to simplify the task of maintenance.

Chapter Review

Implementation and integration activities must be carried out in parallel (Section 13.1). Top-down, bottom-up, and sandwich implementation and integration are described and compared (Sections 13.1.1 through 13.1.3). Implementation and integration of object-oriented products is discussed in Section 13.1.4. Various types of testing must be carried out during the implementation and integration phase (Section 13.2), including product testing (Section 13.4) and acceptance testing (Section 13.5). Integration testing of graphical user interfaces (Section 13.3) can pose special problems. In Section 13.6, CASE tools for the implementation and integration phase are discussed; CASE tools for the complete process are discussed in Section 13.7. Language-centered, structure-oriented, and toolkit environments are introduced in Sections 13.8, 13.9, and 13.10 respectively. The issue of integrated CASE tools is discussed in Section 13.11. Environments for business applications are presented in Section 13.12. Section 13.13 is devoted to public tool infrastructures. Next there is a comparison of environment types (Section 13.14) and a description of metrics for the implementation and integration phase (Section 13.15). The chapter concludes with the MSG Case Study (Section 13.16).

For Further Reading

Selection of test data for integration testing appears in [Harrold and Soffa, 1991]. [Munoz, 1988] describes an approach to product testing. It is important to know how long it will be cost-effective to continue testing a product; solutions to this problem are described in [Brettschneider, 1989] and [Sherer, 1991]. The testing of large-scale products is described in [House and Newman, 1989].

A good starting point for information about CASE environments is [Barstow, Shrobe, and Sandewall, 1984]. Turning to specific environments, some language-centered environments are Interlisp [Teitelman and Masinter, 1981], Smalltalk [Goldberg, 1984], an implementation of an Ada APSE [Archer and Devlin, 1986], and Eiffel [Meyer, 1992b]. Structure-oriented environments include Pecan [Reiss, 1984], FLOW [Dooley and Schach, 1985], and Gandalf [Notkin, 1985; Habermann and Notkin, 1986]. Toolkit environments include the UNIX Programmer's Workbench [Dolotta, Haight, and Mashey, 1984]. There are many technique-based environments, including Software through Pictures [Wasserman and Pircher, 1987].

Every 2 or 3 years, ACM SIGSOFT and SIGPLAN sponsor a Symposium on Practical Software Development Environments. The proceedings provide information on a broad spectrum of toolkits and environments. Also useful are the proceedings of the annual International Workshops on Computer-Aided Software Engineering. Further papers on environments can be found in special issues of various journals, including the May 1992 issue of *IEEE Software*.

With regard to the object-oriented paradigm, [Jorgensen and Erickson, 1994] describes the integration testing of object-oriented software. The September 1994 issue of *Communications of the ACM* contains a number of articles on testing object-oriented software.

Information on integrated CASE tools can be found in the March 1992 issue of *IEEE Software*, and especially [Brown and McDermid, 1992] and [Chen and Norman, 1992]. An earlier article on data stream tool integration is [Reiss, 1990]. Information on AD/Cycle can be found in [Mercurio, Meyers, Nisbet, and Radin, 1990].

Problems

Explain the difference between logic modules and operational modules. **13.1**

Defensive programming is good software engineering practice. At the same time, it **13.2** can prevent operational modules from being tested thoroughly enough for reuse purposes. How can this apparent contradiction be resolved?

What are the similarities between product testing and acceptance testing? What are **13.3** the major differences?

What is the role of SQA during the implementation and integration phase? **13.4**

You are the owner and sole employee of One-Person Software Company. You decide **13.5** that in order to be competitive you must buy CASE tools. You therefore apply for a bank loan for $15,000. Your bank manager asks you for a statement not more than one page in length (and preferably shorter) explaining in lay terms why you need CASE tools. Write the statement.

The newly appointed vice-president for software development of Olde Fashioned **13.6** Software Corporation has hired you to help her change the way the company develops software. There are 650 employees, all writing COBOL code without the assistance of any CASE tools. Write a memo to the vice-president stating what sort of CASE equipment the company should purchase. Carefully justify your choice.

You and a friend decide to start Personal Computer Software Unlimited, developing **13.7** software for personal computers on personal computers. Then a distant cousin dies, leaving you $1 million on condition that you spend the money on a business-oriented environment and the hardware needed to run it, and that you keep the environment for at least 5 years. What do you do, and why?

You are a computer science professor at an excellent small liberal arts college. **13.8** Programming assignments for computer science courses are done on a network of 35 personal computers. The dean asks you whether to use the limited software budget to buy CASE tools, bearing in mind that, unless some sort of site license can be obtained, 35 copies of every CASE tool will have to be purchased. What do you advise?

13.9   You have just been elected mayor of a large city. You discover that no CASE tools are being used to develop software for the city. What do you do?

13.10   (Term Project) Implement and integrate the Osbert Oglesby product (Appendix A). Use the programming language specified by your instructor. Remember to use the black-box test cases you developed in Problem 12.27.

13.11   (Case Study) Starting with the design of Appendix G, code the MSG Case Study in an object-oriented language other than Java.

13.12   (Case Study) Recode the MSG Case Study in pure C, without any C++ features. Although C does not support inheritance, object-based concepts such as encapsulation and information hiding can easily be achieved. How would you implement polymorphism and dynamic binding?

13.13   (Case Study) To what extent is the documentation of the code of Appendix I inadequate? Make any necessary additions.

13.14   (Readings in Software Engineering) Your instructor will distribute copies of [Meyer, 1992a]. Do you agree that "Design by Contract" obviates the need for defensive programming, or do you feel that Meyer's assertion-based scheme is unrealistic in practice?

References

[ANSI/IEEE 990, 1987] "Recommended Practice for Ada as a Program Design Language," ANSI/IEEE 990-1987, American National Standards Institute, Inc., Institute of Electrical and Electronic Engineers, Inc., 1987.

[Archer and Devlin, 1986] J. E. ARCHER, JR., AND M. T. DEVLIN, "Rational's Experience Using Ada for Very Large Systems," *Proceedings of the First International Conference on Ada Programming Language Applications for the NASA Space Station*, NASA, 1986, pp. B2.5.1–B2.5.12.

[Barstow, Shrobe, and Sandewall, 1984] D. R. BARSTOW, H. E. SHROBE, AND E. SANDEWALL (Editors), *Interactive Programming Environments*, McGraw-Hill, New York, 1984.

[Booch, 1994] G. BOOCH, *Object-Oriented Analysis and Design with Applications, Second Edition,* Benjamin/Cummings, Redwood City, CA, 1994.

[Brettschneider, 1989] R. BRETTSCHNEIDER, "Is Your Software Ready for Release?" *IEEE Software* **6** (July 1989), pp. 100, 102, and 108.

[Brown and McDermid, 1992] A. W. BROWN AND J. A. McDERMID, "Learning from IPSE's Mistakes," *IEEE Software* **9** (March 1992), pp. 23–29.

[Chen and Norman, 1992] M. CHEN AND R. J. NORMAN, "A Framework for Integrated CASE," *IEEE Software* **8** (March 1992), pp. 18–22.

[Dart, Ellison, Feiler, and Habermann, 1987] S. A. DART, R. J. ELLISON, P. H. FEILER, AND A. N. HABERMANN, "Software Development Environments," *IEEE Computer* **20** (November 1987), pp. 18–28.

[DoD, 1980] "Requirements for the Programming Environment for the Common High-Order Language, STONEMAN," United States Department of Defense, February 1980.

[Dolotta, Haight, and Mashey, 1984] T. A. DOLOTTA, R. C. HAIGHT, AND J. R. MASHEY, "UNIX Time-Sharing System: The Programmer's Workbench," in: *Interactive Programming Environments,* D. R. Barstow, H. E. Shrobe, and E. Sandewall (Editors), McGraw-Hill, New York, 1984, pp. 353–369.

[Dooley and Schach, 1985] J. W. M. DOOLEY AND S. R. SCHACH, "FLOW: A Software Development Environment Using Diagrams," *Journal of Systems and Software* **5** (August 1985), pp. 203–219.

[Fuggetta, 1993] A. FUGGETTA, "A Classification of CASE Technology," *IEEE Computer* **26** (December 1993), pp. 25–38.

[Goldberg, 1984] A. GOLDBERG, *Smalltalk-80: The Interactive Programming Environment,* Addison-Wesley, Reading, MA, 1984.

[Habermann and Notkin, 1986] A. N. HABERMANN AND D. NOTKIN, "Gandalf: Software Development Environments," *IEEE Transactions on Software Engineering* **SE-12** (December 1986), pp. 1117–1127.

[Harel et al., 1990] D. HAREL, H. LACHOVER, A. NAAMAD, A. PNUELI, M. POLITI, R. SHERMAN, A. SHTULL-TRAURING, AND M. TRAKHTENBROT, "STATEMATE: A Working Environment for the Development of Complex Reactive Systems," *IEEE Transactions on Software Engineering* **16** (April 1990), pp. 403–414.

[Harrold and Soffa, 1991] M. J. HARROLD AND M. L. SOFFA, "Selecting and Using Data for Integration Testing," *IEEE Software* **8** (1991), pp. 58–65.

[House and Newman, 1989] D. E. HOUSE AND W. F. NEWMAN, "Testing Large Software Products," *ACM SIGSOFT Software Engineering Notes* **14** (April 1989), pp. 71–78.

[Jorgensen and Erickson, 1994] P. C. JORGENSEN AND C. ERICKSON, "Object-Oriented Integration Testing," *Communications of the ACM* **37** (September 1994), pp. 30–38.

[Martin, 1990] J. MARTIN, *Information Engineering,* Prentice-Hall, Englewood Cliffs, NJ, 1990.

[Mercurio, Meyers, Nisbet, and Radin, 1990] V. J. MERCURIO, B. F. MEYERS, A. M. NISBET, AND G. RADIN, "AD/Cycle Strategy and Architecture," *IBM Systems Journal* **29** (No. 2, 1990), pp. 170–188.

[Meyer, 1992a] B. MEYER, "Applying 'Design by Contract'," *IEEE Computer* **25** (October 1992), pp. 40–51.

[Meyer, 1992b] B. MEYER, *Eiffel: The Language,* Prentice-Hall, New York, 1992.

[Myers, 1979] G. J. MYERS, *The Art of Software Testing,* John Wiley and Sons, New York, 1979.

[Munoz, 1988] C. U. MUNOZ, "An Approach to Software Product Testing," *IEEE Transactions on Software Engineering* **14** (November 1988), pp. 1589–1596.

[Notkin, 1985] D. NOTKIN, "The GANDALF Project," *Journal of Systems and Software* **5** (May 1985), pp. 91–105.

[Reiss, 1984] S. P. REISS, "Graphical Program Development with PECAN Program Development Systems," *Proceedings of the ACM SIGSOFT/SIGPLAN Software Engineering Symposium on Practical Software Development Environments, ACM SIGPLAN Notices* **19** (May 1984), pp. 30–41.

[Reiss, 1990] S. P. REISS, "Connecting Tools Using Message Passing in the Field Environment," *IEEE Software* **7** (July 1990), pp. 57–66.

[Riehle, 1991] R. RIEHLE, "A Space for CASE," *HP Professional* **5** (July 1991), pp. 40–47.

[Rochkind, 1975] M. J. ROCHKIND, "The Source Code Control System," *IEEE Transactions on Software Engineering* **SE-1** (October 1975), pp. 255–265.

[Rumbaugh et al., 1991] J. RUMBAUGH, M. BLAHA, W. PREMERLANI, F. EDDY, AND W. LORENSEN, *Object-Oriented Modeling and Design,* Prentice-Hall, Englewood Cliffs, NJ, 1991.

[Sherer, 1991] S. A. SHERER, "A Cost-Effective Approach to Testing," *IEEE Software* **8** (March 1991), pp. 34–40.

[Teitelman and Masinter, 1981] W. TEITELMAN AND L. MASINTER, "The Interlisp Programming Environment," in: *Tutorial: Software Development Environments,* A. I. Wasserman (Editor), IEEE Computer Society Press, Washington, DC, 1981, pp. 73–81.

[Thomas, 1989] I. THOMAS, "PCTE Interfaces: Supporting Tools in Software Engineering Environments," *IEEE Software* **6** (November 1989), pp. 15–23.

[Tichy, 1985] W. F. TICHY, "RCS—A System for Version Control," *Software—Practice and Experience* **15** (July 1985), pp. 637–654.

[Wasserman and Pircher, 1987] A. I. WASSERMAN AND P. A. PIRCHER, "A Graphical, Extensible Integrated Environment for Software Development," *Proceedings of the Second ACM SIGSOFT/SIGPLAN Software Engineering Symposium on Practical Software Development Environments, ACM SIGPLAN Notices* **22** (January 1987), pp. 131–142.

[Yourdon, 1989] E. YOURDON, *Modern Structured Analysis,* Yourdon Press, Englewood Cliffs, NJ, 1989.

chapter

14

MAINTENANCE PHASE

Once the product has passed its acceptance test, it is handed over to the client. Any changes after the client has accepted the product constitute maintenance. Because the product consists of more than just the source code, any changes to the documentation, manuals, or other component of the product are also examples of maintenance. Some computer scientists prefer to use the term *evolution* rather than maintenance to indicate that products evolve in time. In fact, there are those who view the entire software life cycle, from beginning to end, as an evolutionary process.

The reader might be surprised that this is a relatively short chapter because a major theme of the book is the vital importance of maintenance. The key point is that maintainability has to be built into a product from the very beginning and must not be compromised at any time during the development process. Thus, in a very real sense, the previous chapters have been devoted to the subject of maintenance. What is described in this chapter is how to ensure that maintainability is not compromised during the maintenance process itself.

14.1 WHY MAINTENANCE IS NECESSARY

There are three main reasons for making changes to a product after it has been delivered to the client. The first reason is to correct any residual faults, whether specification faults, design faults, coding faults, documentation faults, or any other types of faults. This is termed *corrective maintenance*. Surprisingly enough, a study of 69 organizations showed that maintenance programmers spend only 17.5 percent of their time on corrective maintenance [Lientz, Swanson, and Tompkins, 1978]. This is depicted in the pie chart of Figure 14.1. Most of their time, namely 60.5 percent, is spent on the second type of maintenance, *perfective maintenance*. Here, changes are made to the code to improve the effectiveness of the product. For instance, the client may wish to have additional functionality added or might request that the product be modified so that it runs faster. Improving the maintainability of a product is another example of perfective maintenance. The third reason for changing a product is *adaptive maintenance,* changes made to the product in order to react to changes in the environment in which the product

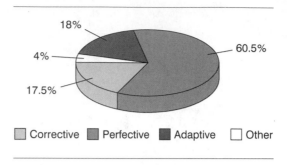

Figure 14.1 Percentage of time devoted to each of the types of maintenance.

operates. For example, a product will almost certainly have to be modified if it is ported to a new compiler, operating system, and/or hardware. If there is a change to the tax code, then a product that prepares tax returns has to be modified accordingly. When the U.S. Postal Service introduced nine-digit ZIP codes in 1981, products that had allowed for only five-digit ZIP codes had to be changed. Adaptive maintenance is thus not requested by a client; instead, it is externally imposed on the client. The study showed that 18 percent of software maintenance was adaptive in nature. The remaining 4 percent of maintenance time was devoted to other types of maintenance that did not fall into the other three categories.

14.2   WHAT IS REQUIRED OF MAINTENANCE PROGRAMMERS

During the software life cycle, more time is spent on maintenance than on any other phase. In fact, on average 67 percent of the total cost of a product can be attributed to maintenance [Lientz, Swanson, and Tompkins, 1978; Zelkowitz, Shaw, and Gannon, 1979]. But many organizations, even today, assign the task of maintenance to beginners and to less competent programmers, leaving the "glamorous" job of product development to better or more experienced programmers.

In fact, maintenance is the most difficult of all aspects of software production. A major reason is that maintenance incorporates aspects of all the other phases of the software process. Consider what happens when a fault report is handed to a maintenance programmer. A fault report is filed if, in the opinion of the user, the product is not working as specified in the user manual. There are a number of possible scenarios. First, there could be nothing wrong at all; perhaps the user has either misunderstood the user manual or is using the product incorrectly. Alternatively, if the fault does lie in the product, it might simply be that the user manual has been badly worded, and that there is nothing wrong with the code itself. Usually, however, the fault is in the code. But before making any changes, the maintenance programmer has to determine exactly where the fault lies, using the fault report filed by the user, the source code—and often nothing else. Thus the maintenance programmer needs to have far above average debugging skills, because the fault could lie anywhere within the product. And the original cause of the fault might lie in the by now nonexistent specification or design documents.

Now suppose that the maintenance programmer has located the fault and must fix it without inadvertently introducing another fault elsewhere in the product, that is, a *regression fault*. If regression faults are to be minimized, detailed documentation for the product as a whole and for each individual module must be available. However, software professionals are notorious for their dislike of paperwork of all kinds, especially documentation, and it is quite common for the documentation to be incomplete, faulty, or totally missing. In these cases the maintenance programmer has to be able to deduce from the source code itself, the only valid form of documentation available, all the information needed to avoid introducing a regression fault.

Having determined the probable fault and tried to correct it, the maintenance programmer must now test that the modification works correctly and that no regression faults have in fact been introduced. In order to check the modification itself, the maintenance programmer must construct special test cases; checking for regression faults is done using the set of test data stored precisely for the purpose of performing regression testing. Then the test cases constructed for the purpose of checking the modification must be added to the set of stored test cases to be used for future regression testing of the modified product. In addition, if changes to the specification and/or design had to be made in order to correct the fault, then these changes must also be checked. Expertise in testing is therefore an additional prerequisite for maintenance programmers. Finally, it is essential that the maintenance programmer document every change. The preceding discussion relates to corrective maintenance. For that task, the maintenance programmer must first and foremost be a superb diagnostician to be able to determine if there is a fault, and if so, an expert technician to be able to fix it.

However, the major maintenance tasks are adaptive and perfective maintenance. To perform these, the maintenance programmer must go through the phases of requirements, specification, design, and implementation and integration, taking the existing product as the starting point. For some types of changes, additional modules have to be designed and implemented. In other cases, changes to the design and implementation of existing modules are needed. Thus, while specifications are frequently produced by specification experts, designs by design experts, and code by programming experts, the maintenance programmer has to be an expert in all three areas. Perfective and adaptive maintenance are adversely affected by a lack of adequate documentation, just as corrective maintenance is. Furthermore, the ability to design suitable test cases and the ability to write good documentation are needed for perfective and adaptive maintenance, just as they are needed for corrective maintenance. Thus none of the forms of maintenance is a task for a less experienced programmer unless a top rank computer professional supervises the process.

From the preceding discussion, it is clear that maintenance programmers have to possess almost every technical skill that a software professional could have. But what does he or she get in return? Maintenance is a thankless task in every way. Maintainers deal with dissatisfied users; if the user were happy with the product it would not need maintenance. Furthermore, the user's problems have frequently been caused by the individuals who developed the product, not the maintainer. The code itself may be badly written, adding to the frustrations of the maintainer. Finally, maintenance is looked down on by many software developers who consider development to be a glamorous job and maintenance to be drudge work fit only for junior programmers or incompetents.

Maintenance can be likened to after-sales service. The product has been delivered to the client. But now there is client dissatisfaction, either because the product does not work correctly, or because it does not do everything that the client currently wants, or because the circumstances for which the product was built have changed in some way. Unless the software organization provides the client with good maintenance service, the client will take his or her future product development business elsewhere. When the client and software group are part of the same organization, and hence are inextricably tied from the viewpoint of future work, a dissatisfied client may use every means, fair or foul, to discredit the software group. This, in turn, leads to an erosion of confidence, from both outside and inside the software group, and to resignations and dismissals. It is important for every software organization to keep its clients happy by providing excellent maintenance service.

For product after product, maintenance is the most challenging phase of software production—and frequently the most thankless.

How can this situation be changed? Managers must assign maintenance tasks to their best programmers. They must make it known that only the finest computer professionals merit maintenance assignments in their organization and pay them accordingly. If management believes that maintenance is a challenge and that good maintenance is critical for the success of the organization, attitudes toward maintenance will slowly improve.

Some of the problems that maintenance programmers face are now highlighted in a case study.

14.3 MAINTENANCE CASE STUDY

In countries with centralized economies, the government controls the distribution and marketing of agricultural products. In one such country, temperate fruits such as peaches, apples, and pears were the responsibility of the Temperate Fruit Committee (TFC). One day, the chairman of the TFC asked a government computer consultant to computerize the operations of the TFC. The chairman informed the consultant that there are exactly seven temperate fruits, namely apples, apricots, cherries, nectarines, peaches, pears, and plums. The database was to be designed for those seven fruits, no more and no less. After all, that was the way that the world was, and the consultant was not to waste time and money allowing for any sort of expandability.

The product was duly delivered to the TFC. About a year later, the chairman summoned the maintenance programmer responsible for the product. "What do you know about kiwi fruit?" asked the chairman. "Nothing," replied the mystified programmer. "Well," said the chairman, "it seems that kiwi fruit is a temperate fruit that has just started to be grown in our country, and the TFC is responsible for it. Please change the product accordingly."

The maintenance programmer discovered that the consultant fortunately had not carried out the chairman's original instructions to the letter. The good practice of allowing for some sort of future expansion was too ingrained, and the consultant had provided a number of unused fields in the relevant database records. By slightly rearranging certain items, the maintenance programmer was able to incorporate kiwi fruit, the eighth temperate fruit, into the product.

Another year went by, and the product functioned well. Then the maintenance programmer was again called to the chairman's office. The chairman was in a good mood. He jovially informed the programmer that the government had reorganized the distribution and marketing of agricultural products. His committee was now responsible for all fruit produced in that country, not just temperate fruit, and so the product now had to be modified to incorporate the 26 additional kinds of fruit on the list he handed to the maintenance programmer. The programmer protested, pointing out that this change would take almost as long as rewriting the product from scratch. "Nonsense," replied the chairman. "You had no trouble adding kiwi fruit. Just do the same thing another 26 times!"

There are a number of important lessons to be learned from this. First, the problem with the product, namely no provision for expansion, was caused by the developer, not the maintainer. The developer made the mistake of obeying the chairman's instruction regarding future expandability of the product, but it was the maintenance programmer who suffered the consequences. In fact, unless he reads this book, the consultant who developed the original product may never realize that his product was anything but a success. This is one of the more annoying aspects of maintenance, in that the maintainer is responsible for fixing other people's mistakes. The person who caused the problem either has other duties or has left the organization, but the maintenance programmer is left holding the baby. Second, the client frequently does not understand that maintenance can be difficult, or in some instances, all but impossible. The problem is exacerbated when the maintenance programmer has successfully carried out previous perfective and adaptive maintenance tasks, but now suddenly protests that a new assignment cannot be done, even though superficially it seems no different from what has been done before with little difficulty. Third, all software development activities must be carried out with an eye on future maintenance. If the consultant had designed the product for an arbitrary number of different kinds of fruit, there would have been no difficulty in incorporating first the kiwi fruit and then the 26 other kinds of fruit. As has been stated many times, maintenance is a vital phase of software production, and the one which consumes the most resources. During product development, it is essential that the development team never forget about the maintenance programmer who will be responsible for the product once it has been installed.

14.4   MANAGEMENT OF MAINTENANCE

Issues regarding management of maintenance are now considered.

14.4.1   FAULT REPORTS

The first thing that is needed when maintaining a product is to set up a mechanism for changing the product. With regard to corrective maintenance, that is, removing residual faults, if the product appears to be functioning incorrectly, then a *fault report* should be filed by the user. This must include enough information to enable the maintenance programmer to recreate the problem, which will usually be some sort of software failure.

Ideally, every fault reported by a user should be fixed immediately. In practice, programming organizations are usually understaffed, and there is a backlog of work, both development and maintenance. If the fault is critical, such as if a payroll product crashes the day before payday or overpays employees or underpays them, immediate corrective action will have to be taken. Otherwise, each fault report must at least receive an immediate preliminary investigation.

The maintenance programmer should first consult the fault report file. This contains all reported faults that have not yet been fixed, together with suggestions for working around them, that is, ways for the user to bypass the portion of the product that apparently is responsible for the failure, until such time as the fault can be fixed. If the fault has previously been reported, any information in the fault report file should be given to the user. But if what the user has reported appears to be a new fault, then the maintenance programmer should study the problem and attempt to find the cause and a way to fix it. In addition, an attempt should be made to find a way to work around the problem, because it may take 6 or 9 months before someone can be assigned to make the necessary changes to the software. In the light of the serious shortage of programmers, and in particular, programmers who are good enough to perform maintenance, suggesting a way to live with the fault until it can be solved is often the only way to deal with fault reports that are true emergencies.

The maintenance programmer's conclusions should then be added to the fault report file, together with any supporting documentation such as listings, designs, and manuals used to arrive at those conclusions. The manager in charge of maintenance should consult the file regularly, prioritizing the various fixes. The file should also contain the client's requests for perfective and adaptive maintenance. The next modification to be made to the product will then be the one with the highest priority. However, it is not a good idea for a new release to address more than one of corrective, perfective, or adaptive maintenance. This should be taken into account when planning maintenance tasks.

When copies of a product have been distributed to a variety of sites, copies of fault reports must be circulated to all users of the product, together with an estimate of when each fault can be fixed. Then if the same failure occurs at another site, the user can consult the relevant fault report to determine if it is possible to work around the fault and when it will be fixed. It would of course be preferable to fix every fault immediately and then distribute a new version of the product to all sites. Given the current worldwide shortage of good programmers and the realities of software maintenance, distributing fault reports is probably the best that can be done.

14.4.2 AUTHORIZING CHANGES TO THE PRODUCT

Once a decision has been made to perform corrective maintenance, a maintenance programmer will be assigned the task of determining the fault that caused the failure and then repairing it. After the code has been changed, the fix must be tested, as must the product as a whole (regression testing). Then the documentation must be updated to reflect the changes. In particular, a detailed description of what was changed, why it was changed, by whom, and when, must be added to the prologue comments of any changed module. If necessary, design and/or specification documents also have to be changed. A similar set of steps is followed when performing perfective or adaptive maintenance; the only real difference is that perfective and adaptive maintenance are initiated by a change in requirements rather than by a fault report.

At this point all that would seem to be needed would be to distribute the new version to the users. But what if the maintenance programmer has not tested the fix adequately? Before the product is distributed, it must be subjected to SQA performed by an independent group, that is, the members of the maintenance SQA group must not report to the same manager as the maintenance programmer; it is important that SQA remain managerially independent (Section 5.1.2).

Reasons were given previously as to why maintenance is difficult. For those same reasons, maintenance is also fault-prone. Testing during the maintenance phase is both difficult and time-consuming, and the SQA group should not underestimate the implications of software maintenance with regard to testing. Once the new version has been approved by SQA, it can be distributed.

Another area in which management must ensure that procedures are carefully followed is when the technique of baselines and private copies (Section 4.6.2) is used. Suppose that a programmer wishes to change class TaxProvision. The programmer freezes the relevant module and makes copies of all other modules that will be needed to perform the required maintenance task; often this will be all the other modules in the product. The programmer makes the necessary changes to TaxProvision, tests them, and the new revision of TaxProvision incorporating the changes is installed in the baseline. But when the modified product is delivered to the user, it immediately crashes. What went wrong is that the maintenance programmer tested the modified version of TaxProvision using his or her private workspace copies, that is, the copies of the other modules that were in the baseline at the time that maintenance of TaxProvision was started. In the meantime, certain other modules were updated by other maintenance programmers working on the same product. The lesson is clear: Before installing a module, it must be tested using the current baseline versions of all the other modules and not the programmer's private versions. This is a further reason for stipulating independent SQA—members of the SQA group simply do not have access to programmers' private workspaces.

14.4.3 ENSURING MAINTAINABILITY

Maintenance is not a one-time effort. A well-written product will go through a series of versions over its lifetime. As a result, it is necessary to plan for maintenance during the entire software process. During the design phase, for example, information hiding techniques (Section 6.6) should be employed; during implementation, variable names should be selected that will be meaningful to future maintenance programmers (Section 12.4). Documentation should be complete and correct, and reflect the current version of every component module of the product.

During the maintenance phase, it is important not to compromise the maintainability that has been built into the product from the very beginning. In other words, just as software development personnel should always be conscious of the inevitable maintenance that will occur, so software maintenance personnel should always be conscious of the equally inevitable future maintenance. The principles established for maintainability during development are equally applicable to the maintenance phase itself.

14.4.4 PROBLEM OF REPEATED MAINTENANCE

One of the more frustrating difficulties of product development is the moving target problem (Section 3.4.1). What can happen is that as fast as the developer constructs the product, the client changes the requirements. Not only is this frustrating to the development team, but the frequent changes can result in a poorly constructed product. In addition, such changes add to the cost of the product. In theory, the way to cope with this is to start by constructing a rapid prototype. Then it does not matter how often the client changes the requirements. Once the client is finally satisfied, the specifications are approved and the product itself is constructed. In practice, there is nothing to stop the client from changing the requirements the day after he or she has finally approved them. The main advantage to prototyping in this situation is that, by presenting the client with a working model, it *may* reduce the number and the frequency of the changes. But if the client is willing to pay the price, nothing can be done to prevent the requirements being changed every Monday and Thursday.

The problem is exacerbated during the maintenance phase. The more a completed product is changed, the more it will deviate from its original design, and the more difficult it will become to make further changes. Under repeated maintenance the documentation is likely to become even less reliable than usual, and the regression testing files may not be up to date. If still more maintenance has to be done, the product as a whole may first have to be completely rewritten using the current version as a prototype.

The problem of the moving target is clearly a management problem. In theory, if management is sufficiently firm with the client and explains the problem at the beginning of the project, then the requirements can be frozen from the time the prototype has been accepted until the product is delivered. Again, after each request for perfective maintenance, the requirements can be frozen for, say, 3 months or 1 year. In practice, it does not work that way. For example, if the client happens to be the president of the corporation and the development organization is the information systems division of that organization, then the president can indeed order changes every Monday and Thursday, and they will be implemented. The old proverb, "he who pays the piper calls the tune," is unfortunately only too relevant in this situation. Perhaps the best that the vice-president for information systems can do is to try to explain to the president the effect on the product of repeated maintenance, and then simply have the complete product rewritten whenever further maintenance would be hazardous to the integrity of the product.

Trying to discourage additional maintenance by ensuring that the requested changes are implemented slowly only has the effect of the relevant personnel being replaced by others who are prepared to do the job faster. In short, if the person who requests the repeated changes has sufficient clout, then there is no solution to the problem of the moving target.

14.5 MAINTENANCE OF OBJECT-ORIENTED SOFTWARE

One of the reasons put forward for using the object-oriented paradigm is that it promotes maintenance. After all, an object is an independent unit of a program. More specifically, a well-designed object exhibits conceptual independence, otherwise known as encapsulation (Section 6.4). Every aspect of the product that relates to the portion of the real world modeled by that object is localized to the object itself. In addition, objects exhibit physical independence; information hiding is employed to ensure that implementation details are not visible outside that object (Section 6.6). The only form of communication permitted is the sending of a message to the object to carry out a specific method.

As a consequence, the argument goes, it will be easy to maintain an object for two reasons. First, conceptual independence means it will be easy to determine which part of a product must be changed in order to achieve a specific maintenance objective, be it enhancement or corrective maintenance. Second, information hiding ensures that a change made to an object will have no impact outside that object, and hence the number of regression faults will be greatly reduced.

In practice, however, the situation is not quite this idyllic. In fact, there are three obstacles that are specific to the maintenance of object-oriented software. One of the problems can be solved through use of appropriate CASE tools, but the others are less tractable. First, consider the Java class hierarchy shown in Figure 14.2. Method displayNode is defined in class UndirectedTree, inherited by class DirectedTree, and then redefined in class RootedTree. It is this redefined version that is inherited by class BinaryTree and class BalancedBinaryTree and is utilized in class BalancedBinaryTree. Thus, a maintenance programmer has to study the complete inheritance hierarchy to understand class BalancedBinaryTree. Worse,

```
class UndirectedTree
{
   . . .
   void displayNode (Node a);
   . . .
}
class DirectedTree : extends UndirectedTree
{
   . . .
}
class RootedTree : extends DirectedTree
{
   . . .
   void displayNode (Node a);
   . . .
}
class BinaryTree : extends RootedTree
{
   . . .
}
class BalancedBinaryTree : extends BinaryTree
{
     Node      hhh;
     displayNode (hhh);
}
```

Figure 14.2   Class hierarchy.

the heirarchy may not be displayed in the linear fashion of Figure 14.2, but will generally be spread over the entire product. Thus, in order to understand what displayNode does in class BalancedBinaryTree, the maintenance programmer may have to peruse a major proportion of the product. This is a far cry from the "independent" object described at the beginning of this section.

The solution to this problem is straightforward, namely, the use of an appropriate CASE tool. Just as a Java compiler can resolve precisely the version of displayNode within instances of class BalancedBinaryTree, so a programming workbench can provide a "flattened" version of a class, that is, a definition of the class with all features inherited directly or indirectly appearing explicitly, with any renaming or redefinition incorporated. Thus, the flattened form of class BalancedBinaryTree of Figure 14.2 includes the definition of displayNode from Class RootedTree. CASE tools for flattening are not restricted to Java. For example, Eiffel incorporates the command **flat** for this purpose [Meyer, 1990].

The second obstacle to maintenance of a product implemented using an object-oriented language is less easy to solve. It arises as a consequence of polymorphism and dynamic binding; these concepts were explained in Section 6.8. An example was given in that section, namely a base class named FileClass, together with three subclasses, namely DiskFileClass, TapeFileClass, and DisketteFileClass. This is shown in Figure 6.30(b), reproduced here for convenience as Figure 14.3. In

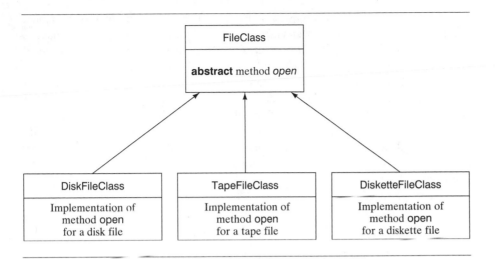

Figure 14.3 Definition of base class FileClass with derived classes DiskFileClass, TapeFileClass, and DisketteFileClass.

base class FileClass, a dummy (**abstract**) method open is declared. Then, a specific implementation of the method appears in each of the three subclasses; each of the methods is given the identical name, that is, open, as shown in Figure 14.3. Suppose that myFile is declared to be an object, an instance of FileClass, and that the code to be maintained contains the message myFile.open (). As a consequence of polymorphism and dynamic binding, at run time myFile could be a member of any of the three derived classes of FileClass, that is, a disk file, a tape file, or a diskette file. Once the run-time system has determined in which derived class it is, the appropriate version of open is invoked.

This can have adverse consequences for maintenance. If a maintenance programmer encounters the call myFile.open () in the code then, in order to understand that part of the product, he or she has to consider what would happen if myFile were an instance of each of the three subclasses. A CASE tool cannot help here because, in general, there is no way to resolve dynamic binding issues using static methods. The only way to determine which of a number of dynamic bindings actually occurs in a particular set of circumstances is to trace through the code, either by running it on a computer or tracing through it manually. Polymorphism and dynamic binding are indeed extremely powerful aspects of object-oriented technology that promote the development of an object-oriented product. However, they can have a deleterious impact on maintenance by forcing the maintenance programmer to investigate a wide variety of possible bindings that might occur at run time, and hence determine which of a number of different methods could be invoked at that point in the code.

The third problem arises as a consequence of inheritance. Suppose a base class exists that does most, but not all, of what is required for the design of a new product. A derived class is now defined, that is, a class that is identical to the base class in many ways, but new features may be added and existing features may be renamed, reimplemented, suppressed, or changed in other ways. Furthermore, these changes may be made without having any effect on the base class or on any other derived classes. However, suppose now that the base class is changed. If this happens, all derived classes are changed in the same way. In other words, the strength of inheritance is that new leaves can be added to the inheritance tree (or graph, if multiple inheritance is supported) without altering any other class in the tree. But if an interior node of the tree is changed in any way, then this change is propagated to all its descendants. Thus, inheritance is another feature of object-oriented technology that can have a major positive influence on development, but a negative impact on maintenance.

14.6   MAINTENANCE SKILLS VERSUS DEVELOPMENT SKILLS

Earlier in this chapter much was said about the skills needed for maintenance. For corrective maintenance, the ability to determine the cause of a failure of a large product was deemed essential. But this skill is not needed exclusively for product maintenance. It is used throughout integration and product testing. Another vital skill is the ability to function effectively without adequate documentation. Again, the documentation is rarely complete while integration and product testing are under way. It was also stressed that skills with regard to specification, design, implementation and integration, and testing are essential for adaptive and perfective maintenance. These activities are also carried out during the development process, and each requires specialized skills if it is to be performed correctly.

In other words, the skills that a maintenance programmer needs are in no way different from those needed by software professionals specializing in other phases of software production. The key point is that a maintenance programmer must not merely be skilled in a broad variety of areas, he or she must be *highly* skilled in *all* those areas. Although the average software developer can specialize in one area of software development such as design or testing, the software maintainer must be a specialist in virtually every area of software production. After all, maintenance is the same as development, only more so.

14.7   REVERSE ENGINEERING

As has been pointed out, it sometimes happens that the only documentation available for maintenance is the source code itself. Under these circumstances, maintaining the code can be extremely difficult. One way of handling this problem is to start with the source code and attempt to recreate the design documents, or even the specifications. This process is called *reverse engineering*.

There are CASE tools that will assist with this process. One of the simplest is a pretty printer (Section 4.4) that may help to display the code more clearly. There are also tools that will construct diagrams, such as flowcharts or structure charts, directly from the source code; these visual aids can help in the process of design recovery.

Once the maintenance team has reconstructed the design, there are two possibilities. One alternative is to attempt to reconstruct the specifications, modify the reconstructed specifications to reflect the necessary changes, and then reimplement the product the usual way. (Within the context of reverse engineering, the usual development process that proceeds from specifications through design to code is called *forward engineering*. The process of reverse engineering followed by forward engineering is sometimes called *reengineering*.) In practice, reconstruction of the specifications is an extremely hard task. More frequently the reconstructed design is modified, and the modified design is then forward engineered.

A related activity that is often performed during the maintenance phase is *restructuring*. Reverse engineering takes the product from a lower level of abstraction to a higher level of abstraction, for example, from code to design. Forward engineering takes the product from a higher level of abstraction to a lower level. Restructuring, however, takes place at the same level. It is the process of improving the product without changing its functionality. Pretty printing is one form of restructuring; so is converting code from unstructured to structured form (Section 12.3). In general, restructuring is performed in order to make the source code (or design, or even the database) easier to maintain.

A worse situation occurs if the source code is lost, and the executable version of the product is all that is available. At first sight it might seem that the only possible way to recreate the source code is to use a disassembler to create assembler code and then to build a tool (that might be termed a *reverse compiler*) to try to recreate the original high-level language code. There are a number of virtually insurmountable problems with this approach. First, the names of the variables have been lost as a consequence of the original compilation. Second, many compilers optimize the code in some way, making it extremely difficult to attempt to recreate the source code. Third, a construct such as a loop in the assembler could correspond to a number of different possible constructs in the source code. In practice, therefore, the existing product is treated as a black box and reverse engineering is used to deduce the specifications from the behavior of the current product. The reconstructed specifications are modified as required, and the new version of the product is then forward engineered.

14.8 TESTING DURING THE MAINTENANCE PHASE

While the product is being developed, many members of the development team have a broad overview of the product as a whole, but as a result of the rapid personnel turnover in the computer industry it is unlikely that members of the maintenance team will previously have been involved in the original development. Thus the maintainer tends to see the product as a set of loosely related modules and is generally not conscious of the fact that a change to one module may seriously affect one or more other modules, and hence the product as a whole. Even if the maintainer wished to understand every aspect of the product, the pressures to fix or to extend the product are generally such that there is no time for the detailed study needed to achieve this. Furthermore, in many cases there is little or no documentation available to assist in gaining that understanding. One way of trying to minimize this difficulty is to use regression testing, that is, testing the changed product against previous test cases to ensure that it still works correctly.

For this reason it is vital to store all test cases, together with their expected outcomes, in machine-readable form. As a result of changes made to the product, certain stored test cases may have to be modified. For example, if salary withholding percentages change as a consequence of tax legislation, then the correct output from a payroll product for each test case involving withholding will change. Similarly, if satellite observations lead to corrections in the latitude and longitude of an island, then the correct output from a product that calculates the position of an aircraft using the coordinates of that island will correspondingly change. Depending on the maintenance performed, some valid test cases will become invalid. But the computations that need to be made to correct the stored test cases are essentially the same computations that would have to be made in order to set up new test data for checking that the maintenance has been correctly performed. No additional work is therefore involved in maintaining the file of test cases and their expected outcomes.

It can be argued that regression testing is a waste of time because regression testing requires the complete product to be retested against a whole host of test cases, most of which apparently have nothing to do with the modules that were modified in the course of product maintenance. The word *apparently* is the key word in the previous sentence. The dangers of unwitting side effects of maintenance (that is, the introduction of regression faults) are too great for that argument to hold water; regression testing is an essential aspect of maintenance in all situations.

14.9 CASE TOOLS FOR THE MAINTENANCE PHASE

It is unreasonable to expect maintenance programmers to keep track manually of the various revision numbers and to assign the next revision number each time a module is updated. Unless the operating system incorporates version control, a version control tool such as the UNIX tool *sccs* (source code control system) [Rochkind, 1975], or *rcs* (revision control system) [Tichy, 1985] is needed. It is equally unreasonable to expect manual control of the freezing technique described in Chapter 4 or any other manual way of ensuring that revisions are updated appropriately. What is needed is a configuration control tool. A typical example of a commercial tool is CCC (change and configuration control). Even if the software organization does not wish to purchase a complete configuration control tool, at the very least a build tool must be used in conjunction with a version control tool.

In Section 14.7 a description was given of some of the categories of CASE tools that can assist in reverse engineering and reengineering. Examples of such tools that assist by creating visual displays of the structure of the product include Battlemap, Teamwork, and Bachman Reengineering Product Set.

JUST IN CASE YOU WANTED TO KNOW

What will the future of software engineering be? Like most people, I have 20–20 hindsight—forecasting the future is much, much harder!

One direction in which software engineering could move is to place far greater stress on formal techniques [Botting, 1994]. Mathematics in general (and discrete mathematics in particular) would play a larger role. Coupled with this, software engineers would have to be certified, in much the same way that other engineers are certified.

Another possibility is intensive reuse. That is to say, software would be built using hundreds of stan-

dard classes incorporating knowledge of data, mathematics, graphics, telecommunications, hardware, and so on. Software development would then largely devolve into choosing and combining these standard classes.

Whether the future lies partially or totally in either of these directions, or whether something totally different from anything currently envisioned is in store for us, one thing is certain: In the future, software engineering will be just as challenging, and just as much fun, as it is at present.

Maintenance is difficult and frustrating. The very least that management can do is to provide the maintenance team with the tools that are needed for efficient and effective product maintenance.

14.10 METRICS FOR THE MAINTENANCE PHASE

The activities of the maintenance phase are essentially specification, design, implementation, integration, testing, and documentation. Thus the metrics that measure these activities are equally applicable to the maintenance phase. For example, the complexity metrics of Section 12.16.2 are relevant to maintenance in that a module with high complexity is a likely candidate for inducing a regression fault. Particular care must therefore be taken in modifying such a module.

In addition, metrics specific to the maintenance phase include measures relating to software fault reports, such as the total number of faults reported, as well as classifications of those faults by severity and by fault type. In addition, information regarding the current status of the fault reports is needed. For example, there is a considerable difference between having 13 critical faults reported and fixed during 1996 and having only 3 critical faults reported during that year but with none of them fixed.

The final Just in Case You Wanted to Know box on this page, deals with the future of software engineering.

Chapter Review

Maintenance is an important and challenging software activity (Sections 14.1 and 14.2). This is illustrated by means of the case study of Section 14.3. Issues relating to the management of maintenance are described (Section 14.4), including the problem of repeated maintenance (Section 14.4.4). The maintenance of object-oriented software is discussed in Section 14.5. The skills that a maintenance programmer needs are the same as those of a developer; the difference is that a developer can specialize in one aspect of the software process, whereas the maintainer must be an expert in all aspects of software production (Section 14.6). A description of reverse engineering is given in Section 14.7. Next follows a description of testing during the maintenance phase (Section 14.8) and CASE tools for maintenance (Section 14.9). Finally, metrics for the maintenance phase are discussed in Section 14.10.

For Further Reading

Sources of information on maintenance in general include [Lientz and Swanson, 1980], [Glass and Noiseux, 1981], [Babich, 1986], and [Parikh, 1988]. [Schneidewind, 1987] is an excellent overview of the state of the art. [Basili, 1990] presents an interesting view of maintenance as a reuse process.

Ways of reducing the cost of maintenance are described in [Guimaraes, 1983]. The impact of the use of objects on maintenance is described in [Henry and Humphrey, 1990] and [Mancl and Havanas, 1990]. Useful material on maintenance can be found in [Longstreet, 1990]. The proceedings of the annual Conference on Software Maintenance are a broadly based source of information on all aspects of maintenance.

The maintenance of object-oriented products is described in [Lejter, Meyers, and Reiss, 1992] and [Wilde, Matthews, and Huitt, 1993]. The use of metrics within the context of maintainability is discussed in [Banker, Datar, Kemerer, and Zwieg, 1993], [Coleman, Ash, Lowther, and Oman, 1994], and [Henry, Henry, Kafura, and Matheson, 1994].

Papers on software maintenance appear in the December 1992 issue of *IEEE Transactions on Software Engineering* and the May 1994 issue of *Communications of the ACM*.

Problems

14.1 Why do you think that the mistake is frequently made of considering software maintenance to be inferior to software development?

14.2 Consider a product that determines whether a computer is virus-free. Describe why such a product is likely to have multiple variations of many of it modules. What are the implications for maintenance? How can the resulting problems be solved?

14.3 Repeat Problem 14.2 for the automated library circulation system of Problem 6.18.

Repeat Problem 14.2 for the automated teller machine (ATM) of Problem 9.2.   **14.4**

Repeat Problem 14.2 for the product of Problem 6.17 that checks whether a bank   **14.5**
statement is correct.

You are the manager in charge of maintenance in a large software organization. What   **14.6**
qualities do you look for when hiring new employees?

What are the implications of maintenance for a one-person software production   **14.7**
organization?

You have been asked to build a computerized fault report file. What sort of data   **14.8**
would you store in the file? What sort of queries could be answered by your tool?
What sort of queries could not be answered by your tool?

You receive a memo from the vice-president for software maintenance of Olde   **14.9**
Fashioned Software Corporation (Problem 13.6) pointing out that for the foreseeable
future Olde Fashioned will have to maintain tens of millions of lines of COBOL code
and asking your advice with regard to CASE tools for such maintenance. What do
you reply?

(Term Project) Suppose that the Osbert Oglesby product has been developed as   **14.10**
specified in Appendix A. Now Osbert notices that, as required, dates of sale and dates
of purchase have the format mm/dd/yy. What changes need to be made to the
product so that it can be used in the twenty-first century?

(Case Study) The Java implementation of Appendix I allows non-digits to be entered   **14.11**
as an investmentID. Correct this and the other faults of this kind in the input
routines.

(Case Study) Improve the aesthetic appearance of all the reports in the Java   **14.12**
implementation of Appendix I by adjusting the alignment of the various components.

(Case Study) Replace the menu-driven input routines in the Java implementation of   **14.13**
Appendix I with a graphical user interface (GUI).

(Readings in Software Engineering) Your instructor will distribute copies of [Basili,   **14.14**
1990]. Do you agree with the assessment of maintenance as a reuse process? Give
reasons for your answer.

References

[Babich, 1986] W. A. BABICH, *Software Configuration Management: Coordination for Team Productivity*, Addison-Wesley, Reading, MA, 1986.

[Banker, Datar, Kemerer, and Zwieg, 1993] R. D. BANKER, S. M. DATAR, C. F. KEMERER, AND D. ZWIEG, "Software Complexity and Maintenance Costs," *Communications of the ACM* **36** (November 1993), pp. 81–94.

[Basili, 1990] V. R. BASILI, "Viewing Maintenance as Reuse-Oriented Software Development," *IEEE Software* **7** (January 1990), pp. 19–25.

[Botting, 1994] R. BOTTING, Personal communication, 1994.

[Coleman, Ash, Lowther, and Oman, 1994] D. COLEMAN, D. ASH, B. LOWTHER, AND P. OMAN, "Using Metrics to Evaluate Software System Maintainability," *IEEE Computer* **27** (August 1994), pp. 44–49.

[Glass and Noiseux, 1981] R. L. GLASS AND R. A. NOISEUX, *Software Maintenance Guidebook,* Prentice-Hall, Englewood Cliffs, NJ, 1981.

[Guimaraes, 1983] T. GUIMARAES, "Managing Application Program Maintenance Expenditures," *Communications of the ACM* **26** (October 1983), pp. 739–746.

[Henry and Humphrey, 1990] S. M. HENRY AND M. HUMPHREY, "A Controlled Experiment to Evaluate Maintainability of Object-Oriented Software," *Proceedings of the IEEE Conference on Software Maintenance*, San Diego, CA, November 1990, pp. 258–265.

[Henry, Henry, Kafura, and Matheson, 1994] J. HENRY, S. HENRY, D. KAFURA, AND L. MATHESON, "Improving Software Maintenance at Martin Marietta," *IEEE Software* **11** (July, 1994), pp. 67–75.

[Lientz and Swanson, 1980] B. P. LIENTZ AND E. B. SWANSON, *Software Maintenance Management: A Study of the Maintenance of Computer Applications Software in 487 Data Processing Organizations*, Addison-Wesley, Reading, MA, 1980.

[Lientz, Swanson, and Tompkins, 1978] B. P. LIENTZ, E. B. SWANSON, AND G. E. TOMPKINS, "Characteristics of Application Software Maintenance," *Communications of the ACM* **21** (June 1978), pp. 466–471.

[Lejter, Meyers, and Reiss, 1992] M. LEJTER, S. MEYERS, AND S. P. REISS, "Support for Maintaining Object-Oriented Programs," *IEEE Transactions on Software Engineering* **18** (December 1992), pp. 1045–1052.

[Longstreet, 1990] D. H. LONGSTREET (Editor), *Software Maintenance and Computers,* IEEE Computer Society Press, Los Alamitos, CA, 1990.

[Mancl and Havanas, 1990] D. MANCL AND W. HAVANAS, "A Study of the Impact of C++ on Software Maintenance," *Proceedings of the IEEE Conference on Software Maintenance*, San Diego, CA, November 1990, pp. 63–69.

[Meyer, 1990] B. MEYER, "Lessons from the Design of the Eiffel Libraries," *Communications of the ACM* **33** (September 1990), pp. 68–88.

[Parikh, 1988] G. PARIKH (Editor), *Techniques of Program and System Maintenance*, Second Edition, QED Information Services, Wellesley, MA, 1988.

[Rochkind, 1975] M. J. ROCHKIND, "The Source Code Control System," *IEEE Transactions on Software Engineering* **SE-1** (October 1975), pp. 255–265.

[Schneidewind, 1987] N. F. SCHNEIDEWIND, "The State of Software Maintenance," *IEEE Transactions on Software Engineering* **SE-13** (March 1987), pp. 303–310.

[Tichy, 1985] W. F. TICHY, "RCS—A System for Version Control," *Software—Practice and Experience* **15** (July 1985), pp. 637–654.

[Wilde, Matthews, and Huitt, 1993] N. WILDE, P. MATTHEWS, AND R. HUITT, "Maintaining Object-Oriented Software," *IEEE Software* **10** (January 1993), pp. 75–80.

[Zelkowitz, Shaw, and Gannon, 1979] M. V. ZELKOWITZ, A. C. SHAW, AND J. D. GANNON, *Principles of Software Engineering and Design*, Prentice-Hall, Englewood Cliffs, NJ, 1979.

epilogue

JAVA: A CASE STUDY IN SOFTWARE ENGINEERING

In 1991, Sun Microsystems, Inc. decided to expand into the world of consumer electronics. First they developed a personal digital assistant (PDA). This was a small hand-held computer, similar to the Apple Newton, that incorporated a cellular telephone and fax. James Gosling started developing the software for this PDA in C++. However, he soon realized that C++ software may not be reliable or secure, as pointed out in the Just in Case You Wanted to Know box on page 399. He was therefore forced to design his own language, now called Java.

Sales of the first version of the Newton were disappointing, so Sun dropped the PDA project. They decided instead to use their new language in a different consumer product, this time interactive television. Again, Java was to be used for an embedded real-time system. However, this project, too, was terminated before completion. Sun now had what seemed to be an excellent programming language but with no obvious use for it. After considerable brainstorming, it became clear that a language that is appropriate for consumer electronic products like a PDA or interactive television is equally suited to World Wide Web software.

In fact, the qualities of Java that make it the language of choice for Web software are precisely those qualities that make Java a case study in software engineering, including portability, security, and robustness. These qualities are now briefly discussed.

Java and Modularity   The fact that Java was used to illustrate the modularity concepts of Chapter 6 indicates that Java supports the partition of a large program into modules. Specifically, a Java application program consists of a number of classes. If the program is properly designed, these classes will reflect encapsulation (Section 6.4) and information hiding (Section 6.6). Java is a pure object-oriented language, so it does not support separate functions or procedures. Instead, modules of this type are implemented as methods within classes.

In Java, encapsulation and information hiding can be enhanced by grouping sets of related classes into **package**s. Unless a visibility modifier such as **private** is used, attributes ("instance variables") and methods are accessible to all objects within the same package but are invisible outside that package. Like other forms of encapsulation and information hiding, packages can promote maintainability.

Some languages like C++ support multiple inheritance. That is, a class can inherit from more than one superclass. Multiple inheritance can be a powerful abstraction technique. However, it also can make software extremely complicated. For example, if two superclasses both contain a field with the same name, the resulting ambiguity has to be resolved.

Java supports only single inheritance. However, the effect of multiple inheritance can be achieved via Java interfaces. An interface is similar to an Ada **header**; it is an abstract description of a set of methods. A class that implements an interface must provide an implementation of each of the methods that appear in that interface. A Java class can inherit implementations from only one superclass but can implement many interfaces, thereby achieving abstraction, the major benefit of multiple inheritance, without its potential problems.

Java and Structured Programming   Java supports the three control structures of structured programming (Section 12.3). Unlike C and C++, there is no **goto** statement in Java.[1] There is essentially no need for a **goto** because Java supports the labeled **break** and **continue** statements outlined in this subsection as well as the **try . . . catch** statement described later.

The **break** statement in C and C++ transfers control out of the nearest enclosing **for, while, do,** or **switch** statement. The (unlabeled) **break** statement in Java is essentially identical to its C or C++ counterpart.[2] In addition, however, Java allows such enclosing statements to bear a label. A labeled **break** statement, that is, the keyword **break** followed by the name of a label, causes control to be transferred out of the specified labeled enclosing statement (as opposed to the nearest enclosing statement in the unlabeled case).

Similarly, the **continue** statement in C and C++ and the (unlabeled) **continue** statement in Java cause control to be transferred to the end of the nearest enclosing **for, while,** or **do** statement; loop iteration then proceeds. The labeled **continue** statement in Java transfers control to the end of the specified enclosing statement, analogously to the behavior of the labeled **break** statement.

The Java **continue** and **break** statements do not obey either of the two definitions of structured programming in Section 12.3.2. Furthermore, it is hard to argue that they make Java code more readable, which is the true aim of structured programming, as explained at the end of Section 12.3.2. Readability is reduced because the labeled **continue** and the labeled **break** statement are counterintuitive; in neither case is control transferred to the label itself.

Java and Portability   Java is a truly portably language. Unlike most other languages, Java is usually not compiled down to machine code. Instead, Java source is translated into *bytecode* by javac, the Java compiler; the bytecode version is then interpreted by java, the bytecode interpreter. Thus, in order to be able to run a Java program on a new machine, all that is needed is to port the Java bytecode interpreter (*runtime system*) to the new machine, a comparatively easy task. Most World Wide

---

[1]More precisely, **goto** is a reserved word in Java but it is not used in the current release of Java.
[2]For the sake of simplicity, the Java **finally** clause is ignored in this discussion.

Web browsers now incorporate a Java interpreter. Bytecode applets (small application programs) transmitted over the Web can then be run on the user's machine.

It is certainly true that interpreted code runs more slowly than compiled code, sometimes by a factor of 5 or even 10. In some cases this is not important. For example, the MSG case study of Chapters 7 through 14 is an interactive program, so slowness caused by interpretation is hardly detectable. However, in other cases the speed of a program is of critical importance. In such cases, it is necessary to write a Java compiler that will generate machine code for the target machine, thus sacrificing portability in the interests of execution time. One way to simplify this task is to use java2c, a compiler that translates Java source code into C source code, which can then be compiled using an optimizing C compiler. Thus, even though Java is usually interpreted, this does not mean that it can never be executed in the usual way.

As discussed in Section 12.12.2, numerical incompatibility can pose an obstacle to portability. This problem does not arise in Java. In all implementations, type **int** is a signed two's complement 32-bit integer, and **float** conforms to IEEE Standard 754 for 32-bit floating point numbers [ANSI/IEEE 754, 1985]. This is another example of the way that Java was designed from the outset for true portability.

The compiler that translates Java into bytecodes is itself written in Java, thus providing yet another form of portability. Thus, when porting Java to a new architecture there is no need to modify the Java compiler for that new environment. The bytecode interpreter is written in ANSI C (Section 12.10.4) and all but complies with POSIX (Section 12.12.2). Finally, unlike Ada, there are no implementation-dependent parts in the Java language specification.

Java and Security   Unlike C++, Java does not support explicit pointer variables. As explained in the Just in Case You Wanted to Know Box on page 399, one danger of pointer variables is that they can be used to access addresses within the operating system. This is a favorite stratagem used by perpetrators of computer viruses. If the virus is able to execute privileged instructions within the operating system, it can essentially do anything. However, because Java does not support pointer variables, this cannot happen in a Java program.

Even without explicit pointer variables, it is possible to access memory illegally if a bytecode has been doctored appropriately. Java precludes this sort of security attack as well; the java interpreter checks each bytecode before interpreting it. There is still one loophole, however. A malefactor can modify the Java bytecode interpreter to disable this bytecode checking. Thus, the system manager should carefully monitor the Java interpreter (as well as all other system software) to make sure that a so-called Trojan Horse [Thompson, 1984] has not been introduced.

There are other problems that can be caused by improper or incorrect use of pointer variables. For example, in a language such as Pascal that supports dynamic data structures, the command new (ptr_var) causes an area of memory to be set aside; variable ptr_var points to this area of memory. If ptr_var is now immediately assigned to some other address, that area of memory is now inaccessible and cannot be used by the application program (standard Pascal does not support a garbage collector). Similar problems arise in C and C++. More seriously, it is possible to deallocate a record too soon, that is, while there are still pointers that point to that record. Again, this cannot happen in Java because Java does not support explicit pointer variables.

Java and Reliability   One way to ensure that a program is reliable is to implement it in a strongly typed language. In such a language, every variable has to be of a specific type, a variable can take on only those values that are permitted for that type, and the only operations that can be performed on that variable are operations permitted for variables of that type. One consequence is that when a method is invoked within a strongly typed language, the type of each actual parameter has to match that of the corresponding formal parameter (see Section 4.4). Unfortunately, C is not strongly typed. Furthermore, even though C++ supports strong typing, it does not enforce it; recall that a C++ compiler accepts virtually every C program. Java, on the other hand, is a strongly typed language. The types of all variables and methods and their arguments have to be declared. Also, the type of each parameter of a method is checked by the Java compiler. In addition, Java offers only limited automatic type coercion; explicit type cases are generally needed. The Java verifier (part of the run-time system) also enforces strong type checking, as does the Java loader.

Consider again the issue of dynamic variables mentioned in the previous subsection. Certain languages such as Pascal, C, and C++ that support the creation of dynamic variables require explicit deletion of these dynamic variables after use so that memory can be freed for reuse by new dynamic variables. Other languages (including LISP and Smalltalk) that support dynamic variables have an automatic garbage collector that releases memory when it is no longer being used for a dynamic variable, that is, when there is no longer a pointer to that variable. This makes programming easier and simpler. However, invocation of the garbage collector by the run-time system can slow down execution. Java is a multithreaded language; more than one execution stream can proceed in parallel. Automatic garbage collection is therefore performed in the background as a low-priority task in parallel with the user's application program. In this way, Java users have the advantage of automatic garbage collection implemented in a way that interferes minimally with execution of an application program.

Another reason for the reliability of Java application software is that the basic Java system (compiler and interpreter) occupies fewer than 250 Kbytes. The number of faults is proportional to the size of the software (Section 12.16.2). The compilation and interpretation of Java bytecodes is therefore more likely to be fault-free than the compilation of code by a large compiler followed by its execution in a large run-time environment.

As pointed out in the Just in Case You Wanted to Know box on page 132, run-time checking of array subscripts is important for reliability. Arrays as such are not defined in C and C++. Instead, a pointer to the first element of the array is used. This is doubly dangerous because pointers are implicitly insecure and the lack of an explicit array construct precludes bounds checking. Java, on the other hand, supports both arrays and array bounds checking.

Another way that Java supports reliability is exception handling. As pointed out in Section 12.23, real-time software frequently has to run untended (that is, without a computer operator) and must consequently be able to recover automatically from a variety of emergencies and exceptional conditions. As described in more detail in Section 12.3, Java supports exception handling by means of the **try . . . catch** construct. If an exception is caught within a **try . . . catch** block, control is passed to the statement after the **catch,** thus affording the method in question the opportunity to recover from the exception. The **throw** statement is used to select the appropriate exception handler.

Java and Constants   Java is a pure object-oriented language. Thus, it does not support constants as such. Instead, constants have to be defined as **final** variables within a class. It is somewhat confusing for a constant to be defined as a "variable."

Unlike C and C++, Java also does not support macros such as **#define** that can be used, in conjunction with a preprocessor, to declare the value of a constant. There is a good reason for this. Java applets are designed to be independent programs loaded over the Internet. Java therefore does not support header files or other components that need to be available in conjunction with otherwise stand-alone programs.

Java and Object Orientation   Java supports the five basic elements of an object-oriented language described in Chapter 6, namely, classes, objects, inheritance, polymorphism, and dynamic binding. Java is a pure object-oriented language; it does not support the classical paradigm. Thus there are no functions or procedures, only methods or classes.

Protagonists of a hybrid object-oriented language like C++ that supports both the classical paradigm and the object-oriented paradigm point out that it is easy for a C programmer to move to C++. After all, C is a subset of C++, so all that the programmer needs to learn are the object-oriented aspects of C++. However, it is equally easy for that programmer to slip back into the classical paradigm. Java, on the other hand, supports only the object-oriented paradigm and so, the argument goes, programmers are forced to develop object-oriented software. The fallacy here is that there is more to the object-oriented paradigm than using the keyword **class.** That is, unless a product has been developed using object-oriented analysis (Chapter 9) and object-oriented design (Section 11.8), it will not be object oriented, no matter what programming language is used.

Thus, the jury is still out as to whether it is better to learn the object-oriented paradigm gradually while moving from C to C++ or from COBOL to OO-COBOL, or whether it is better to use a pure object-oriented language like Java or Smalltalk from the start.

Java and Reusability   All object-oriented programming languages support reuse via inheritance of classes. In addition, mechanisms such as templates (in C++) and generics (in Ada) provide reuse at a higher level of abstraction. A *template* or *generic* is a module that is defined in terms of parameters. The generic is then instantiated for a particular set of parameters. For example, a generic sort is defined in terms of elements of an arbitrary type. A programmer can then instantiate a sort for integers or a sort for insurance policy records.

Java does not directly support templates of this kind. Java interfaces (described in the first subsection) are similar to templates, but they are less flexible and less powerful than templates. Nevertheless, they do provide a level of abstraction that can increase maintainability and reusability.

Java and Visibility   Up to now, it might seem that Java is the ideal programming language and is in every way superior to C++. This is not the case. Indeed, there are many features of Java that can be improved. Furthermore, there are instances in which C++ is superior to Java. For example, consider access rules.

In C++, there are three *access specifiers:* **public**, **protected**, and **private**. If an attribute is defined to be **public**, then it can be accessed from anywhere within the product. A **protected** attribute is accessible from within an instance of the class in which it is defined as well as from within an instance of a subclass of that class. Finally, a **private** attribute can be accessed only from within an instance of the class in which it is defined. If no access specifier is explicitly given, the default is **private**. Identical rules apply to methods.[3]

In Java, however, there are five types of access and the rules are more convoluted than in C++ because Java classes can be grouped into **package**s of related classes. The simplest visibility modifier is **public**. As in C++, if a Java attribute is declared to be **public** it can be accessed from anywhere within the product. A **protected** attribute is accessible from anywhere within the package in which that attribute is declared; in addition, a subclass in a different package can access attributes inherited from its superclass, but cannot access attributes of instances of the superclass itself. A **private protected** attribute is accessible from within an instance of the class in which it is defined as well as within an instance of a subclass of that class. As with **protected**, a **private protected** attribute cannot access attributes of instances of its superclass. A **private** attribute can be accessed only from within an instance of the class in which it is defined. The default is yet another accessibility type, one that has no name. This default type allows access from anywhere within the package in which it is defined. Again, identical rules apply to methods.

Another area where C++ is superior to Java is the declaration of constants. In C++, the reserved word **const** is used to declare a constant; for example,

const float sales_tax = 6.0;

The corresponding Java statement is

public static final float salesTax = (**float**) 6.0;

It is to be hoped that this and other awkward constructs will be improved in the next release of Java.

---

[3]The description in this paragraph is somewhat oversimplified; **friend**s have been ignored, and so have *access declarations,* which modify the basic access rules.

There are many sources of information on Java, including books, articles in research journals, and technical articles that can be downloaded over the Internet. Almost invariably, a major theme of this material is that Java is the language of the World Wide Web. It is certainly true that features such as its reliability, security, portability, and the small size of Java compilers and interpreters make Java the ideal language for interchanging code (and especially bytecode) over the Internet. At the same time, it is important to realize that many (but not all) of these features were part of Java before the existence of the World Wide Web. That is, Java is the language of the Internet because it was well designed from the start, *not* because it was specifically designed for Internet use. In other words, Java is indeed a case study in software engineering.

References

[ANSI/IEEE 754, 1985] "Standard for Binary Floating Point Arithmetic," ANSI/IEEE 754, American National Standards Institute, Inc., Institute of Electrical and Electronic Engineers, Inc., 1985.

[Thompson, 1984] K. THOMPSON, "Reflections on Trusting Trust," *Communications of the ACM* **27** (November 1984), pp. 761–763.

OSBERT OGLESBY—ART DEALER

Osbert Oglesby is a noted art dealer. He specializes in buying and selling French Impressionist paintings, but he will buy any piece of art if he thinks he can make a profit when he sells it in his gallery, *Les Objets d'Orient*.

Lately, however, Osbert has been losing money. After having carefully analyzed his business records, he concludes that he has been overpaying for paintings. He decides that he needs a software product, running on a portable computer, that he can use to determine the maximum price he should pay for a painting. (Osbert plans to take the computer when he views a painting in a client's home or office.) The input to the program is the painting classification (masterpiece, masterwork,[1] other), together with the data needed to compute the price for that classification of painting.

Osbert commissions a computer scientist to devise an algorithm for determining the maximum price he should pay for a painting. Here is the algorithm:

- A masterpiece: Scan auction records for the most similar work by the same artist. Use the auction purchase price of the most similar work as the base price. (For the definition of similarity, see below.) The maximum purchase price is found by adding 8.5 percent to the base price, compounded annually, for each year since that auction.

- A masterwork: First, compute the maximum purchase price as if it were a masterpiece by the same artist. Then, if the picture was painted in the 20th century, multiply this figure by 0.25, otherwise multiply it by $(20 - c) / (21 - c)$, where c is the century in which the work was painted ($12 < c < 20$).

- Other: Measure the dimensions of the canvas. The maximum purchase price is given by the formula $F * A$, where F is a constant for that painter (fashionability coefficient) and A is the area of the canvas in square centimeters. If there is no fashionability coefficient for that painter, Osbert will not buy the painting.

In the case of masterpieces and masterworks, the coefficient of similarity between two paintings is computed as follows:

Score 1 for a match on medium, otherwise 0.

Score 1 for a match on subject, otherwise 0.

Add these two numbers, multiply by the area of the smaller of the two paintings, and divide by the area of the larger of the two.

The resulting number is the coefficient of similarity.

---

[1] A masterwork is an inferior work by an artist who has previously painted a masterpiece.

If the coefficient of similarity between the painting under consideration and the paintings in the file of auction data is zero, then Osbert will not buy that masterwork or masterpiece.

The program must include a file of artists and their corresponding F values. The value of F can vary from month to month, depending on the current fashionability of an artist, so the file must be implemented to allow Osbert to perform regular updates. The program must also include a file containing data on auction sales of masterpieces. This file will include the name of artist, title of painting, date of painting, date of auction (assumed to be in this century), sale price, and type of work. The type of work consists of three components, namely medium (oil, watercolor, or other), dimensions (height and width), and subject (portrait, still-life, landscape, or other). This file is updated regularly by an outside source and is never modified by Osbert.

For each painting he has bought since introducing his scheme, Osbert needs to record the following:

Description of painting

    First name of artist (followed by ? if there is uncertainty)

    Last name of artist (followed by ? if there is uncertainty)

    Title of work (followed by ? if there is uncertainty)

    Date of work (yyyy, followed by ? if there is uncertainty)

    Classification (masterpiece, masterwork, other)

    Height (cm)

    Width (cm)

    Medium (oil, watercolor, other)

    Subject (portrait, still-life, landscape, other)

Date of purchase (mm/dd/yy)

Name of seller

Address of seller

Maximum purchase price determined by algorithm

Actual purchase price

Target selling price (2.15 times the purchase price)

If the piece has been sold, then add:

    Date of sale (mm/dd/yy)

    Name of buyer

    Address of buyer

    Actual selling price

Question marks in the first four fields are to be ignored when determining similarity. They should be included, however, in the three reports described below. All three reports are to be generated on demand and must incorporate sales and purchases during the past year. That is to say, Osbert wishes a report generated at any time on April 6, 1997, to cover the period from April 6, 1996, through April 6, 1997. The product should pause after every 20 lines of text to allow Osbert to view each report one screen at a time.

A report is needed to display all the paintings purchased during the past year. The output should be in the following order: classification type, purchase date, artist's last name, painting title, suggested maximum purchase price, and actual purchase price. Any painting purchased for more than the maximum purchase price computed by the algorithm must be flagged (by placing an asterisk before the classification type). This report must be sorted by classification, and by date of purchase within classification. The average ratio of the actual purchase price to the algorithm's suggested maximum purchase price, for all the paintings in the report, should be displayed at the end of the report.

A second report should display the paintings that have been sold during the past year. The output should be in the following order: classification type, sale date, artist's last name, painting title, target selling price, and actual selling price. Any painting sold at a price of 5 percent or more below the target selling price must be flagged. This report must be sorted by classification, and by date of sale within classification. The average ratio of the actual selling price to the target selling price for all of the paintings in the report should be displayed at the end of the report.

Finally, Osbert is keen to detect new trends in the art market as soon as possible. He is particularly interested in determining when higher prices than expected are consistently paid for a particular artist's work, so that he can buy up paintings by that artist before others notice the trend. He therefore requires a report that shows artists whose works have been sold at a price that has exceeded the target selling price in every instance during the past year. For an artist to appear in this report, at least two of his or her works must have been sold in that period. The names of the relevant artists (if any) should be in alphabetical order. Each name should appear on one line of the screen. The various works sold must appear on successive lines, in order of date of sale. For each work, the date of sale, classification type, painting title, target selling price, and actual selling price must appear, in that order.

B

SOFTWARE ENGINEERING RESOURCES

There are two good ways to get more information on software engineering topics, namely by reading journals and conference proceedings, and via the Internet.

There are journals dedicated exclusively to software engineering, such as *IEEE Transactions on Software Engineering*. There are also journals of a more general nature, such as *Communications of the ACM*, in which significant articles on software engineering are published. For reasons of space, only a selection of journals of both classes appears below. The journals have been chosen on a subjective basis, namely, those which the author has found to be the most useful.

ACM Computing Surveys
ACM Guide to the Computing Literature
ACM SIGAda Ada Letters
ACM SIGCHI Bulletin
ACM SIGPLAN Letters
ACM SIGSOFT Software Engineering Notes
ACM Transactions on Computer Systems
ACM Transactions on Programming Languages and Systems
ACM Transactions on Software Engineering and Methodology
Communications of the ACM
Computer Journal
Computing Reviews
IBM Journal of Research and Development
IBM Systems Journal
IEEE Computer
IEEE Software
IEEE Transactions on Computers
IEEE Transactions on Software Engineering
Java Report
Journal of Object-Oriented Programming
Journal of Software Maintenance: Research and Practice
Journal of Systems and Software
Software Engineering Journal
Software—Practice and Experience

In addition, there are many conferences whose proceedings contain important articles on software engineering topics. Again, a subjective selection appears below. Most of the conferences are commonly referred to by their acronym or name of sponsoring organization; these appear in parentheses.

ACM SIGPLAN Annual Conference (SIGPLAN)

ACM SIGSOFT Symposium on the Foundations of Software Engineering (FSE)

Conference on Object-Oriented Programming Systems, Languages, and Applications (OOPSLA)

Conference on Software Maintenance (CSM)

Human Factors in Computing Systems (CHI)

International Computer Software and Applications Conference (COMPSAC)

International Conference on Software Engineering (ICSE)

International Software Process Workshop

International Symposium on Software Testing and Analysis (ISSTA)

International Workshop on Software Configuration Management (SCM)

International Workshop on Software Reusability (IWSR)

International Workshop on Software Specification and Design (IWSSD)

The Internet is another valuable source of information on software engineering. With regard to Usenet news groups, the following two have been consistently useful to the author:

```
comp.object
comp.software-eng
```

Other newsgroups that sometimes have items that the author finds relevant include the following:

```
comp.lang.ada
comp.lang.c++
comp.lang.java
comp.software.testing
comp.specification
comp.specification.z
```

New newsgroups are continually being formed, so the reader should scan the list of available groups to see if something worthwhile has been formed since the time of writing.

In addition, many organizations maintain information online that can be accessed via mechanisms such as anonymous ftp, Gopher, WAIS, or World Wide Web (www). With regard to the latter, the World Wide Web Virtual Library for Software Engineering can be found at http://ricis.cl.uh.edu/virt-lib/soft-eng.html. An especially valuable source is the Software Engineering Institute at Carnegie-Mellon University. Documents can be obtained by anonymous ftp from ftp.sei.cmu.edu.

C

MSG Case Study: Rapid Prototype

This appendix contains the rapid prototype for the MSG Case Study. It is written in Java, for the reasons mentioned in Section 7.15.

```java
import java.io.*;
import java.util.*;

/********************************************************************************
 *
 *                              Class InvestmentRecord
 *
 ********************************************************************************/

class InvestmentRecord
{
    public String          number;
    public String          name;
    public float           ret;
    public Date            date;
} // InvestmentRecord


/********************************************************************************
 *
 *                          Class MSGPrototypeApplication
 *
 ********************************************************************************/

class MSGPrototypeApplication
{
    public static void main (String args[])
    {
        MSGPrototype thisApplication = new MSGPrototype ();

        thisApplication.initialize ();
        thisApplication.clearScreen ();
        thisApplication.mainMenu ();
    } // main

} // class MSGPrototypeApplication


/********************************************************************************
 *
 *                              Class MSGPrototype
 *
 ********************************************************************************/

class MSGPrototype
{
    public static final int NUM_RECORDS = 11;

    public InvestmentRecord portfolio[] = new InvestmentRecord[NUM_RECORDS];

/********************************************************************************
 *
 *    Because this is a rapid prototype, an array of records has been used.
 *    In the actual implementation, a dynamic data structure is needed
 *    because it is not known how many investments there will be.
 *
 ********************************************************************************/
```

```java
public void clearScreen ()
//
// Clear the screen
//
{
    //
    // Implementation-dependent code to clear the screen
    //

} // clearScreen
```

//--

```java
public void initialize ()
//
// Initialize investments
//
{
    for (int i = 0; i < NUM_RECORDS; i++)
    {
        portfolio[i] = new InvestmentRecord ();
        portfolio[i].number = "000000000000";
    }
} // initialize
```

//--

```java
public void addInvestment ()
//
// Allows user to add investments
//
{
    try
    {
        int             current = 0;
        char            c;
        boolean         found = false;
        StringBuffer    input;

        while (!found || (current == NUM_RECORDS))
        {
            if (portfolio[current].number.compareTo ("000000000000") == 0)
                found = true;
            else
                current++;
        }

        clearScreen ();

        System.out.println ("Enter investment number (12 digits): ");
        input = new StringBuffer ();
        while ((c = (char) System.in.read ()) != '\n')
        {
            input.append (c);
        }
        portfolio[current].number = input.toString ();
```

```
            System.out.println ("Enter name: ");
            input = new StringBuffer ();
            while ((c = (char) System.in.read ()) != '\n')
            {
                input.append (c);
            }
            portfolio[current].name = input.toString ();

            System.out.println ("Enter estimated annual return: ");
            input = new StringBuffer ();
            while ((c = (char) System.in.read ()) != '\n')
            {
                input.append (c);
            }
            Float tempFloat = new Float (input.toString ());
            portfolio[current].ret = tempFloat.floatValue ();

            portfolio[current].date = new Date ();

        }
        catch (Exception e)
        {
            System.out.println ("addinvestment error: " + e);
        }

    } // addInvestment

//-------------------------------------------------------------------------------------------

    public void modifyInvestment ()
    //
    // Allows user to modify investments
    //
    {
        try
        {
            int            current;
            char           c;
            byte           choice[] = new byte[10];
            boolean        found;
            StringBuffer   input;

            clearScreen ();

            System.out.println ("\n\n");
            System.out.println ("Enter investment number of investment to be modified: ");
            input = new StringBuffer ();
            while ((c = (char) System.in.read ()) != '\n')
            {
                input.append (c);
            }

            found = false;
            current = 0;
            while (!found && (current < NUM_RECORDS))
            {
                if (portfolio[current].number.compareTo (input.toString ()) == 0)
                    found = true;
```

```
                    else current = current + 1;
        }

    if (!found)
        System.out.println ("Record not found");
    else
    {
        System.out.println ("\n\n");
        System.out.println ("          1. Investment Number \n");
        System.out.println ("          2. Investment Name \n");
        System.out.println ("          3. Estimated Annual Ret \n");
        System.out.println ("\n\n");

        System.out.println (" Select field to be modified ");
        System.in.read (choice);

        System.out.println ("\n\n");

        switch ( (char) choice[0])
        {
            case '1':
                System.out.println ("Enter investment number (12 digits): ");
                input = new StringBuffer ();
                while ((c = (char) System.in.read ()) != '\n')
                {
                    input.append (c);
                }
                portfolio[current].number = input.toString ();
                break;

            case '2':
                System.out.println ("Enter investment name: ");
                input = new StringBuffer ();
                while ((c = (char) System.in.read ()) != '\n')
                {
                    input.append (c);
                }
                portfolio[current].name = input.toString ();
                break;

            case '3':
                System.out.println ("Enter estimated annual return: ");
                input = new StringBuffer ();
                while ((c = (char) System.in.read ()) != '\n')
                {
                    input.append (c);
                }
                Float tempFloat = new Float (input.toString ());
                portfolio[current].ret = tempFloat.floatValue ();
                portfolio[current].date = new Date ();
                break;
        } // switch

    } // else

}
catch (Exception e)
{
```

```
              }

     } // modifyInvestment
//------------------------------------------------------------------------------------------------------------------

     public void deleteInvestment ()
     //
     // Allows user to delete investments
     //
     {
          try
          {
               int              current;
               char             c;
               boolean          found;
               StringBuffer     input;

               clearScreen ();

               System.out.println ("\n\n");
               System.out.println ("Enter investment # of investment to be deleted: ");
               input = new StringBuffer ();
               while ((c = (char) System.in.read ()) != '\n')
               {
                    input.append (c);
               }

               found = false;
               current = 1;
               while (!found && (current < NUM_RECORDS))
               {
                    if (portfolio[current].number.compareTo (input.toString ()) == 0)
                         found = true;
                    else
                         current = current + 1;
               }

               if (!found)
                    System.out.println ("Record not found\n");
               else
               {
                    portfolio[current].number = new String ("000000000000");
                    System.out.println ("Record deleted");
               }

          }
          catch (Exception e)
          {
          }

     } // deleteInvestment

//------------------------------------------------------------------------------------------------------------------

     public void addMortgage ()
     //
     // Allows user to add mortgage
```

```
//
{
    try
    {
        byte            c[] = new byte[10];

        System.out.println ("Not yet implemented.  Press ENTER to continue");
        System.in.read (c);

    }
    catch (Exception e)
    {
    }

} // addMortgage
```

//--

```
public void modifyMortgage ()
//
// Allows user to modify mortgage
//
{
    try
    {
        byte            c[] = new byte[10];

        System.out.println ("Not yet implemented.  Press ENTER to continue");
        System.in.read (c);

    }
    catch (Exception e)
    {
    }

} // modifyMortgage
```

//--

```
public void deleteMortgage ()
//
// Allows user to delete mortgage
//
{
    try
    {

        byte            c[] = new byte[10];

        System.out.println ("Not yet implemented.  Press ENTER to continue");
        System.in.read (c);

    }
    catch (Exception e)
    {
    }

} // deleteMortgage
```

```
//-----------------------------------------------------------------------------------

public void mortgageMenu ()
//
// Allows user to select operations on mortgage information
//
{
    try
    {
        byte            choice[] = new byte[10];
        boolean         done = false;

        while (!done)
        {
            clearScreen ();

            System.out.println ("\n\n\n\n");
            System.out.println ("                    MORTGAGE MENU");
            System.out.println ("\n\n");
            System.out.println ("              1. Add Mortgage data");
            System.out.println ();
            System.out.println ("              2. Modify Mortgage data");
            System.out.println ();
            System.out.println ("              3. Delete Mortgage data");
            System.out.println ();
            System.out.println ("              4. Return to Main Menu");
            System.out.println ("\n\n");

            System.out.println ("    Enter your selection and press <ENTER> ");
            System.in.read (choice);

            switch ( (char) choice[0])
            {
                case '1':
                    addMortgage ();
                    break;

                case '2':
                    modifyMortgage ();
                    break;

                case '3':
                    deleteMortgage ();
                    break;

                case '4':
                case '\n':
                    done = true;
                    break;

                default:
                    System.out.println ("\n\n");
                    System.out.println ("Incorrect selection, try again \n");
                    break;
            } // switch
        }
```

```
        }
        catch (Exception e)
        {
        }

    } // mortgageMenu
```

//--

```
    public void opexpensesMenu ()
    //
    // Allows user to select operations on operating expenses
    //
    {
        try
        {
            byte            c[] = new byte[10];

            System.out.println ("Not yet implemented.  Press ENTER to continue");
            System.in.read (c);

        }
        catch (Exception e)
        {
        }

    } // opexpensesMenu
```

//--

```
    public void investmentMenu ()
    //
    // Allows user to select operations on investment information
    //
    {
        try
        {
            byte            choice[] = new byte[10];
            boolean         done = false;

            while (!done)
            {
                clearScreen ();

                System.out.println ("\n\n\n\n");
                System.out.println ("                    INVESTMENT MENU \n");
                System.out.println ("\n\n");
                System.out.println ("                    1. Add Investment data \n");
                System.out.println ("                    2. Modify Investment data \n");
                System.out.println ("                    3. Delete Investment data \n");
                System.out.println ("                    4. Return to Main Menu \n\n");

                System.out.println ("            Enter your selection and press <ENTER> ");
                System.in.read (choice);

                switch ( (char) choice[0])
                {
                    case '1':
```

```
                addInvestment ();
                break;

            case '2':
                modifyInvestment ();
                break;

            case '3':
                deleteInvestment ();
                break;

            case '4':
            case '\n':
                done = true;
                break;

            default:
                System.out.println (" Choice is out of range ");
                break;
            }
        }

    }
    catch (Exception e)
    {
    }

} // investmentMenu
```

//--

```
    public void investmentListing ()
    //
    // Prints the investment report
    //
    {
        try
        {
            byte            c[] = new byte[10];

            clearScreen ();

            System.out.println ("\n\n");
            System.out.println ("               INVESTMENTS REPORT");
            System.out.println ("          MARTHA STOCKTON GREENGAGE FOUNDATION");
            System.out.println ("               Investments Listing");
            System.out.println ();
            System.out.println ("Item No.\t\tItem Name\tEstimated\tDate Estimated");
            System.out.println ("\t\t\t\tAnnual Ret\tAnnual Ret Updated");
            System.out.println ("------------------------------------------------------------------------------\n");

            for (int counter = 0; counter < NUM_RECORDS; counter++)
            {
                if (portfolio[counter].number.compareTo ("000000000000") != 0 )
                {
                    System.out.print (portfolio[counter].number + "\t\t");
                    System.out.print (portfolio[counter].name + "\t\t");
                    System.out.print (portfolio[counter].ret + "\t\t");
```

```
                    System.out.print ((portfolio[counter].date.getMonth () + 1) + "/");
                    System.out.print (portfolio[counter].date.getDate () + "/");
                    System.out.println (portfolio[counter].date.getYear ());
                }
            }

            System.out.println ("\n\n");
            System.out.println ("      Press ENTER to return to main menu");
            System.in.read (c);

        }
        catch (Exception e)
        {
        }

    } // investmentListing

//-------------------------------------------------------------------------------------------------------------------

    public void report ()
    //
    // Runs all the report programs
    //
    {
        try
        {
            byte           choice[] = new byte[10];
            boolean        done = false;

            while (!done)
            {
                clearScreen ();

                System.out.println ("\n\n");
                System.out.println ("                MARTHA STOCKTON GREENGAGE FOUNDATION");
                System.out.println ("                    REPORTS");
                System.out.println ();
                System.out.println ("          1. Listing of all Investments");
                System.out.println ();
                System.out.println ("          2. Listing of all Mortgages");
                System.out.println ();
                System.out.println ("          3. Results of weekly computations");
                System.out.println ();
                System.out.println ("          4. Return to Main Menu");
                System.out.println ("\n\n");

                System.out.println ("          Enter your choice and press <ENTER> ");
                System.in.read (choice);

                switch ( (char) choice[0])
                {
                    case '1':
                        investmentListing ();
                        break;

                    case '2':
                        clearScreen ();
```

```
                    System.out.println ("\n\n");
                    System.out.println ("      LIST OF ALL MORTGAGES\n");
                    System.out.println ("   This report is not implemented in the prototype\n");
                    System.out.println ("\n\n\n\n");

                    System.out.println ("    Press <ENTER> to return to the menu ");
                    System.in.read (choice);
                    break;

                case '3':
                    clearScreen ();

                    System.out.println ("\n\n");
                    System.out.println ("      WEEKLY COMPUTATION REPORTS \n");
                    System.out.println ("   This report is not implemented in the prototype \n");
                    System.out.println ("\n\n\n\n");

                    System.out.println ("    Press <ENTER> to return to the menu ");
                    System.in.read (choice);
                    break;

                case '4':
                case '\n':
                    done = true;
                    break;

                default:
                    System.out.println (" Choice is out of range \n");
                    break;
            } // switch

        } // while

    }
    catch (Exception e)
    {
    }

} // report

//--------------------------------------------------------------------------------------------------------

public void mainMenu ()
{
    try
    {
        byte            choice[] = new byte[10];
        boolean         done = false;

        while (!done)
        {
            clearScreen ();

            System.out.println ("\n\n\n\n");
            System.out.println ("      MARTHA STOCKTON GREENGAGE FOUNDATION");
            System.out.println ("\n\n");
            System.out.println ("      1. Maintain Investment data\n");
            System.out.println ("      2. Maintain Operating Expenses data\n");
```

```
        System.out.println ("        3. Maintain Mortgage data\n");
        System.out.println ("        4. Produce a report\n");
        System.out.println ("        5. Quit \n\n");

        System.out.println ("        Enter your choice and press <ENTER>: ");
        System.in.read (choice);

        switch ( (char) choice[0])
        {
            case '1':
                investmentMenu ();
                break;

            case '2':
                opexpensesMenu ();
                break;

            case '3':
                mortgageMenu ();
                break;

            case '4':
                report ();
                break;

            case '5':
            case '\n':
                done = true;
                break;

            default:
                System.out.println (" Choice is out of range ");
                break;
        }
    }

    }
    catch (Exception e)
    {
    }

    } // mainMenu

} // class MSGPrototype
```

MSG CASE STUDY:
STRUCTURED SYSTEMS ANALYSIS

Step 1. Draw the Data Flow Diagram   See Figure 8.27.

Step 2. Decide What Sections to Computerize and How   Computerize complete product online. However, if the weekly computation regarding availability of funds to purchase homes turns out to be time consuming, it may be better to perform it in batch the night before it is required.

Step 3. Put in the Details of the Data Flows

   investment details
      investment number
      investment name
      expected return (9 + 2 digits)
      date expected return updated (8 characters)
   mortgage details
      mortgage number (12 digits)
      mortgage name
      price (6 + 2 digits)
      date mortgage issued (8 characters)
      weekly income (6 + 2 digits)
      date weekly income was updated (8 characters)
      annual property tax (5 + 2 digits)
      annual insurance premium (5 + 2 digits)
      mortgage balance (6 + 2 digits)
   expected mortgage payments for week (9 + 2 digits)
   income details
      expected income for week (9 + 2 digits)
   expected grants for week (9 + 2 digits)
   annual operating expenses (9 + 2 digits)
   expected total return on investments (9 + 2 digits)
   available funds for week (9 + 2 digits)

Step 4. Define the Logic of the Processes

verify transaction type and validity
  Determine that transaction is either *add, modify*, or *delete*
  Obtain relevant data

add
  If item already exists, print error message
  If item does not exist, add new item to appropriate data store

modify
  If item already exists, perform modification to item in data store
  If item does not exist, print error message

delete
  If item already exists, prompt "Are you sure?"
    If yes, delete item from data store
    If no, cancel request
  If item does not exist, print error message

generate listing of mortgages
  For each mortgage in MORTGAGE DATA
    Print mortgage details

generate listing of investments
  For each investment in INVESTMENT DATA
    Print investment details

compute total expected return on investments
  For each investment in INVESTMENT DATA
    Add expected return to expected total return on investments

compute expected income, mortgage payments, and grants for week
  expected income for week = expected total return on investments / 52
  For each mortgage in MORTGAGE DATA
    Add expected mortgage payment for week (if any) to expected mortgage payments for week
    Add the expected grant for week (if any) to expected grants for week
  Update GRANT DATA

compute availability of funds and generate funds report data
  Obtain expected grants for week from GRANT DATA
  Obtain annual operating expenses from EXPENSES DATA
  available funds for week = expected income for week
                          − annual operating expenses / 52
                          + expected mortgage payments for week
                          − expected grants for week

Step 5. Define the Data Stores

EXPENSES DATA
annual operating expenses [defined in Step 3]

GRANT DATA
expected grants for week [defined in Step 3]

INCOME DATA
expected mortgage payments for week [defined in Step 3]
expected income for week [defined in Step 3]

INVESTMENT DATA
investment details [defined in Step 3]

MORTGAGE DATA
mortgage details [defined in Step 3]

RETURN DATA
mortgage details [defined in Step 3]

All files are sequential, and hence there is no DIAD.

Step 6. Define the Physical Resources

EXPENSES DATA
Sequential file
Stored on disk

GRANT DATA
Sequential file
Stored on disk

INCOME DATA
Sequential file
Stored on disk

INVESTMENT DATA
Sequential file
Stored on disk

MORTGAGE DATA
Sequential file
Stored on disk

RETURN DATA
Sequential file
Stored on disk

Step 7. Determine the Input/Output Specifications   Input screens will be designed
for the following processes:

*add investment, delete investment, modify investment, add
mortgage, delete mortgage, modify mortgage, update annual
operating expenses*

The following reports will be printed:

list of investments, list of mortgages, available funds for week

The screens and reports of the rapid prototype will be used as a basis for the above. The exact format of all screens and reports is subject to approval by MSG.

Step 8. Perform Sizing   Less than 1 Megabyte of storage is needed for the software. If there are 50 investments and 1000 mortgages, about 20 Megabytes may be needed for data storage.

Step 9. Determine the Hardware Requirements

Personal computer with hard disk, monitor, and keyboard.

Cartridge tape for backup.

Laser printer for reports.

E

MSG CASE STUDY:
OBJECT-ORIENTED ANALYSIS

The complete object-oriented analysis of the MSG Case Study is presented in Section 9.6.

MSG CASE STUDY:
SOFTWARE PROJECT MANAGEMENT PLAN

The document presented here is a SPMP for development of the MSG product by a small software organization consisting of three individuals, namely Andy, the owner of the company, and two software engineers, Bob and Cathy.

1. Introduction

1.1. Project Overview   The objective of this project is to develop a software product that will assist the Martha Stockton Greengage Foundation (MSG) in making decisions regarding home mortgages for married couples. The product will allow the client to add, modify, and delete information regarding the Foundation's investments, operating expenses, and individual mortgage information. The product will perform the required calculations in these areas and produce reports listing investments, mortgages, and weekly operating expenses.

    The time, budget, and personnel requirements are as follows:

Requirements phase (1 week, two team members, $2400)

Specifications (analysis) phase (1 week, two team members, $2400)

Planning phase (1 week, two team members, $2400)

Design phase (2 weeks, two team members, $4800)

Implementation phase (3 weeks, three team members, $10,800)

Integration phase (2 weeks, three team members, $7200)

[*The implementation and integration phases will be combined, as described in Chapter 13.*]

The total development time is 10 weeks and the total internal cost is $30,000.

1.2 Project Deliverables   The complete source code with user and operations manuals will be delivered 10 weeks after the project commences. The client will be responsible for acquiring the recommended hardware and system software by the time the product is delivered.

1.3. Evolution of the SPMP   All changes in the SPMP must be agreed to by Andy before they are implemented. All changes should be documented in order to keep the SPMP correct and up-to-date.

1.4. Reference materials   Our company coding, documentation, and testing standards.

1.5. Definitions and Acronyms
MSG—Martha Stockton Greengage Foundation; the Foundation is our client
SPMP—software project management plan

2. Project Organization

2.1. Process Model   The software process model to be used is the waterfall model with rapid prototyping. The specifications were written by Bob and Cathy and verified by the client at meetings between Andy and the client. The design task will be shared between Bob and Cathy, and Andy will check the overall design. Coding will also be performed by Bob and Cathy. Bob and Cathy will test each other's code and Andy will conduct integration testing. Extensive testing will then be done by all three. The time required for all these activities is outlined in the Introduction.

2.2. Organizational Structure   The development team consists of Andy (owner), and Bob and Cathy (software engineers).

2.3. Organizational Boundaries and Interfaces   All the work on this project will be performed by Andy, Bob, and Cathy. Andy will meet weekly with the client to report progress and discuss possible changes and modifications. Any major changes which will affect the milestones or the budget will have to be approved by Andy, and documented. There will be no outside SQA personnel involved. The benefits of having someone other than the individual who carried out the development task to do the testing will be accomplished by having each person's work products tested by someone else.

2.4. Project Responsibilities   Each member is responsible for the quality of the module he or she codes. Andy will handle the mortgage modules, Bob will write the investment modules, and Cathy will work on the operating expenses modules. Andy will oversee module integration and overall quality of the product and will liaise with the client.

3. Managerial Process

3.1. Managerial Objectives and Priorities   The overall objective is to deliver a fault-free product on time and within the budget. If this cannot be achieved, a fault-free product will be delivered as soon as possible after the due date.

The three team members will work separately on their assigned modules. Andy's assigned role will be to monitor the daily progress of the other two, oversee integration, be responsible for overall quality, and interact with the client. Team members will meet at the end of each day and discuss problems and progress. Formal meetings with the client will be held at the end of each week to report progress and determine if any changes need to be made. Andy will ensure that schedule and budget requirements are met. Risk management will also be Andy's responsibility.

Minimizing faults and maximizing user friendliness will be Andy's priorities. Andy is also responsible for all documentation and has to ensure that it is up-to-date.

3.2. Assumptions, Dependencies, and Constraints   Contraints are listed in the specification document. They include the following:

The deadline must be met.

The budget constraints must be met.

The product must be reliable.

The product must meet the acceptance criteria.

The architecture must be open so that additional modules may be added later.

The product must conform to the client's hardware.

The product must be user friendly.

3.3. Risk Management   The risk factors and the tracking mechanisms are as follows:

There is no existing software with which the new product can be compared. Accordingly, it will not be possible to run the product in parallel with an existing one. Therefore, the product should be subjected to extensive testing.

The client is assumed to be inexperienced with computers. Special attention was therefore paid to the specification phase and communication with the client. The product has to be made as user friendly as possible.

There is always the possibility of a major design fault, so extensive testing will be done during the design phase. Also, each of the team members will initially test his or her own code and then test the code of another member. Andy will be responsible for integration testing.

The product must meet the specified storage requirements and response times. This should not be a major problem because of the small size of the product, but it will be monitored by Andy throughout development.

There is a slim chance of hardware failure in which case another machine will be leased. If there is a fault in the compiler, it will be replaced. These are covered in the warranties received from the hardware and compiler suppliers.

3.4. Monitoring and Controlling Mechanisms   Andy will be responsible for all review and auditing. This will be accomplished through daily meetings with the team members. At each meeting, Bob and Cathy will present the day's progress and problems. Andy will determine if they are progressing as expected and if they are following the specifications and the SPMP. Any major problems faced by the team members will immediately be reported to Andy.

3.5. Staffing Plan   Andy is needed for the entire 10 weeks, for the first 5 weeks only in a managerial capacity and the second 5 weeks as both manager and programmer. Bob and Cathy are needed for the entire 10 weeks.

4. Technical Process

4.1. Methods, Tools, and Techniques   The waterfall model with rapid prototyping has been used to date, and will continue to be used. The rapid prototype was written in Java. The specifications were drawn up using object-oriented analysis (Chapter 9). Object-oriented design (Section 11.8) will be used. Source code will be written in Java and run under UNIX on a personal computer. Documentation and coding will be done in accordance with company standards.

4.2. Software Documentation   Software documentation will follow company standards. Reviews of documentation will be conducted by Andy at the completion of each phase of the process model. This will ensure that all the documentation for a particular phase is complete by the time the next phase is started.

4.3. Project Support Functions   Quality assurance will be performed as described in section 2.1 of this document.

5. Work Packages, Schedule, and Budget

5.1. Work Packages   Modules (or more precisely, methods) to add, modify, and delete mortgages and investments are needed. Other routines are needed to compute weekly expenses and determine how much money is available for the purchase of new homes. In addition, reports listing mortgages, investments, and current expenses are to be produced. Each of these modules will be created independently. The team members will be in constant communication; this should ensure that the modules are compatible.

5.2. Dependencies   As specified in the process model. Specifically, no phase will be started until the work products of the previous phase have been approved by Andy.

5.3. Resource Requirements   Three personal computers running under UNIX, together with standard UNIX tools.

5.4. Budget and Resource Allocation   The budget for each phase is as follows:

Requirements phase:	$2400
Object-oriented analysis phase:	$2400
Planning phase:	$2400
Object-oriented design phase:	$4800
Implementation phase:	$10,800
Integration phase:	$7200
Total:	$30,000

5.5. Schedule

Week 1:	Met with client, determined requirements. Produced rapid prototype. Client and users approved rapid prototype.
Week 2:	Wrote object-oriented analysis document. Inspected object-oriented analysis document, client approved document.
Week 3:	Produced SPMP, inspected SPMP.
Week 4, 5:	Object-oriented design document, object-oriented design inspection, detailed design document, detailed design inspection.
Week 6, 7, 8:	Implementation and inspection of each module, module testing and documentation.
Week 9, 10:	Integration of each module, inspection of individual modules, product testing, documentation check.

Additional Components

Security: A password will be needed to use the product.

Training: Training will be done by Andy at time of delivery. Because the product is straightforward to use, one day is sufficient for training. Andy will answer questions at no cost for the first year of use.

Product Maintenance: Corrective maintenance will be done by the team at no cost for a period of 12 months. A separate contract will be drawn up regarding enhancement.

MSG Case Study: Design

The architectural (object-oriented) design appears in Section 11.16, together with a small sample of the detailed design.

The complete detailed design is given below. To assist the reader, the methods of the MSG product are listed alphabetically by class name, and by method name within class name. There are 51 methods in all; a table containing the 14 data access methods appears at the end, after the tables containing the detailed designs of the other 37 methods.

Class name	*FinancialInstrument*
Method name	*deleteRecord*
Modifiers, type	**public void**
Arguments	none
Error messages	If record to be deleted does not exist
Files accessed	none
Files changed	none
Methods called	*findRecord, performDeletion*
Narrative	Prompts user to enter ID of record to be deleted. Calls *findRecord* to find the specified record, then calls *performDeletion* to delete record. Finally, reports that record has been deleted.

Class name	*FinancialInstrument*
Method name	*inputNewRecord*
Modifiers, type	**public void**
Arguments	none
Error messages	none
Files accessed	none
Files changed	none
Methods called	*obtainNewData, putRecord, displayRecord*
Narrative	Calls *obtainNewData* to obtain data for new record to be added, *putRecord* to insert record in appropriate file, and *displayRecord* to display record to user.

Class name	*Investment*
Method name	*changeInvestmentField*
Modifiers, type	**public void**
Arguments	**char**
Error messages	none
Files accessed	none
Files changed	none
Methods called	none
Narrative	Gets new input for field in investment record to be changed. Input is character corresponding to field to be changed.

Class name	*Investment*
Method name	*displayRecord*
Modifiers, type	**public void**
Arguments	none
Error messages	none
Files accessed	none
Files changed	none
Methods called	none
Narrative	Displays the names of the fields of an investment and their values.

Class name	*Investment*
Method name	*findRecord*
Modifiers, type	**public boolean**
Arguments	String
Error messages	none
Files accessed	investment.dat
Files changed	none
Methods called	*readRecord*
Narrative	Attempts to locate a specific investment record. Returns **true** if investment exists, otherwise **false**.

Class name	*Investment*
Method name	*obtainNewData*
Modifiers, type	**public void**
Arguments	none
Error messages	none
Files accessed	none
Files changed	none
Methods called	*readInvestmentData*
Narrative	Reads an investment record by calling method *readInvestmentData.*

Class name	*Investment*
Method name	*performDeletion*
Modifiers, type	**public void**
Arguments	none
Error messages	none
Files accessed	investment.dat, investment.tmp
Files changed	investment.tmp
Methods called	*readRecord, writeRecord*
Narrative	Performs actual deletion of an investment record by copying entire investment.dat file, with the exception of record to be deleted, into investment.tmp. It then deletes investment.dat and changes name of investment.tmp to investment.dat. Reading and writing of records is accomplished by calling *readRecord* and *writeRecord,* respectively.

Class name	*Investment*
Method name	*produceInvestmentReport*
Modifiers, type	**public void**
Arguments	none
Error messages	If no investments exist
Files accessed	investment.dat
Files changed	investment.dat
Methods called	*readRecord, displayRecord*
Narrative	Reads records from investment.dat by calling *readRecord* and then displays them by calling *displayRecord.*

Class name	*Investment*
Method name	*putRecord*
Modifiers, type	**public void**
Arguments	none
Error messages	none
Files accessed	investment.dat, investment.tmp
Files changed	investment.tmp
Methods called	*readRecord, writeRecord*
Narrative	Writes a new investment record to investment.tmp, ordered by investmentID.

Class name	*Investment*
Method name	*readInvestmentData*
Modifiers, type	**public void**
Arguments	none
Error messages	If investment ID is not valid
Files accessed	none
Files changed	none
Methods called	none
Narrative	Obtains input data for all fields of an investment.

Class name	*Investment*
Method name	*readRecord*
Modifiers, type	**public void**
Arguments	RandomAccessFile
Error messages	none
Files accessed	RandomAccessFile (input variable)
Files changed	none
Methods called	none
Narrative	Reads an investment from RandomAccessFile.

Class name	*Investment*
Method name	*totalWeeklyReturnOnInvestment*
Modifiers, type	**public float**
Arguments	none
Error messages	none
Files accessed	investment.dat
Files changed	none
Methods called	*readRecord*
Narrative	Reads through investment.dat by calling *readRecord*. Computes total weekly return on investments by summing annual returns on investments and dividing by 52.

Class name	*Investment*
Method name	*updateRecord*
Modifiers, type	**public void**
Arguments	none
Error messages	If investment entered does not exist. If invalid choice is entered.
Files accessed	none
Files changed	none
Methods called	*findRecord, changeInvestmentField, displayRecord*
Narrative	Solicits from user the investment record to be modified and field to be changed. Then, it locates that record using *findRecord*. Finally, calls *changeInvestment Field* to implement desired change and *displayRecord* to display changed record. Loops until all desired field changes have been made to the record.

Class name	*Investment*
Method name	*writeRecord*
Modifiers, type	**public void**
Arguments	RandomAccessFile
Error messages	none
Files accessed	none
Files changed	RandomAccessFile (input variable)
Methods called	none
Narrative	Writes an investment to specified file.

Class name	*Mortgage*
Method name	*changeMortgageField*
Modifiers, type	**public void**
Arguments	**char**
Error messages	none
Files accessed	none
Files changed	none
Methods called	none
Narrative	Gets new input for field in mortgage record to be changed. Input is character corresponding to field to be changed.

Class name	*Mortgage*
Method name	*displayRecord*
Modifiers, type	**public void**
Arguments	none
Error messages	none
Files accessed	none
Files changed	none
Methods called	none
Narrative	Displays the names of the fields of a mortgage and their values.

Class name	*Mortgage*
Method name	*findRecord*
Modifiers, type	**public boolean**
Arguments	String
Error messages	none
Files accessed	mortgage.dat
Files changed	none
Methods called	*readRecord*
Narrative	Attempts to locate a specific mortgage record. Returns true if the mortgage exists, otherwise false.

Class name	*Mortgage*
Method name	*obtainNewData*
Modifiers, type	**public void**
Arguments	none
Error messages	none
Files accessed	none
Files changed	none
Methods called	*readMortgageData*
Narrative	Gets the data for a new mortgage by calling method *readMortgageData*.

Class name	*Mortgage*
Method name	*performDeletion*
Modifiers, type	**public void**
Arguments	none
Error messages	none
Files accessed	mortgage.dat, mortgage.tmp
Files changed	mortgage.tmp
Methods called	*readRecord, writeRecord*
Narrative	Performs actual deletion of a mortgage record by copying entire mortgage.dat file, with the exception of record to be deleted, into mortgage.tmp. It then deletes mortgage.dat and changes name of mortgage.tmp to mortgage.dat. Reading and writing of records is accomplished by calling *readRecord* and *writeRecord*, respectively.

Class name	*Mortgage*
Method name	*produceMortgageReport*
Modifiers, type	**public void**
Arguments	none
Error messages	If no mortgages exist
Files accessed	mortgage.dat
Files changed	none
Methods called	*readRecord, displayRecord*
Narrative	Reads records from mortgage.dat by calling *readRecord* and then displays them by calling *displayRecord*.

Class name	*Mortgage*
Method name	*putRecord*
Modifiers, type	**public void**
Arguments	none
Error messages	none
Files accessed	mortgage.dat, mortgage.tmp
Files changed	mortgage.tmp
Methods called	*readRecord, writeRecord*
Narrative	Writes a new mortgage record to a file order by investmentID.

Class name	*Mortgage*
Method name	*readMortgageData*
Modifiers, type	**public void**
Arguments	none
Error messages	If mortgage number is invalid.
Files accessed	none
Files changed	none
Methods called	none
Narrative	Obtains input data for all fields of a mortgage.

Class name	*Mortgage*
Method name	*readRecord*
Modifiers, type	**public void**
Arguments	RandomAccessFile
Error messages	none
Files accessed	RandomAccessFile (input variable)
Files changed	none
Methods called	none
Narrative	Reads a mortgage from RandomAccessFile.

Class name	*Mortgage*
Method name	*totalWeeklyNetPayments*
Modifiers, type	**public float**
Arguments	none
Error messages	none
Files accessed	mortgage.dat
Files changed	none
Methods called	*readRecord*
Narrative	Reads through mortgage.dat by calling *readRecord*. Computes total weekly net payments by summing total weekly mortgages and subtracting total weekly grants.

Class name	*Mortgage*
Method name	*updateRecord*
Modifiers, type	**public void**
Arguments	none
Error messages	If mortgage does not exist. If invalid choice is entered.
Files accessed	none
Files changed	none
Methods called	*findRecord, changeMortgageField, displayRecord*
Narrative	Solicits from user the mortgage record to be modified and field to be changed. Then, it locates that record using *findRecord*. Finally, calls *changeMortgageField* to implement desired change and *displayRecord* to display changed record. Loops until all desired field changes have been made to the record.

Class name	*Mortgage*
Method name	*writeRecord*
Modifiers, type	**public void**
Arguments	RandomAccessFile
Error messages	none
Files accessed	none
Files changed	RandomAccessFile (input variable)
Methods called	none
Narrative	Writes a mortgage to specified file.

Class name	*MSGApplication*
Method name	*InitializeApplication*
Modifiers, type	**private static void**
Arguments	none
Error messages	none
Files accessed	opexp.dat
Files changed	none
Methods called	*MSGApplication.setAnnualOperatingExpenses*
Narrative	Initializes annual operating expenses from file opexp.dat, if it exists. If file does not exist, annual operating expenses are set to 0.0 by calling *MSGApplication.setAnnualOperatingExpenses.*

Class name	*MSGApplication*
Method name	*main*
Modifiers, type	**public static void**
Arguments	String
Error messages	none
Files accessed	none
Files changed	none
Methods called	*MSGApplication.InitializeApplication,* *MSGUtilities.displayMainMenu*
Narrative	Drives entire product. First performs initialization by calling *MSG Application.InitializeApplication*, then calls *MSGUtilities.displayMainMenu* to solicit user's choice.

Class name	*MSGApplication*
Method name	*setAnnualOperatingExpenses*
Modifiers, type	**public static void**
Arguments	**float**
Error messages	none
Files accessed	opexp.dat
Files changed	opexp.dat
Methods called	none
Narrative	Validates new annual operating expenses, writes data to opexp.dat for use in the current execution.

Class name	*MSGUtilities*
Method name	*clearScreen*
Modifiers, type	**public static void**
Arguments	none
Error messages	none
Files accessed	none
Files changed	none
Methods called	none
Narrative	Clears the user's screen.

Class name	*MSGUtilities*
Method name	*displayInvestmentMenu*
Modifiers, type	**public static void**
Arguments	none
Error messages	If invalid choice is entered.
Files accessed	none
Files changed	none
Methods called	*Investment.inputNewRecord, Investment.updateRecord, Investment.deleteRecord*
Narrative	Displays investment menu, offering user choice of adding, modifying, or deleting an investment; calls appropriate method. User may also choose to return to main menu.

Class name	*MSGUtilities*
Method name	*displayMainMenu*
Modifiers, type	**public static void**
Arguments	none
Error messages	If an invalid choice is entered.
Files accessed	none
Files changed	none
Methods called	*MSGUtilities.displayInvestmentMenu,* *MSGUtilities.displayMortgageMenu,* *MSGUtilities.displayReportMenu,* *updateAnnualOperatingExpenses*
Narrative	Displays main menu that drives product, offering user choice of investment data, mortgage data, operating expenses, or report; calls appropriate method. User may also choose to quit.

Class name	*MSGUtilities*
Method name	*displayMortgageMenu*
Modifiers, type	**public static void**
Arguments	none
Error messages	If invalid choice is entered.
Files accessed	none
Files changed	none
Methods called	*Mortgage.inputNewRecord,* *Mortgage.updateRecord,* *Mortgage.deleteRecord*
Narrative	Displays mortgage menu, offering user choice of adding, modifying, or deleting a mortgage; calls appropriate method. User may also choose to return to main menu.

Class name	*MSGUtilities*
Method name	*displayReportMenu*
Modifiers, type	**public static void**
Arguments	none
Error messages	If an invalid choice is entered.
Files accessed	none
Files changed	none
Methods called	*Investment.produceInvestmentReport, Mortgage.produceMortgageReport, MSGUtilities.fundsAvailable*
Narrative	Displays report menu, offering user choice of investment report, mortgage report, or funds availability report; calls appropriate method. User may also choose to return to main menu.

Class name	*MSGUtilities*
Method name	*fundsAvailable*
Modifiers, type	**public static void**
Arguments	none
Error messages	none
Files accessed	none
Files changed	none
Methods called	*Investment.totalWeeklyReturnOnInvestment, Mortgage.totalWeeklyNetPayments*
Narrative	Computes total funds available. Annual operating expenses are divided by 52 to yield total weekly operating expenses. Expected weekly return on investments is obtained by calling method *Investment.totalWeeklyReturnOnInvestment.* Expected total net weekly payments (mortgages less grants) is obtained by calling *Mortgage.totalWeeklyNetPayments.* Amount available is then expected weekly return on investments less expected weekly operating expenses plus total weekly net payments. This quantity is then printed out.

Class name	*MSGUtilities*
Method name	*parseDate*
Modifiers, type	**public static** Date
Arguments	String
Error messages	none
Files accessed	none
Files changed	none
Methods called	none
Narrative	Parses string in format mm/dd/yy and returns a Date corresponding to that string.

Class name	*MSGUtilities*
Method name	*updateAnnualOperatingExpenses*
Modifiers, type	**void**
Arguments	none
Error messages	none
Files accessed	none
Files changed	none
Methods called	*MSGApplication.setAnnualOperatingExpenses*
Narrative	Solicits new annual operating expenses from user, then sets that value by calling *MSGApplication.setAnnualOperatingExpenses*.

Data Access Methods

Following the usual object-oriented convention, the name of each of the 14 data access methods (that is, methods that return the value of an instance variable) has the form getXyz, where Xyz is the name of the instance variable returned by that access method. The type of the data member is the type of the value returned by the corresponding data access method. This is reflected in the table below:

Class	Data Access Methods
MSGApplication	**public static float** *getAnnualOperatingExpenses*
Investment	**public** String *getInvestmentID* **public** String *getInvestmentName* **public float** *getExpectedAnnualReturn* **public** Date *getExpectedAnnualReturnUpdated*
Mortgage	**public** String *getMortgageID* **public** String *getMortgageName* **public float** *getPrice* **public** Date *getDateMortgageIssued* **public float** *getCurrentWeeklyIncome* **public** Date *getWeeklyIncomeUpdated* **public float** *getAnnualPropertyTax* **public float** *getAnnualInsurancePremium* **public float** *getMortgageBalance*

MSG CASE STUDY: BLACK-BOX TEST CASES

Using equivalence classes and boundary value analysis as well as functional analysis, the following black box test cases have been created for the MSG product.

Equivalence classes and boundary value analysis:

Investment information:

Equivalence classes for item number.

1. Character instead of digit	Error (not a number)
2. < 12 digits	Acceptable
3. 12 digits	Acceptable
4. > 12 digits	Error (too many digits)

Equivalence classes for item name.

1. First character not alphabetic	Error
2. < 1 character	Error
3. ≥ 1 character	Acceptable

Equivalence classes for estimated annual return and expected annual operating expenses.

1. < $0.00	Error
2. $0.00	Acceptable
3. $0.01	Acceptable
4. Between $0.01 and $999,999,999.97	Acceptable
5. $999,999,999.98	Acceptable
6. $999,999,999.99	Acceptable
7. $1,000,000,000.00	Error
8. > $1,000,000,000.00	Error
9. Character instead of digit	Error (not a number)

Mortgage information:

Equivalence classes for **account number** are same as for **item number** above.

Equivalence classes for last name of mortgagees (husband/wife have same last name).

1.	First character not alphabetic	Error
2.	< 1 character	Error
3.	≥ 1 character	Acceptable

Equivalence classes for last names of husband (husband/wife have different last names—we refer to names of husband and wife as **hn** and **wn**, respectively).

1.	First character **hn** not alphabetic, **wn** any	Error
2.	First character **wn** not alphabetic, **hn** any	Error
3.	< 1 character in **hn**, **wn** any	Error
4.	< 1 character in **wn**, **hn** any	Error
5.	1 character in **hn**, **wn** any	Acceptable
6.	≥ 1 character in **wn**, **hn** any	Acceptable

Equivalence classes for original price of home, current family income, and mortgage balance.

1.	< $0.00	Error
2.	$0.00	Acceptable
3.	$0.01	Acceptable
4.	Between $0.01 and $999,999.98	Acceptable
5.	$999,999.98	Acceptable
6.	$999,999.99	Acceptable
7.	$1,000,000.00	Error
8.	> $1,000,000.00	Error
9.	Character instead of digit	Error (not a number)

Equivalence classes for annual property tax and annual home-owner's premium.

1.	< $0.00	Error
2.	$0.00	Acceptable
3.	$0.01	Acceptable

4. Between $0.01 and $99,999.98	Acceptable
5. $99,999.98	Acceptable
6. $99,999.99	Acceptable
7. $100,000.00	Error
8. > $100,000.00	Error
9. Character instead of digit	Error (not a number)

Functional Testing:

The functions outlined in the specifications document are used to create test cases.

1. Add a mortgage
2. Add an investment
3. Modify a mortgage
4. Modify an investment
5. Delete a mortgage
6. Delete an investment
7. Update operating expenses
8. Compute funds to purchase houses
9. Print list of mortgages
10. Print list of investments

In addition to these direct tests, it is necessary to perform these additional tests.

11. Attempt to add a mortgage that is already on file
12. Attempt to add an investment that is already on file
13. Attempt to delete a mortgage that is not on file
14. Attempt to delete an investment that is not on file
15. Attempt to modify a mortgage that is not on file
16. Attempt to modify an investment that is not on file
17. Attempt to delete twice a mortgage that is already on file
18. Attempt to delete twice an investment that is already on file
19. Attempt to update each field of a mortgage twice and check that the second version is stored
20. Attempt to update each field of an investment twice and check that the second version is stored
21. Attempt to update operating expenses twice and check that the second version is stored

MSG CASE STUDY: SOURCE CODE

In the solution presented below, no use is made of any nonstandard screen capabilities, with the exception of method **clearscreen** in class **MSGUtilities**, the implementation of which is system-dependent.

To aid the reader, an alphabetical list of the 51 methods in the implementation of the MSG product appears in Figure I.1.

class MSGApplication

class MSGUtilities

Figure I.1   Alphabetical list of methods in implementation of MSG product.

```
import java.io.*;
import java.util.*;

/*********************************************************************************
 *
 *                                    Class MSGApplication
 *
 *********************************************************************************/

class MSGApplication
{
    //
    // Class variables—constants and parameters
    //
    static final float  WEEKS_IN_YEAR                       = (float) 52.0;
    static final float  INTEREST_RATE                       = (float) 0.04;
    static final float  MAXIMUM_PERC_OF_INCOME              = (float) 0.28;
    static final int    NUMBER_OF_MORTGAGE_PAYMENTS         = 1560;


    //
    // Class variable—other
    //
    private static float        annualOperatingExpenses;        // annual operating expenses


    //
    // Data access method
    //
    public static float getAnnualOperatingExpenses ()
    {
        return annualOperatingExpenses;
    }


    //
    // Class methods
    //
    public static void setAnnualOperatingExpenses (float newAnnualOperatingExpenses)
    //
    // Validates new annual operating expenses, writes data to opexp.dat
    // for use in the current execution.
    //
    {
        try
        {
            if (newAnnualOperatingExpenses >= 0.0)
            {
                File            operatingExpensesFile = new File ("opexp.dat");
                                            // file containing annual operating expenses
                FileOutputStream newFileOutput = new FileOutputStream (operatingExpensesFile);
                                            // output stream for newPrintStream
                PrintStream     newFilePrint = new PrintStream (newFileOutput);
                                            // to output newAnnualOperatingExpenses

                newFilePrint.println (newAnnualOperatingExpenses);
                newFilePrint.close ();
                newFileOutput.close ();

                annualOperatingExpenses = newAnnualOperatingExpenses;
            }
```

```
        }
        catch (Exception e)
        {
            System.out.println ("***** Error: MSGApplication.setAnnualOperatingExpenses () "
                    + "*****");
            System.out.println ("\t" + e);
        }
    } // setAnnualOperatingExpenses ()
```

//--

```
    private static void initializeApplication ()
    //
    // initializeApplication initializes annual operating expenses from file opexp.dat, if it exists.
    // If file does not exist, annual operating expenses are set to 0.0 by calling
    // setAnnualOperatingExpenses
    //
    {
        try
        {
            File                operatingExpensesFile = new File ("opexp.dat");
                                                // file containing annual operating expenses

            if (!operatingExpensesFile.exists ())
            {
                setAnnualOperatingExpenses ( (float) 0.0);
            }
            else
            {
                RandomAccessFile    inFile = new RandomAccessFile (operatingExpensesFile, "r");
                char                c;              // character entered by user
                StringBuffer        input = new StringBuffer ();
                                                // buffer for line of characters

                while ((c = (char) inFile.read ()) != '\n')
                {
                    input.append (c);
                }
                Float tempFloat = new Float (input.toString ());
                annualOperatingExpenses = tempFloat.floatValue ();

                inFile.close ();
            }
        }
        catch (Exception e)
        {
            System.out.println ("***** Error: MSGApplication.initializeApplication () *****");
            System.out.println ("\t" + e);
        }
    } // initializeApplication ()
```

//--

```
    public static void main (String args[])
    //
    // main method of MSG product
    //First performs initialization by calling initializeApplication,
    // then calls displayMainMenu to solicit user's choice.
```

```
    //
    {
        initializeApplication ();
        MSGUtilities.displayMainMenu ();
    } // main ()

} // class MSGApplication

/***********************************************************************************
 *
 *                                    Class MSGUtilities
 *
 ***********************************************************************************/

class MSGUtilities
{
    //
    // Class methods
    //
    public static void updateAnnualOperatingExpenses ()
    //
    // updateAnnualOperatingExpenses obtains the new annual operating expenses from user, validates,
    // and then writes the data to the operating expenses file.
    //
    {
    try
        {
            char            c;                          // character entered by user
            StringBuffer    input;                      // buffer for line of characters
            float           newAnnualOperatingExpenses;
                                                        // for storing user's response

        MSGUtilities.clearScreen ();

        System.out.println ("\nEnter new annual operating expenses:");
        input = new StringBuffer ();
        while ((c = (char) System.in.read ()) != '\n')
        {
            input.append (c);
        }
        Float tempFloat = new Float (input.toString ());
        newAnnualOperatingExpenses = tempFloat.floatValue ();

        MSGApplication.setAnnualOperatingExpenses (newAnnualOperatingExpenses);
        }
    catch (Exception e)
        {
        System.out.println ("***** Error: MSGUtil.updateAnnualOperatingExpenses () *****");
        System.out.println ("\t" + e);
        }
    } // updateAnnualOperatingExpenses ()


//----------------------------------------------------------------------------------------

    public static void fundsAvailable ()
    //
    // fundsAvailable computes total funds available for purchasing new mortgages in
    // the current week.
```

```
//
{
    try
    {
        float               expectedWeeklyInvestmentReturn = (float) 0.0;
                                        // expected weekly investment return
        float               expectedTotalWeeklyNetPayments = (float) 0.0;
                                        // expected total mortgage payments less total weekly grants

        Investment          inv = new Investment ();       // investment record
        Mortgage            mort = new Mortgage ();         // mortgage record

        expectedWeeklyInvestmentReturn = inv.totalWeeklyReturnOnInvestment ();
        expectedTotalWeeklyNetPayments = mort.totalWeeklyNetPayments ();

        System.out.println ("Funds available: " + (expectedWeeklyInvestmentReturn -
                (MSGApplication.getAnnualOperatingExpenses () /
                MSGApplication.WEEKS_IN_YEAR) +
                expectedTotalWeeklyNetPayments));

        System.out.println ("\n\n\n Press ENTER to continue ...");
        int                 c;
        c = System.in.read ();
    }
    catch (Exception e)
    {
        System.out.println ("***** Error: MSGUtilities.fundsAvailable () *****");
        System.out.println ("\t" + e);
    }
} // fundsAvailable ()
```

//---

```
public static void clearScreen ()
//
// clearScreen clears the screen
//
{
    int                     i;      // loop counter representing the number of blank lines to be printed

    //
    // Implementation-dependent code to clear the screen should replace the code
    // given below.
    //
    for (i = 0; i < 26; i++)
    {
        System.out.println ();
    }
} // clearScreen ()
```

//---

```
public static void displayMainMenu ()
//
// displayMainMenu displays main menu that drives product, offering the user choice
// of investment data, mortgage data, operating expenses, or reports; the appropriate
// method is then called, namely displayInvestmentMenu, displayMortgageMenu,
// updateAnnualOperatingExpenses, or displayReportMenu, respectively.
```

```java
// The user may also choose to quit
//
{
    boolean             done;                               // terminates while loop
    byte                choice[] = new byte[10];            // user's choice

    done = false;

    while (!done)
    {
        MSGUtilities.clearScreen ();

        System.out.println ("\t           MAIN MENU\n\n");
        System.out.println ("\t MARTHA STOCKTON GREENGAGE FOUNDATION\n\n")
        System.out.println ("\t        1. Investment Data\n");
        System.out.println ("\t        2. Mortgage Data\n");
        System.out.println ("\t        3. Operating Expenses\n");
        System.out.println ("\t        4. Produce Reports\n");
        System.out.println ("\t        5. Quit\n\n");
        System.out.println ("Enter your choice and press <ENTER>: ");

        try
        {
            System.in.read (choice);

            switch ( (char) choice[0])
            {
                case '1':
                    MSGUtilities.displayInvestmentMenu ();
                    break;

                case '2':
                    MSGUtilities.displayMortgageMenu ();
                    break;

                case '3':
                    MSGUtilities.updateAnnualOperatingExpenses ();
                    break;

                case '4':
                    MSGUtilities.displayReportMenu ();
                    break;

                case '5':
                case '\n':
                    done = true;
                    break;

                default:
                    System.out.println ("\n\nNot a valid choice\n");
                    System.out.println ("Press <ENTER> to return to menu...");
                    System.in.read (choice);
                    break;
            }
        }
        catch (Exception e)
        {
            System.out.println ("***** Error: MSGUtilities.displayMainMenu () *****");
```

```
                    System.out.println ("\t" + e);
             }
          }
    } // displayMainMenu ()

//------------------------------------------------------------------------------------------------------------------------

    public static void displayInvestmentMenu ()
    //
    // displayInvestmentMenu displays investment, offering the user the
    // choice of adding, modifying, or deleting an investment; the appropriate
    // method is then called, namely inputNewRecord, updateRecord, or
    // deleteRecord, respectively. The user may also choose to return to main menu.
    //
    {
        boolean        done;                            // terminates while loop
        byte           choice[] = new byte[10];         // user's choice
        Investment     inv = new Investment ();         // investment record

        done = false;

        while (!done)
        {
            MSGUtilities.clearScreen ();

            System.out.println ("\t             INVESTMENTS\n\n");
            System.out.println ("\t MARTHA STOCKTON GREENGAGE FOUNDATION\n\n");
            System.out.println ("\t        1. Add an investment\n");
            System.out.println ("\t        2. Modify an investment\n");
            System.out.println ("\t        3. Delete an investment\n");
            System.out.println ("\t        4. Exit to main menu\n\n");
            System.out.println ("Enter your choice and press <ENTER>: ");

            try
            {
                System.in.read (choice);

                switch ( (char) choice[0])
                {
                    case '1':
                        MSGUtilities.clearScreen ();
                        inv.inputNewRecord ();
                        break;

                    case '2':
                        MSGUtilities.clearScreen ();
                        inv.updateRecord ();
                        break;

                    case '3':
                        MSGUtilities.clearScreen ();
                        inv.deleteRecord ();
                        break;

                    case '4':
                    case '\n':
                        done = true;
                        break;
```

```
                        default:
                            System.out.println ("\n\nNot a valid choice\n");
                            System.out.println ("Press <ENTER> to return to menu...");
                            System.in.read (choice);
                            break;
                    }
                }
                catch (Exception e)
                {
                    System.out.println ("***** Error: MSGUtilities.displayInvestmentMenu () *****");
                    System.out.println ("\t" + e);
                }
            }
        } // displayInvestmentMenu ()


//--------------------------------------------------------------------------------------------------------------------------------


        public static void displayMortgageMenu ()
        //
        // displayMortgageMenu displays mortgage menu, offering the user the
        // choice of adding, modifying, or deleting a mortgage; the appropriate
        // method is then called, namely inputNewRecord, updateRecord, or
        // deleteRecord, respectively  The user may also choose to return to main menu.
        //
        {
            boolean           done;                          // terminates while-loop
            byte              choice[] = new byte[10];        // user's choice
            Mortgage          mort = new Mortgage ();         // mortgage record

            done = false;

            while (!done)
            {
                MSGUtilities.clearScreen ();

                System.out.println ("\t            MORTGAGES\n\n");
                System.out.println ("\t MARTHA STOCKTON GREENGAGE FOUNDATION\n\n");
                System.out.println ("\t      1. Add a mortgage\n");
                System.out.println ("\t      2. Modify a mortgage\n");
                System.out.println ("\t      3. Delete a mortgage\n");
                System.out.println ("\t      4. Exit to main menu\n");
                System.out.println ("Enter your choice and press <ENTER>: ") ;

                try
                {
                    System.in.read (choice);

                    switch ( (char) choice[0])
                    {
                        case '1':
                            MSGUtilities.clearScreen ();
                            mort.inputNewRecord ();
                            break;

                        case '2':
                            MSGUtilities.clearScreen ();
                            mort.updateRecord ();
```

```java
                        break;

            case '3':
                MSGUtilities.clearScreen ();
                mort.deleteRecord ();
                break;

            case '4':
            case '\n':
                done = true;
                break;

            default:
                System.out.println ("\n\nNot a valid choice\n");
                System.out.println ("Press <ENTER> to return to menu...");
                System.in.read (choice);
                break;
            }
        }
        catch (Exception e)
        {
            System.out.println ("***** Error: MSGUtilities.displayMortgageMenu () *****");
            System.out.println ("\t" + e);
        }
    }
} // displayMortgageMenu ()
```

//--

```java
    public static void displayReportMenu ()
    //
    // displayReportMenu displays report menu, offering the user the choice of
    // investment report, mortgage report, or funds availability report;
    // the appropriate method is then called, namely produceInvestmentReport,
    // produceMortgageReport, or fundsAvailable, respectively.
    // The user may also choose to return to main menu.
    //
    {
        boolean     done;                       // terminates while loop
        byte        choice[] = new byte[10];    // user's choice
        Investment  inv = new Investment ();    // investment record
        Mortgage    mort = new Mortgage ();     // mortgage record

        done = false;

        while (!done)
        {
            MSGUtilities.clearScreen ();

            System.out.println ("\t              REPORTS\n\n");
            System.out.println ("\t  MARTHA STOCKTON GREENGAGE FOUNDATION\n\n");
            System.out.println ("\t      1. List of investments\n");
            System.out.println ("\t      2. List of mortgages\n");
            System.out.println ("\t      3. Funds available\n");
            System.out.println ("\t      4. Exit to main menu\n");
            System.out.println ("Enter your choice and press <ENTER>: ");

            try
```

```
        {
            System.in.read (choice);

            switch ( (char) choice[0])
            {
                case '1':
                    inv.produceInvestmentReport ();
                    break;

                case '2':
                    mort.produceMortgageReport ();
                    break;

                case '3':
                    MSGUtilities.fundsAvailable ();
                    break;

                case '4':
                case '\n':
                    done = true;
                    break;

                default:
                    System.out.println ("\n\nNot a valid choice\n");
                    System.out.println ("Press <ENTER> to return to menu...");
                    System.in.read (choice);
                    break;
            }
        }
        catch (Exception e)
        {
            System.out.println ("***** Error: MSGUtilities.displayReportMenu () *****");
            System.out.println ("\t" + e);
        }
    }
} // displayReportMenu ()

//------------------------------------------------------------------------------------------------------

    public static Date parseDate (String s)
    //
    // parseDate parses a string of the form mm/dd/yy and creates a new Date
    //
    {
        int             theMonth = -1;          // for storing mm
        int             theDay = -1;            // for storing dd
        int             theYear = -1;           // for storing yy
        int             i = 0;                  // position within string s
        int             c = -1;                 // character being tested
        int             prevc = 0;              // previous character
        int             n = -1;                 // for converting characters to integers

syntax:
        {
            if (s == null)
                break syntax;

            int             limit = s.length ();        // number of characters in s
```

```java
        while (i < limit)
        {
            c = s.charAt (i);
            i++;

            if (c == '/')
            {
                prevc = c;
                continue;
            }
            else if ('0' <= c && c <= '9')
            {
                n = c - '0';
                while (i < limit && '0' <= (c = s.charAt (i)) && c <= '9')
                {
                    n = n * 10 + c - '0';
                    i++;
                }
                if (prevc == 0)
                    theMonth = n;
                else if (prevc == '/' && theDay > 0)
                    theYear = n;
                else
                    theDay = n;
            }
            else
                break syntax;
        } // while

        Date              goodDate = new Date (theYear, theMonth - 1, theDay);

        return goodDate;
    }
    throw new IllegalArgumentException ();
} // parseDate ()

} // class MSGUtilities

/**********************************************************************************************
 *
 *                              Class FinancialInstrument
 *
 **********************************************************************************************/

abstract class FinancialInstrument
{
    //
    // Abstract methods
    //
    public abstract void readRecord (RandomAccessFile fileName);
    public abstract void displayRecord ();
    public abstract void obtainNewData ();
    public abstract void performDeletion ();
    public abstract void putRecord ();
    public abstract void updateRecord ();
    public abstract void writeRecord (RandomAccessFile fileName);
    public abstract boolean findRecord (String findRecordID);
```

```
//
// Instance methods
//
public void deleteRecord ()
//
// deleteRecord deletes a FinancialInstrument.
//
{
    try
    {
        char            c;                              // character entered by user
        StringBuffer    input = new StringBuffer ();
                                                        // buffer for line of characters
        boolean         done = false;                   // tells when user is done entering information
        boolean         found = false;                  // tells when an investment has been found
        byte            choice[] = new byte[10];        // for storing user's response
        while (!found && !done)
        {
            System.out.println ("Please enter the number of the " + getClass ().getName () +
                " to be updated (12 digits): ");
            while ((c = (char) System.in.read ()) != '\n')
            {
                input.append (c);
            }
            found = findRecord (input.toString ());

            if (!found)
            {
                System.out.println (getClass ().getName () + " " + input.toString () +
                    " was not found.");
                System.out.println ("Would you like to enter another " + getClass ().getName ()
                    + "?");
                System.in.read (choice);

                if (( (char) choice[0]) == 'n')
                {
                    done = true;
                }
            }
        }
        if (!found)
        {
            return;
        }
        performDeletion ();
        System.out.println ("\nThe record has been deleted.");
        System.out.println ("\n\n\n Press ENTER to continue ...");
        c = (char) System.in.read ();
    }
    catch (Exception e)
    {
        System.out.println ("***** Error: FinancialInstrument.deleteRecord () *****");
        System.out.println ("\t" + e);
    }
} // deleteRecord

//----------------------------------------------------------------------------------------------------------
```

```
        public void inputNewRecord ()
        //
        // inputNewRecord adds a new investment/mortgage record.
        //
        {
            try
            {
                int              c;                          // character entered by user

                obtainNewData ();
                putRecord ();
                System.out.println ("\nThe following record was inserted\n");
                displayRecord ();
                System.out.println ("\n\n\n Press ENTER to continue ...");
                c = System.in.read ();

            }
            catch (Exception e)
            {
                System.out.println ("***** Error: FinancialInstrument.inputNewRecord () *****");
                System.out.println ("\t" + e);
            }
        } // inputNewRecord

} // class FinancialInstrument

/*****************************************************************************
 *
 *                                 Class Investment
 *
 *****************************************************************************/

class Investment extends FinancialInstrument
{
    //
    // Instance variables
    //
    private String          investmentID;                   // investment ID (characters)
    private String          investmentName;                 // investment name
    private float           expectedAnnualReturn;
                                                // expected annual return on investment
    private Date            expectedAnnualReturnUpdated;
                                                // date expected annual return updated

    //
    // Data access methods
    //
    public String getInvestmentID () { return investmentID; }
    public String getInvestmentName () { return investmentName; }
    public float getExpectedAnnualReturn () { return expectedAnnualReturn; }
    public Date getExpectedAnnualReturnUpdated () { return expectedAnnualReturnUpdated; }

    //
    // Instance methods
    //
    public float totalWeeklyReturnOnInvestment ()
    //
```

```
// totalWeeklyReturnOnInvestment reads records from the investments
// file and computes totalAnnualReturn by summing each expectedAnnualReturn
// on investments and dividing by WEEKS_IN_YEAR.
//
{
try
    {
        File                investmentFile = new File ("investment.dat");

        float               totalAnnualReturn = (float) 0.0;
                                                    // total annual return on investments

        if (investmentFile.exists ())
            {
            RandomAccessFile inFile = new RandomAccessFile (investmentFile, "r");

            while (inFile.getFilePointer () != inFile.length ())
                {
                readRecord (inFile);
                totalAnnualReturn += expectedAnnualReturn;
                }
            inFile.close ();
            }
        return (totalAnnualReturn / MSGApplication.WEEKS_IN_YEAR);
    }
catch (Exception e)
    {
    System.out.println ("***** Error: Investment.totalWeeklyReturnOnInvestment () *****");
    System.out.println ("***** Returned a value of 0 *****");
    System.out.println ("\t" + e);

    return (float) 0.0;
    }
} // totalWeeklyReturnOnInvestment
```

//---

```
public boolean findRecord (String findInvestmentID)
//
// findRecord locates a given investment record if it exists.
// Returns true if the investment is located, otherwise false.
//
{
    try
        {
        File                investmentFile = new File ("investment.dat");

        boolean             found = false;              // result of comparison

        if (investmentFile.exists ())
            {
            RandomAccessFile inFile = new RandomAccessFile (investmentFile, "r");

            while (!found && (inFile.getFilePointer () != inFile.length ()))
                {
                readRecord (inFile);

                if (investmentID.compareTo (findInvestmentID) == 0) found = true;
```

```
            }
            inFile.close ();
        }
        return found;
    }
    catch (Exception e)
    {
        System.out.println ("***** Error: Investment.findRecord () *****");
        System.out.println ("\t" + e);

        return false;
    }
} // findRecord
```

//--

```
    public void readRecord (RandomAccessFile fileName)
    //
    // readRecord reads an investment record from fileName.
    // Assumes that the existence of fileName has already been established.
    //
    {
        try
        {
            String              inputString = new String ();      // for storing investment record
            int                 i = 0;                            // position in record

            inputString = fileName.readLine ();

            StringBuffer        input = new StringBuffer ();       // for storing field within record

            while (inputString.charAt (i) != 'l')
            {
                input.append (inputString.charAt (i));
                i++;
            }
            investmentID = input.toString ();
            i++;

            input = new StringBuffer ();
            while (inputString.charAt (i) != 'l')
            {
                input.append (inputString.charAt (i));
                i++;
            }
            investmentName = input.toString ();
            i++;

            input = new StringBuffer ();
            while (inputString.charAt (i) != 'l')
            {
                input.append (inputString.charAt (i));
                i++;
            }
            Float tempFloat = new Float (input.toString ());
            expectedAnnualReturn = tempFloat.floatValue ();
            i++;
```

```
        input = new StringBuffer ();
        while (i < inputString.length ())
        {
            input.append (inputString.charAt (i));
            i++;
        }
        expectedAnnualReturnUpdated = new Date (input.toString ());

    }
    catch (Exception e)
    {
        System.out.println ("***** Error: Investment.readRecord () *****");
        System.out.println ("\t" + e);
    }
} // readRecord
```

//--

```
public void writeRecord (RandomAccessFile fileName)
//
// writeRecord writes an investment record to fileName.
//
{
    try
    {
        fileName.writeBytes (investmentID + "|" + investmentName + "|");
        fileName.writeBytes (expectedAnnualReturn + "|");
        fileName.writeBytes (expectedAnnualReturnUpdated.toString () + "\n");
    }
    catch (Exception e)
    {
        System.out.println ("***** Error: Investment.writeRecord () *****");
        System.out.println ("\t" + e);
    }
} // writeRecord
```

//--

```
public void displayRecord ()
//
// displayRecord displays the contents of an investment record.
//
{
    System.out.print ("Investment ID: " + investmentID);
    System.out.println ("\tInvestment Name: " + investmentName);
    System.out.println ("Expected return: " + expectedAnnualReturn);
    System.out.print (" Date expected return was updated: ");
    System.out.print ((expectedAnnualReturnUpdated.getMonth () + 1) + "/");
    System.out.print (expectedAnnualReturnUpdated.getDate () + "/");
    System.out.println (expectedAnnualReturnUpdated.getYear ());
} // displayRecord
```

//--

```
public void obtainNewData ()
//
// Reads a new investment record by calling readInvestmentData.
//
```

```
    {
        readInvestmentData ();
    } // obtainNewData

//----------------------------------------------------------------------------------------------------

    public void performDeletion ()
    //
    // performDeletion performs the actual deletion of an investment record from a file.
    //
    {
        try
        {
            File                investmentFile = new File ("investment.dat");
            File                tempInvestmentFile = new File ("investment.tmp");

            Investment          inv = new Investment ();        // record to be checked

            if (!investmentFile.exists ())
            {
                return;
            }

            RandomAccessFile inFile = new RandomAccessFile (investmentFile, "r");
            RandomAccessFile outFile = new RandomAccessFile (tempInvestmentFile, "rw");

            while (inFile.getFilePointer () != inFile.length ())
            {
                inv.readRecord (inFile);

                if (investmentID.compareTo (inv.getInvestmentID ()) != 0)
                {
                    inv.writeRecord (outFile);
                }
            }

            inFile.close ();
            outFile.close ();

            investmentFile.delete ();
            tempInvestmentFile.renameTo (investmentFile);
        }
        catch (Exception e)
        {
            System.out.println ("***** Error: Investment.performDeletion () *****");
            System.out.println ("\t" + e);
        }
    } // performDeletion

//----------------------------------------------------------------------------------------------------

    public void produceInvestmentReport ()
    //
    // produceInvestmentReport generates the investment report.
    //
    {
        try
        {
```

```
        File                investmentFile = new File ("investment.dat");

        int                 i = 0;                        // used for screen clearing

    if (investmentFile.exists ())
    {
        RandomAccessFile inFile = new RandomAccessFile (investmentFile, "r");

        while (inFile.getFilePointer () != inFile.length ())
        {
            //
            // pause the screen after every three investments
            //
            if (((i % 4) == 0) && (i != 0))
            {
                System.out.println ();
                System.out.println ();
                System.out.println (" Press <ENTER> to view the next screen...");
                System.in.read ();
            }

            //
            // display a header message after every third printing
            //
            if ((i % 4) == 0)
            {
                MSGUtilities.clearScreen ();

                System.out.println ();
                System.out.println ();
                System.out.println ("\t      Martha Stockton Greengage Foundation");
                System.out.println ("\t              INVESTMENT REPORT\n");
            }

            System.out.println ("------------------------------------------------------------------------");

            readRecord (inFile);

            displayRecord ();

            i++;
        }

        inFile.close ();
    }
    else
    {
        System.out.println ("\nNo investments currently exist.");
    }

    System.out.println ("\n\n Press ENTER to continue ...");
    int                 c;
    c = System.in.read ();

}
catch (Exception e)
{
    System.out.println ("***** Error: Investment.produceInvestmentReport () *****");
```

```
            System.out.println ("\t" + e);
        }
    } // produceInvestmentReport

//----------------------------------------------------------------------------------------------------------------------

    public void putRecord ()
    //
    // putRecord writes an individual investment record into a file, ordered by investmentID.
    //
    {
        try
        {
            File                investmentFile = new File ("investment.dat");
                                                        // file of investments
            File                tempInvestmentFile = new File ("investment.tmp");
                                                        // temporary file for investments

            Investment          inv = new Investment ();    // record read, then written
            boolean             found = false;              // terminates while-loop

            RandomAccessFile newFile = new RandomAccessFile (tempInvestmentFile, "rw");

            if (!investmentFile.exists ())
            {
                writeRecord (newFile);
            }
            else
            {
                RandomAccessFile oldFile = new RandomAccessFile (investmentFile, "r");

                int compareInvestments;
                                            // to find correct place for the new investment

                while (oldFile.getFilePointer () != oldFile.length ())
                {
                    inv.readRecord (oldFile);

                    compareInvestments = investmentID.compareTo (inv.getInvestmentID ());

                    if ((!found) && (compareInvestments < 0))
                    {
                        writeRecord (newFile);
                        inv.writeRecord (newFile);
                        found = true;
                    }
                    else if (compareInvestments == 0)
                    {
                        writeRecord (newFile);
                        found = true;
                    } else
                    {
                        inv.writeRecord (newFile);
                    }
                } // while

                if (!found) writeRecord (newFile);
```

```
                oldFile.close ();
            } // else

        newFile.close ();

        investmentFile.delete ();
        tempInvestmentFile.renameTo (investmentFile);

    }
    catch (Exception e)
    {
        System.out.println ("***** Error: Investment.putRecord () *****");
        System.out.println ("\t" + e);
    }

} // putRecord
```

//--

```
public void readInvestmentData ()
//
// readInvestmentData obtains input data for all fields of an investment record.
//
{
    try
    {
        char                c;                              // character entered by user
        StringBuffer        input = new StringBuffer ();    // buffer for line of characters
        boolean             valid = false;                  // used to validate length of ID

        while (!valid)
        {
            System.out.println ("Enter investment number (12 digits): ");
            input = new StringBuffer ();
            while ((c = (char) System.in.read ()) != '\n')
            {
                input.append (c);
            }
            valid = (input.toString ().length () <= 12);

            if (!valid)
                System.out.println ("\n\nThe investment number must be 12 digits long.");
        }
        investmentID = input.toString ();

        System.out.println ("Enter investment name: ");
        input = new StringBuffer ();
        while ((c = (char) System.in.read ()) != '\n')
        {
            input.append (c);
        }
        investmentName = input.toString ();

        System.out.println ("Enter expected annual return: ");
        input = new StringBuffer ();
        while ((c = (char) System.in.read ()) != '\n')
        {
            input.append (c);
```

```
            }
            Float newFloat = new Float (input.toString ());
            expectedAnnualReturn = newFloat.floatValue ();

            expectedAnnualReturnUpdated = new Date ();
        }
        catch (Exception e)
        {
            System.out.println ("***** Error: Investment.readInvestmentData () *****");
            System.out.println ("\t" + e);
        }
    } // readInvestmentData

//-------------------------------------------------------------------------------------------

    public void updateRecord ()
    //
    // updateRecord modifies an investment record.
    //
    {
        try
        {
            char            option = '0';              // # of field to be changed
            boolean         done = false;              // terminates while-loop
            boolean         found = false;             // tells if investment is found
            char            c;                         // character entered by user
            StringBuffer    input = new StringBuffer ();   // buffer for line of characters
            byte            choice[] = new byte[10];   // user's choice

            while (!found && !done)
            {
                System.out.println ("Please enter the number of the investment to be" +
                        " updated (12 digits): ");

                input = new StringBuffer ();
                while ((c = (char) System.in.read ()) != '\n')
                {
                    input.append (c);
                }

                found = findRecord (input.toString ());

                if (!found)
                {
                    System.out.println ("Investment " + input.toString () + " was not found.");
                    System.out.println ("Would you like to enter another investment?");
                    System.in.read (choice);

                    if (( (char) choice[0]) == 'n')
                    {
                        done = true;
                    }
                }
            }

            if (!found)
            {
                return;
```

```
        }

        while (!done)
        {
            while (!done)
            {
                MSGUtilities.clearScreen ();

                System.out.println ("\t        UPDATE INVESTMENTS\n\n");
                System.out.println ("\t MARTHA STOCKTON GREENGAGE FOUNDATION\n\n");
                System.out.println ("\t        1. Update investment name\n");
                System.out.println ("\t        2. Update expected return\n");
                System.out.println ("\t        3. Exit to investment menu\n\n");
                System.out.println ("Enter your choice and press <ENTER>: ");

                try
                {
                    System.in.read (choice);

                    switch ( (char) choice[0])
                    {
                        case '1':
                            option = '1';
                            break;

                        case '2':
                            option = '2';
                            break;

                        case '3':
                        case '\n':
                            done = true;
                            break;

                        default:
                            System.out.println ("\n\nNot a valid choice\n");
                            System.out.println ("Press <ENTER> to return to menu...");
                            System.in.read (choice);
                            break;
                    }
                }
                catch (Exception e)
                {
                    System.out.println ("***** Error: Investment.updateRecord () *****");
                    System.out.println ("\t" + e);
                }

                if (!done)
                {
                    changeInvestmentField (option);
                    displayRecord ();

                    System.out.println ("\n\n Press ENTER to continue ...");
                    c = (char) System.in.read ();
                }
            }
        }
```

```
            putRecord ();
        }
        catch (Exception e)
        {
            System.out.println ("***** Error: Investment.updateRecord () *****");
            System.out.println ("\t" + e);
        }
    } // updateRecord
```

//---

```
    public void changeInvestmentField (char investmentFieldNumber)
    //
    // changeInvestmentField gets new input for field in investment record to be changed.
    //
    {
        try
        {
            char            c;                          // character entered by user
            StringBuffer    input = new StringBuffer (); // buffer for line of characters

            switch (investmentFieldNumber)
            {
                case '1':
                    System.out.println ("\n\nOld investment name: " + investmentName);
                    System.out.println ("Enter new investment name: ");
                    while ((c = (char) System.in.read ()) != '\n')
                    {
                        input.append (c);
                    }
                    investmentName = input.toString ();
                    break;

                case '2':
                    System.out.println ("\n\nOld expected return: " + expectedAnnualReturn);
                    System.out.println ("Enter new expected return: ");
                    while ((c = (char) System.in.read ()) != '\n')
                    {
                        input.append (c);
                    }
                    Float tempFloat = new Float (input.toString ());
                    expectedAnnualReturn = tempFloat.floatValue ();
                    expectedAnnualReturnUpdated = new Date ();
            } // switch
        }
        catch (Exception e)
        {
            System.out.println ("***** Error: Investment.changeInvestmentField () *****");
            System.out.println ("\t" + e);
        }
    } // changeInvestmentField

} // class Investment
```

```
/********************************************************************************
 *
 *                              Class Mortgage
 *
```

```
************************************************************************************/

class Mortgage extends FinancialInstrument
{
    //
    // Instance variables
    //
    private String        mortgageID;                  // mortgage ID (stored as chars)
    private String        mortgageeName;               // names of mortgagees
    private float         price;                        // price paid for mortgaged property
    private Date          dateMortgageIssued;           // date mortgage was issued
    private float         currentWeeklyIncome;          // weekly income of mortgagees
    private Date          weeklyIncomeUpdated;          // date weekly income updated
    private float         annualPropertyTax;            // annual property tax
    private float         annualInsurancePremium;       // annual insurance premium
    private float         mortgageBalance;              // mortgage balance


    //
    // Data access methods
    //
    public String getMortgageID () { return mortgageID; }
    public String getMortgageeName () { return mortgageeName; }
    public float getPrice () { return price; }
    public Date getDateMortgageIssued () { return dateMortgageIssued; }
    public float getCurrentWeeklyIncome () { return currentWeeklyIncome; }
    public Date getWeeklyIncomeUpdated () { return weeklyIncomeUpdated; }
    public float getAnnualPropertyTax () { return annualPropertyTax; }
    public float getAnnualInsurancePremium () { return annualInsurancePremium; }
    public float getMortgageBalance () { return mortgageBalance; }


    //
    // Instance methods
    //
    public float totalWeeklyNetPayments ()
    //
    // Computes the net total weekly payments made by the mortgagees, that is,
    // the expected total weekly mortgage amount less the expected total weekly grants.
    //
    {
        try
        {
            File              mortgageFile = new File ("mortgage.dat");
                                                        // file of mortgage records

            float             expectedTotalWeeklyMortgages = (float) 0.0;
                                                        // expected total weekly mortgages
            float             expectedTotalWeeklyGrants = (float) 0.0;
                                                        // expected total weekly grants
            float             capitalRepayment = (float) 0.0;
                                                        // capital repayment
            float             interestPayment = (float) 0.0;   // interest payment
            float             escrowPayment = (float) 0.0;    // escrow payment
            float             tempMortgage = (float) 0.0;     // temporary mortgage payment
            float             maximumPermittedMortgagePayment = (float) 0.0;
                                                        // maximum a family is allowed to pay

            if (mortgageFile.exists ())
            {
```

```
            RandomAccessFile inFile = new RandomAccessFile (mortgageFile, "r");

        while (inFile.getFilePointer () != inFile.length ())
        {
            readRecord (inFile);

            capitalRepayment = price /
                MSGApplication.NUMBER_OF_MORTGAGE_PAYMENTS;

            interestPayment = mortgageBalance * MSGApplication.INTEREST_RATE /
                MSGApplication.WEEKS_IN_YEAR ;

            escrowPayment = (annualPropertyTax + annualInsurancePremium) /
                MSGApplication.WEEKS_IN_YEAR;

            tempMortgage = capitalRepayment + interestPayment + escrowPayment;

            expectedTotalWeeklyMortgages += tempMortgage;

            maximumPermittedMortgagePayment = currentWeeklyIncome *
                MSGApplication.MAXIMUM_PERC_OF_INCOME;

            if (tempMortgage > maximumPermittedMortgagePayment)
                expectedTotalWeeklyGrants += tempMortgage -
                    maximumPermittedMortgagePayment;
        }

        inFile.close ();
    }   // if

    return (expectedTotalWeeklyMortgages - expectedTotalWeeklyGrants);
}
catch (Exception e)
{
    System.out.println ("***** Error: Mortgage.totalWeeklyNetPayments () *****");
    System.out.println ("\t" + e);
    return ( (float) 0.0);
}
} // totalWeeklyNetPayments

//-------------------------------------------------------------------------------------------------

public boolean findRecord (String findMortgageID)
//
// findRecord locates a given mortgage record if it exists.
// Returns true if the mortgage is located, otherwise false.
//
{
    try
    {
        File            mortgageFile = new File ("mortgage.dat");
                                                    // file of mortgage records

        boolean         found = false;              // result of comparison

        if (mortgageFile.exists ())
        {
            RandomAccessFile inFile = new RandomAccessFile (mortgageFile, "r");
```

```java
                    while (!found && (inFile.getFilePointer () != inFile.length ()))
                    {
                        readRecord (inFile);

                        if (mortgageID.compareTo (findMortgageID) == 0) found = true;
                    }
                    inFile.close ();
                }
                return found;
            }
        catch (Exception e)
            {
            System.out.println ("***** Error: Mortgage.findRecord () *****");
            System.out.println ("\t" + e);

            return false;
            }
    } // findRecord
```

//---

```java
    public void readRecord (RandomAccessFile fileName)
    //
    // readRecord reads a mortgage record from fileName.
    // Assumes that the existence of fileName has already been established.
    //
    {
        try
        {
            String              inputString = new String ();      // for storing mortgage record
            int                 i = 0;                            // position within string

            inputString = fileName.readLine ();

            StringBuffer input = new StringBuffer ();
            while (inputString.charAt (i) != '|')
            {
                input.append (inputString.charAt (i));
                i++;
            }
            mortgageID = input.toString ();
            i++;

            input = new StringBuffer ();
            while (inputString.charAt (i) != '|')
            {
                input.append (inputString.charAt (i));
                i++;
            }
            mortgageeName = input.toString ();
            i++;

            input = new StringBuffer ();
            while (inputString.charAt (i) != '|')
            {
                input.append (inputString.charAt (i));
                i++;
```

```
}
Float tempFloat = new Float (input.toString ());
price = tempFloat.floatValue ();
i++;

input = new StringBuffer ();
while (inputString.charAt (i) != '|')
{
    input.append (inputString.charAt (i));
    i++;
}
dateMortgageIssued = new Date (input.toString ());
i++;

input = new StringBuffer ();
while (inputString.charAt (i) != '|')
{
    input.append (inputString.charAt (i));
    i++;
}
tempFloat = new Float (input.toString ());
currentWeeklyIncome = tempFloat.floatValue ();
i++;

input = new StringBuffer ();
while (inputString.charAt (i) != '|')
{
    input.append (inputString.charAt (i));
    i++;
}
weeklyIncomeUpdated = new Date (input.toString ());
i++;

input = new StringBuffer ();
while (inputString.charAt (i) != '|')
{
    input.append (inputString.charAt (i));
    i++;
}
tempFloat = new Float (input.toString ());
annualPropertyTax = tempFloat.floatValue ();
i++;

input = new StringBuffer ();
while (inputString.charAt (i) != '|')
{
    input.append (inputString.charAt (i));
    i++;
}
tempFloat = new Float (input.toString ());
annualInsurancePremium = tempFloat.floatValue ();
i++;

input = new StringBuffer ();
while (i < inputString.length ())
{
    input.append (inputString.charAt (i));
    i++;
```

```
            }
            tempFloat = new Float (input.toString ());
            mortgageBalance = tempFloat.floatValue ();
            i++;
        }
        catch (Exception e)
        {
            System.out.println ("***** Error: Mortgage.readRecord () *****");
            System.out.println ("\t" + e);
        }
    } // readRecord
```

//---

```
    public void writeRecord (RandomAccessFile fileName)
    //
    // readRecord writes a mortgage record to specified file.
    //
    {
        try
        {
            fileName.writeBytes (mortgageID + "|" + mortgageeName + "|");
            fileName.writeBytes (price + "|" + dateMortgageIssued.toString () + "|");
            fileName.writeBytes (currentWeeklyIncome + "|" + weeklyIncomeUpdated.toString () + "|");
            fileName.writeBytes (annualPropertyTax + "|" + annualInsurancePremium + "|");
            fileName.writeBytes (mortgageBalance + "\n");
        }
        catch (Exception e)
        {
            System.out.println ("***** Error: Mortgage.writeRecord () *****");
            System.out.println ("\t" + e);
        }
    } // writeRecord
```

//---

```
    public void displayRecord ()
    //
    // displayRecord displays the names of the fields of a mortgage record and their values.
    //
    {
        System.out.print ("Mortgage ID: " + mortgageID);
        System.out.println ("\tMortgagee Name: " + mortgageeName);
        System.out.println ("Price :" + price);

        System.out.print (" Date mortgage issued: ");
        System.out.print ((dateMortgageIssued.getMonth () + 1) + "/");
        System.out.print (dateMortgageIssued.getDate () + "/");
        System.out.println (dateMortgageIssued.getYear ());

        System.out.println ("Current weekly income: " + currentWeeklyIncome);

        System.out.print (" Date weekly income updated: ");
        System.out.print ((weeklyIncomeUpdated.getMonth () + 1) + "/");
        System.out.print (weeklyIncomeUpdated.getDate () + "/");
        System.out.println (weeklyIncomeUpdated.getYear ());

        System.out.print ("Annual property tax: " + annualPropertyTax);
```

```
            System.out.println ("\t\tAnnual insurance premium: " + annualInsurancePremium);
            System.out.println ("Mortgage balance: " + mortgageBalance);
    } // displayRecord
```

//--

```
    public void obtainNewData ()
    //
    // obtainNewData reads a new mortgage record by calling readMortgageData.
    //
    {
        readMortgageData ();
    } // obtainNewData
```

//--

```
    public void performDeletion ()
    //
    // performDeletion performs the actual deletion of a mortgage record from a file.
    //
    {
        try
        {
            File                mortgageFile = new File ("mortgage.dat");
                                                        // file of mortgage records
            File                tempMortgageFile = new File ("mortgage.tmp");
                                                        // temporary file of mortgage records

            Mortgage            mort = new Mortgage ();         // record to be checked

            if (!mortgageFile.exists ())
            {
                return;
            }

            RandomAccessFile inFile = new RandomAccessFile (mortgageFile, "r");
            RandomAccessFile outFile = new RandomAccessFile (tempMortgageFile, "rw");

            while (inFile.getFilePointer () != inFile.length ())
            {
                mort.readRecord (inFile);

                if (mortgageID.compareTo (mort.getMortgageID ()) != 0)
                {
                    mort.writeRecord (outFile);
                }
            }

            inFile.close ();
            outFile.close ();

            mortgageFile.delete ();
            tempMortgageFile.renameTo (mortgageFile);
        }
        catch (Exception e)
        {
            System.out.println ("***** Error: Mortgage.performDeletion () *****");
            System.out.println ("\t" + e);
```

```
        }
    } // performDeletion

//-----------------------------------------------------------------------------

    public void produceMortgageReport ()
    //
    // produceMortgageReport generates the mortgage report.
    //
    {
        try
        {
            File                mortgageFile = new File ("mortgage.dat");
                                                                // file of mortgage records
            int                 i = 0;                          // used for screen clearing

            if (mortgageFile.exists ())
            {
                RandomAccessFile inFile = new RandomAccessFile (mortgageFile, "r");

                while (inFile.getFilePointer () != inFile.length ())
                {
                    //
                    // pause the screen after every three mortgages
                    //
                    if (((i % 2) == 0) && (i != 0))
                    {
                        System.out.println ();
                        System.out.println ();
                        System.out.println (" Press <ENTER> to view the next screen...");
                        System.in.read ();
                    }

                    //
                    // display a header message after every third mortgage
                    //
                    if ((i % 2) == 0)
                    {
                        MSGUtilities.clearScreen ();

                        System.out.println ();
                        System.out.println ();
                        System.out.println ("\t       Martha Stockton Greengage Foundation");
                        System.out.println ("\t              MORTGAGE REPORT\n");
                    }

                    System.out.println ("-----------------------------------------------------------------------");

                    readRecord (inFile);

                    displayRecord ();

                    i++;
                }

                inFile.close ();
            }
            else
```

```
                {
                        System.out.println ("\nNo mortgages currently exist.");
                }

                System.out.println ("\n\n Press ENTER to continue ...");
                int                     c;
                c = System.in.read ();
        }
        catch (Exception e)
        {
        System.out.println ("***** Error: Mortgage.produceMortgageReport () *****");
        System.out.println ("\t" + e);
        }
} // produceMortgageReport
```

//--

```
public void putRecord ()
//
// putRecord writes an individual mortgage record into a file, ordered by mortgageID.
//
{
        try
        {
                File            mortgageFile = new File ("mortgage.dat");
                                                        // file of mortgage records
                File            tempMortgageFile = new File ("mortgage.tmp");
                                                        // temporary file of mortgage records

                Mortgage        mort = new Mortgage ();        // record read, then written
                boolean         found = false;                 // terminates while-loop

                RandomAccessFile newFile = new RandomAccessFile (tempMortgageFile, "rw");

                if (!mortgageFile.exists ())
                {
                        writeRecord (newFile);
                }
                else
                {
                        RandomAccessFile oldFile = new RandomAccessFile (mortgageFile, "r");

                        int             compareMortgages;      // to find correct place for the new mortgage

                        while (oldFile.getFilePointer () != oldFile.length ())
                        {
                                mort.readRecord (oldFile);

                                compareMortgages = mortgageID.compareTo (mort.getMortgageID ());

                                if ((!found) && (compareMortgages < 0))
                                {
                                        writeRecord (newFile);
                                        mort.writeRecord (newFile);
                                        found = true;
                                }
                                else if (compareMortgages == 0)
                                {
```

```
                        writeRecord (newFile);
                        found = true;
                    }
                    else
                    {
                        mort.writeRecord (newFile);
                    }
                } // while

                if (!found) writeRecord (newFile);

                oldFile.close ();
            }

            newFile.close ();

            mortgageFile.delete ();
            tempMortgageFile.renameTo (mortgageFile);
        }
        catch (Exception e)
        {
            System.out.println ("***** Error: Mortgage.putRecord () *****");
            System.out.println ("\t" + e);
        }
    } // putRecord

//------------------------------------------------------------------------------------------------

    public void readMortgageData ()
    //
    // readMortgageData asks user to enter information for the fields of a mortgage.
    //
    {
        try
        {
            char            c;                              // character entered by user
            StringBuffer    input = new StringBuffer ();     // buffer for line of characters
            boolean         valid = false;                   // used to validate length of ID

            while (!valid)
            {
                System.out.println ("Enter mortgage number (12 digits): ");
                input = new StringBuffer ();
                while ((c = (char) System.in.read ()) != '\n')
                {
                    input.append (c);
                }
                valid = (input.toString ().length () <= 12);

                if (!valid)
                    System.out.println ("\n\nThe mortgage number must be 12 digits.");
            }
            mortgageID = input.toString ();

            System.out.println ("Enter mortgagee name: ");
            input = new StringBuffer ();
            while ((c = (char) System.in.read ()) != '\n')
            {
```

```
                input.append (c);
        }
        mortgageeName = input.toString ();

        System.out.println ("Enter price of home: ");
        input = new StringBuffer ();
        while ((c = (char) System.in.read ()) != '\n')
        {
                input.append (c);
        }
        Float tempFloat = new Float (input.toString ());
        price = tempFloat.floatValue ();

        System.out.println ("Enter date mortgage was issued (mm/dd/yy): ");
        input = new StringBuffer ();
        while ((c = (char) System.in.read ()) != '\n')
        {
                input.append (c);
        }
        dateMortgageIssued = MSGUtilities.parseDate (input.toString ());

        System.out.println ("Enter current weekly income: ");
        input = new StringBuffer ();
        while ((c = (char) System.in.read ()) != '\n')
        {
                input.append (c);
        }
        tempFloat = new Float (input.toString ());
        currentWeeklyIncome = tempFloat.floatValue ();

        weeklyIncomeUpdated = new Date ();

        System.out.println ("Enter annual property tax: ");
        input = new StringBuffer ();
        while ((c = (char) System.in.read ()) != '\n')
        {
                input.append (c);
        }
        tempFloat = new Float (input.toString ());
        annualPropertyTax = tempFloat.floatValue ();

        System.out.println ("Enter mortgage balance: ");
        input = new StringBuffer ();
        while ((c = (char) System.in.read ()) != '\n')
        {
                input.append (c);
        }
        tempFloat = new Float (input.toString ());
        mortgageBalance = tempFloat.floatValue ();
    }
    catch (Exception e)
    {
        System.out.println ("***** Error: Mortgage.readMortgageData () *****");
        System.out.println ("\t" + e);
    }
} // readMortgageData

//-----------------------------------------------------------------------------------------------------
```

```
public void updateRecord ()
//
// updateRecord modifies a mortgage record.
//
{
    try
    {
        char            option = '0';              // # of field to be changed
        boolean         done = false;              // terminates while-loop
        boolean         found = false;             // tells if mortgage is found
        char            c;                         // character entered by user
        StringBuffer    input = new StringBuffer ();   // buffer for line of characters
        byte            choice[] = new byte[10];   // user's choice

        while (!found && !done)
        {
            System.out.println ("Please enter the number of the mortgage to be" +
                    " updated (12 digits): ");
            input = new StringBuffer ();
            while ((c = (char) System.in.read ()) != '\n')
            {
                input.append (c);
            }

            found = findRecord (input.toString ());

            if (!found)
            {
                System.out.println ("Mortgage " + input.toString () + " was not found.");
                System.out.println ("Would you like to enter another mortgage?");
                System.in.read (choice);

                if (( (char) choice[0]) == 'n')
                {
                    done = true;
                }
            }
        }

        if (!found)
        {
            return;
        }

        while (!done)
        {
            while (!done)
            {
                MSGUtilities.clearScreen ();

                System.out.println ("\t       UPDATE MORTGAGES\n\n");
                System.out.println ("\t MARTHA STOCKTON GREENGAGE FOUNDATION\n\n");
                System.out.println ("\t    1. Update mortgagee name\n");
                System.out.println ("\t    2. Update price of home\n");
                System.out.println ("\t    3. Update date mortgage issued\n");
                System.out.println ("\t    4. Update current weekly income\n");
                System.out.println ("\t    5. Update property tax\n");
```

```
System.out.println ("\t       6. Update insurance premium\n");
System.out.println ("\t       7. Update mortgage balance\n");
System.out.println ("\t       8. Exit to mortgage menu\n\n");
System.out.println ("Enter your choice and press <ENTER>: ");

try
{
    System.in.read (choice);

    switch ( (char) choice[0])
    {
        case '1':
            option = '1';
            break;

        case '2':
            option = '2';
            break;

        case '3':
            option = '3';
            break;

        case '4':
            option = '4';
            break;

        case '5':
            option = '5';
            break;

        case '6':
            option = '6';
            break;

        case '7':
            option = '7';
            break;

        case '8':
        case '\n':
            done = true;
            break;

        default:
            System.out.println ("\n\nNot a valid choice\n");
            System.out.println ("Press <ENTER> to return to menu...");
            System.in.read (choice);
            break;
    }
}
catch (Exception e)
{
    System.out.println ("***** Error: Mortgage.updateRecord () *****");
    System.out.println ("\t" + e);
}

if (!done)
```

```
                {
                    changeMortgageField (option);
                    displayRecord ();

                    System.out.println ("\n\n Press ENTER to continue ...");
                    c = (char) System.in.read ();
                }
            }
        }
        putRecord ();
    }
    catch (Exception e)
    {
        System.out.println ("***** Error: Mortgage.updateRecord () *****");
        System.out.println ("\t" + e);
    }
} // updateRecord
```

//---

```
    public void changeMortgageField (char mortgageFieldNumber)
    //
    // changeMortgageField gets new input for field in mortgage record to be changed.
    //
    {
        try
        {
            char            c;                          // character entered by user
            StringBuffer    input = new StringBuffer (); // buffer for line of characters
            Float           tempFloat;

            switch (mortgageFieldNumber)
            {
                case '1':
                    System.out.println ("\n\nOld mortgagee name: " + mortgageeName);
                    System.out.println ("Enter new mortgagee name: ");
                    while ((c = (char) System.in.read ()) != '\n')
                    {
                        input.append (c);
                    }
                    mortgageeName = input.toString ();
                    break;

                case '2':
                    System.out.println ("\n\nOld price: " + price);
                    System.out.println ("Enter new price of home: ");
                    while ((c = (char) System.in.read ()) != '\n')
                    {
                        input.append (c);
                    }
                    tempFloat = new Float (input.toString ());
                    price = tempFloat.floatValue ();
                    break;

                case '3':
                    System.out.print ("\n\nOld mortgage date: ");
                    System.out.print ((dateMortgageIssued.getMonth () + 1) + "/");
                    System.out.print (dateMortgageIssued.getDate () + "/");
```

```
            System.out.println (dateMortgageIssued.getYear ());
            System.out.println ("Enter date the mortgage was issued (mm/dd/yy):");
            while ((c = (char) System.in.read ()) != '\n')
            {
                input.append (c);
            }
            dateMortgageIssued = MSGUtilities.parseDate (input.toString ());
            break;

        case '4':
            System.out.println ("\n\nOld weekly income: " + currentWeeklyIncome);
            System.out.println ("Enter current weekly income:");
            while ((c = (char) System.in.read ()) != '\n')
            {
                input.append (c);
            }
            tempFloat = new Float (input.toString ());
            currentWeeklyIncome = tempFloat.floatValue ();
            weeklyIncomeUpdated = new Date ();
            break;

        case '5':
            System.out.println ("\n\nOld annual property tax: " + annualPropertyTax);
            System.out.println ("Enter new annual property tax:");
            while ((c = (char) System.in.read ()) != '\n')
            {
                input.append (c);
            }
            tempFloat = new Float (input.toString ());
            annualPropertyTax = tempFloat.floatValue ();
            break;

        case '6':
            System.out.println ("\n\nOld insurance premium: " + annualInsurancePremium);
            System.out.println ("Enter new annual insurance premium:");
            while ((c = (char) System.in.read ()) != '\n')
            {
                input.append (c);
            }
            tempFloat = new Float (input.toString ());
            annualInsurancePremium = tempFloat.floatValue ();
            break;

        case '7':
            System.out.println ("\n\nOld mortgagee balance: " + mortgageBalance);
            System.out.println ("Enter new mortgage balance:");
            while ((c = (char) System.in.read ()) != '\n')
            {
                input.append (c);
            }
            tempFloat = new Float (input.toString ());
            mortgageBalance = tempFloat.floatValue ();
    } // switch
}
catch (Exception e)
{
    System.out.println ("***** Error: Mortgage.changeMortgageField () *****");
    System.out.println ("\t" + e);
```

```
        }
    } // changeMortgageField

} // class Mortgage
```

BIBLIOGRAPHY

The chapter number in parentheses denotes the chapter in which the item has been referenced.

[Abrial, 1980] J.-R. ABRIAL, "The Specification Language Z: Syntax and Semantics," Oxford University Computing Laboratory, Programming Research Group, Oxford, UK, April 1980. (Chapter 8)

[Abowd, Allen, and Garlan, 1993] G. ABOWD, R. ALLEN, AND D. GARLAN, "Using Style to Understand Descriptions of Software Architecture," *Proceedings of the First ACM SIGSOFT Symposium on the Foundations of Software Engineering, ACM SIGSOFT Software Engineering Notes* **18** (December 1993), pp. 9–20. (Chapter 11)

[Ackerman, Buchwald, and Lewski, 1989] A. F. ACKERMAN, L. S. BUCHWALD, AND F. H. LEWSKI, "Software Inspections: An Effective Verification Process," *IEEE Software* **6** (May 1989), pp. 31–36. (Chapter 5)

[Alavi, 1984] M. ALAVI, "An Assessment of the Prototyping Approach to Information Systems Development," *Communications of the ACM* **27** (June 1984), pp. 556–563. (Chapter 7)

[Albrecht, 1979] A. J. ALBRECHT, "Measuring Application Development Productivity," *Proceedings of the IBM SHARE/GUIDE Applications Development Symposium,* Monterey, CA, October 1979, pp. 83–92. (Chapter 10)

[Albrecht and Gaffney, 1983] A. J. ALBRECHT AND J. E. GAFFNEY, JR., "Software Function, Source Lines of Code, and Development Effort Prediction: A Software Science Validation," *IEEE Transactions on Software Engineering* **SE-9** (November 1983), pp. 639–648. (Chapter 10)

[Alford, 1985] M. ALFORD, "SREM at the Age of Eight; The Distributed Computing Design System," *IEEE Computer* **18** (April 1985), pp. 36–46. (Chapter 8)

[Anger, Munson, and Rodriguez, 1994] F. D. ANGER, J. C. MUNSON, AND R. V. RODRIGUEZ, "Temporal Complexity and Software Faults," *Proceedings of the 5th International Symposium on Software Reliability Engineering,* Monterey, CA, November 1994, pp. 115–125. (Chapter 11)

[ANSI X3.9, 1977] "Programming Language FORTRAN," ANSI X3.9-1977, American National Standards Institute, Inc., 1977. (Chapter 12)

[ANSI X3.159, 1989] "The Programming Language C," ANSI X3.159-1989, American National Standards Institute, Inc., 1989. (Chapter 12)

[ANSI/IEEE 754, 1985] "Standard for Binary Floating Point Arithmetic," ANSI/IEEE 754, American National Standards Institute, Inc., Institute of Electrical and Electronic Engineers, Inc., 1985. (Chapter 12, Epilogue)

[ANSI/IEEE 770X3.97, 1983] "Pascal Computer Programming Language," ANSI/IEEE 770X3.97-1983, American National Standards Institute, Inc., Institute of Electrical and Electronic Engineers, Inc., 1983. (Chapter 12)

[ANSI/IEEE 829, 1983] "Software Test Documentation," ANSI/IEEE 829-1983, American National Standards Institute, Inc., Institute of Electrical and Electronic Engineers, Inc., 1983. (Chapter 10)

[ANSI/IEEE 990, 1987] "Recommended Practice for Ada as a Program Design Language," ANSI/IEEE 990-1987, American National Standards Institute, Inc., Institute of Electrical and Electronic Engineers, Inc., 1987. (Chapter 13)

[ANSI/MIL-STD-1815A, 1983] "Reference Manual for the Ada Programming Language," ANSI/MIL-STD-1815A, American National Standards Institute, Inc., United States Department of Defense, 1983. (Chapter 12)

[Apple, 1984] *Macintosh Pascal User's Guide,* Apple Computer, Inc., Cupertino, CA 1984. (Chapter 4)

[Archer and Devlin, 1986] J. E. ARCHER, JR., AND M. T. DEVLIN, "Rational's Experience Using Ada for Very Large Systems," *Proceedings of the First International Conference on Ada Programming Language Applications for the NASA Space Station,* NASA, 1986, pp. B2.5.1–B2.5.12. (Chapter 13)

[Aron, 1983] J. D. ARON, *The Program Development Process. Part II. The Programming Team,* Addison-Wesley, Reading, MA, 1983. (Chapter 12)

[August, 1991] J. H. AUGUST, *Joint Application Design: The Group Session Approach to System Design,* Yourdon Press, Englewood Cliffs, NJ, 1991. (Chapter 7)

[Baber, 1987] R. L. BABER, *The Spine of Software: Designing Provably Correct Software: Theory and Practice,* John Wiley and Sons, New York, 1987. (Chapter 5)

[Babich, 1986] W. A. BABICH, *Software Configuration Management: Coordination for Team Productivity,* Addison-Wesley, Reading, MA, 1986. (Chapters 4 and 14)

[Baker, 1972] F. T. BAKER, "Chief Programmer Team Management of Production Programming," *IBM Systems Journal* **11** (No. 1, 1972), pp. 56–73. (Chapter 12)

[Balda and Gustafson, 1990] D. M. BALDA AND D. A. GUSTAFSON, "Cost Estimation Models for the Reuse and Prototype Software Development Life Cycles," *ACM SIGSOFT Software Engineering Notes* **15** (July 1990), pp. 42–50. (Chapter 10)

[Balzer, 1985] R. BALZER, "A 15 Year Perspective on Automatic Programming," *IEEE Transactions on Software Engineering* **SE-11** (November 1985), pp. 1257–1268. (Chapter 8)

[Bamford and Deibler, 1993a] R. C. BAMFORD AND W. J. DEIBLER, II, "Comparing, Contrasting ISO 9001 and the SEI Capability Maturity Model," *IEEE Computer* **26** (October 1993), pp. 68–70. (Chapter 3)

[Bamford and Deibler, 1993b] R. C. BAMFORD AND W. J. DEIBLER, II, "A Detailed Comparison of the SEI Software Maturity Levels and Technology Stages to the Requirements for ISO 9001 Registration," Software Systems Quality Consulting, San Jose, CA, 1993. (Chapter 3)

[Banker, Datar, Kemerer, and Zwieg, 1993] R. D. BANKER, S. M. DATAR, C. F. KEMERER, AND D. ZWIEG, "Software Complexity and Maintenance Costs," *Communications of the ACM* **36** (November 1993), pp. 81–94. (Chapter 14)

[Barnard and Price, 1994] J. BARNARD AND A. PRICE, "Managing Code Inspection Information," *IEEE Software* **11** (March 1994), pp. 59–69. (Chapter 12)

[Barnes and Bollinger, 1991] B. H. BARNES AND T. B. BOLLINGER, "Making Reuse Cost-Effective," *IEEE Software* **8** (January 1991), pp. 13–24. (Chapter 6)

[Barstow, Shrobe, and Sandewall, 1984] D. R. BARSTOW, H. E. SHROBE, AND E. SANDEWALL (Editors), *Interactive Programming Environments,* McGraw-Hill, New York, 1984. (Chapter 13)

[Basili, 1990] V. R. BASILI, "Viewing Maintenance as Reuse-Oriented Software Development," *IEEE Software* **7** (January 1990), pp. 19–25. (Chapter 14)

[Basili and Hutchens, 1983] V. R. BASILI AND D. H. HUTCHENS, "An Empirical Study of a Syntactic Complexity Family," *IEEE Transactions on Software Engineering* **SE-9** (November 1983), pp. 664–672. (Chapter 12)

[Basili and Musa, 1991] V. R. BASILI AND J. D. MUSA, "The Future Engineering of Software: A Management Perspective," *IEEE Computer* **24** (September 1991), pp. 90–96. (Chapter 1)

[Basili and Selby, 1987] V. R. BASILI AND R. W. SELBY, "Comparing the Effectiveness of Software Testing Strategies," *IEEE Transactions on Software Engineering* **SE-13** (December 1987), pp. 1278–1296. (Chapter 12)

[Basili and Weiss, 1984] V. R. BASILI AND D. M. WEISS, "A Methodology for Collecting Valid Software Engineering Data," *IEEE Transactions on Software Engineering* **SE-10** (November 1984), pp. 728–738. (Chapter 12)

[Behrens, 1983] C. A. BEHRENS, "Measuring the Productivity of Computer Systems Development Activities with Function Points," *IEEE Transactions on Software Engineering* **SE-9** (November 1983), pp. 648–652. (Chapter 10)

[Beizer, 1990] B. BEIZER, *Software Testing Techniques,* Second Edition, Van Nostrand Reinhold, New York, 1990. (Chapters 2, 5, 11, and 12)

[Berard, 1993] E. V. BERARD, *Essays on Object-Oriented Software Engineering, Volume I,* Prentice-Hall, Englewood Cliffs, NJ. 1993. (Chapter 9)

[Berry, 1978] D. M. BERRY, Personal Communication, 1978. (Chapter 6)

[Berry, 1985] D. M. BERRY, "On the Application of Ada and Its Tools to the Information Hiding Decomposition Methodology for the Design of Software Systems," in: *Methodologies for Computer System Design,* W. K. Giloi and B. D. Shriver (Editors), Elsevier North-Holland, Amsterdam, 1985, pp. 308–321. (Chapter 6)

[Berry and Wing, 1985] D. M. BERRY AND J. M. WING, "Specifying and Prototyping: Some Thoughts on Why They are Successful," in: *Formal Methods and Software Development, Proceedings of the International Joint Conference on Theory and Practice of Software Development, Volume 2,* Springer-Verlag, Berlin, 1985, pp. 117–128. (Chapter 5)

[Bersoff and Davis, 1991] E. H. BERSOFF AND A. M. DAVIS, "Impacts of Life Cycle Models on Software Configuration Management," *Communications of the ACM* **34** (August 1991), pp. 104–118. (Chapter 4)

[Berzins, Gray, and Naumann, 1986] V. BERZINS, M. GRAY, AND D. NAUMANN, "Abstraction-Based Software Developments," *Communications of the ACM* **29** (May 1986), pp. 402–415. (Chapter 6)

[Bhandari et al., 1994] I. BHANDARI, M. J. HALLIDAY, J. CHAAR, R. CHILLAREGE, K. JONES, J. S. ATKINSON, C. LEPORI-COSTELLO, P. Y. JASPER, E. D. TARVER, C. C. LEWIS, AND M. YONEZAWA, "In-Process Improvement through Defect Data Interpretation," *IBM Systems Journal* **33** (No. 1, 1994), pp. 182–214. (Chapter 1)

[Bias, 1991] R. BIAS, "Walkthroughs: Efficient Collaborative Testing," *IEEE Software* **8** (September 1991), pp. 94–95. (Chapter 11)

[Biggerstaff and Perlis, 1989] T. J. BIGGERSTAFF AND A. J. PERLIS (Editors), *Software Reusability, Volumes I and II,* ACM Press, New York, 1989. (Chapter 6)

[Bishop, 1994] M. BISHOP, Usenet posting <2p8pab$rv0@source.asset.com> on comp.software-eng, April 22, 1994. (Chapter 3)

[Bjørner, 1987] D. BJØRNER, "On the Use of Formal Methods in Software Development," *Proceedings of the Ninth International Conference on Software Engineering,* Monterey, CA, March 1987, pp. 17–29. (Chapter 8)

[Blaha, Premerlani, and Rumbaugh, 1988] M. R. BLAHA, W. J. PREMERLANI, AND J. E. RUMBAUGH, "Relational Database Design Using an Object-Oriented Methodology," *Communications of the ACM* **31** (April 1988), pp. 414–427. (Chapter 6)

[Blair, Murphy, Schach, and McDonald, 1988] J. A. BLAIR, L. C. MURPHY, S. R. SCHACH, AND C. W. McDONALD, "Rapid Prototyping, Bottom-Up Design, and Reusable Modules: A Case Study," *ACM Mid-Southeast Summer Meeting,* Nashville, TN, May 1988. (Chapter 7)

[Boehm, 1976] B. W. BOEHM, "Software Engineering," *IEEE Transactions on Computers* **C-25** (December 1976), pp. 1226–1241. (Chapters 1 and 2)

[Boehm, 1979] B. W. BOEHM, "Software Engineering, R & D Trends and Defense Needs," in: *Research Directions in Software Technology,* P. Wegner (Editor), The MIT Press, Cambridge, MA, 1979. (Chapter 1)

[Boehm, 1980] B. W. BOEHM, "Developing Small-Scale Application Software Products: Some Experimental Results," *Proceedings of the Eighth IFIP World Computer Congress,* October 1980, pp. 321–326. (Chapter 1)

[Boehm, 1981] B. W. BOEHM, *Software Engineering Economics,* Prentice-Hall, Englewood Cliffs, NJ, 1981. (Chapters 1, 3, and 10)

[Boehm, 1984a] B. W. BOEHM, "Verifying and Validating Software Requirements and Design Specifications," *IEEE Software* **1** (January 1984), pp. 75–88. (Chapter 5)

[Boehm, 1984b] B. W. BOEHM, "Software Engineering Economics," *IEEE Transactions on Software Engineering* **SE-10** (January 1984), pp. 4–21. (Chapter 10)

[Boehm, 1988] B. W. BOEHM, "A Spiral Model of Software Development and Enhancement," *IEEE Computer* **21** (May 1988), pp. 61–72. (Chapter 3)

[Boehm, 1991] B. W. BOEHM, "Software Risk Management: Principles and Practices," *IEEE Software* **8** (January 1991), pp. 32–41. (Chapter 3)

[Boehm, Gray, and Seewaldt, 1984] B. W. BOEHM, T. E. GRAY, AND T. SEEWALDT, "Prototyping Versus Specifying: A Multi-Project Experiment," *IEEE Transactions on Software Engineering* **SE-10** (May 1984), pp. 290–303. (Chapter 7)

[Boehm and Papaccio, 1988] B. W. BOEHM AND P. N. PAPACCIO, "Understanding and Controlling Software Costs," *IEEE Transactions on Software Engineering* **14** (October 1988), pp. 1462–1477. (Chapters 1 and 2)

[Boehm, Penedo, Stuckle, Williams, and Pyster, 1984] B. W. BOEHM, M. H. PENEDO, E. D. STUCKLE, R. D. WILLIAMS, AND A. B. PYSTER, "A Software Development Environment for Improving Productivity," *IEEE Computer* **17** (June 1984), pp. 30–44. (Chapters 3 and 10)

[Böhm and Jacopini, 1966] C. BÖHM AND G. JACOPINI, "Flow Diagrams, Turing Machines, and Languages with Only Two Formation Rules," *Communications of the ACM* **9** (May 1966), pp. 366–371. (Chapter 12)

[Bollinger and McGowan, 1991] T. BOLLINGER AND C. MCGOWAN, "A Critical Look at Software Capability Evaluations," *IEEE Software* **8** (July 1991), pp. 25–41. (Chapter 3)

[Bologna, Quirk, and Taylor, 1985] S. BOLOGNA, W. J. QUIRK, AND J. R. TAYLOR, "Simulation and System Validation," in: *Verification and Validation of Real-Time Software*, W. J. Quirk (Editor), Springer-Verlag, Berlin, 1985, pp. 179–201. (Chapter 12)

[Booch, 1994] G. BOOCH, *Object-Oriented Analysis and Design with Applications, Second Edition,* Benjamin/Cummings, Redwood City, CA, 1994. (Chapters 3, 9, 11, and 13)

[Botting, 1994] R. BOTTING, Personal communication, 1994. (Chapter 14)

[Brady, 1977] J. M. BRADY, *The Theory of Computer Science,* Chapman and Hall, London, 1977. (Chapter 8)

[Brandl, 1990] D. L. BRANDL, "Quality Measures in Design: Finding Problems before Coding," *ACM SIGSOFT Software Engineering Notes* **15** (January 1990), pp. 68–72. (Chapter 11)

[Branstad and Powell, 1984] M. BRANSTAD AND P. B. POWELL, "Software Engineering Project Standards," *IEEE Transactions on Software Engineering* **SE-10** (January 1984), pp. 73–78. (Chapter 10)

[Bratley, Fox, and Schrage, 1987] P. BRATLEY, B. L. FOX, AND L. E. SCHRAGE, *Guide to Simulation,* Second Edition, Springer-Verlag, New York, 1987. (Chapter 8)

[Brettschneider, 1989] R. BRETTSCHNEIDER, "Is Your Software Ready for Release?" *IEEE Software* **6** (July 1989), pp. 100, 102, and 108. (Chapter 13)

[Brooks, 1975] F. P. BROOKS, JR., *The Mythical Man-Month: Essays in Software Engineering,* Addison-Wesley, Reading, MA, 1975. (Chapters 1, 2, 7, and 12)

[Brooks, 1986] F. P. BROOKS, JR., "No Silver Bullet," in: *Information Processing '86,* H.-J. Kugler (Editor), Elsevier North-Holland, New York, 1986. Reprinted in: *IEEE Computer* **20** (April 1987), pp. 10–19. (Chapter 2)

[Brown and McDermid, 1992] A. W. BROWN AND J. A. MCDERMID, "Learning from IPSE's Mistakes," *IEEE Software* **9** (March 1992), pp. 23–29. (Chapter 13)

[Browne, 1994] D. BROWNE, *STUDIO: STructured User-interface Design for Interaction Optimization,* Prentice-Hall, Englewood Cliffs, NJ, 1994. (Chapter 7)

[Bruegge, Blythe, Jackson, and Shufelt, 1992] B. BRUEGGE, J. BLYTHE, J. JACKSON, AND J. SHUFELT, "Object-Oriented Modeling with OMT," *Proceedings of the Conference on Object-Oriented Programming, Languages, and Systems, OOPSLA '92, ACM SIGPLAN Notices* **27** (October 1992), pp. 359–376. (Chapter 6)

[Bruno and Marchetto, 1986] G. BRUNO AND G. MARCHETTO, "Process-Translatable Petri Nets for the Rapid Prototyping of Process Control Systems," *IEEE Transactions on Software Engineering* **SE-12** (February 1986), pp. 346–357. (Chapter 8)

[Budd, 1991] T. A. BUDD, *An Introduction to Object-Oriented Programming*, Addison-Wesley, Reading, MA, 1991. (Chapter 1)

[Bush, 1990] M. BUSH, "Improving Software Quality: The Use of Formal Inspections at the Jet Propulsion Laboratory," *Proceedings of the 12th International Conference on Software Engineering,*

Nice, France, March 1990, pp. 196–199. (Chapter 5)

[Caldiera and Basili, 1991] G. CALDIERA AND V. R. BASILI, "Identifying and Qualifying Reusable Software Components," *IEEE Computer* **24** (February 1991), pp. 61–70. (Chapter 6)

[Cameron, 1986] J. R. CAMERON, "An Overview of JSD," *IEEE Transactions on Software Engineering* **SE-12** (February 1986), pp. 222–240. (Chapter 11)

[Cameron, 1988] J. CAMERON, *JSP & JSD—The Jackson Approach to Software Development,* Second Edition, IEEE Computer Society Press, Washington, DC, 1988. (Chapter 11)

[Capper, Colgate, Hunter, and James, 1994] N. P. CAPPER, R. J. COLGATE, J. C. HUNTER, AND M. F. JAMES, "The Impact of Object-Oriented Technology on Software Quality: Three Case Histories," *IBM Systems Journal* **33** (No. 1, 1994), pp. 131–157. (Chapters 1, 6, 7, and 9)

[Card, McGarry, and Page, 1987] D. N. CARD, F. E. MCGARRY, AND G. T. PAGE, "Evaluating Software Engineering Technologies," *IEEE Transactions on Software Engineering* **SE-13** (July 1987), pp. 845–851. (Chapters 1 and 2)

[Carlson, Druffel, Fisher, and Whitaker, 1980] W. E. CARLSON, L. E. DRUFFEL, D. A. FISHER, AND W. A. WHITAKER, "Introducing Ada," *Proceedings of the ACM Annual Conference, ACM 80,* Nashville, TN 1980, pp. 263–271. (Chapter 12)

[Chandrasekharan, Dasarathy, and Kishimoto, 1985] M. CHANDRASEKHARAN, B. DASARATHY, AND Z. KISHIMOTO, "Requirements-Based Testing of Real-Time Systems: Modeling for Testability," *IEEE Computer* **18** (April 1985), pp. 71–80. (Chapter 8)

[Charette, 1989] R. N. CHARETTE, *Software Engineering Risk Analysis and Management,* McGraw-Hill, New York, 1989. (Chapter 3)

[Chen, 1976] P. CHEN, "The Entity-Relationship Model—Toward a Unified View of Data," *ACM Transactions on Database Systems* **1** (March 1976), pp. 9–36. (Chapter 8)

[Chen, 1983] P. P.-S. CHEN, "ER—A Historical Perspective and Future Directions," in: *Entity Relationship Approach to Software Engineering,* C. G. Davis (Editor), North-Holland, Amsterdam, 1983. (Chapter 8)

[Chen and Norman, 1992] M. CHEN AND R. J. NORMAN, "A Framework for Integrated CASE," *IEEE Software* **8** (March 1992), pp. 18–22. (Chapter 13)

[Chidamber and Kemerer, 1994] S. R. CHIDAMBER AND C. F. KEMERER, "A Metrics Suite for Object Oriented Design," *IEEE Transactions on Software Engineering* **20** (June 1994), pp. 476–493. (Chapter 11)

[Chow, 1985] T. S. CHOW (Editor), *Tutorial: Software Quality Assurance: A Practical Approach,* IEEE Computer Society Press, Washington, DC, 1985. (Chapter 5)

[Clarke, Podgurski, Richardson, and Zeil, 1989] L. A. CLARKE, A. PODGURSKI, D. J. RICHARDSON, AND S. J. ZEIL, "A Formal Evaluation of Data Flow Path Selection Criteria," *IEEE Transactions on Software Engineering* **15** (November 1989), pp. 1318–1332. (Chapter 12)

[Coad and Yourdon, 1991a] P. COAD AND E. YOURDON, *Object-Oriented Analysis, Second Edition,* Yourdon Press, Englewood Cliffs, NJ, 1991. (Chapter 9)

[Coad and Yourdon, 1991b] P. COAD AND E. YOURDON, *Object-Oriented Design,* Yourdon Press, Englewood Cliffs, NJ, 1991. (Chapters 9 and 11)

[Cobb, 1985] R. H. COBB, "In Praise of 4GLs," *Datamation* **31** (July 15, 1985), pp. 90–96. (Chapter 12)

[Cobb and Mills, 1990] R. H. COBB AND H. D. MILLS, "Engineering Software under Statistical Quality Control," *IEEE Software* **7** (November 1990), pp. 44–54. (Chapter 12)

[Coleman, Ash, Lowther, and Oman, 1994] D. COLEMAN, D. ASH, B. LOWTHER, AND P. OMAN, "Using Metrics to Evaluate Software System Maintainability," *IEEE Computer* **27** (August 1994), pp. 44–49. (Chapters 1 and 14)

[Coleman et al., 1994] D. COLEMAN, P. ARNOLD, S. BODOFF, C. DOLLIN, H. GILCHRIST, F. HAYES AND P. JEREMAES, *Object-Oriented Development: The Fusion Method,* Prentice-Hall, Englewood Cliffs, NJ, 1994. (Chapter 9)

[Coleman, Hayes, and Bear, 1992] D. COLEMAN, F. HAYES, AND S. BEAR, "Introducing Objectcharts or How to Use Statecharts in Object-Oriented Design," *IEEE Transactions on Software*

Engineering **18** (January 1992), pp. 9–18. (Chapters 8 and 9)

[Connell and Shafer, 1989] J. L. CONNELL AND L. SHAFER, *Structured Rapid Prototyping: An Evolutionary Approach to Software Development*, Yourdon Press, Englewood Cliffs, NJ, 1989. (Chapters 3 and 7)

[Conte, Dunsmore, and Shen, 1986] S. D. CONTE, H. E. DUNSMORE, AND V. Y. SHEN, *Software Engineering Metrics and Models,* Benjamin/Cummings, Menlo Park, CA, 1986. (Chapters 4, 10, and 12)

[Coolahan and Roussopoulos, 1983] J. E. COOLAHAN, JR., AND N. ROUSSOPOULOS, "Timing Requirements for Time-Driven Systems Using Augmented Petri Nets," *IEEE Transactions on Software Engineering* **SE-9** (September 1983), pp. 603–616. (Chapter 8)

[Coomber and Childs, 1990] C. J. COOMBER AND R. E. CHILDS, "A Graphical Tool for the Prototyping of Real-Time Systems," *ACM SIGSOFT Software Engineering Notes* **15** (April 1990), pp. 70–82. (Chapter 7)

[Côté, Bourque, Oligny, and Rivard, 1988] V. CÔTÉ, P. BOURQUE, S. OLIGNY, AND N. RIVARD, "Software Metrics: An Overview of Recent Results," *Journal of Systems and Software* **8** (March 1988), pp. 121–131. (Chapter 4)

[Coulter, 1983] N. S. COULTER, "Software Science and Cognitive Psychology," *IEEE Transactions on Software Engineering* **SE-9** (March 1983), pp. 166–171. (Chapters 4, 10, and 12)

[Cox, 1986] B. J. COX, *Object-Oriented Programming: An Evolutionary Approach,* Addison-Wesley, Reading, MA, 1986. (Chapter 6)

[Cox, 1990] B. J. COX, "There *Is* a Silver Bullet," *Byte* **15** (October 1990), pp. 209–218. (Chapter 2)

[Crossman, 1982] T. D. CROSSMAN, "Inspection Teams, Are They Worth It?" *Proceedings of the Second National Symposium on EDP Quality Assurance,* Chicago, November 1982. (Chapter 12)

[Currit, Dyer, and Mills, 1986] P. A. CURRIT, M. DYER, AND H. D. MILLS, "Certifying the Reliability of Software," *IEEE Transactions on Software Engineering* **SE-12** (January 1986), pp. 3–11. (Chapter 3)

[Dahl, Dijkstra, and Hoare, 1972] O.-J. DAHL, E. W. DIJKSTRA, AND C. A. R. HOARE, *Structured*

Programming, Academic Press, New York, 1972. (Chapter 5)

[Dahl, Myrhaug, and Nygaard, 1973] O.-J DAHL, B. MYRHAUG, AND K. NYGAARD, *SIMULA begin,* Auerbach, Philadelphia, 1973. (Chapter 6)

[Dahl and Nygaard, 1966] O.-J DAHL AND K. NYGAARD, "SIMULA—An ALGOL-Based Simulation Language," *Communications of the ACM* **9** (September 1966), pp. 671–678. (Chapter 6)

[Daly, 1977] E. B. DALY, "Management of Software Development," *IEEE Transactions on Software Engineering* **SE-3** (May 1977), pp. 229–242. (Chapter 1)

[Dart, Ellison, Feiler, and Habermann, 1987] S. A. DART, R. J. ELLISON, P. H. FEILER, AND A. N. HABERMANN, "Software Development Environments," *IEEE Computer* **20** (November 1987), pp. 18–28. (Chapters 8 and 13)

[Dasarathy, 1985] B. DASARATHY, "Timing Constraints of Real-Time Systems: Constructs for Expressing Them, Methods of Validating Them," *IEEE Transactions on Software Engineering* **SE-11** (January 1985), pp. 80–86. (Chapter 12)

[Dasgupta and Pearce, 1972] A. K. DASGUPTA AND D. W. PEARCE, *Cost-Benefit Analysis,* Macmillan, London, 1972. (Chapter 4)

[Date, 1990] C. J. DATE, *An Introduction to Database Systems*, Fifth Edition, Addison-Wesley, Reading, MA, 1990. (Chapter 12)

[Davis, 1993] A. M. DAVIS, "Software Requirements: Objects, Functions, and States," Revised Edition, Prentice-Hall, Englewood Cliffs, NJ, 1993. (Chapter 7)

[Davis, Bersoff, and Comer, 1988] A. M. DAVIS, E. H. BERSOFF, AND E. R. COMER, "A Strategy for Comparing Alternative Software Development Life Cycle Models," *IEEE Transactions on Software Engineering* **14** (October 1988), pp. 1453–1461. (Chapter 3)

[Dawood, 1994] M. DAWOOD, "It's Time for ISO 9000," *CrossTalk* (March 1994) pp. 26–28. (Chapter 3)

[de Champeaux and Faure, 1992] D. DE CHAMPEAUX AND P. FAURE, "A Comparative Study of Object-Oriented Analysis Methods," *Journal of Object-Oriented Programming* **5** (March/April 1992), pp. 21–33. (Chapter 9)

[Delisle and Garlan, 1990] N. DELISLE AND D. GARLAN, "A Formal Description of an Oscilloscope," *IEEE Software* **7** (September 1990), pp. 29–36. (Chapter 8)

[Delisle and Schwartz, 1987] N. DELISLE AND M. SCHWARTZ, "A Programming Environment for CSP," *Proceedings of the Second ACM SIGSOFT/ SIGPLAN Software Engineering Symposium on Practical Software Development Environments, ACM SIGPLAN Notices* **22** (January 1987), pp. 34–41. (Chapter 8)

[DeMarco, 1978] T. DEMARCO, *Structured Analysis and System Specification*, Yourdon Press, New York, 1978. (Chapter 8)

[DeMarco, 1986] T. DEMARCO, *Controlling Software Projects: Management, Measurement, and Estimation*, Second Edition, Yourdon Press, Englewood Cliffs, NJ, 1986. (Chapter 10)

[DeMarco and Lister, 1987] T. DEMARCO AND T. LISTER, *Peopleware: Productive Projects and Teams*, Dorset House, New York, 1987. (Chapters 1 and 12)

[DeMarco and Lister, 1989] T. DEMARCO AND T. LISTER, "Software Development: The State of the Art vs. State of the Practice," *Proceedings of the 11th International Conference on Software Engineering*, Pittsburgh, May 1989, pp. 271–275. (Chapters 1 and 2)

[DeMillo, Lipton, and Perlis, 1979] R. A. DEMILLO, R. J. LIPTON, AND A. J. PERLIS, "Social Processes and Proofs of Theorems and Programs," *Communications of the ACM* **22** (May 1979), pp. 271–280. (Chapter 5)

[DeMillo, Lipton, and Sayward, 1978] R. A. DEMILLO, R. J. LIPTON, AND F. G. SAYWARD, "Hints on Test Data Selection: Help for the Practicing Programmer," *IEEE Computer* **11** (April 1978), pp. 34–43. (Chapter 5)

[Deming, 1986] W. E. DEMING, *Out of the Crisis*, MIT Center for Advanced Engineering Study, Cambridge, MA, 1986. (Chapter 3)

[Deo, 1983] N. DEO, *System Simulation with Digital Computer*, Prentice-Hall, Englewood Cliffs, NJ, 1983. (Chapter 10)

[DeRemer and Kron, 1976] F. DEREMER AND H. H. KRON, "Programming-in-the-Large versus Programming-in-the-Small," *IEEE Transactions on Software Engineering* **SE-2** (June 1976), pp. 80–86. (Chapter 4)

[Dijkstra, 1968a] E. W. DIJKSTRA, "Go To Statement Considered Harmful," *Communications of the ACM* **11** (March 1968), pp. 147–148. (Chapter 12)

[Dijkstra, 1968b] E. W. DIJKSTRA, "The Structure of the 'THE' Multiprogramming System," *Communications of the ACM* **11** (May 1968), pp. 341–346. (Chapter 6)

[Dijkstra, 1968c] E. W. DIJKSTRA, "A Constructive Approach to the Problem of Program Correctness," *BIT* **8** (No. 3, 1968), pp. 174–186. (Chapter 5)

[Dijkstra, 1972] E. W. DIJKSTRA, "The Humble Programmer," *Communications of the ACM* **15** (October 1972), pp. 859–866. (Chapter 5)

[Dijkstra, 1976] E. W. DIJKSTRA, *A Discipline of Programming*, Prentice-Hall, Englewood Cliffs, NJ, 1976. (Chapters 4 and 5)

[Diller, 1990] A. DILLER, *Z: An Introduction to Formal Methods*, John Wiley and Sons, Chichester, UK, 1990. (Chapter 8)

[Dion, 1993] R. DION, "Process Improvement and the Corporate Balance Sheet," *IEEE Software* **10** (July 1993), pp. 28–35. (Chapter 3)

[Dix, Finlay, Abowd, and Beale, 1993] A. DIX, J. FINLAY, G. ABOWD, AND R. BEALE, *Human–Computer Interaction*, Prentice-Hall, Englewood Cliffs, NJ, 1993. (Chapter 7)

[DoD, 1980] "Requirements for the Programming Environment for the Common High-Order Language, STONEMAN," United States Department of Defense, February 1980. (Chapter 13)

[Dolotta, Haight, and Mashey, 1984] T. A. DOLOTTA, R. C. HAIGHT, AND J. R. MASHEY, "UNIX Time-Sharing System: The Programmer's Workbench," in: *Interactive Programming Environments*, D. R. Barstow, H. E. Shrobe, and E. Sandewall (Editors), McGraw-Hill, New York, 1984, pp. 353–369. (Chapter 13)

[Doolan, 1992] E. P. DOOLAN, "Experience with Fagan's Inspection Method," *Software—Practice and Experience* **22** (February 1992), pp. 173–182. (Chapters 5 and 8)

[Dooley and Schach, 1985] J. W. M. DOOLEY AND S. R. SCHACH, "FLOW: A Software Development

Environment Using Diagrams," *Journal of Systems and Software* **5** (August 1985), pp. 203–219. (Chapters 4 and 13)

[Dreger, 1989] J. B. DREGER, *Function Point Analysis,* Prentice-Hall, Englewood Cliffs, NJ, 1989. (Chapter 10)

[Dunn, 1984] R. H. DUNN, *Software Defect Removal,* McGraw-Hill, New York, 1984. (Chapters 5 and 11)

[Dunn and Ullman, 1982] R. DUNN AND R. ULLMAN, *Quality Assurance for Computer Software,* McGraw-Hill, New York, 1982. (Chapter 5)

[Dyer, 1992] M. DYER, *The Cleanroom Approach to Quality Software Development,* John Wiley and Sons, New York, 1992. (Chapters 5 and 12)

[Elshoff, 1976] J. L. ELSHOFF, "An Analysis of Some Commercial PL/I Programs," *IEEE Transactions on Software Engineering* **SE-2** (June 1976), 113–120. (Chapter 1)

[Endres, 1975] A. ENDRES, "An Analysis of Errors and their Causes in System Programs," *IEEE Transactions on Software Engineering* **SE-1** (June 1975), pp. 140–149. (Chapter 12)

[Fagan, 1974] M. E. FAGAN, "Design and Code Inspections and Process Control in the Development of Programs," Technical Report IBM-SSD TR 21.572, IBM Corporation, December 1974. (Chapter 1)

[Fagan, 1976] M. E. FAGAN, "Design and Code Inspections to Reduce Errors in Program Development," *IBM Systems Journal* **15** (No. 3, 1976), pp. 182–211. (Chapters 5, 8 and 11)

[Fagan, 1986] M. E. FAGAN, "Advances in Software Inspections," *IEEE Transactions on Software Engineering* **SE-12** (July 1986), pp. 744–751. (Chapters 5 and 11)

[Faulk and Parnas, 1988] S. R. FAULK AND D. L. PARNAS, "On Synchronization in Hard-Real-Time Systems," *Communications of the ACM* **31** (March 1988), pp. 274–287. (Chapter 11)

[Feldman, 1979] S. I. FELDMAN, "Make—A Program for Maintaining Computer Programs," *Software—Practice and Experience* **9** (April 1979), pp. 225–265. (Chapter 4)

[Feldman, 1981] M. B. FELDMAN, "Data Abstraction, Structured Programming, and the Practicing

Programmer," *Software—Practice and Experience* **11** (July 1981), pp. 697–710. (Chapter 6)

[Fenton, 1994] N. FENTON, "Software Measurement: A Necessary Scientific Basis," *IEEE Transactions on Software Engineering* **20** (March 1994), pp. 199–206. (Chapter 4)

[Ferrentino and Mills, 1977] A. B. FERRENTINO AND H. D. MILLS, "State Machines and Their Semantics in Software Engineering," *Proceedings of the First International Computer Software and Applications Conference, COMPSAC '77*, Chicago, 1977, pp. 242–251. (Chapter 8)

[Fichman and Kemerer, 1992] R. G. FICHMAN AND C. F. KEMERER, "Object-Oriented and Conventional Analysis and Design Methodologies: Comparison and Critique," *IEEE Computer* **25** (October 1992), pp. 22–39. (Chapters 9 and 11)

[Fisher, 1976] D. A. FISHER, "A Common Programming Language for the Department of Defense—Background and Technical Requirements," Report P–1191, Institute for Defense Analyses, Arlington, VA, 1976. (Chapter 12)

[Flanagan, 1996] D. FLANAGAN, *Java in a Nutshell,* O'Reilly and Associates, Sebastopol, CA, 1996. (Chapters 6 and 11)

[Fowler, 1986] P. J. FOWLER, "In-Process Inspections of Workproducts at AT&T," *AT&T Technical Journal* **65** (March/April 1986), pp. 102–112. (Chapter 5)

[Freeman, 1987] P. FREEMAN (Editor), *Tutorial: Software Reusability,* IEEE Computer Society Press, Washington, DC, 1987. (Chapter 6)

[Freeman and Wasserman, 1983] P. FREEMAN AND A. J. WASSERMAN (Editor), *Tutorial: Software Design Techniques,* Fourth Edition, IEEE Computer Society Press, Washington, DC, 1983. (Chapter 11)

[Freiman and Park, 1979] F. R. FREIMAN AND R. E. PARK, "PRICE Software Model—Version 3: An Overview," *Proceedings of the IEEE-PINY Workshop on Quantitative Software Models*, October 1979, pp. 32–41. (Chapter 10)

[Fuggetta, 1993] A. FUGGETTA, "A Classification of CASE Technology," *IEEE Computer* **26** (December 1993), pp. 25–38. (Chapters 4 and 13)

[Fuggetta and Picco, 1994] A. FUGGETTA AND G. P. PICCO, "An Annotated Bibliography on Software Process Improvement," *ACM SIGSOFT Software*

Engineering Notes **19** (July 1994), pp. 66–68. (Chapter 3)

[Gane, 1989] C. GANE, *Rapid System Development: Using Structured Techniques and Relational Technology,* Prentice-Hall, Englewood Cliffs, NJ, 1989. (Chapters 3 and 7)

[Gane and Sarsen, 1979] C. GANE AND T. SARSEN, *Structured Systems Analysis: Tools and Techniques,* Prentice-Hall, Englewood Cliffs, NJ, 1979. (Chapters 8 and 11)

[Garcia-Molina, Germano, and Kohler, 1984] H. GARCIA-MOLINA, F. GERMANO, JR., AND W. H. KOHLER, "Debugging a Distributed Computer System," *IEEE Transactions on Software Engineering* **SE-10** (March 1984), pp. 210–219. (Chapter 12)

[Gargaro and Pappas, 1987] A. GARGARO AND T. L. PAPPAS, "Reusability Issues and Ada," *IEEE Software* **4** (July 1987), pp. 43–51. (Chapter 6)

[Garman, 1981] J. R. GARMAN, "The 'Bug' Heard 'Round the World," *ACM SIGSOFT Software Engineering Notes* **6** (October 1981), pp. 3–10. (Chapter 12)

[Gause and Weinberg, 1990] D. C. GAUSE AND G. M. WEINBERG, *Are Your Lights On? How to Figure Out What the Problem Is,* Dorset House, New York, 1990. (Chapter 7)

[Gelperin and Hetzel, 1988] D. GELPERIN AND B. HETZEL, "The Growth of Software Testing," *Communications of the ACM* **31** (June 1988), pp. 687–695. (Chapter 5)

[Ghezzi and Mandrioli, 1987] C. GHEZZI AND D. MANDRIOLI, "On Eclecticism in Specifications: A Case Study Centered around Petri Nets," *Proceedings of the Fourth International Workshop on Software Specification and Design,* Monterey, CA, 1987, pp. 216–224. (Chapter 8)

[Gibbs, 1994] W. W. GIBBS, "Software's Chronic Crisis," *Scientific American* **271** (September 1994), pp. 86–95. (Chapter 1)

[Gibson and Jackson, 1987] C. F. GIBSON AND B. B. JACKSON, *The Information Imperative: Managing the Impact of Information Technology on Business and People*, Lexington Books, Lexington, MA, 1987. (Chapter 7)

[Gifford and Spector, 1987] D. GIFFORD AND A. SPECTOR, "Case Study: IBM's System/360-370

Architecture," *Communications of the ACM* **30** (April 1987), pp. 292–307. (Chapter 12)

[Gilb, 1988] T. GILB, *Principles of Software Engineering Management,* Addison-Wesley, Wokingham, UK, 1988. (Chapter 3)

[Glass, 1982] R. L. GLASS, "Real-Time Checkout: The 'Source Error First' Approach," *Software—Practice and Experience* **12** (January 1982), pp. 77–83. (Chapter 12)

[Glass, 1983] R. L. GLASS (Editor), *Real-Time Software,* Prentice-Hall, Englewood Cliffs, NJ, 1983. (Chapter 12)

[Glass and Noiseux, 1981] R. L. GLASS AND R. A. NOISEUX, *Software Maintenance Guidebook*, Prentice-Hall, Englewood Cliffs, NJ, 1981. (Chapter 14)

[Goel, 1985] A. L. GOEL, "Software Reliability Models: Assumptions, Limitations, and Applicability," *IEEE Transactions on Software Engineering* **SE-11** (December 1985), pp. 1411–1423. (Chapter 12)

[Goldberg, 1984] A. GOLDBERG, *Smalltalk-80: The Interactive Programming Environment,* Addison-Wesley, Reading, MA, 1984. (Chapter 13)

[Goldberg, 1986] R. GOLDBERG, "Software Engineering: An Emerging Discipline," *IBM Systems Journal* **25** (No. 3/4, 1986), pp. 334–353. (Chapters 1 and 2)

[Goldberg and Robson, 1989] A. GOLDBERG AND D. ROBSON, *Smalltalk-80: The Language,* Addison-Wesley, Reading, MA, 1989. (Chapters 6 and 11)

[Gomaa, 1986] H. GOMAA, "Software Development of Real-Time Systems," *Communications of the ACM* **29** (July 1986), pp. 657–668. (Chapter 11)

[Goodenough, 1979] J. B. GOODENOUGH, "A Survey of Program Testing Issues," in: *Research Directions in Software Technology,* P. Wegner (Editor), The MIT Press, Cambridge, MA, 1979, pp. 316–340. (Chapter 5)

[Goodenough and Gerhart, 1975] J. B. GOODENOUGH AND S. L. GERHART, "Toward a Theory of Test Data Selection," *Proceedings of the Third International Conference on Reliable Software,* Los Angeles, 1975, pp. 493–510. Also published in *IEEE Transactions on Software Engineering* **SE-1** (June 1975), pp. 156–173. Revised version: J. B. Goodenough, and S. L. Gerhart, "Toward a

Theory of Test Data Selection: Data Selection Criteria," in: *Current Trends in Programming Methodology, Volume 2*. R. T. Yeh (Editor), Prentice-Hall, Englewood Cliffs, NJ, 1977, pp. 44–79. (Chapters 5 and 8)

[Gordon, 1979] M. J. C. GORDON, *The Denotational Description of Programming Languages: An Introduction*, Springer-Verlag, New York, 1979. (Chapter 8)

[Gordon and Bieman, 1995] V. S. GORDON AND J. M. BIEMAN, "Rapid Prototyping Lessons Learned," *IEEE Software* **12** (January 1995). pp. 85–95. (Chapter 7)

[Grady, 1992] R. B. GRADY, *Practical Software Metrics for Project Management and Process Improvement*, Prentice-Hall, Englewood Cliffs, NJ, 1992. (Chapters 4 and 12)

[Grady, 1994] R. B. GRADY, "Successfully Applying Software Metrics," *IEEE Computer* **27** (September 1994), pp. 18–25. (Chapter 1)

[Grant, 1985] F. J. GRANT, "The Downside of 4GLs," *Datamation* **31** (July 15, 1985), pp. 99–104. (Chapter 12)

[Gremillion, 1984] L. L. GREMILLION, "Determinants of Program Repair Maintenance Requirements," *Communications of the ACM* **27** (August 1984), pp. 826–832. (Chapter 12)

[Guha, Lang, and Bassiouni, 1987] R. K. GUHA, S. D. LANG, AND M. BASSIOUNI, "Software Specification and Design Using Petri Nets," *Proceedings of the Fourth International Workshop on Software Specification and Design*, Monterey, CA, April 1987, pp. 225–230. (Chapter 8)

[Guimaraes, 1983] T. GUIMARAES, "Managing Application Program Maintenance Expenditures," *Communications of the ACM* **26** (October 1983), pp. 739–746. (Chapter 14)

[Guimaraes, 1985] T. GUIMARAES, "A Study of Application Program Development Techniques," *Communications of the ACM* **28** (May 1985), pp. 494–499. (Chapter 12)

[Guttag, 1977] J. GUTTAG, "Abstract Data Types and the Development of Data Structures," *Communications of the ACM* **20** (June 1977), pp. 396–404. (Chapter 6)

[Habermann and Notkin, 1986] A. N. HABERMANN AND D. NOTKIN, "Gandalf: Software Development Environments," *IEEE Transactions on Software Engineering* **SE-12** (December 1986), pp. 1117–1127. (Chapter 13)

[Hall, 1990] A. HALL, "Seven Myths of Formal Methods," *IEEE Software* **7** (September 1990) pp. 11–19. (Chapter 8)

[Halstead, 1977] M. H. HALSTEAD, *Elements of Software Science*, Elsevier North-Holland, New York, 1977. (Chapters 10 and 12)

[Hamer and Frewin, 1982] P. G. HAMER AND G. D. FREWIN, "M. H. Halstead's Software Science—A Critical Examination," *Proceedings of the Sixth International Conference on Software Engineering*, Tokyo, 1982, pp. 197–205. (Chapter 10)

[Hansen, 1983] K. HANSEN, *Data Structured Program Design*, Ken Orr and Associates, Topeka, KS, 1983. (Chapter 11)

[Harel, 1987] D. HAREL, "Statecharts: A Visual Formalism for Complex Systems," *Science of Computer Programming* **8** (June 1987), pp. 231–274. (Chapter 8)

[Harel, 1992] D. HAREL, "Biting the Silver Bullet," *IEEE Computer* **25** (January 1992), pp. 8–24. (Chapter 2)

[Harel et al., 1990] D. HAREL, H. LACHOVER, A. NAAMAD, A. PNUELI, M. POLITI, R. SHERMAN, A. SHTULL-TRAURING, AND M. TRAKHTENBROT, "STATEMATE: A Working Environment for the Development of Complex Reactive Systems," *IEEE Transactions on Software Engineering* **16** (April 1990), pp. 403–414. (Chapters 8 and 13)

[Harrold and Soffa, 1991] M. J. HARROLD AND M. L. SOFFA, "Selecting and Using Data for Integration Testing," *IEEE Software* **8** (March 1991), pp. 58–65. (Chapter 13)

[Harrold, McGregor, and Fitzpatrick, 1992] M. J. HARROLD, J. D. MCGREGOR, AND K. J. FITZPATRICK, "Incremental Testing of Object-Oriented Class Structures," *Proceedings of the 14th International Conference on Software Engineering*, Melbourne, Australia, May 1992, pp. 68–80. (Chapter 12)

[Hatley and Pirbhai, 1987] D. J. HATLEY AND I. A. PIRBHAI, *Strategies for Real-Time System Specification*, Dorset House, New York, 1987. (Chapter 11)

[Helmer-Hirschberg, 1966] O. HELMER-HIRSCHBERG, *Social Technology*, Basic Books, New York, 1966. (Chapter 10)

[Henderson-Sellers and Edwards, 1990] B. HENDERSON-SELLERS AND J. M. EDWARDS, "The Object-Oriented Systems Life Cycle," *Communications of the ACM* **33** (September 1990), pp. 142–159. (Chapters 3 and 9)

[Henry and Humphrey, 1990] S. M. HENRY AND M. HUMPHREY, "A Controlled Experiment to Evaluate Maintainability of Object-Oriented Software," *Proceedings of the IEEE Conference on Software Maintenance*, San Diego, CA, November 1990, pp. 258–265. (Chapter 14)

[Henry and Kafura, 1981] S. M. HENRY AND D. KAFURA, "Software Structure Metrics Based on Information Flow," *IEEE Transactions on Software Engineering* **SE-7** (September 1981), pp. 510–518. (Chapter 11)

[Henry and Selig, 1990] S. HENRY AND C. SELIG, "Predicting Source-Code Complexity at the Design Stage," *IEEE Software* **7** (March 1990), pp. 36–44, (Chapter 11)

[Henry, Henry, Kafura, and Matheson, 1994] J. HENRY, S. HENRY, D. KAFURA, AND L. MATHESON, "Improving Software Maintenance at Martin Marietta," *IEEE Software* **11** (July 1994), pp. 67–75. (Chapter 14)

[Hetzel, 1988] W. C. HETZEL, *The Complete Guide to Software Testing*, Second Edition, QED Information Systems, Wellesley, MA, 1988. (Chapter 5)

[Hicks and Card, 1994] M. HICKS AND D. CARD, "Tales of Process Improvement," *IEEE Software* **11** (January 1994), pp. 114–115. (Chapter 3)

[Hoare, 1969] C. A. R. HOARE, "An Axiomatic Basis for Computer Programming," *Communications of the ACM* **12** (October 1969), pp. 576–583. (Chapter 5)

[Hoare, 1981] C. A. R. HOARE, "The Emperor's Old Clothes," *Communications of the ACM* **24** (February 1981), pp. 75–83. (Chapter 5)

[Hoare, 1985] C. A. R. HOARE, *Communicating Sequential Processes*, Prentice-Hall International, Englewood Cliffs, NJ, 1985. (Chapter 8)

[Hoare, 1987] C. A. R. HOARE, "An Overview of Some Formal Methods for Program Design," *IEEE Computer* **20** (September 1987), pp. 85–91. (Chapter 11)

[Honiden, Kotaka, Kishimoto, 1993] S. HONIDEN, N. KOTAKA, AND Y. KISHIMOTO, "Formalizing Specification Modeling in OOA," *IEEE Software* **10** (January 1993), pp. 54–66. (Chapter 9)

[Houghton, 1984] R. C. HOUGHTON, JR., "Online Help Systems: A Conspectus," *Communications of the ACM* **27** (February 1984), pp. 126–133. (Chapter 4)

[House and Newman, 1989] D. E. HOUSE AND W. F. NEWMAN, "Testing Large Software Products," *ACM SIGSOFT Software Engineering Notes* **14** (April 1989), pp. 71–78. (Chapter 13)

[Howden, 1987] W. E. HOWDEN, *Functional Program Testing and Analysis*, McGraw-Hill, New York, 1987. (Chapter 12)

[Hsia, Davis, and Kung, 1993] P. HSIA, A. DAVIS, AND D. KUNG, "Status Report: Requirements Engineering," *IEEE Software* **10** (November 1993), pp. 75–79. (Chapter 7)

[Humphrey, 1989] W. S. HUMPHREY, *Managing the Software Process*, Addison-Wesley, Reading, MA, 1989. (Chapter 3)

[Humphrey, 1995] W. S. HUMPHREY, *A Discipline for Software Engineering*, Addison-Wesley, Reading, MA, 1995 (Chapter 3)

[Humphrey, Snider, and Willis, 1991] W. S. HUMPHREY, T. R. SNIDER, AND R. R. WILLIS, "Software Process Improvement at Hughes Aircraft," *IEEE Software* **8** (July 1991), pp. 11–23. (Chapter 3)

[Hwang, 1981] S.-S. V. HWANG, "An Empirical Study in Functional Testing, Structural Testing, and Code Reading Inspection," Scholarly Paper 362, Department of Computer Science, University of Maryland, College Park, MD, 1981. (Chapter 12)

[IEEE 610.12, 1990] "A Glossary of Software Engineering Terminology," IEEE 610.12-1990, Institute of Electrical and Electronic Engineers, Inc., 1990. (Chapter 5)

[IEEE 1028, 1988] "Standard for Software Reviews and Audits," IEEE 1028, Institute of Electrical and Electronic Engineers, Inc., 1988. (Chapter 5)

[IEEE 1058.1, 1987] "Standard for Software Project Management Plans," IEEE 1058.1, Institute of Electrical and Electronic Engineers, Inc., 1987. (Chapter 10)

[ISO 9000–3, 1991] "ISO 9000–3, Guidelines for the Application of ISO 9001 to the Development,

Supply, and Maintenance of Software,"
International Organization for Standardization,
Geneva, 1991. (Chapter 3)

[ISO 9001, 1987] "ISO 9001, Quality Systems—Model
for Quality Assurance in Design/Development,
Production, Installation, and Servicing,"
International Organization for Standardization,
Geneva, 1987. (Chapter 3)

[ISO-7185, 1980] "Specification for the Computer
Programming Language Pascal," ISO-7185,
International Standards Organization, 1980.
(Chapter 12)

[ISO/IEC 8652, 1995] "Programming Language Ada:
Language and Standard Libraries," ISO/IEC 8652,
International Organization for Standardization,
International Electrotechnical Commission, 1995.
(Chapters 6, 11, and 12)

[IWSSD, 1986] Call for Papers, Fourth International
Workshop on Software Specification and Design,
ACM SIGSOFT Software Engineering Notes **11**
(April 1986), pp. 94–96. (Chapter 8)

[Jackson, 1975] M. A. JACKSON, *Principles of Program
Design,* Academic Press, New York, 1975.
(Chapter 11)

[Jackson, 1983] M. A. JACKSON, *System Development*,
Prentice-Hall, Englewood Cliffs, NJ, 1983.
(Chapters 8 and 11)

[Jacob, 1985] R. J. K. JACOB, "A State Transition
Diagram Language for Visual Programming,"
IEEE Computer **18** (August 1985), pp. 51–59.
(Chapter 8)

[Jacobson, Christerson, Jonsson, and Overgaard, 1992]
I. JACOBSON, M. CHRISTERSON, P. JONSSON, AND G.
OVERGAARD, *Object-Oriented Software
Engineering: A Use Case Driven Approach*, ACM
Press, New York, 1992. (Chapters 9 and 11)

[Jain, 1991] R. JAIN, *The Art of Computer Systems
Performance Analysis: Techniques for
Experimental Design, Measurement, Simulation,
and Modeling*, John Wiley and Sons, New York,
1991. (Chapter 8)

[Jeffrey, Low, and Barnes, 1993] D. R. JEFFREY, G. C.
LOW, AND M. BARNES, "A Comparison of Function
Point Counting Techniques," *IEEE Transactions
on Software Engineering* **19** (May 1993), pp. 529–
532. (Chapter 10)

[Jensen and Wirth, 1975] K. JENSEN AND N. WIRTH,
Pascal User Manual and Report, Second Edition,
Springer-Verlag, New York, 1975. (Chapter 12)

[Johnson, 1979] S. C. JOHNSON, "A Tour through the
Portable C Compiler," Seventh Edition, UNIX
Programmer's Manual, Bell Laboratories, Murray
Hill, NJ, January 1979. (Chapter 12)

[Johnson and Ritchie, 1978] S. C. JOHNSON AND D. M.
RITCHIE, "Portability of C Programs and the UNIX
System," *Bell System Technical Journal* **57** (No.
6, Part 2, 1978), pp. 2021–2048. (Chapter 12)

[Jones, 1978] T. C. JONES, "Measuring Programming
Quality and Productivity," *IBM Systems Journal*
17 (No. 1, 1978), pp. 39–63. (Chapters 5 and 6)

[Jones, 1984] T. C. JONES, "Reusability in
Programming: A Survey of the State of the Art,"
IEEE Transactions on Software Engineering **SE-
10** (September 1984), pp. 488–494. (Chapter 6)

[Jones, 1986a] C. JONES, *Programming Productivity*,
McGraw-Hill, New York, 1986. (Chapters 10
and 12)

[Jones, 1986b] C. B. JONES, *Systematic Software
Development Using VDM*, Prentice-Hall,
Englewood Cliffs, NJ, 1986. (Chapter 8)

[Jones, 1987] C. JONES, Letter to the Editor, *IEEE
Computer* **20** (December 1987), p. 4. (Chapter 10)

[Joos, 1994] R. JOOS, "Software Reuse at Motorola,"
IEEE Software **11** (September 1994), pp. 42–47.
(Chapter 6)

[Jorgensen and Erikson, 1994] P. C. JORGENSEN AND C.
ERIKSON, "Object-Oriented Integration Testing,"
Communications of the ACM **37** (September
1994), pp. 30–38. (Chapter 13)

[Josephson, 1992] M. JOSEPHSON, *Edison, A Biography*,
John Wiley and Sons, New York, 1992.
(Chapter 1)

[Juran, 1988] J. M. JURAN, *Juran on Planning for
Quality*, Macmillan, New York, 1988. (Chapter 3)

[Kampen, 1987] G. R. KAMPEN, "An Eclectic
Approach to Specification," *Proceedings of the
Fourth International Workshop on Software
Specification and Design*, Monterey, CA, April
1987, pp. 178–182. (Chapter 8)

[Kan et al., 1994] S. H. KAN, S D. DULL, D. N.
AMUNDSON, R. J. LINDNER, AND R. J. HEDGER,
"AS/400 Software Quality Management," *IBM*

Systems Journal **33** (No. 1, 1994), pp. 62–88. (Chapter 1)

[Kelly and Sherif, 1992] J. C. KELLY AND J. S. SHERIF, "A Comparison of Four Design Methods for Real-Time Software Development," *Information and Software Technology* **34** (February 1992), pp. 74–82 (Chapter 11)

[Kelly, Sherif, and Hops, 1992] J. C. KELLY, J. S. SHERIF, AND J. HOPS, "An Analysis of Defect Densities Found during Software Inspections," *Journal of Systems and Software* **17** (January 1992), pp. 111–117. (Chapters 1 and 5)

[Kemerer, 1987] C. F. KEMERER, "An Empirical Validation of Software Cost Estimation Models," *Communications of the ACM* **30** (May 1987), pp. 416–429. (Chapter 10)

[Kemerer, 1993] C. F. KEMERER, "Reliability of Function Points Measurement: A Field Experiment," *Communications of the ACM* **36** (February 1993), pp. 85–97. (Chapter 10)

[Kemerer and Porter, 1992] C. F. KEMERER AND B. S. PORTER, "Improving the Reliability of Function Point Measurement: An Empirical Study," *IEEE Transactions on Software Engineering* **18** (November 1992), pp. 1011–1024. (Chapter 10)

[Kernighan and Plauger, 1974] B. W. KERNIGHAN AND P. J. PLAUGER, *The Elements of Programming Style,* McGraw-Hill, New York, 1974. (Chapter 12)

[Kernighan and Ritchie, 1978] B. W. KERNIGHAN AND D. M. RITCHIE, *The C Programming Language*, Prentice-Hall, Englewood Cliffs, NJ, 1978. (Chapter 12)

[King, 1988] D. KING, *Creating Effective Software: Computer Program Design Using the Jackson Methodology*, Prentice-Hall, Englewood Cliffs, NJ, 1988. (Chapter 11)

[King and Schrems, 1978] J. L. KING AND E. L. SCHREMS, "Cost-Benefit Analysis in Information Systems Development and Operation," *ACM Computer Surveys* **10** (March 1978), pp. 19–34. (Chapter 4)

[Kitchenham and Känsälä, 1993] B. KITCHENHAM AND K. KÄNSÄLÄ, "Inter-Item Correlations among Function Points," *Proceedings of the Fifteenth International Conference on Software Engineering,* Baltimore, MD, May 1993, pp. 477–480. (Chapter 10)

[Kitchenham, Pickard, and Linkman, 1990] B. A. KITCHENHAM, L. M. PICKARD, AND S. J. LINKMAN, "An Evaluation of Some Design Metrics," *Software Engineering Journal* **5** (January 1990), pp. 50–58. (Chapter 11)

[Kitson and Masters, 1993] D. H. KITSON AND S. M. MASTERS, "An Analysis of SEI Software Process Assessment Results: 1987–1991," *Proceedings of the Fifteenth International Conference on Software Engineering*, Baltimore, MD, May 1993, pp. 68–77. (Chapter 3)

[Klunder, 1988] D. KLUNDER, "Hungarian Naming Conventions," Technical Report, Microsoft Corporation, Redmond, WA, January 1988. (Chapter 12)

[Kmielcik et al., 1984] J. KMIELCIK ET AL., "SCR Methodology User's Manual," Grumman Aerospace Corporation, Report SRSR-A6-84-002, 1984. (Chapter 11)

[Knuth, 1968] D. E. KNUTH, *The Art of Computer Programming, Volume I, Fundamental Algorithms,* Addison-Wesley, Reading, MA, 1968. (Chapter 8)

[Knuth, 1974] D. E. KNUTH, "Structured Programming with **go to** Statements," *ACM Computing Surveys* **6** (December 1974), pp. 261–301. (Chapters 6 and 12)

[Korson and McGregor, 1990] T. KORSON AND J. D. MCGREGOR, "Understanding Object-Oriented: A Unifying Paradigm," *Communications of the ACM* **33** (September 1990), pp. 40–60. (Chapter 6)

[Kramer, 1994] J. KRAMER, "Distributed Software Engineering," *Proceedings of the 16th International Conference on Software Engineering*, Sorrento, Italy, May 1994, pp. 253–263. (Chapters 8 and 11)

[Kurki-Suonio, 1993] R. KURKI-SUONIO, "Stepwise Design of Real-Time Systems," *IEEE Transactions on Software Engineering* **19** (January 1993), pp. 56–69. (Chapter 4)

[Lamport, 1980] L. LAMPORT, " 'Sometime' Is Sometimes 'Not Never': On the Temporal Logic of Programs," *Proceedings of the Seventh Annual ACM Symposium on Principles of Programming Languages*, Las Vegas, NV, 1980, pp. 174–185. (Chapter 5)

[Landis et al., 1992] L. LANDIS, S. WALIGARA, F. MCGARRY, ET AL., "Recommended Approach to Software Development: Revision 3," Technical Report SEL-81-305, Software Engineering Laboratory, Greenbelt, MD, June 1992. (Chapter 3)

[Landwehr, 1983] C. E. LANDWEHR, "The Best Available Technologies for Computer Security," *IEEE Computer* **16** (July 1983), pp. 86–100. (Chapter 5)

[Lanergan and Grasso, 1984] R. G. LANERGAN AND C. A. GRASSO, "Software Engineering with Reusable Designs and Code," *IEEE Transactions on Software Engineering* **SE-10** (September 1984), pp. 498–501. (Chapter 6)

[Lantz, 1985] K. E. LANTZ, *The Prototyping Methodology*, Prentice-Hall, Englewood Cliffs, NJ, 1985. (Chapters 3 and 7)

[Leavenworth, 1970] B. LEAVENWORTH, Review #19420, *Computing Reviews* **11** (July 1970), pp. 396–397. (Chapters 5 and 8)

[Lecarme and Gart, 1986] O. LECARME AND M. P. GART, *Software Portability*, McGraw-Hill, New York, 1986. (Chapter 12)

[Lederer and Prasad, 1992] A. L. LEDERER AND J. PRASAD, "Nine Management Guidelines for Better Cost Estimating," *Communications of the ACM* **35** (February 1992), pp. 51–59. (Chapter 10)

[Ledgard, 1975] H. LEDGARD, *Programming Proverbs*, Hayden Books, Rochelle Park, NJ, 1975. (Chapter 12)

[Lejter, Meyers, and Reiss, 1992] M. LEJTER, S. MEYERS, AND S. P. REISS, "Support for Maintaining Object-Oriented Programs," *IEEE Transactions on Software Engineering* **18** (December 1992), pp. 1045–1052. (Chapter 14)

[Leveson and Turner, 1993] N. G. LEVESON AND C. S. TURNER, "An Investigation of the Therac-25 Accidents," *IEEE Computer* **26** (July 1993), pp. 18–41. (Chapter 1)

[Levi and Agrawala, 1990] S.-T. LEVI AND A. K. AGRAWALA, *Real Time System Design,* McGraw-Hill, New York, 1990. (Chapter 11)

[Licker, 1985] P. S. LICKER, *The Art of Managing Software Development People*, John Wiley and Sons, New York, 1985. (Chapter 12)

[Lientz and Swanson, 1980] B. P. LIENTZ AND E. B. SWANSON, *Software Maintenance Management: A Study of the Maintenance of Computer Applications Software in 487 Data Processing Organizations,* Addison-Wesley, Reading, MA, 1980. (Chapter 14)

[Lientz, Swanson, and Tompkins, 1978] B. P. LEINTZ, E. B. SWANSON, AND G. E. TOMPKINS, "Characteristics of Application Software Maintenance," *Communications of the ACM* **21** (June 1978), pp. 466–471. (Chapters 1 and 14)

[Lim, 1994] W. C. LIM, "Effects of Reuse on Quality, Productivity, and Economics," *IEEE Software* **11** (September 1994), pp. 23–30. (Chapters 6 and 10)

[Linger, 1980] R. C. LINGER, "The Management of Software Engineering. Part III. Software Design Practices," *IBM Systems Journal* **19** (No. 4, 1980), pp. 432–450. (Chapter 8)

[Linger, 1994] R. C. LINGER, "Cleanroom Process Model," *IEEE Software* **11** (March 1994), pp. 50–58. (Chapter 12)

[Linger, Mills, and Witt, 1979] R. C. LINGER, H. D. MILLS, AND B. I. WITT, *Structured Programming: Theory and Practice,* Addison-Wesley, Reading, MA, 1979. (Chapter 5)

[Liskov and Guttag, 1986] B. LISKOV AND J. GUTTAG, *Abstraction and Specification in Program Development,* The MIT Press, Cambridge, MA, 1986. (Chapter 6)

[Liskov, Snyder, Atkinson, and Schaffert, 1977] B. LISKOV, A. SNYDER, R. ATKINSON, AND C. SCHAFFERT, "Abstraction Mechanisms in CLU," *Communications of the ACM* **20** (August 1977), pp. 564–576. (Chapter 12)

[Liskov and Zilles, 1974] B. LISKOV AND S. ZILLES, "Programming with Abstract Data Types," *ACM SIGPLAN Notices* **9** (April 1974), pp. 50–59. (Chapter 6)

[Littlewood and Strigini, 1992] B. LITTLEWOOD AND L. STRIGINI, "The Risks of Software," *Scientific American* **267** (November 1992), pp. 62–75. (Chapter 1)

[London, 1971] R. L. LONDON, "Software Reliability through Proving Programs Correct," *Proceedings of the IEEE International Symposium on Fault-Tolerant Computing*, March 1971. (Chapters 5 and 8)

[Longstreet, 1990] D. H. LONGSTREET (Editor), *Software Maintenance and Computers,* IEEE Computer Society Press, Los Alamitos, CA, 1990. (Chapter 14)

[Low and Jeffrey, 1990] G. C. LOW AND D. R. JEFFREY, "Function Points in the Estimation and Evaluation of the Software Process," *IEEE Transactions on Software Engineering* **16** (January 1990), pp. 64–71. (Chapter 10)

[Luckham and von Henke, 1985] D. C. LUCKHAM AND F. W. VON HENKE, "An Overview of Anna, a Specification Language for Ada," *IEEE Software* **2** (March 1985), pp. 9–22. (Chapter 8)

[Luqi, 1989] LUQI, "Software Evolution through Rapid Prototyping," *IEEE Computer* **22** (May 1989), pp. 13–25. (Chapter 7)

[Luqi and Royce, 1992] LUQI AND W. ROYCE, "Status Report: Computer-Aided Prototyping," *IEEE Software* **9** (November 1992), pp. 77–81. (Chapters 3 and 7)

[Mackenzie, 1980] C. E. MACKENZIE, *Coded Character Sets: History and Development,* Addison-Wesley, Reading, MA, 1980. (Chapter 12)

[Mancl and Havanas, 1990] D. MANCL AND W. HAVANAS, "A Study of the Impact of C++ on Software Maintenance," *Proceedings of the IEEE Conference on Software Maintenance,* San Diego, CA, November 1990, pp. 63–69. (Chapter 14)

[Manna, 1974] Z. MANNA, *Mathematical Theory of Computation,* McGraw-Hill, New York, 1974. (Chapter 5)

[Manna and Pnueli, 1992] Z. MANNA AND A. PNUELI, *The Temporal Logic of Reactive and Concurrent Systems,* Springer-Verlag, New York, 1992. (Chapter 5)

[Manna and Waldinger, 1978] Z. MANNA AND R. WALDINGER, "The Logic of Computer Programming," *IEEE Transactions on Software Engineering* **SE-4** (1978), pp. 199–229. (Chapter 5)

[Mantei, 1981] M. MANTEI, "The Effect of Programming Team Structures on Programming Tasks," *Communications of the ACM* **24** (March 1981), pp. 106–113. (Chapter 12)

[Mantei and Teorey, 1988] M. M. MANTEI AND T. J. TEOREY, "Cost/Benefit Analysis for Incorporating Human Factors in the Software Development Lifecycle," *Communications of the ACM* **31** (April 1988), pp. 428–439. (Chapter 3)

[Martin, 1985] J. MARTIN, *Fourth-Generation Languages, Volumes I, II, and III,* Prentice-Hall, Englewood Cliffs, NJ, 1985. (Chapter 12)

[Martin, 1990] J. MARTIN, *Information Engineering,* Prentice-Hall, Englewood Cliffs, NJ, 1990. (Chapter 13)

[Martin and McClure, 1985] J. P. MARTIN AND C. MCCLURE, *Diagramming Techniques for Analysts and Programmers,* Prentice-Hall, Englewood Cliffs, NJ, 1985. (Chapters 8 and 11)

[Martin and Odell, 1992] J. MARTIN AND J. J. ODELL, *Object-Oriented Analysis and Design,* Prentice-Hall, Englewood Cliffs, NJ, 1992. (Chapters 9 and 11)

[Mason and Carey, 1983] R. E. A. MASON AND T. T. CAREY, "Prototyping Interactive Information Systems," *Communications of the ACM* **26** (May 1983), pp. 347–354. (Chapter 7)

[Mathis, 1986] R. F. MATHIS, "The Last 10 Percent," *IEEE Transactions on Software Engineering* **SE-12** (June 1986), pp. 705–712. (Chapters 1 and 2)

[Matsumoto, 1984] Y. MATSUMOTO, "Management of Industrial Software Production," *IEEE Computer* **17** (February 1984), pp. 59–72. (Chapter 6)

[Matsumoto, 1987] Y. MATSUMOTO, "A Software Factory: An Overall Approach to Software Production," in: *Tutorial: Software Reusability,* P. Freeman (Editor), Computer Society Press, Washington, DC, 1987, pp. 155–178. (Chapter 6)

[Mays, 1994] R. G. MAYS, "Forging a Silver Bullet from the Essence of Software," *IBM Systems Journal* **33** (No. 1, 1994) pp. 20–45. (Chapter 2)

[McCabe, 1976] T. J. MCCABE, "A Complexity Measure," *IEEE Transactions on Software Engineering* **SE-2** (December 1976), pp. 308–320. (Chapters 11 and 12)

[McCabe, 1983] T. J. MCCABE, *Structural Testing,* IEEE Computer Society Press, Los Angeles, 1983. (Chapter 12)

[McCabe and Butler, 1989] T. J. MCCABE AND C. W. BUTLER, "Design Complexity Measurement and Testing," *Communications of the ACM* **32** (December 1989), pp. 1415–1425. (Chapter 12)

[McConnell, 1993] S. MCCONNELL, *Code Complete: A Practical Handbook of Software Construction,*

Microsoft Press, Redmond, WA, 1993. (Chapter 12)

[Mellor, 1994] P. MELLOR, "CAD: Computer-Aided Disaster," Technical Report, Centre for Software Reliability, City University, London, UK, July 1994. (Chapter 1)

[Mercurio, Meyers, Nisbet, and Radin, 1990] V. J. MERCURIO, B. F. MEYERS, A. M. NISBET, AND G. RADIN, "AD/Cycle Strategy and Architecture," *IBM Systems Journal* **29** (No. 2, 1990), pp. 170–188. (Chapter 13)

[Metzger, 1981] P. W. METZGER, *Managing a Programming Project*, Second Edition, Prentice-Hall, Englewood Cliffs, NJ, 1981. (Chapter 12)

[Meyer, 1985] B. MEYER, "On Formalism in Specifications," *IEEE Software* **2** (January 1985), pp. 6–26. (Chapter 8)

[Meyer, 1986] B. MEYER, Genericity versus Inheritance," *Proceedings of the Conference on Object-Oriented Programming Systems, Languages and Applications, ACM SIGPLAN Notices* **21** (November 1986), pp. 391–405. (Chapter 6)

[Meyer, 1987] B. MEYER, "Reusability: The Case for Object-Oriented Design," *IEEE Software* **4** (March 1987), pp. 50–64. (Chapter 6)

[Meyer, 1990] B. MEYER, "Lessons from the Design of the Eiffel Libraries," *Communications of the ACM* **33** (September 1990), pp. 68–88. (Chapters 6, 11, and 14)

[Meyer, 1992a] B. MEYER, "Applying 'Design by Contract'," *IEEE Computer* **25** (October 1992), pp. 40–51. (Chapters 1, 6, and 13)

[Meyer, 1992b] B. MEYER, *Eiffel: The Language*, Prentice-Hall, New York, 1991. (Chapters 5, 6, 11, and 13)

[Miller, 1956] G. A. MILLER, "The Magical Number Seven, Plus or Minus Two: Some Limits on Our Capacity for Processing Information," *The Psychological Review* **63** (March 1956), pp. 81–97. (Chapter 4)

[Mills, 1988] H. D. MILLS, "Stepwise Refinement and Verification in Box-Structured Systems," *IEEE Computer* **21** (June 1988), pp. 23–36. (Chapter 4)

[Mills, Basili, Gannon, and Hamlet, 1987] H. D. MILLS, V. R. BASILI, J. D. GANNON, AND R. G. HAMLET, *Principles of Computer Programming: A Mathematical Approach*, Allyn and Bacon, Newton, MA, 1987. (Chapter 5)

[Mills, Dyer, and Linger, 1987] H. D. MILLS, M. DYER, AND R. C. LINGER, "Cleanroom Software Engineering," *IEEE Software* **4** (September 1987), pp. 19–25. (Chapter 12)

[Mills, Linger, and Hevner, 1987] H. D. MILLS, R. C. LINGER, AND A. R. HEVNER, "Box Structured Information Systems," *IBM Systems Journal* **26** (No. 4, 1987), pp. 395–413. (Chapter 4)

[Mishan, 1982] E. J. MISHAN, *Cost-Benefit Analysis: An Informal Introduction,* Third Edition, George Allen & Unwin, London, 1982. (Chapter 4)

[Misra and Jalics, 1988] S. K. MISRA AND P. J. JALICS, "Third-Generation versus Fourth-Generation Software Development," *IEEE Software* **5** (July 1988), pp. 8–14. (Chapter 12)

[Moder, Phillips, and Davis, 1983] J. J. MODER, C. R. PHILLIPS, AND E. W. DAVIS, *Project Management with CPM, PERT, and Precedence Diagramming*, Third Edition, Van Nostrand Reinhold, New York, 1983. (Chapter 10)

[Monarchi and Puhr, 1992] D. E. MONARCHI AND G. I. PUHR, "A Research Typology for Object-Oriented Analysis and Design," *Communications of the ACM* **35** (September 1992), pp. 35–47. (Chapters 9 and 11)

[Mooney, 1990] J. D. MOONEY, "Strategies for Supporting Application Portability," *IEEE Computer* **23** (November 1990), pp. 59–70. (Chapter 12)

[Moran, 1981] T. P. MORAN (Editor), Special Issue: The Psychology of Human-Computer Interaction, *ACM Computing Surveys* **13** (March 1981). (Chapter 4)

[Munoz, 1988] C. U. MUNOZ, "An Approach to Software Product Testing," *IEEE Transactions on Software Engineering* **14** (November 1988), pp. 1589–1596. (Chapter 13)

[Musa and Everett, 1990] J. D. MUSA AND W. W. EVERETT, "Software-Reliability Engineering: Technology for the 1990s," *IEEE Software* **7** (November 1990), pp. 36–43. (Chapter 12)

[Musa, Iannino, and Okumoto, 1987] J. D. MUSA, A. IANNINO, AND K. OKUMOTO, *Software Reliability: Measurement, Prediction, Application*, McGraw-Hill, New York, 1987. (Chapters 4 and 12)

[Myers, 1975] G. J. MYERS, *Reliable Software through Composite Design*, Petrocelli/Charter, New York, 1975. (Chapter 6)

[Myers, 1976] G. J. MYERS, *Software Reliability: Principles and Practices*, Wiley-Interscience, New York, 1976. (Chapter 12)

[Myers, 1978a] G. J. MYERS, "A Controlled Experiment in Program Testing and Code Walkthroughs/Inspections," *Communications of the ACM* **21** (September 1978), pp. 760–768. (Chapter 12)

[Myers, 1978b] G. J. MYERS, *Composite/Structured Design*, Van Nostrand Reinhold, New York, 1978. (Chapter 6)

[Myers, 1979] G. J. MYERS, *The Art of Software Testing*, John Wiley and Sons, New York, 1979. (Chapters 5, 12, and 13)

[Myers, 1989] W. MYERS, "Allow Plenty of Time for Large-Scale Software," *IEEE Software* **6** (July 1989), pp. 92–99. (Chapter 10)

[Myers, 1992] W. MYERS, "Good Software Practices Pay Off—or Do They?", *IEEE Software* **9** (March 1992), pp. 96–97. (Chapter 4)

[Myers and Rosson, 1992] B. A. MYERS AND M. B. ROSSON, "Survey on User Interface Programming," *Proceedings of ACM SIGCHI Conference on Human Factors in Computing Systems*, Monterey, CA, May 1992, pp. 195–202. (Chapter 7)

[Naur, 1964] P. NAUR, "The Design of the GIER ALGOL Compiler," in: *Annual Review in Automatic Programming, Volume 4*, Pergamon Press, Oxford, UK, 1964, pp. 49–85. (Chapter 8)

[Naur, 1969] P. NAUR, "Programming by Action Clusters, *BIT* **9** (No. 3, 1969), pp. 250–258. (Chapters 5 and 8)

[Naur, Randell, and Buxton, 1976] P. NAUR, B. RANDELL, AND J. N. BUXTON (Editors), *Software Engineering: Concepts and Techniques: Proceedings of the NATO Conferences,* Petrocelli-Charter, New York, 1976. (Chapter 1)

[Neumann, 1980] P. G. NEUMANN, Letter from the Editor, *ACM SIGSOFT Software Engineering Notes* **5** (July 1980), p. 2. (Chapter 1)

[Neumann, 1986] P. G. NEUMANN, "On Hierarchical Design of Computer Systems for Critical Applications," *IEEE Transactions on Software Engineering* **SE-12** (September 1986), pp. 905–920. (Chapter 6)

[New, 1992] R. NEW, Personal Communication, 1992. (Chapter 5)

[Nielsen, 1993] J. NIELSEN, "Iterative User-Interface Design," *IEEE Computer* **26** (November 1993), pp. 32–41. (Chapter 7)

[Nissen and Wallis, 1984] J. NISSEN AND P. WALLIS (Editors), *Portability and Style in Ada*, Cambridge University Press, Cambridge, UK, 1984. (Chapters 6 and 12)

[NIST 151, 1988] "POSIX: Portable Operating System Interface for Computer Environments," Federal Information Processing Standard 151, National Institute of Standards and Technology, Washington, DC, 1988. (Chapter 12)

[Nix and Collins, 1988] C. J. NIX AND B. P. COLLINS, "The Use of Software Engineering, Including the Z Notation, in the Development of CICS," *Quality Assurance* **14** (September 1988), pp. 103–110. (Chapter 8)

[Norden, 1958] P. V. NORDEN, "Curve Fitting for a Model of Applied Research and Development Scheduling," *IBM Journal of Research and Development* **2** (July 1958), pp. 232–248. (Chapter 10)

[Norusis, 1982] M. J. NORUSIS, *SPSS Introductory Guide: Basic Statistics and Operations,* McGraw-Hill, New York, 1982. (Chapter 6)

[Notkin, 1985] D. NOTKIN, "The GANDALF Project," *Journal of Systems and Software* **5** (May 1985), pp. 91–105. (Chapter 13)

[Oest, 1986] O. N. OEST, "VDM From Research to Practice," *Proceedings of the IFIP Congress, Information Processing '86,* 1986, pp. 527–533. (Chapter 8)

[Orr, 1981] K. ORR, *Structured Requirements Definition*, Ken Orr and Associates, Inc., Topeka, KS, 1981. (Chapters 8 and 11)

[Ottenstein, 1979] L. M OTTENSTEIN, "Quantitative Estimates of Debugging Requirements," *IEEE Transactions on Software Engineering* **SE-5** (September 1979), pp. 504–514. (Chapter 12)

[Parikh, 1988] G. PARIKH (Editor), *Techniques of Program and System Maintenance,* Second

Edition, QED Information Services, Wellesley, MA, 1988. (Chapter 14)

[Parnas, 1971] D. L. PARNAS, "Information Distribution Aspects of Design Methodology," *Proceedings of the IFIP Congress*, Ljubljana, Yugoslavia, 1971, pp. 339–344. (Chapters 6 and 11)

[Parnas, 1972a] D. L. PARNAS, "A Technique for Software Module Specification with Examples," *Communications of the ACM* **15** (May 1972), pp. 330–336. (Chapters 6 and 11)

[Parnas, 1972b] D. L. PARNAS, "On the Criteria to Be Used in Decomposing Systems into Modules," *Communications of the ACM* **15** (December 1972), pp. 1053–1058. (Chapters 6 and 11)

[Parnas, 1979] D. L. PARNAS, "Designing Software for Ease of Extension and Contraction," *IEEE Transactions on Software Engineering* **SE-5** (March 1979), pp. 128–138. (Chapter 2)

[Parnas, 1990] D. L. PARNAS, "Education for Computing Professionals," *IEEE Computer* **23** (January 1990), pp. 17–22. (Chapter 1)

[Parnas, 1994] D. L. PARNAS, "Software Aging," *Proceedings of the 16th International Conference on Software Engineering,* Sorrento, Italy, May 1994, pp. 279–287. (Chapter 1)

[Parnas, Clements, and Weiss, 1985] D. L. PARNAS, P. C. CLEMENTS, AND D. M. WEISS, "The Modular Structure of Complex Systems," *IEEE Transactions on Software Engineering* **SE-11** (March 1985), pp. 259–266. (Chapter 6)

[Parnas and Weiss, 1987] D. L. PARNAS AND D. M. WEISS, "Active Design Reviews: Principles and Practices," *Journal of Systems and Software* **7** (December 1987), pp. 259–265. (Chapter 11)

[Paulk, 1995] M. C. PAULK, "How ISO 9001 Compares with the CMM," *IEEE Software* **12** (January 1995), pp. 74–83. (Chapter 3)

[Paulk, Curtis, Chrissis, and Weber, 1993] M. C. PAULK, B. CURTIS, M. B. CHRISSIS, AND C. V. WEBER, "Capability Maturity Model for Software, Version 1.1," Report CMU/SEI-93-TR-24, ADA263403, Software Engineering Institute, Carnegie Mellon University, Pittsburgh, February 1993. (Chapter 3)

[Paulk et al, 1993] M. C. PAULK, C. V. WEBER, S. GARCIA, M. B. CHRISSIS, AND M. BUSH, "Key Practices of the Capability Maturity Model,

Version 1.1," Report CMU/SEI-93-TR-25, ADA263432, Software Engineering Institute, Carnegie Mellon University, Pittsburgh, February 1993. (Chapter 3)

[Perry, 1983] W. E. PERRY, *A Structured Approach to Systems Testing*, Prentice-Hall, Englewood Cliffs, NJ, 1983. (Chapter 11)

[Perry and Kaiser, 1990] D. E. PERRY AND G. E. KAISER, "Adequate Testing and Object-Oriented Programming," *Journal of Object-Oriented Programming* **2** (January/February 1990), pp. 13–19. (Chapter 12)

[Peterson, 1981] J. L. PETERSON, *Petri Net Theory and the Modeling of Systems,* Prentice-Hall, Englewood Cliffs, NJ, 1981. (Chapter 8)

[Petri, 1962] C. A. PETRI, "Kommunikation mit Automaten," Ph.D. Dissertation, University of Bonn, Germany, 1962. (In German.) (Chapter 8)

[Petschenik, 1985] N. H. PETSCHENIK, "Practical Priorities in System Testing," *IEEE Software* **2** (September 1985), pp. 18–23. (Chapter 12)

[Phillips, 1986] J. PHILLIPS, *The NAG Library: A Beginner's Guide*, Clarendon Press, Oxford, UK, 1986. (Chapter 6)

[Pittman, 1993] M. PITTMAN, "Lessons Learned in Managing Object-Oriented Development, *IEEE Software* **10** (January 1993), pp. 43–53. (Chapter 10)

[Pollack, Hicks, and Harrison, 1971] S. L. POLLACK, H. T. HICKS, JR., AND W. J. HARRISON, *Decision Tables: Theory and Practice*, Wiley-Interscience, New York, NY, 1971. (Chapter 8)

[Ponder and Bush, 1994] C. PONDER AND B. BUSH, "Polymorphism Considered Harmful," *ACM SIGSOFT Software Engineering Notes* **19** (April 1994), pp. 35–38. (Chapter 6)

[Poston and Bruen, 1987] R. M. POSTON AND M. W. BRUEN, "Counting Down to Zero Software Failures," *IEEE Software* **4** (September 1987), pp. 54–61. (Chapter 5)

[Preece, 1994] J. PREECE, *Human-Computer Interaction*, Addison-Wesley, Reading, MA, 1994. (Chapter 7)

[Prieto-Díaz, 1991] R. PRIETO-DÍAZ, "Implementing Faceted Classification for Software Reuse," *Communications of the ACM* **34** (May 1991), pp. 88–97. (Chapter 6)

[Prieto-Díaz, 1993] R. PRIETO-DÍAZ, "Status Report: Software Reusability," *IEEE Software* **10** (May 1993), pp. 61–66. (Chapter 6)

[Prieto-Díaz and Freeman, 1987] R. PRIETO-DÍAZ AND P. FREEMAN, "Classifying Software for Reusability," *IEEE Software* **4** (January 1987), pp. 6–16. (Chapter 6)

[Putnam, 1978] L. H. PUTNAM, "A General Empirical Solution to the Macro Software Sizing and Estimating Problem," *IEEE Transactions on Software Engineering* **SE-4** (July 1978), pp. 345–361. (Chapter 10)

[Quirk, 1983] W. J. QUIRK, "Recent Developments in the SPECK Specification System," Report CSS.146, Harwell, UK, 1983. (Chapter 12)

[Quirk, 1985] W. J. QUIRK (Editor), *Verification and Validation of Real-Time Software,* Springer-Verlag, Berlin, 1985. (Chapter 12)

[Rajlich, 1985] V. RAJLICH, "Stepwise Refinement Revisited," *Journal of Systems and Software* **5** (February 1985), pp. 81–88. (Chapter 4)

[Rajlich, 1994] V. RAJLICH, "Decomposition/ Generalization Methodology for Object-Oriented Programming," *Journal of Systems and Software* **24** (February, 1994), pp. 181–186. (Chapter 3)

[Rapps and Weyuker, 1985] S. RAPPS AND E. J. WEYUKER, "Selecting Software Test Data Using Data Flow Information," *IEEE Transactions on Software Engineering* **SE-11** (April 1985), pp. 367–375. (Chapter 12)

[Reifer, 1986] D. J. REIFER (Editor), *Tutorial: Software Management,* Third Edition, IEEE Computer Society Press, Washington, DC, 1986. (Chapter 10)

[Reiss, 1984] S. P. REISS, "Graphical Program Development with PECAN Program Development Systems," *Proceedings of the ACM SIGSOFT/ SIGPLAN Software Engineering Symposium on Practical Software Development Environments, ACM SIGPLAN Notices* **19** (May 1984), pp. 30–41. (Chapter 13)

[Reiss, 1990] S. P. REISS, "Connecting Tools Using Message Passing in the Field Environment," *IEEE Software* **7** (July 1990), pp. 57–66. (Chapter 13)

[Rettig, 1994] M. RETTIG, "Prototyping for Tiny Fingers," *Communications of the ACM* **37** (April 1994), pp. 21–27. (Chapter 7)

[Riehle, 1991] R. RIEHLE, "A Space for CASE," *HP Professional* **5** (July 1991), pp. 40–47. (Chapter 13)

[Rifkin, 1993] S. RIFKIN, Usenet posting <1993Mar1.201334.20244@seas.gwu.edu> on comp.software-eng, March 1, 1993. (Chapter 3)

[Rochkind, 1975] M. J. ROCHKIND, "The Source Code Control System," *IEEE Transactions on Software Engineering* **SE-1** (October 1975), pp. 255–265. (Chapters 4, 13, and 14)

[Ross, 1985] D. T. ROSS, "Applications and Extensions of SADT," *IEEE Computer* **18** (April 1985), pp. 25–34. (Chapter 8)

[Royce, 1970] W. W. ROYCE, "Managing the Development of Large Software Systems: Concepts and Techniques," *1970 WESCON Technical Papers, Western Electric Show and Convention,* Los Angeles, August 1970, pp. A/ 1-1–A/1-9. Reprinted in *Proceedings of the 11th International Conference on Software Engineering,* Pittsburgh, May 1989, pp. 328–338. (Chapter 3)

[Rumbaugh et al., 1991] J. RUMBAUGH, M. BLAHA, W. PREMERLANI, F. EDDY, AND W. LORENSEN, *Object-Oriented Modeling and Design,* Prentice-Hall, Englewood Cliffs, NJ, 1991. (Chapters 9, 11, and 13)

[Russell, 1991] G. W. RUSSELL, "Experience with Inspection in Ultralarge-Scale Developments," *IEEE Software* **8** (January 1991), pp. 25–31. (Chapter 5)

[Sackman, 1970] H. SACKMAN, *Man–Computer Problem Solving: Experimental Evaluation of Time-Sharing and Batch Processing,* Auerbach, Princeton, NJ, 1970. (Chapter 10)

[Sackman, Erikson, and Grant, 1968] H. SACKMAN, W. J. ERIKSON, AND E. E. GRANT, "Exploratory Experimental Studies Comparing Online and Offline Programming Performance," *Communications of the ACM* **11** (January 1968), pp. 3–11. (Chapter 10)

[Saiedien and Kuzara, 1995] H. SAIEDIEN AND R. KUZARA, "SEI Capability Maturity Model's Impact on Contractors," *IEEE Computer* **28** (January 1995), pp. 16–26. (Chapter 3)

[Sammet, 1978] J. E. SAMMET, "The Early History of COBOL," *Proceedings of the History of*

Programming Languages Conference, Los Angeles, 1978, pp. 199–276. (Chapter 12)

[Schach, 1992] S. R. Schach, *Software Reuse: Past, Present, and Future*, Videotape, 150 mins, US-VHS format. IEEE Computer Society Press, Los Alamitos, CA, November 1992. (Chapter 6)

[Schach, 1994] S. R. Schach, "The Economic Impact of Software Reuse on Maintenance," *Journal of Software Maintenance: Research and Practice* **6** (July/August 1994), pp. 185–196. (Chapters 6 and 10)

[Schach, 1996] S. R. Schach, "The Cohesion and Coupling of Objects," *Journal of Object-Oriented Programming* **8** (January 1966), pp. 48–50. (Chapter 6)

[Schach and Stevens-Guille, 1979] S. R. Schach and P. D. Stevens-Guille, "Two Aspects of Computer-Aided Design," *Transactions of the Royal Society of South Africa* **44** (Part 1, 1979), 123–126. (Chapter 6)

[Schach and Wood, 1986] S. R. Schach and P. T. Wood, "An Almost Path-Free Very High-Level Interactive Data Manipulation Language for a Microcomputer-Based Database System," *Software—Practice and Experience* **16** (March 1986), pp. 243–268. (Chapter 7)

[Scheffer, Stone, and Rzepka, 1985] P. A. Scheffer, A. H. Stone, III, and W. E. Rzepka, "A Case Study of SREM," *IEEE Computer* **18** (April 1985), pp. 47–54. (Chapter 8)

[Schneidewind, 1987] N. F. Schneidewind, "The State of Software Maintenance," *IEEE Transactions on Software Engineering* **SE-13** (March 1987), pp. 303–310. (Chapter 14)

[Scholtz et al., 1993] J. Scholtz, S. Chidamber, R. Glass, A. Goerner, M. B. Rosson, M. Stark, and I. Vessey, "Object-Oriented Programming: The Promise and the Reality," *Journal of Systems and Software* **23** (November 1993), pp. 199–204. (Chapter 1)

[Schulmeyer and McManus, 1987] G. G. Schulmeyer and J. I. McManus (Editors), *Handbook of Software Quality Assurance*, Van Nostrand Reinhold, New York, 1987. (Chapter 5)

[Schwartz and Delisle, 1987] M. D. Schwartz and N. M. Delisle, "Specifying a Lift Control System with CSP," *Proceedings of the Fourth International Workshop in Software Specification and Design,* Monterey, CA, April 1987, pp. 21–27. (Chapter 8)

[Seitz, 1985] C. L. Seitz, "The Cosmic Cube," *Communications of the ACM* **28** (January 1985), pp. 22–33. (Chapter 12)

[Selby, 1989] R. W. Selby, "Quantitative Studies of Software Reuse," in: *Software Reusability. Volume II: Applications and Experience*, T. J. Biggerstaff and A. J. Perlis (Editors), ACM Press, New York, 1989, pp. 213–233. (Chapter 6)

[Selby, Basili, and Baker, 1987] R. W. Selby, V. R. Basili, and F. T. Baker, "Cleanroom Software Development: An Empirical Evaluation," *IEEE Transactions on Software Engineering* **SE-13** (September 1987), pp. 1027–1037. (Chapters 3 and 12)

[Shapiro, 1994] F. R. Shapiro, "The First Bug," *Byte* **19** (April 1994), p. 308. (Chapter 1)

[Shaw, 1984] M. Shaw, "Abstraction Techniques in Modern Programming Languages," *IEEE Software* **1** (October 1984), pp. 10–26. (Chapter 6)

[Shaw, 1990] M. Shaw, "Prospects for an Engineering Discipline of Software," *IEEE Software* **7** (November 1990), pp. 15–24. (Chapter 1)

[Shen, Conte, and Dunsmore, 1983] V. Y. Shen, S. D. Conte, and H. E. Dunsmore, "Software Science Revisited: A Critical Analysis of the Theory and Its Empirical Support," *IEEE Transactions on Software Engineering* **SE-9** (March 1983), pp. 155–165. (Chapter 10)

[Shepperd, 1988a] M. J. Shepperd, "An Evaluation of Software Product Metrics," *Information and Software Technology* **30** (No. 3, 1988), pp. 177–188. (Chapters 10 and 12)

[Shepperd, 1988b] M. J. Shepperd, "A Critique of Cyclomatic Complexity as a Software Metric," *Software Engineering Journal* **3** (March 1988), pp. 30–36. (Chapter 12)

[Shepperd, 1990] M. Shepperd, "Design Metrics: An Empirical Analysis," *Software Engineering Journal* **5** (January 1990), pp. 3–10. (Chapter 11)

[Shepperd and Ince, 1994] M. Shepperd and D. C. Ince, "A Critique of Three Metrics," *Journal of Systems and Software* **26** (September 1994), pp. 197–210. (Chapters 10 and 12)

[Sherer, 1991] S. A. SHERER, "A Cost-Effective Approach to Testing," *IEEE Software* **8** (March 1991), pp. 34–40. (Chapter 13)

[Shlaer and Mellor, 1988] S. SHLAER AND S. MELLOR, *Object-Oriented Systems Analysis: Modeling the World in Data*, Yourdon Press, Englewood Cliffs, NJ, 1988. (Chapter 9)

[Shlaer and Mellor, 1992] S. SHLAER AND S. MELLOR, *Object Lifecycles: Modeling the World in States*, Yourdon Press, Englewood Cliffs, NJ, 1992. (Chapters 9 and 11)

[Shneiderman, 1980] B. SHNEIDERMAN, *Software Psychology: Human Factors in Computer and Information Systems*, Winthrop Publishers, Cambridge, MA, 1980. (Chapter 1)

[Shneiderman and Mayer, 1975] B. SHNEIDERMAN AND R. MAYER, "Towards a Cognitive Model of Programmer Behavior," Technical Report TR-37, Indiana University, Bloomington, IN, 1975. (Chapter 6)

[Shooman, 1983] M. L. SHOOMAN, *Software Engineering: Design, Reliability, and Management*, McGraw-Hill, New York, 1983. (Chapter 12)

[Shriver and Wegner, 1987] B. SHRIVER AND P. WEGNER (Editors), *Research Directions in Object-Oriented Programming*, The MIT Press, Cambridge, MA, 1987. (Chapter 6)

[Silberschatz and Galvin, 1994] A SILBERSCHATZ AND P. B. GALVIN, *Operating System Concepts*, Fourth Edition, Addison-Wesley, Reading, MA, 1994. (Chapters 8, 11, and 12)

[Smith, Kotik, and Westfold, 1985] D. R. SMITH, G. B. KOTIK, AND S. J. WESTFOLD, "Research on Knowledge-Based Software Environments at the Kestrel Institute," *IEEE Transactions on Software Engineering* **SE-11** (November 1985), pp. 1278–1295. (Chapter 8)

[Snyder, 1993] A. SNYDER, "The Essence of Objects: Concepts and Terms," *IEEE Software* **10** (January 1993), pp. 31–42. (Chapters 1 and 6)

[Sobell, 1995] M. G. SOBELL, *A Practical Guide to the UNIX System*, Third Edition, Benjamin/Cummings, Menlo Park, CA, 1995. (Chapter 4)

[Spivey, 1988] J. M. SPIVEY, *Understanding Z: A Specification Language and Its Informal Semantics*, Cambridge University Press, Cambridge, UK, 1988. (Chapter 8)

[Spivey, 1990] J. M. SPIVEY, "Specifying a Real-Time Kernel," *IEEE Software* **7** (September 1990), pp. 21–28. (Chapter 8)

[Spivey, 1992] J. M. SPIVEY, *The Z Notation: A Reference Manual*, Prentice-Hall, New York, 1992. (Chapters 3 and 8)

[Stefik and Bobrow, 1986] M. STEFIK AND D. G. BOBROW, "Object-Oriented Programming: Themes and Variations," *The AI Magazine* **6** (No. 4, 1986), pp. 40–62. (Chapter 6)

[Stephenson, 1976] W. E. STEPHENSON, "An Analysis of the Resources Used in Safeguard System Software Development," Bell Laboratories, Draft Paper, August 1976. (Chapter 1)

[Sternbach and Okuda, 1991] R. STERNBACH AND M. OKUDA, *Star Trek: The Next Generation, Technical Manual*, Pocket Books, New York, 1991. (Chapter 2)

[Stevens, Myers, and Constantine, 1974] W. P. STEVENS, G. J. MYERS, AND L. L. CONSTANTINE, "Structured Design," *IBM Systems Journal* **13** (No. 2, 1974), pp. 115–139. (Chapter 6)

[Stroustrup, 1991] B. STROUSTRUP, *The C++ Programming Language*, Second Edition, Addison-Wesley, Reading, MA, 1991. (Chapters 6, 11, and 12)

[Symons, 1991] C. R. SYMONS, *Software Sizing and Estimating: Mk II FPA*, John Wiley and Sons, Chichester, UK, 1991. (Chapter 10)

[Takahashi and Kamayachi, 1985] M. TAKAHASHI AND Y. KAMAYACHI, "An Empirical Study of a Model for Program Error Prediction," *Proceedings of the Eighth International Conference on Software Engineering*, London, 1985, pp. 330–336. (Chapter 12)

[Tamir, 1980] M. TAMIR, "ADI: Automatic Derivation of Invariants," *IEEE Transactions on Software Engineering* **SE-6** (January 1980), pp. 40–48. (Chapter 5)

[Tanenbaum, 1981] A. S. TANENBAUM, "Network Protocols," *ACM Computing Surveys* **13** (December 1981), pp. 453–489. (Chapter 12)

[Tanenbaum, 1990] A. S. TANENBAUM, *Structured Computer Organization*, Third Edition, Prentice-Hall, Englewood Cliffs, NJ, 1990. (Chapter 6)

[Teichrow and Hershey, 1977] D. TEICHROW AND E. A. HERSHEY, III "PSL/PSA: A Computer-Aided Technique for Structured Documentation and Analysis of Information Processing Systems," *IEEE Transactions on Software Engineering* **SE-3** (January 1977), pp. 41–48. (Chapter 8)

[Teitelbaum and Reps, 1981] T. TEITELBAUM AND T. REPS, "The Cornell Program Synthesizer: A Syntax-Directed Programming Environment," *Communications of the ACM* **24** (September 1981), pp. 563–573. (Chapter 4)

[Teitelman and Masinter, 1981] W. TEITELMAN AND L. MASINTER, "The Interlisp Programming Environment," in: *Tutorial: Software Development Environments*, A. I. Wasserman (Editor), IEEE Computer Society Press, Washington, DC, 1981, pp. 73–81. (Chapter 13)

[Thayer, 1988] R. H. THAYER (Editor), *Tutorial: Software Engineering Management*, IEEE Computer Society Press, Washington, DC, 1988. (Chapter 10)

[Thayer and Dorfman, 1990] R. THAYER AND M. DORFMAN, *Tutorial: System and Software Requirements Engineering*, IEEE Computer Society Press, Los Alamitos, CA, 1990. (Chapter 7)

[Thomas, 1989] I. THOMAS, "PCTE Interfaces: Supporting Tools in Software Engineering Environments," *IEEE Software* **6** (November 1989), pp. 15–23. (Chapter 13)

[Thompson, 1984] K. THOMPSON, "Reflections on Trusting Trust," *Communications of the ACM* **27** (November 1984), pp. 761–763. (Epilogue)

[Tichy, 1985] W. F. TICHY, "RCS—A System for Version Control," *Software—Practice and Experience* **15** (July 1985), pp. 637–654. (Chapters 4, 13, and 14)

[Tracz, 1979] W. TRACZ, "Computer Programming and the Human Thought Process," *Software—Practice and Experience* **9** (February 1979), pp. 127–137. (Chapter 4)

[Tracz, 1988] W. J. TRACZ, "Software Reuse Myths," *ACM SIGSOFT Software Engineering Notes* **13** (January 1988), pp. 17–21. (Chapter 6)

[Tracz, 1994] W. TRACZ, "Software Reuse Myths Revisited," *Proceedings of the 16th International Conference on Software Engineering*, Sorrento, Italy, May 1994, pp. 271–272. (Chapter 6)

[Trammel, Binder, and Snyder, 1992] C. J. TRAMMEL, L. H. BINDER, AND C. E. SNYDER, "The Automated Production Control Documentation System: A Case Study in Cleanroom Software Engineering," *ACM Transactions on Software Engineering and Methodology* **1** (January 1992), pp. 81–94. (Chapters 5 and 12)

[Turner, 1994] C. D. TURNER, "State-Based Testing: A New Method for Testing Object-Oriented Programs," Ph.D. Thesis, Computer Science Division, University of Durham, Durham, UK, November 1994. (Chapter 12)

[van der Poel and Schach, 1983] K. G. VAN DER POEL AND S. R. SCHACH, "A Software Metric for Cost Estimation and Efficiency Measurement in Data Processing System Development," *Journal of Systems and Software* **3** (September 1983), pp. 187–191. (Chapters 10 and 12)

[van Wijngaarden et al., 1975] A. VAN WIJNGAARDEN, B. J. MAILLOUX, J. E. L. PECK, C. H. A. KOSTER, M. SINTZOFF, C. H. LINDSEY, L. G. L. T. MEERTENS, AND R. G. FISKER, "Revised Report on the Algorithmic Language ALGOL 68," *Acta Informatica* **5** (1975), pp. 1–236. (Chapter 2)

[Verner and Tate, 1988] J. VERNER AND G. TATE, "Estimating Size and Effort in Fourth-Generation Development," *IEEE Software* **5** (July 1988), pp. 15–22. (Chapter 12)

[Volta, 1993] L. G. VOLTA, JR., "DOES EVERY INSPECTION NEED A MEETING?" *Proceedings of the First ACM SIGSOFT Symposium on the Foundations of Software Engineering, ACM SIGSOFT Software Engineering Notes* **18** (December 1993), pp. 107–114. (Chapter 5)

[Wahl and Schach, 1988] N. J. WAHL AND S. R. SCHACH, "A Methodology and Distributed Tool for Debugging Dataflow Programs," *Proceedings of the Second Workshop on Software Testing, Verification, and Analysis,* Banff, Canada, July 1988, pp. 98–105. (Chapter 12)

[Walker, 1992] I. J. WALKER, "Requirements of an Object-Oriented Design Method," *Software Engineering Journal* **7** (March 1992), pp. 102–113. (Chapter 11)

[Wallis, 1982] P. J. L. WALLIS, *Portable Programming*, John Wiley and Sons, New York, 1982. (Chapter 12)

[Walsh, 1979] T. J. WALSH, "A Software Reliability Study Using a Complexity Measure," *Proceedings of the AFIPS National Computer Conference*, New York, 1979, pp. 761–768. (Chapter 12)

[Ward and Mellor, 1985] P. T. WARD AND S. MELLOR, *Structured Development for Real-Time Systems. Volumes 1, 2, and 3*, Yourdon Press, New York, 1985. (Chapter 11)

[Warnier, 1976] J. D. WARNIER, *Logical Construction of Programs*, Van Nostrand Reinhold, New York, 1976. (Chapter 11)

[Warnier, 1981] J. D. WARNIER, *Logical Construction of Systems*, Van Nostrand Reinhold, New York, 1981. (Chapters 8 and 11)

[Wasserman, 1985] A. I. WASSERMAN, "Extending State Transition Diagrams for the Specification of Human-Computer Interaction," *IEEE Transactions on Software Engineering* SE-11 (August 1985), pp. 699–713. (Chapter 8)

[Wasserman and Pircher, 1987] A. I. WASSERMAN AND P. A. PIRCHER, "A Graphical, Extensible Integrated Environment for Software Development," *Proceedings of the Second ACM SIGSOFT/ SIGPLAN Software Engineering Symposium on Practical Software Development Environments*, *ACM SIGPLAN Notices* 22 (January 1987), pp. 131–142. (Chapter 13)

[Weinberg, 1971] G. M. WEINBERG, *The Psychology of Computer Programming*, Van Nostrand Reinhold, New York, 1971. (Chapters 1 and 12)

[Weller, 1993] E. F. WELLER, "Lessons from Three Years of Inspection Data," *IEEE Software* 10 (September 1993), pp. 38–45. (Chapter 5)

[Weyuker, 1988a] E. J. WEYUKER, "An Empirical Study of the Complexity of Data Flow Testing," *Proceedings of the Second Workshop on Software Testing, Verification, and Analysis*, Banff, Canada, July 1988, pp. 188–195. (Chapter 12)

[Weyuker, 1988b] E. J. WEYUKER, "Evaluating Software Complexity Measures," *IEEE Trans. on Software Engineering* 14 (September 1988), pp. 1357–1365. (Chapters 10 and 12)

[Whitgift, 1991] D. WHITGIFT, *Methods and Tools for Software Configuration Management*, John Wiley and Sons, New York, 1991. (Chapter 4)

[Wiest and Levy, 1977] J. D. WIEST AND F. K. LEVY, *A Management Guide to PERT/CPM: With GERT/ PDM/DCPM and other Networks*, Second Edition, Prentice-Hall, Englewood Cliffs, NJ, 1977. (Chapter 10)

[Wildblood, 1990] A. WILDBLOOD, "Ada Reuse: The Promises Ring True," *Defense Science* 9 (April 1990), pp. 38–39. (Chapter 6)

[Wilde, Matthews, and Huitt, 1993] N. WILDE, P. MATTHEWS, AND R. HUITT, "Maintaining Object-Oriented Software," *IEEE Software* 10 (January 1993), pp. 75–80. (Chapters 12 and 14)

[Wing, 1990] J. WING, "A Specifier's Introduction to Formal Methods," *IEEE Computer* 23 (September 1990), pp. 8–24. (Chapter 8)

[Wirfs-Brock, Wilderson, and Wiener, 1990] R. WIRFS-BROCK, B. WILKERSON, AND L. WIENER, *Designing Object-Oriented Software*, Prentice-Hall, Englewood Cliffs, NJ, 1990. (Chapters 1 and 11)

[Wirth, 1971] N. WIRTH, "Program Development by Stepwise Refinement," *Communications of the ACM* 14 (April 1971), pp. 221–227. (Chapters 4 and 5)

[Wirth, 1975] N. WIRTH, *Algorithms + Data Structures = Programs*, Prentice-Hall, Englewood Cliffs, NJ, 1975. (Chapter 4)

[Wohlwend and Rosenbaum, 1993] H. WOHLWEND AND S. ROSENBAUM, "Software Improvements in an International Company," *Proceedings of the 15th International Conference on Software Engineering*, Baltimore, MD, May 1993, pp. 212–220. (Chapter 3)

[Wolberg, 1983] J. R. WOLBERG, *Conversion of Computer Software*, Prentice-Hall, Englewood Cliffs, NJ, 1983. (Chapter 12)

[Wong, 1984] C. WONG, "A Successful Software Development," *IEEE Transactions on Software Engineering* SE-10 (November 1984), pp. 714–727. (Chapter 3)

[Woodcock, 1989] J. WOODCOCK, "Calculating Properties of Z Specifications," *ACM SIGSOFT Software Engineering Notes* 14 (July 1989), pp. 43–54. (Chapter 8)

[Woodward, Hedley, and Hennell, 1980] M. R. WOODWARD, D. HEDLEY, AND M. A. HENNELL, "Experience with Path Analysis and Testing of Programs," *IEEE Transactions on Software Engineering* **SE-6** (May 1980), pp. 278–286. (Chapter 12)

[World Book Encyclopedia, 1992] *World Book Encyclopedia*, World Book-Childcraft International, Inc., Chicago, 1992, Volume N–O, pp. 558–559. (Chapter 9)

[Yau and Tsai, 1986] S. S. YAU AND J. J.-P. TSAI, "A Survey of Software Design Techniques," *IEEE Transactions on Software Engineering* **SE-12** (June 1986), pp. 713–721. (Chapter 11)

[Young and Gregory, 1972] D. M. YOUNG AND R. T. GREGORY, *A Survey of Numerical Mathematics, Volume I*, Addison-Wesley, Reading, MA, 1972. (Chapter 6)

[Yourdon, 1989] E. YOURDON, *Modern Structured Analysis*, Yourdon Press, Englewood Cliffs, NJ, 1989. (Chapters 4, 8, and 11)

[Yourdon, 1992] E. YOURDON, *Decline and Fall of the American Programmer*, Yourdon Press, Englewood Cliffs, NJ, 1992. (Chapters 1 and 2)

[Yourdon and Constantine, 1979] E. YOURDON AND L. L. CONSTANTINE, *Structured Design: Fundamentals of a Discipline of Computer Program and Systems Design*, Prentice-Hall, Englewood Cliffs, NJ, 1979. (Chapters 6, 8, and 11)

[Zage and Zage, 1993] W. M. ZAGE AND D. M. ZAGE, "Evaluating Design Metrics on Large-Scale Software," *IEEE Software* **10** (July 1993), pp. 75–81. (Chapter 11)

[Zelkowitz, Shaw, and Gannon, 1979] M. V. ZELKOWITZ, A. C. SHAW, AND J. D. GANNON, *Principles of Software Engineering and Design*, Prentice-Hall, Englewood Cliffs, NJ, 1979. (Chapters 1 and 14)

AUTHOR INDEX

This index includes only authors and references cited in the actual text.

SUBJECT INDEX

A

abstract data type, 149, 166–168, 169, 420
  definition, 166
abstract data type design, 347
abstract method, 175, 359, 475
abstraction, 161–166, 322–323
acceptance criteria, 223
acceptance testing, 11, 41, 114, 448, 449–450
accidental reuse, 178
action, 333
action-oriented design, 324–332, 352–353
  comparison with data-oriented design, object-oriented design, 352–353
activity, 304, 312–315
  critical, 312–315
  definition, 304
AD/Cycle, 456
Ada, Countess of Lovelace, 402
Ada, 17, 48, 98, 132, 141, 153, 173, 213, 232, 255, 296, 369, 398, 401–403, 406, 457, 485
  history 402
Ada, 83 401
Ada, 95 346, 401
Ada compiler, validation, 401–403
Ada Design Language (ADL), 451
Ada Joint Program Office (AJPO) 401, 403
Ada programming support environment (APSE), 451
Ada reference manual, 398, 401, 402
Ada standard, 401–403
adaptive maintenance, 11, 96, 465, 467, 470, 471, 476
  definition, 465
  time spent on, 466
ADF, 373

ADW, 91, 257, 457
aggregation, 173
Aide-de-Camp, 102, 450
ALGOL, 60 49, 128, 132, 372
all-definition-use-path coverage, 415
alpha testing, 41
alter verb, 150
ambiguity, 35, 56, 224
analysis, 11, 36, (see also specification)
Analyst/Designer, 91, 257, 356, 453
analytic network modeling, 223
Anna, 254
APL, 49
applet, 1
architectural design, 11, 21, 39, 322–327, 329–341, 344–350, 352–353
ASCII, 397
assembler, 296, 372, 375, 405, 425, 477
assert statement, 131
assertion, 124–127, 131
  definition, 124
association, 173
AT & T Bell Laboratories, 399
attribute, 24, 172, 269, 421

B

Bachman Product Set, 457, 478
back-end CASE tool, 91, 356
back-end tool integration, 456
back-up programmer, 389–390, 391
baseline, 101, 471–472
  definition, 101, 305
BASIC, 368
Battlemap, 478
beta testing, 41
black box testing, 309, 408, 411–414, 418–420, 448
Borland, 41

bottom-up implementation and integration, 444–445
  advantages, 444–445
  disadvantages, 445
boundary value analysis, 412–413
branch coverage, 414–415
bridge, 7–9
Brooks's Law, 386
budget, 37, 291, 305
bug, 23, 24, 387
build, 61–66
build tool, 102–103, 478
build-and-fix model, 53–54, 63, 64, 206, 213, 269
business-oriented environment, 456–457
bytecode, 484, 489

C

C, 17, 102, 132, 141, 155, 161, 162, 174, 346, 370, 399, 400, 401, 405, 457, 483–488
  history 399
C standard, 401
C++, 24, 98, 102, 132, 141, 155, 171, 173, 179, 181, 213, 346, 370, 371, 382, 399, 401, 483–488
  history, 399
  popularity, 371
C++ standard, 401
C^3I software, 235
C^4I software, 209
CA-Tellaplan, 315
capability maturity model (CMM), 71–76, 458
CASE, 82, 90–103, 179, 207, 212–213, 231, 257–258, 282–283, 297, 312–315, 356–357, 429, 447, 450–458, 473, 474, 476, 478–479
  scope, 92–96, 450